Houghton
[…]in
[…]ourt

GO MATH!

Volume 2

Made in the United States
Text printed on
recycled paper

Houghton
Mifflin
Harcourt

GO MATH!

Printed in the U.S.A.

ISBN 978-0-544-43272-7

15 0928 22 21 20 19

4500760104 D E F G

Dear Students and Families,

Welcome to **Go Math!**, Grade 1! In this exciting mathematics program, there are hands-on activities to do and real-world problems to solve. Best of all, you will write your ideas and answers right in your book. In **Go Math!**, writing and drawing on the pages helps you think deeply about what you are learning, and you will really understand math!

By the way, all of the pages in your **Go Math!** book are made using recycled paper. We wanted you to know that you can Go Green with **Go Math!**

Sincerely,

The Authors

Made in the United States
Text printed on recycled paper

GO MATH!

Authors

Juli K. Dixon, Ph.D.
Professor, Mathematics Education
University of Central Florida
Orlando, Florida

Edward B. Burger, Ph.D.
President, Southwestern University
Georgetown, Texas

Steven J. Leinwand
Principal Research Analyst
American Institutes for Research (AIR)
Washington, D.C.

Contributor

Rena Petrello
Professor, Mathematics
Moorpark College
Moorpark, CA

Matthew R. Larson, Ph.D.
K-12 Curriculum Specialist for Mathematics
Lincoln Public Schools
Lincoln, Nebraska

Martha E. Sandoval-Martinez
Math Instructor
El Camino College
Torrance, California

English Language Learners Consultant

Elizabeth Jiménez
CEO, GEMAS Consulting
Professional Expert on English Learner Education
Bilingual Education and Dual Language
Pomona, California

VOLUME I

Operations and Algebraic Thinking

Common Core **Critical Area** Developing understanding of addition, subtraction, and strategies for addition and subtraction within 20

Critical Area

GO DIGITAL

Go online! Your math lessons are interactive. Use *i*Tools, Animated Math Models, the Multimedia *e*Glossary, and more.

Chapter 1 Overview

In this chapter, you will explore and discover answers to the following **Essential Questions**:

- How can you model adding within 10?
- How do you show adding to a group?
- How do you model putting together?
- How do you show adding in any order?

Chapter 2 Overview

In this chapter, you will explore and discover answers to the following **Essential Questions**:

- How can you subtract numbers from 10 or less?
- How do you model taking apart?
- How do you show taking from a group?
- How do you subtract to compare?

Personal Math Trainer
Online Assessment and Intervention

Chapter 3 Overview

In this chapter, you will explore and discover answers to the following **Essential Questions**:

- How do you solve addition problems?
- What strategies can you use to add facts?
- Why can you add in any order?
- How can you add three numbers?

Practice and Homework

Lesson Check and Spiral Review in every lesson

3 Addition Strategies 127

Domain Operations and Algebraic Thinking

COMMON CORE STATE STANDARDS 1.OA.A.2, 1.OA.B.3, 1.OA.C.5, 1.OA.C.6

Chapter 4 Overview

In this chapter, you will explore and discover answers to the following **Essential Questions**:

- How do you solve subtraction problems?
- What strategies can you use to subtract facts?
- How can an addition fact help you solve a related subtraction fact?
- How can you make a ten to help you subtract?

4 Subtraction Strategies 207

Domain Operations and Algebraic Thinking

COMMON CORE STATE STANDARDS 1.OA.A.1, 1.OA.B.4, 1.OA.C.5, 1.OA.C.6

5 Addition and Subtraction Relationships 251

Domain Operations and Algebraic Thinking

COMMON CORE STATE STANDARDS 1.OA.A.1, 1.OA.C.6, 1.OA.D.7, 1.OA.D.8

Chapter 5 Overview

In this chapter, you will explore and discover answers to the following **Essential Questions**:

- How can relating addition and subtraction help you to learn and understand facts within 20?
- How do addition and subtraction undo each other?
- What is the relationship between related facts?
- How can you find unknown numbers in related facts?

Critical Area

GO DIGITAL

Go online! Your math lessons are interactive. Use *i*Tools, Animated Math Models, the Multimedia *e*Glossary, and more.

Chapter 6 Overview

In this chapter, you will explore and discover answers to the following **Essential Questions**:

- How do you use place value to model, read, and write numbers to 120?
- What ways can you use tens and ones to model numbers to 120?
- How do numbers change as you count by tens to 120?

Personal Math Trainer
Online Assessment and Intervention

VOLUME 2

Number and Operations in Base Ten

Common Core **Critical Area** Developing understanding of whole number relationships and place value, including grouping in tens and ones

6 Count and Model Numbers 327

Domain Number and Operations in Base Ten

COMMON CORE STATE STANDARDS 1.NBT.A.1, 1.NBT.B.2, 1.NBT.B.2a, 1.NBT.B.2b, 1.NBT.B.2c, 1.NBT.B.3

7 Compare Numbers 395

Domain Number and Operations in Base Ten

COMMON CORE STATE STANDARDS 1.NBT.B.3, 1.NBT.C.5

8 Two-Digit Addition and Subtraction 433

Domains Operations and Algebraic Thinking
Number and Operations in Base Ten

COMMON CORE STATE STANDARDS 1.OA.C.6, 1.NBT.C.4, 1.NBT.C.6

Chapter 7 Overview

In this chapter, you will explore and discover answers to the following **Essential Questions**:

- How do you use place value to compare numbers?
- What ways can you use tens and ones to compare two-digit numbers?
- How can you find 10 more and 10 less than a number?

Practice and Homework

Lesson Check and Spiral Review in every lesson

Chapter 8 Overview

In this chapter, you will explore and discover answers to the following **Essential Questions**:

- How can you add and subtract two-digit numbers?
- What ways can you use tens and ones to add and subtract two-digit numbers?
- How can making a ten help you add a two-digit number and a one-digit number?

Critical Area

GO DIGITAL

Go online! Your math lessons are interactive. Use *i*Tools, Animated Math Models, the Multimedia *e*Glossary, and more.

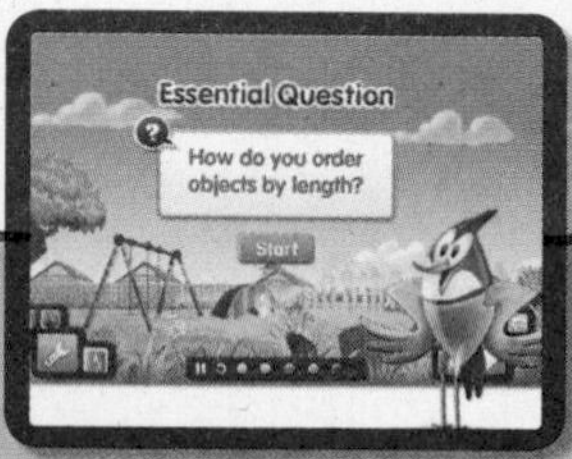

Chapter 9 Overview

In this chapter, you will explore and discover answers to the following **Essential Questions**:

- How can you measure a length and tell time?
- How can you describe using paper clips to measure the length of an object?
- How can you use the hour and minute hands of a clock to tell time to the hour and to the half hour?

Personal Math Trainer
Online Assessment and Intervention

Measurement and Data

Common Core **Critical Area** Developing understanding of linear measurement and measuring lengths as iterating length units

9 Measurement 509

Domain Measurement and Data

COMMON CORE STATE STANDARDS 1.MD.A.1, 1.MD.A.2, 1.MD.B.3

10 Represent Data 571

Domain Measurement and Data

COMMON CORE STATE STANDARDS 1.MD.C.4

Chapter 10 Overview

In this chapter, you will explore and discover answers to the following **Essential Questions**:

- How can graphs and charts help you organize, represent, and interpret data?
- How can you look at a graph or chart to tell the most or least popular item without counting?
- How are tally charts, picture graphs, and bar graphs alike? How are they different?
- How can you compare information recorded in a graph?

Practice and Homework

Lesson Check and Spiral Review in every lesson

Critical Area

GO DIGITAL

Go online! Your math lessons are interactive. Use *i*Tools, Animated Math Models, the Multimedia *e*Glossary, and more.

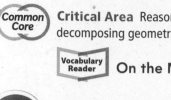

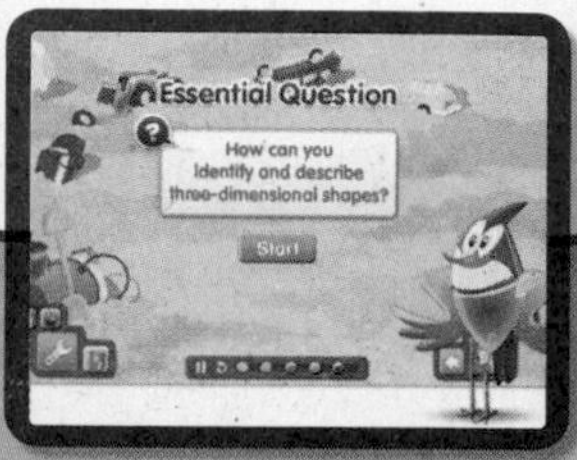

Chapter 11 Overview

In this chapter, you will explore and discover answers to the following **Essential Questions**:

- How can you identify and describe three-dimensional shapes?
- How can you combine three-dimensional shapes to make new shapes?
- How can you use a combined shape to make a new shape?
- What two-dimensional shapes are on three-dimensional shapes?

Chapter 12 Overview

In this chapter, you will explore and discover answers to the following **Essential Questions**:

- How do you sort and describe two-dimensional shapes?
- How can you describe two-dimensional shapes?
- How can you identify equal and unequal parts in two-dimensional shapes?

Geometry

Common Core **Critical Area** Reasoning about attributes of, and composing and decomposing geometric shapes

11 Three-Dimensional Geometry 629

Domain Geometry

COMMON CORE STATE STANDARDS 1.G.A.1, 1.G.A.2

12 Two-Dimensional Geometry 667

Domain Geometry

COMMON CORE STATE STANDARDS 1.G.A.1, 1.G.A.2, 1.G.A.3

Around the Neighborhood

written by John Hudson

Common Core CRITICAL AREA Developing understanding of whole number relationships and place value, including grouping in tens and ones

The mail carrier brings letters to Mr. and Mrs. Jones. How many letters does she bring?

_____ ◯ _____ ◯ _____

Social Studies

How do mail carriers help us?

The mail carrier brings packages to the fire station. Then she brings more packages. How many packages does she bring?

_____ ◯ _____ ◯ _____

Social Studies

How do firefighters help us?

It is time for lunch. The mail carrier eats in the park. How many boys and girls are playing?

_____ ◯ _____ ◯ _____

Social Studies

How do parents help us?

The mail carrier brings 12 packages to the police station. "This person has moved," says the police officer. "You need to take these back." How many packages does the officer keep?

____ ◯ ____ ◯ ____

Social Studies

How do police officers help us?

The mail carrier stops at City Hall.
She brings 8 letters for the mayor.
She brings 4 letters for the city clerk.
How many letters does she bring?

_____ ◯ _____ ◯ _____

Social Studies

How do city workers help us?

Name ______________________________________

Write About the Story

One day, Mr. and Mrs. Jones each got the same number of letters. They got 12 letters in all. Draw the two groups of letters.

Vocabulary Review

add
difference
doubles
subtract
sum

Mr. Jones

Mrs. Jones

Letters for Mr. Jones	Letters for Mrs. Jones

Write the number sentence. _____ ◯ _____ ◯ _____

WRITE Math Describe your number sentence. Use a vocabulary word.

____

____

How Many Letters?

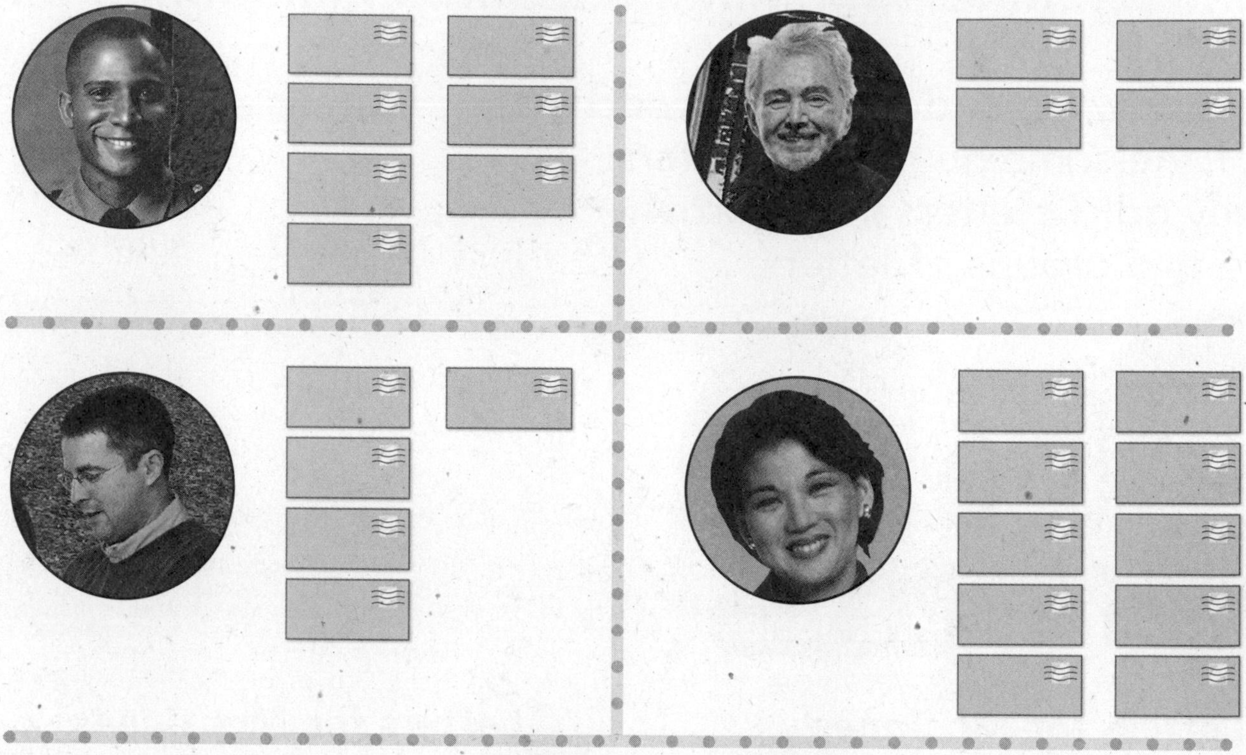

1. How many letters do  and  have in all?

_____ ◯ _____ ◯ _____

2. How many more letters does  have than ?

_____ ◯ _____ ◯ _____

3. Circle the two that have 11 letters in all.

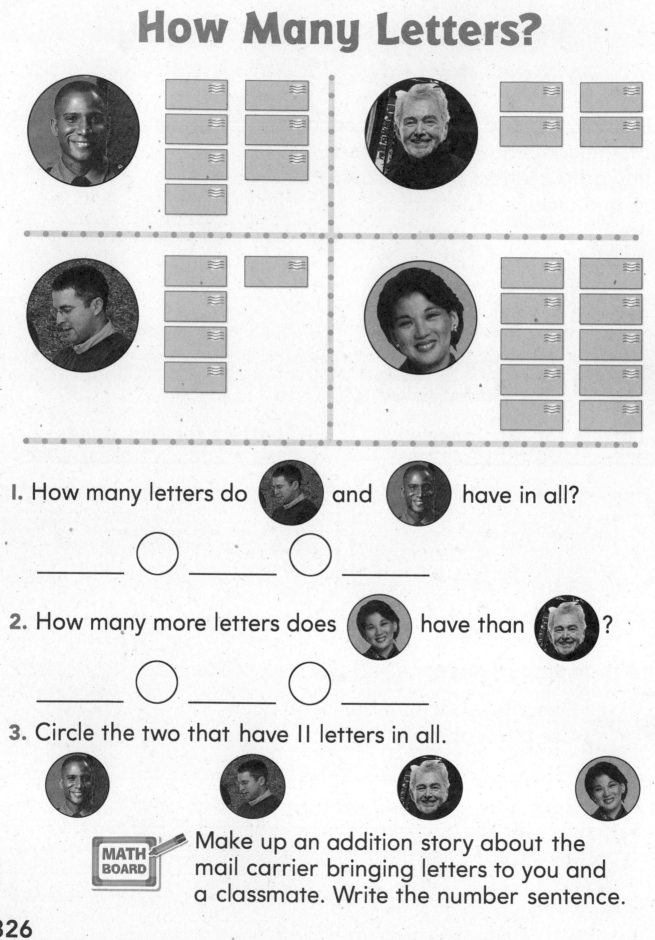

MATH BOARD Make up an addition story about the mail carrier bringing letters to you and a classmate. Write the number sentence.

Chapter 6

Count and Model Numbers

Curious About Math with Curious George

Dan and May like apples.
They buy 15 apples in all.
If Dan buys 10 apples, how many apples does May buy?

Name ______________________

Show What You Know

Personal Math Trainer
Online Assessment and Intervention

Explore Numbers 6 to 9

Count how many. Circle the number. (K.CC.B.4)

1. 

6

7

2. 

8

9

Count Groups to 20

Circle groups of 10. Write how many. (1.NBT.A.1)

3. 

____

4. 

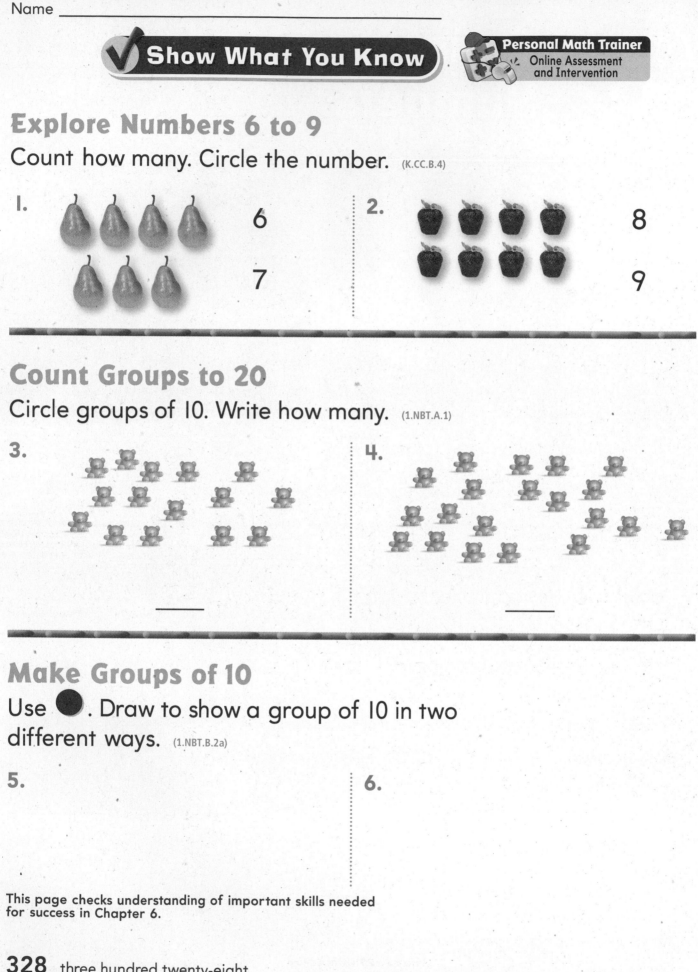

____

Make Groups of 10

Use ●. Draw to show a group of 10 in two different ways. (1.NBT.B.2a)

5.

6.

This page checks understanding of important skills needed for success in Chapter 6.

Name ______________________

Vocabulary Builder

Review Words	
one	two
three	four
five	six
seven	eight
nine	ten

Visualize It

Draw pictures in the box to show the number.

two — [ ]

nine — [ ]

five — [ ]

Understand Vocabulary

Write a review word to name the number.

1.  ______________

2. 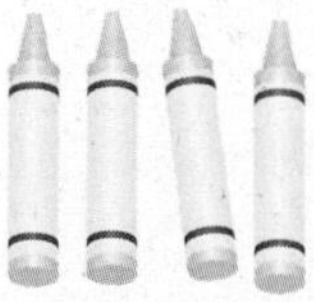 ______________

3. 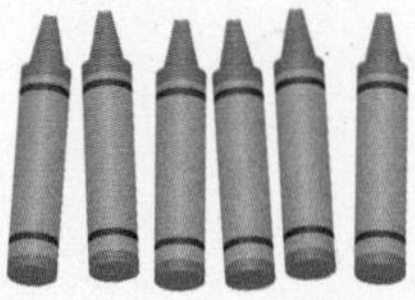 ______________

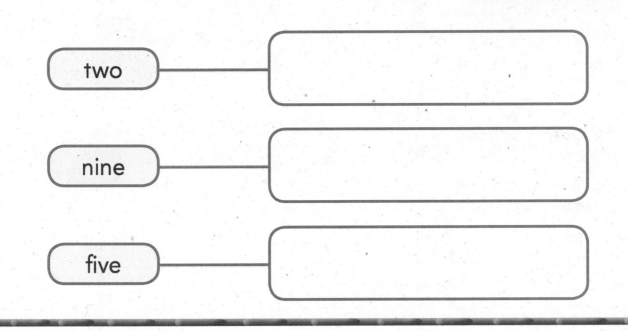

GO DIGITAL
• Interactive Student Edition
• Multimedia eGlossary

Chapter 6

Game Show the Numbers

Materials • [pawn] and [pawn] • [spinner 1–6]
• 20 [counters] • [ten frame]

Play with a partner.

1. Put your [pawn] on START.
2. Spin the [spinner]. Move your [pawn] that many spaces.
3. Read the number. Use [counters] to show the number on a ten frame.
4. Have your partner count the [counters] to check your answer. If you are not correct, lose a turn.
5. The first player to get to END wins.

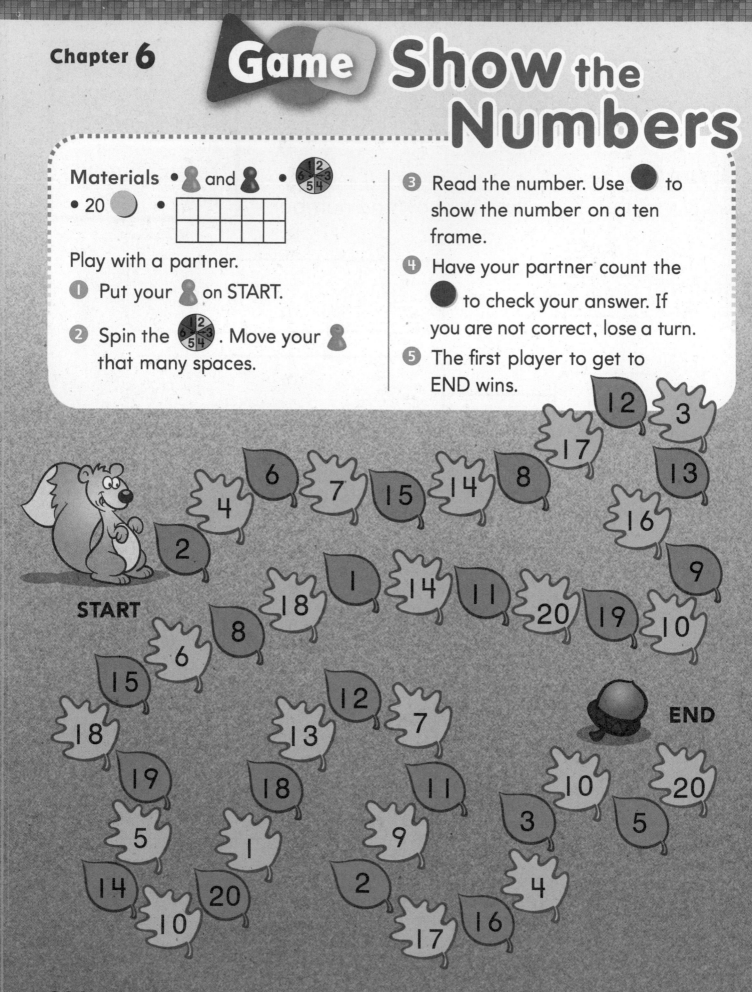

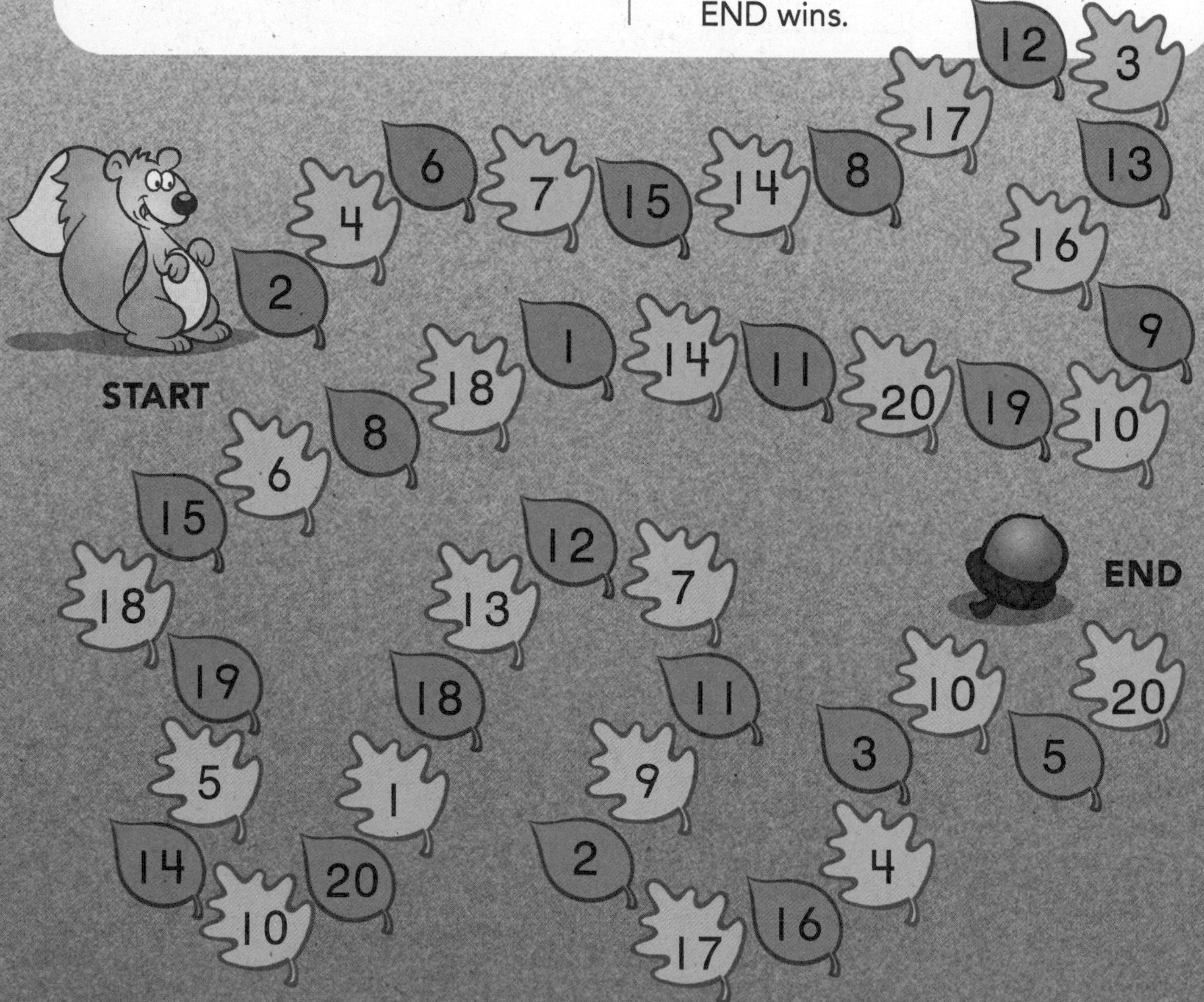

Chapter 6 Vocabulary

addend sumando 2	**difference** diferencia 13
digit dígito 14	**hundred** centena 29
ones unidades 39	**subtract** restar 52
sum suma o total 54	**ten** decena 57

9 − 4 = 5

The **difference** is 5.

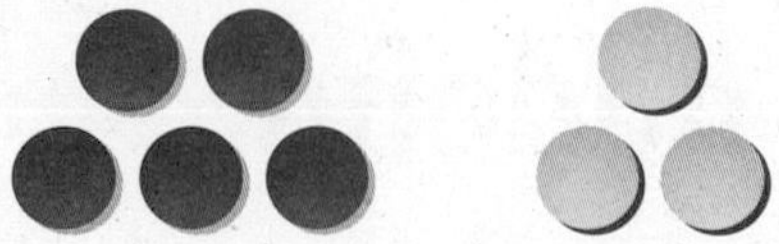

5 + 3 = 8

addends

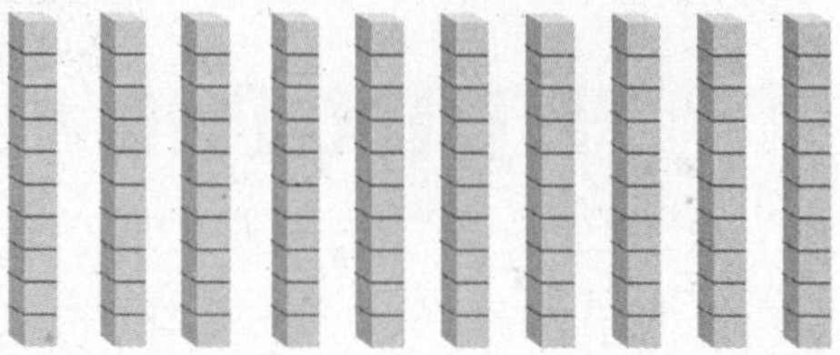

10 tens is the same as 1 **hundred**.

13 is a two-digit number.

The 1 in 13 means 1 ten.

The 3 in 13 means 3 ones.

5 − 2 = 3

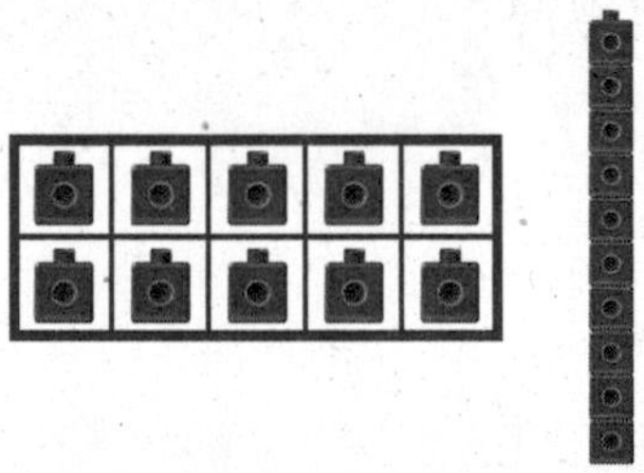

10 **ones** = 1 ten

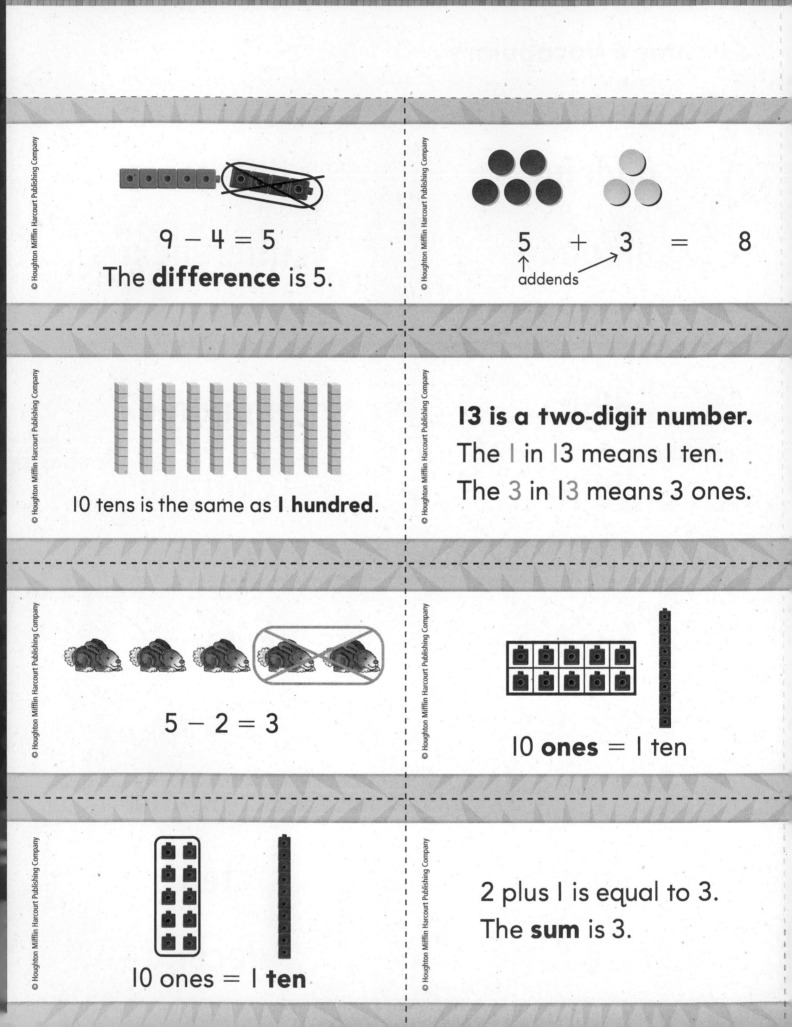

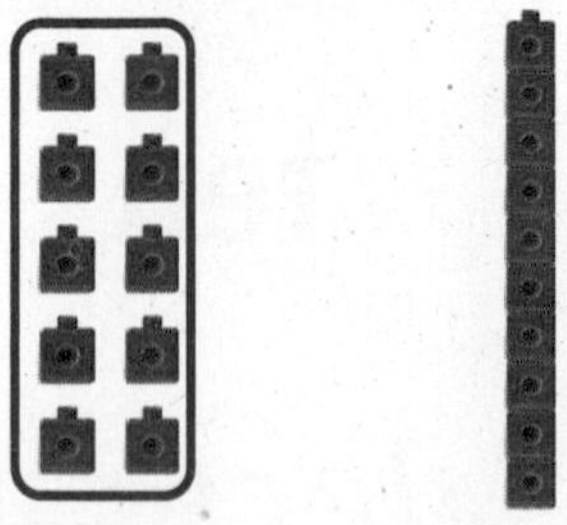

10 ones = 1 **ten**

2 plus 1 is equal to 3.

The **sum** is 3.

Game

Going to Town

Word Box
- addend
- difference
- digit
- hundred
- ones
- subtract
- sum
- ten

For 2 players

Materials

- 1
- 1
- 1
- clue cards

How to Play

1. Put your on START.
2. Toss the to take a turn. Move that many spaces.
3. If you land on one of these spaces:

   Red Space Take a Clue Card. Answer the question. If you are correct, move ahead 1. Return the Clue Card to the bottom of the pile.

   Blue Space Read the word. Tell what it means, or give an example. If you are correct, move ahead 1.

   Green Space Follow the directions in the space.
4. The first player to reach FINISH wins.

Game

DIRECTIONS 2 players. Take turns to play. • To take a turn, toss the [cube]. Move that many spaces • Follow the directions for the space where you land. • First player to reach FINISH wins.

MATERIALS • 1 [connecting cube] per player • 1 [number cube] • 1 set of clue cards

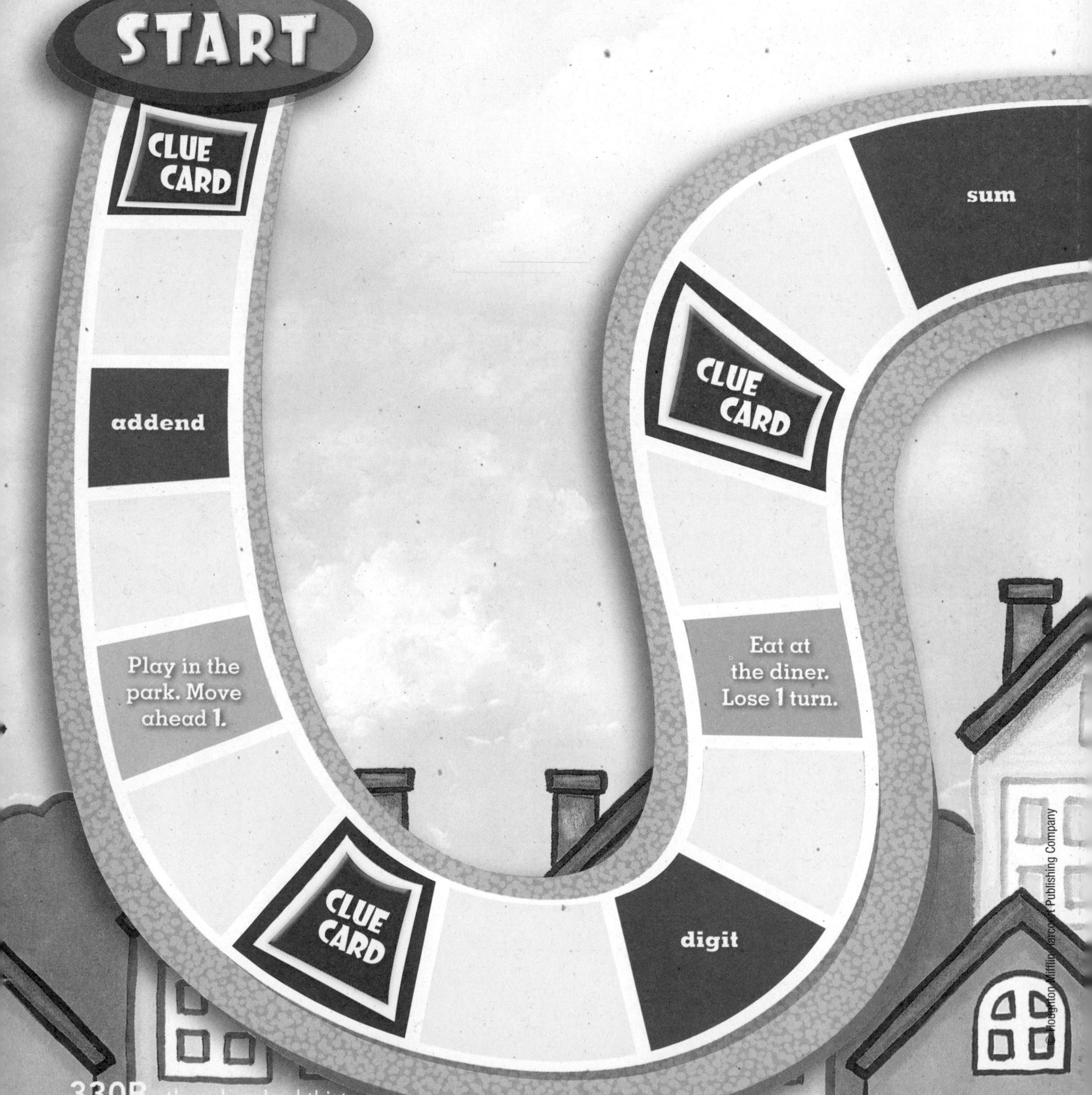

Game
FINISH
Shop at the market. Take another turn.
CLUE CARD
difference
Go to the library. Trade places with another player.
CLUE CARD
subtract
Wait at the post office. Go back 1.

Journal

The Write Way

Reflect

Choose one idea. Draw and write about it.

- Tell how you can use a counting chart to solve problems.
- Explain two ways that you can show a number as tens and ones.

Name ____________________

Count by Ones to 120

Essential Question How can knowing a counting pattern help you count to 120?

Common Core **Number and Operations in Base Ten—1.NBT.A.1**
MATHEMATICAL PRACTICES
MP5, MP7, MP8

Listen and Draw Real World

Write the missing numbers.

21	22	23	24	25	26	27	28	29	30
31	32	33	34	35	36	37	38	39	40
41	42	43	44	45	46	47	48	49	50
51	52	53	54	55	56	57	58	59	60
61	62	63	64	65	66	67	68	69	70
71	72	73	74	75	76	77	78	79	80
81	82	83	84	85	86	87	88	89	90
91	92	93	94	95	96	97	98	99	100

FOR THE TEACHER • Read the following problem. Debbie saw this page in a puzzle book. Two rows of numbers are missing. Use what you know about counting to write the missing numbers.

Math Talk MATHEMATICAL PRACTICES 7

Look for Structure
Explain how you know which numbers are missing.

Model and Draw

Count forward.
Write the numbers.

1	2	3	4	5	6	7	8	9	10
11	12	13	14	15	16	17	18	19	20
21	22	23	24	25	26	27	28	29	30
31	32	33	34	35	36	37	38	39	40
41	42	43	44	45	46	47	48	49	50
51	52	53	54	55	56	57	58	59	60
61	62	63	64	65	66	67	68	69	70
71	72	73	74	75	76	77	78	79	80
81	82	83	84	85	86	87	88	89	90
91	92	93	94	95	96	97	98	99	100
101	102	103	104	105	106	107	108	109	110
111	112	113	114	115	116	117	118	119	120

10, 11, ____, ____, ____

100, 101, ____, ____, ____

110, 111, ____, ____, ____

Share and Show MATH BOARD

Use a Counting Chart. Count forward.
Write the numbers.

Look for a pattern to help you write the numbers.

1. 114, ____, ____, ____, ____, ____, ____

2. 51, ____, ____, ____, ____, ____, ____

3. 94, ____, ____, ____, ____, ____, ____

4. 78, ____, ____, ____, ____, ____, ____

✓5. 35, ____, ____, ____, ____, ____, ____

✓6. 104, ____, ____, ____, ____, ____, ____

Name ________________________________

On Your Own

MATHEMATICAL PRACTICE 7 **Look for a Pattern**

Use a Counting Chart. Count forward.
Write the numbers.

7. 19, ___, ___, ___, ___, ___, ___, ___, ___

8. 98, ___, ___, ___, ___, ___, ___, ___, ___

9. 60, ___, ___, ___, ___, ___, ___, ___, ___

10. 27, ___, ___, ___, ___, ___, ___, ___, ___

11. 107, ___, ___, ___, ___, ___, ___, ___, ___

12. THINK SMARTER Use a Counting Chart to write the numbers counting forward.

___, ___, ___, ___, ___, 120

Math on the Spot

13. THINK SMARTER There is an unknown number in the sequence counting forward. The number is greater than 51. The number is less than 53. What is the unknown number?

___

Problem Solving • Applications (Real World)

WRITE Math

Use a Counting Chart. Draw and write numbers to solve.

14. GO DEEPER The bag has 99 buttons. Draw more buttons so there are 105 buttons in all. Write the numbers as you count.

15. THINK SMARTER The bag has 56 buttons. How many more buttons do you need to add to the bag to have 64 buttons?

____ buttons

16. THINK SMARTER Tito counts 105 cubes. Then he counts forward some more cubes. Write the numbers.

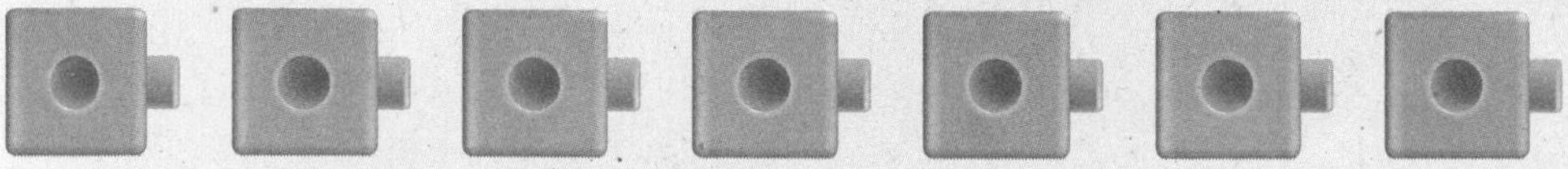

105, ____, ____, ____, ____, ____, ____

TAKE HOME ACTIVITY • Take a walk with your child. Count aloud together as you take 120 steps.

Name ______________________________

Count by Ones to 120

Common Core — **COMMON CORE STANDARD—1.NBT.A.1**
Extend the counting sequence.

Use a Counting Chart. Count forward. Write the numbers.

1. 40, ____, ____, ____, ____, ____, ____, ____, ____

2. 55, ____, ____, ____, ____, ____, ____, ____, ____

3. 37, ____, ____, ____, ____, ____, ____, ____, ____

4. 98, ____, ____, ____, ____, ____, ____, ____, ____

Problem Solving — Real World

Use a Counting Chart. Draw and write numbers to solve.

5. The bag has 111 marbles. Draw more marbles so there are 117 marbles in all. Write the numbers as you count.

6. WRITE Math Choose a number between 90 and 110. Write the number. Then count forward to write the next 5 numbers.

____

____

____

Lesson Check (1.NBT.A.1)

1. Count forward. Write the missing number.

110, 111, 112, ____, 114

Spiral Review (1.OA.A.1)

2. Solve. Write the number.
There are 6 bees. 2 bees fly away. How many bees are there now?

____ bees

3. Solve. Draw a model to explain.
There are 8 children. 6 children are boys. The rest are girls. How many children are girls?

____ girls

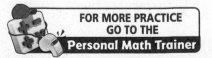

Name ______________________

Count by Tens to 120

Essential Question How do numbers change as you count by tens to 120?

Common Core **Number and Operations in Base Ten—1.NBT.A.1**

MATHEMATICAL PRACTICES MP2, MP5, MP8

Listen and Draw

Start on 10. Count forward by tens.
Color each number as you say it.

1	2	3	4	5	6	7	8	9	10
11	12	13	14	15	16	17	18	19	20
21	22	23	24	25	26	27	28	29	30
31	32	33	34	35	36	37	38	39	40
41	42	43	44	45	46	47	48	49	50
51	52	53	54	55	56	57	58	59	60
61	62	63	64	65	66	67	68	69	70
71	72	73	74	75	76	77	78	79	80
81	82	83	84	85	86	87	88	89	90
91	92	93	94	95	96	97	98	99	100

FOR THE TEACHER • Ask children: How do you count by tens? Starting at 10 on the hundred chart, have children count forward by tens, coloring each additional ten as they count.

Math Talk

MATHEMATICAL PRACTICES 8

Generalize Which numbers in the hundred chart did you color? Explain.

Model and Draw

Start on 3. Count by tens.

1	2	3	4	5	6	7	8	9	10
11	12	13	14	15	16	17	18	19	20
21	22	23	24	25	26	27	28	29	30
31	32	33	34	35	36	37	38	39	40
41	42	43	44	45	46	47	48	49	50
51	52	53	54	55	56	57	58	59	60
61	62	63	64	65	66	67	68	69	70
71	72	73	74	75	76	77	78	79	80
81	82	83	84	85	86	87	88	89	90
91	92	93	94	95	96	97	98	99	100
101	102	103	104	105	106	107	108	109	110
111	112	113	114	115	116	117	118	119	120

THINK
When you count by tens, each number is ten more.

3, 13, 23, 33, ____, ____, ____, ____, ____, ____, ____, ____

Share and Show

MATH BOARD

Use a Counting Chart to count by tens.
Write the numbers.

1. Start on 17.

17, ____, ____, ____, ____, ____, ____, ____, ____

✓2. Start on 1.

1, ____, ____, ____, ____, ____, ____, ____, ____

✓3. Start on 39.

39, ____, ____, ____, ____, ____, ____, ____, ____

Name ____________________

On Your Own

MATHEMATICAL PRACTICE 5 **Use Patterns** Use a Counting Chart. Count by tens. Write the numbers.

4. 40, ____, ____, ____, ____, ____, ____, ____, ____

5. 15, ____, ____, ____, ____, ____, ____, ____, ____

6. 28, ____, ____, ____, ____, ____, ____, ____, ____

7. 6, ____, ____, ____, ____, ____, ____, ____, ____

8. 14, ____, ____, ____, ____, ____, ____, ____, ____

9. 32, ____, ____, ____, ____, ____, ____, ____, ____

10. THINKSMARTER If you start on 43 and count by tens, what number is after 73 and before 93?

____

11. You say me when you start on 21 and count by tens. I am after 91. I am before 111. What number am I?

____

Problem Solving • Applications Real World

WRITE Math

GO DEEPER Use what you know about a Counting Chart to write the missing numbers.

12.

6			
16			
		28	29

13.

		54	55
		64	
72			

14.

			15
32			

15.

97	98		

16. THINK SMARTER Use a Counting Chart. Count by tens. Match each number on the left to a number that is 10 more.

57 •	• 103
73 •	• 67
77 •	• 87
93 •	• 83

TAKE HOME ACTIVITY • Write these numbers: 2, 12, 22, 32, 42. Ask your child to tell you the next 5 numbers.

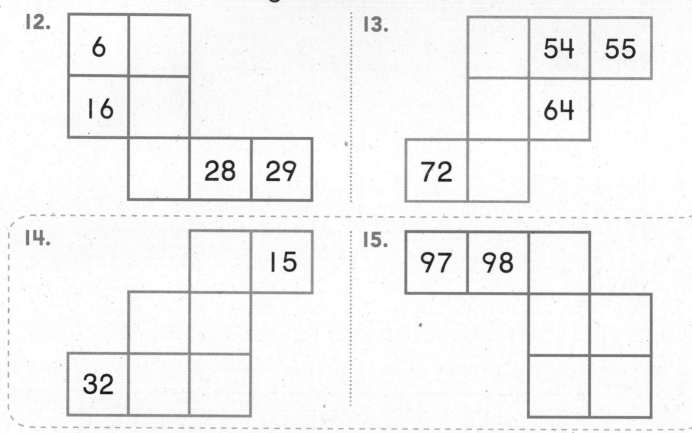

Name ______________________

Count by Tens to 120

COMMON CORE STANDARD—1.NBT.A.1
Extend the counting sequence.

Use a Counting Chart.
Count by tens.
Write the numbers.

1. 1, ___, ___, ___, ___, ___, ___, ___, ___, ___

2. 14, ___, ___, ___, ___, ___, ___, ___, ___, ___

3. 7, ___, ___, ___, ___, ___, ___, ___, ___, ___

4. 29, ___, ___, ___, ___, ___, ___, ___, ___, ___

5. 5, ___, ___, ___, ___, ___, ___, ___, ___, ___

6. 12, ___, ___, ___, ___, ___, ___, ___, ___, ___

7. 26, ___, ___, ___, ___, ___, ___, ___, ___, ___

Problem Solving Real World

Solve.

8. I am after 70.
I am before 90.
You say me when you count by tens.
What number am I? ___

9. WRITE Math Use numbers to explain the pattern you see when you count forward by tens.

____

____

____

Lesson Check (1.NBT.A.1)

1. Count by tens.
Write the missing numbers.

44, 54, 64, ______, ______, 94

Spiral Review (1.OA.C.6)

2. Use the model. Write to show how you make a ten. Then add.

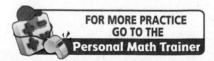

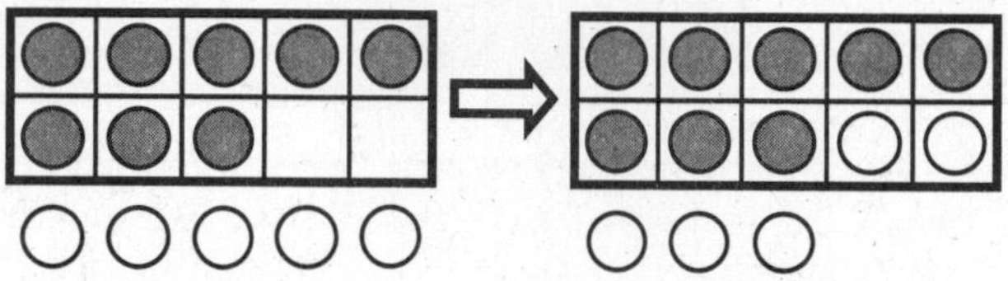

___ + ___ + ___

___ + ___ = ___

So, ___ + ___ = ___

3. Write a number sentence to complete the related facts.

$9 + 6 = 15$ $15 - 6 = 9$

$6 + 9 = 15$ [ ]

Name ______________________________

Understand Ten and Ones

Essential Question How can you use different ways to write a number as ten and ones?

Common Core **Number and Operations in Base Ten—1.NBT.B.2b**

MATHEMATICAL PRACTICES
MP3, MP5, MP6

Listen and Draw

Real World · Hands On

Use ■ to model the problem.
Draw the ■ to show your work.

FOR THE TEACHER • Read the problem. Tim has 10 books. He gets 2 more books. How many books does Tim have now?

Math Talk · MATHEMATICAL PRACTICES 5

Use Tools How does your picture show the books Tim has?

Model and Draw

13 is a two-**digit** number.
The 1 in 13 means 1 **ten**.
The 3 in 13 means 3 **ones**.

THINK
10 ones and 3 ones
is the same as
1 ten 3 ones.

1 ten 3 ones

10 + 3

13

Share and Show MATH BOARD

Use the model. Write the number three different ways.

1. 

____ ten ____ ones

____ + ____

____

2. 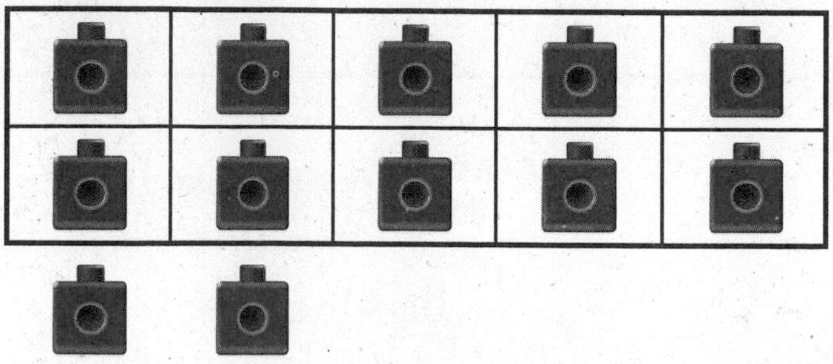

____ ten ____ ones

____ + ____

____

Name ______________________

On Your Own

MATHEMATICAL PRACTICE 6 **Make Connections**

Use the model. Write the number three different ways.

3.

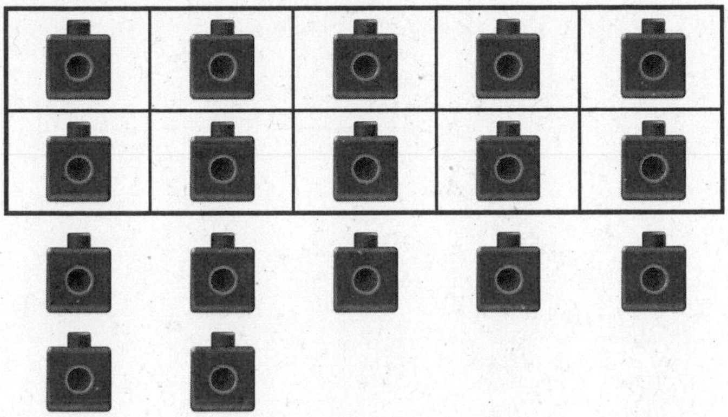

____ ten ____ ones

____ + ____

____

4.

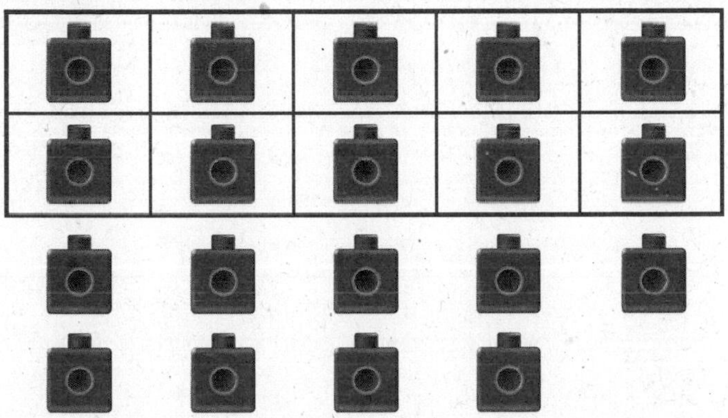

____ ten ____ ones

____ + ____

____

5. GO DEEPER Draw cubes to show the number. Write the missing numbers.

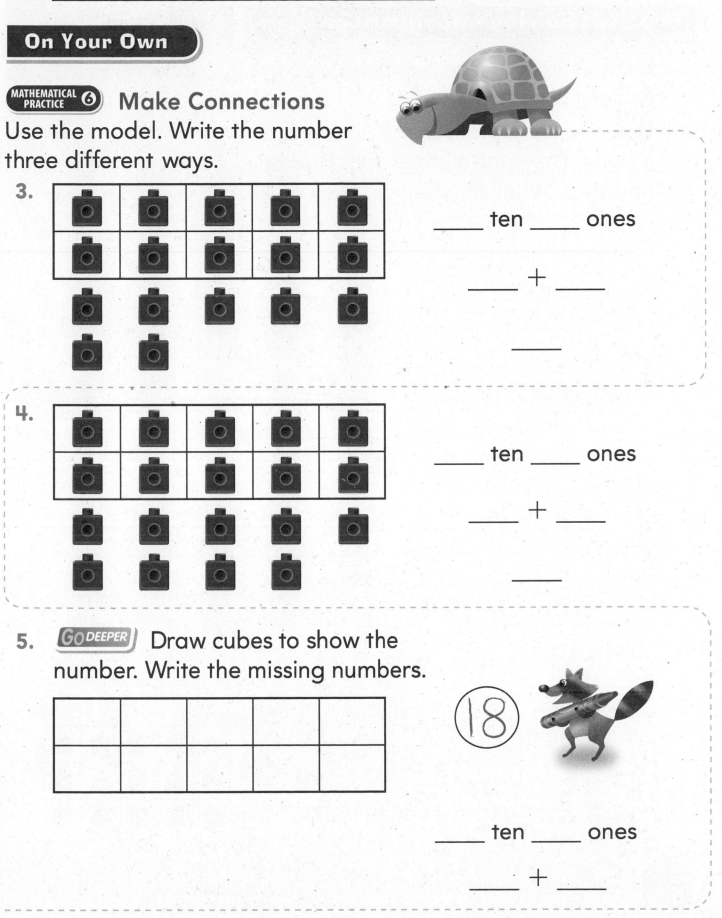

18

____ ten ____ ones

____ + ____

Problem Solving • Applications Real World

WRITE Math

Draw cubes to show the number. Write the number three different ways.

6. David has 1 ten and 3 ones. Abby has 6 ones. They put all their tens and ones together. What number did they make?

____ ten ____ ones

____ + ____

____

7. THINK SMARTER Karen has 7 ones. Jimmy has 9 ones. They put all their ones together. What number did they make?

Math on the Spot

____ ten ____ ones

____ + ____

____

8. THINK SMARTER Does the number match the model?

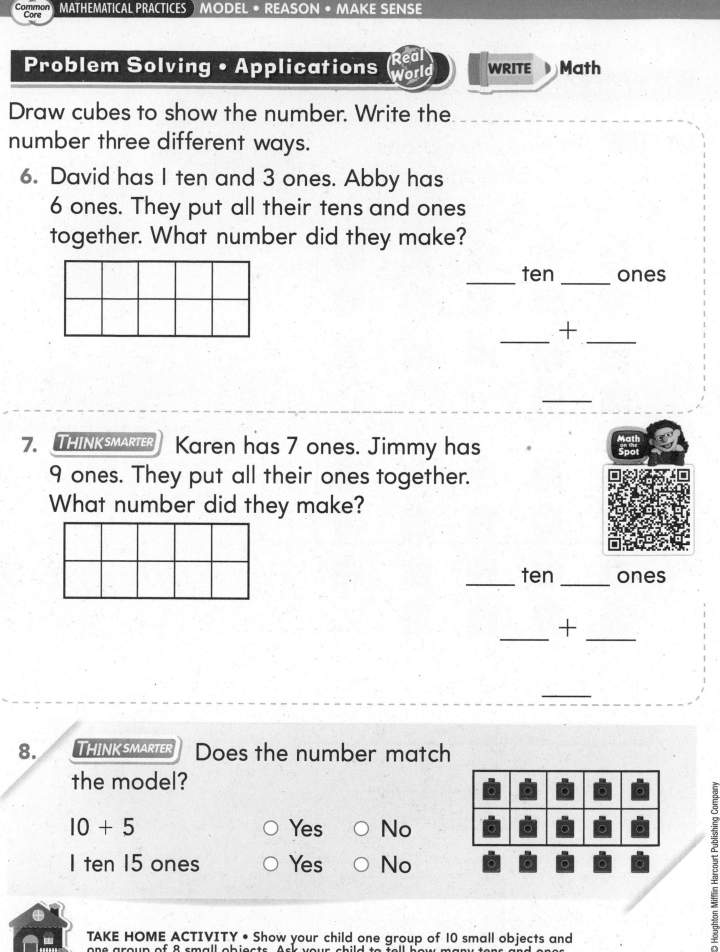

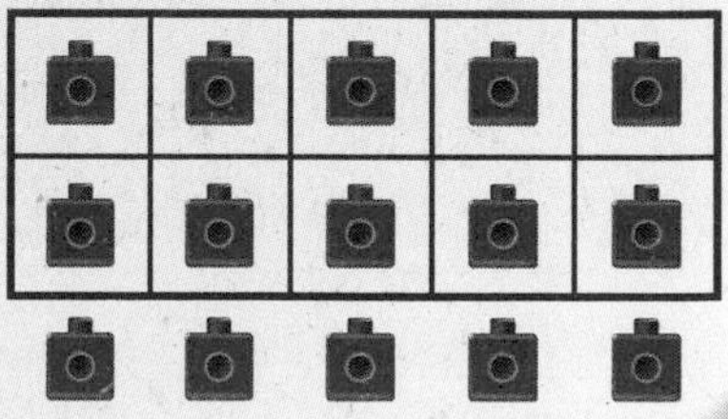

10 + 5	○ Yes	○ No
1 ten 15 ones	○ Yes	○ No

TAKE HOME ACTIVITY • Show your child one group of 10 small objects and one group of 8 small objects. Ask your child to tell how many tens and ones there are and say the number. Repeat with other numbers from 11 to 19.

Name ______________________________

Understand Ten and Ones

Common Core — **COMMON CORE STANDARD—1.NBT.B.2b**
Understand place value.

Use the model. Write the number three different ways.

1.

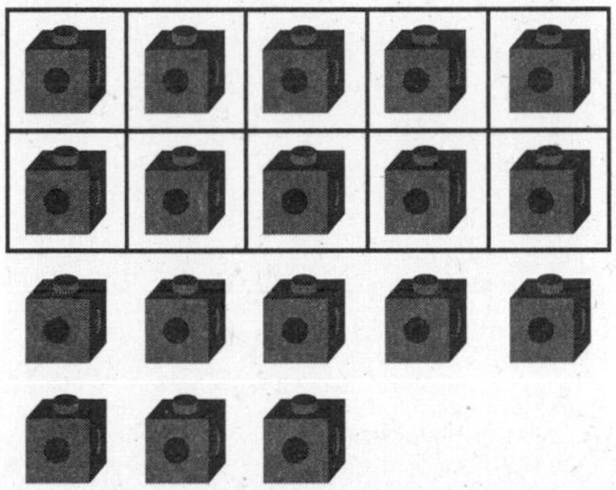

____ ten ____ ones

____ + ____

____

Problem Solving — Real World

Draw cubes to show the number.
Write the number different ways.

Rob has 7 ones. Nick has 5 ones. They put all their ones together. What number did they make?

2.

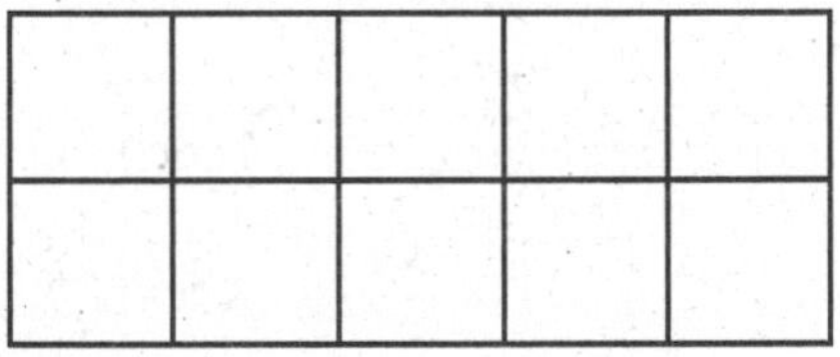

____ ten ____ ones

____ + ____

____

3. WRITE Math Show twelve in four different ways. Use words, pictures, and numbers.

____

____

____

Lesson Check (1.NBT.B.2b)

1. Use the model. Write the number three different ways.

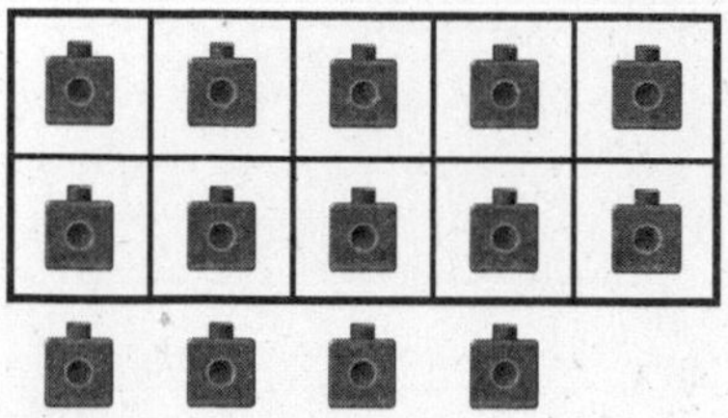

____ ten ____ ones

____ + ____ = ____

____

Spiral Review (1.OA.C.6)

2. Use the model. Write the addition sentence. What number sentence does this model show?

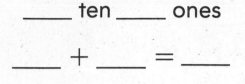

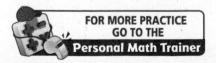

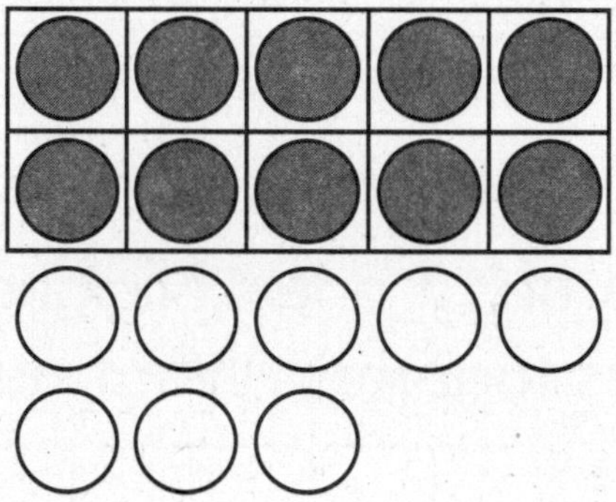

____ + ____ = ____

3. Write two subtraction facts related to $7 + 5 = 12$.

____ − ____ = ____

____ − ____ = ____

FOR MORE PRACTICE GO TO THE **Personal Math Trainer**

Name ______________________________

Make Ten and Ones

Essential Question How can you show a number as ten and ones?

Common Core **Number and Operations in Base Ten—1.NBT.B.2b**

MATHEMATICAL PRACTICES
MP2, MP3, MP4, MP6

Listen and Draw

Real World · Hands On

Use cubes to model the problem.
Draw cubes to show your work.

Draw to show the group of ten another way.

Math Talk MATHEMATICAL PRACTICES 3

Compare How are the pictures the same? How are the pictures different?

FOR THE TEACHER • Read the problem. Destiny has 10 cubes. How can she show 1 ten?

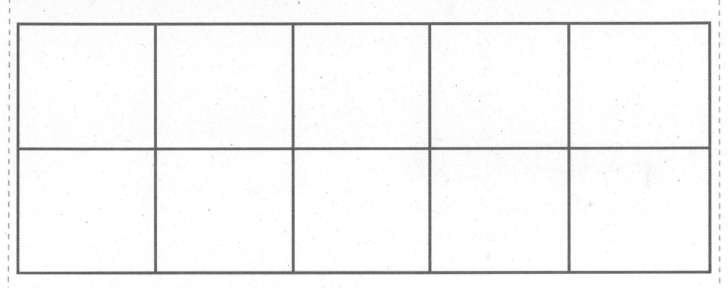

Model and Draw

You can group 10 ■ to make 1 ten.

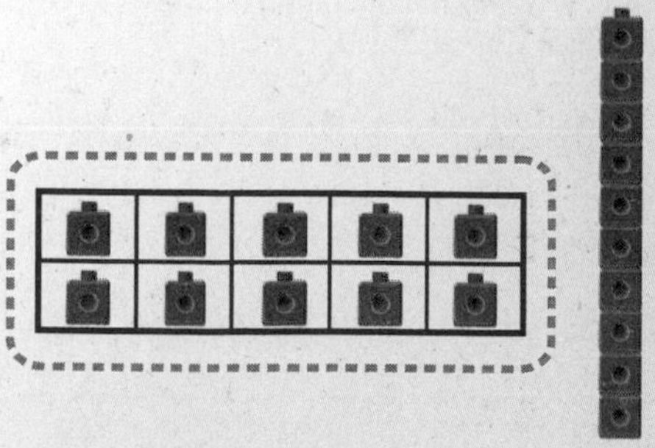

10 ones = 1 ten

Draw a quick picture to show 1 ten.

1 ten

Share and Show MATH BOARD

Use ■. Make groups of ten and ones.
Draw your work. Write how many.

1.

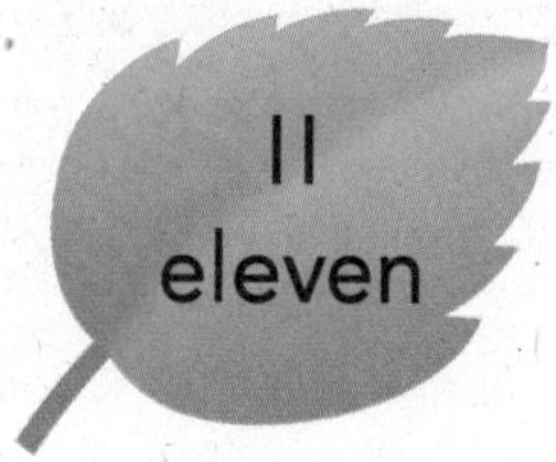

1 ten 1 one

2.

____ ten ____ ones

✔ 3.

____ ten ____ ones

✔ 4.

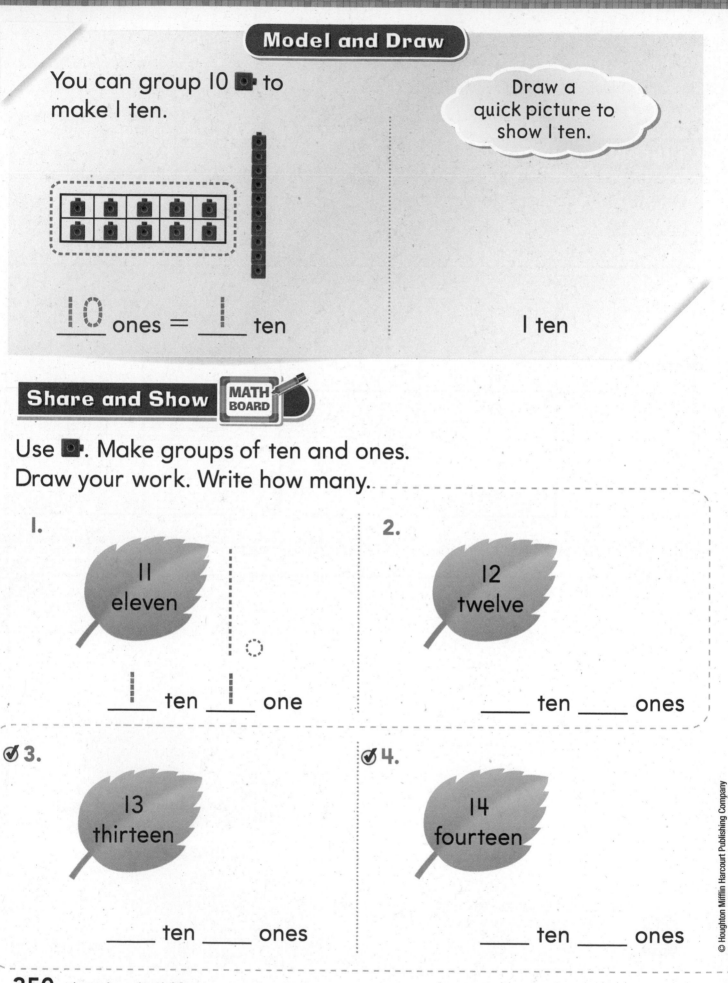

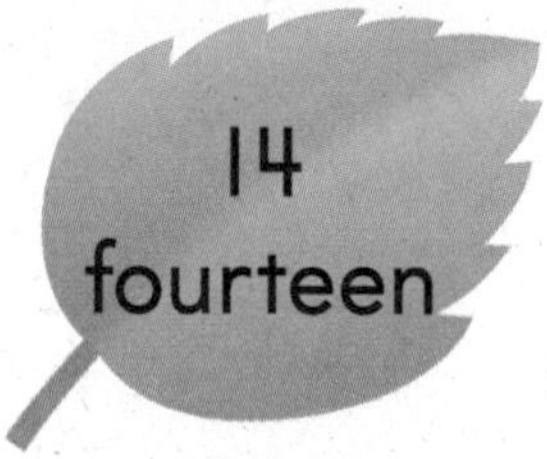

____ ten ____ ones

Name ____________________

On Your Own

MATHEMATICAL PRACTICE 6 **Compare** Use ■. Make groups of ten and ones. Draw your work. Write how many.

5. 15
fifteen

____ ten ____ ones

6. 16
sixteen

____ ten ____ ones

7. 17
seventeen

____ ten ____ ones

8. 18
eighteen

____ ten ____ ones

9. 19
nineteen

____ ten ____ ones

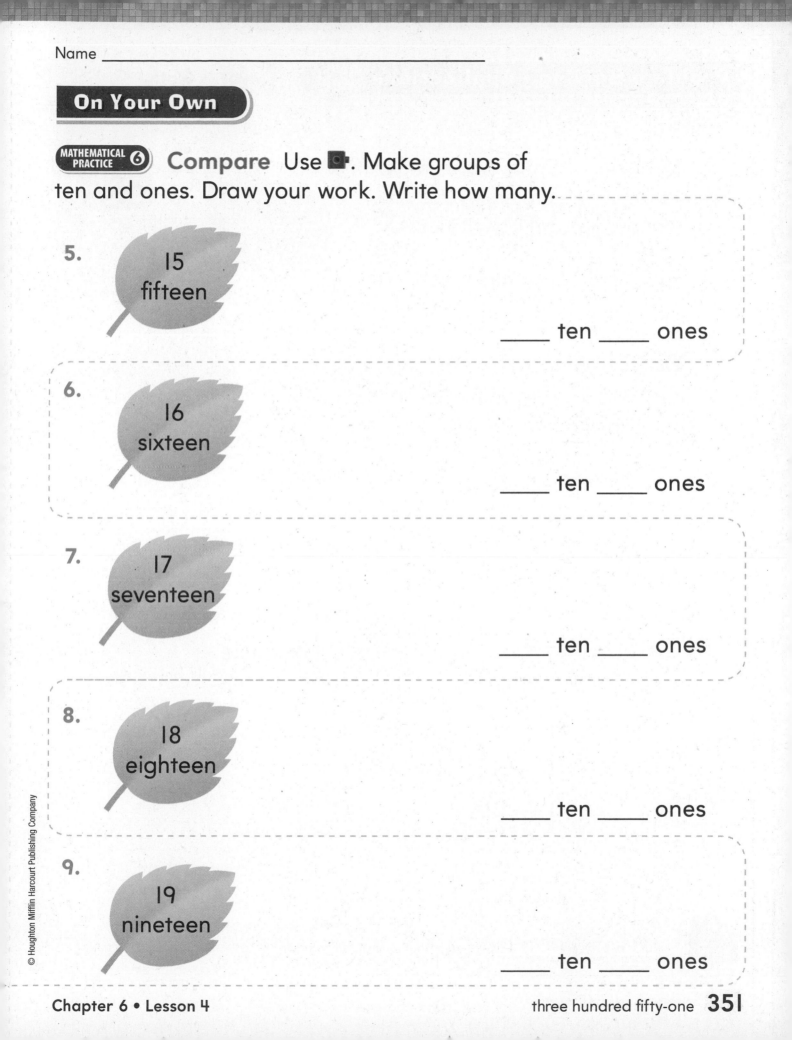

Problem Solving • Applications Real World

WRITE Math

Solve.

10. THINK SMARTER Emily wants to write ten and ones to show 20. What does Emily write?

Math on the Spot

____ ten ____ ones

11. GO DEEPER Gina thinks of a number that has 7 ones and 1 ten. What is the number? Draw to show your work.

____

12. Ben drew this picture to show a number. What is the number?

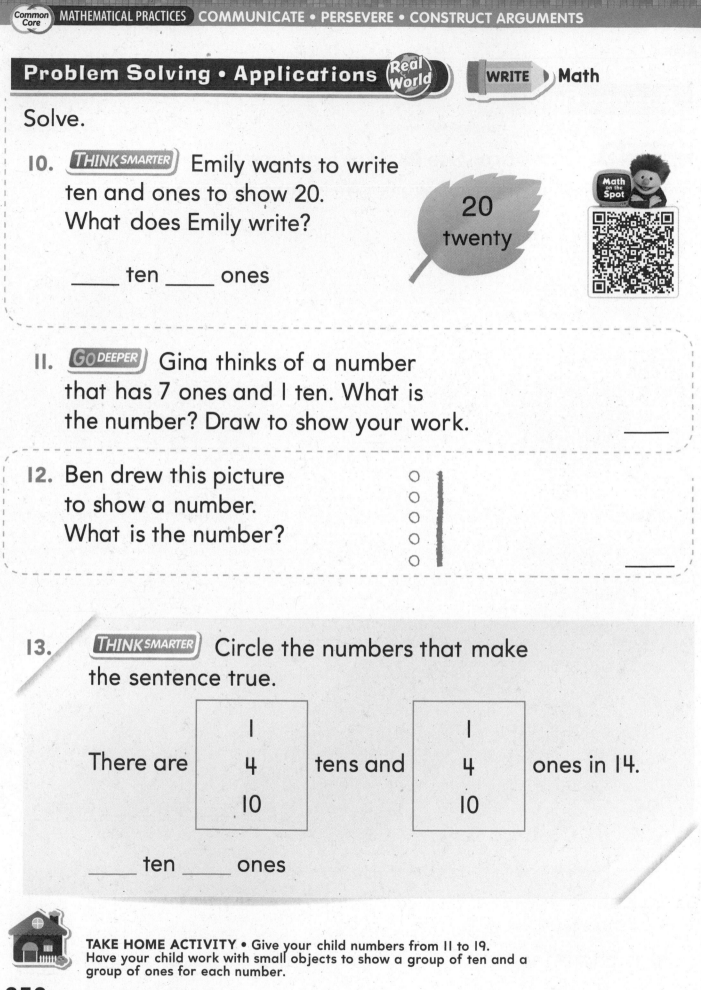

____

13. THINK SMARTER Circle the numbers that make the sentence true.

There are [1 / 4 / 10] tens and [1 / 4 / 10] ones in 14.

____ ten ____ ones

TAKE HOME ACTIVITY • Give your child numbers from 11 to 19. Have your child work with small objects to show a group of ten and a group of ones for each number.

Name ______________________________

Make Ten and Ones

COMMON CORE STANDARD—1.NBT.B.2b
Understand place value.

Use [cube]. Make groups of ten and ones. Draw your work. Write how many.

1. 14
fourteen

____ ten ____ ones

2. 12
twelve

____ ten ____ ones

3. 15
fifteen

____ ten ____ ones

4. 18
eighteen

____ ten ____ ones

Problem Solving (Real World)

Solve.

5. Tina thinks of a number that has 3 ones and 1 ten. What is the number? ____

6. WRITE Math Choose a number from 11 to 19. Write the number and number word. Use words and pictures to show how many tens and ones.

Lesson Check (1.NBT.B.2b)

1. How many tens and ones make 17? Write the numbers.

____ ten ____ ones

Spiral Review (1.OA.A.1, 1.OA.C.6)

2. Use the model. Write the addition sentence. What number sentence does this model show?

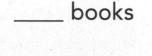

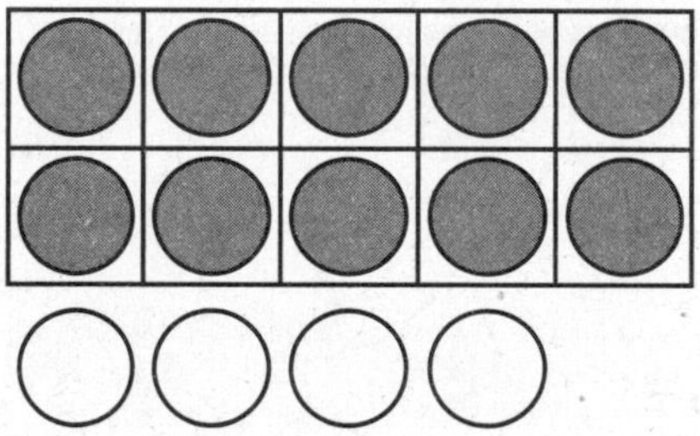

____ + ____ = ____

3. Choose a way to solve. Draw or write to explain. Ben has 17 books. He gives some away. He has 8 left. How many books does he give away?

____ books

FOR MORE PRACTICE GO TO THE Personal Math Trainer

Name ______________________________

Tens

Essential Question How can you model and name groups of ten?

Common Core **Number and Operations in Base Ten—1.NBT.B.2a, 1.NBT.B.2c**
MATHEMATICAL PRACTICES MP4, MP7, MP8

Listen and Draw Real World Hands On

Use ■ to solve the riddle.
Draw and write to show your work.

Math Talk MATHEMATICAL PRACTICES 7

Look for Structure What did you do to solve the first riddle?

FOR THE TEACHER • Read the following riddles. I am thinking of a number that is the same as 1 ten and 4 ones. What is my number? I am thinking of a number that is the same as 1 ten and 0 ones. What is my number?

Model and Draw

You can group ones to make tens.

Draw a quick picture to show the tens.

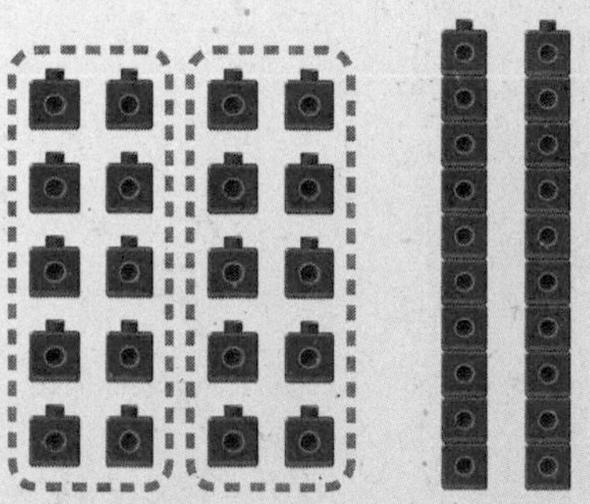

20 ones = 2 tens 0 ones

2 tens = 20
twenty

Share and Show

MATH BOARD

Use ■. Make groups of ten.
Write the tens and ones.

Draw the tens.
Count by tens.

1. 

30 ones = ____ tens ____ ones

____ tens = ____
thirty

2. 

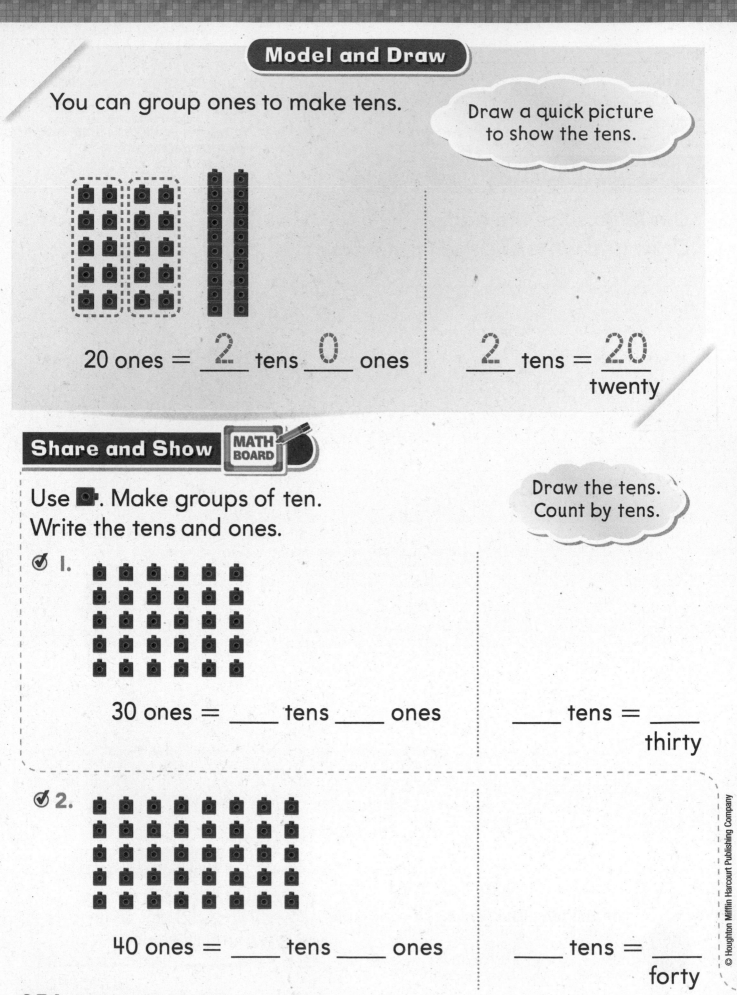

40 ones = ____ tens ____ ones

____ tens = ____
forty

Name ______________________________

On Your Own

Draw the tens.
Count by tens.

MATHEMATICAL PRACTICE 8 **Use Repeated Reasoning**

Use ■. Make groups of ten. Write the tens and ones.

3. 50 ones

____ tens ____ ones

____ tens = ____ fifty

4. 60 ones

____ tens ____ ones

____ tens = ____ sixty

5. 70 ones

____ tens ____ ones

____ tens = ____ seventy

6. 80 ones

____ tens ____ ones

____ tens = ____ eighty

7. 90 ones

____ tens ____ ones

____ tens = ____ ninety

8. THINK SMARTER 100 ones

Math on the Spot

____ tens ____ ones

____ tens = ____ hundred

Name ______________________________

✓ Mid-Chapter Checkpoint

Personal Math Trainer
Online Assessment and Intervention

Concepts and Skills

Use a Counting Chart. Count forward. Write the numbers. (1.NBT.A.1)

1. 63, 64, ____, ____, ____
2. 108, 109, ____, ____, ____

Use a Counting Chart. Count by tens. Write the numbers. (1.NBT.A.1)

3. 42, 52, ____, ____, ____
4. 79, 89, ____, ____, ____

5. Use the model. Write the number three different ways. (1.NBT.B.2b)

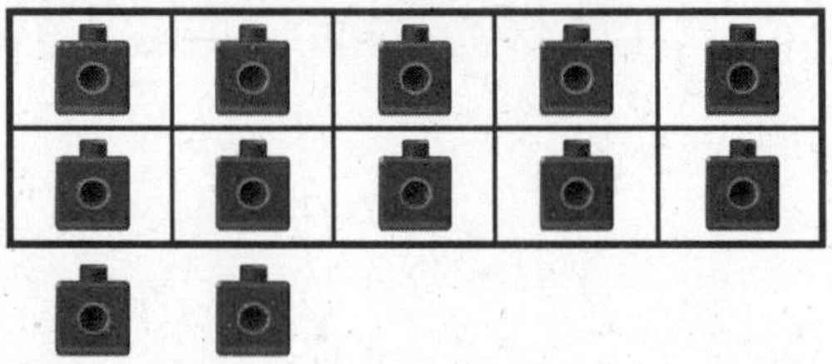

____ ten ____ ones

____ + ____

____

Use ▪. Make groups of ten and ones. Draw your work. Write how many. (1.NBT.B.2b)

6.

____ ten ____ ones

7. THINK SMARTER Choose all the ways that name the model.

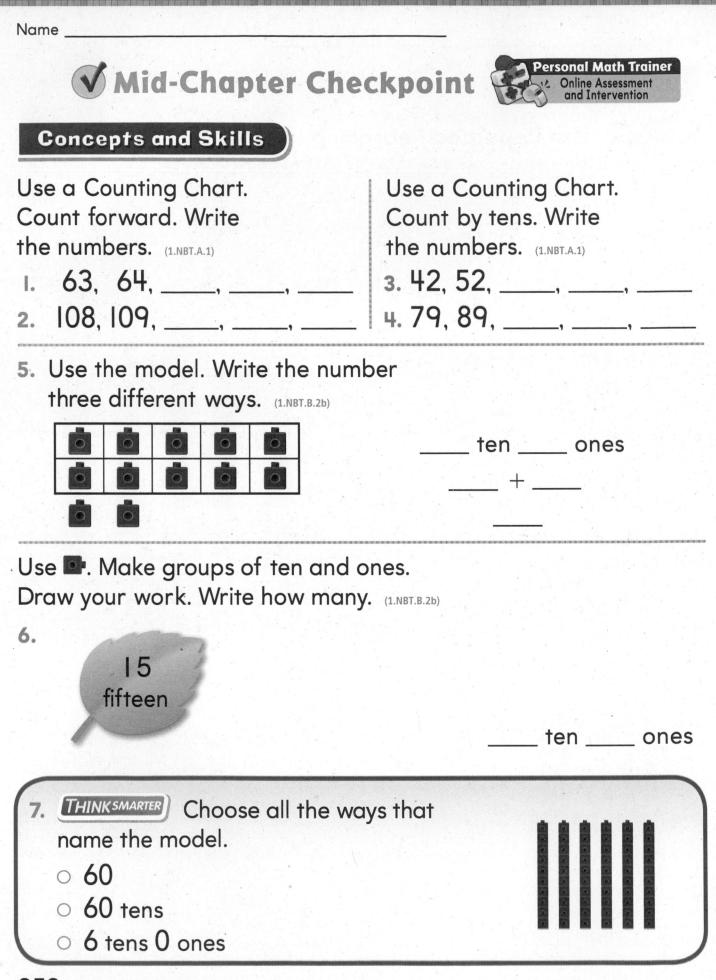

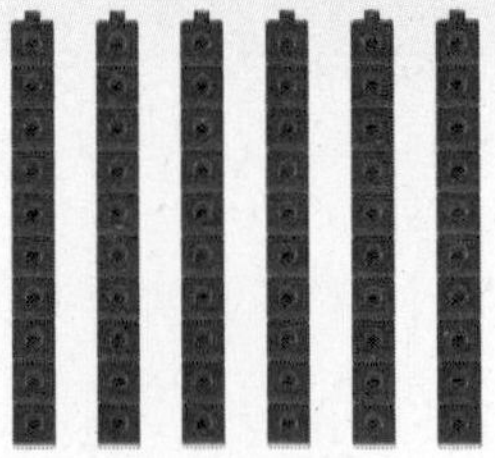

○ 60
○ 60 tens
○ 6 tens 0 ones

Name ____________________

Tens

COMMON CORE STANDARDS—1.NBT.B.2a, 1.NBT.B.2c
Understand place value.

Use ▢. Make groups of ten. Write the tens and ones.

1. 90 ones

____ tens = ____ ones

____ tens = ____ ninety

2. 50 ones

____ tens = ____ ones

____ tens = ____ fifty

3. 40 ones

____ tens = ____ ones

____ tens = ____ forty

Problem Solving Real World

Look at the model. Write the number.

4. What number does the model show?

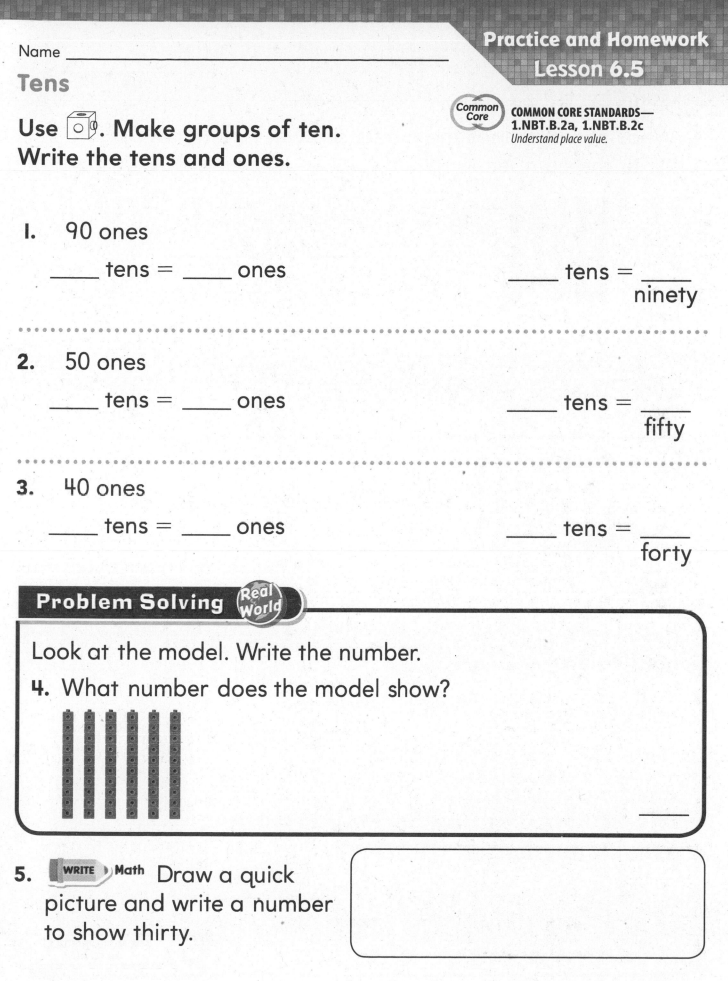

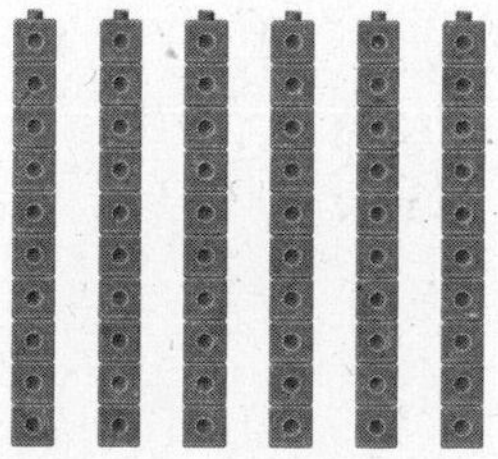

____

5. WRITE Math Draw a quick picture and write a number to show thirty.

Lesson Check (1.NBT.B.2a, 1.NBT.B.2c)

1. What number does the model show?
Write the number.

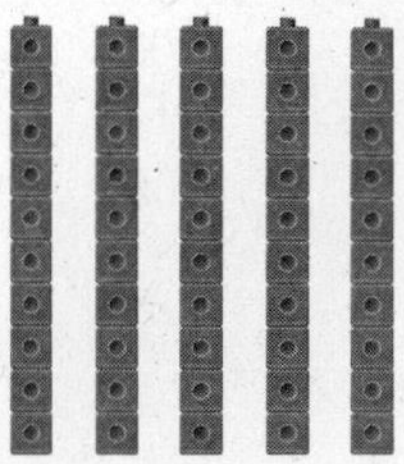

____ tens = ____

2. What number does the model show?
Write the number.

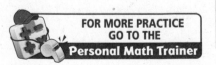

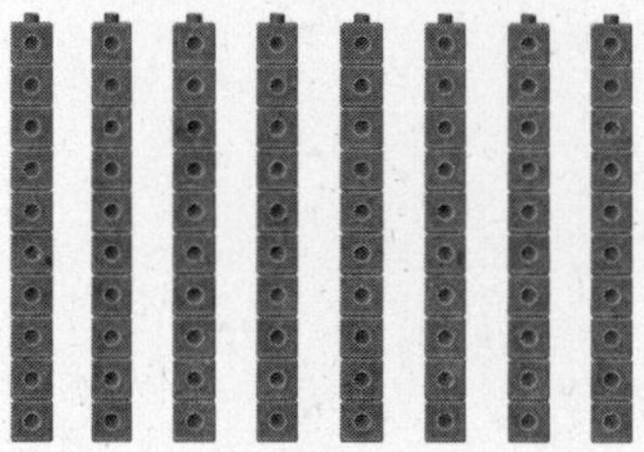

____ tens = ____

Spiral Review (1.OA.B.3, 1.OA.D.8)

3. Write the missing number.

$$6 + \square = 13$$

4. What is the sum for 3 + 3 + 4?

____

FOR MORE PRACTICE GO TO THE Personal Math Trainer

Name ________________________________

Tens and Ones to 50

HANDS ON
Lesson 6.6

Essential Question How can you group cubes to show a number as tens and ones?

Common Core **Number and Operations in Base Ten—1.NBT.B.2**
MATHEMATICAL PRACTICES
MP4, MP5, MP6

Listen and Draw

Hands On

Use ▪ to model the number.
Draw ▪ to show your work.

Tens	Ones

Math Talk MATHEMATICAL PRACTICES 4

Model How did you figure out how many tens and ones are in 23?

FOR THE TEACHER • Ask children to use 23 cubes and show them as tens and ones.

Model and Draw

The 2 in 24 means 2 tens.

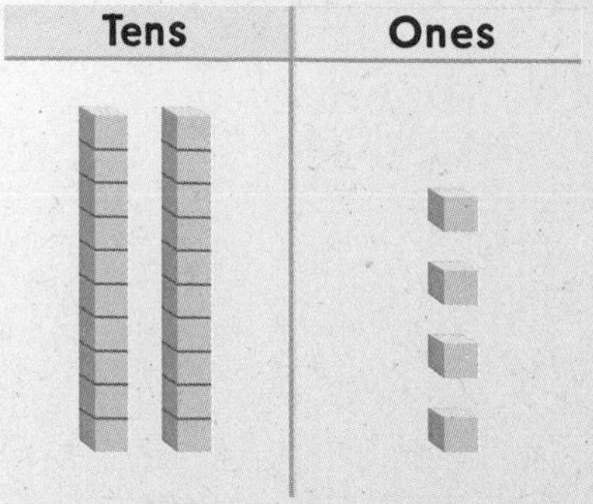

2 tens 4 ones = 24

The 2 in 42 means 2 ones.

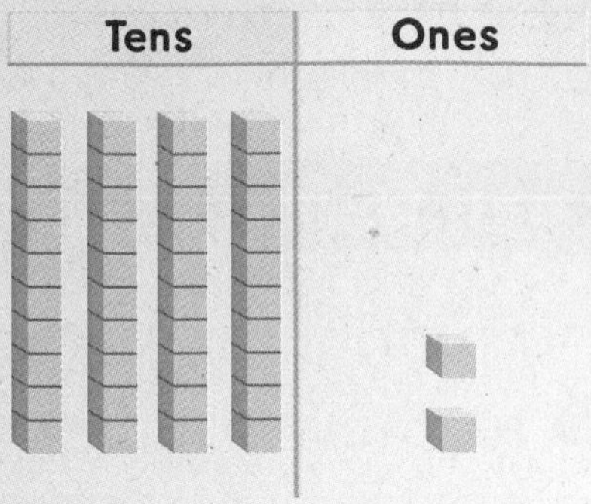

4 tens 2 ones = 42

Share and Show MATH BOARD

Use your MathBoard and  to show the tens and ones. Write the numbers.

1.

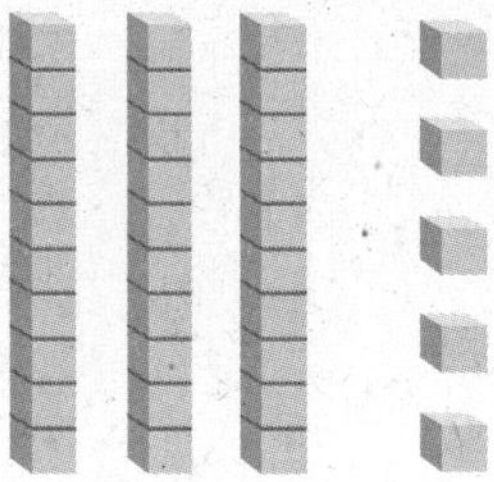

_____ tens _____ ones = _____

2.

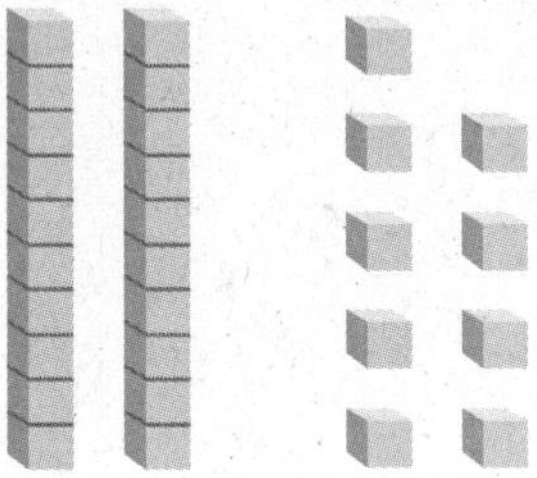

_____ tens _____ ones = _____

✓3.

_____ tens _____ ones = _____

✓4.

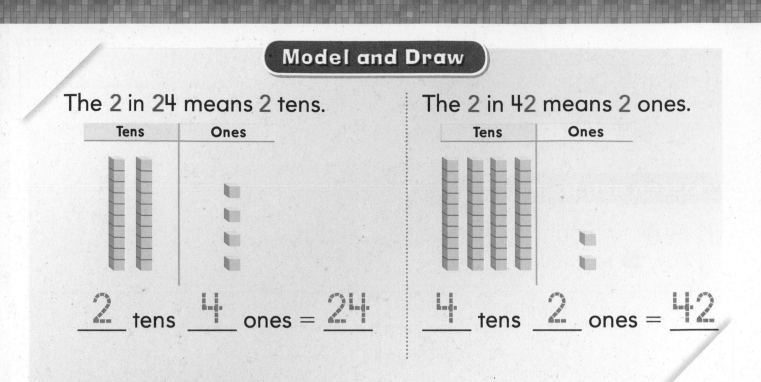

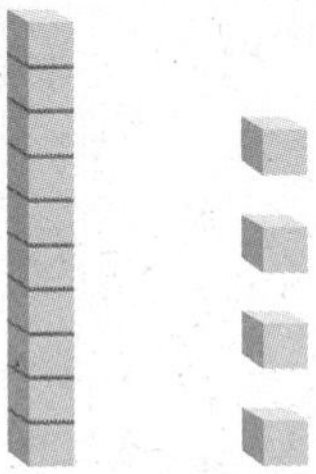

_____ ten _____ ones = _____

Name ______________________

On Your Own

MATHEMATICAL PRACTICE 6 **Make Connections**

Write the numbers.

5. 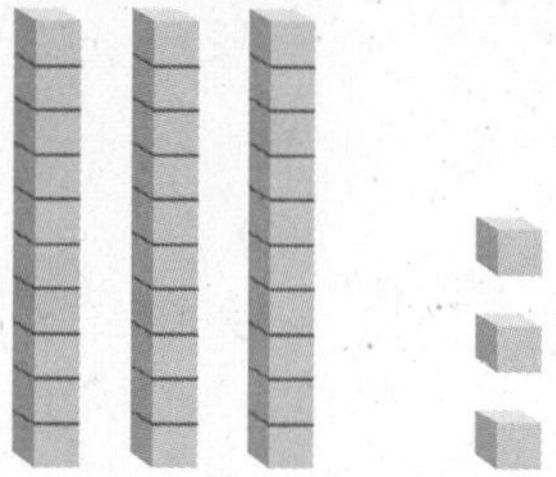

____ tens ____ ones = ____

6. 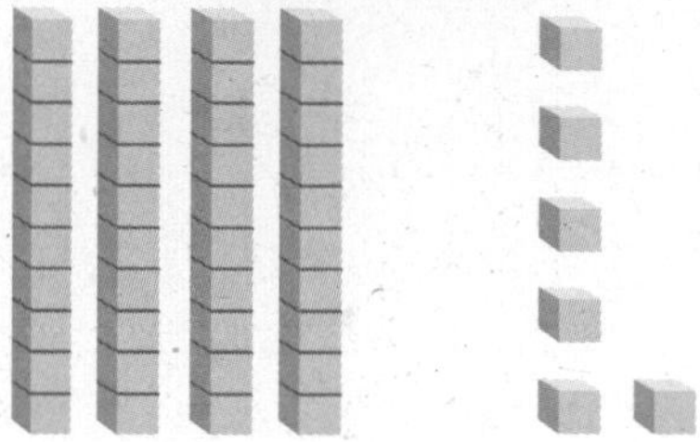

____ tens ____ ones = ____

7. 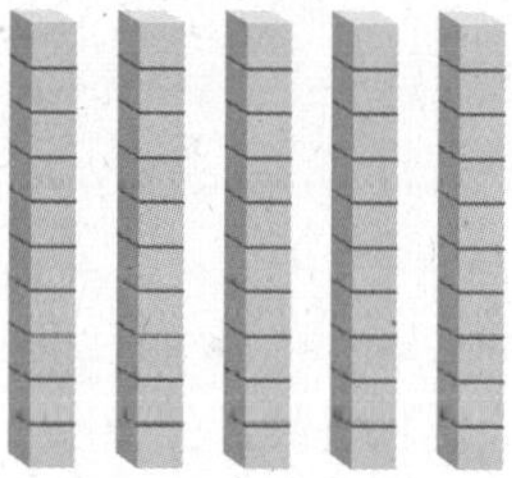

____ tens ____ ones = ____

8. 

____ tens ____ ones = ____

9. GO DEEPER Mary drew tens and ones to show 32.
She made a mistake.
Draw a correct quick picture to show 32.
Write the numbers.

Tens	Ones

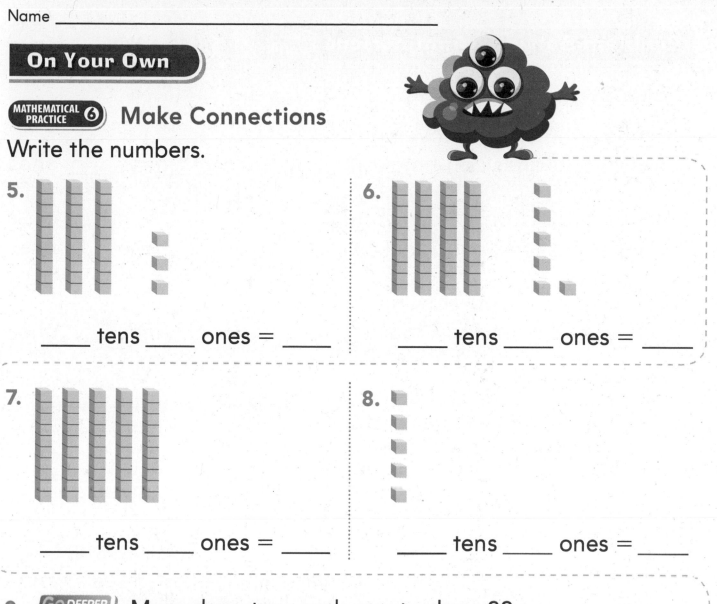

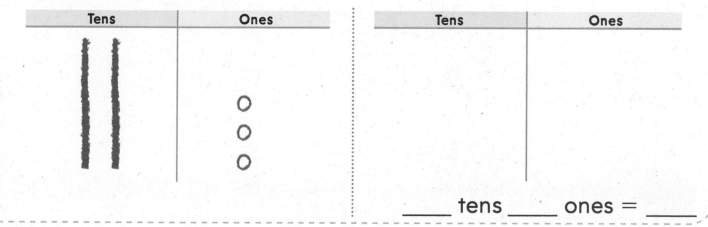

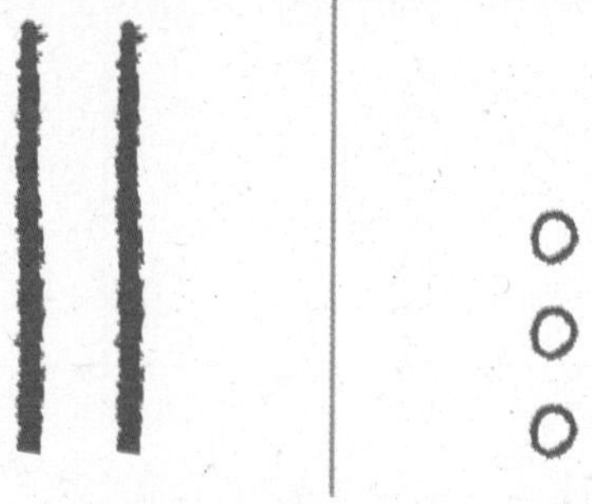

Tens	Ones

____ tens ____ ones = ____

Problem Solving • Applications Real World WRITE Math

Solve. Write the numbers.

10. I have 46 cubes. How many tens and ones can I make? _____ tens _____ ones

11. I have 32 cubes. How many tens and ones can I make? _____ tens _____ ones

12. I have 28 cubes. How many tens and ones can I make? _____ tens _____ ones

13. **THINK SMARTER** I am a number less than 50. I have 8 ones and some tens. What numbers could I be?

14. **THINK SMARTER +** There are 35 ▪. Jun says that there are 3 ones and 5 tens. Rob says that there are 3 tens and 5 ones. Who is correct? Circle the name.

Jun Rob

How can you draw to show 35?

🏠 **TAKE HOME ACTIVITY** • Write a two-digit number from 20 to 50, such as 26. Ask your child to tell which digit names the tens and which digit names the ones. Repeat with different numbers.

Name ______________________________

Tens and Ones to 50

Practice and Homework
Lesson 6.6

COMMON CORE STANDARDS—1.NBT.B.2
Understand place value.

Write the numbers.

1.

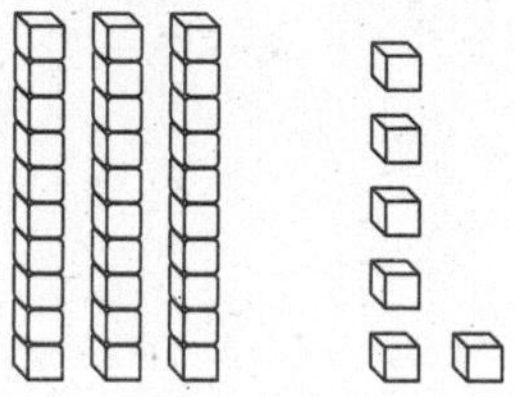

____ tens ____ ones = ____

2.

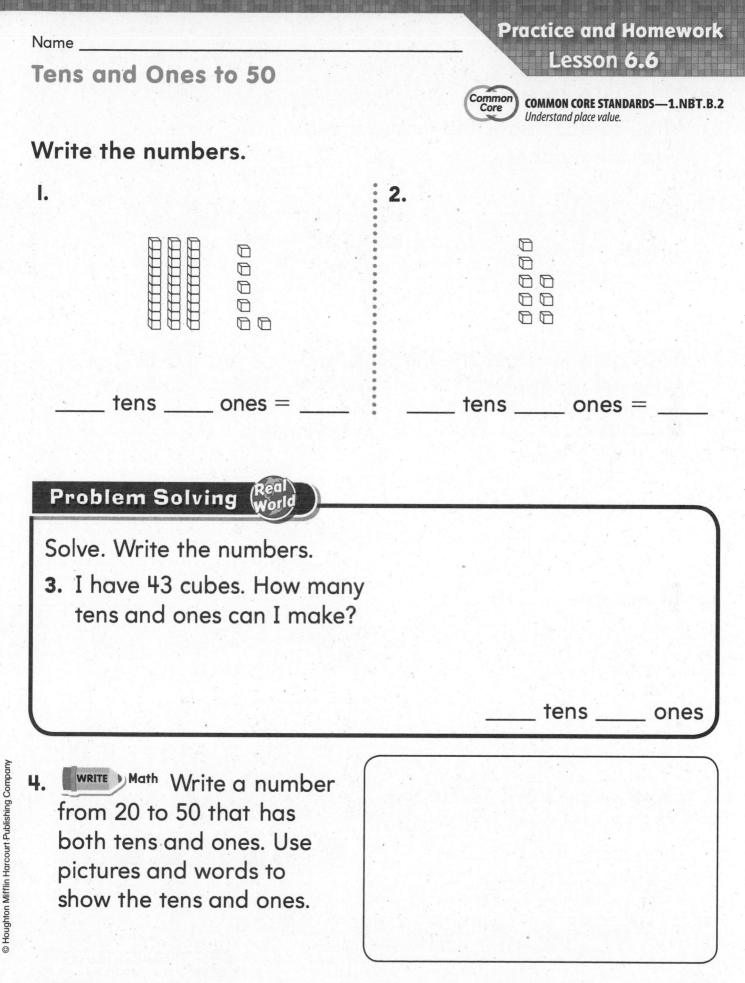

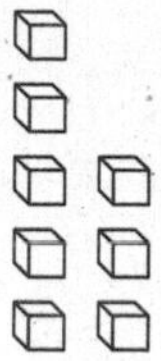

____ tens ____ ones = ____

Problem Solving Real World

Solve. Write the numbers.

3. I have 43 cubes. How many tens and ones can I make?

____ tens ____ ones

4. WRITE Math Write a number from 20 to 50 that has both tens and ones. Use pictures and words to show the tens and ones.

Lesson Check (1.NBT.B.2)

1. What number does the model show?
Write the numbers.

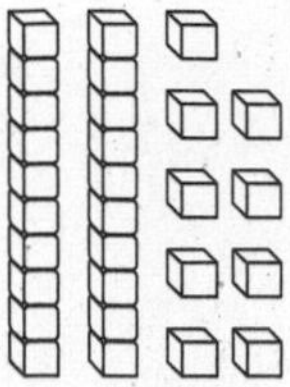

____ tens ____ ones = ____

2. What number does the model show?
Write the numbers.

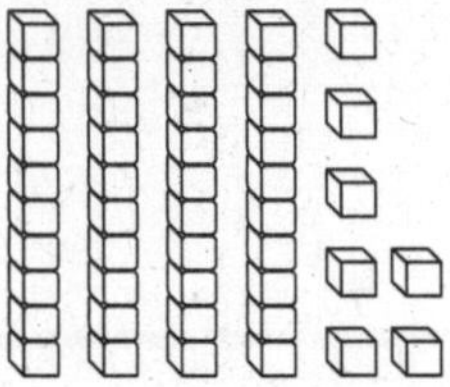

____ tens ____ ones = ____

Spiral Review (1.OA.A.1, 1.OA.C.6)

3. Write the sum.

$$\begin{array}{r} 6 \\ +\ 3 \\ \hline \end{array}$$

4. Show taking from. Circle the part you take from the group. Then cross it out.
Write the difference.

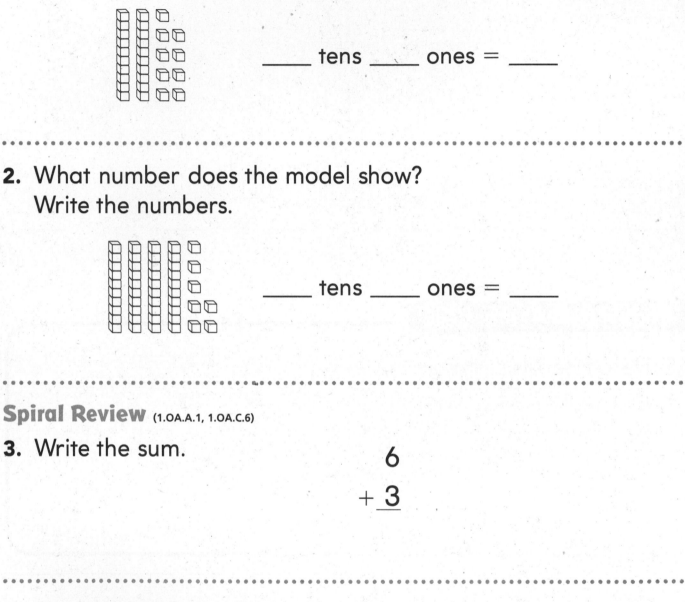

$6 - 4 =$ ____

FOR MORE PRACTICE GO TO THE
Personal Math Trainer

Name ______________________________

HANDS ON
Lesson 6.7

Tens and Ones to 100

Essential Question How can you show numbers to 100 as tens and ones?

Common Core **Number and Operations in Base Ten—1.NBT.B.2**
MATHEMATICAL PRACTICES
MP.2, MP.4, MP.6

Listen and Draw

Use [tens block] [ones block] to model the number.
Draw a quick picture to show your work.

25

50

52

Math Talk MATHEMATICAL PRACTICES 2

Reasoning How did you figure out how many tens and ones are in 52?

FOR THE TEACHER • Ask children to use base-ten blocks to show how many tens and ones there are in 25, 50, and 52.

Model and Draw

The number just after 99 is 100.
10 tens is the same as 1 **hundred**.

Draw quick pictures to show 99 and 100.

9 tens 9 ones = 99

10 tens 0 ones = 100

Share and Show

MATH BOARD

Use your MathBoard and  to show the tens and ones. Write the numbers.

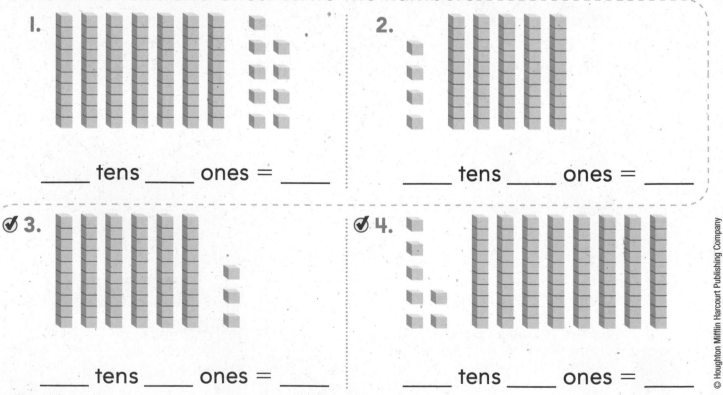

1. 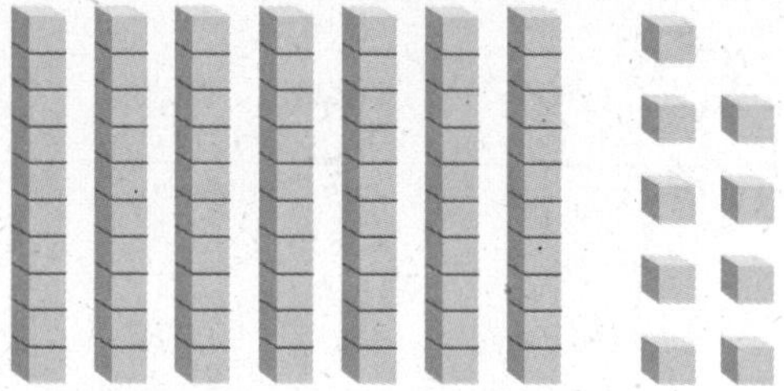

____ tens ____ ones = ____

2. 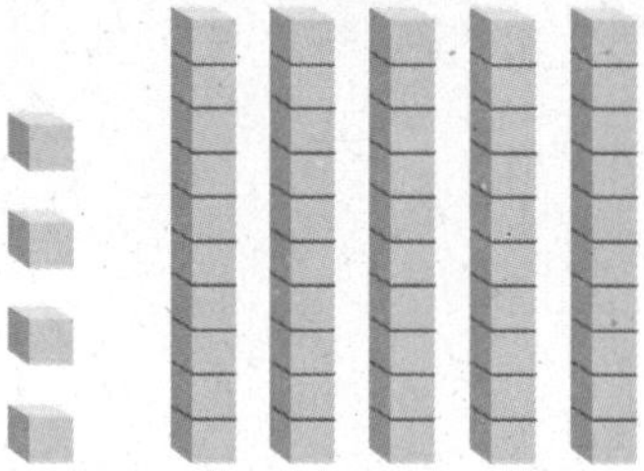

____ tens ____ ones = ____

✓ 3. 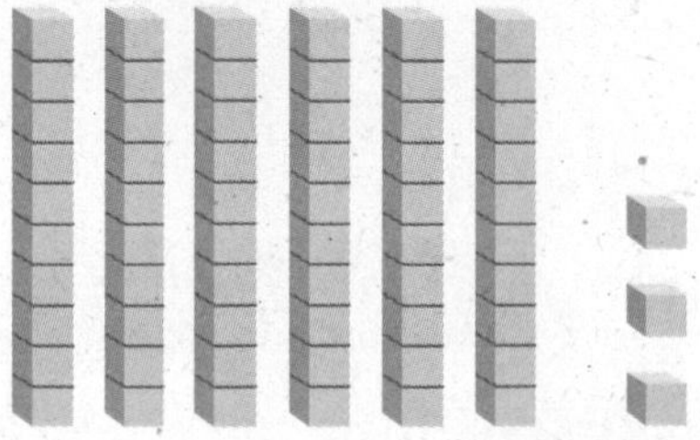

____ tens ____ ones = ____

✓ 4. 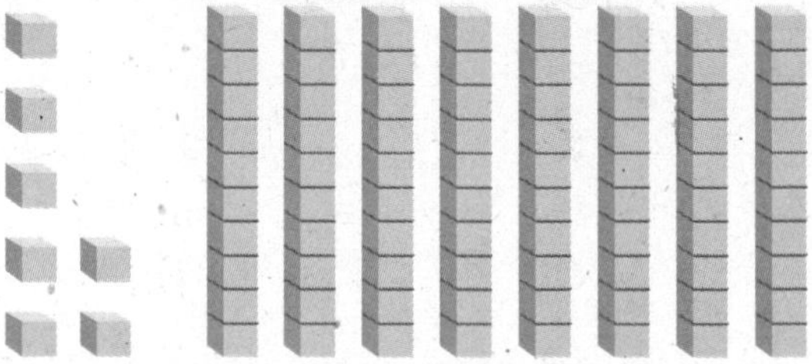

____ tens ____ ones = ____

Name ____________________

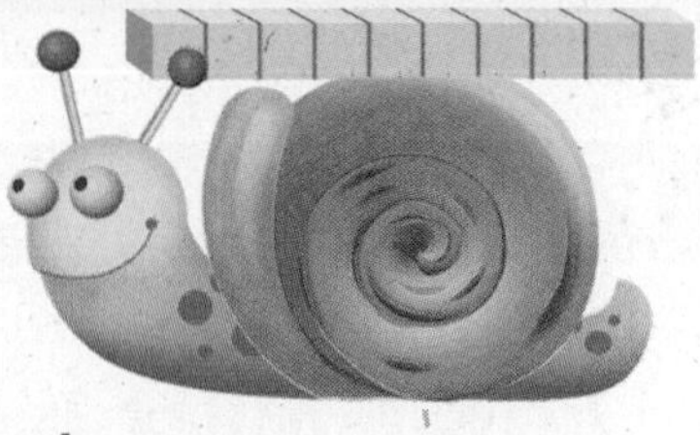

On Your Own

MATHEMATICAL PRACTICE 2 **Reason Quantitatively** Write the numbers.

5. 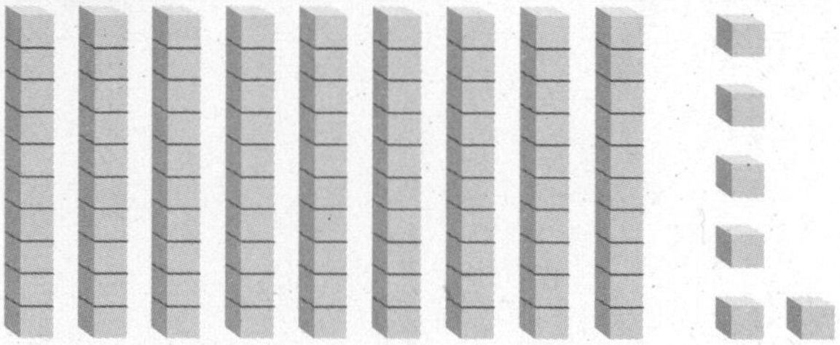

____ tens ____ ones = ____

6. 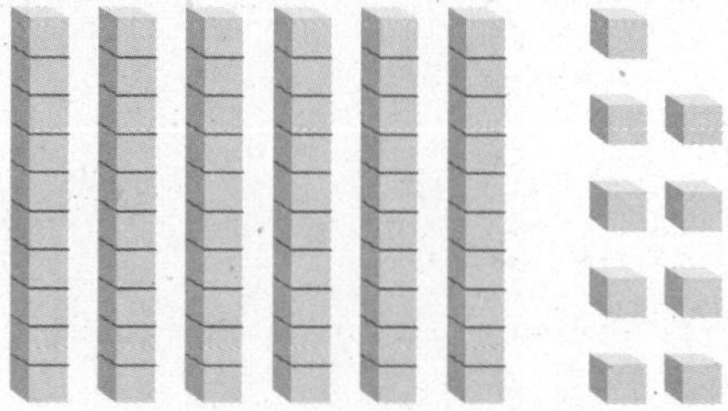

____ tens ____ ones = ____

7. 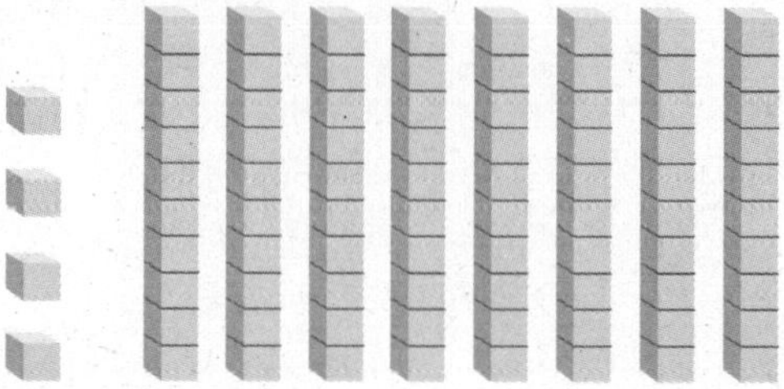

____ tens ____ ones = ____

8. 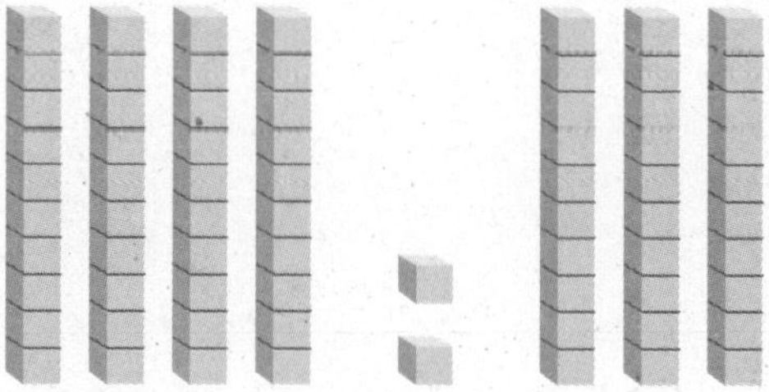

____ tens ____ ones = ____

9. 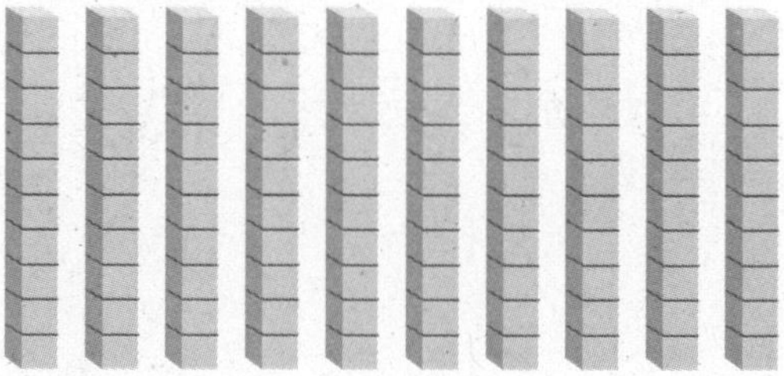

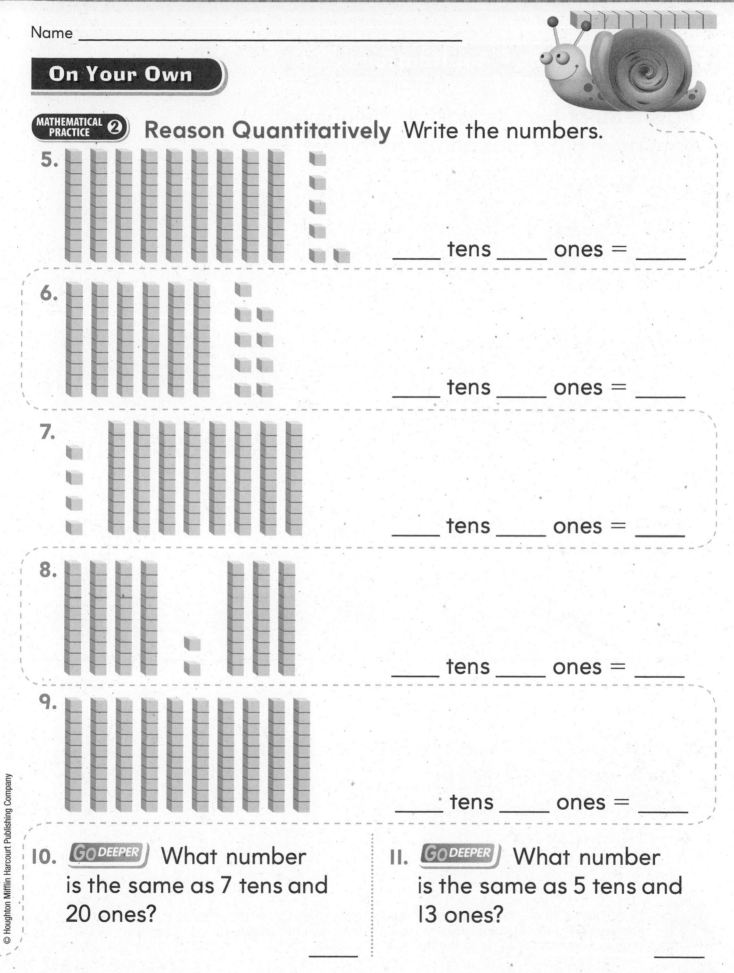

____ tens ____ ones = ____

10. GO DEEPER What number is the same as 7 tens and 20 ones?

____

11. GO DEEPER What number is the same as 5 tens and 13 ones?

____

Problem Solving • Applications Real World

WRITE Math

Draw a quick picture to show the number.
Write how many tens and ones there are.

12. Edna has 82 stamps.

____ tens ____ ones

13. Amy has 79 beads.

____ tens ____ ones

14. THINKSMARTER Moe has a group of 70 red feathers and 30 brown feathers.

Math on the Spot

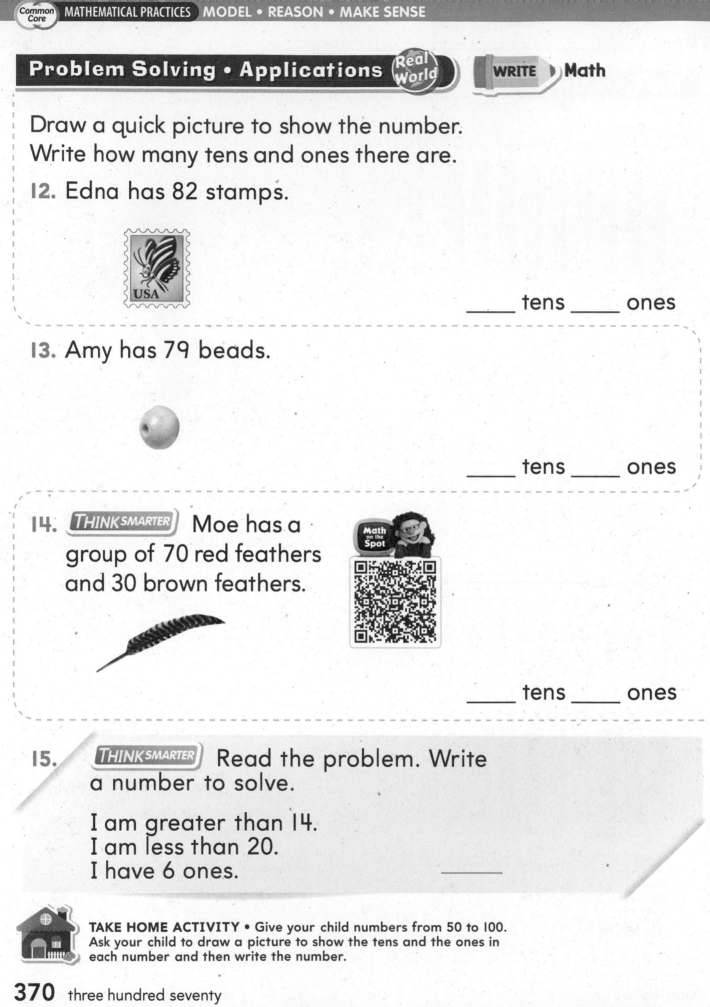

____ tens ____ ones

15. THINKSMARTER Read the problem. Write a number to solve.

I am greater than 14.
I am less than 20.
I have 6 ones. ______

TAKE HOME ACTIVITY • Give your child numbers from 50 to 100. Ask your child to draw a picture to show the tens and the ones in each number and then write the number.

Name ____________________

Tens and Ones to 100

Common Core — **COMMON CORE STANDARDS—1.NBT.B.2**
Understand place value.

Write the numbers.

1. 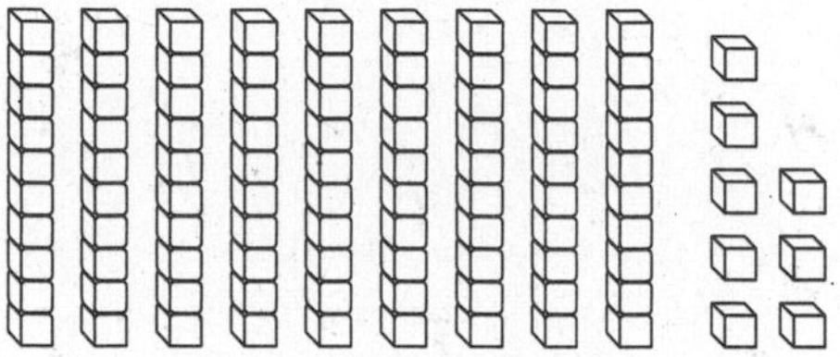

____ tens ____ ones = ____

2. 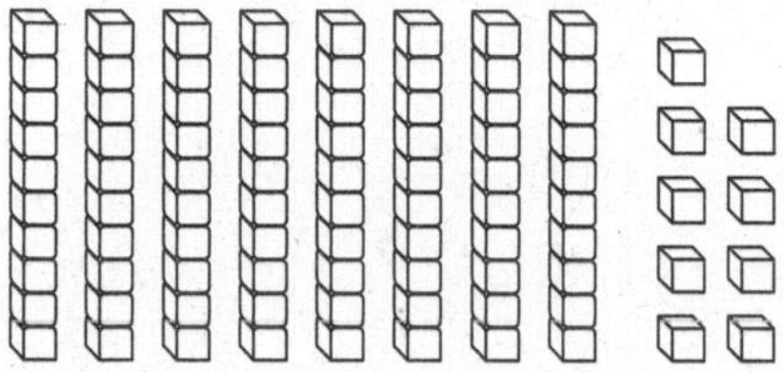

____ tens ____ ones = ____

3. 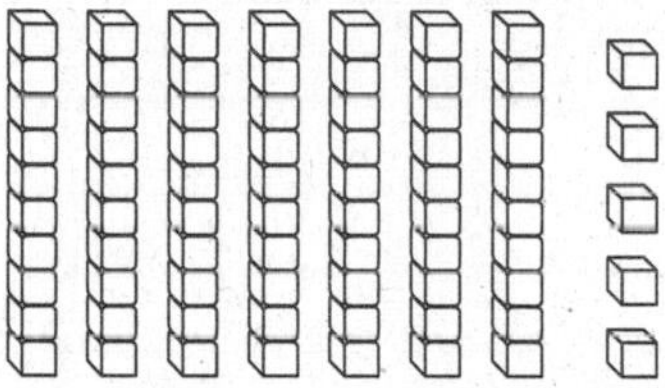

____ tens ____ ones = ____

Problem Solving — Real World

Draw a quick picture to show the number.
Write how many tens and ones there are.

4. Inez has 57 shells.

____ tens ____ ones

5. WRITE Math Use words and pictures to show 59 and 95.

Lesson Check (1.NBT.B.2)

1. What number has 10 tens 0 ones?

____

2. What number does the model show? Write the numbers.

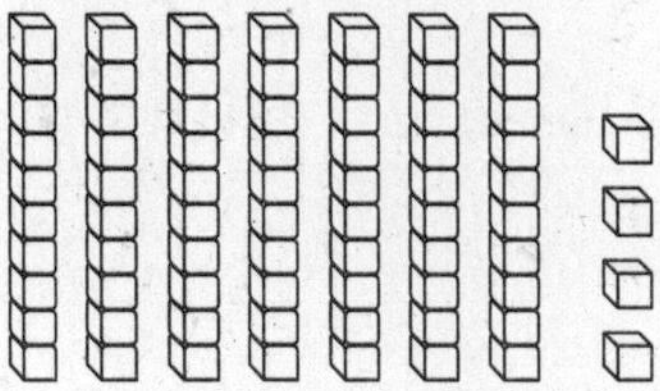

____ tens ____ ones = ____

Spiral Review (1.OA.B.3, 1.OA.C.5)

3. Barry knows that 6 + 5 = 11. What other addition fact does he know? Write the new fact.

____ + ____ = ____

4. Count on to solve 2 + 6. Write the sum.

2 + 6 = ____

Name ______________________

Problem Solving • Show Numbers in Different Ways

Essential Question How can making a model help you show a number in different ways?

Common Core Number and Operations in Base Ten—1.NBT.B.2a, 1.NBT.B.3
MATHEMATICAL PRACTICES
MP1, MP4, MP6, MP7

Gary and Jill both want 23 stickers for a class project. There are 3 sheets of 10 stickers and 30 single stickers on the table. How could Gary and Jill each take 23 stickers?

Unlock the Problem Real World

What do I need to find?

two different ways to make a number

What information do I need to use?

The number is 23.

Show how to solve the problem.

Gary

Tens	Ones

23

=

Jill

Tens	Ones

23

HOME CONNECTION • Showing the number with base-ten blocks helps your child explore different ways to combine tens and ones.

Try Another Problem

Use ▭▭▭ ▪ to show the number two different ways. Draw both ways.

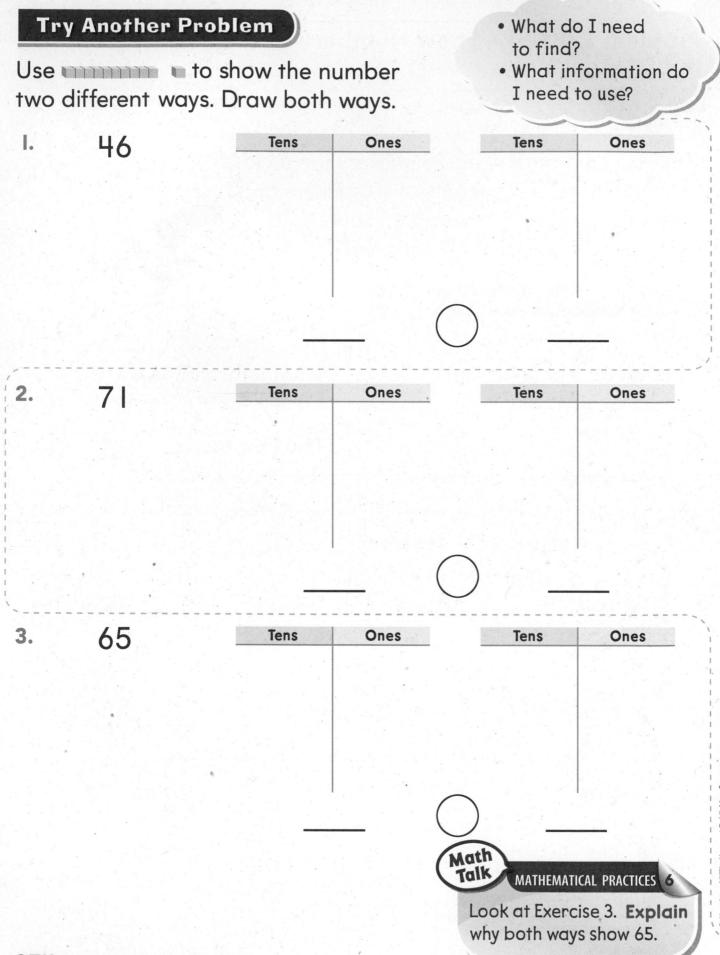

> • What do I need to find?
> • What information do I need to use?

1. 46

Tens	Ones

Tens	Ones

_____ ◯ _____

2. 71

Tens	Ones

Tens	Ones

_____ ◯ _____

3. 65

Tens	Ones

Tens	Ones

_____ ◯ _____

Math Talk

MATHEMATICAL PRACTICES 6

Look at Exercise 3. **Explain** why both ways show 65.

Name ______________________________

Share and Show MATH BOARD

Use ▭ ▪ to show the number two different ways. Draw both ways.

4. 59

Tens	Ones

Tens	Ones

_____ ◯ _____

5. 34

Tens	Ones

Tens	Ones

_____ ◯ _____

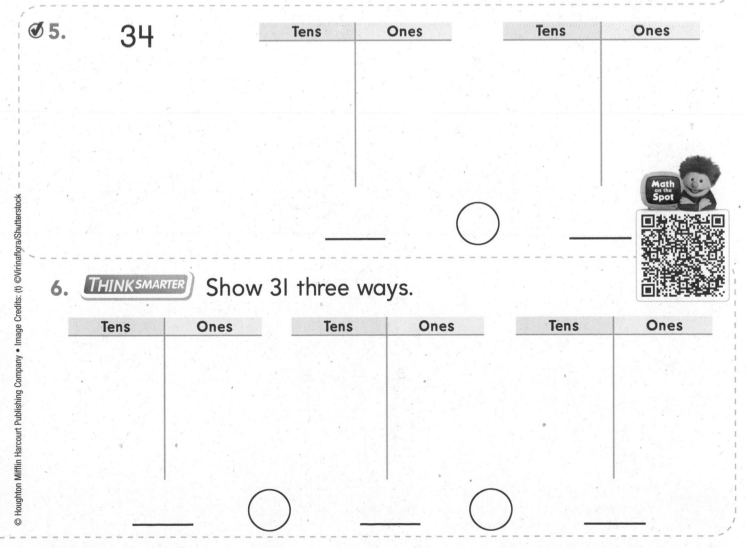

6. THINKSMARTER Show 31 three ways.

Tens	Ones

Tens	Ones

Tens	Ones

_____ ◯ _____ ◯ _____

On Your Own

WRITE Math

Write a number sentence to solve. Draw to explain.

7. MATHEMATICAL PRACTICE 4 **Write an Equation**
Felix invites 15 friends to his party. Some friends are girls. 8 friends are boys. How many friends are girls?

____ ○ ____ ○ ____ girls

GO DEEPER Solve. Write the numbers.

8. I am a number less than 35.
I have 3 tens and some ones.
What numbers can I be?

____

Personal Math Trainer

9. THINK SMARTER + Choose all the ways that show the same number.

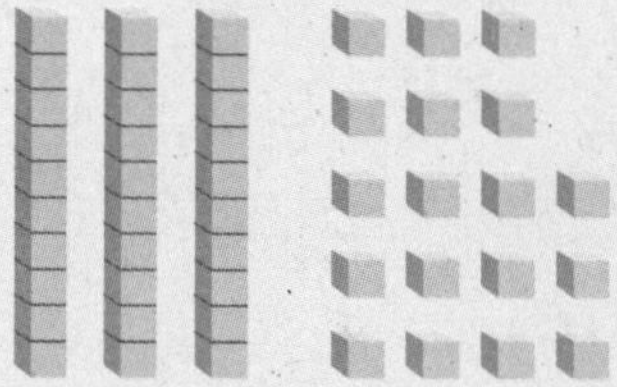

○ 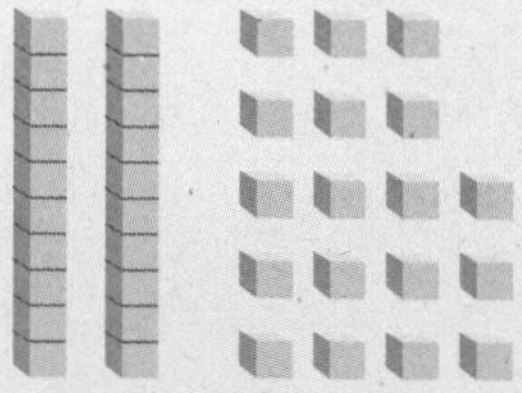

○ 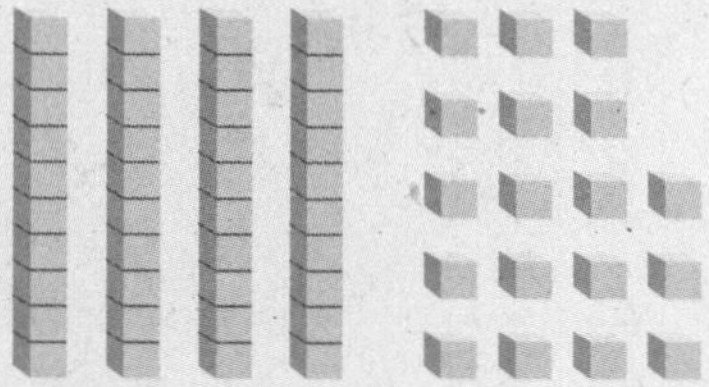

○ 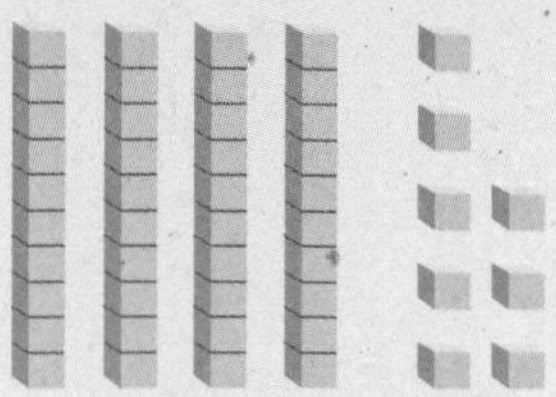

○ 

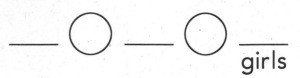

TAKE HOME ACTIVITY • Have your child draw quick pictures to show the number 56 two ways.

Name ______________________

Problem Solving • Show Numbers in Different Ways

COMMON CORE STANDARDS—1.NBT.B.2a, 1.NBT.B.3 *Understand place value.*

Use [tens rod] [ones cube] to show the number two different ways. Draw both ways.

1. 62

Tens	Ones

Tens	Ones

_____ ◯ _____

2. 38

Tens	Ones

Tens	Ones

_____ ◯ _____

3. WRITE Math Draw to show 55 three different ways.

Lesson Check (1.NBT.B.2a, 1.NBT.B.3)

1. What number does each model show? Write the numbers.

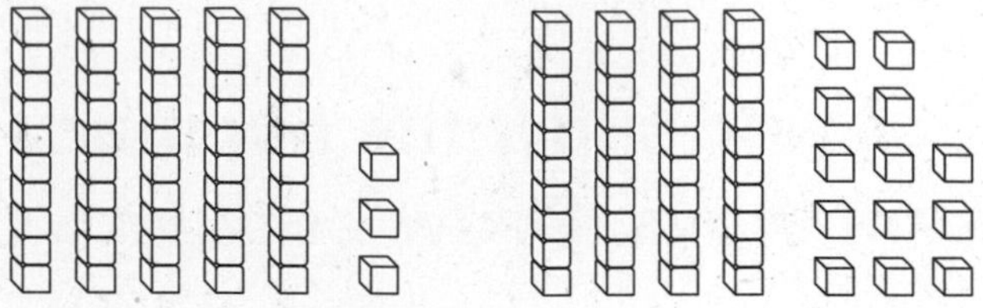

_____ = _____

2. What number does the model show? Write the number.

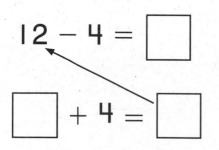

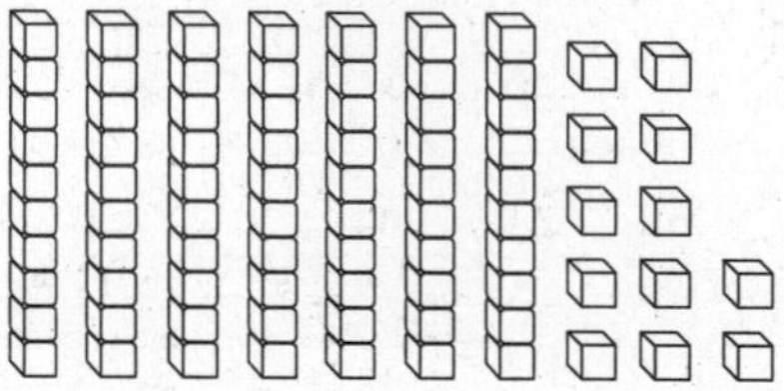

_____

Spiral Review (1.OA.C.6)

3. Subtract to solve. Then add to check your answer.

$12 - 4 = \square$

$\square + 4 = \square$

4. Write two ways to make 15.

15 = _____ + _____   15 = _____ + _____

FOR MORE PRACTICE GO TO THE **Personal Math Trainer**

Name ______________________________

Model, Read, and Write Numbers from 100 to 110

Essential Question How can you model, read, and write numbers from 100 to 110?

Common Core **Number and Operations in Base Ten—1.NBT.A.1**

MATHEMATICAL PRACTICES
MP.4, MP.5, MP.7

Listen and Draw Real World

Use  .

Circle a number to answer the question.

1	2	3	4	5	6	7	8	9	10
11	12	13	14	15	16	17	18	19	20
21	22	23	24	25	26	27	28	29	30
31	32	33	34	35	36	37	38	39	40
41	42	43	44	45	46	47	48	49	50
51	52	53	54	55	56	57	58	59	60
61	62	63	64	65	66	67	68	69	70
71	72	73	74	75	76	77	78	79	80
81	82	83	84	85	86	87	88	89	90
91	92	93	94	95	96	97	98	99	100

Math Talk **MATHEMATICAL PRACTICES 7**

Look for Structure
Why is 100 to the right of 99 on the hundred chart? Why is 100 below 90?

FOR THE TEACHER • Have children locate each number on the hundred chart. What number is the same as 30 ones? What number is the same as 10 tens? What number is the same as 8 tens 7 ones? What number has 1 more one than 52? What number has 1 more ten than 65?

Model and Draw

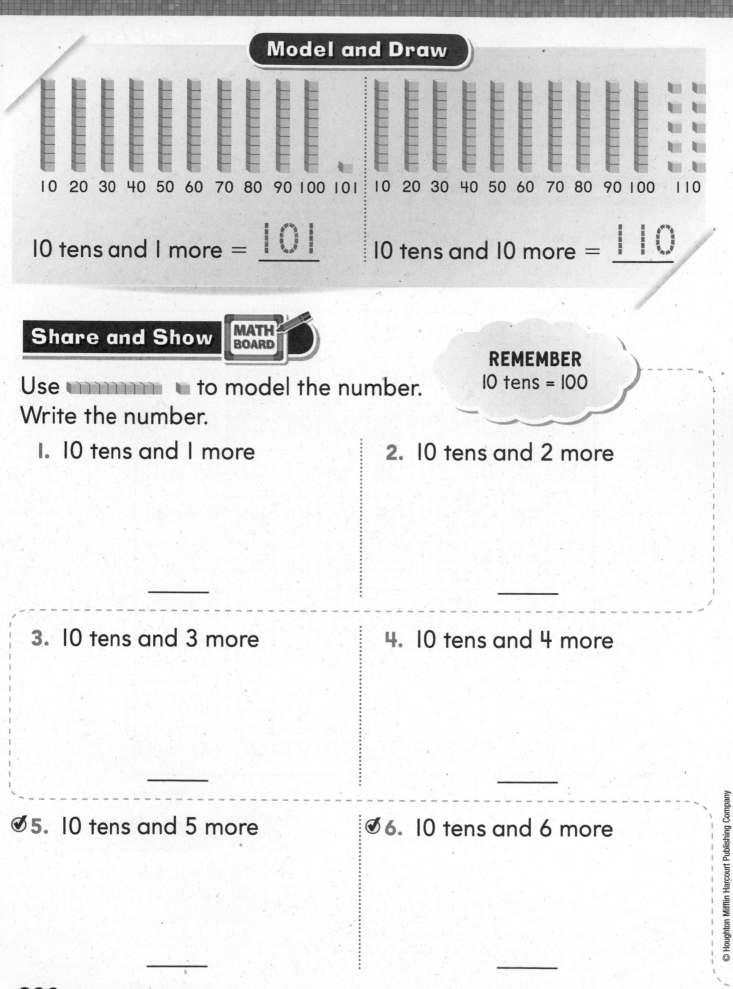

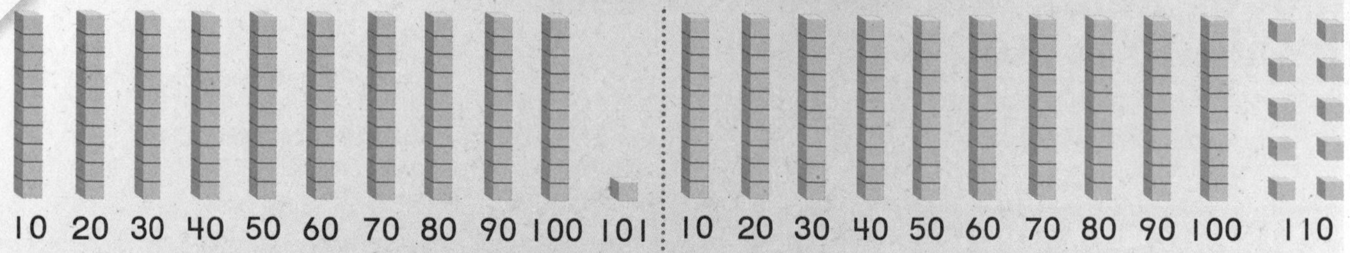

10 tens and 1 more = 101

10 tens and 10 more = 110

Share and Show MATH BOARD

REMEMBER
10 tens = 100

Use to model the number.
Write the number.

1. 10 tens and 1 more ____

2. 10 tens and 2 more ____

3. 10 tens and 3 more ____

4. 10 tens and 4 more ____

5. 10 tens and 5 more ____

6. 10 tens and 6 more ____

Name ______________________

On Your Own

MATHEMATICAL PRACTICE 4 **Model Mathematics**

Use  to model the number.
Write the number.

7. 10 tens and 7 more ______

8. 10 tens and 8 more ______

9. 10 tens and 9 more ______

10. 10 tens and 10 more ______

11. THINK SMARTER 11 tens ______

Math on the Spot

Write the number.

12.

______

13.

______

14.

______

15.

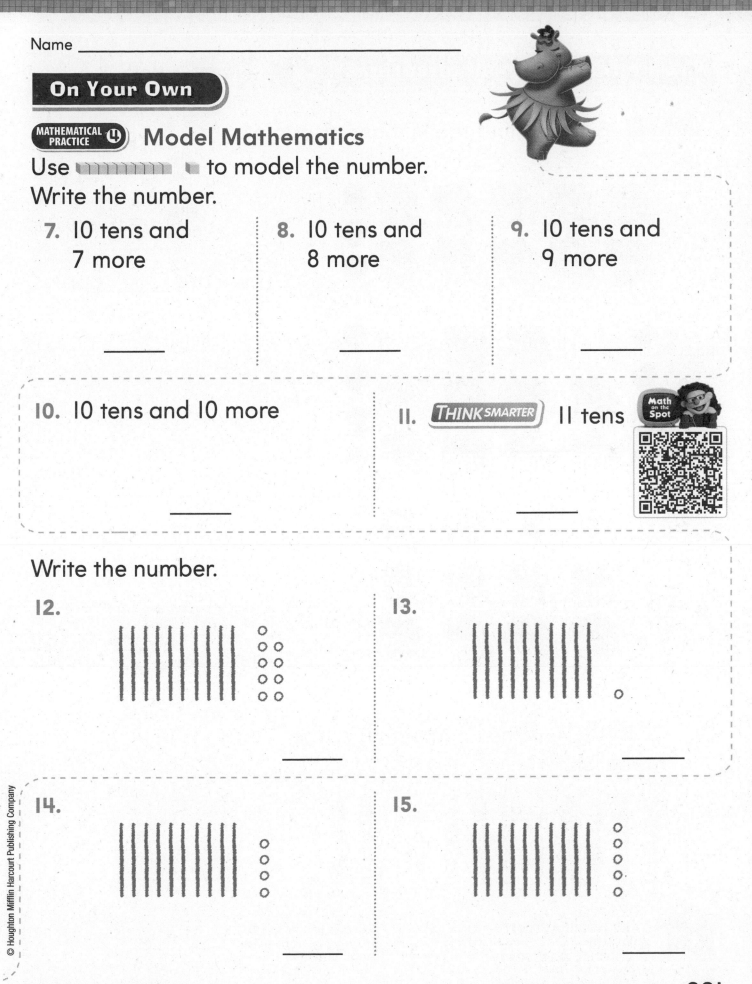

______

Problem Solving • Applications Real World

WRITE Math

GO DEEPER Solve to find the number of apples.

THINK

= 1 apple

=10 apples

16.

There are _____ apples.

17.

There are _____ apples.

18.

There are _____ apples.

19. THINK SMARTER What number does the model show?

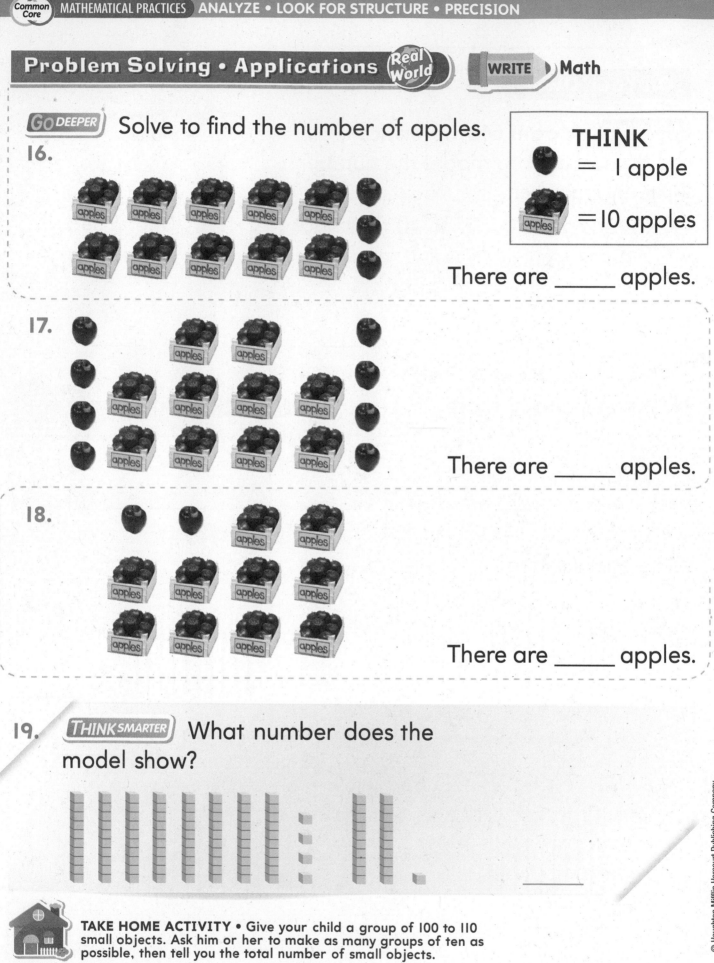

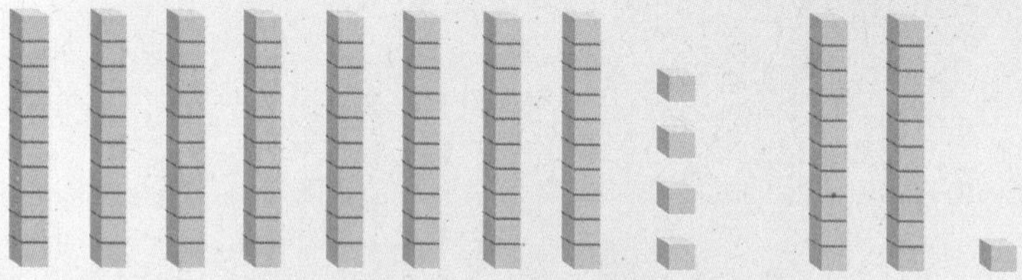

_____

TAKE HOME ACTIVITY • Give your child a group of 100 to 110 small objects. Ask him or her to make as many groups of ten as possible, then tell you the total number of small objects.

Name ___________________________

Model, Read, and Write Numbers from 100 to 110

Common Core — **COMMON CORE STANDARDS—1.NBT.A.1**
Understand place value.

Use 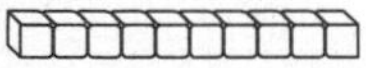  to show the number.
Write the number.

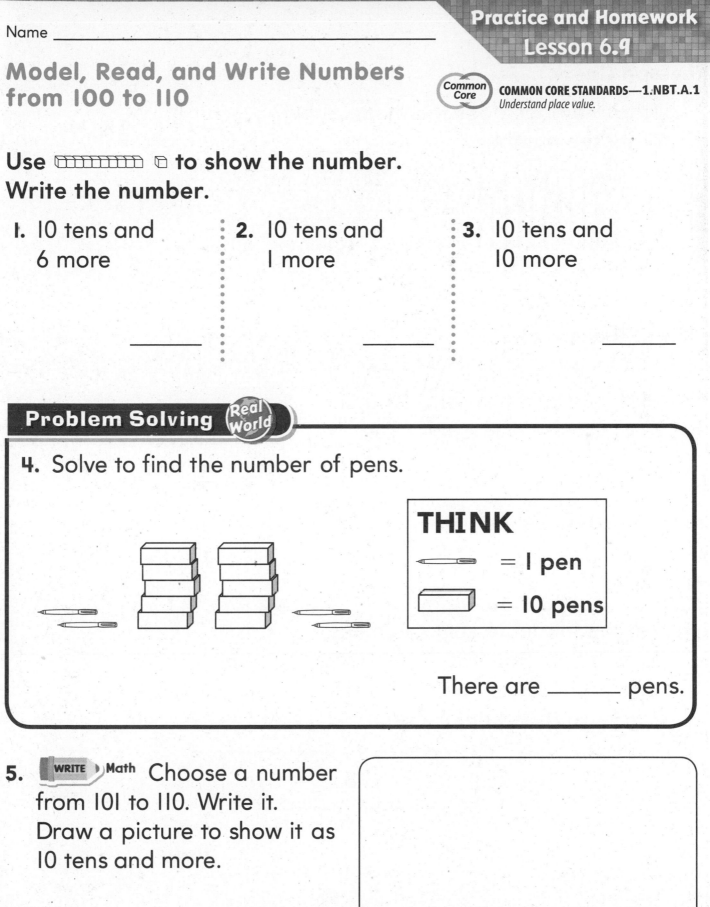

1. 10 tens and 6 more ______

2. 10 tens and 1 more ______

3. 10 tens and 10 more ______

Problem Solving — Real World

4. Solve to find the number of pens.

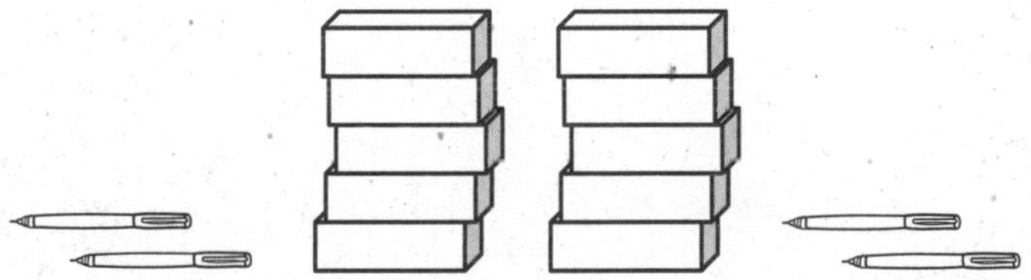

THINK

 = 1 pen

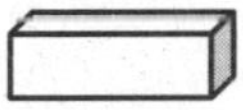 = 10 pens

There are ______ pens.

5. WRITE Math Choose a number from 101 to 110. Write it. Draw a picture to show it as 10 tens and more.

Lesson Check (1.NBT.A.1)

1. What number does the model show? Write the number.

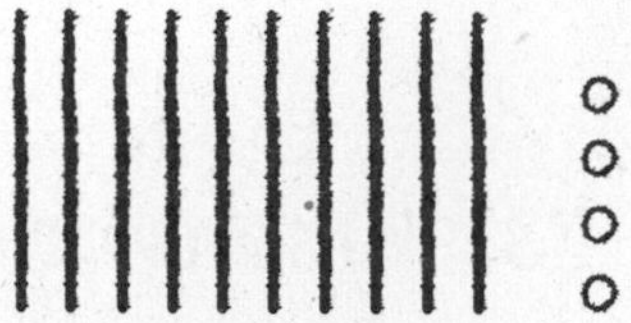

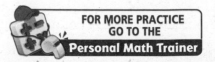

_____

Spiral Review (1.OA.A.1)

2. Show taking from. Circle the part you take from the group. Then cross it out. Write the difference.

$4 - 3 =$ _____

3. Use the model to solve. Ken has 8 toy trains. Ron has 3 toy trains. How many fewer toy trains does Ron have than Ken?

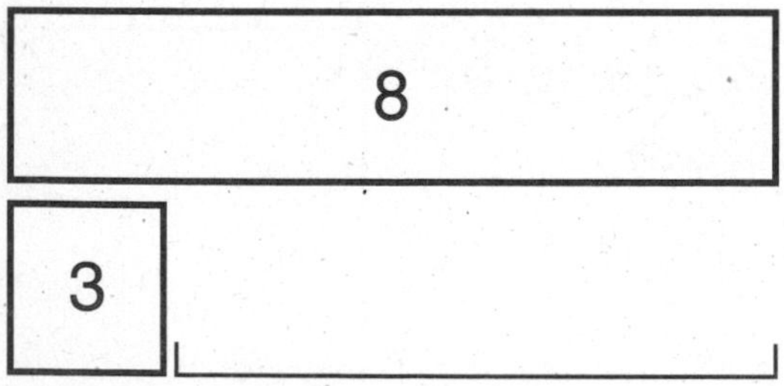

_____

Name ____________________

Model, Read, and Write Numbers from 110 to 120

Essential Question How can you model, read, and write numbers from 110 to 120?

Common Core **Number and Operations in Base Ten—1.NBT.A.1**

MATHEMATICAL PRACTICES
MP2, MP4, MP6

Listen and Draw (Real World)

How many shells are there?

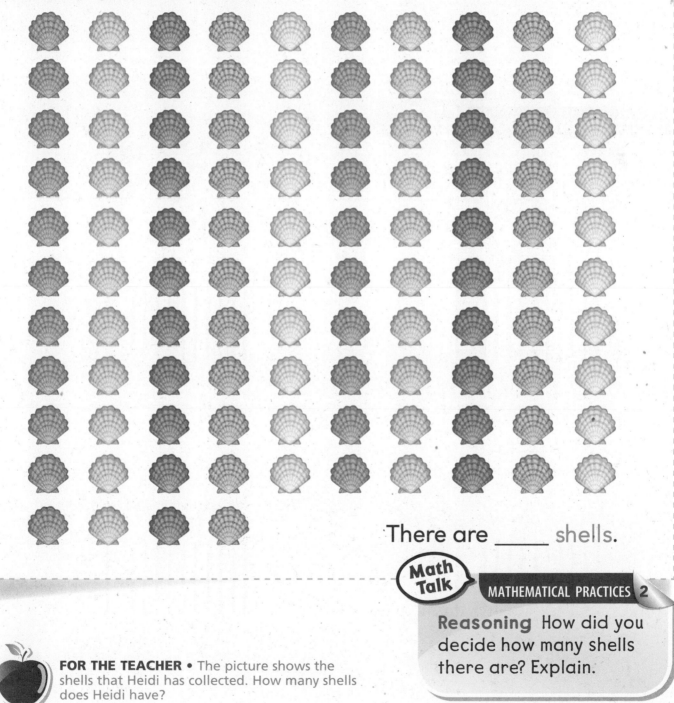

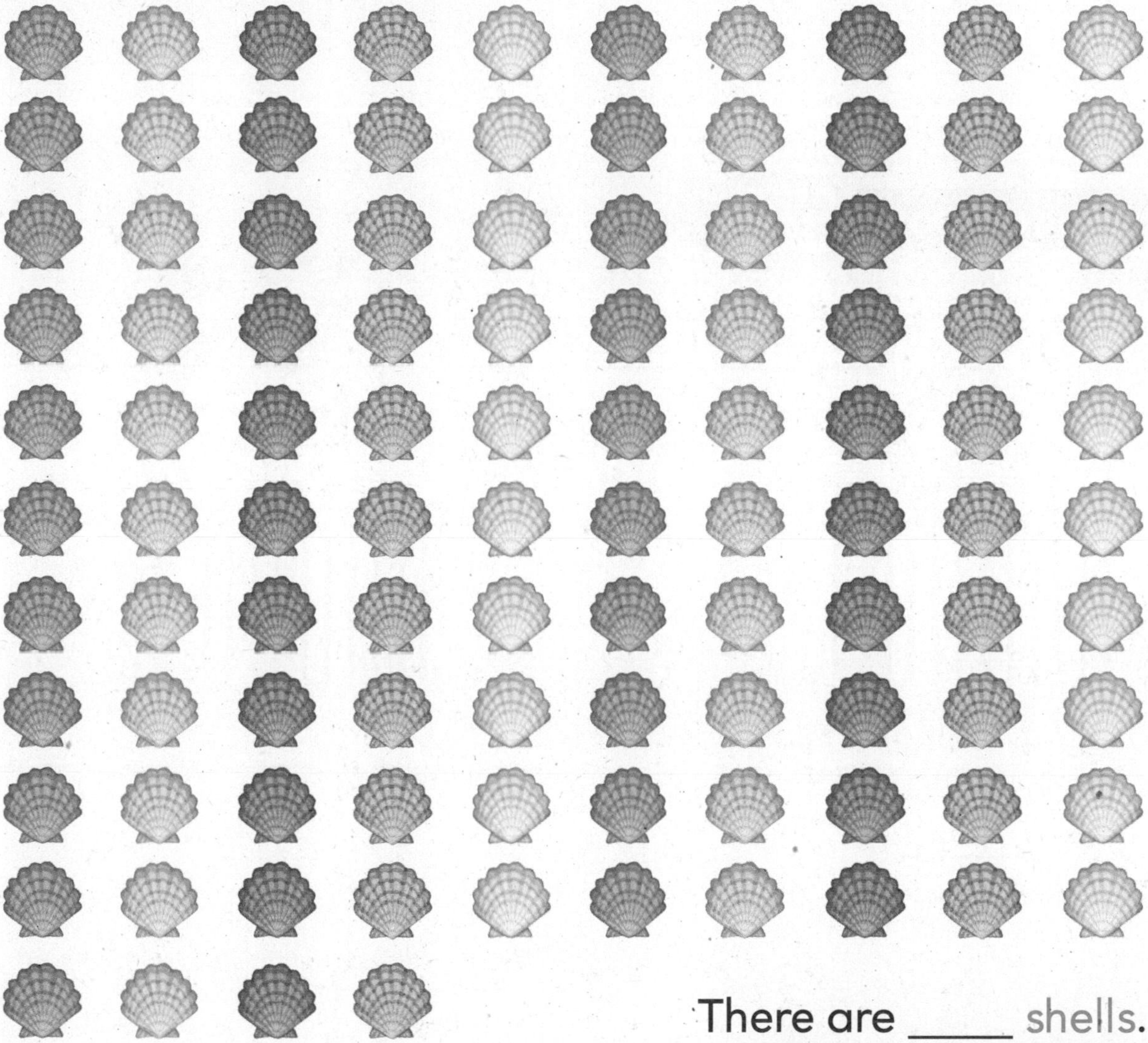

There are _____ shells.

Math Talk MATHEMATICAL PRACTICES 2

Reasoning How did you decide how many shells there are? Explain.

FOR THE TEACHER • The picture shows the shells that Heidi has collected. How many shells does Heidi have?

Model and Draw

11 tens is 110.

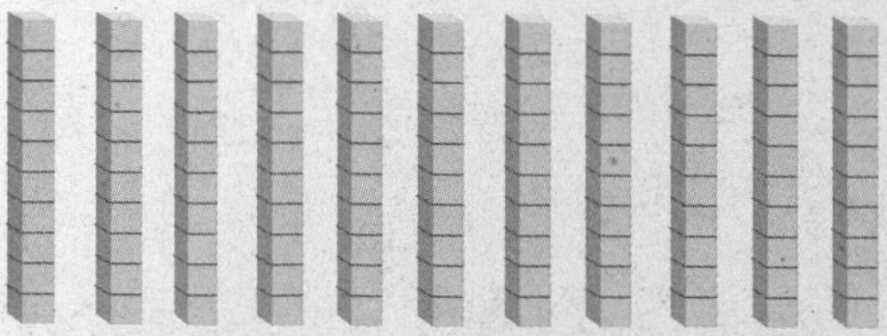

110

12 tens is 120.

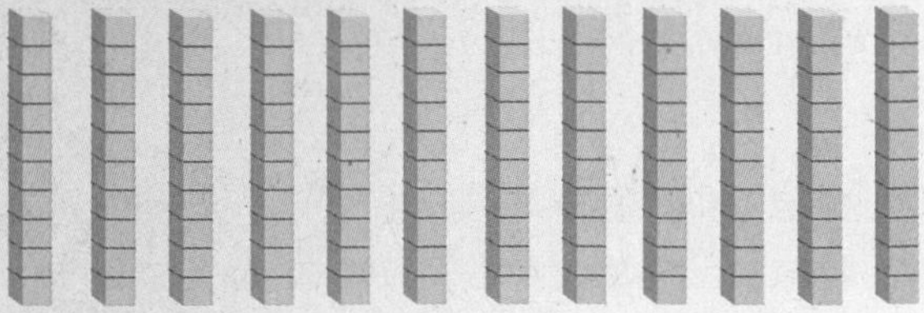

120

Share and Show

MATH BOARD

Use tens and ones to model the number.
Write the number.

1.

111

2.

____

3.

____

4.

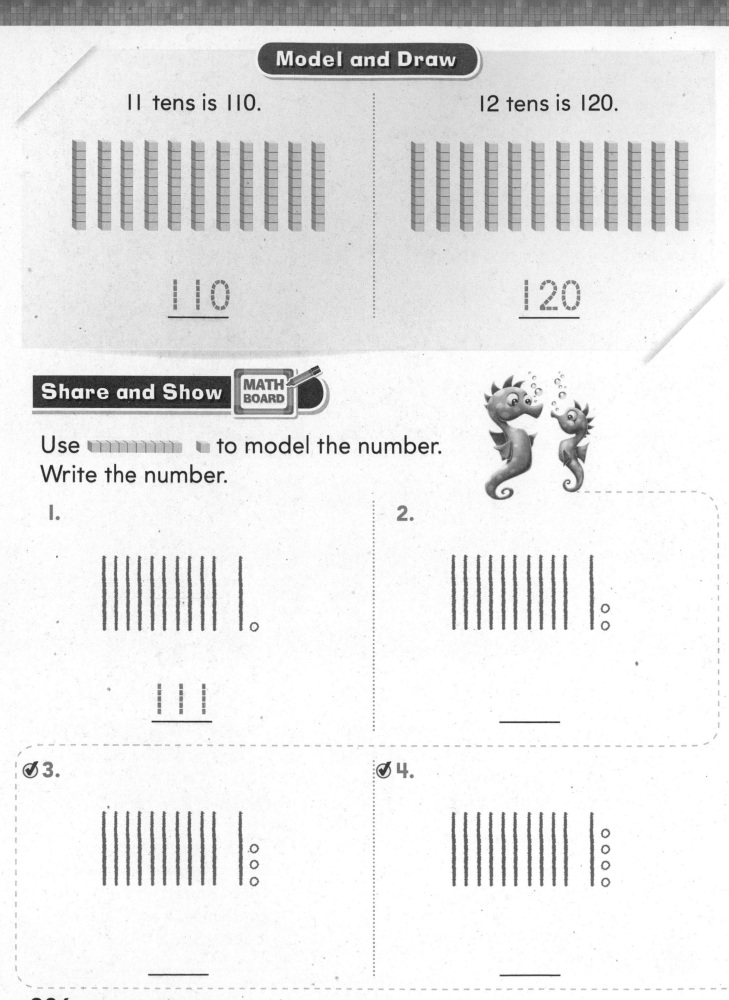

____

Name ______________________________

On Your Own

MATHEMATICAL PRACTICE 4 **Model Mathematics**

Use to model the number.
Write the number.

5.

_____

6.

_____

7.

_____

8.

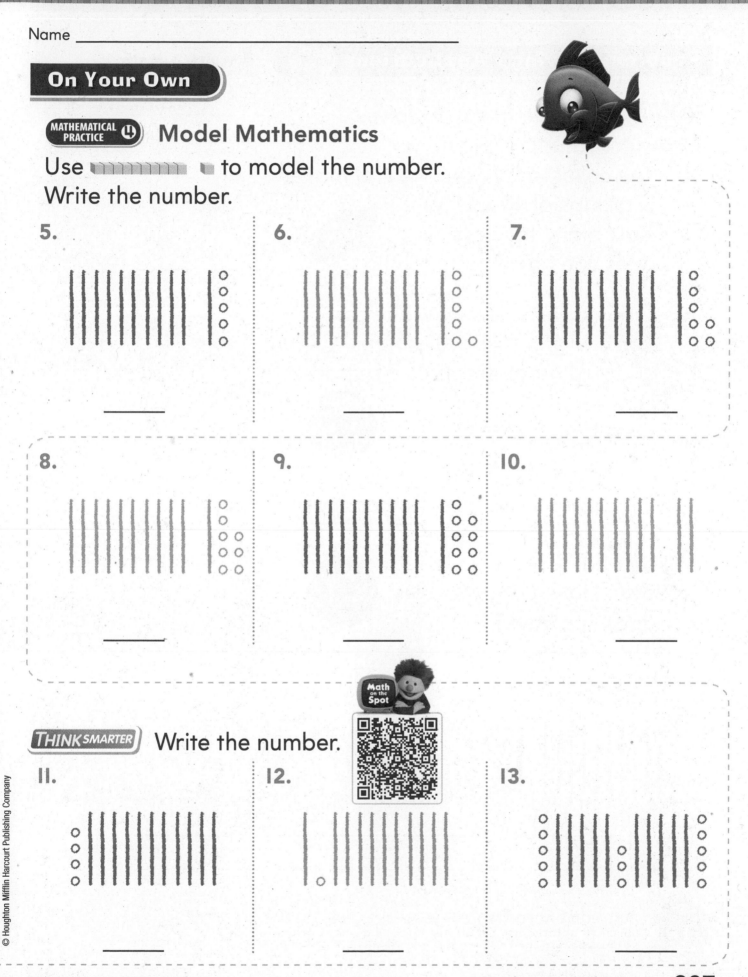

_____

9.

_____

10.

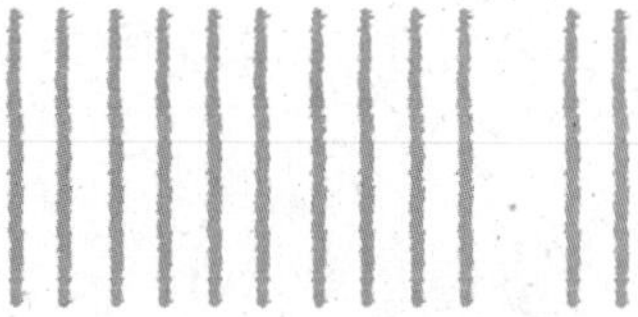

_____

THINK SMARTER Write the number.

11.

_____

12.

_____

13.

_____

Problem Solving • Applications Real World

WRITE Math

GO DEEPER Choose a way to solve.
Draw or write to explain.

14. Joe collects toy cars. He can make 11 groups of 10 toy cars. How many toy cars does Joe have?

_____ toy cars

15. Cindy collects buttons. She can make 11 groups of 10 buttons and one more group of 7 buttons. How many buttons does Cindy have?

_____ buttons

16. Lee collects marbles. He can make 11 groups of 10 marbles and has 2 marbles left over. How many marbles does Lee have?

_____ marbles

17. THINK SMARTER Finish the drawing to show 119.

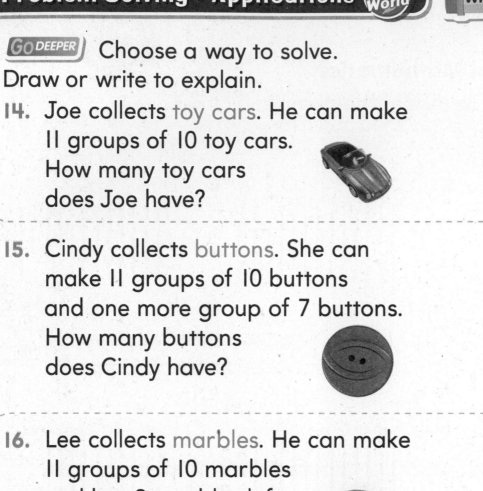

Write to explain.

TAKE HOME ACTIVITY • Give your child a group of 100 to 120 small objects. Ask him or her to make as many groups of ten as possible and then tell you the total number of small objects.

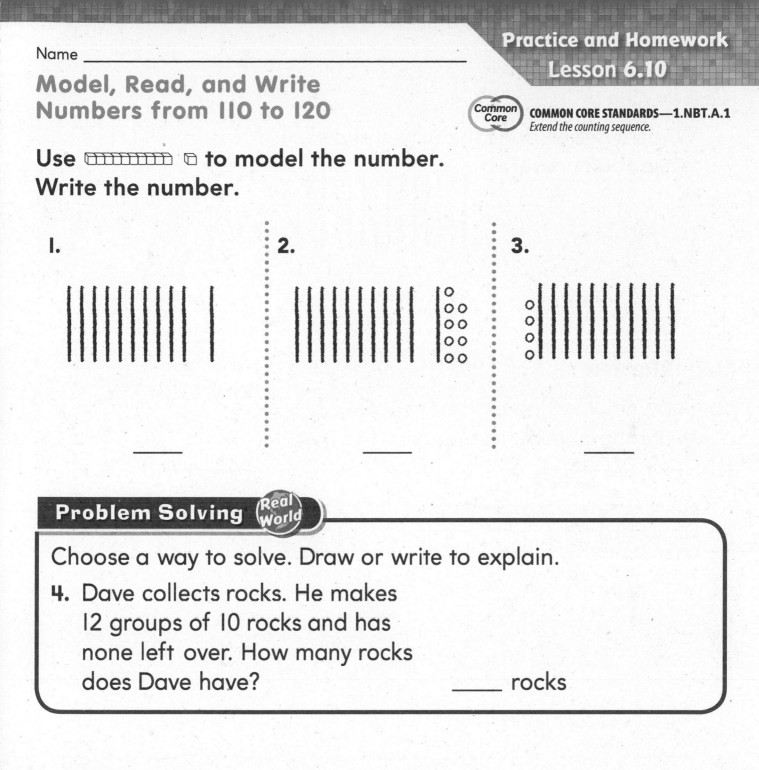

Name ______________________________

Model, Read, and Write Numbers from 110 to 120

Practice and Homework
Lesson 6.10

Common Core **COMMON CORE STANDARDS—1.NBT.A.1**
Extend the counting sequence.

Use 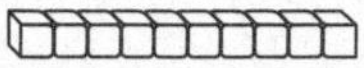  to model the number.
Write the number.

1.

____

2.

____

3.

____

Problem Solving Real World

Choose a way to solve. Draw or write to explain.

4. Dave collects rocks. He makes 12 groups of 10 rocks and has none left over. How many rocks does Dave have?

____ rocks

5. WRITE Math Choose a number from 111 to 120. Write the number. Draw a picture to show it as tens and ones.

Lesson Check (1.NBT.A.1)

I. What number does the model show?
Write the number.

|||||||||| o
 o
 o
 o o
 o o

..

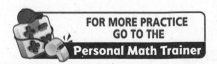

Spiral Review (1.OA.C.6)

2. Show how to make a ten to solve 13 − 7.
Write the number sentence.

$$\underline{\quad} - \underline{\quad} - \underline{\quad}$$

$$\underline{\quad} - \underline{\quad} = \underline{\quad}$$

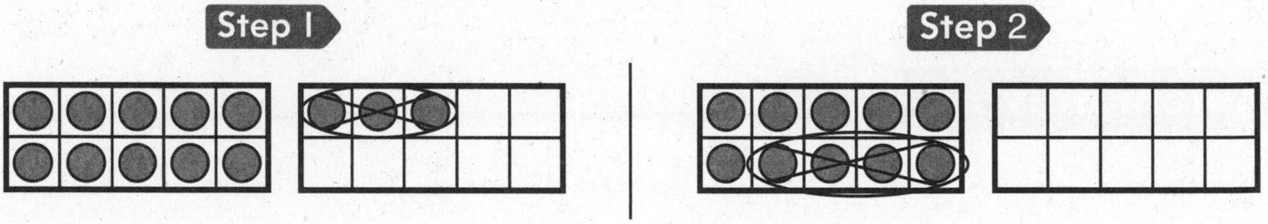

So, 13 − 7 = ____.

..

3. What is the difference?
Write the number.

$$\begin{array}{r} 9 \\ -\ 4 \\ \hline \end{array}$$

© Houghton Mifflin Harcourt Publishing Company

FOR MORE PRACTICE
GO TO THE
Personal Math Trainer

Name ____________________

Chapter 6 Review/Test

Personal Math Trainer
Online Assessment and Intervention

1. Felix counts 46 cubes. Then he counts forward some more cubes. Write the numbers.

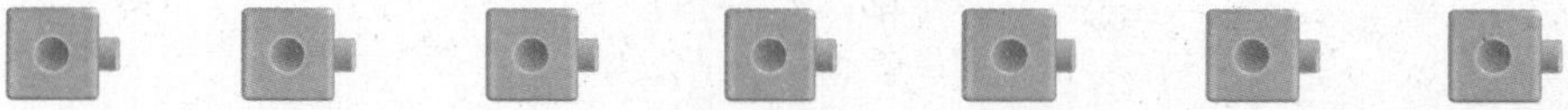

46, ____, ____, ____, ____, ____, ____, ____

2. Count by tens. Match each number on the left to a number that is 10 more.

35 •	• 69
49 •	• 59
59 •	• 75
65 •	• 45
57 •	• 67

GO DIGITAL Assessment Options Chapter Test

3. Does the number match the model? Choose Yes or No.

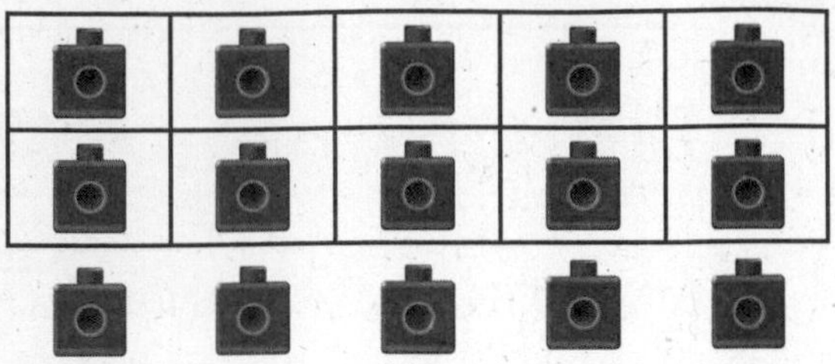

10 + 10	○ Yes	○ No
1 ten 4 ones	○ Yes	○ No
1 ten 5 ones	○ Yes	○ No
10 + 5	○ Yes	○ No

4. Circle the numbers that make the sentence true.

There are [1 / 2 / 10] tens and [1 / 2 / 10] ones in 12.

5. Choose all the ways that name the model.

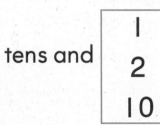

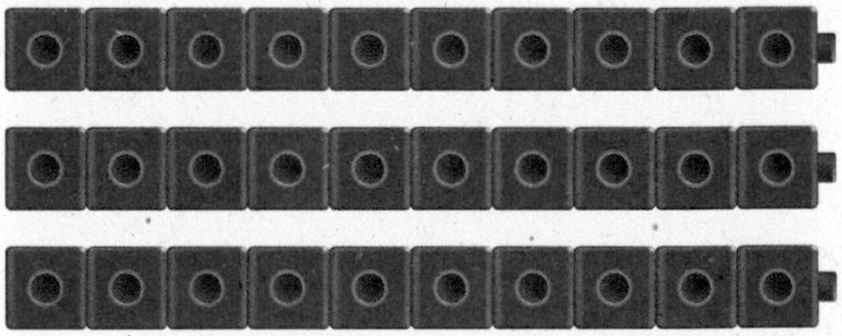

○ 3 ones

○ 3 tens

○ 3 tens 0 ones

○ 30

Name ___________________________

6. There are 42 cubes. Lisa says that there are 4 tens and 2 ones. Elena says there are 2 tens and 4 ones. Who is correct? Circle the name.

Lisa Elena

How can you draw to show 42?

7. Read the problem. Write a number to solve.

I am greater than 27.
I am less than 30.
I have 9 ones.

Personal Math Trainer

8. THINK SMARTER + Choose all the ways that show the same number.

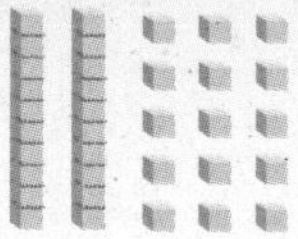

○ 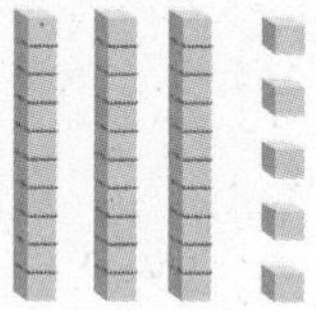

○ 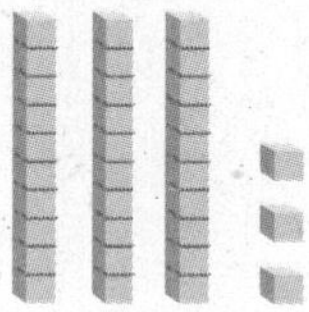

○ 

○ 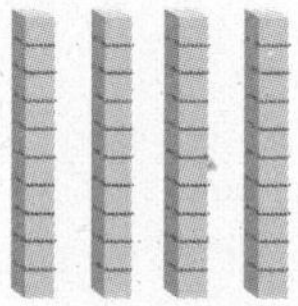

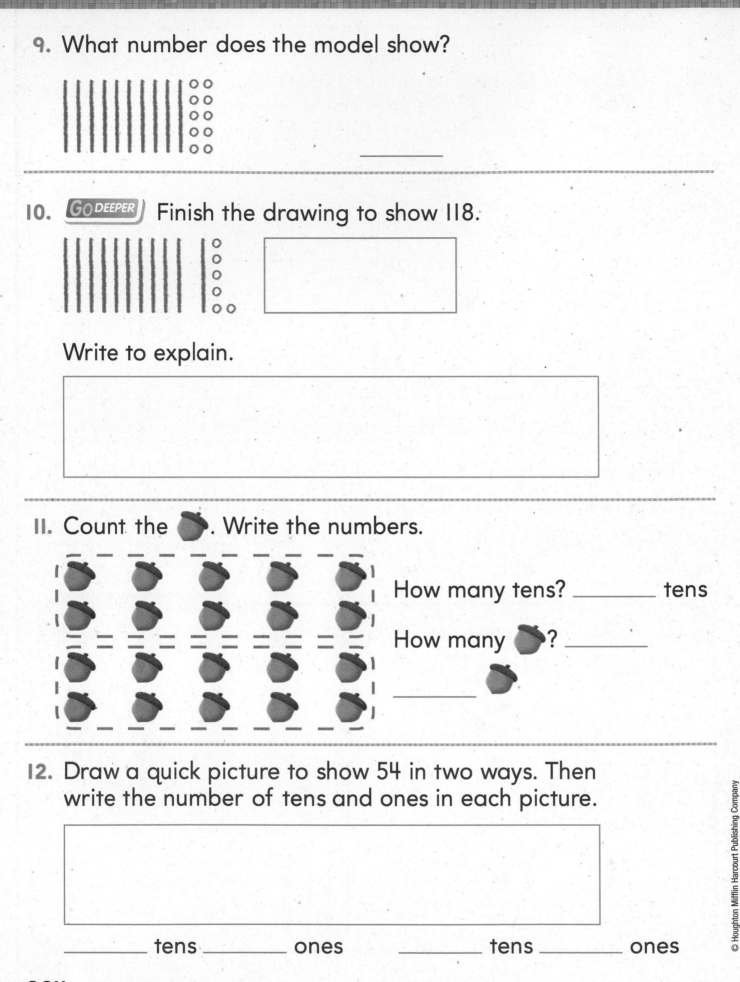

9. What number does the model show?

______

10. GO DEEPER Finish the drawing to show 118.

Write to explain.

11. Count the acorns. Write the numbers.

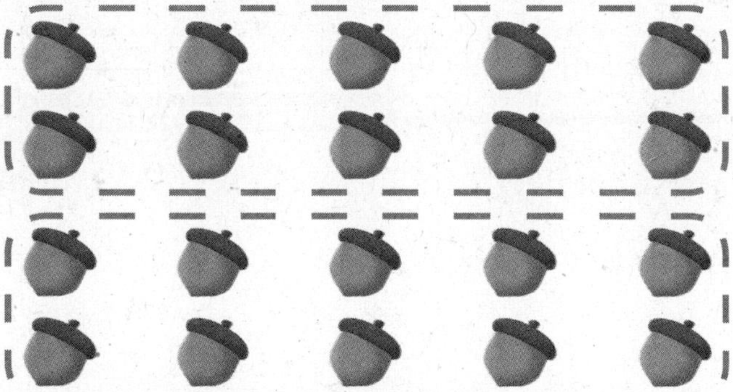

How many tens? ______ tens

How many acorns? ______

______ acorns

12. Draw a quick picture to show 54 in two ways. Then write the number of tens and ones in each picture.

______ tens ______ ones ______ tens ______ ones

Chapter 7

Compare Numbers

Curious About Math with Curious George

How many colors do you see in the kite? Name the number that is one more.

Name ______________________________

Show What You Know

Personal Math Trainer
Online Assessment and Intervention

Model More

Draw lines to match.
Circle the set that has more. (K.CC.C.6)

1.

2.

More, Fewer

3. Circle the row that has more. (K.CC.C.6)

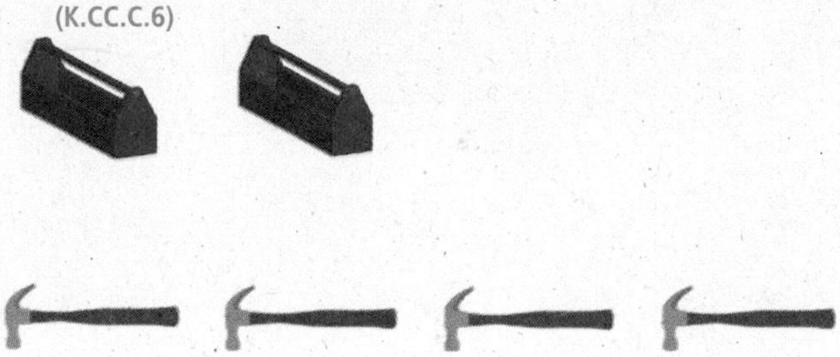

4. Circle the row that has fewer. (K.CC.C.6)

Draw Equal Groups

5. Draw a ball for each glove. (1.OA.D.7)

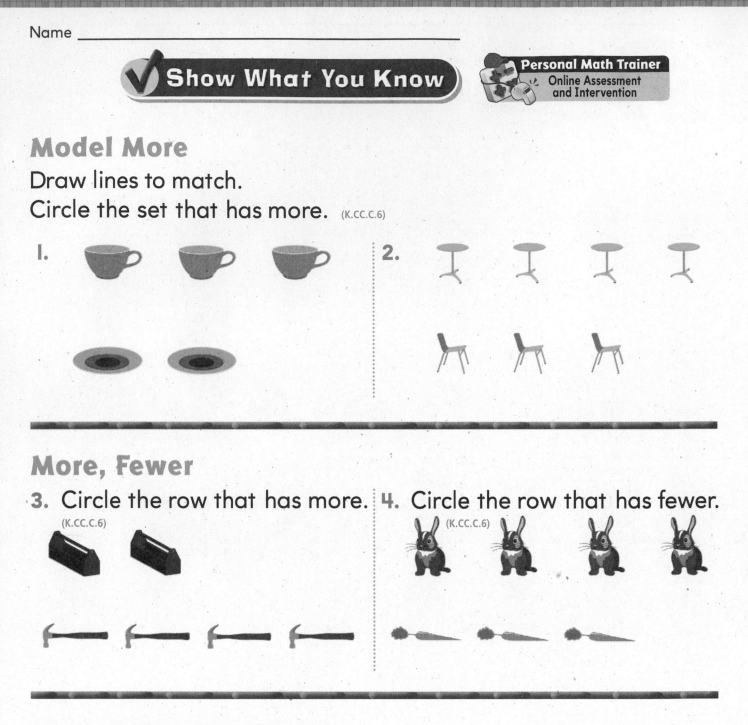

This page checks understanding of important skills needed for success in Chapter 7.

Name ______________________

Vocabulary Builder

Review Words

Review Words
fewer
more
same

Visualize It

Draw pictures in the box to show **more, fewer,** or the **same** number.

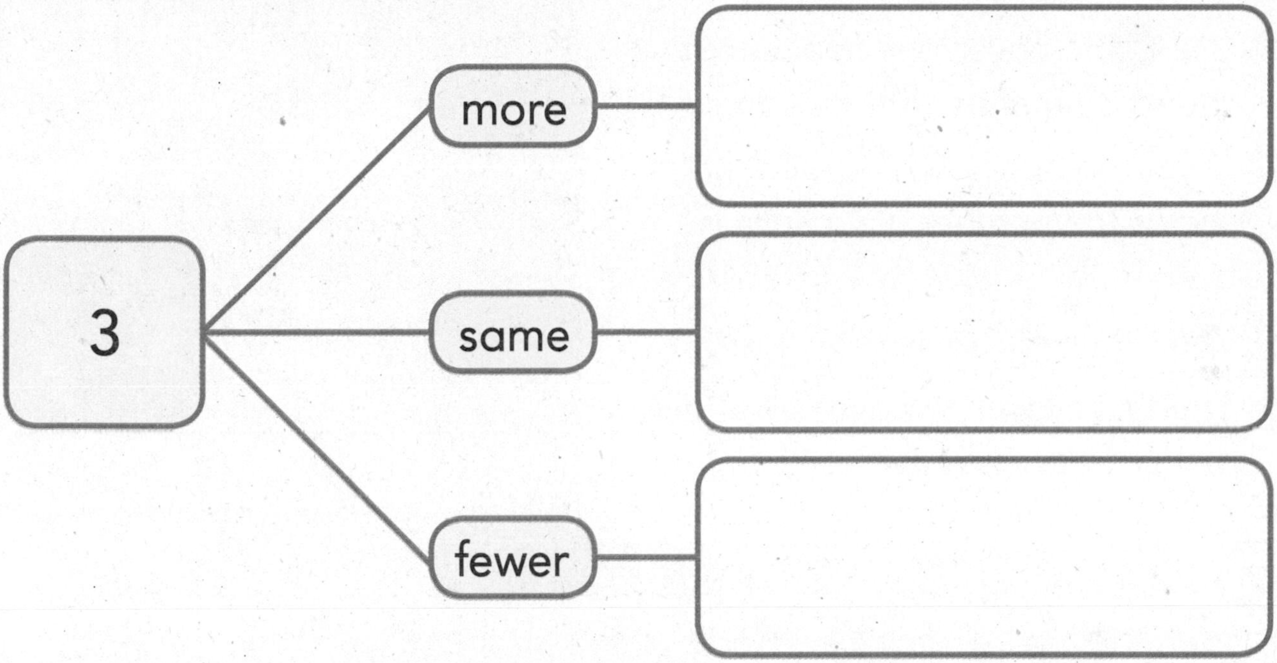

Understand Vocabulary

Complete the sentences with review words.

1. I see 2 white cats and 4 yellow cats. I see ____________ yellow cats than white cats.

2. Dave has 9 grapes. Ann has 6 grapes. Ann has ____________ grapes than Dave.

3. 5 ducks and 5 swans are at the pond. There are the ____________ number of ducks and swans.

GO DIGITAL
• Interactive Student Edition
• Multimedia eGlossary

Chapter 7

Game Rainy Day Bingo

Materials • • 9 • 9

Play with a partner.

1. Toss the .
2. Use to cover one space that shows a number that is 1 more.
3. If you do not have a space that shows the number, your turn is over.
4. The other player takes a turn.
5. The first player to cover all of his or her spaces wins.

Player 1		
4	5	2
3	6	4
2	5	7

Player 2		
6	2	3
4	7	6
5	3	7

Chapter 7 Vocabulary

add sumar 1	**difference** diferencia 13
fewer menos 19	**is greater than (>)** es mayor que (>) 31
is less than (<) es menor que (<) 32	**more** más 38
subtract restar 52	**sum** suma o total 54

9 − 4 = 5

The **difference** is 5.

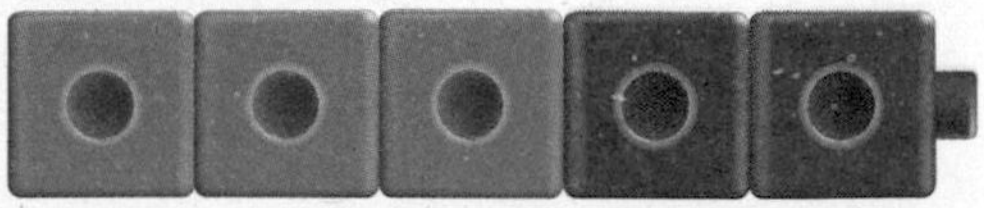

3 + 2 = 5

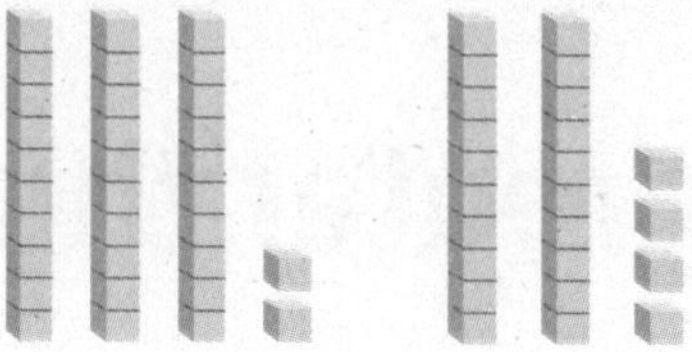

32 > 24

32 **is greater than** 24.

3 **fewer** 

5 − 3 = 2

There are **more**  .

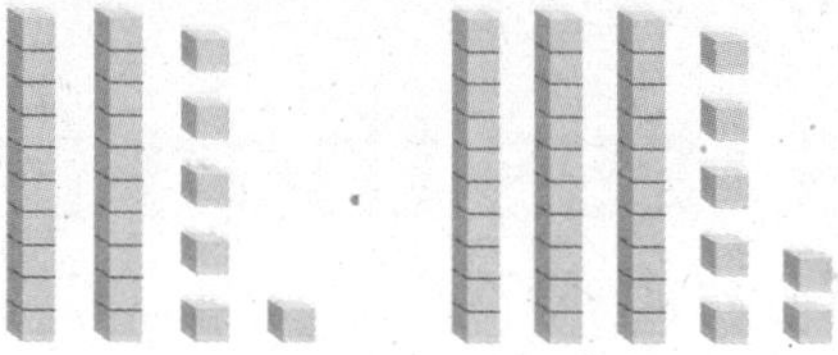

26 < 37

26 **is less than** 37.

2 plus 1 is equal to 3.

The **sum** is 3.

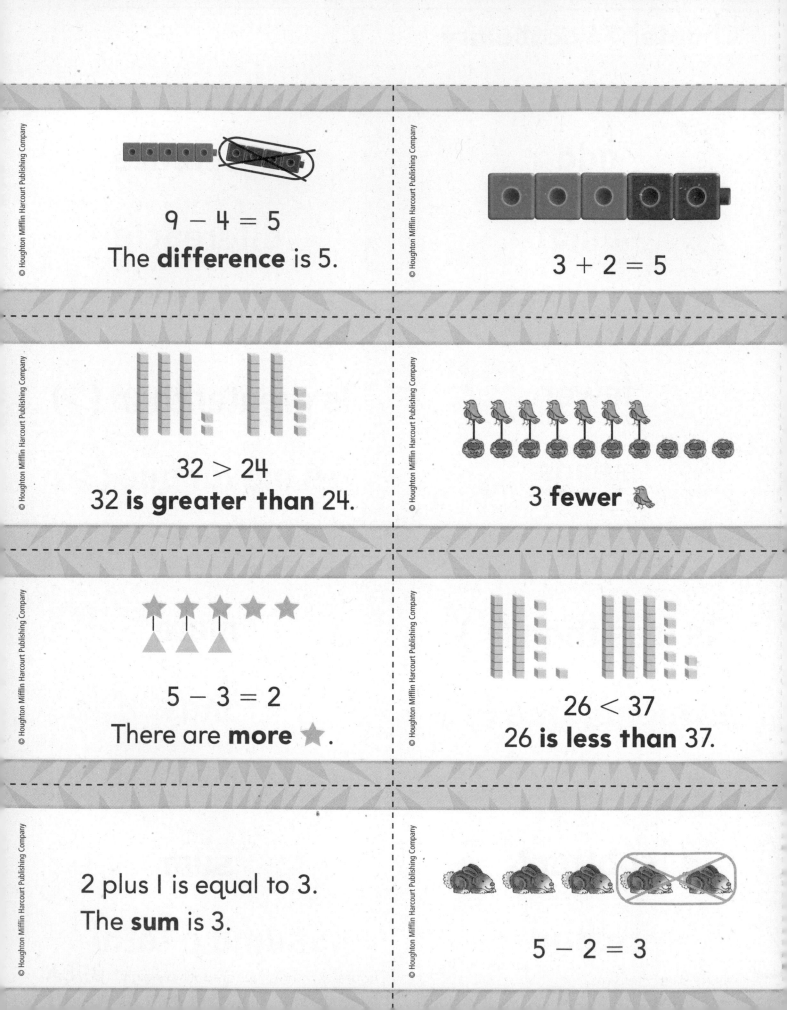

5 − 2 = 3

Game

Guess the Word

Word Box
add
difference
fewer
is greater than (>)
is less than (<)
more
subtract
sum

Materials

timer

How to Play

Play with a partner.

1. Choose a math word from the Word Box. Do not tell your partner.
2. Set the timer.
3. Give a one-word clue.
4. Your partner tries to guess the secret word.
5. Repeat with a new one-word clue until your partner guesses correctly or time runs out.
6. Take turns.
7. The first player to correctly guess 5 words wins.

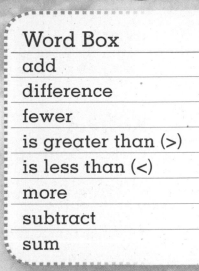

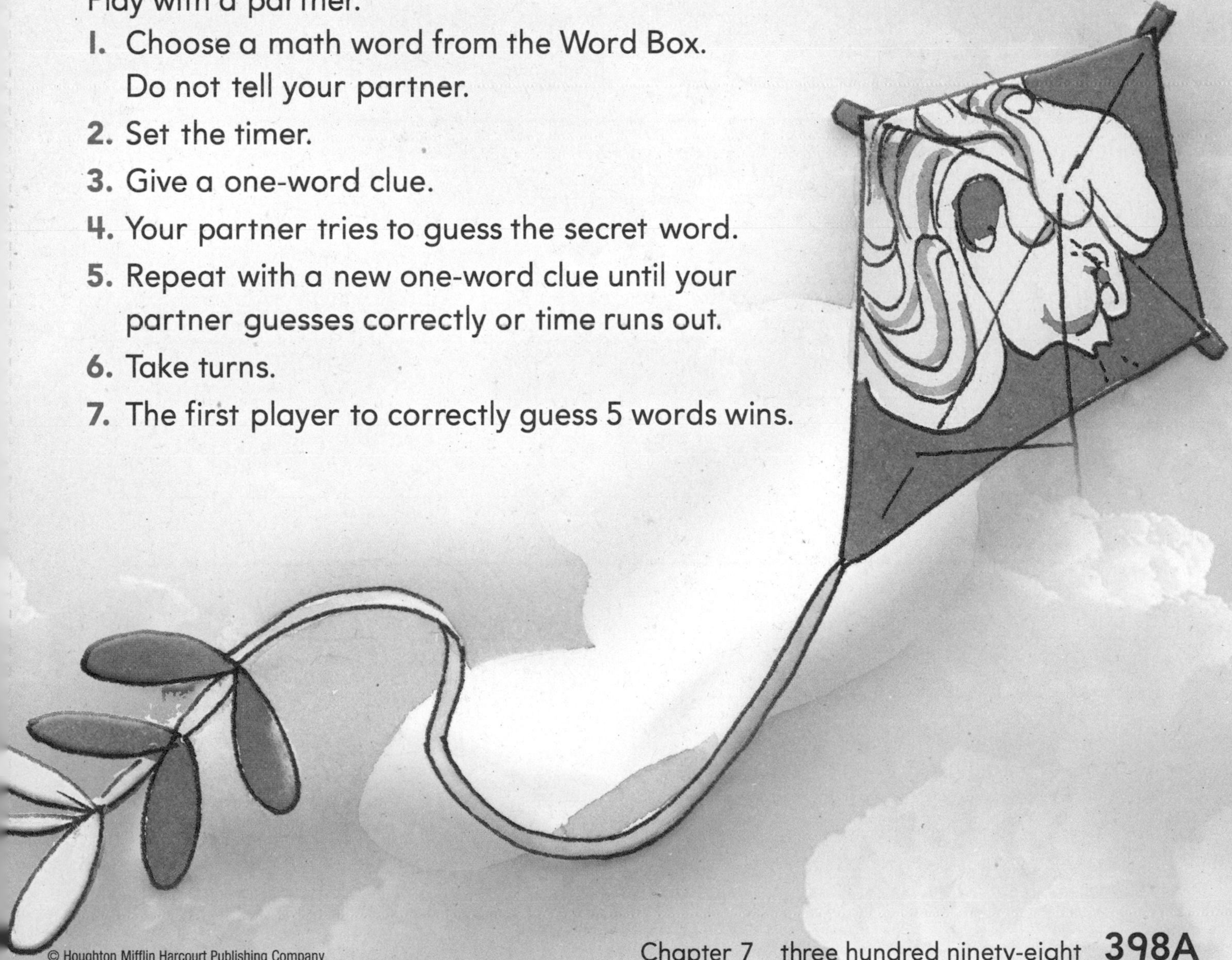

Journal

The Write Way

Reflect

Choose one idea. Draw and write about it.

- Write two questions you have about comparing numbers.
- Explain how to compare 43 and 35.

Name _____

Algebra • Greater Than

Essential Question How can you compare two numbers to find which is greater?

Common Core
Number and Operations in Base Ten—1.NBT.B.3
MATHEMATICAL PRACTICES
MP5, MP7

Listen and Draw

Use ▭▭▭▭▭ ▫ or an *i* Tool to solve.
Draw quick pictures to show your work.

Tens	Ones

Math Talk
MATHEMATICAL PRACTICES 5

How did you **use tools** to decide which number is greater?

FOR THE TEACHER • Read the problem. Which number is greater, 65 or 56? Have children use base-ten blocks and draw quick pictures to solve.

Model and Draw

To compare 25 and 17, first compare the tens.

If the tens are the same, compare the ones.

2 tens are more than 1 ten.

7 ones are more than 5 ones.

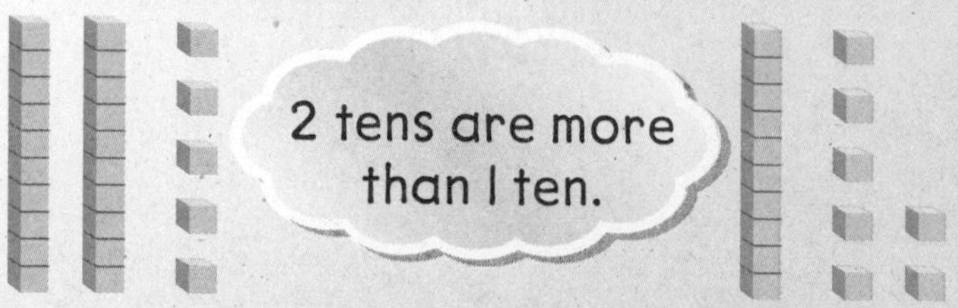

__25__ **is greater than** __17__ .

__25__ **>** __17__

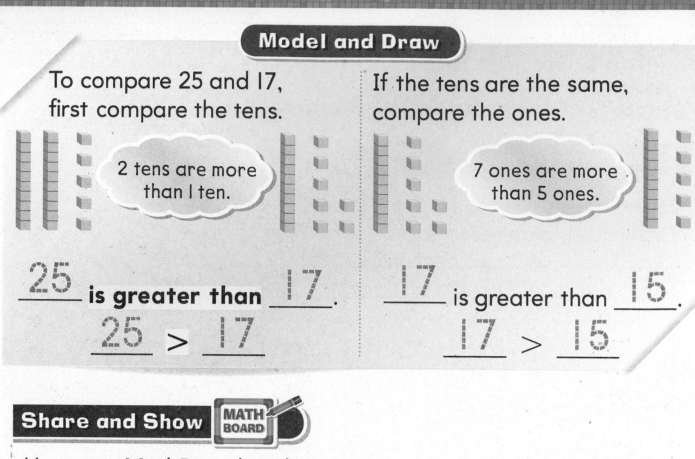

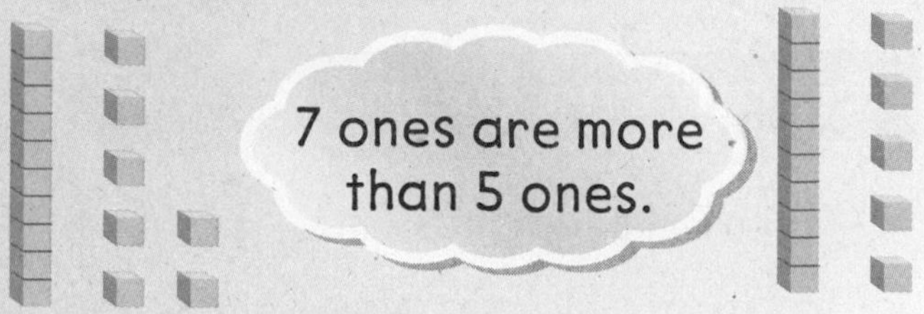

__17__ is greater than __15__ .

__17__ **>** __15__

Share and Show

MATH BOARD

Use your MathBoard and ▭▭▭▭ to show each number.

	Circle the greater number.	Did tens or ones help you decide?	Write the numbers.
1.	62 (65)	tens (ones)	__65__ is greater than __62__ . __65__ > __62__
✓2.	84 48	tens ones	___ is greater than ___ . ___ > ___
✓3.	72 70	tens ones	___ is greater than ___ . ___ > ___

© Houghton Mifflin Harcourt Publishing Company

Name ______________________________

On Your Own

MATHEMATICAL PRACTICE 5 **Use a Concrete Model**

Use [tens block] [ones block] if you need to.

	Circle the greater number.	Did tens or ones help you decide?	Write the numbers.
4.	57 75	tens ones	____ is greater than ____. ____ > ____
5.	94 98	tens ones	____ is greater than ____. ____ > ____

Write or draw to solve.

6. THINK SMARTER Pam and Jake play a game for points. Pam's points are 1 ten 6 ones. Jake's points are 1 one 6 tens. Who has the greater number of points?

Math on the Spot

____

7. GO DEEPER John has 51 cards. Paul has 32 cards. George has a number of cards greater than either Paul or John. How many cards might George have?

____ cards

Problem Solving • Applications Real World

WRITE Math

8. THINK SMARTER Color the balloons that show numbers greater than 56.

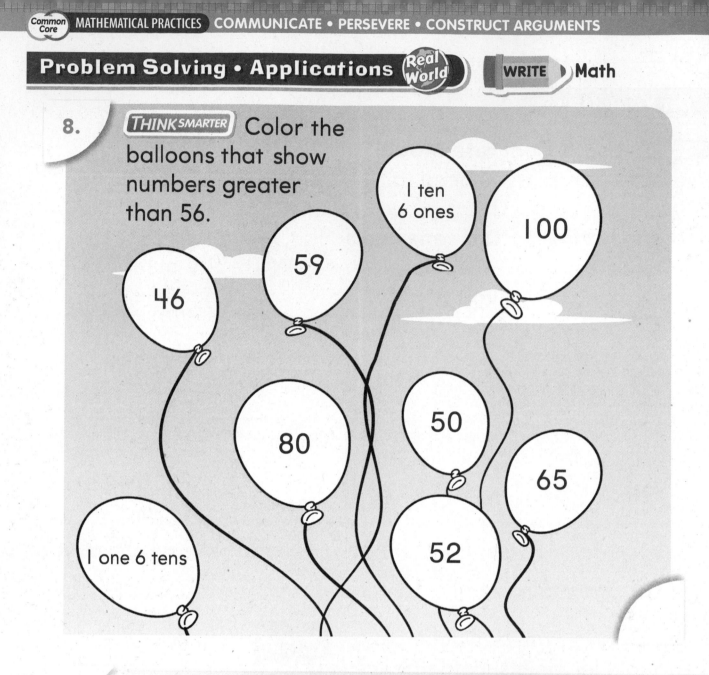

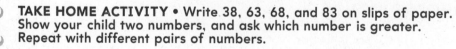

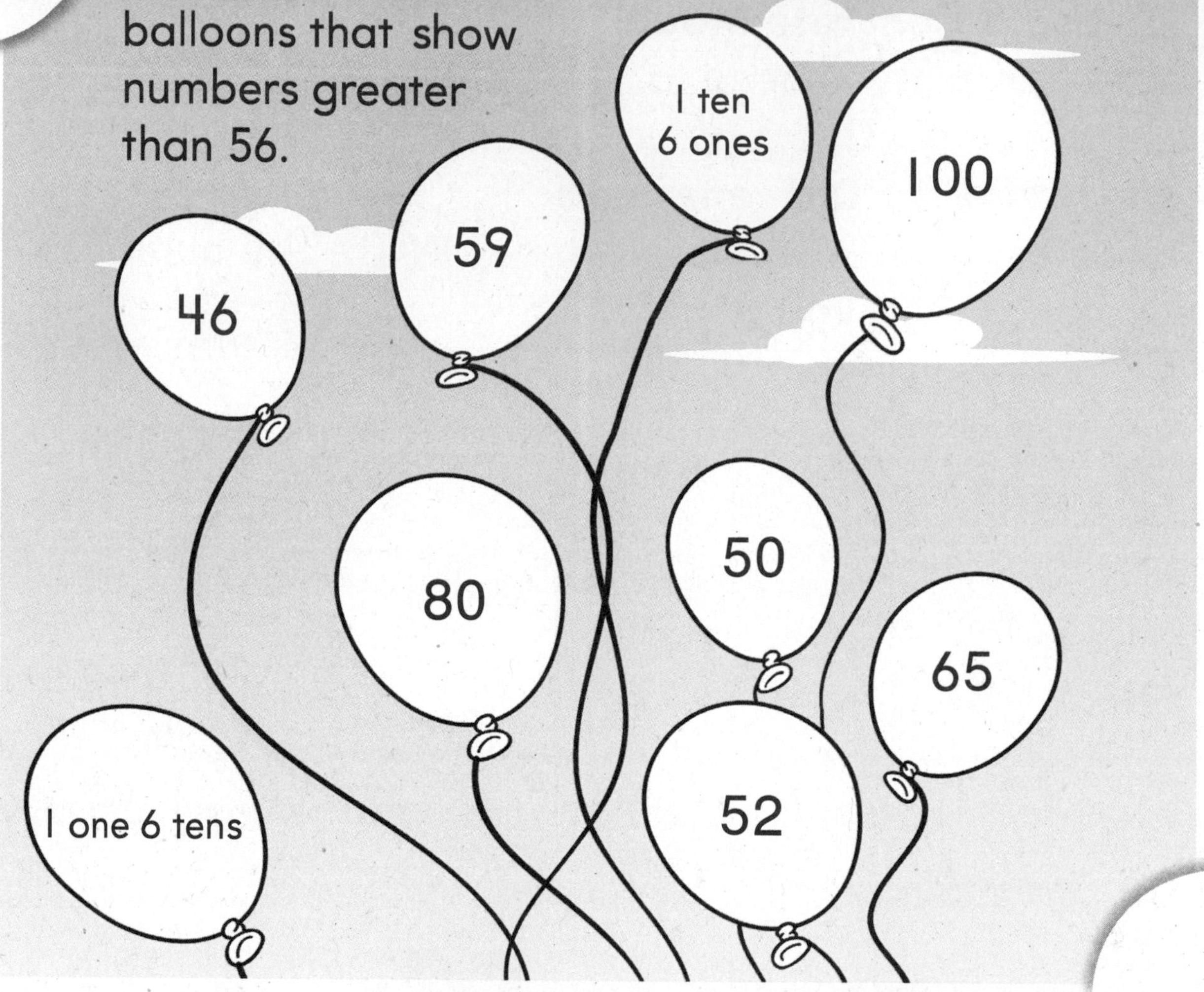

9. THINK SMARTER Compare. Is the math sentence true? Choose Yes or No.

37 is greater than 43.	○ Yes	○ No
41 is greater than 39.	○ Yes	○ No
48 > 52	○ Yes	○ No
86 > 68	○ Yes	○ No

TAKE HOME ACTIVITY • Write 38, 63, 68, and 83 on slips of paper. Show your child two numbers, and ask which number is greater. Repeat with different pairs of numbers.

Algebra • Greater Than

COMMON CORE STANDARDS—1.NBT.B.3
Understand place value.

Use if you need to.

Circle the greater number.	Did tens or ones help you decide?	Write the numbers.
1. 22 42	tens ones	____ is greater than ____. ____ > ____
2. 46 64	tens ones	____ is greater than ____. ____ > ____
3. 88 86	tens ones	____ is greater than ____. ____ > ____

Problem Solving Real World

4. Color the blocks that show numbers greater than 47.

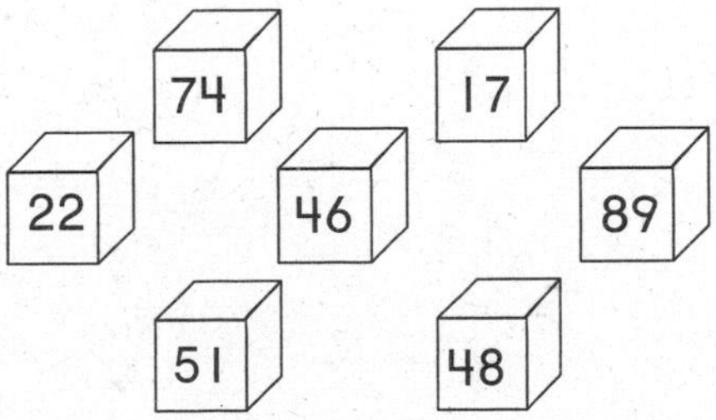

5. WRITE Math Write a number that is greater than 29. Draw quick pictures to explain.

Lesson Check (1.NBT.B.3)

1. Circle the number that is greater than 65.
Write the numbers.

37 49 56 66

____ is greater than ____.

____ > ____

2. Circle the number that is greater than 29.
Write the numbers.

19 20 28 92

____ is greater than ____.

____ > ____

Spiral Review (1.OA.C.6, 1.NBT.A.1)

3. What is 5 + 7? Write the sum.

$5 + 7 =$ ____

4. Count forward. Write the number that is missing.

110, 111, ____, 113, 114

FOR MORE PRACTICE GO TO THE **Personal Math Trainer**

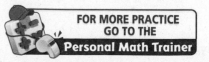

Name ____________________

Algebra • Less Than

Essential Question How can you compare two numbers to find which is less?

Common Core **Number and Operations in Base Ten—1.NBT.B.3**
MATHEMATICAL PRACTICES
MP3, MP5, MP7

Listen and Draw

Hands On

Use to solve. Draw quick pictures to show your work.

Tens	Ones

Math Talk MATHEMATICAL PRACTICES 3

Compare How does your drawing show which number is less? Explain.

FOR THE TEACHER • Read the problem. Which number is less, 22 or 28? Have children use base-ten blocks to solve.

Model and Draw

Compare numbers to find which is less.

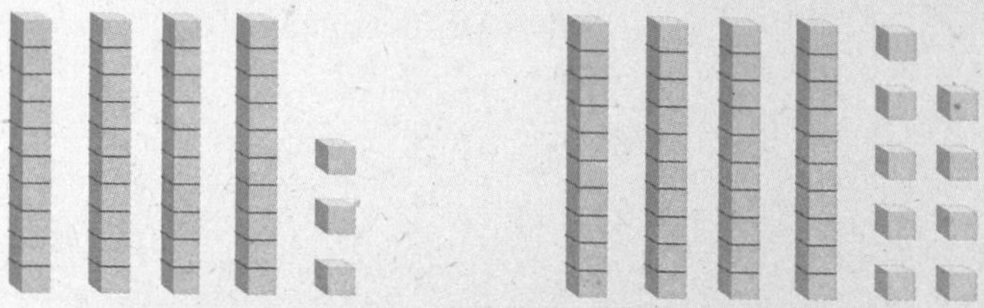

43 is less than 49.

43 < 49

How do you know which number is less?

Share and Show

MATH BOARD

Use your MathBoard and [tens] [ones] to show each number.

	Circle the number that is less.	Did tens or ones help you decide?	Write the numbers.
1.	39 (36)	tens (ones)	36 is less than 39. 36 < 39
✓2.	80 94	tens ones	____ is less than ____. ____ < ____
✓3.	57 54	tens ones	____ is less than ____. ____ < ____

Name ______________________________

On Your Own

MATHEMATICAL PRACTICE 5 **Use a Concrete Model**

GO DEEPER Use [tens and ones blocks] if you need to.

	Circle the number that is less.	Did tens or ones help you decide?	Write the numbers.
4.	47 48	tens ones	____ is less than ____. ____ < ____
5.	82 28	tens ones	____ is less than ____. ____ < ____
6.	96 90	tens ones	____ is less than ____. ____ < ____
7.	23 32	tens ones	____ is less than ____. ____ < ____

Write a number to solve.

8. THINK SMARTER Ella has 22 beads. Lauren has fewer beads than Ella. How many beads might Lauren have?

____ beads

Problem Solving • Applications Real World

WRITE Math

Write a number to solve.

9. THINK SMARTER Nan makes the number 46. Marty makes a number that is less than 46. What could be a number Marty makes?

_____

10. THINK SMARTER Jack makes the number 92. Kit makes a number that has fewer ones than 92. What could be a number Kit makes?

Math on the Spot

_____

11. THINK SMARTER Write a number that is less than 67.

How do you know your number is less than 67?

_____

_____

TAKE HOME ACTIVITY • Write 47, 54, 57, and 74 on slips of paper. Show your child two numbers, and ask which number is less. Repeat with different pairs of numbers.

Name ____________________

Algebra • Less Than

Common Core
COMMON CORE STANDARD—1.NBT.B.3
Understand place value.

Use [tens] [ones] if you need to.

Circle the number that is less.	Did tens or ones help you decide?	Write the numbers.
1. 34 36	tens ones	____ is less than ____. ____ < ____
2. 75 57	tens ones	____ is less than ____. ____ < ____
3. 80 89	tens ones	____ is less than ____. ____ < ____

Problem Solving Real World

Write a number to solve.

4. Lori makes the number 74. Gabe makes a number that is less than 74. What could be a number Gabe makes? ____

5. WRITE Math Write a number that is less than 41. Draw quick pictures to explain.

Lesson Check (1.NBT.B.3)

1. Circle the number that is less than 52.
Write the numbers.

25 52 64 88

____ is less than ____.

____ < ____

2. Circle the number that is less than 76.
Write the numbers.

100 81 77 59

____ is less than ____.

____ < ____

Spiral Review (1.NBT.A.1, 1.NBT.B.2)

3. What number does the model show? Write the number.

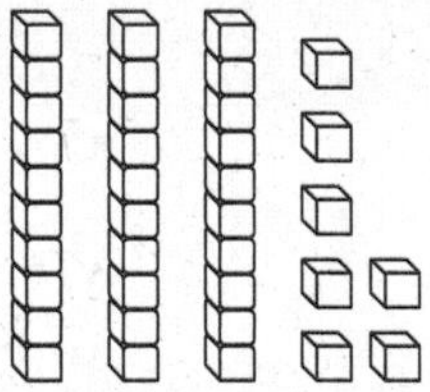

____ tens ____ ones = ____

4. Count by tens.
Write the missing numbers.

8, 18, 28, ____, ____, 58

Name ______________________________________

Algebra • Use Symbols to Compare

Essential Question How can you use symbols to show how numbers compare?

Common Core **Number and Operations in Base Ten—1.NBT.B.3** *Also 1.OA.D.7*

MATHEMATICAL PRACTICES
MP1, MP4, MP8

Listen and Draw

Hands On

Use tens and ones. Draw quick pictures to show your work. Write the numbers to compare.

___ $<$ 36	___ $=$ 36	___ $>$ 36

FOR THE TEACHER • Have children use base-ten blocks to show a number less than 36, a number equal to 36, and a number greater than 36.

Math Talk — MATHEMATICAL PRACTICES 4

Represent Compare 47 and 32 in two ways. What two symbols do you use?

Model and Draw

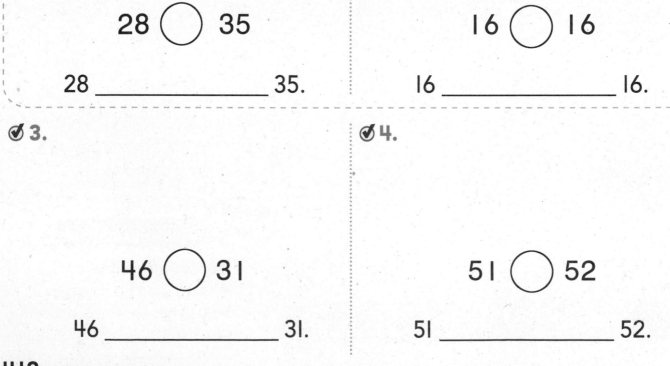

$21 < 24$

21 is less than 24.

$24 = 24$

24 is equal to 24.

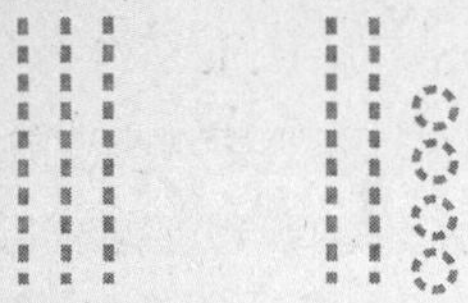

$30 > 24$

30 is greater than 24.

Share and Show MATH BOARD

Use ▭ ▫. Draw to show each number.
Write $<$, $>$, or $=$. Complete the sentence.

1.

28 ◯ 35

28 ______________ 35.

2.

16 ◯ 16

16 ______________ 16.

✓3.

46 ◯ 31

46 ______________ 31.

✓4.

51 ◯ 52

51 ______________ 52.

Name ____________________

On Your Own

REMEMBER
< is less than
> is greater than
= is equal to

MATHEMATICAL PRACTICE 4 **Use Symbols**

GO DEEPER Write <, >, or =.
Draw a quick picture if you need to.

5. 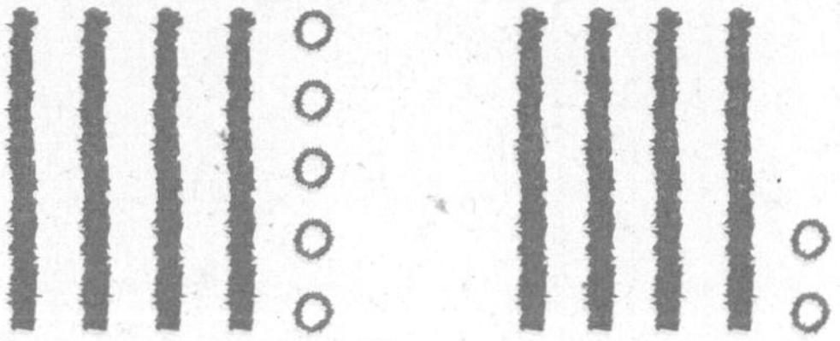

45 (>) 42

6. 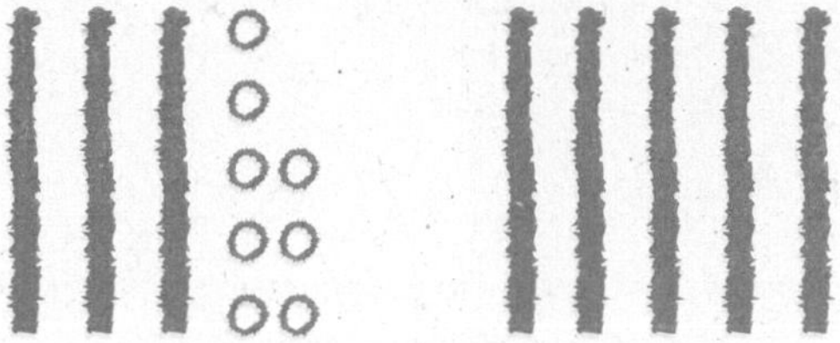

38 ◯ 50

7. 90 ◯ 93

8. 87 ◯ 87

9. 64 ◯ 59

10. THINK SMARTER Gill and Rob win tokens in a game. Gill has 86 tokens. Rob has 61 tokens. 70 tokens are needed for a prize. Who has enough tokens for a prize? Write the number.

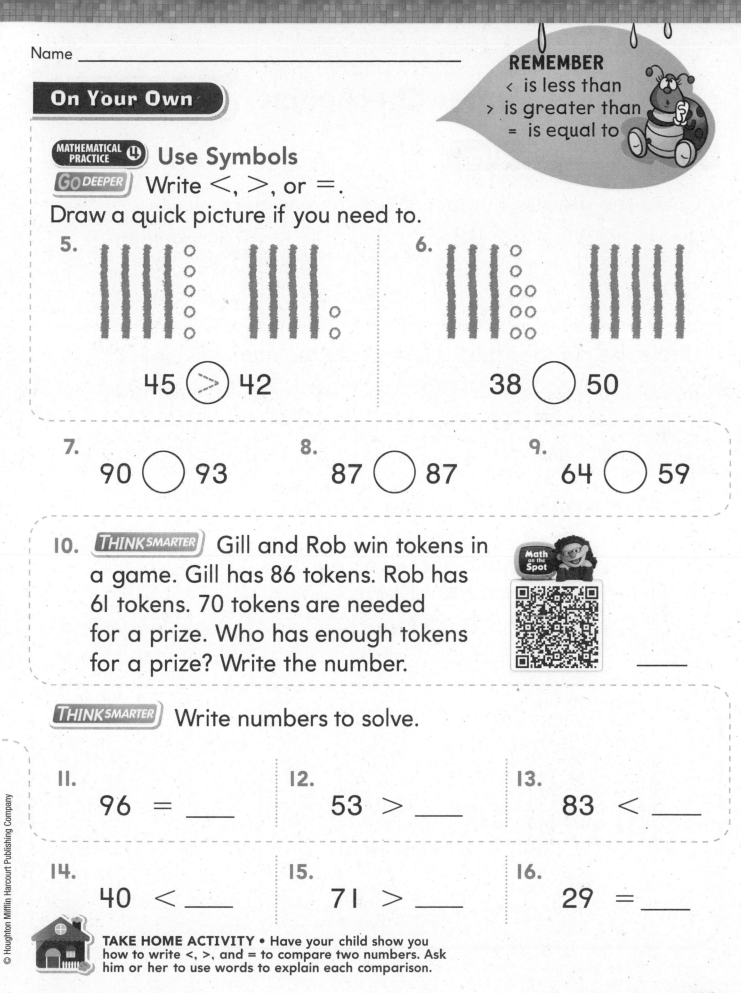

____

THINK SMARTER Write numbers to solve.

11. 96 = ____

12. 53 > ____

13. 83 < ____

14. 40 < ____

15. 71 > ____

16. 29 = ____

TAKE HOME ACTIVITY • Have your child show you how to write <, >, and = to compare two numbers. Ask him or her to use words to explain each comparison.

Name ______________________________

Mid-Chapter Checkpoint

Personal Math Trainer
Online Assessment and Intervention

Concepts and Skills

Circle the greater number. Write the numbers. (1.NBT.B.3)

1. 38 83

___ is greater than ___.

___ > ___

Circle the number that is less. Write the numbers. (1.NBT.B.3)

2. 61 29

___ is less than ___.

___ < ___

3. Matt scores 34 points and wins the game. Lee scores points and does not win. The number of Lee's points is less than the number of Matt's points. Is Lee's score 49 or 29? (1.NBT.B.3) ___

4. THINK SMARTER Circle the symbol that makes the math sentence true. (1.NBT.B.3)

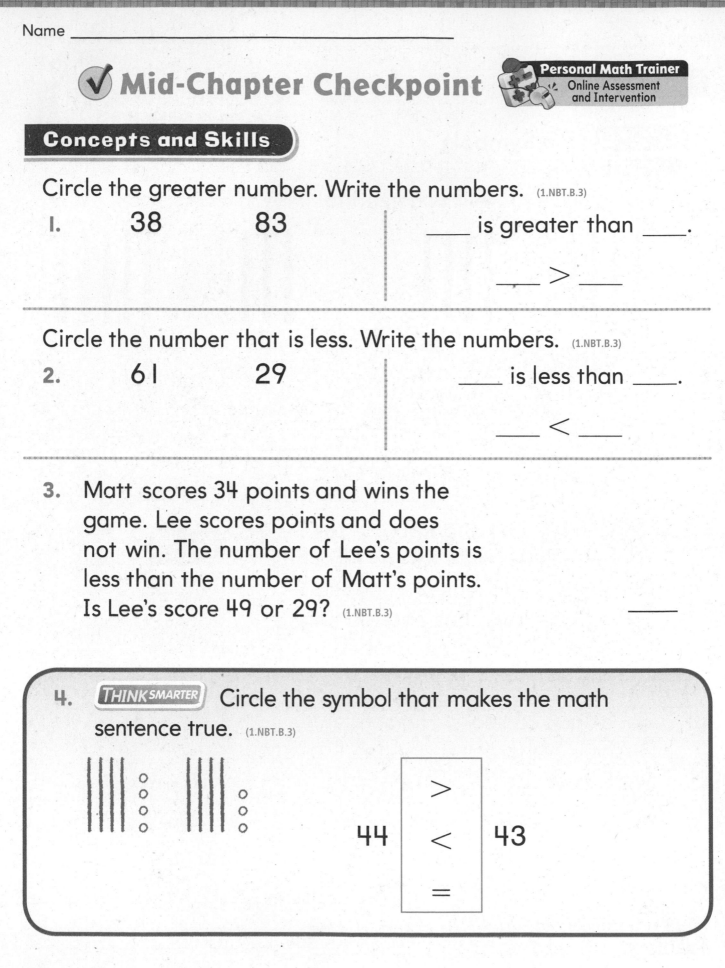

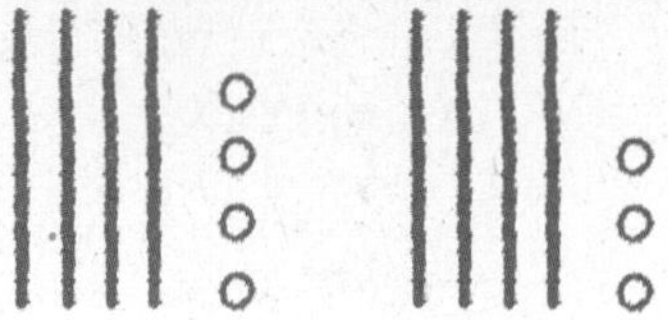

44 [> / < / =] 43

Name ____________________________________

Algebra • Use Symbols to Compare

Common Core **COMMON CORE STANDARD—1.NBT.B.3**
Understand place value.

Write <, >, or =.
Draw a quick picture if you need to.

1.

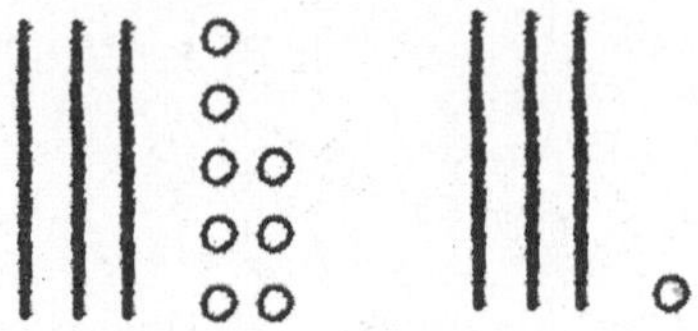

38 ◯ 31

2.

26 ◯ 42

3. 88 ◯ 78

4. 77 ◯ 77

5. 91 ◯ 89

6. 80 ◯ 82

7. 33 ◯ 44

8. 51 ◯ 60

Problem Solving Real World

Write <, >, or = to solve. Circle your answer.

9. Tracey has 26 shells. Heba has 29 shells. Who has a greater number of shells?

Tracey   Heba

29 ◯ 26

10. WRITE Math Choose some numbers to compare to 55. Use <, >, and =.

____

____

Lesson Check (1.NBT.B.3)

1. Compare each pair of numbers. Write <, >, or =.

22 ◯ 28 | 28 ◯ 28 | 22 ◯ 22 | 28 ◯ 22

2. Compare each pair of numbers. Write <, >, or =.

78 ◯ 87 | 78 ◯ 78 | 87 ◯ 78 | 87 ◯ 87

Spiral Review (1.NBT.B.2, 1.NBT.B.2b)

3. What number does the model show? Write the number.

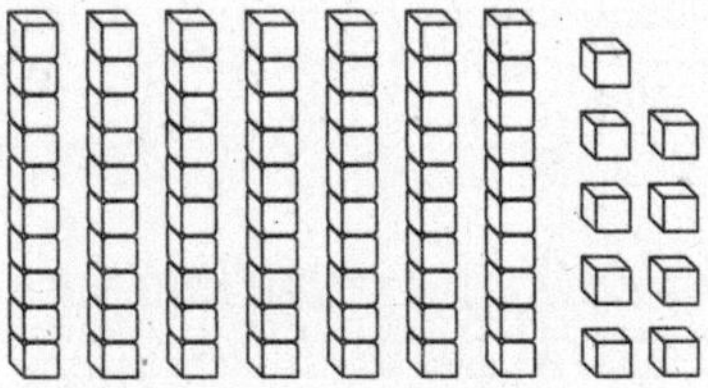

____ tens ____ ones = ____

4. Use the model. Write the number three different ways.

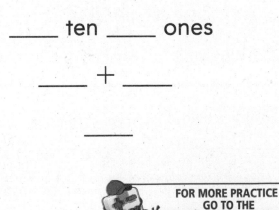

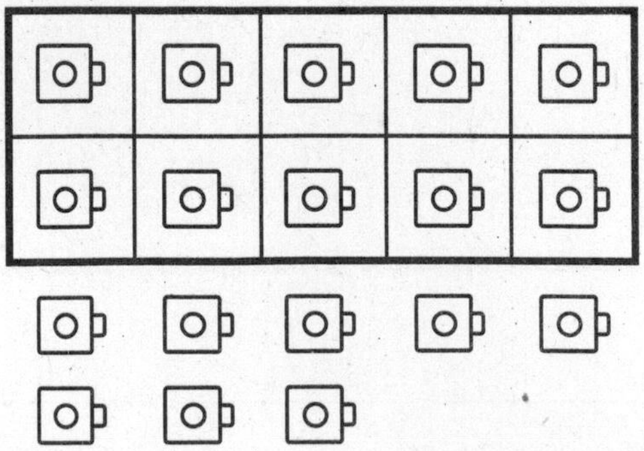

____ ten ____ ones

____ + ____

____

Name ______________________

Problem Solving • Compare Numbers

Essential Question How can making a model help you compare numbers?

Common Core **Number and Operations in Base Ten—1.NBT.B.3**
MATHEMATICAL PRACTICES MP2, MP4, MP6

Cassidy has the number cards shown below. She gives away the cards with numbers less than 49 or greater than 53. Which number cards does Cassidy have now?

Unlock the Problem

What do I need to find?

the number cards that Cassidy has now

What information do I need to use?

number cards $<$ 49 or $>$ 53

Show how to solve the problem.

47	48	51	52	54

Cassidy has number cards 51, 52.

HOME CONNECTION • Your child made a model of the problem. The numbers crossed out are less than 49 or greater than 53. The remaining numbers are the solution to the problem.

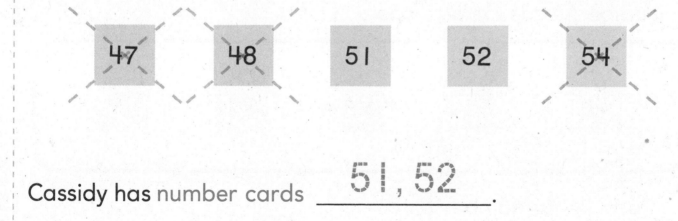

Try Another Problem

Make a model to solve.

- What do I need to find?
- What information do I need to use?

1. Tony has these number cards. He gives away the cards with numbers less than 16 or greater than 19. Cross those out. Which number cards does Tony have now?

15	17	18	20	22

Tony has number cards ______________.

2. Carol has these number cards. She keeps the cards with numbers greater than 98 or less than 95. Circle the number cards Carol keeps.

90	91	96	97	99

Carol keeps number cards ______________.

Math Talk MATHEMATICAL PRACTICES 4

Model Explain how you can find the number cards Tony has now.

Name ____________________________

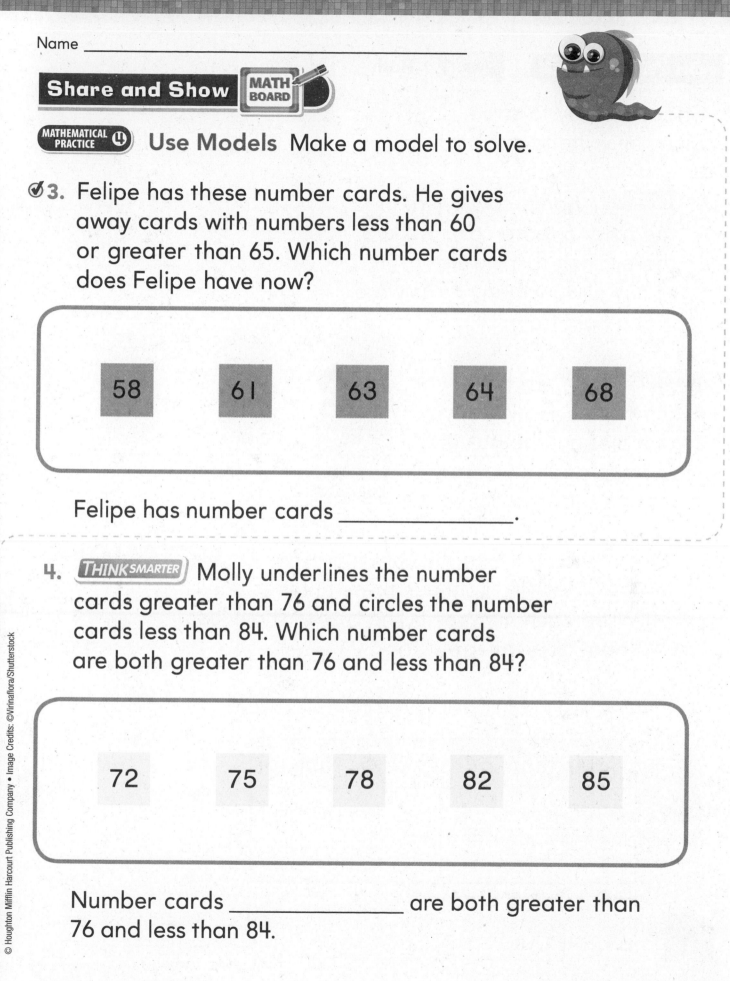

Share and Show MATH BOARD

MATHEMATICAL PRACTICE 4 **Use Models** Make a model to solve.

✓3. Felipe has these number cards. He gives away cards with numbers less than 60 or greater than 65. Which number cards does Felipe have now?

58	61	63	64	68

Felipe has number cards ______________.

4. THINKSMARTER Molly underlines the number cards greater than 76 and circles the number cards less than 84. Which number cards are both greater than 76 and less than 84?

72	75	78	82	85

Number cards ______________ are both greater than 76 and less than 84.

On Your Own

WRITE Math

Choose a way to solve.
Draw or write to explain.

5. GO DEEPER Some cows were in the field. 6 more cows walked there. Then there were 13 cows. How many cows were in the field before?

____ cows

6. THINK SMARTER Ed has 6 marbles. How many marbles can he put in a red cup and how many can he put in a blue cup?

Math on the Spot

____ + ____ = 6

Personal Math Trainer

7. THINK SMARTER + Lani has these number cards. Write each number in the box to show **less than** 24 or **greater than** 24.

22 27 23 21 25

less than 24	greater than 24

TAKE HOME ACTIVITY • Ask your child to tell you a number that is greater than 59 and a number less than 59.

Name ______________________

Problem Solving • Compare Numbers

Common Core — COMMON CORE STANDARD—1.NBT.B.3
Understand place value.

Make a model to solve.

1. Ava has these number cards. She gives away cards with numbers less than 34 or greater than 38. Cross those out. Which number cards does Ava have now?

32	33	35	37	39

Ava has number cards ________.

2. Ron has these number cards. He keeps the cards with numbers greater than 60 or less than 56. Circle the number cards Ron keeps.

54	57	58	59	61

Ron keeps number cards ________.

3. WRITE Math Write your own problem. Choose a secret number. Write clues about the number using the words *is greater than* and *is less than.*

____

____

Lesson Check (1.NBT.B.3)

1. Juan crosses out the numbers that are less than 45 or greater than 50. Circle the numbers that are left.

43	44	46	49	52

Spiral Review (1.OA.C.5, 1.OA.C.6)

2. Count back 3.
Write the difference.

$9 - 3 =$ ____

3. Write the numbers to complete the related facts.

$4 + 7 = 11$ $\qquad$ $11 - 4 = 7$

$7 + 4 = 11$ $\qquad$ ____ $-$ ____ $=$ ____

FOR MORE PRACTICE GO TO THE **Personal Math Trainer**

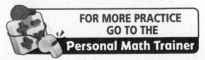

Name ______________________________

10 Less, 10 More

Essential Question How can you identify numbers that are 10 less or 10 more than a number?

Common Core **Number and Operations in Base Ten—1.NBT.C.5**

MATHEMATICAL PRACTICES
MP1, MP2, MP3, MP6

Listen and Draw

Real World · Hands On

Use  to solve. Draw quick pictures to show your work.

Pat

___

Tony

___

Jan

___

Math Talk MATHEMATICAL PRACTICES 6

What number has one less 10 than 12? **Explain.**

FOR THE TEACHER • Read the following problem. Tony has 2 boxes of markers and 2 more markers. Pat has 10 fewer markers than Tony. Jan has 10 more markers than Tony. How many markers does each child have?

Model and Draw

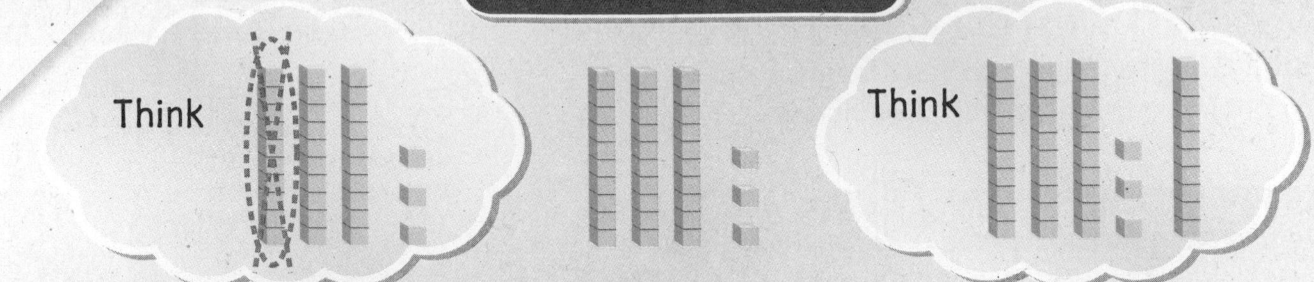

23　　33　　43

____ is 10 less than 33.　　____ is 10 more than 33.

Share and Show MATH BOARD

Use mental math. Write the numbers that are 10 less and 10 more.

1. 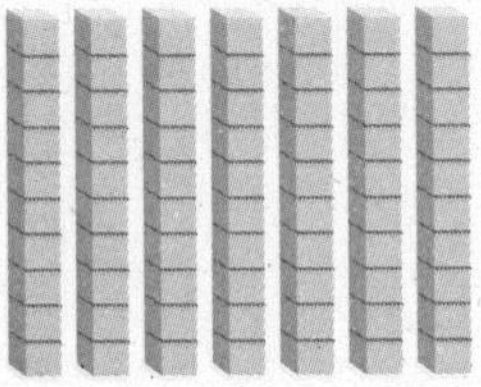

☐ 70 ☐

2. 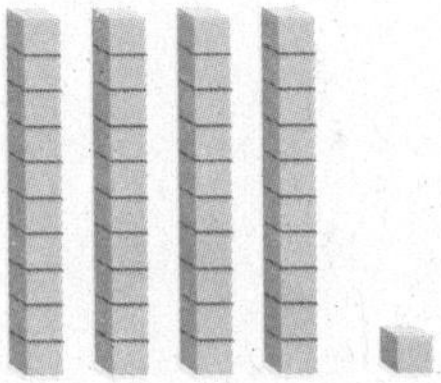

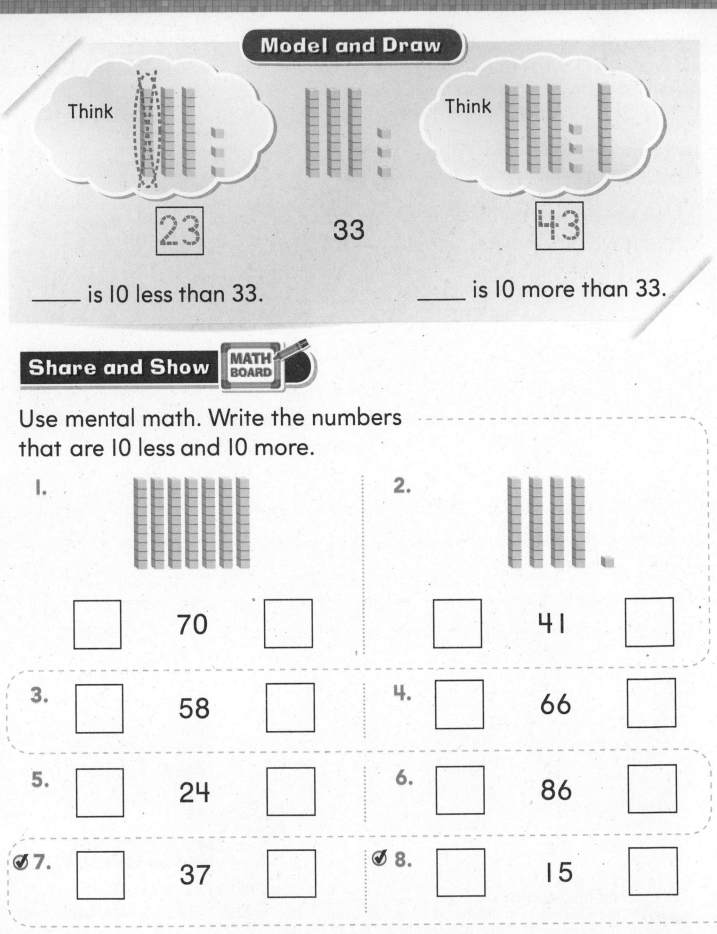

☐ 41 ☐

3. ☐ 58 ☐

4. ☐ 66 ☐

5. ☐ 24 ☐

6. ☐ 86 ☐

✓ 7. ☐ 37 ☐

✓ 8. ☐ 15 ☐

Name ____________________

On Your Own

MATHEMATICAL PRACTICE 3 **Apply** Use mental math.
Complete the chart. Explain your method.

	10 Less		10 More
9.	____	39	____
10.	____	75	____
11.	____	64	____
12.	____	90	____
13.	____	43	____
14.	11	____	____
15.	____	____	26

16. THINK SMARTER Solve.
I have 89 rocks. I want to collect 10 more. How many rocks will I have then?

Math on the Spot

____ rocks

Problem Solving • Applications Real World

WRITE Math

Choose a way to solve. Draw or write to show your work.

17. The plant has 4 fewer ladybugs on it than the tree. The tree has 7 ladybugs on it. How many ladybugs are on the plant?

____ ladybugs

18. Amy has 7 ribbons. Charlotte has 9 ribbons. How many more ribbons does Charlotte have than Amy?

____ more ribbons

19. GO DEEPER Margo has 28 stamps. Chet has 10 more stamps than Margo. Luis has 10 more stamps than Chet. How many stamps does Luis have?

____ stamps

Personal Math Trainer

20. THINK SMARTER + Draw a quick picture to show a number that is 10 less than the model.

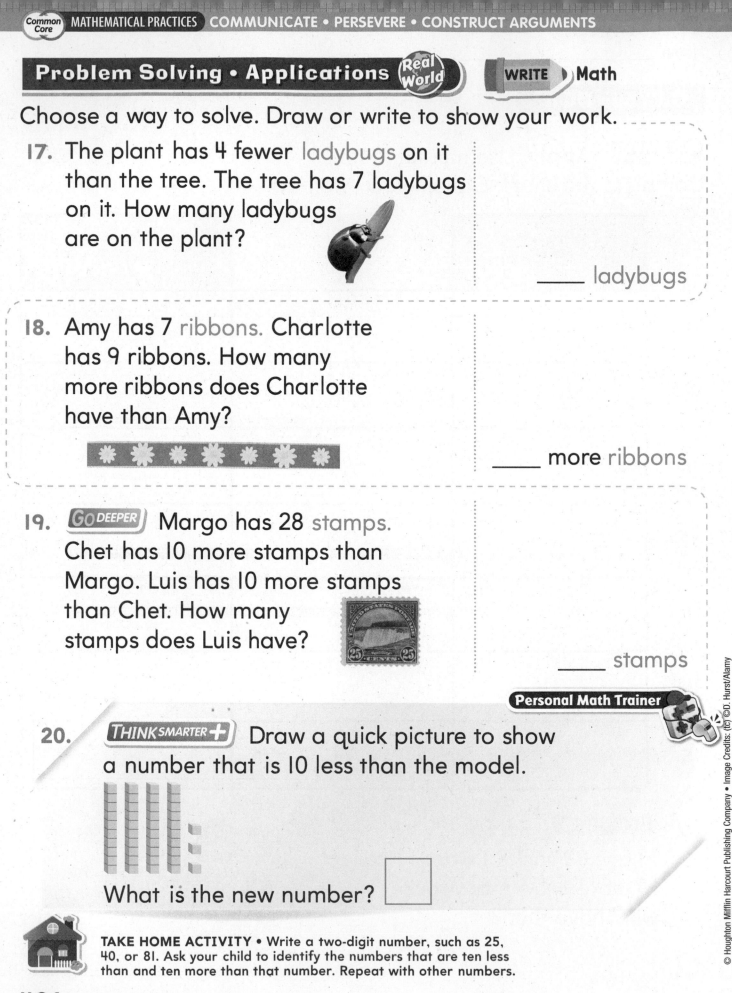

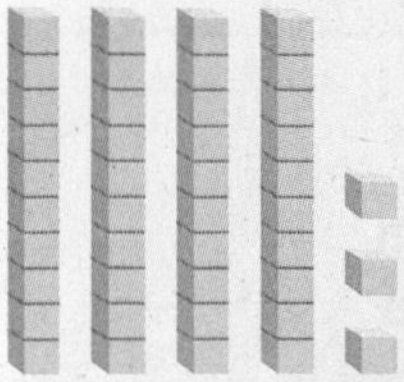

What is the new number? ☐

TAKE HOME ACTIVITY • Write a two-digit number, such as 25, 40, or 81. Ask your child to identify the numbers that are ten less than and ten more than that number. Repeat with other numbers.

Name ______________________________

10 Less, 10 More

COMMON CORE STANDARD—1.NBT.C.5
Use place value understanding and properties of operations to add and subtract.

Use mental math.
Complete the chart.

	10 Less		10 More
1.	____	48	____
2.	____	83	____
3.	8	____	____
4.	____	____	47

Problem Solving Real World

Choose a way to solve. Draw or write to show your work.

5. Jim has 16 books. Doug has 10 fewer books than Jim. How many books does Doug have?

______ books

6. WRITE Math Choose a number from 10 to 90. Draw and write to show the numbers that are 10 less and 10 more than your number.

Lesson Check (1.NBT.C.5)

1. What number is 10 less than 67?
Write the number.

_____

2. What number is 10 more than 39?
Write the number.

_____

Spiral Review (1.NBT.B.2b, 1.NBT.B.2c)

3. How many tens and ones make this number?
Write how many.

_____ ten _____ ones

4. What number does the model show?
Write the number.

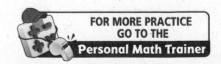

_____ tens = _____

Name ______________________

Chapter 7 Review/Test

Personal Math Trainer
Online Assessment and Intervention

1. Compare. Is the math sentence true? Choose Yes or No.

54 is greater than 45.	○ Yes	○ No
37 is greater than 29.	○ Yes	○ No
$29 > 43$	○ Yes	○ No
$55 > 45$	○ Yes	○ No

2. Choose all the numbers that are less than 71.

○ 62 ○ 80 ○ 70 ○ 49

3. Circle the symbol that makes the math sentence true.

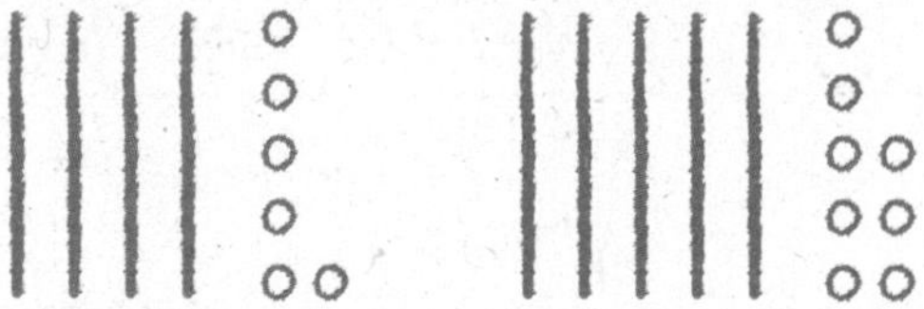

46 [$>$ / $<$ / $=$] 58

GO DIGITAL Assessment Options Chapter Test

4. Megan has these number cards. Write each number in the box to show **less than** 33 or **greater than** 33.

37 34 31 35 32

less than 33	greater than 33

5. Use mental math. Complete the chart.

10 Less		10 More
____	33	____
____	57	____

6. Write a number that is less than 30.

How do you know your number is less than 30?

Name ___________________________

7. Choose all the math sentences that are true.

- ○ $35 < 47$
- ○ $24 = 39$
- ○ $14 > 41$
- ○ $48 = 48$
- ○ $23 > 21$

8. James circles the numbers that are **less than** 87 or **greater than** 91. Which numbers does James circle?

86 88 89 90 92

James circles _____ and _____.

Personal Math Trainer

9. THINKSMARTER+ Draw a quick picture to show a number that is 10 more than the model.

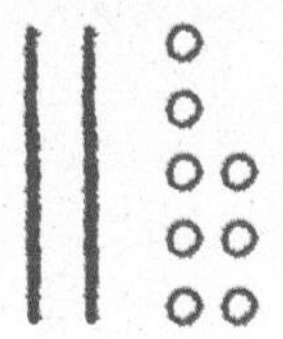

10. Compare. Is the math sentence true?
Choose Yes or No.

49 is greater than 57.	○ Yes	○ No
54 is greater than 53.	○ Yes	○ No
60 > 50	○ Yes	○ No
72 > 68	○ Yes	○ No

11. GO DEEPER Write <, >, or = to compare the numbers.

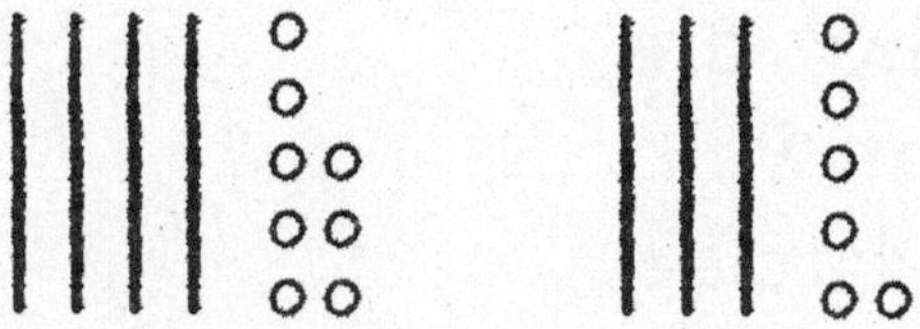

48 ______ 36

How do the drawings help you compare
the numbers?

12. Circle the words that make the sentence true.

88 is greater than / less than / equal to 90.

Chapter 8 Two-Digit Addition and Subtraction

Curious About Math with Curious George

There are 4 boxes of oranges on a table. Each box holds 10 oranges. How many oranges are there?

Name ______________________________

Show What You Know

Personal Math Trainer
Online Assessment and Intervention

Add and Subtract

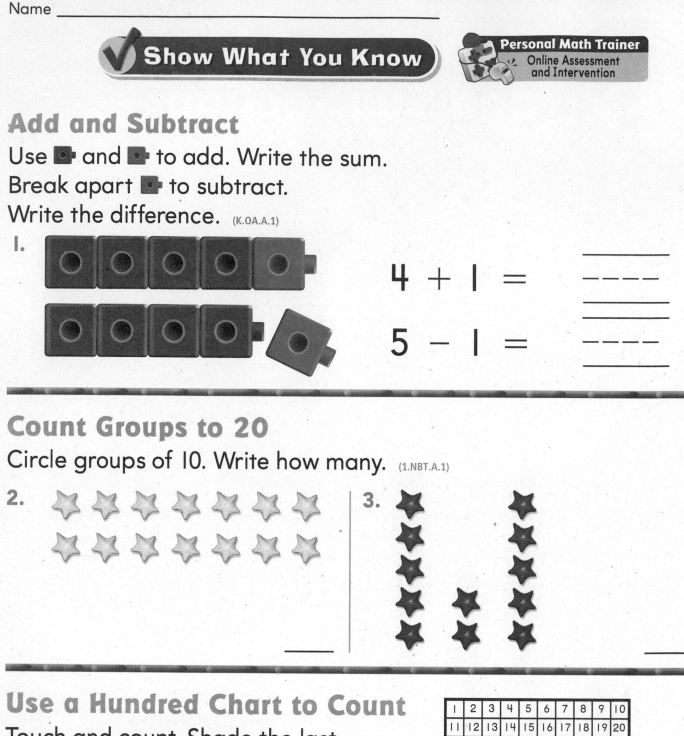

Use and to add. Write the sum.
Break apart to subtract.
Write the difference. (K.OA.A.1)

1.

4 + 1 = ____

5 − 1 = ____

Count Groups to 20

Circle groups of 10. Write how many. (1.NBT.A.1)

2.

____

3.

____

Use a Hundred Chart to Count

Touch and count. Shade the last number counted. (1.NBT.A.1)

4. Start at 1 and count to 20.
5. Start at 30 and count to 56.
6. Start at 77 and count to 93.

1	2	3	4	5	6	7	8	9	10
11	12	13	14	15	16	17	18	19	20
21	22	23	24	25	26	27	28	29	30
31	32	33	34	35	36	37	38	39	40
41	42	43	44	45	46	47	48	49	50
51	52	53	54	55	56	57	58	59	60
61	62	63	64	65	66	67	68	69	70
71	72	73	74	75	76	77	78	79	80
81	82	83	84	85	86	87	88	89	90
91	92	93	94	95	96	97	98	99	100

This page checks understanding of important skills needed for success in Chapter 8.

Name ___________________________

Vocabulary Builder

Review Words
add
subtract
sum
difference

Visualize It

Sort the review words from the box.

Put Together

____
____
____

Take Apart

____
____
____

Understand Vocabulary

Use a review word to complete each sentence.

1. 8 is the ____________ for 17 – 9.

2. 17 is the ____________ for 8 + 9.

3. When you ____________ 4 to 8, you find the sum.

4. When you ____________ 4 from 8, you find the difference.

GO DIGITAL • Interactive Student Edition • Multimedia eGlossary

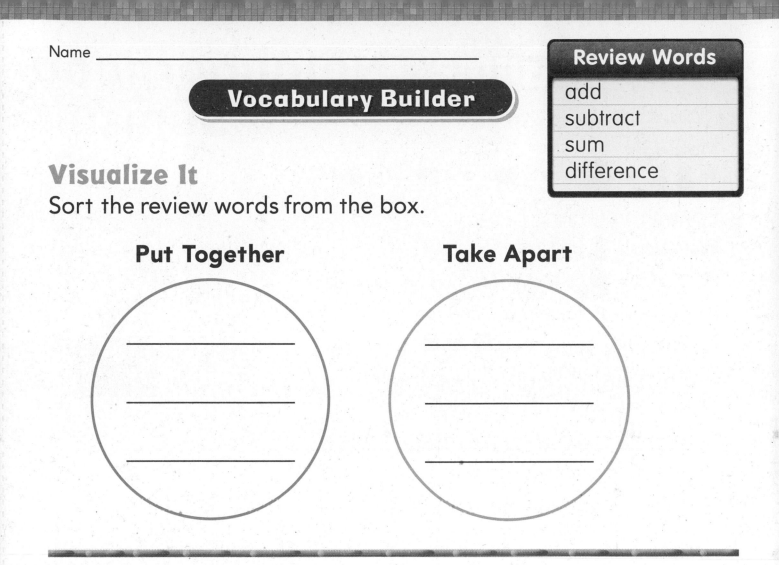

Game Neighborhood Sums

Materials

- 🟉 2 playing pieces • spinner (1, 2, 3) • 9 cubes • 9 cubes • 9 cubes

Play with a partner.

1. Put your playing piece on START.
2. Spin the spinner. Move that number of spaces.
3. Make a ten to help you find the sum.
4. The other player uses cubes to check.
5. If you are not correct, you lose a turn.
6. The first player to get to END wins.

2 4 +8	Move ahead one space.	4 9 +6	4 4 +6	9 1 +6	END
4 6 +3	5 3 +7	9 7 +1	Move back one space.	3 7 +7	5 8 +5
					6 6 +4
	START	2 4 +8	Move ahead one space.	6 1 +9	8 8 +2

Chapter 8 Vocabulary

add sumar 1	**addition sentence** enunciado de suma 3
difference diferencia 13	**fewer** menos 19
more más 38	**subtract** restar 52
subtraction sentence enunciado de resta 53	**sum** suma o total 54

4 + 2 = 6

is an **addition sentence.**

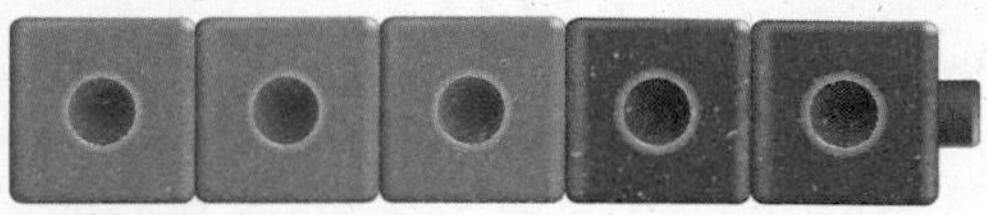

3 + 2 = 5

3 **fewer**

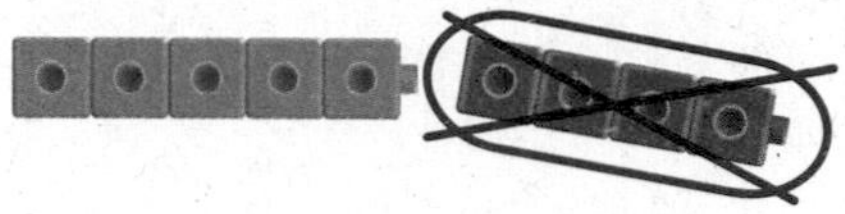

9 − 4 = 5

The **difference** is 5.

5 − 2 = 3

5 − 3 = 2

There are **more** .

2 plus 1 is equal to 3.

The **sum** is 3.

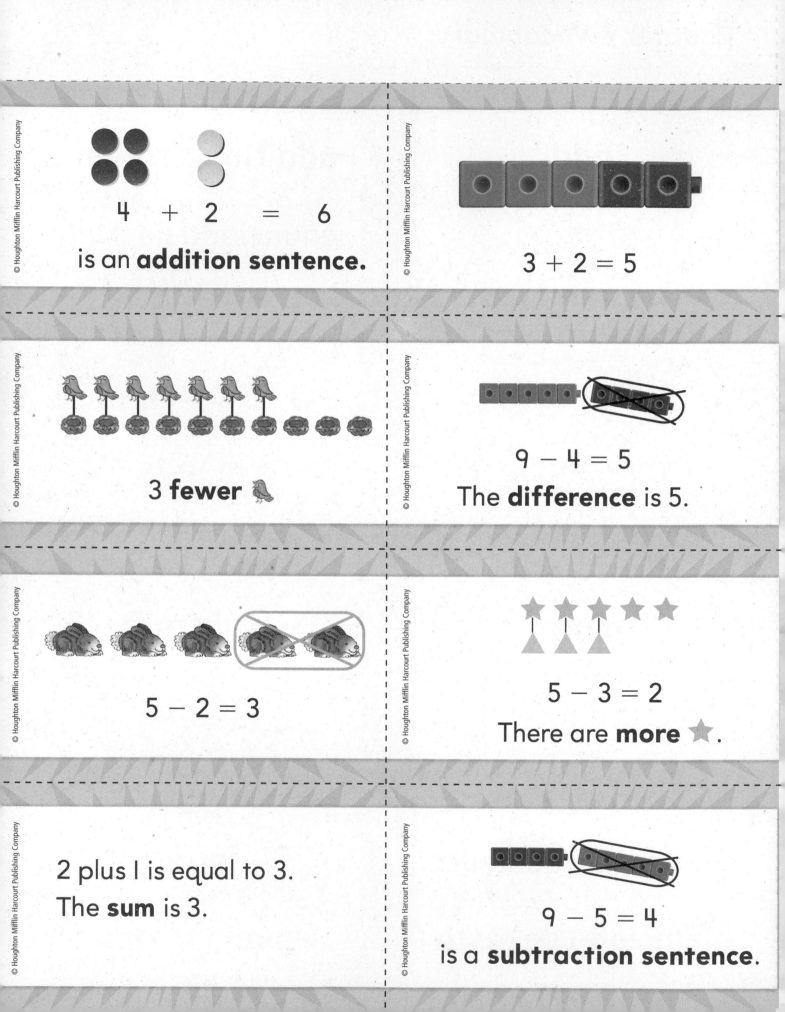

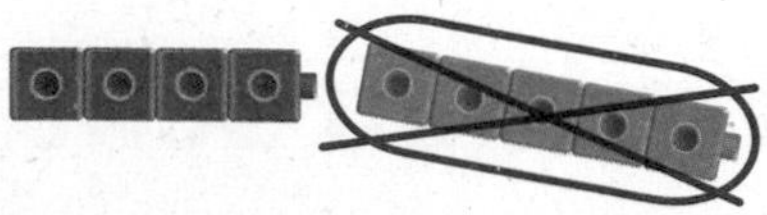

9 − 5 = 4

is a **subtraction sentence**.

Game

Bingo

Word Box
add
addition sentence
difference
fewer
more
subtract
subtraction sentence
sum

Materials

- 1 set of word cards
- 18 ●

How to Play

Play with a partner.

1. Mix the cards. Put the cards in a pile with the blank side up.
2. Take a card. Read the word.
3. Find the matching word on your bingo board. Cover the word with a ●. Put the card at the bottom of the pile.
4. The other player takes a turn.
5. The first player to cover 3 spaces in a line wins. The line may go across or down.

Player 1

fewer	add	more
addition sentence	BINGO	sum
subtraction sentence	difference	subtract

Player 2

subtraction sentence	addition sentence	fewer
add	BINGO	difference
subtract	more	sum

The Write Way

Reflect

Choose one idea. Draw and write about it.

- Write sentences that include at least two of these terms.

  add **subtract** **addition sentence** **subtraction sentence**

- Explain how you would solve this problem.

$$53 + 20 = \_\_\_\_$$

Name ______________________________

Add and Subtract Within 20

Essential Question What strategies can you use to add and subtract?

Common Core **Operations and Algebraic Thinking—1.OA.C.6**

MATHEMATICAL PRACTICES
MP1, MP3, MP6

Listen and Draw (Real World)

What is 5 + 4?
Use a strategy to solve the addition fact. Draw to show your work.

5 + 4 = ____

FOR THE TEACHER • Have children choose and model a strategy to solve the addition fact. Then have them draw to show their work.

Math Talk MATHEMATICAL PRACTICES 3

Apply What strategy did you use to find the answer?

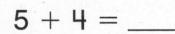

Model and Draw

Think of a strategy you can use to add or subtract.

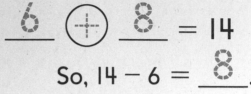

What is $14 - 6$?

I can use a related fact.

$\underline{6} \oplus \underline{8} = 14$

So, $14 - 6 = \underline{8}$.

Share and Show

MATH BOARD

Add or subtract.

1. $5 + 3 =$ ____
2. $10 - 5 =$ ____
3. $3 + 6 =$ ____
4. $12 - 5 =$ ____
5. $15 - 9 =$ ____
6. $5 + 7 =$ ____
7. $8 + 7 =$ ____
8. $9 - 7 =$ ____
9. $5 + 5 =$ ____
10. $12 - 7 =$ ____
11. $18 - 9 =$ ____
12. $9 + 4 =$ ____
13. $2 + 7 =$ ____
14. $5 - 1 =$ ____
15. $9 + 1 =$ ____
16. $7 - 6 =$ ____
17. ✓ $13 - 4 =$ ____
18. ✓ $2 + 6 =$ ____

Name ______________________________

On Your Own

MATHEMATICAL PRACTICE 3 **Apply** Add or subtract.

19. $\begin{array}{r} 14 \\ -\ 5 \\ \hline \end{array}$	20. $\begin{array}{r} 2 \\ +10 \\ \hline \end{array}$	21. $\begin{array}{r} 3 \\ +3 \\ \hline \end{array}$	22. $\begin{array}{r} 14 \\ -\ 8 \\ \hline \end{array}$	23. $\begin{array}{r} 8 \\ +9 \\ \hline \end{array}$	24. $\begin{array}{r} 6 \\ -3 \\ \hline \end{array}$
25. $\begin{array}{r} 6 \\ -5 \\ \hline \end{array}$	26. $\begin{array}{r} 2 \\ +8 \\ \hline \end{array}$	27. $\begin{array}{r} 0 \\ +5 \\ \hline \end{array}$	28. $\begin{array}{r} 10 \\ -\ 2 \\ \hline \end{array}$	29. $\begin{array}{r} 9 \\ +9 \\ \hline \end{array}$	30. $\begin{array}{r} 5 \\ -4 \\ \hline \end{array}$
31. $\begin{array}{r} 8 \\ -8 \\ \hline \end{array}$	32. $\begin{array}{r} 10 \\ +\ 1 \\ \hline \end{array}$	33. $\begin{array}{r} 4 \\ +7 \\ \hline \end{array}$	34. $\begin{array}{r} 9 \\ -3 \\ \hline \end{array}$	35. $\begin{array}{r} 1 \\ +8 \\ \hline \end{array}$	36. $\begin{array}{r} 17 \\ -\ 9 \\ \hline \end{array}$
37. $\begin{array}{r} 13 \\ -\ 7 \\ \hline \end{array}$	38. $\begin{array}{r} 6 \\ +5 \\ \hline \end{array}$	39. $\begin{array}{r} 10 \\ +\ 2 \\ \hline \end{array}$	40. $\begin{array}{r} 14 \\ -\ 9 \\ \hline \end{array}$	41. $\begin{array}{r} 10 \\ +10 \\ \hline \end{array}$	42. $\begin{array}{r} 11 \\ -\ 3 \\ \hline \end{array}$

43. THINK SMARTER Jamal thinks of an addition fact. The sum is 15. One addend is 8. What is a fact Jamal could be thinking of?

Math on the Spot

____ ◯ ____ ◯ ____

Problem Solving • Applications Real World

WRITE Math

Solve. Write or draw to explain.

44. THINK SMARTER There are 9 ants on a rock. Some more ants get on the rock. Now there are 18 ants on the rock. How many more ants got on the rock?

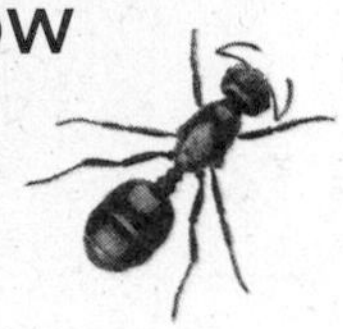

____ more ants

45. GO DEEPER Fill in the blanks. Write a number sentence to solve.

Lin sees ____ bees. Some bees flew away. Now there are ____ bees. How many bees flew away?

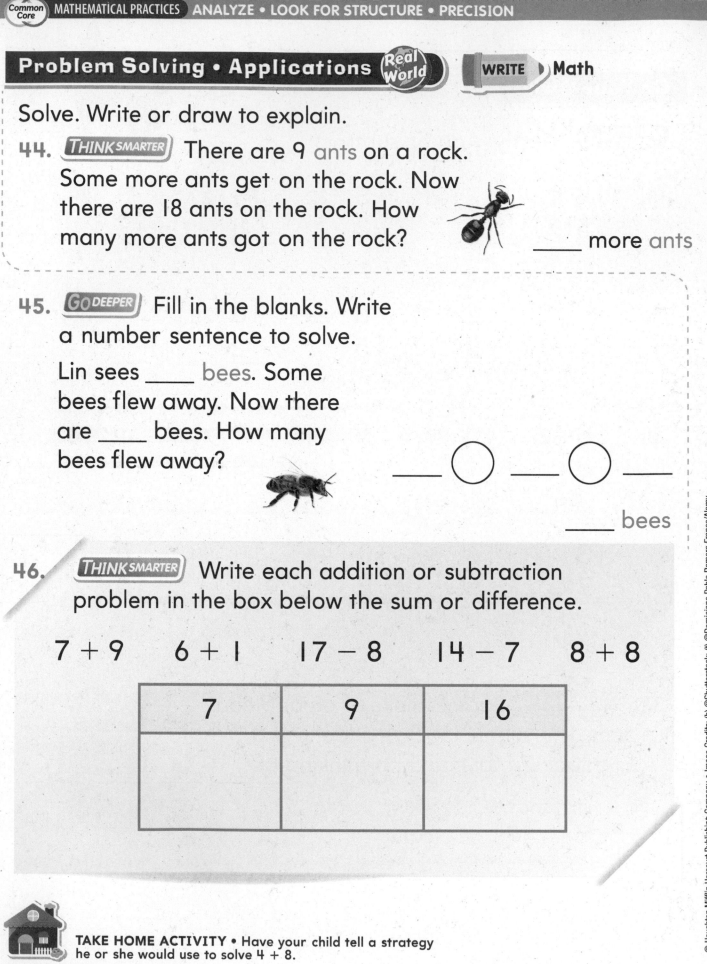

____ ◯ ____ ◯ ____

____ bees

46. THINK SMARTER Write each addition or subtraction problem in the box below the sum or difference.

7 + 9   6 + 1   17 − 8   14 − 7   8 + 8

7	9	16

TAKE HOME ACTIVITY • Have your child tell a strategy he or she would use to solve 4 + 8.

Name ____________________

Add and Subtract Within 20

Common Core **COMMON CORE STANDARD—1.OA.C.6**
Add and subtract within 20.

Add or subtract.

1. $6 + 0$	2. $11 - 2$	3. $4 + 5$	4. $9 + 8$	5. $4 + 10$	6. $14 - 9$
7. $7 + 4$	8. $8 - 5$	9. $10 - 10$	10. $6 + 7$	11. $18 - 9$	12. $15 - 6$

Problem Solving Real World

Solve. Draw or write to explain.

13. Jesse has 4 shells. He finds some more. Now he has 12 shells. How many more shells did Jesse find?

_____ more shells

14. WRITE Math Write an addition or subtraction fact. Then write a strategy you could use to add or subtract.

____

____

____

____

Lesson Check (1.OA.C.6)

1. What is the sum?
Write the number.

$8 + 5 =$ ____

2. What is the difference?
Write the number.

$11 - 4 =$ ____

Spiral Review (1.NBT.B.3)

3.

Circle the greater number.	Did tens or ones help you decide?	Write the numbers.
43 46	tens ones	____ is greater than ____. ____ $>$ ____

4.

Circle the number that is less.	Did tens or ones help you decide?	Write the numbers.
69 84	tens ones	____ is less than ____. ____ $<$ ____

FOR MORE PRACTICE GO TO THE **Personal Math Trainer**

Name ____________________

Add Tens

Essential Question How can you add tens?

Common Core **Number and Operations in Base Ten—1.NBT.C.4**
MATHEMATICAL PRACTICES MP2, MP7

Listen and Draw (Real World)

Choose a way to show the problem.
Draw a quick picture to show your work.

Math Talk MATHEMATICAL PRACTICES 2

Reasoning Why will there be no ones in your answer when you add 20 + 30?

FOR THE TEACHER • Read the following problems. Barb has 20 baseball cards. Ed has 30 baseball cards. How many baseball cards do they have? Kyle has 40 baseball cards. Kim has 50 baseball cards. How many baseball cards do they have?

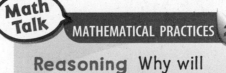

Model and Draw

How can you find 30 + 40?

30 + 40 = 70

____ tens

Share and Show MATH BOARD

Use [tens rod] [unit cube]. Draw to show tens.
Write the sum. Write how many tens.

1. 20 + 40 = 60

____ tens

2. 30 + 30 = 60

____ tens

3. 40 + 50 = 90

____ tens

4. 50 + 30 = 80

____ tens

Name ______________________________

On Your Own

MATHEMATICAL PRACTICE 2 **Represent a Problem** Draw to show tens. Write the sum. Write how many tens.

5. 40 + 40 = ____

____ tens

6. 70 + 20 = ____

____ tens

7. 10 + 80 = ____

____ tens

8. 60 + 30 = ____

____ tens

9. GO DEEPER Draw two groups of tens you can add to get a sum of 50. Write the number sentence.

____ ◯ ____ ◯ ____

Problem Solving • Applications Real World

WRITE Math

10. THINK SMARTER Complete the web. Write the missing addend to get a sum of 90.

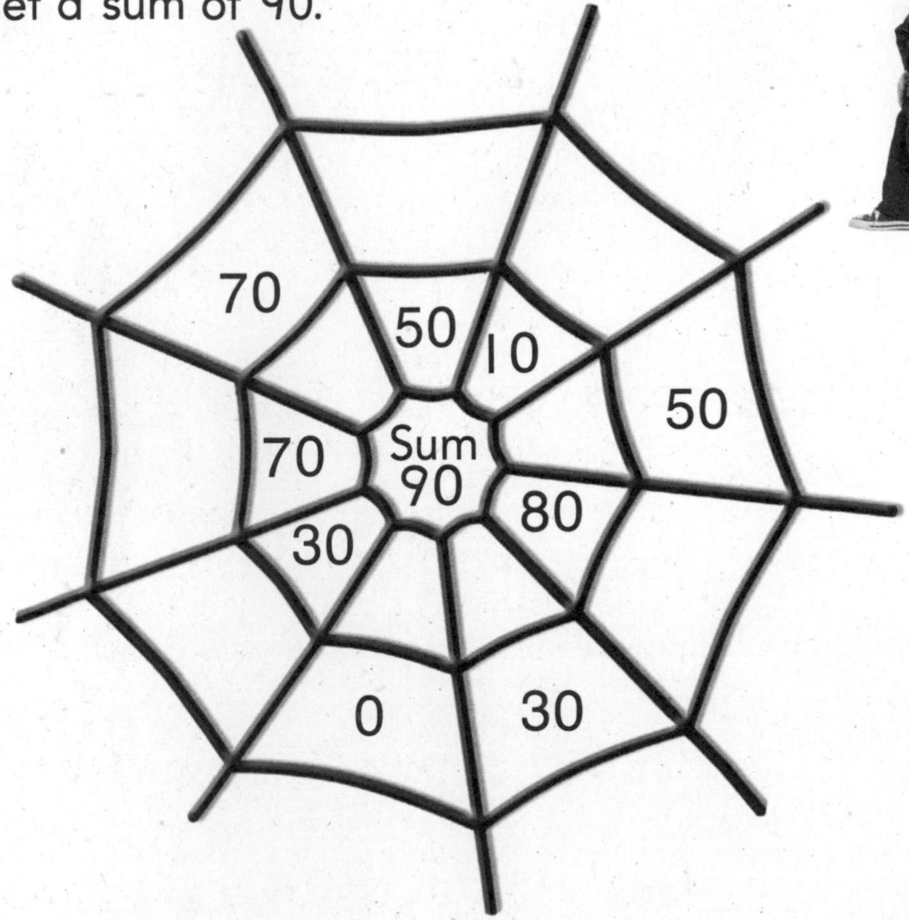

11. THINK SMARTER Choose all the ways that name the model.

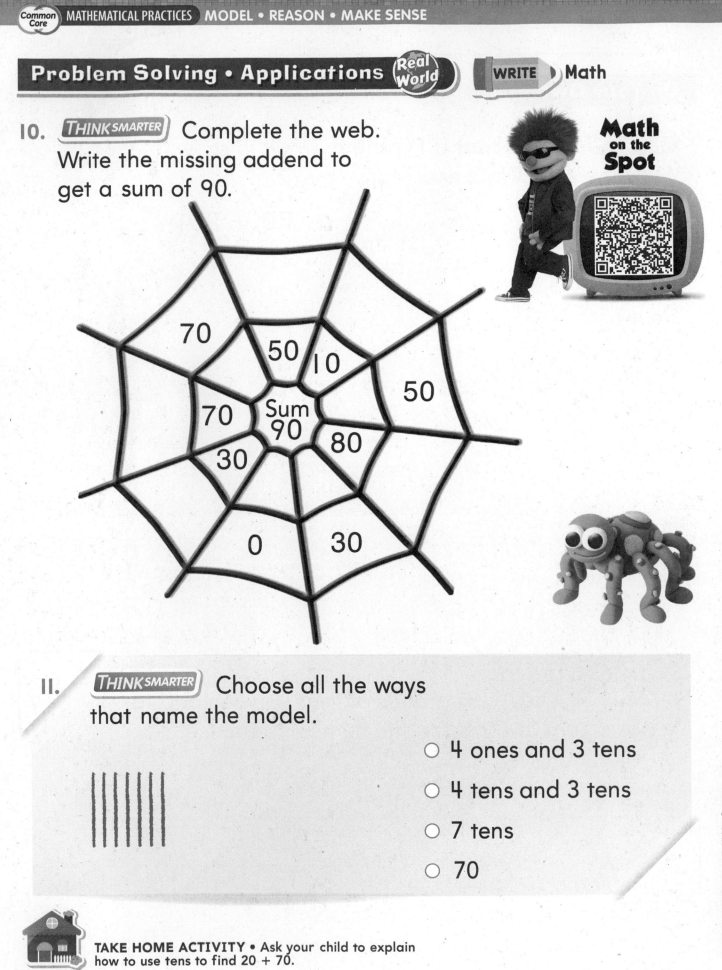

○ 4 ones and 3 tens

○ 4 tens and 3 tens

○ 7 tens

○ 70

TAKE HOME ACTIVITY • Ask your child to explain how to use tens to find 20 + 70.

Name ______________________

Add Tens

Practice and Homework Lesson 8.2

Common Core **COMMON CORE STANDARD—1.NBT.C.4** *Use place value understanding and properties of operations to add and subtract.*

Draw to show tens. Write the sum. Write how many tens.

1. 10 + 30 = ____

____ tens

2. 30 + 30 = ____

____ tens

3. 60 + 10 = ____

____ tens

4. 10 + 70 = ____

____ tens

Problem Solving Real World

Draw tens to solve.

5. Drew makes 20 posters. Tia makes 30 posters. How many posters do they make?

____ posters

6. Regina read 40 pages. Alice read 50 pages. How many pages did they read?

____ pages

7. WRITE Math Choose an addition problem from the spider web on page 446. Draw a quick picture and write the number sentence.

Lesson Check (1.NBT.C.4)

1. What is the sum?
 Write the number.

$$20 + 30 = \underline{}$$

2. What is the sum?
 Write the number.

$$30 + 10 = \underline{}$$

Spiral Review (1.OA.C.6, 1.NBT.B.3)

3. Write a doubles fact that can help you solve $6 + 5 = 11$.

$$\underline{} + \underline{} = \underline{}$$

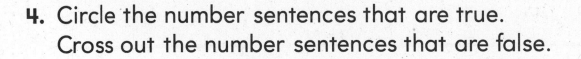

4. Circle the number sentences that are true.
 Cross out the number sentences that are false.

$$30 > 10 \qquad 30 < 10 \qquad 10 > 30 \qquad 10 < 30$$

FOR MORE PRACTICE
GO TO THE
Personal Math Trainer

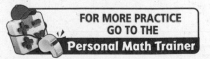

Name ______________________________

Subtract Tens

Essential Question How can you subtract tens?

Common Core **Number and Operations in Base Ten—1.NBT.C.6**

MATHEMATICAL PRACTICES
MP3, MP4, MP6, MP8

Listen and Draw Real World

Choose a way to show the problem.
Draw a quick picture to show your work.

Math Talk MATHEMATICAL PRACTICES 4

Represent How does your picture show the first problem?

FOR THE TEACHER • Read the following problems. Tara has 30 seashells. 20 shells are big. The rest are small. How many small shells does she have? Sammy has 50 shells. He gives 30 shells to his friend. How many shells does Sammy have now?

Model and Draw

How can you find 80 − 30?

80 − 30 = 50

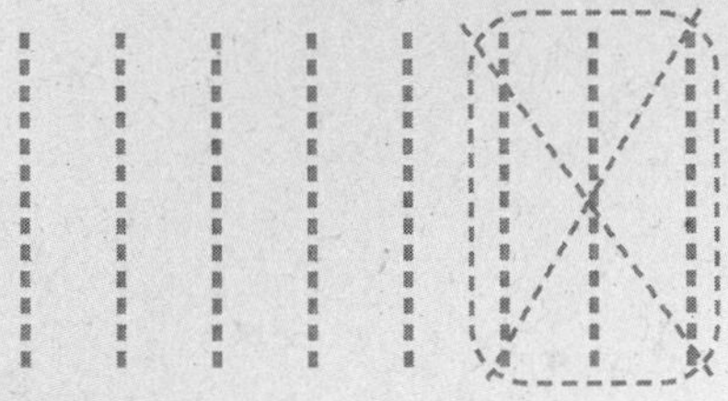

____ tens

Share and Show

MATH BOARD

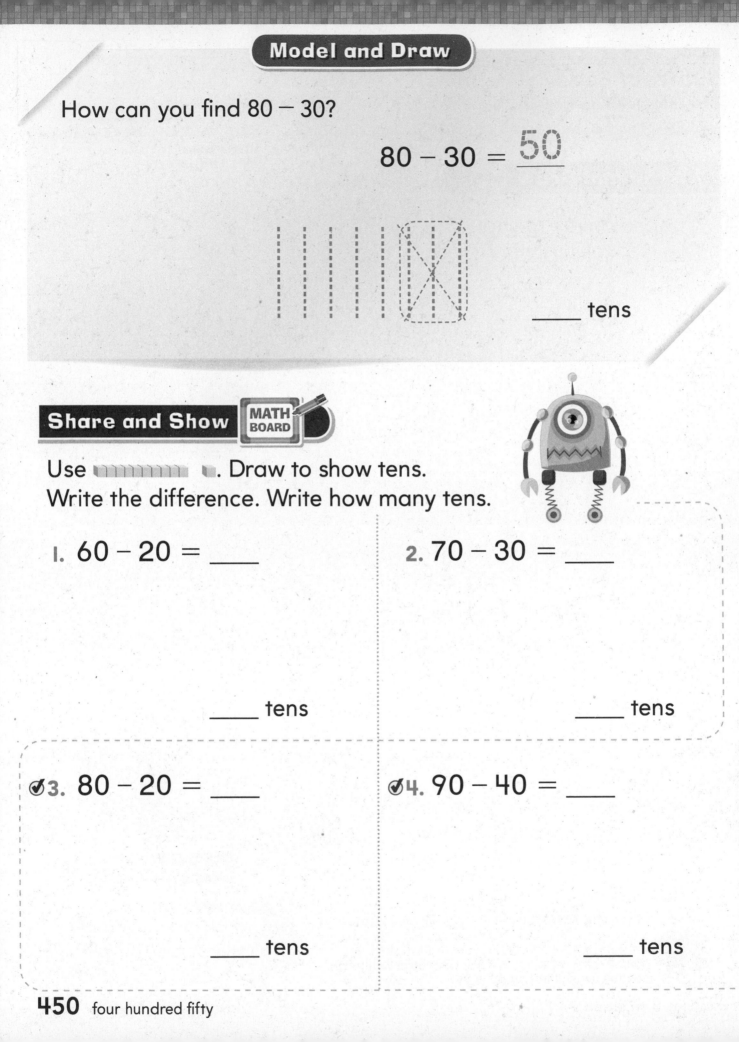

Use ▭ ▫. Draw to show tens.
Write the difference. Write how many tens.

1. 60 − 20 = ____

____ tens

2. 70 − 30 = ____

____ tens

✓3. 80 − 20 = ____

____ tens

✓4. 90 − 40 = ____

____ tens

Name ______________________________

On Your Own

MATHEMATICAL PRACTICE 6 **Make Connections** Draw to show tens. Write the difference. Write how many tens.

5. 80 − 40 = ____

____ tens

6. 90 − 70 = ____

____ tens

7. 70 − 50 = ____

____ tens

8. 30 − 30 = ____

____ tens

THINK SMARTER Solve.

9. Jeff has 40 pennies. He gives some to Jill. He has 10 pennies left. How many pennies does Jeff give to Jill?

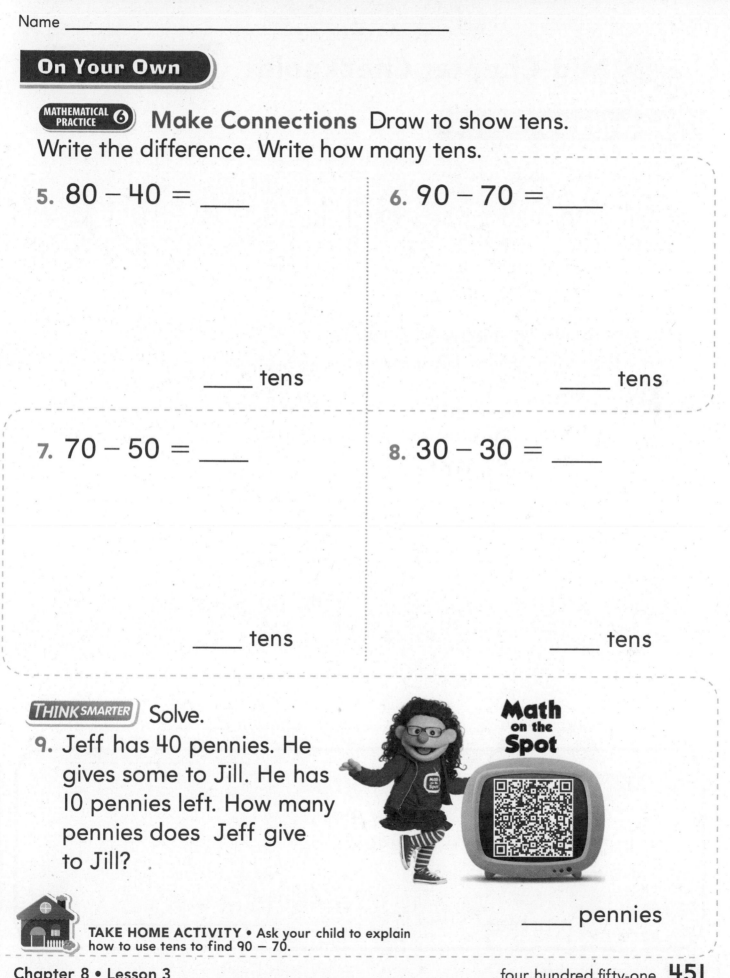

____ pennies

TAKE HOME ACTIVITY • Ask your child to explain how to use tens to find 90 − 70.

Name ______________________________

Mid-Chapter Checkpoint

Personal Math Trainer
Online Assessment and Intervention

Concepts and Skills

Add or subtract. (1.OA.C.6)

1. $4 + 8 =$ ____
2. $15 - 7 =$ ____
3. $9 - 6 =$ ____
4. $3 + 1 =$ ____
5. $10 + 6 =$ ____
6. $11 - 2 =$ ____

Use tens and ones. Draw to show tens.
Write the sum. Write how many tens. (1.NBT.C.4)

7. $30 + 50 =$ ____

____ tens

8. $40 + 20 =$ ____

____ tens

Use tens and ones. Draw to show tens.
Write the difference. Write how many tens. (1.NBT.C.6)

9. $90 - 20 =$ ____

____ tens

10. $60 - 40 =$ ____

____ tens

11. THINK SMARTER Mike has 60 marbles. He gives 20 to Kathy. How many marbles does Mike have left? Show your work. (1.NBT.C.6)

______ marbles

Name ______________________

Subtract Tens

Common Core

COMMON CORE STANDARD—1.NBT.C.6
Use place value understanding and properties of operations to add and subtract.

Draw to show tens. Write the difference. Write how many tens.

1. 40 − 10 = ____

____ tens

2. 80 − 40 = ____

____ tens

Problem Solving Real World

Draw tens to solve.

3. Mario has 70 baseball cards.
He gives 30 to Lisa.
How many baseball cards does Mario have left?

____ baseball cards

4. WRITE Math Draw a picture to show how to solve 50 − 40.

Lesson Check (1.NBT.C.6)

1. What is the difference?
Write the number.

$60 - 20 =$ ____

2. What is the difference?
Write the number.

$70 - 30 =$ ____

Spiral Review (1.OA.C.6, 1.NBT.B.3)

3. Use ○ ● and a ten frame. Show both addends. Draw to make ten. Then write a new fact. Add.

$$\begin{array}{r} 9 \\ +\ 4 \\ \hline \end{array}$$

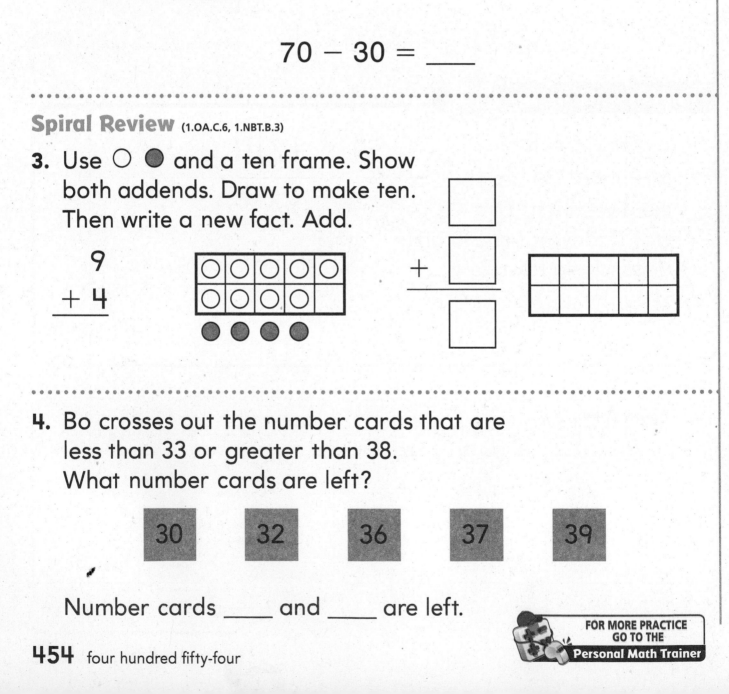

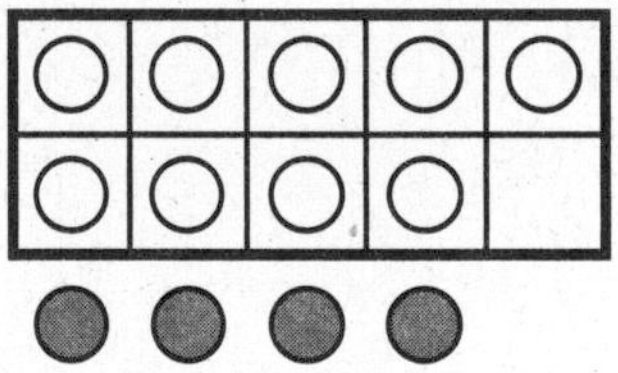

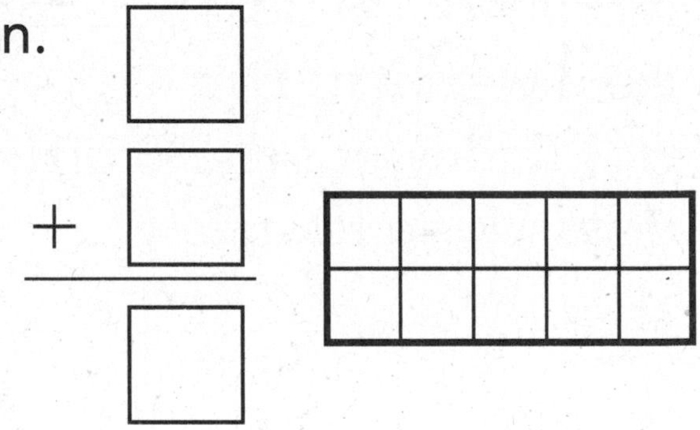

4. Bo crosses out the number cards that are less than 33 or greater than 38.
What number cards are left?

30 32 36 37 39

Number cards ____ and ____ are left.

Name ______________________

Use a Hundred Chart to Add

Essential Question How can you use a hundred chart to count on by ones or tens?

Common Core **Number and Operations in Base Ten—1.NBT.C.4**
MATHEMATICAL PRACTICES MP4, MP5, MP6

Listen and Draw Real World

Use the hundred chart to solve the problems.

1	2	3	4	5	6	7	8	9	10
11	12	13	14	15	16	17	18	19	20
21	22	23	24	25	26	27	28	29	30
31	32	33	34	35	36	37	38	39	40
41	42	43	44	45	46	47	48	49	50
51	52	53	54	55	56	57	58	59	60
61	62	63	64	65	66	67	68	69	70
71	72	73	74	75	76	77	78	79	80
81	82	83	84	85	86	87	88	89	90
91	92	93	94	95	96	97	98	99	100

FOR THE TEACHER • Read the following problems. Alice picks 12 flowers. Then she picks 4 more flowers. How many flowers does Alice pick? Ella picks 10 strawberries. Then she picks 20 more strawberries. How many strawberries does Ella pick?

Math Talk MATHEMATICAL PRACTICES 6

Explain how you can use a hundred chart to find each sum.

Model and Draw

Count on a hundred chart to find a sum.

1	2	3	4	5	6	7	8	9	10
11	12	13	14	15	16	17	18	19	20
21	22	23	24	25	26	27	28	29	30
31	32	33	34	35	36	37	38	39	40
41	42	43	44	45	46	47	48	49	50
51	52	53	54	55	56	57	58	59	60
61	62	63	64	65	66	67	68	69	70
71	72	73	74	75	76	77	78	79	80
81	82	83	84	85	86	87	88	89	90
91	92	93	94	95	96	97	98	99	100

Start at **24.**
Count on four ones.
25, 26, 27, 28

$24 + 4 =$ 28

Start at **31.**
Count on four tens.
41, 51, 61, 71

$31 + 40 =$ 71

Share and Show MATH BOARD

Use the hundred chart to add.
Count on by ones or tens.

1. $42 + 7 =$ ____

2. $57 + 30 =$ ____

✓3. $91 + 5 =$ ____

✓4. $18 + 50 =$ ____

Name ________________________________

On Your Own

How can you use the hundred chart to find each sum?

1	2	3	4	5	6	7	8	9	10
11	12	13	14	15	16	17	18	19	20
21	22	23	24	25	26	27	28	29	30
31	32	33	34	35	36	37	38	39	40
41	42	43	44	45	46	47	48	49	50
51	52	53	54	55	56	57	58	59	60
61	62	63	64	65	66	67	68	69	70
71	72	73	74	75	76	77	78	79	80
81	82	83	84	85	86	87	88	89	90
91	92	93	94	95	96	97	98	99	100

32 + 5 = ___

48 + 30 = ___

MATHEMATICAL PRACTICE 5 **Use Appropriate Tools**

Use the hundred chart to add.
Count on by ones or tens.

5. 13 + 70 = ___

6. 22 + 6 = ___

7. 71 + 3 = ___

8. 49 + 50 = ___

9. 53 + 4 = ___

10. 25 + 40 = ___

11. GO DEEPER Solve. Show your work.

31 + 20 + 40 = ___

Problem Solving • Applications Real World

WRITE Math

Choose a way to solve. Draw or write to show your work.

12. THINK SMARTER Rae put 20 books away. She put 20 more books away, then 11 more. How many books did Rae put away?

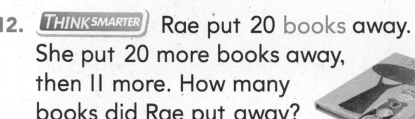

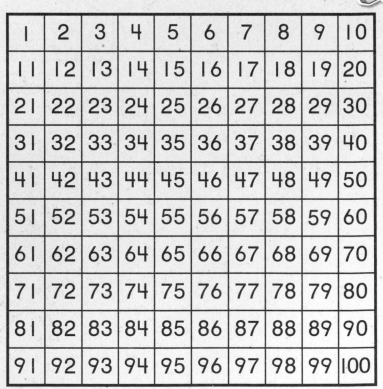

____ books

Personal Math Trainer

13. THINK SMARTER + Use the hundred chart to add. Count on by ones or tens.

$62 + 9 =$ ____

1	2	3	4	5	6	7	8	9	10
11	12	13	14	15	16	17	18	19	20
21	22	23	24	25	26	27	28	29	30
31	32	33	34	35	36	37	38	39	40
41	42	43	44	45	46	47	48	49	50
51	52	53	54	55	56	57	58	59	60
61	62	63	64	65	66	67	68	69	70
71	72	73	74	75	76	77	78	79	80
81	82	83	84	85	86	87	88	89	90
91	92	93	94	95	96	97	98	99	100

Explain how you used the chart to find the sum.

TAKE HOME ACTIVITY • On a piece of paper, write 36 + 40. Ask your child to explain how to use the hundred chart to count on by tens to find the sum.

Name ______________________

Use a Hundred Chart to Add

Common Core — **COMMON CORE STANDARD—1.NBT.C.4**
Use place value understanding and properties of operations to add and subtract.

**Use the hundred chart to add.
Count on by ones or tens.**

1	2	3	4	5	6	7	8	9	10
11	12	13	14	15	16	17	18	19	20
21	22	23	24	25	26	27	28	29	30
31	32	33	34	35	36	37	38	39	40
41	42	43	44	45	46	47	48	49	50
51	52	53	54	55	56	57	58	59	60
61	62	63	64	65	66	67	68	69	70
71	72	73	74	75	76	77	78	79	80
81	82	83	84	85	86	87	88	89	90
91	92	93	94	95	96	97	98	99	100

1. $47 + 2 =$ ______

2. $26 + 50 =$ ______

3. $22 + 5 =$ ______

4. $4 + 85 =$ ______

Problem Solving (Real World)

Choose a way to solve. Draw or write to show your work.

5. 17 children are on the bus. Then 20 more children get on the bus. How many children are on the bus now?

______ children

6. WRITE Math Write a number sentence to add 6 ones to 21. Write a number sentence to add 6 tens to 21.

____

____

____

Lesson Check (1.NBT.C.4)

1. What is the sum?
Write the number.

42 + 50 = ____

1	2	3	4	5	6	7	8	9	10
11	12	13	14	15	16	17	18	19	20
21	22	23	24	25	26	27	28	29	30
31	32	33	34	35	36	37	38	39	40
41	42	43	44	45	46	47	48	49	50
51	52	53	54	55	56	57	58	59	60
61	62	63	64	65	66	67	68	69	70
71	72	73	74	75	76	77	78	79	80
81	82	83	84	85	86	87	88	89	90
91	92	93	94	95	96	97	98	99	100

2. What is the sum?
Write the number.

11 + 8 = ____

Spiral Review (1.OA.D.8, 1.NBT.C.5)

3. Use mental math.
What number is ten less than 52?
Write the number.

____

4. Write an addition fact that helps you solve 16 − 9.

____ + ____ = ____

FOR MORE PRACTICE GO TO THE **Personal Math Trainer**

Name ______________________

Use Models to Add

HANDS ON
Lesson 8.5

Essential Question How can models help you add ones or tens to a two-digit number?

Common Core **Number and Operations in Base Ten—1.NBT.C.4**
MATHEMATICAL PRACTICES
MP4, MP6

Listen and Draw Real World

Draw to show how you can find the sum.

14 + 5 = ____

Math Talk MATHEMATICAL PRACTICES 4

Model Explain how you found the sum.

FOR THE TEACHER • Read the following problem. Amir counts 14 cars as they go by. Then he counts 5 more cars. How many cars does Amir count?

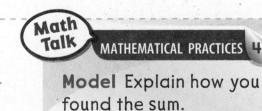

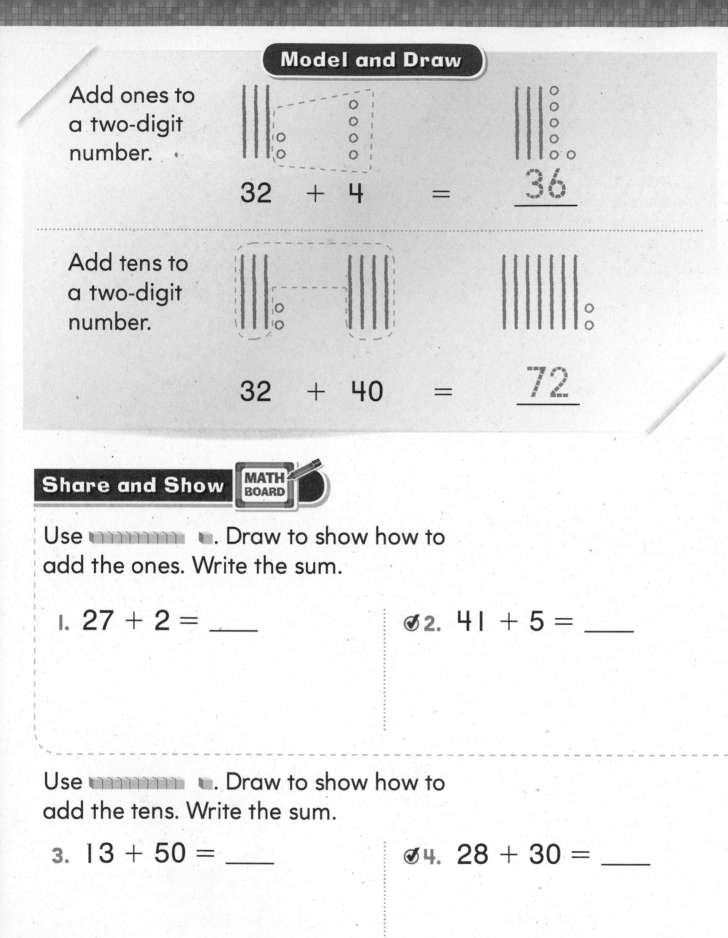

Model and Draw

Add ones to a two-digit number.

32 + 4 = 36

Add tens to a two-digit number.

32 + 40 = 72

Share and Show

MATH BOARD

Use  . Draw to show how to add the ones. Write the sum.

1. 27 + 2 = ____

✓2. 41 + 5 = ____

Use 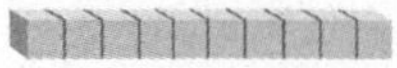 . Draw to show how to add the tens. Write the sum.

3. 13 + 50 = ____

✓4. 28 + 30 = ____

Name ________________________

On Your Own

MATHEMATICAL PRACTICE 4 Use Models

Use  and your MathBoard.
Add the ones or tens. Write the sum.

5. $65 + 3 =$ ____

6. $81 + 8 =$ ____

7. $54 + 20 =$ ____

8. $32 + 10 =$ ____

9. $95 + 2 =$ ____

10. $25 + 60 =$ ____

11. $2 + 54 =$ ____

12. $70 + 29 =$ ____

GO DEEPER Make a sum of 45. Draw a quick picture. Write the number sentence.

13. Add ones to a two-digit number.

____ + ____ $= 45$

14. Add tens to a two-digit number.

____ + ____ $= 45$

Problem Solving • Applications Real World

WRITE Math

Choose a way to solve. Draw or write to show your work.

15. Rita picks 63 strawberries. Then she picks 30 more. How many strawberries does Rita pick?

____ strawberries

16. THINK SMARTER Kenny planted two rows of corn. He used 20 seeds in each row. He has 18 seeds left. How many seeds of corn did Kenny have?

Math on the Spot

____ seeds

17. There are 7 oak trees and 32 pine trees in the park. How many trees are in the park?

____ trees

18. THINK SMARTER Use the model. Draw to show how to add the tens.

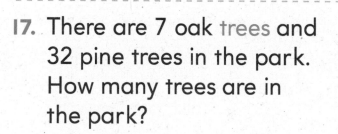

42 + 20 = ____

TAKE HOME ACTIVITY • Give your child the addition problems 25 + 3 and 25 + 30. Ask your child to explain how to solve each problem.

Name ______________________

Use Models to Add

COMMON CORE STANDARD—1.NBT.C.4
Use place value understanding and properties of operations to add and subtract.

Use [tens] [ones] and your MathBoard. Add the ones or tens. Write the sum.

1. 44 + 5 = ____
2. 16 + 70 = ____
3. 78 + 20 = ____
4. 52 + 7 = ____
5. 2 + 13 = ____
6. 73 + 4 = ____
7. 65 + 3 = ____
8. 20 + 25 = ____
9. 49 + 30 = ____
10. 81 + 8 = ____

Problem Solving Real World

Solve. Draw or write to explain.

11. Maria has 21 marbles.
She buys a bag of 20 marbles.
How many marbles does
Maria have now?

____ marbles

12. WRITE Math Write a story problem about 40 apples and 17 pears.

____

____

____

Lesson Check (1.NBT.C.4)

1. What is the sum?
Write the number.

$$62 + 30 = ____$$

2. What is the sum?
Write the number.

$$37 + 2 = ____$$

Spiral Review (1.OA.C.6, 1.NBT.A.1)

3. Write two ways to make 15.

$____ + ____ = 15$

$____ + ____ = 15$

4. What number does the model show?

____

FOR MORE PRACTICE GO TO THE **Personal Math Trainer**

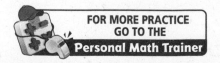

Name ______________________________

HANDS ON
Lesson 8.6

Make Ten to Add

Essential Question How can making a ten help you add a two-digit number and a one-digit number?

Common Core **Number and Operations in Base Ten—1.NBT.C.4**
MATHEMATICAL PRACTICES
MP2, MP5

Listen and Draw

Real World

Hands On

Use . Draw to show how you can find the sum.

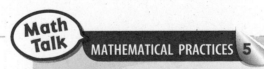

21 + 6 = ____.

Math Talk MATHEMATICAL PRACTICES 5

Use Tools Explain how your model shows the sum of 21 + 6.

FOR THE TEACHER • Read the following problem. Sally has 21 stickers in her sticker book. She gets 6 more stickers. How many stickers does Sally have now?

Model and Draw

Make a ten to find 37 + 8.

What can I add to 7 to make 10?

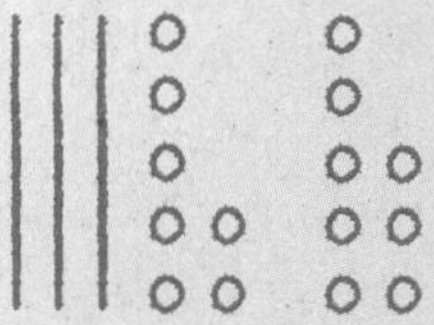

37 + 8

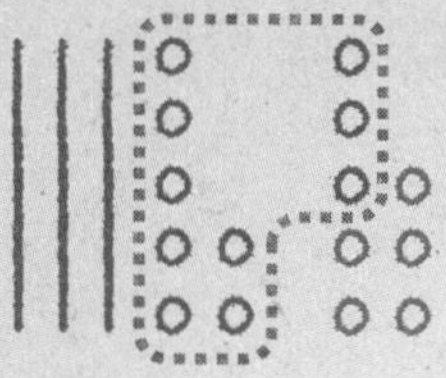

37 + 3 + 5

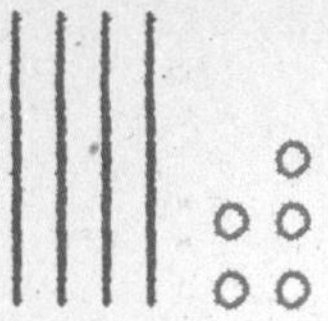

40 + 5

40 + 5 = 45

So, 37 + 8 = 45.

Share and Show

MATH BOARD

Use . Draw to show how you make a ten. Find the sum.

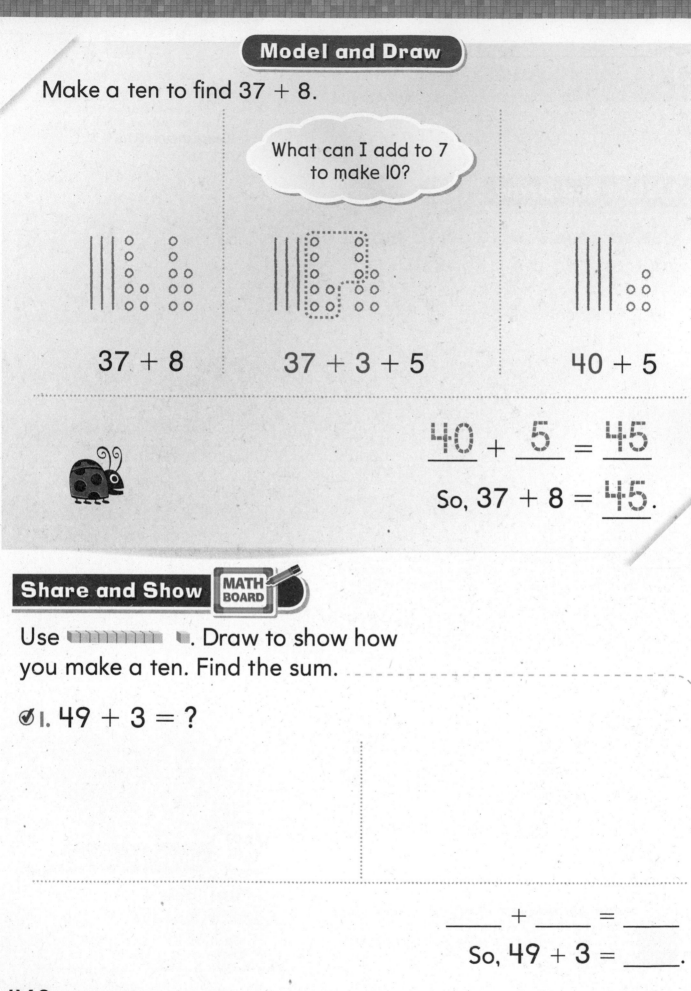

✓ 1. 49 + 3 = ?

____ + ____ = ____

So, 49 + 3 = ____.

Name ________________________________

On Your Own

MATHEMATICAL PRACTICE 5 **Use a Concrete Model**

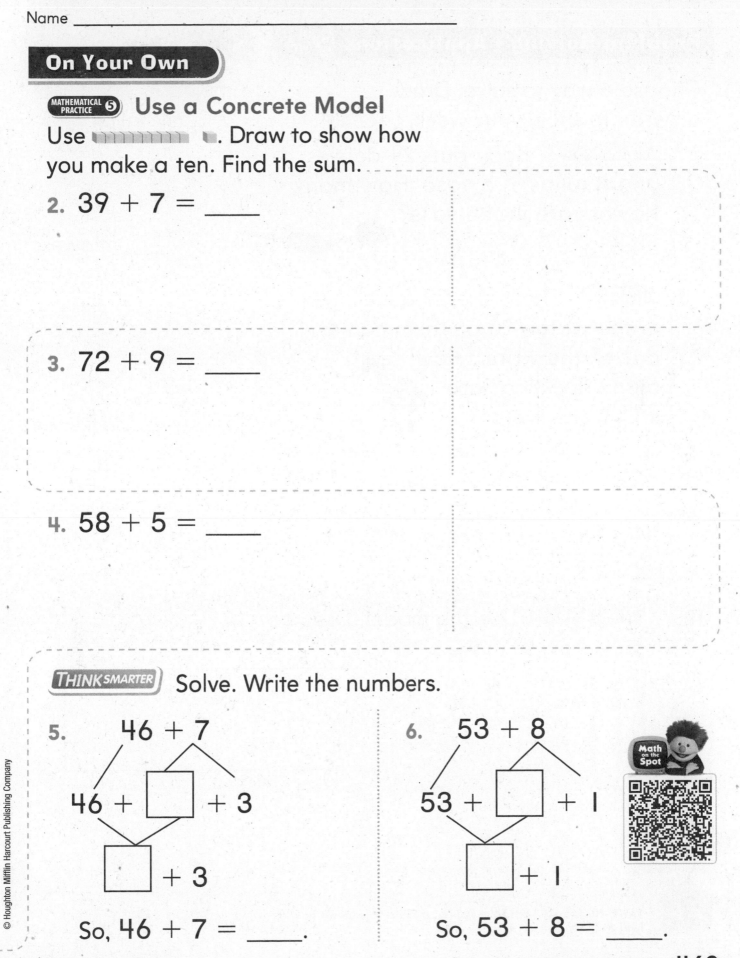

Use tens and ones blocks. Draw to show how you make a ten. Find the sum.

2. $39 + 7 =$ ____

3. $72 + 9 =$ ____

4. $58 + 5 =$ ____

THINKSMARTER Solve. Write the numbers.

5. $46 + 7$

$46 + \square + 3$

$\square + 3$

So, $46 + 7 =$ ____.

6. $53 + 8$

$53 + \square + 1$

$\square + 1$

So, $53 + 8 =$ ____.

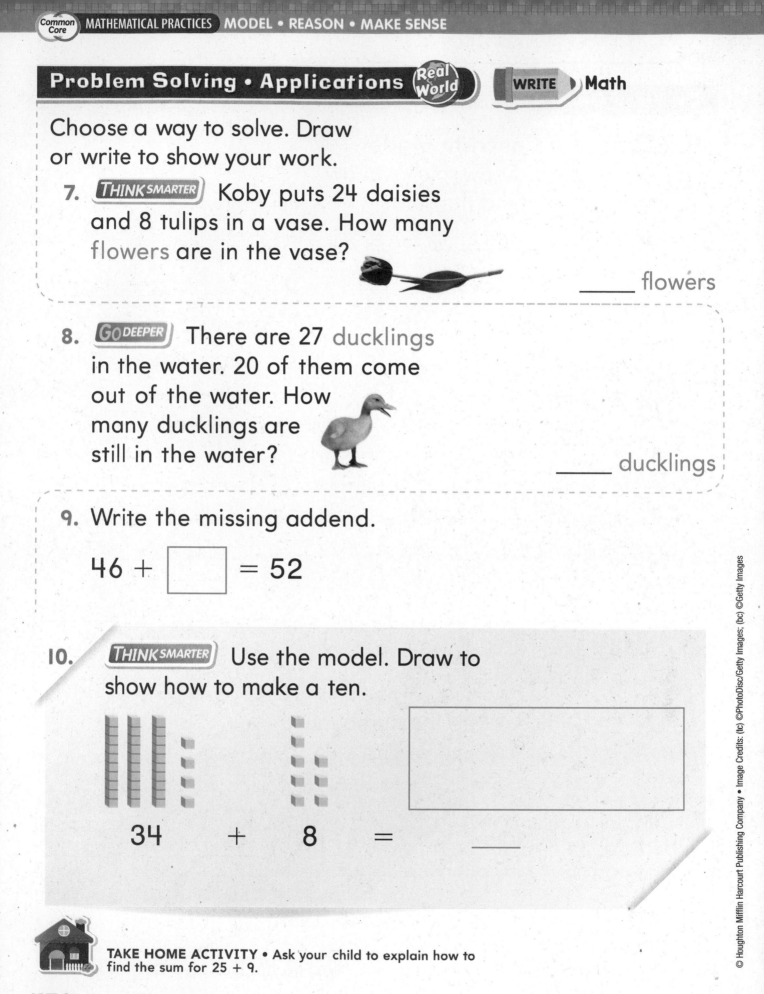

Problem Solving • Applications Real World

WRITE Math

Choose a way to solve. Draw or write to show your work.

7. THINK SMARTER Koby puts 24 daisies and 8 tulips in a vase. How many flowers are in the vase?

____ flowers

8. GO DEEPER There are 27 ducklings in the water. 20 of them come out of the water. How many ducklings are still in the water?

____ ducklings

9. Write the missing addend.

46 + ☐ = 52

10. THINK SMARTER Use the model. Draw to show how to make a ten.

☐

34 + 8 = ____

TAKE HOME ACTIVITY • Ask your child to explain how to find the sum for 25 + 9.

Name ______________________________

Make Ten to Add

Common Core

COMMON CORE STANDARD—1.NBT.C.4
Use place value understanding and properties of operations to add and subtract.

Use [tens] [ones]. Draw to show how you make a ten. Find the sum.

1. 26 + 5 = ______

2. 68 + 4 = ______

Problem Solving Real World

Choose a way to solve. Draw or write to show your work.

3. Debbie has 27 markers. Sal has 9 markers. How many markers do they have?

______ markers

4. WRITE Math Use words or pictures to explain how to solve 44 + 7.

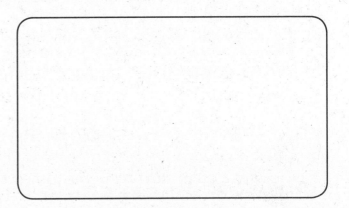

Lesson Check (1.NBT.C.4)

1. What is the sum?
Write the number.

$$47 + 6 = \_\_\_\_$$

2. What is the sum?
Write the number.

$$84 + 8 = \_\_\_\_$$

Spiral Review (1.OA.D.7, 1.NBT.A.1)

3. What number does the model show?
Write the number.

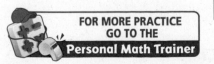

____

4. Write a number to make the sentence true.

$$5 + 4 = 10 - \_\_\_\_$$

Name ________________________________

Use Place Value to Add

Essential Question How can you model tens and ones to help you add two-digit numbers?

Common Core **Number and Operations in Base Ten—1.NBT.C.4**

MATHEMATICAL PRACTICES
MP1, MP2, MP6, MP7

Listen and Draw Real World Hands On

Model the problem with tens and ones.
Draw a quick picture to show your work.

Tens	Ones

Math Talk MATHEMATICAL PRACTICES 1

Describe How many tens? How many ones? How many in all?

FOR THE TEACHER • Read the following problem. Cameron has 30 old stamps and 25 new stamps. How many stamps does Cameron have?

Model and Draw

How can you use tens and ones to add?

$$\begin{array}{r} 35 \\ +38 \\ \hline \end{array}$$

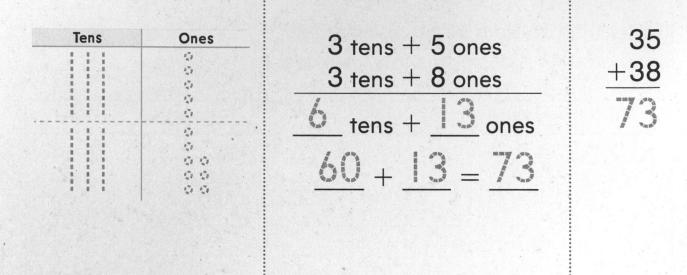

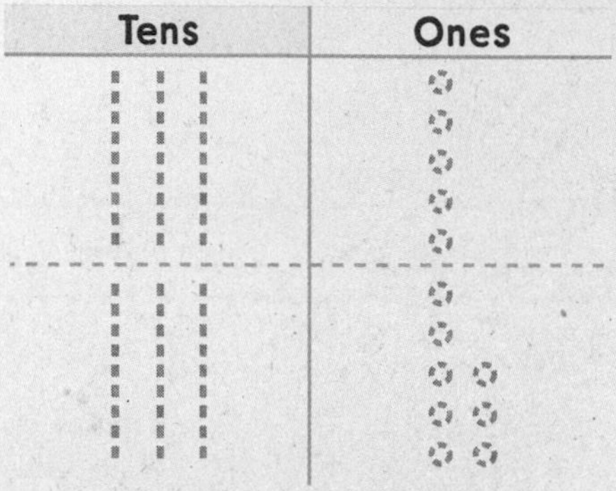

3 tens + 5 ones
3 tens + 8 ones

6 tens + 13 ones

60 + 13 = 73

$$\begin{array}{r} 35 \\ +38 \\ \hline 73 \end{array}$$

Share and Show MATH BOARD

Draw a quick picture.
Use tens and ones to add.

1.

$$\begin{array}{r} 81 \\ +14 \\ \hline \end{array}$$

Tens	Ones

8 tens + 1 one
1 ten + 4 ones

____ tens + ____ ones

____ + ____ = ____

$$\begin{array}{r} 81 \\ +14 \\ \hline \end{array}$$

Name ______________________

On Your Own

MATHEMATICAL PRACTICE 6 **Make Connections**

Draw a quick picture. Use tens and ones to add.

2. $\begin{array}{r} 43 \\ +37 \\ \hline \end{array}$

Tens	Ones

4 tens + 3 ones
3 tens + 7 ones
____ tens + ____ ones

____ + ____ = ____

$\begin{array}{r} 43 \\ +37 \\ \hline \end{array}$

3. $\begin{array}{r} 62 \\ +23 \\ \hline \end{array}$

Tens	Ones

6 tens + 2 ones
2 tens + 3 ones
____ tens + ____ ones

____ + ____ = ____

$\begin{array}{r} 62 \\ +23 \\ \hline \end{array}$

THINK SMARTER Solve.

4. 28 + 17

28 + ____ + 15

____ + 15 = ____

So, 28 + 17 = ____.

Math on the Spot

5. 59 + 13

59 + ____ + 12

____ + 12 = ____

So, 59 + 13 = ____.

6. THINK SMARTER Draw a quick picture to solve. Han has 37 shells. Jonah has 15 shells. How many shells do they have?

Tens	Ones

____

Problem Solving • Applications Real World

WRITE Math

7. THINK SMARTER Draw a quick picture to solve. Kim has 24 marbles. Al has 47 marbles. How many marbles do they have?

____ marbles

Tens	Ones

8. GO DEEPER Choose two addends from 11 to 49. Draw them. Add in any order to solve.

Addend **Addend**

____ + ____ = ____

____ + ____ = ____

9. THINK SMARTER Write the addition that the model shows. Solve.

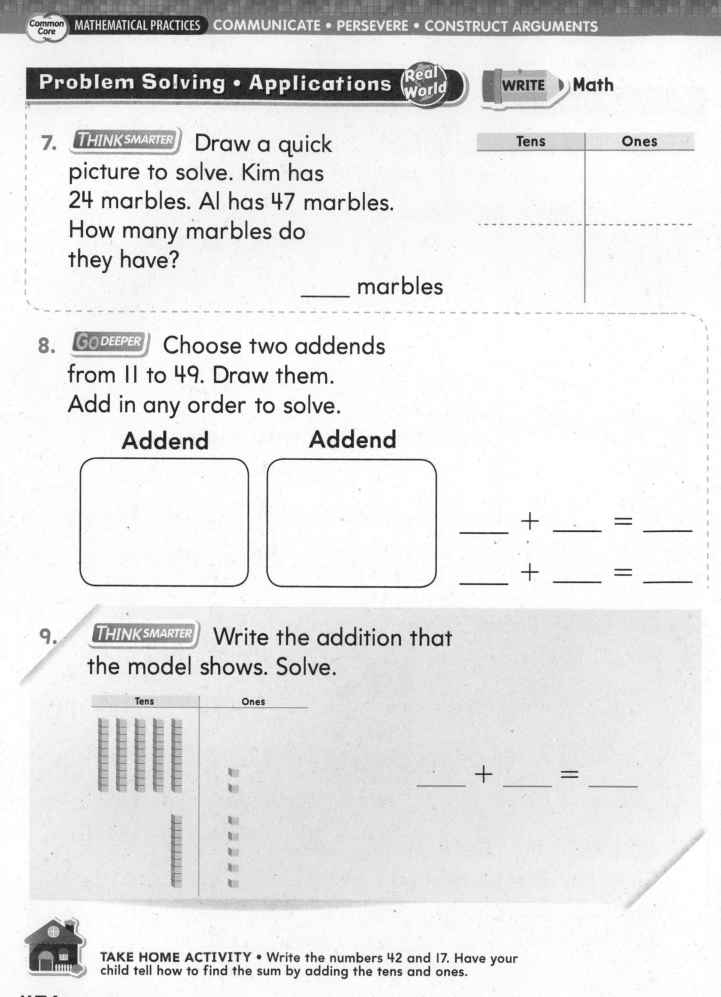

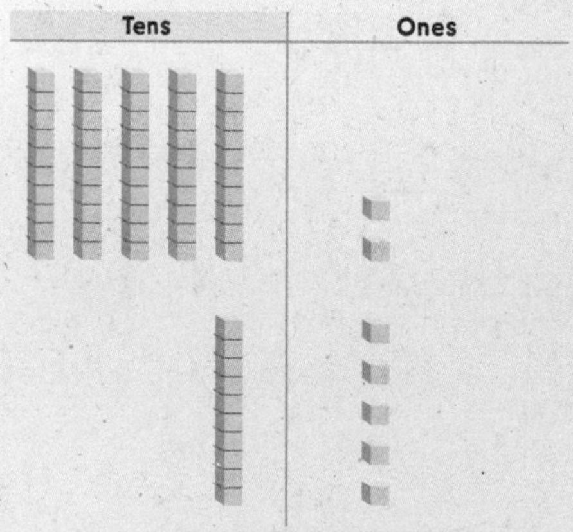

____ + ____ = ____

TAKE HOME ACTIVITY • Write the numbers 42 and 17. Have your child tell how to find the sum by adding the tens and ones.

Name ______________________

Use Place Value to Add

Common Core COMMON CORE STANDARD—1.NBT.C.4
Use place value understanding and properties of operations to add and subtract.

Draw a quick picture. Use tens and ones to add.

1. 31 + 26

Tens	Ones

3 tens + 1 one
2 tens + 6 ones

____ tens + ____ ones

____ + ____ = ____

31 + 26

2. 54 + 34

Tens	Ones

5 tens + 4 ones
3 tens + 4 ones

____ tens + ____ ones

____ + ____ = ____

54 + 34

Problem Solving (Real World)

3. Write two addition sentences you can use to find the sum. Then solve.

Addend

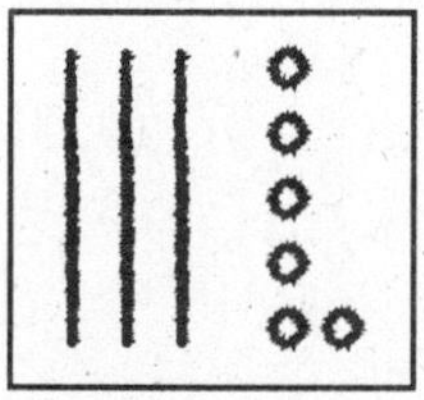

Addend

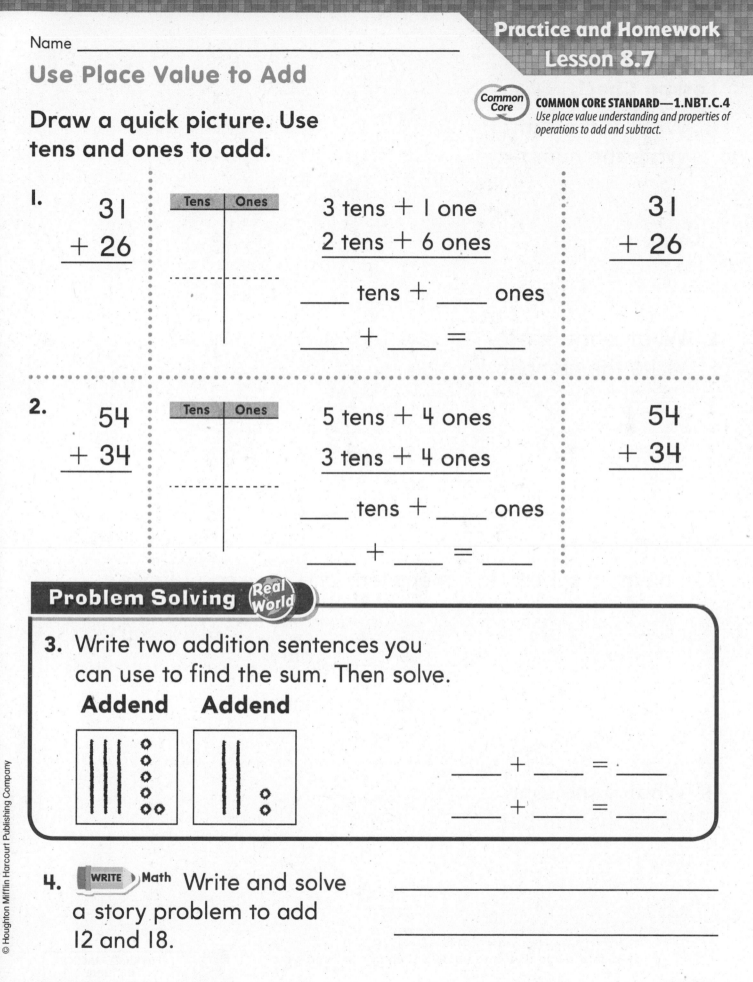

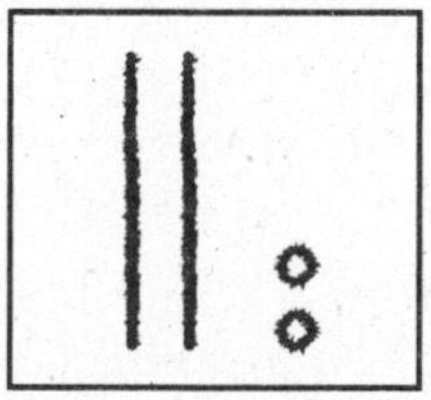

____ + ____ = ____

____ + ____ = ____

4. WRITE Math Write and solve a story problem to add 12 and 18.

____

____

Lesson Check (1.NBT.C.4)

1. What is the sum?
   Write the number.

$$\begin{array}{r} 42 \\ +\ 31 \\ \hline \end{array}$$

2. What is the sum?
   Write the number.

$$\begin{array}{r} 23 \\ +\ 12 \\ \hline \end{array}$$

Spiral Review (1.OA.C.6, 1.NBT.B.2)

3. I have 28 cubes. How many tens and ones can I make?

____ tens ____ ones

____ ten ____ ones

4. What is the sum?
   Write the number.

$$\begin{array}{r} 5 \\ +\ 5 \\ \hline \end{array}$$

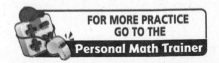

Name ____________________

Problem Solving • Addition Word Problems

Essential Question How can drawing a picture help you explain how to solve an addition problem?

Common Core **Number and Operations in Base Ten—1.NBT.C.4**
MATHEMATICAL PRACTICES MP1, MP2, MP6, MP8

Kelly gets 6 new toy cars.
He already has 18 toy cars.
How many does he have now?

Unlock the Problem

What do I need to find?

how many ____toy cars____ Kelly has now

What information do I need to use?

Kelly has ____18____ cars.

He gets ____6____ more cars.

Show how to solve the problem.

____

HOME CONNECTION • Being able to show and explain how to solve a problem helps your child build on their understanding of addition.

Try Another Problem

Draw and write to solve.
Explain your reasoning.

- What do I need to find?
- What information do I need to use?

1. Aisha picks 60 blueberries to make a pie. Then she picks 12 more to eat. How many blueberries does Aisha pick?

____ blueberries

2. Yuri collects 21 cans for the school food drive. Leo collects 36 cans. How many cans do Yuri and Leo collect?

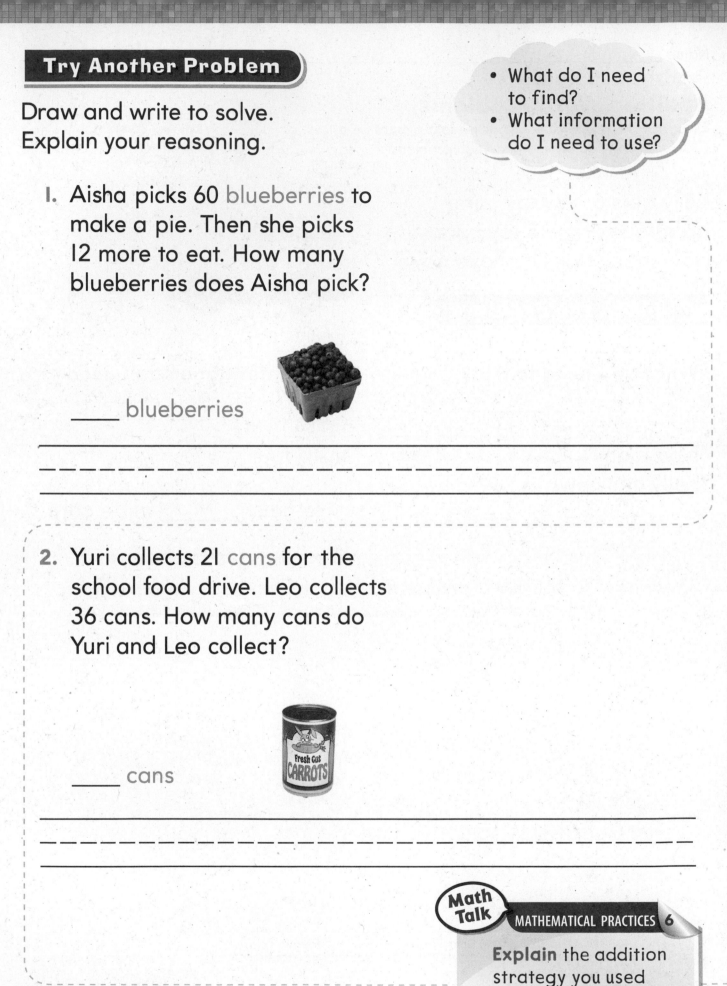

____ cans

Math Talk MATHEMATICAL PRACTICES 6

Explain the addition strategy you used to solve Exercise 1.

Name ______________________________

Share and Show MATH BOARD

MATHEMATICAL PRACTICE 2 **Use Reasoning**

Draw and write to solve.

3. Tyra sees 48 geese in the field. Then she sees 17 more geese in the sky. How many geese does Tyra see?

____ geese

4. Jade paints 35 circles and 45 triangles in art class. How many shapes does Jade paint?

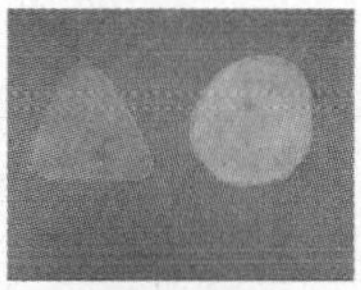

____ shapes

5. THINK SMARTER It takes 10 hops to get across the yard. How many hops does it take to get across the yard and back?

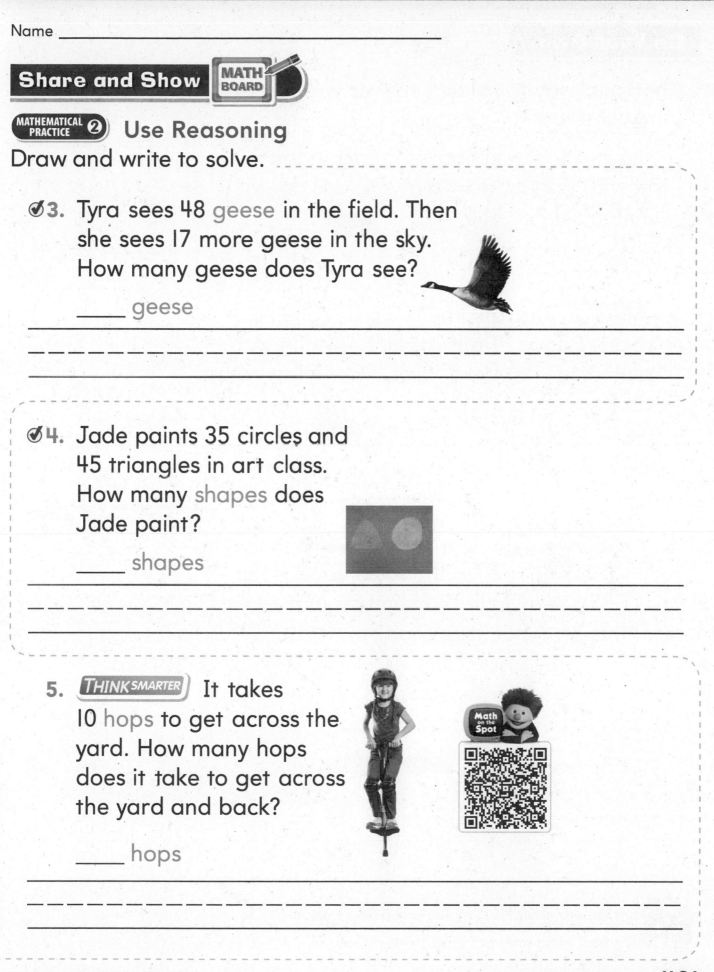

Math on the Spot

____ hops

On Your Own

Choose a way to solve. Draw or write to explain.

6. THINK SMARTER Julian sells 3 books of tickets for the school fair. Each book has 20 tickets. How many tickets does Julian sell?

____ tickets

7. GO DEEPER I have some red roses and pink roses. I have 14 red roses. I have 8 more pink roses than red roses. How many roses do I have?

____ roses

Personal Math Trainer

8. THINK SMARTER + Ella sees 27 . She sees 28 . How many   does Ella see? Circle the number that makes this sentence true.

Ella sees [48 / 51 / 55]   in all.

TAKE HOME ACTIVITY • Ask your child to solve 16 + 7, 30 + 68, and 53 + 24. Ask him or her to explain how they solved each problem.

Name ______________________________

Problem Solving • Addition Word Problems

COMMON CORE STANDARD—1.NBT.C.4
Use place value understanding and properties of operations to add and subtract.

Draw and write to solve. Explain your reasoning.

1. Jean has 10 fish. She gets 4 more fish. How many fish does she have now?

____ fish

2. Courtney buys 2 bags of apples. Each bag has 20 apples. How many apples does she buy?

____ apples

3. John bakes 18 blueberry muffins and 12 banana muffins for the bake sale. How many muffins does he bake?

____ muffins

4. WRITE Math Draw a picture to show how to find 12 + 37.

Lesson Check (1.NBT.C.4)

1. Amy has 9 books about dogs.
She has 13 books about cats.
How many books does she
have about dogs and cats?
Solve. Show your work. Write the number.

____ books

Spiral Review (1.OA.B.3, 1.OA.C.6)

2. What is the sum for $4 + 2 + 4$?
Write the number.

____

3. Solve. Use the ten frame to make a
ten to help you subtract. Ray has
14 pens. 8 are black. The rest
are blue. How many pens are blue?

____ blue pens

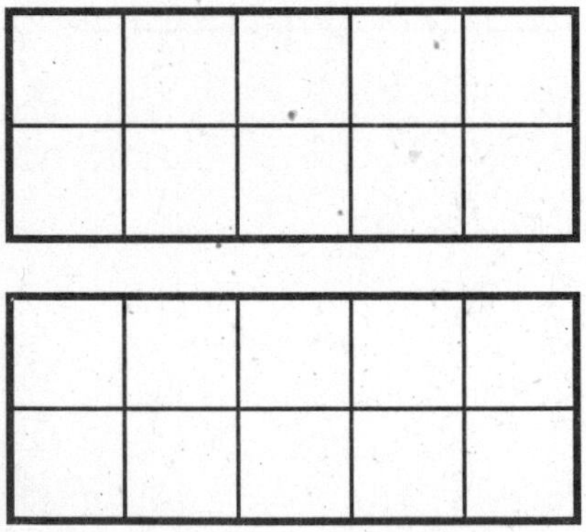

Name ____________________

Related Addition and Subtraction

Essential Question How can you use a hundred chart to show the relationship between addition and subtraction?

Common Core **Number and Operations in Base Ten—1.NBT.C.4**
MATHEMATICAL PRACTICES MP2, MP3, MP7

Listen and Draw Real World

Use the hundred chart to solve the problems.

1	2	3	4	5	6	7	8	9	10
11	12	13	14	15	16	17	18	19	20
21	22	23	24	25	26	27	28	29	30
31	32	33	34	35	36	37	38	39	40
41	42	43	44	45	46	47	48	49	50
51	52	53	54	55	56	57	58	59	60
61	62	63	64	65	66	67	68	69	70
71	72	73	74	75	76	77	78	79	80
81	82	83	84	85	86	87	88	89	90
91	92	93	94	95	96	97	98	99	100

Math Talk MATHEMATICAL PRACTICES 3

Apply Describe how you can use a hundred chart to find the sum and the difference.

FOR THE TEACHER • Read the following problems. Trevor collects 38 acorns. He collects 10 more acorns. How many acorns does Trevor have now? Trevor has 48 acorns. He gives 10 acorns to his brother. How many acorns does Trevor have now?

Model and Draw

You can use a hundred chart to find a sum and a difference.

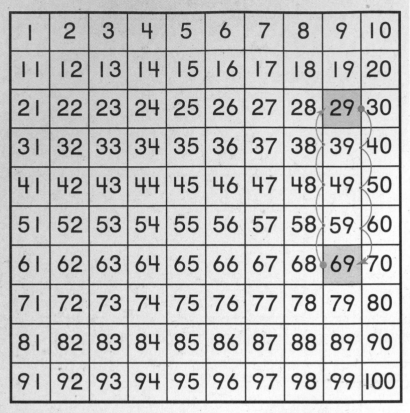

1	2	3	4	5	6	7	8	9	10
11	12	13	14	15	16	17	18	19	20
21	22	23	24	25	26	27	28	29	30
31	32	33	34	35	36	37	38	39	40
41	42	43	44	45	46	47	48	49	50
51	52	53	54	55	56	57	58	59	60
61	62	63	64	65	66	67	68	69	70
71	72	73	74	75	76	77	78	79	80
81	82	83	84	85	86	87	88	89	90
91	92	93	94	95	96	97	98	99	100

Start at **29**. Count on four tens.
39, 49, 59, 69

$29 + 40 =$ 69

Start at **69**. Count back four tens.
59, 49, 39, 29

$69 - 40 =$ 29

Share and Show

MATH BOARD

Use the hundred chart to add and subtract. Count on and back by tens.

1. $56 + 20 =$ ____

$76 - 20 =$ ____

2. $48 + 50 =$ ____

$98 - 50 =$ ____

Name ______________________

On Your Own

How can you use the hundred chart to find the sum and the difference?

$28 + 60 =$ ___

$88 - 60 =$ ___

1	2	3	4	5	6	7	8	9	10
11	12	13	14	15	16	17	18	19	20
21	22	23	24	25	26	27	28	29	30
31	32	33	34	35	36	37	38	39	40
41	42	43	44	45	46	47	48	49	50
51	52	53	54	55	56	57	58	59	60
61	62	63	64	65	66	67	68	69	70
71	72	73	74	75	76	77	78	79	80
81	82	83	84	85	86	87	88	89	90
91	92	93	94	95	96	97	98	99	100

MATHEMATICAL PRACTICE 7 **Look for a Pattern** Use the hundred chart to add and subtract. Count on and back by tens.

3. $36 + 30 =$ ___

$66 - 30 =$ ___

4. $73 + 10 =$ ___

$83 - 10 =$ ___

5. $25 + 70 =$ ___

$95 - 70 =$ ___

6. $18 + 40 =$ ___

$58 - 40 =$ ___

7. THINK SMARTER Solve.

There are 73 bees in a hive. 10 bees fly away. Then 10 more bees fly into the hive. How many bees are in the hive now?

Math on the Spot

___ bees

Problem Solving • Applications Real World

WRITE Math

Solve. Draw or write to show your work.

8. THINK SMARTER There are 38 ants on a rock. 10 move to the grass. 10 walk up a tree. How many ants are on the rock now?

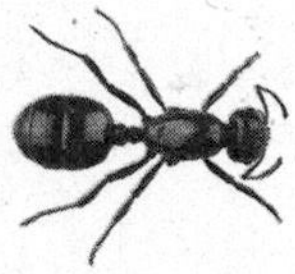

____ ants

9. GO DEEPER There are 27 birds at the park. 50 more birds come. Then 50 fly away. How many birds are at the park now?

____ birds

10. THINK SMARTER Match the math sentences that count on and back by tens.

$25 + 40 = ?$	$65 + 20 = ?$	$45 + 30 = ?$
•	•	•
•	•	•
$65 - 40 = ?$	$75 - 30 = ?$	$85 - 20 = ?$

TAKE HOME ACTIVITY • On slips of paper, write 36 + 40 and 76 – 40. Ask your child to explain how to use the hundred chart to count on and back by tens to find the sum and the difference.

Name ______________________

Related Addition and Subtraction

Common Core COMMON CORE STANDARDS—1.NBT.C.4
Use place value understanding and properties of operations to add and subtract.

Use the hundred chart to add and subtract. Count on and back by tens.

1. 16 + 60 = ______

   76 − 60 = ______

2. 61 + 30 = ______

   91 − 30 = ______

3. 64 + 20 = ______

   84 − 20 = ______

1	2	3	4	5	6	7	8	9	10
11	12	13	14	15	16	17	18	19	20
21	22	23	24	25	26	27	28	29	30
31	32	33	34	35	36	37	38	39	40
41	42	43	44	45	46	47	48	49	50
51	52	53	54	55	56	57	58	59	60
61	62	63	64	65	66	67	68	69	70
71	72	73	74	75	76	77	78	79	80
81	82	83	84	85	86	87	88	89	90
91	92	93	94	95	96	97	98	99	100

Problem Solving Real World

Choose a way to solve. Draw or write to show your work.

4. There are 53 leaves in a tree. 20 leaves blow away. How many leaves are left in the tree?

   ______ leaves

5. WRITE Math Write a number sentence to subtract 3 tens from 93.

   ____

   ____

Lesson Check (1.NBT.C.4)

1. What is 78 − 20?
Write the number.

____

2. What is 37 + 50?
Write the number.

____

1	2	3	4	5	6	7	8	9	10
11	12	13	14	15	16	17	18	19	20
21	22	23	24	25	26	27	28	29	30
31	32	33	34	35	36	37	38	39	40
41	42	43	44	45	46	47	48	49	50
51	52	53	54	55	56	57	58	59	60
61	62	63	64	65	66	67	68	69	70
71	72	73	74	75	76	77	78	79	80
81	82	83	84	85	86	87	88	89	90
91	92	93	94	95	96	97	98	99	100

Spiral Review (1.OA.A.1, 1.OA.B.3)

3. Use the model.
What is the difference of 7 − 3?
Write the number.

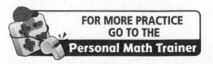

$7 - 3 = $ ____

4. What is the sum for 0 + 7?
Write the number.

____

Name ______________________________

Practice Addition and Subtraction

Essential Question What different ways can you use to add and subtract?

Common Core **Number and Operations in Base Ten— 1.NBT.C.4, 1.NBT.C.6** *Also 1.OA.C.6*

MATHEMATICAL PRACTICES MP1, MP2, MP3, MP8

Listen and Draw (Real World)

Draw to show the problem.
Then solve.

___ ○ ___ ○ ___

Math Talk MATHEMATICAL PRACTICES 1

Describe How did you solve the problem?

FOR THE TEACHER • Read the following problem. The class collects paper bags for an art project. Ron brings 7 more bags than Ben. Ben brings 35 bags. How many bags does Ron bring?

Model and Draw

What ways have you learned to add and subtract?

$5 + 9 =$ ＿＿＿

> **THINK**
> 9 + 5 is the same as 10 + ＿? .

$50 - 30 =$ ＿＿＿

> **THINK**
> 5 tens − 3 tens.

$51 + 21 =$ ＿＿＿

> **THINK**
> 5 tens + 2 tens.
> 1 one + 1 one.

Share and Show MATH BOARD

Add or subtract.

1. $30 + 60 =$ ＿＿＿

2. $73 + 5 =$ ＿＿＿

3. $10 - 4 =$ ＿＿＿

4. $29 + 4 =$ ＿＿＿

5. $9 + 9 =$ ＿＿＿

6. $5 + 6 =$ ＿＿＿

7. $25 + 54 =$ ＿＿＿

8. $15 - 8 =$ ＿＿＿

9. $40 + 10 =$ ＿＿＿

10. $40 - 10 =$ ＿＿＿

11. $14 - 7 =$ ＿＿＿

12. $90 - 70 =$ ＿＿＿

13. $86 + 12 =$ ＿＿＿

14. $1 + 9 =$ ＿＿＿

15. $6 + 7 =$ ＿＿＿

16. $9 - 2 =$ ＿＿＿

17. ✓ $8 + 31 =$ ＿＿＿

18. ✓ $50 + 11 =$ ＿＿＿

Name ______________________________

On Your Own

MATHEMATICAL PRACTICE 8 **Use Repeated Reasoning** Add or subtract.

19. $\begin{array}{r} 12 \\ -\ 3 \\ \hline \end{array}$	20. $\begin{array}{r} 10 \\ +10 \\ \hline \end{array}$	21. $\begin{array}{r} 7 \\ +42 \\ \hline \end{array}$	22. $\begin{array}{r} 41 \\ +36 \\ \hline \end{array}$
23. $\begin{array}{r} 8 \\ +10 \\ \hline \end{array}$	24. $\begin{array}{r} 16 \\ +\ 7 \\ \hline \end{array}$	25. $\begin{array}{r} 6 \\ -6 \\ \hline \end{array}$	26. $\begin{array}{r} 3 \\ +8 \\ \hline \end{array}$
27. $\begin{array}{r} 64 \\ +\ 3 \\ \hline \end{array}$	28. $\begin{array}{r} 60 \\ -30 \\ \hline \end{array}$	29. $\begin{array}{r} 2 \\ +7 \\ \hline \end{array}$	30. $\begin{array}{r} 5 \\ -1 \\ \hline \end{array}$
31. $\begin{array}{r} 13 \\ -\ 5 \\ \hline \end{array}$	32. $\begin{array}{r} 52 \\ +40 \\ \hline \end{array}$	33. $\begin{array}{r} 3 \\ +2 \\ \hline \end{array}$	34. $\begin{array}{r} 30 \\ +50 \\ \hline \end{array}$

Solve. Write or draw to explain.

35. THINK SMARTER Lara collects 8 more stamps than Samson. Samson collects 39 stamps. How many stamps does Lara collect?

_____ stamps

Problem Solving • Applications Real World

WRITE Math

Solve. Write or draw to explain.

36. THINK SMARTER Jane drew some stars. Then she drew 9 more stars. Now there are 19 stars. How many stars did Jane draw first?

Math on the Spot

____ stars

37. THINK SMARTER Adel drew 10 more stars than Charlie. Charlie drew 24 stars. How many stars did Adel draw?

____ stars

38. GO DEEPER Write three ways to get a sum of 49.

____ ◯ ____ = 49

____ ◯ ____ = 49

____ ◯ ____ = 49

39. THINK SMARTER Find the sum of 23 and 30. Use any way to add.

$$23 + 30 = \_\_\_\_$$

Explain how you solved the problem.

TAKE HOME ACTIVITY • Have your child explain how he or she solved Exercise 36.

Name ______________________

Practice Addition and Subtraction

COMMON CORE STANDARDS—1.NBT.C.4, 1.NBT.C.6 *Use place value understanding and properties of operations to add and subtract.*

Add or subtract.

1. $\begin{array}{r} 20 \\ +\ 20 \\ \hline \end{array}$

2. $\begin{array}{r} 90 \\ -\ 30 \\ \hline \end{array}$

3. $\begin{array}{r} 52 \\ +\ 4 \\ \hline \end{array}$

4. $\begin{array}{r} 62 \\ +\ 21 \\ \hline \end{array}$

5. $\begin{array}{r} 39 \\ -\ 10 \\ \hline \end{array}$

6. $\begin{array}{r} 8 \\ +\ 2 \\ \hline \end{array}$

7. $\begin{array}{r} 47 \\ +\ 34 \\ \hline \end{array}$

8. $\begin{array}{r} 4 \\ -\ 0 \\ \hline \end{array}$

9. $\begin{array}{r} 49 \\ -\ 6 \\ \hline \end{array}$

10. $\begin{array}{r} 64 \\ +\ 30 \\ \hline \end{array}$

Problem Solving Real World

Solve. Write or draw to explain.

11. Andrew read 17 pages of his book before dinner. He read 9 more pages after dinner. How many pages did he read?

____ pages

12. WRITE Math Write two ways you could use to find 5 + 8.

____

____

____

____

Lesson Check (1.NBT.C.4, 1.NBT.C.6)

1. What is the sum of 20 + 18?
Write the sum.

20 + 18 = ____

2. What is the difference of 90 − 50?
Write the difference.

90 − 50 = ____

Spiral Review (1.OA.A.1, 1.OA.C.6)

3. Use the model. What number sentence does this model show? Write the number sentence that the model shows.

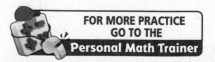

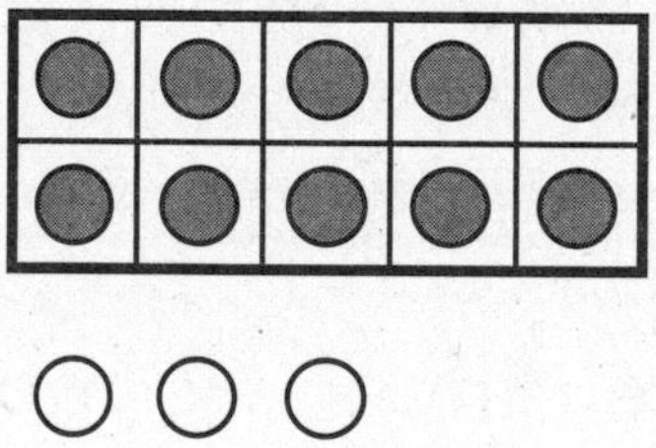

____ + ____ = ____

4. Solve. Mo had some toys. He gave 6 away. Now he has 6 toys. How many toys did Mo start with?

____ toys

Name ____________________

Chapter 8 Review/Test

Personal Math Trainer
Online Assessment and Intervention

1. Write each addition or subtraction problem in the box below the answer.

7 + 2   3 + 3   15 − 9   8 + 6   14 − 5

6	9	14

2. Choose all the ways that name the model.

- ○ 2 tens and 3 tens
- ○ 20 + 30
- ○ 5
- ○ 50

3. Sasha has 70 stickers. She uses 40 of them. How many stickers are left? Show your work.

_____ stickers

Personal Math Trainer

4. THINKSMARTER+ Use the hundred chart to add. Count on by ones or tens.

37 + 5 = ____

Explain how you used the chart to find the sum.

1	2	3	4	5	6	7	8	9	10
11	12	13	14	15	16	17	18	19	20
21	22	23	24	25	26	27	28	29	30
31	32	33	34	35	36	37	38	39	40
41	42	43	44	45	46	47	48	49	50
51	52	53	54	55	56	57	58	59	60
61	62	63	64	65	66	67	68	69	70
71	72	73	74	75	76	77	78	79	80
81	82	83	84	85	86	87	88	89	90
91	92	93	94	95	96	97	98	99	100

5. Use the model. Draw to show how to add the tens.

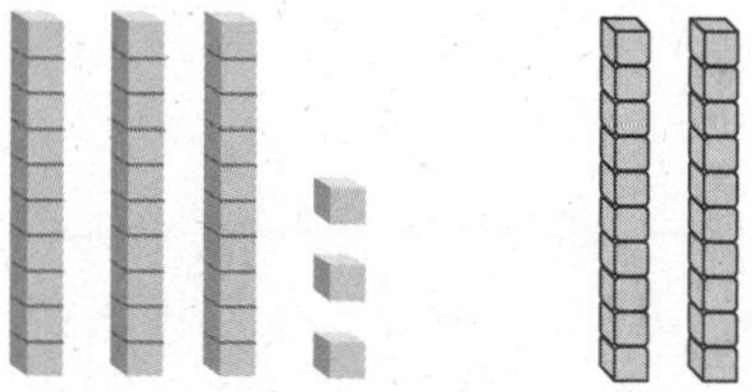

33 + 20 = ____

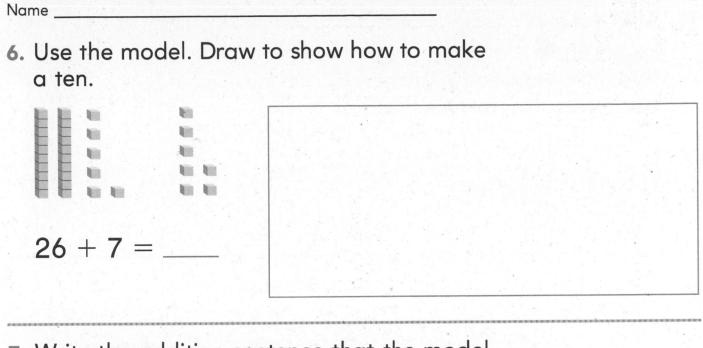

Name ______________________________

6. Use the model. Draw to show how to make a ten.

26 + 7 = ____

7. Write the addition sentence that the model shows. Solve.

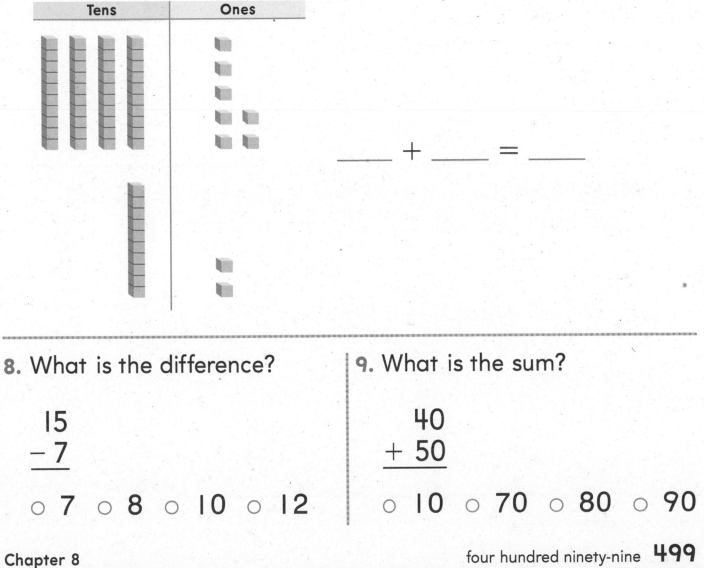

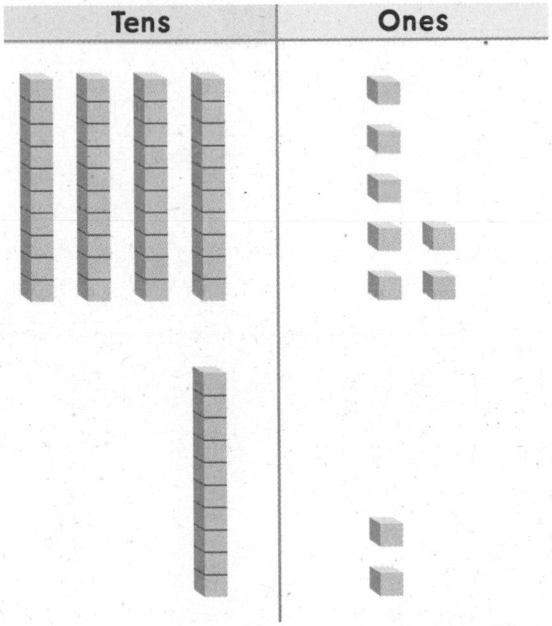

____ + ____ = ____

8. What is the difference?

$$\begin{array}{r} 15 \\ -\ 7 \\ \hline \end{array}$$

○ 7 ○ 8 ○ 10 ○ 12

9. What is the sum?

$$\begin{array}{r} 40 \\ +\ 50 \\ \hline \end{array}$$

○ 10 ○ 70 ○ 80 ○ 90

10. Luis has 16 .

He has 38 .

How many leaves does Luis have? Circle the number that makes the sentence true.

Luis has [48 / 54 / 59] leaves.

---

11. Match the math sentences that count on and back by tens.

38 + 30 = ?	48 + 40 = ?	38 + 20 = ?
•	•	•
•	•	•
58 − 20 = ?	68 − 30 = ?	88 − 40 = ?

---

12. GO DEEPER Find the sum of 62 and 15. Use any way to add.

62 + 15 = ____

Explain how you solved the problem.

All Kinds of Weather

written by Margie Sigman

Common Core CRITICAL AREA Developing understanding of linear measurement and measuring lengths as iterating length units

In rainy weather,

We play together.

Things We Use for Rainy Weather

raincoats					
umbrellas					

Use ● to complete the graph.

How many raincoats do you see? ____

How many umbrellas do you see? ____

SCIENCE

Describe rainy weather.

In sunny weather,

We play together.

Things We Use for Sunny Weather

sun hats					
sunglasses					

Use ● to complete the graph.

How many sunglasses do you see? ____

How many sun hats do you see? ____

SCIENCE

Describe sunny weather.

Whatever the weather,

We play together.

SCIENCE

Describe the weather shown here.

Name ______________________

Write About the Story

Use ●. Show some sun hats and sunglasses in each category on the graph.

Vocabulary Review
category
classify
graph

Things We Use for Sunny Weather

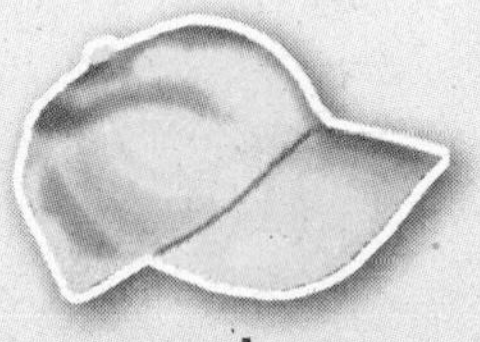

sun hats

sunglasses

WRITE Math Write a sentence telling how many sun hats there are. Write a sentence telling how many sunglasses there are.

More or Fewer?

1. Show more raincoats than umbrellas.
Use ● in each category.

Things We Use for Rainy Weather

 raincoats					
 umbrellas					

2. Show fewer raincoats than umbrellas.
Use ● in each category.

Things We Use for Rainy Weather

 raincoats					
 umbrellas					

MATH BOARD Write a story problem about raincoats and umbrellas. Tell how to classify each item in the correct category.

Chapter 9 Measurement

What objects in the picture are shorter than the arch?

Name ______________________________

Show What You Know

Personal Math Trainer
Online Assessment and Intervention

Bigger and Smaller

Circle the bigger object. (K.MD.A.1)

1. 

Circle the smaller object. (K.MD.A.1)

2. 

Compare Length

Circle the longer object.
Draw a line under the shorter object. (K.MD.A.1)

3. 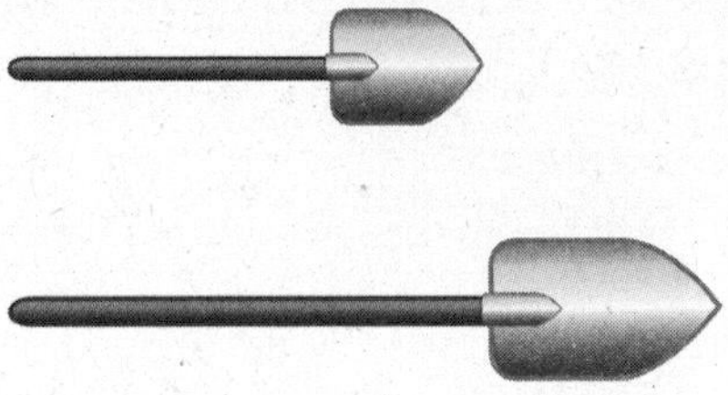

4. 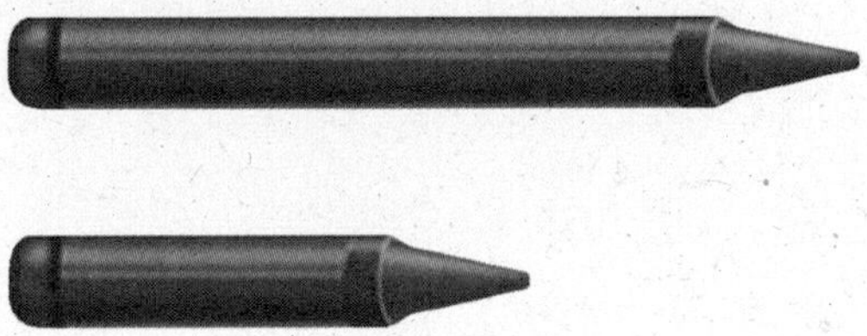

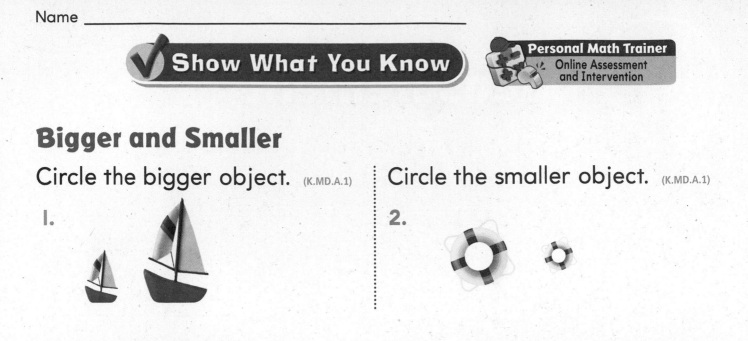

Numbers 1 to 10

Write each number in order to 10. (1.NBT.A.1)

5. 1 ☐ ☐ ☐ ☐ ☐ ☐ ☐ ☐ 10

This page checks understanding of important skills needed for success in Chapter 9.

Name ______________________

Review Words	
nine	ten
eleven	twelve
long	longer
short	shorter

Vocabulary Builder

Visualize It

Sort the review words from the box.

length	sort	numbers
long		nine
______		______
______		______
______		______

Understand Vocabulary

Complete the sentences with the correct word.

1. A crayon is ______________ than a marker.
2. A toothbrush is ______________ than a paper clip.

Write the name below the number.

3. 9 ________ 10 ________ 11 ________ 12 ________

GO DIGITAL • Interactive Student Edition • Multimedia eGlossary

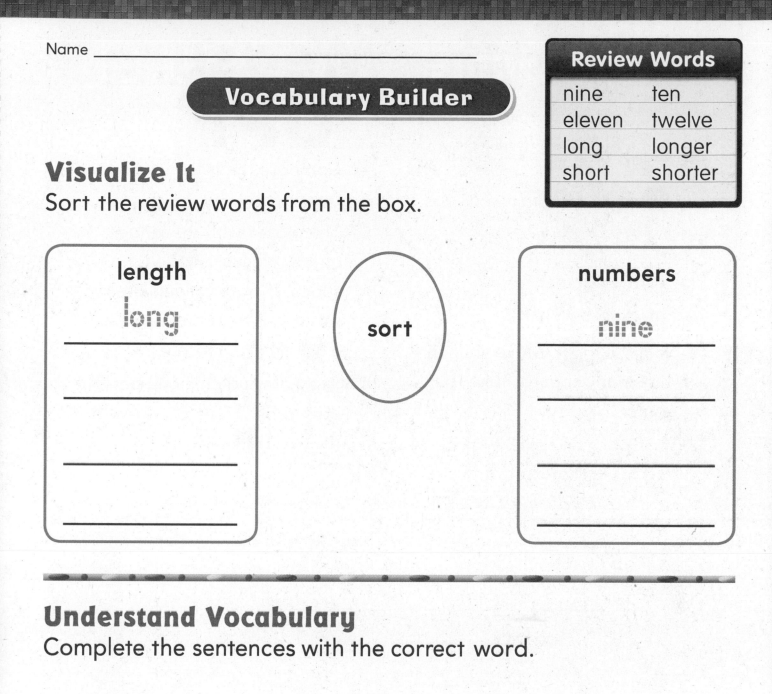

Game Measure UP!

Materials

- • 12 ● ● • 2 ▭ • 2 ✏
- • 2 ▱ • 2 🖍 • 2 ✂ • 2 🖌

Play with a partner.

① Put 👤👤 on START.

② Spin the 🕐. Move your 👤 that many spaces. Take that object.

③ Your partner spins, moves, and takes that object.

④ Compare the lengths of the two objects.

⑤ The player with the longer object places a ● on the space. If both objects are the same length, both players put a ● on the board.

⑥ Keep playing until one person gets to END. The player with the most ● wins.

START

END

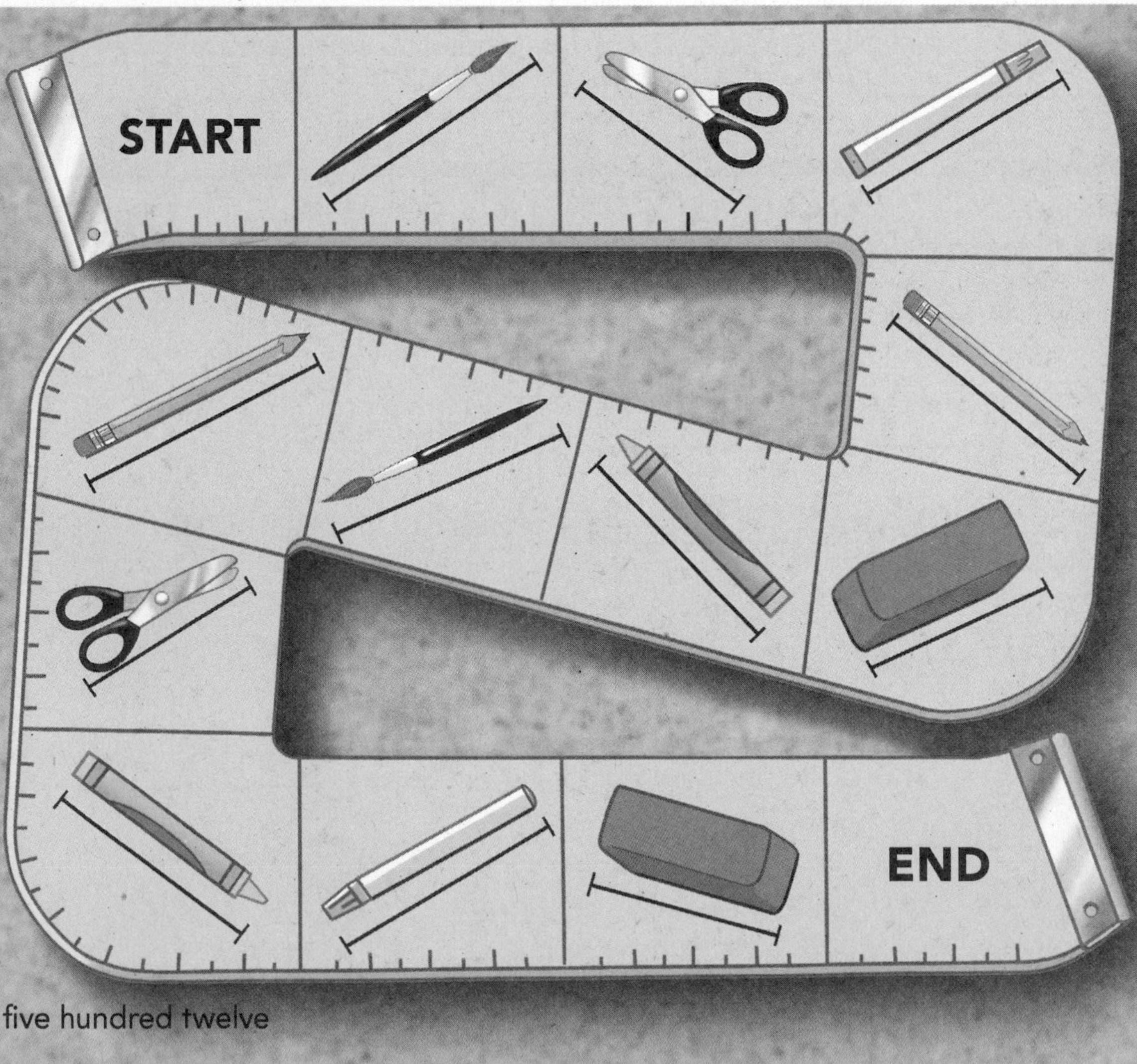

Chapter 9 Vocabulary

half hour media hora 23	**hour** hora 27
hour hand horario 28	**longest** el más largo 33
minute hand minutero 36	**minutes** minutos 37
more más 38	**shortest** el más corto 48

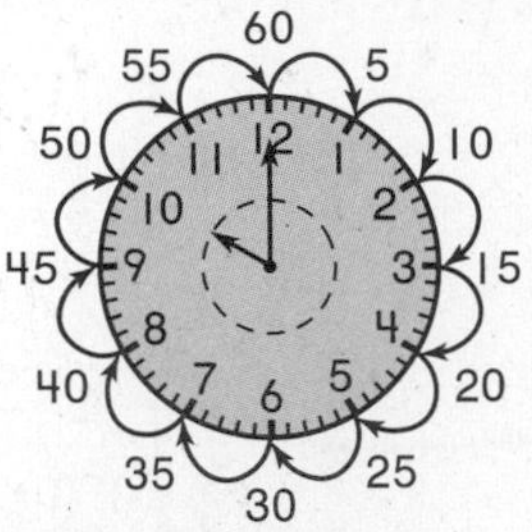

An **hour** has 60 minutes.

© Houghton Mifflin Harcourt Publishing Company

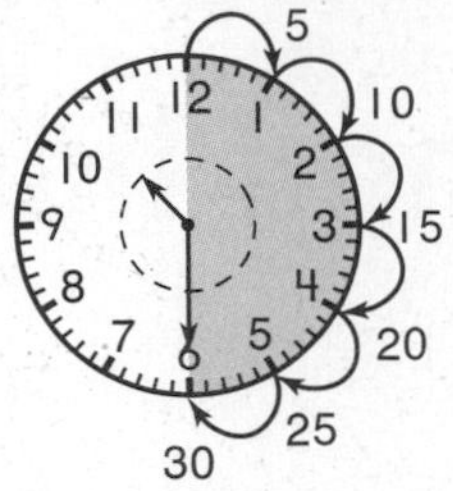

A **half hour** has 30 minutes.

© Houghton Mifflin Harcourt Publishing Company

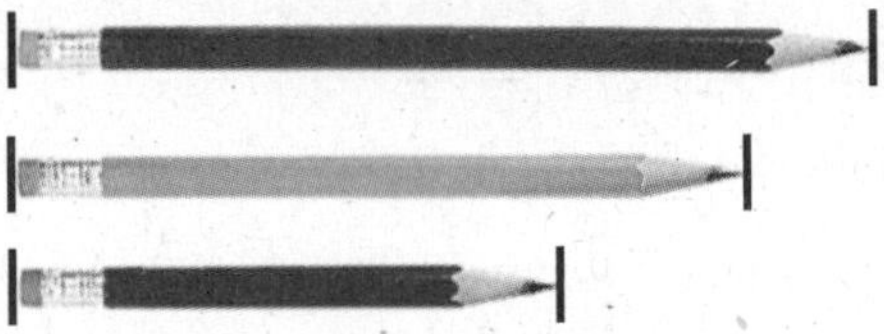

© Houghton Mifflin Harcourt Publishing Company

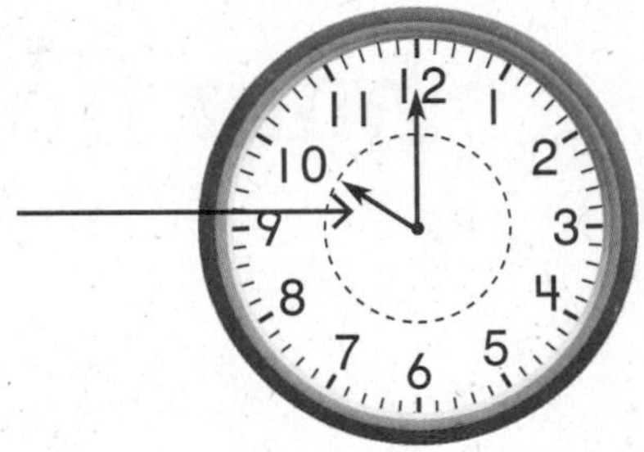

© Houghton Mifflin Harcourt Publishing Company

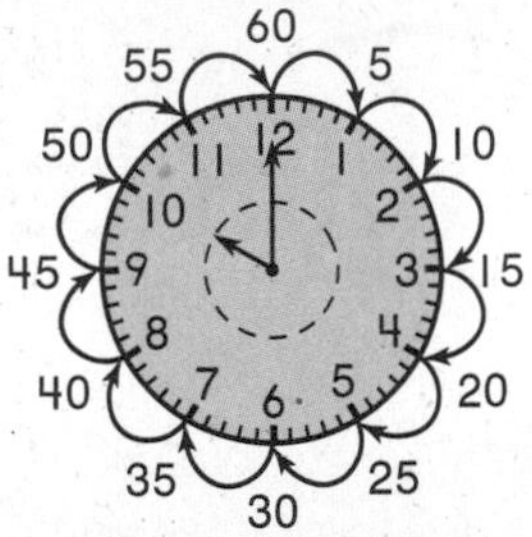

An hour has 60 **minutes**.

© Houghton Mifflin Harcourt Publishing Company

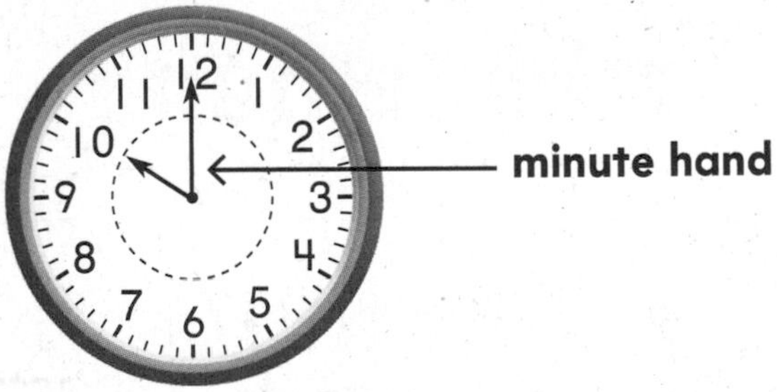

© Houghton Mifflin Harcourt Publishing Company

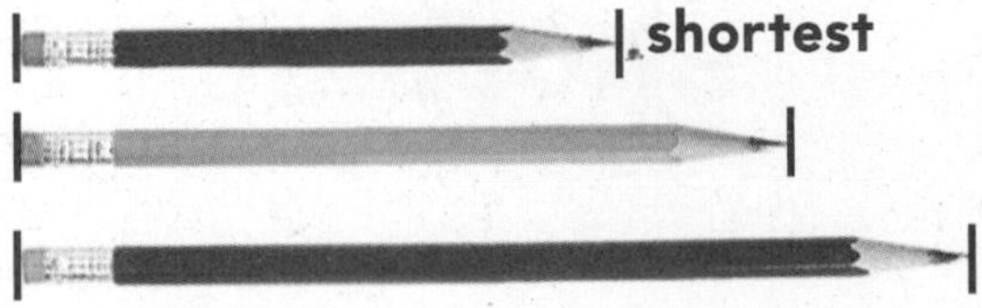

© Houghton Mifflin Harcourt Publishing Company

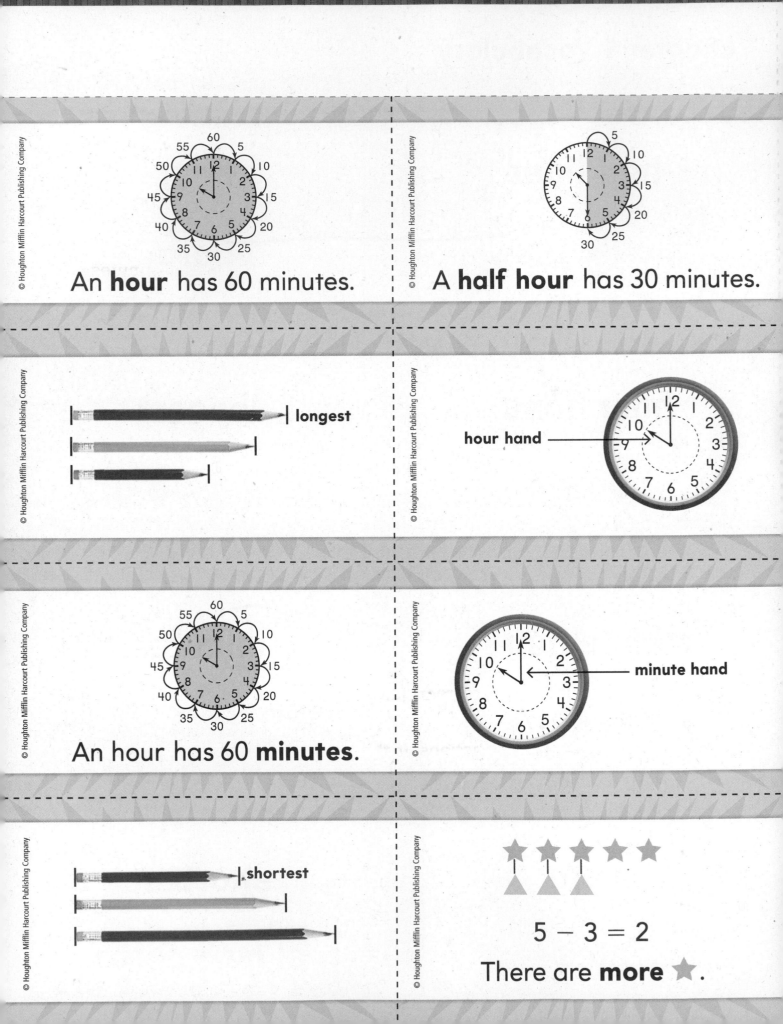

$5 - 3 = 2$

There are **more** ★.

Going to a Weather Station

Word Box

- half hour
- hour
- hour hand
- longest
- minute hand
- minutes
- more
- shortest

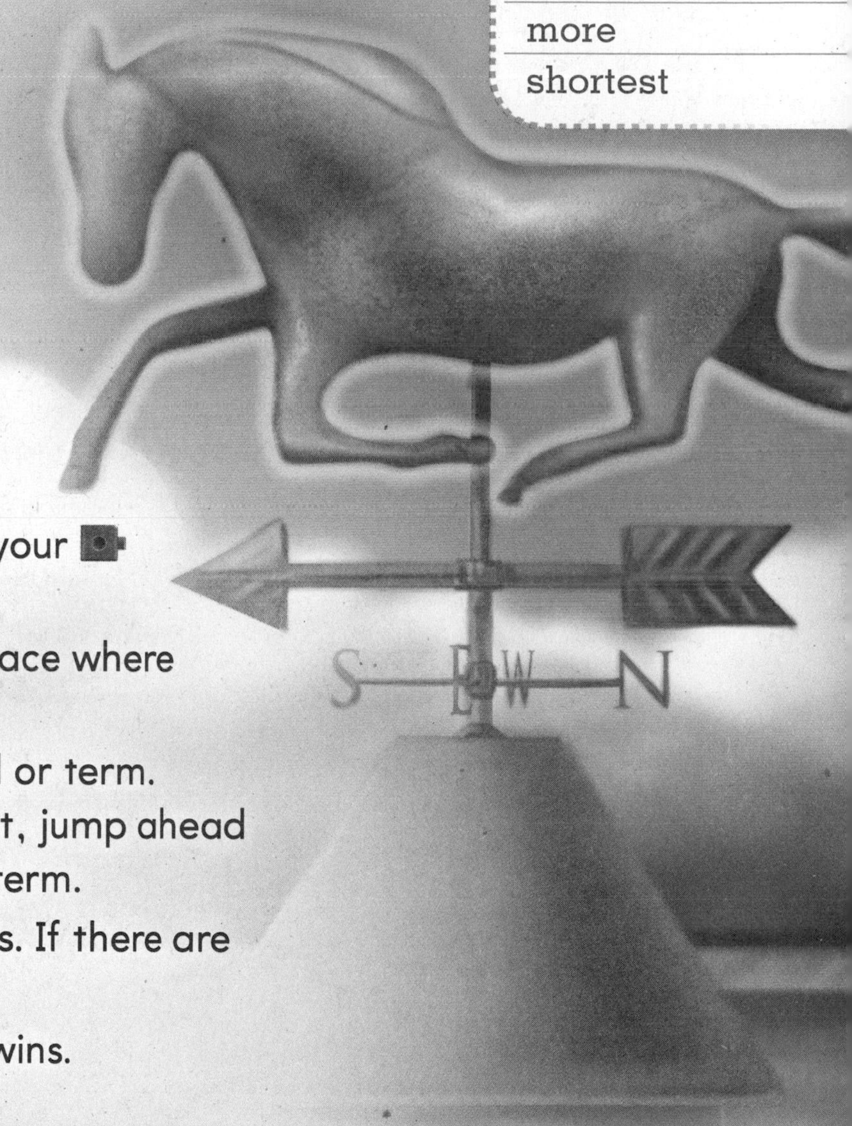

Materials

- 1 ▪
- 1 ▪
- 1 die

How to Play

1. Each player puts a ▪ on START.
2. Toss the die to take a turn. Move your ▪ that many spaces.
3. Follow these directions for the space where you land.

   White Space Read the math word or term. Tell its meaning. If you are correct, jump ahead to the next space with the same term.

   Green Space Follow the directions. If there are no directions, stay where you are.
4. The first player to reach FINISH wins.

HOW TO PLAY

1. Put your on START.
2. Toss the and move your that many spaces.
3. If you land on one of these spaces:

White Space Explain the math word or term, or use it in a sentence. If your answer is correct, jump ahead to the next space with that word or term.
Green Space Follow the directions in the space. If there are no directions, don't move.

4. The first player to reach FINISH wins.

MATERIALS

• 1 • 1 • 1

Game
Go back to
half hour
shortest
more
minutes
half hour
hour
hour hand
longest
minute hand
shortest
more
minutes
minute hand
longest
shortest
half hour
Go back to
hour
hour hand
minute hand
longest
hour hand
hour
half hour
minute hand
minutes
more
shortest

The Write Way

Reflect

Choose one idea. Draw and write about it.

- Julia has to measure an object. She does not have a ruler. Tell what Julia could do to solve her problem.
- Explain why it is important to learn how to tell time.

Name ______________________________

Order Length

Essential Question How do you order objects by length?

HANDS ON
Lesson 9.1

Common Core **Measurement and Data—1.MD.A.1**
MATHEMATICAL PRACTICES
MP1, MP3, MP6

Listen and Draw Real World Hands On

Use objects to show the problem.
Draw to show your work.

Math Talk MATHEMATICAL PRACTICES 3

Compare the straw and the key. Which is longer? Which is shorter? How do you know?

FOR THE TEACHER • Read the problem. Have children use classroom objects to act it out. Rosa has something that is longer than the drinking straw. She has another object that is shorter than the key. What objects might she have?

Model and Draw

Order three pieces of yarn from **shortest** to **longest**. Draw the missing piece of yarn.

shortest

longest

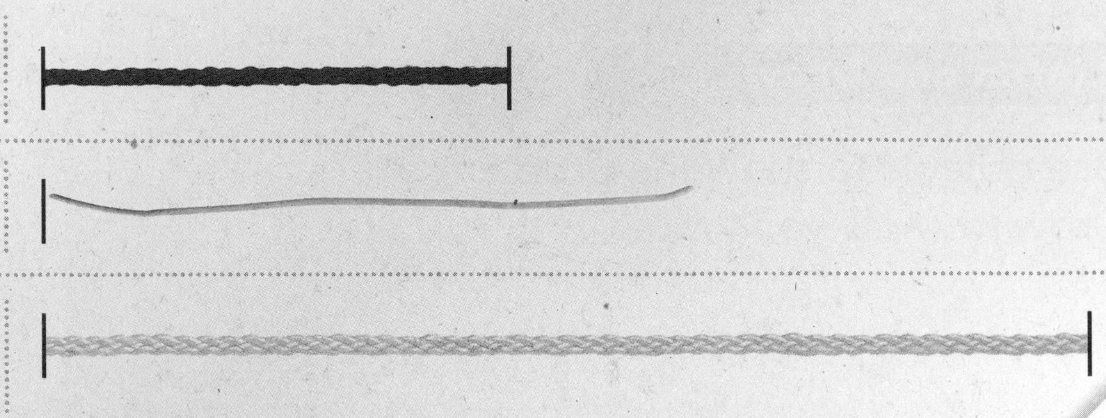

Share and Show

MATH BOARD

Draw three lines in order from **shortest** to **longest**.

1. **shortest**

2.

3. **longest**

Draw three lines in order from **longest** to **shortest**.

✓4. **longest**

✓5.

✓6. **shortest**

Name ____________________

On Your Own

MATHEMATICAL PRACTICE 3 **Compare Representations**

Draw three crayons in order from **shortest** to **longest**.

7. **shortest** |

8. |

9. **longest** |

Draw three crayons in order from **longest** to **shortest**.

10. **longest** |

11. |

12. **shortest** |

13. THINKSMARTER Complete each sentence.

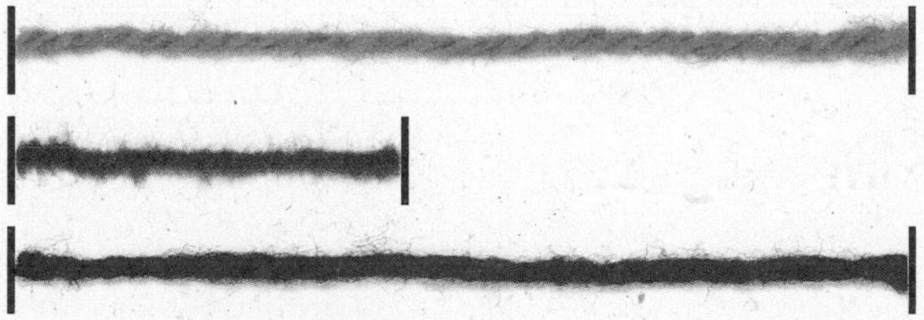

The ___Bigy___ yarn is the shortest.

The ___gred___ yarn and the ___red___ yarn are the same length.

Problem Solving • Applications Real World

WRITE Math

Solve.

14. GO DEEPER Draw four objects in order from shortest to longest.

Objects

15. THINK SMARTER The string is shorter than the ribbon. The chain is shorter than the ribbon. Circle the longest object.

Math on the Spot

string

ribbon

chain

16. THINK SMARTER Match each word on the left to a drawing on the right.

shortest

longest

TAKE HOME ACTIVITY • Show your child three different lengths of objects, such as three pencils or spoons. Ask him or her to order the objects from shortest to longest.

Name ______________________

Order Length

Common Core

COMMON CORE STANDARD—1.MD.A.1
Measure lengths indirectly and by iterating length units.

Draw three markers in order from longest to shortest.

1. longest

2.

3. shortest

Problem Solving Real World

Solve.

4. Fred has the shortest toothbrush in the bathroom. Circle Fred's toothbrush.

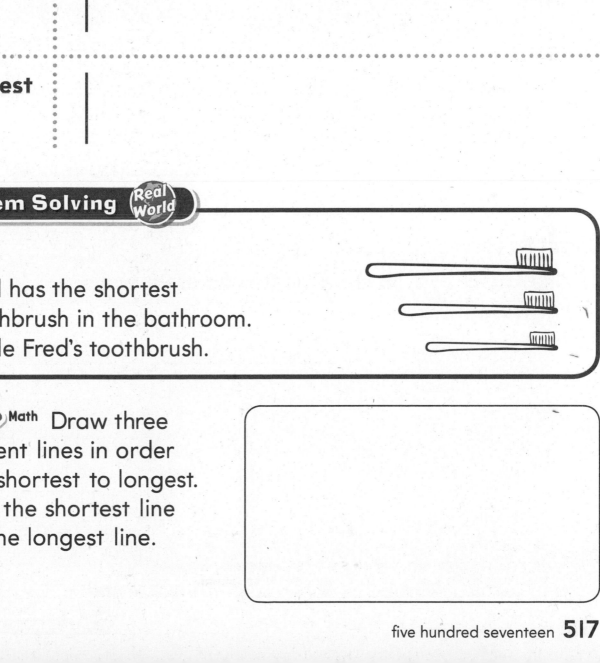

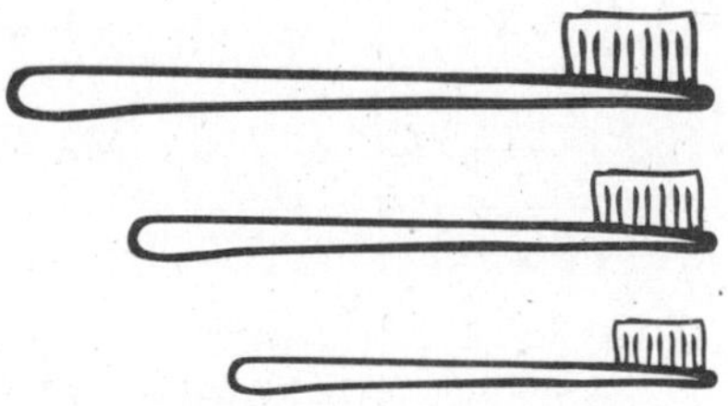

5. WRITE Math Draw three different lines in order from shortest to longest. Label the shortest line and the longest line.

Lesson Check (1.MD.A.1)

1. Draw three crayons in order from longest to shortest.

2. Draw three paint brushes in order from shortest to longest.

Spiral Review (1.NBT.B.2a, 1.NBT.B.3)

3. Use to show 22 two different ways. Draw both ways.

Tens	Ones

Tens	Ones

FOR MORE PRACTICE GO TO THE **Personal Math Trainer**

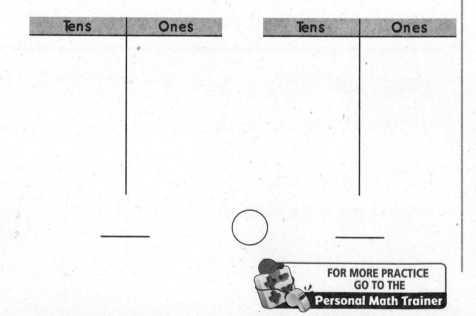

Name ______________________________

Indirect Measurement

Essential Question How can you compare lengths of three objects to put them in order?

Common Core **Measurement and Data—1.MD.A.1**
MATHEMATICAL PRACTICES MP1, MP3, MP4

Listen and Draw

Real World

Clue 1: A yellow string is shorter than a blue string.

Clue 2: The blue string is shorter than a red string.

Clue 3: The yellow string is shorter than the red string.

yellow

blue

red

Math Talk MATHEMATICAL PRACTICES 4

Represent How did the clues help you draw the strings in the correct order?

FOR THE TEACHER • Read the clues. Have children use the MathBoard to draw each clue. Then have children draw the strings in order from shortest to longest.

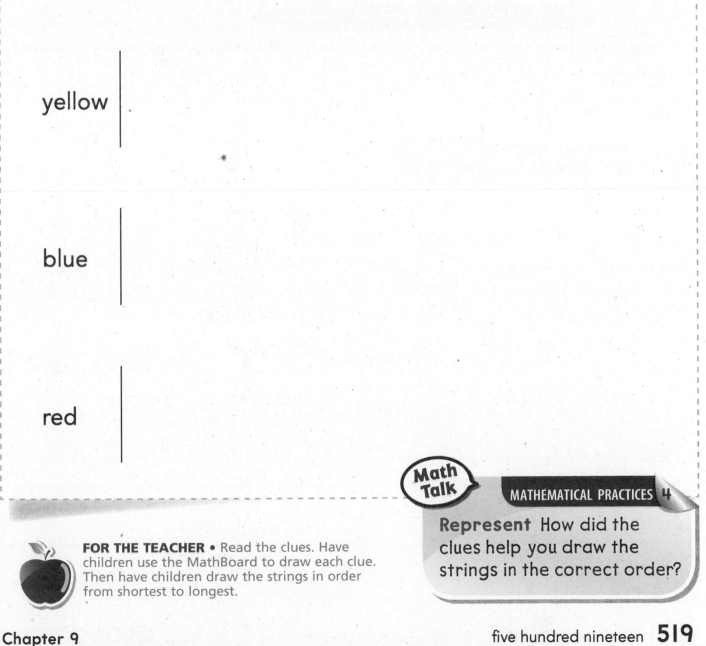

Model and Draw

Use the clues. Write **shorter** or **longer** to complete the sentence. Then draw to prove your answer.

Clue 1: A green pencil is longer than an orange pencil.

Clue 2: The orange pencil is longer than a brown pencil.

So, the green pencil is longer than the brown pencil.

brown	
orange	
green	

Share and Show

MATH BOARD

Use the clues. Write **shorter** or **longer** to complete the sentence. Then draw to prove your answer.

1. Clue 1: A red line is shorter than a blue line.
   Clue 2: The blue line is shorter than a purple line.

   So, the red line is ______________ than the purple line.

red	
blue	
purple	

Name ______________________________

On Your Own

MATHEMATICAL PRACTICE 1 **Analyze Relationships** Use the clues. Write **shorter** or **longer** to complete the sentence. Then draw to prove your answer.

2. Clue 1: A green line is shorter than a pink line.
Clue 2: The pink line is shorter than a blue line.

So, the green line is ____________ than the blue line.

green	
pink	
blue	

3. Clue 1: An orange line is longer than a yellow line.
Clue 2: The yellow line is longer than a red line.

So, the orange line is ____________ than the red line.

red	
yellow	
orange	

Problem Solving • Applications Real World

WRITE Math

4. THINK SMARTER The ribbon is longer than the yarn. The yarn is longer than the string. The yarn and the pencil are the same length. Draw the lengths of the objects next to their labels.

Math on the Spot

ribbon	
yarn	
pencil	
string	

5. THINK SMARTER Is the first line longer than the second line? Choose Yes or No.

○ Yes ○ No

○ Yes ○ No

○ Yes ○ No

TAKE HOME ACTIVITY • Show your child the length of one object. Then show your child an object that is longer and an object that is shorter than the first object.

Name ______________________________

Indirect Measurement

Common Core
COMMON CORE STANDARD—1.MD.A.1
Measure lengths indirectly and by iterating length units.

Read the clues. Write shorter or longer to complete the sentence. Then draw to prove your answer.

1. Clue 1: A piece of yarn is longer than a ribbon.
Clue 2: The ribbon is longer than a crayon.
So, the yarn is ________ than the crayon.

yarn	
ribbon	
crayon	

Problem Solving Real World

Solve. Draw or write to explain.

2. Megan's pencil is shorter than Tasha's pencil.
Tasha's pencil is shorter than Kim's pencil.
Is Megan's pencil shorter or longer than Kim's pencil? ________

3. WRITE Math Use different colors to draw 3 lines that are different lengths. Then write a sentence comparing their lengths.

Lesson Check (1.MD.A.1)

1. A black line is longer than a gray line. The gray line is longer than a white line. Is the black line shorter or longer than the white line? Draw to prove your answer.

____

Spiral Review (1.NBT.C.4)

2. What is the sum? Write the number.

$42 + 20 =$ ____

FOR MORE PRACTICE GO TO THE Personal Math Trainer

Name ______________________________

Use Nonstandard Units to Measure Length

Essential Question How do you measure length using nonstandard units?

Common Core Measurement and Data—1.MD.A.2
MATHEMATICAL PRACTICES
MP1, MP2, MP6, MP8

Listen and Draw

Real World · Hands On

Use ■. Draw to show the problem.

FOR THE TEACHER • Read the problem. Jimmy sees that his boat is about 6 color tiles long. Draw Jimmy's boat. Draw the color tiles to show how you measured.

Math Talk MATHEMATICAL PRACTICES 2

Reasoning How do you draw the boat to be the right length?

Model and Draw

You can use  to measure length.
Write how many.

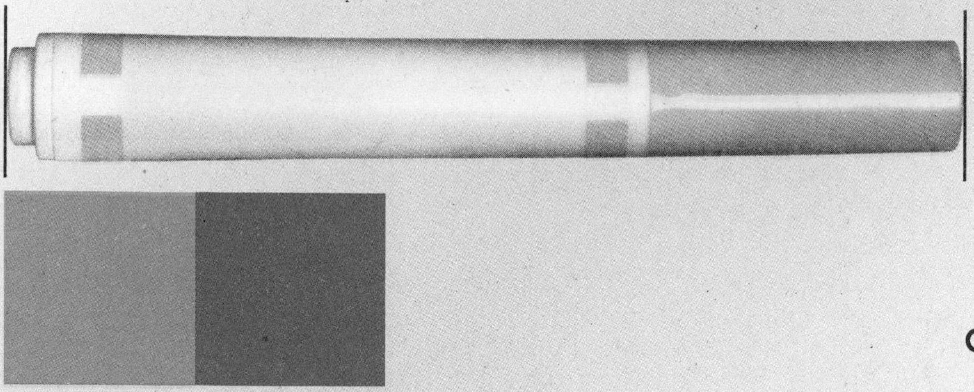

about ____ 

Share and Show

MATH BOARD

Use real objects. Use  to measure.

1. 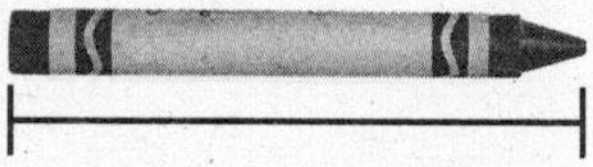

about ____ 

2. 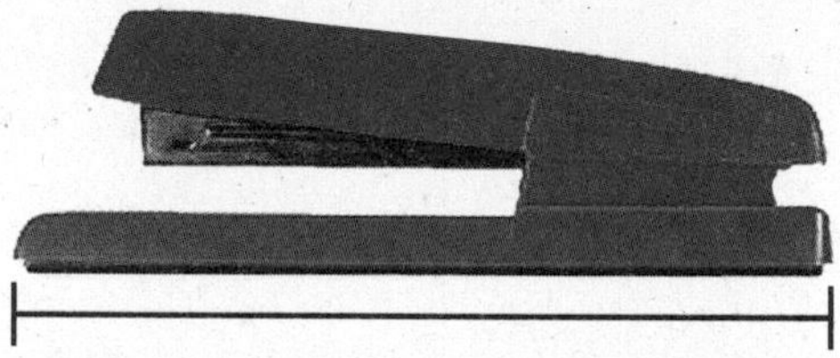

about ____ 

✓3. 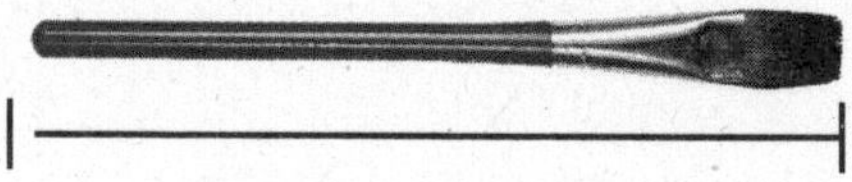

about ____ 

✓4. 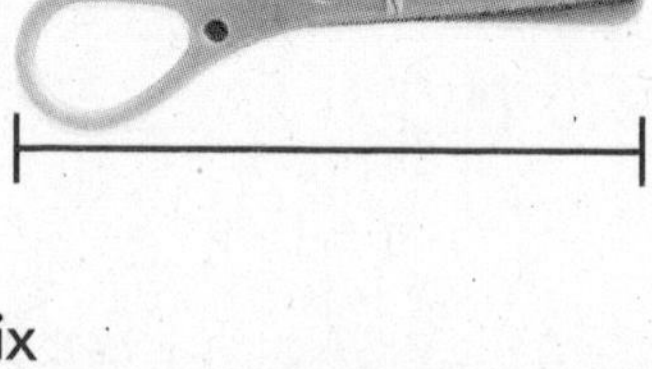

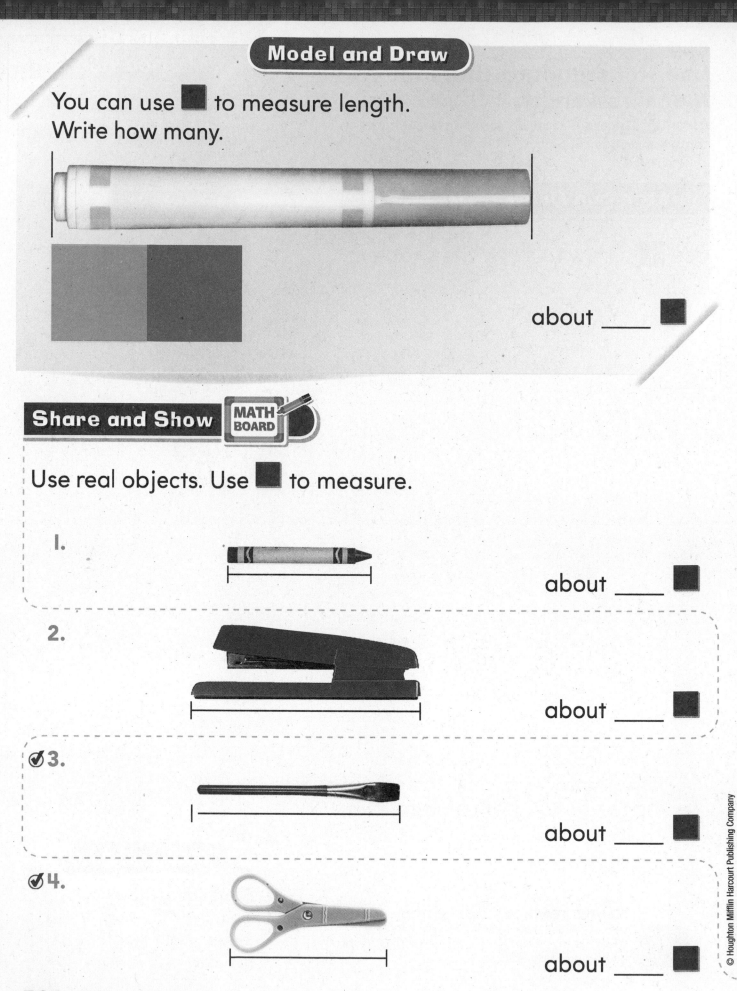

about ____

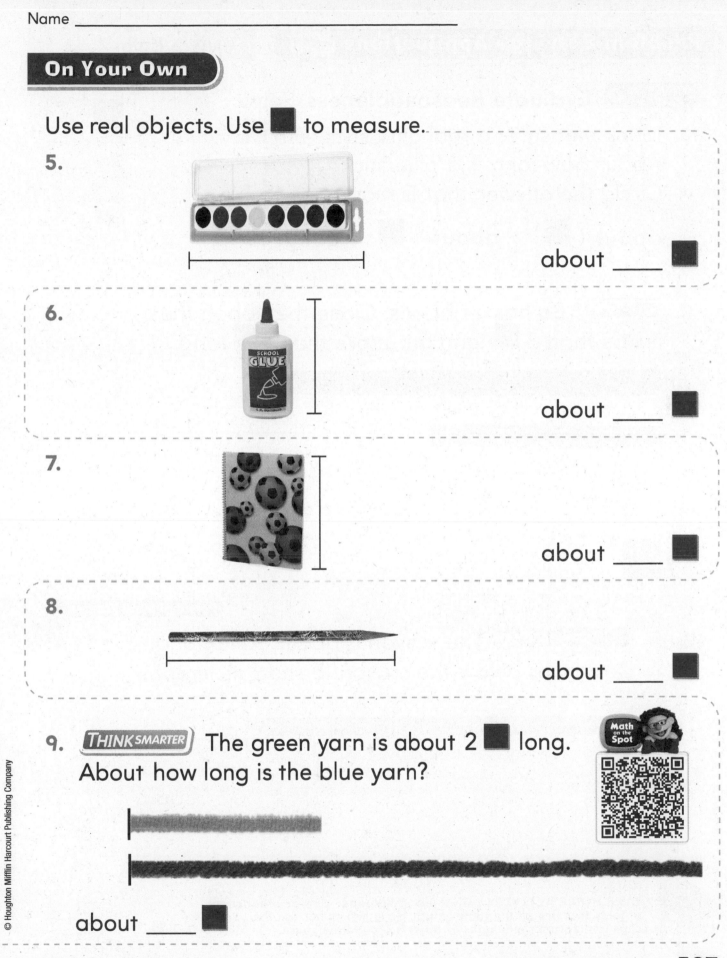

Name ______________________

On Your Own

Use real objects. Use ■ to measure.

5.

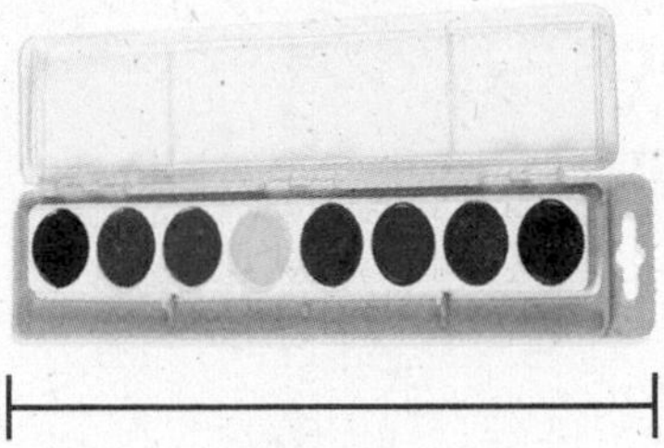

about ____ ■

6.

about ____ ■

7.

about ____ ■

8.

about ____ ■

9. THINKSMARTER The green yarn is about 2 ■ long. About how long is the blue yarn?

about ____ ■

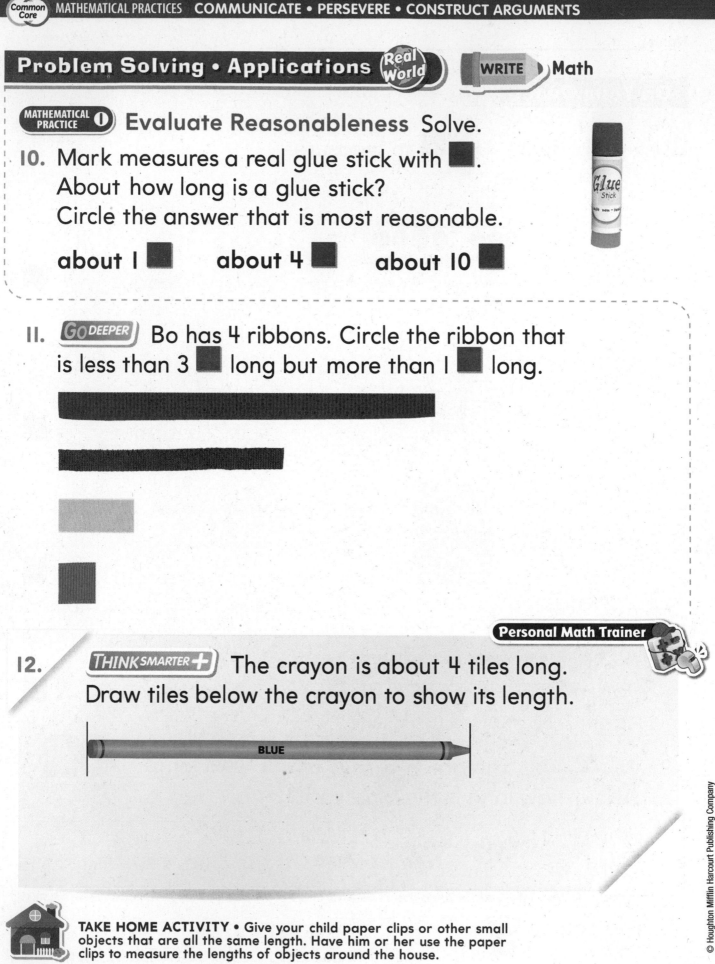

Problem Solving • Applications Real World

WRITE Math

MATHEMATICAL PRACTICE 1 **Evaluate Reasonableness** Solve.

10. Mark measures a real glue stick with ■.
About how long is a glue stick?
Circle the answer that is most reasonable.

about 1 ■ **about 4 ■** **about 10 ■**

11. GO DEEPER Bo has 4 ribbons. Circle the ribbon that is less than 3 ■ long but more than 1 ■ long.

12. THINK SMARTER + The crayon is about 4 tiles long. Draw tiles below the crayon to show its length.

Personal Math Trainer

TAKE HOME ACTIVITY • Give your child paper clips or other small objects that are all the same length. Have him or her use the paper clips to measure the lengths of objects around the house.

Use Nonstandard Units to Measure Length

Common Core COMMON CORE STANDARD—1.MD.A.2
Measure lengths indirectly and by iterating length units.

Use real objects. Use to measure.

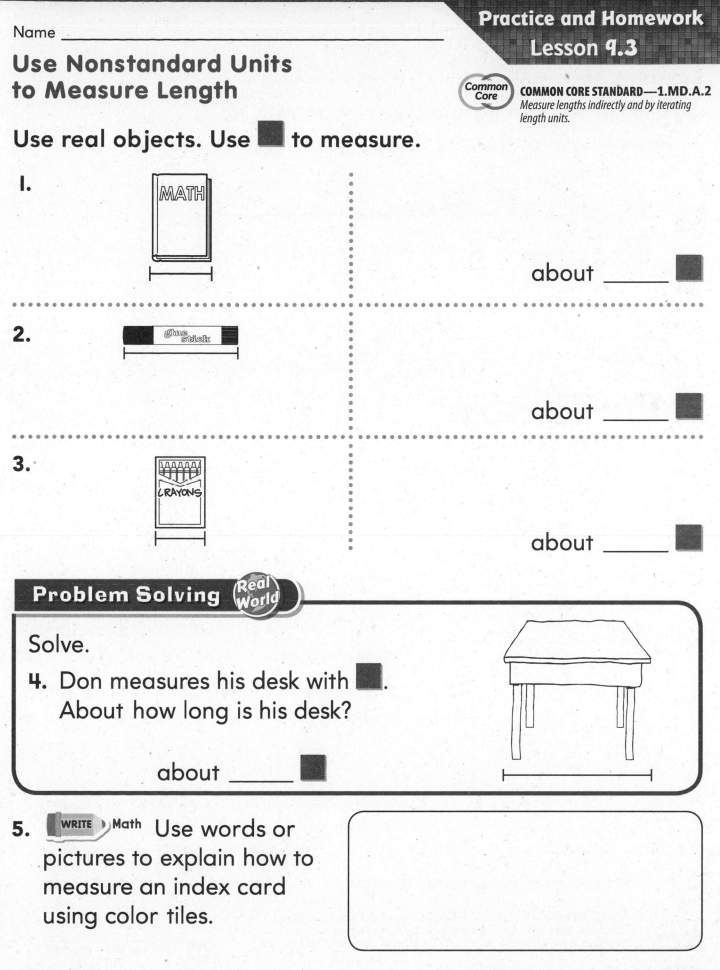

1.
MATH

about _____ ▪

2.
glue Stick

about _____ ▪

3.
CRAYONS

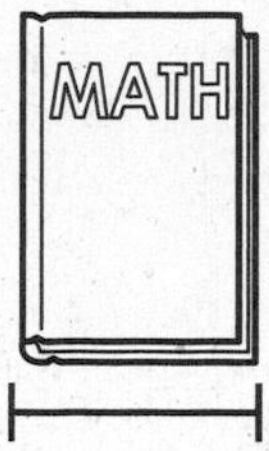

about _____ ▪

Problem Solving Real World

Solve.

4. Don measures his desk with ▪.
About how long is his desk?

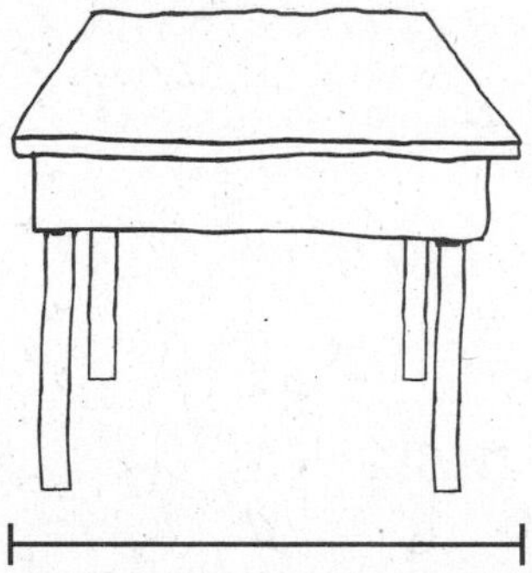

about _____ ▪

5. WRITE Math Use words or pictures to explain how to measure an index card using color tiles.

Lesson Check (1.MD.A.2)

1. Use ■. Kevin measures the ribbon with ■. About how long is the ribbon?

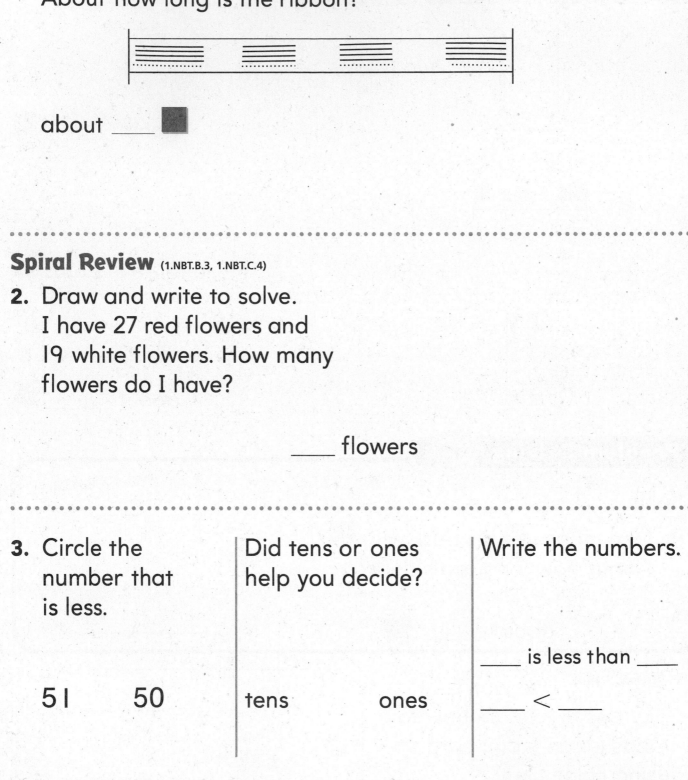

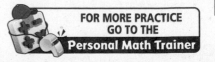

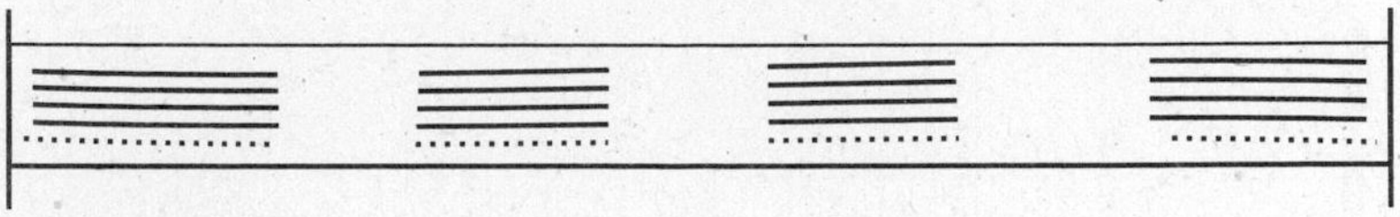

about ____ ■

Spiral Review (1.NBT.B.3, 1.NBT.C.4)

2. Draw and write to solve. I have 27 red flowers and 19 white flowers. How many flowers do I have?

____ flowers

3. Circle the number that is less.

51 50

Did tens or ones help you decide?

tens ones

Write the numbers.

____ is less than ____

____ < ____

FOR MORE PRACTICE GO TO THE Personal Math Trainer

Name ______________________________________

Make a Nonstandard Measuring Tool

Essential Question How do you use a nonstandard measuring tool to measure length?

Common Core **Measurement and Data—1.MD.A.2**
MATHEMATICAL PRACTICES
MP2, MP3, MP5

Listen and Draw (Real World)

Circle the name of the child who measured correctly.

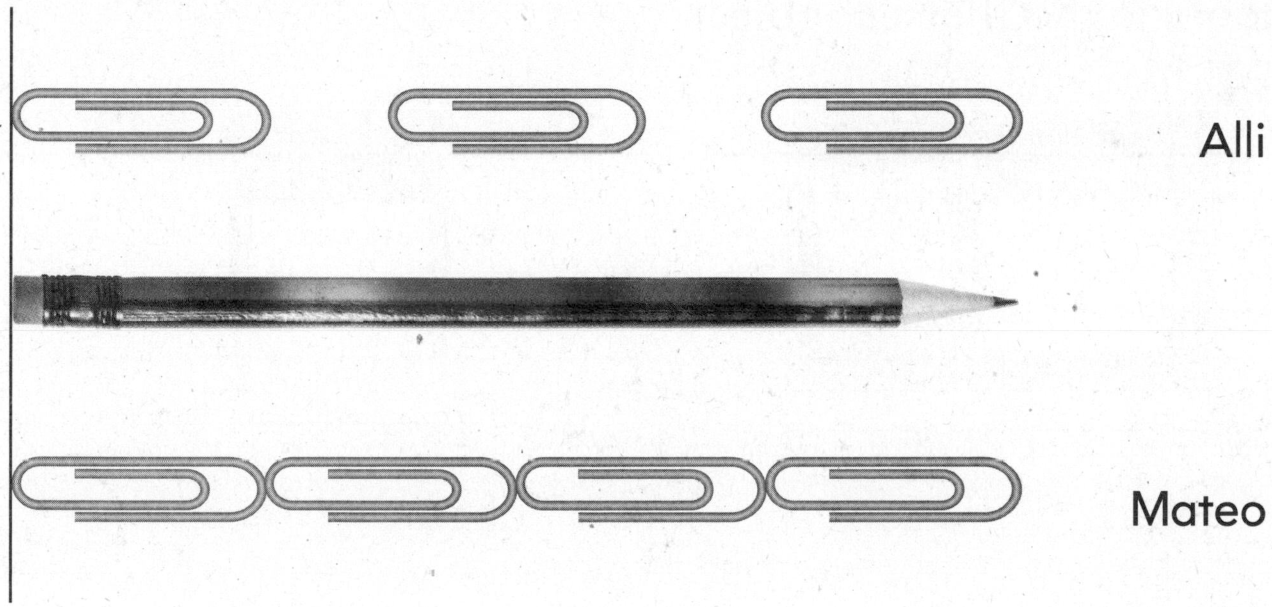

Math Talk MATHEMATICAL PRACTICES 5

Use Tools Explain how you know who measured correctly.

FOR THE TEACHER • Read the problem. Mateo and Alli measure the same pencil. Mateo says it is about 4 paper clips long. Alli says it is about 3 paper clips long. Circle the name of the child who measured correctly.

Model and Draw

Make your own paper clip measuring tool like the one on the shelf. Measure the length of a door. About how long is the door?

about ____ 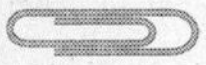

Share and Show

MATH BOARD

Use real objects and the measuring tool you made. Measure. Circle the longest object. Underline the shortest object.

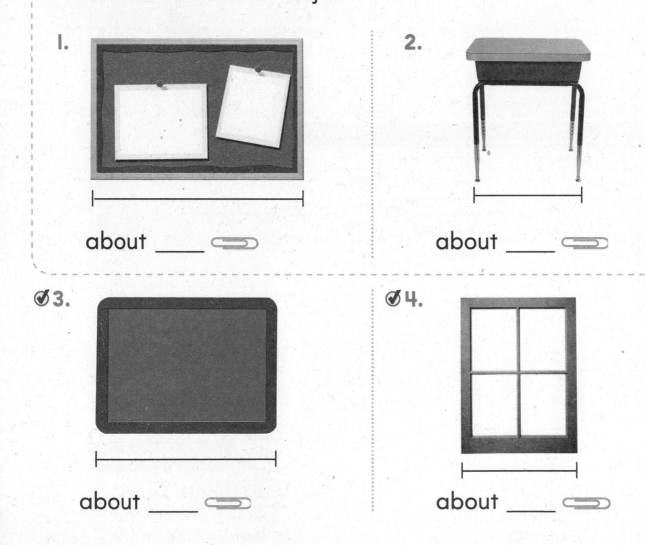

1.

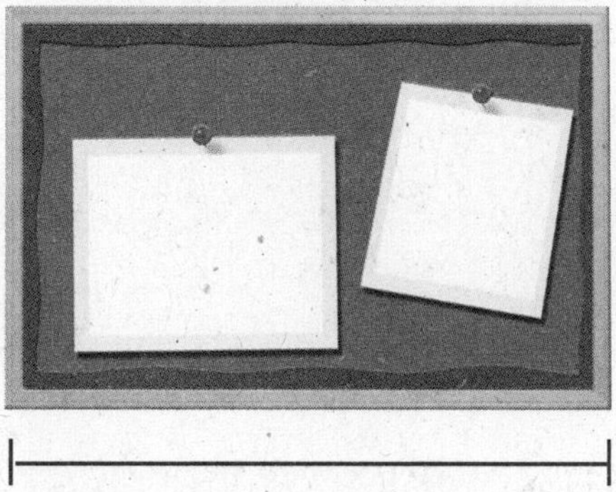

about ____ 

2.

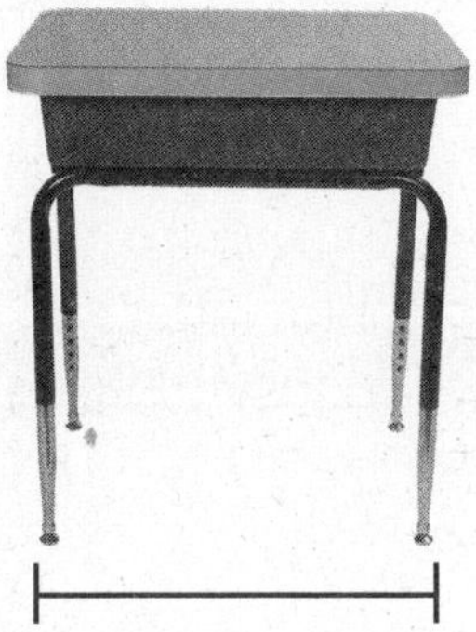

about ____ 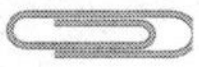

✓3.

about ____ 

✓4.

about ____ 

Name ____________________

On Your Own

MATHEMATICAL PRACTICE 5 **Use Appropriate Tools**

Use the measuring tool you made.
Measure real objects.

5. 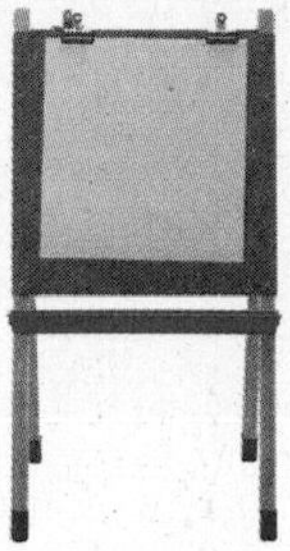

about ____ (paper clips)

6. 

about ____ (paper clips)

7. 

about ____ (paper clips)

8. 

about ____ (paper clips)

9. **GO DEEPER** Cody measured his real lunch box. It is about 10 (paper clips) long. About how long is Cody's real pencil?

about ____ (paper clips)

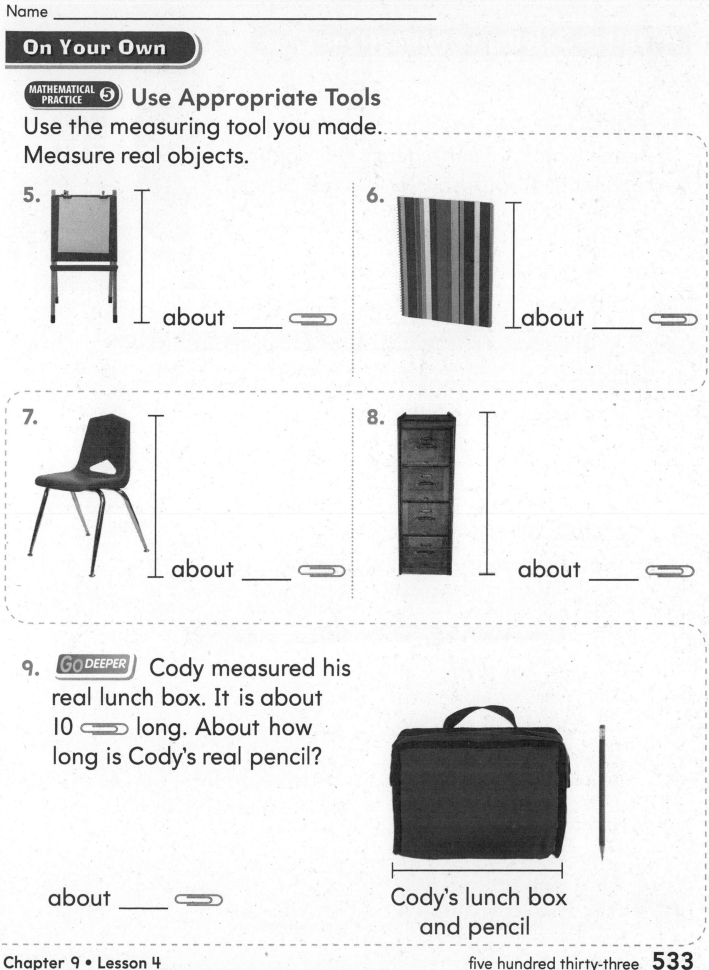

Cody's lunch box and pencil

Problem Solving • Applications Real World

WRITE Math

Solve.

10. THINKSMARTER Lisa tried to measure the pencil. She thinks the pencil is 5 paper clips long. About how long is the pencil?

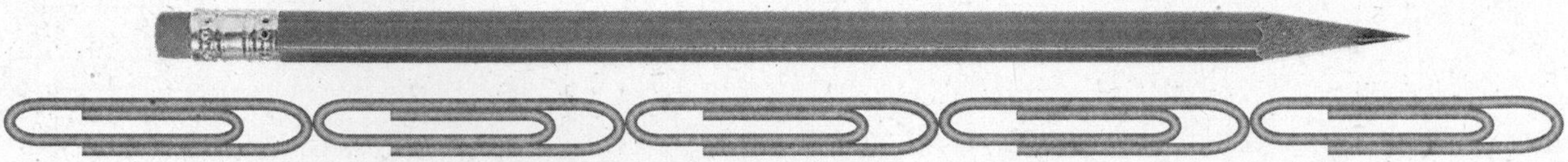

about ____ 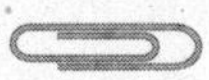

11. THINKSMARTER Use the  below. About how long is the paintbrush?

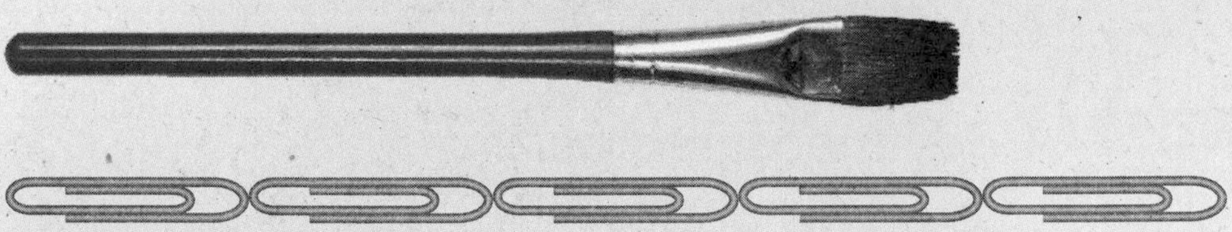

about ____ 

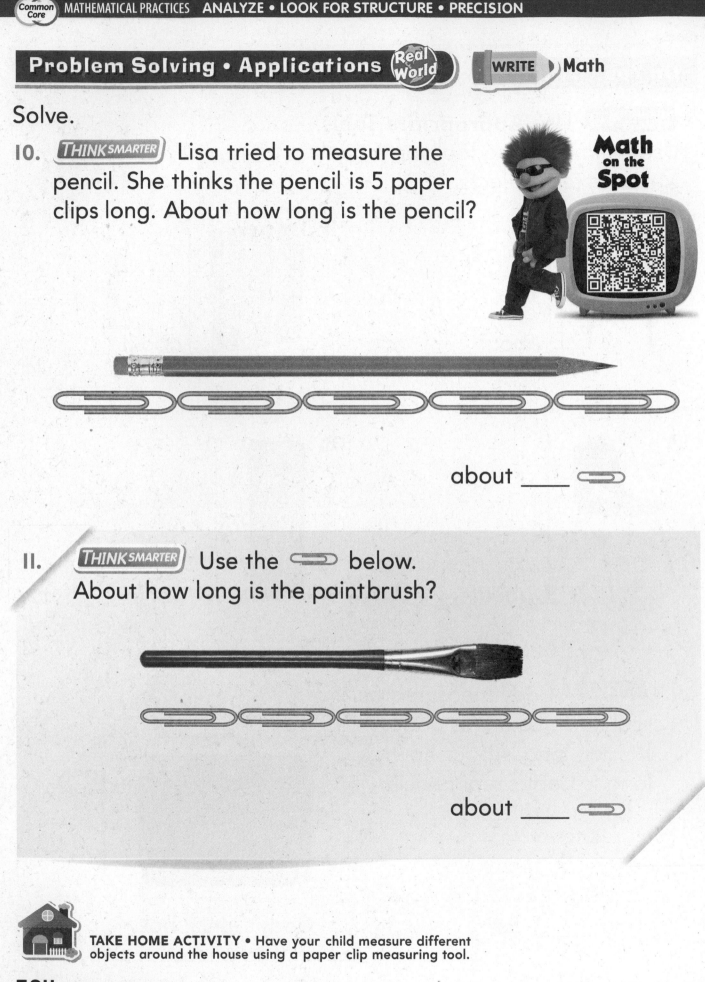

TAKE HOME ACTIVITY • **Have your child measure different objects around the house using a paper clip measuring tool.**

Name ______________________________

Make a Nonstandard Measuring Tool

Common Core

COMMON CORE STANDARD—1.MD.A.2
Measure lengths indirectly and by iterating length units.

Use the measuring tool you made. Measure real objects.

1.

about ______

2.

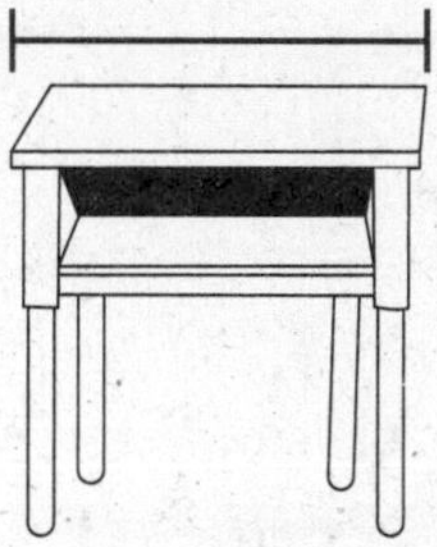

about ______

3.

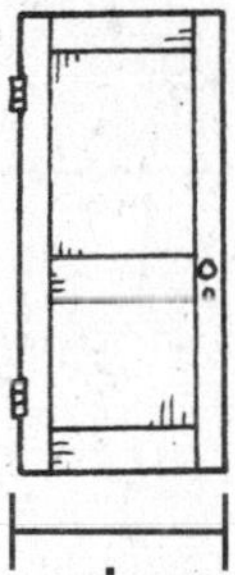

about ______

4.

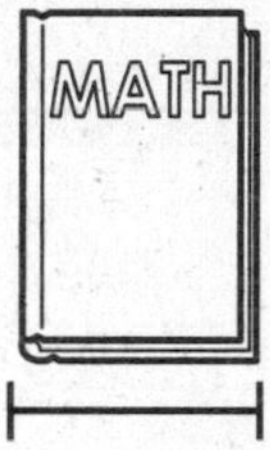

about ______

5.

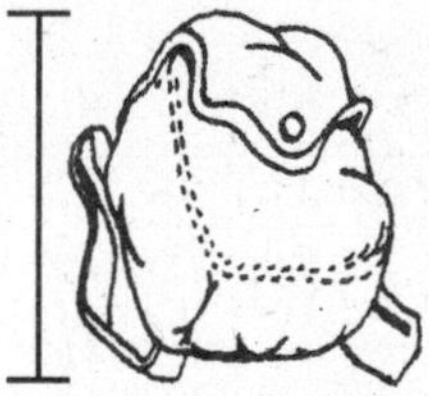

about ______

6.

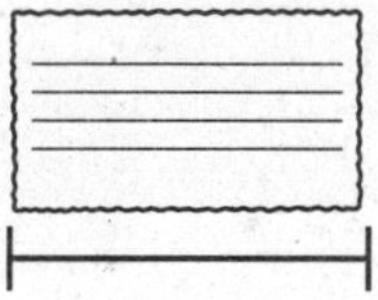

about ______

7. WRITE Math Use words or pictures to explain how to measure a table using a paper clip measuring tool.

Lesson Check (1.MD.A.2)

1. Use the  below. Circle the string that is about 4 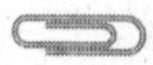 long.

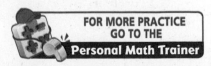

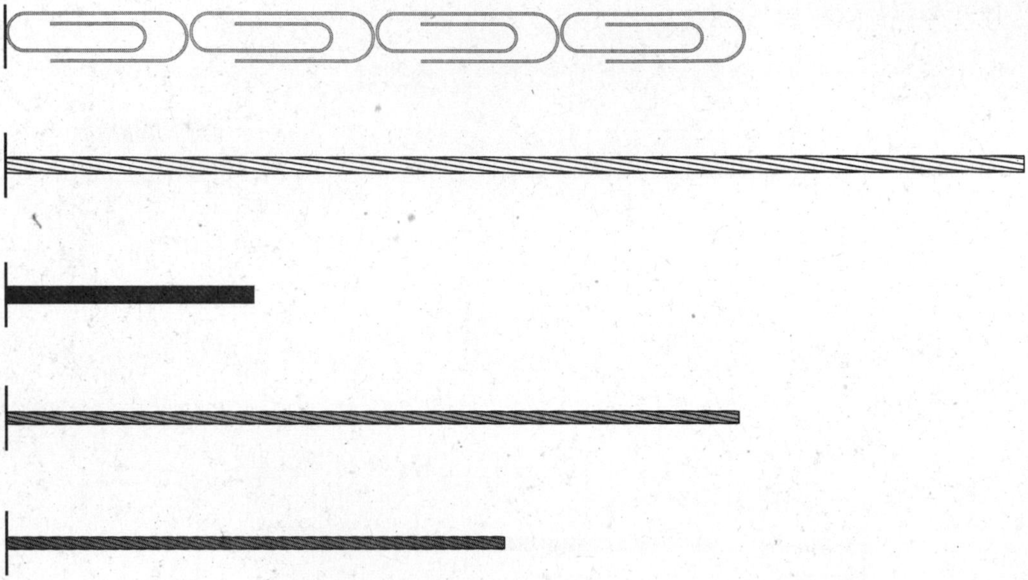

Spiral Review (1.OA.A.1, 1.NBT.B.3)

2. Ty crosses out the number cards that are greater than 38 and less than 34. What numbers are left?

33	35	37	39	40

____ and ____

---

3. There are 12 books. 4 books are large. The rest are small. Write a number sentence that shows how to find the number of small books.

____ − ____ = ____

Name ______________________

Problem Solving • Measure and Compare

Essential Question How can acting it out help you solve measurement problems?

Common Core **Measurement and Data—1.MD.A.2**
MATHEMATICAL PRACTICES MP1, MP3

The blue ribbon is about 4 long. The red ribbon is 1 long. The green ribbon is 2 longer than the red ribbon. Measure and draw the ribbons in order from **shortest** to **longest**.

Unlock the Problem

Hands On

What do I need to find?

order the ribbons from shortest to longest

What information do I need to use?

Measure the ribbons using paper clips.

Show how to solve the problem.

HOME CONNECTION • Have your child act out a measurement problem by finding the lengths of 3 objects and ordering them from shortest to longest.

Try Another Problem

Zack has 3 ribbons. The yellow ribbon is about 4 long. The orange ribbon is 3 shorter than the yellow ribbon. The blue ribbon is 2 longer than the yellow ribbon.

- What do I need to find?
- What information do I need to use?

Measure and draw the ribbons in order from **longest** to **shortest**.

1.

about ____

2.

about ____

3.

about ____

Math Talk MATHEMATICAL PRACTICES 3

Compare How many paper clips shorter is the orange ribbon than the blue ribbon?

Name ______________________________

Share and Show MATH BOARD

Solve. Draw or write to explain.

✓4. GO DEEPER Lisa measures her shoe to be about 5  long. Measure and draw an object that is 3  shorter than her shoe. Measure and draw an object that is 2  longer than her shoe.

Personal Math Trainer

5. THINK SMARTER + Noah measures a marker to be about 4  long and a pencil to be about 6  long. Draw an object that is 1  longer than the marker and 1  shorter than the pencil.

Math on the Spot

TAKE HOME ACTIVITY • Have your child explain how he or she solved Exercise 4.

Name ______________________________

Mid-Chapter Checkpoint

Personal Math Trainer
Online Assessment and Intervention

Concepts and Skills

Draw three crayons in order from **shortest** to **longest**. (1.MD.A.1)

1.

shortest	
longest	

Use ■ to measure. (1.MD.A.2)

2. 

about ____ ■

3. THINK SMARTER Kiley measures a package with her paper clip measuring tool. About how long is the package? Circle your answer. (1.MD.A.2)

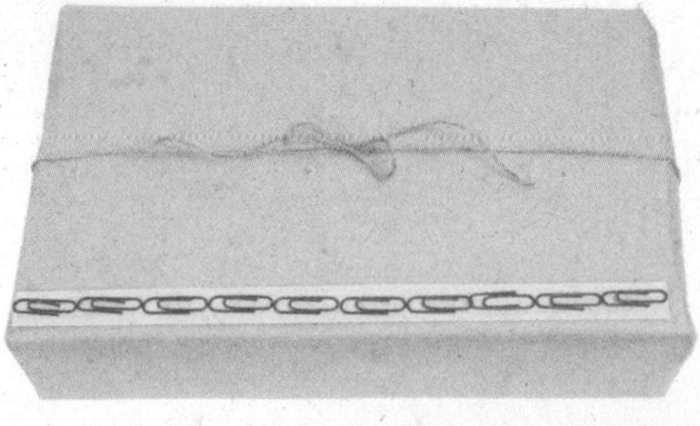

about

1
5
10
20

📎

Name ______________________________

Problem Solving • Measure and Compare

Common Core

COMMON CORE STANDARD—1.MD.A.2
Measure lengths indirectly and by iterating length units.

The blue string is about 3 long. The green string is 2 longer than the blue string. The red string is 1 shorter than the blue string. Measure and draw the strings in order from **longest** to **shortest**.

1.

about ____

2.

about ____

3.

about ____

Problem Solving Real World

4. Sandy has a ribbon about 4 long. She cut a new ribbon 2 longer. Measure and draw the two ribbons.

The new ribbon is about ____ long.

5. WRITE Math Measure and draw to show a blue crayon and a green crayon that is about 1 paper clip longer.

Lesson Check (1.MD.A.2)

1. Mia measures a stapler with her paper clip ruler. About how long is the stapler?

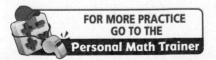

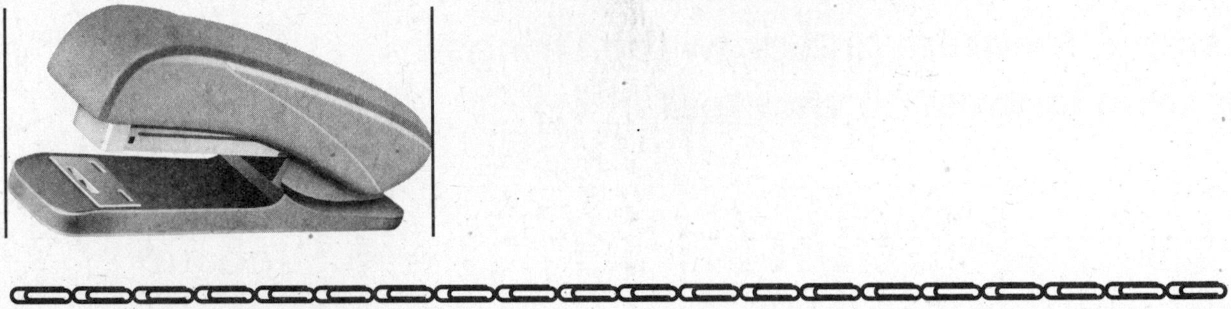

about ____ paper clips

Spiral Review (1.OA.C.6, 1.NBT.C.5)

2. What is the unknown number? Write the number.

$$4 + \_\_\_ = 13$$

3. Count by tens. What numbers are missing? Write the numbers.

17, 27, ______, ______, 57, 67

FOR MORE PRACTICE GO TO THE Personal Math Trainer

Name ______________________________

Time to the Hour

Essential Question How do you tell time to the hour on a clock that has only an hour hand?

Common Core **Measurement and Data—1.MD.B.3**
MATHEMATICAL PRACTICES MP5, MP6, MP7

Listen and Draw (Real World)

Start at 1.
Write the unknown numbers.

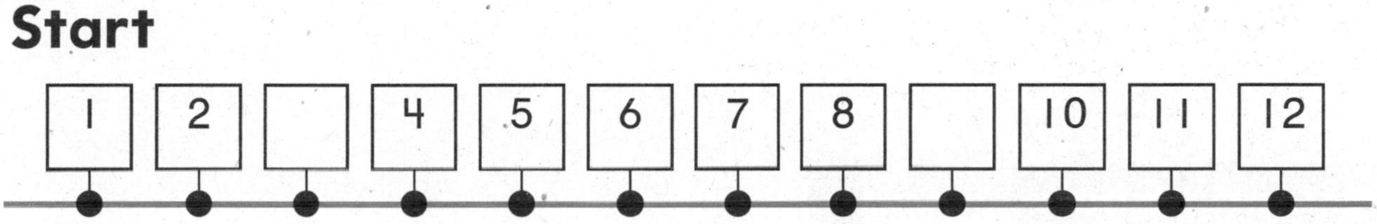

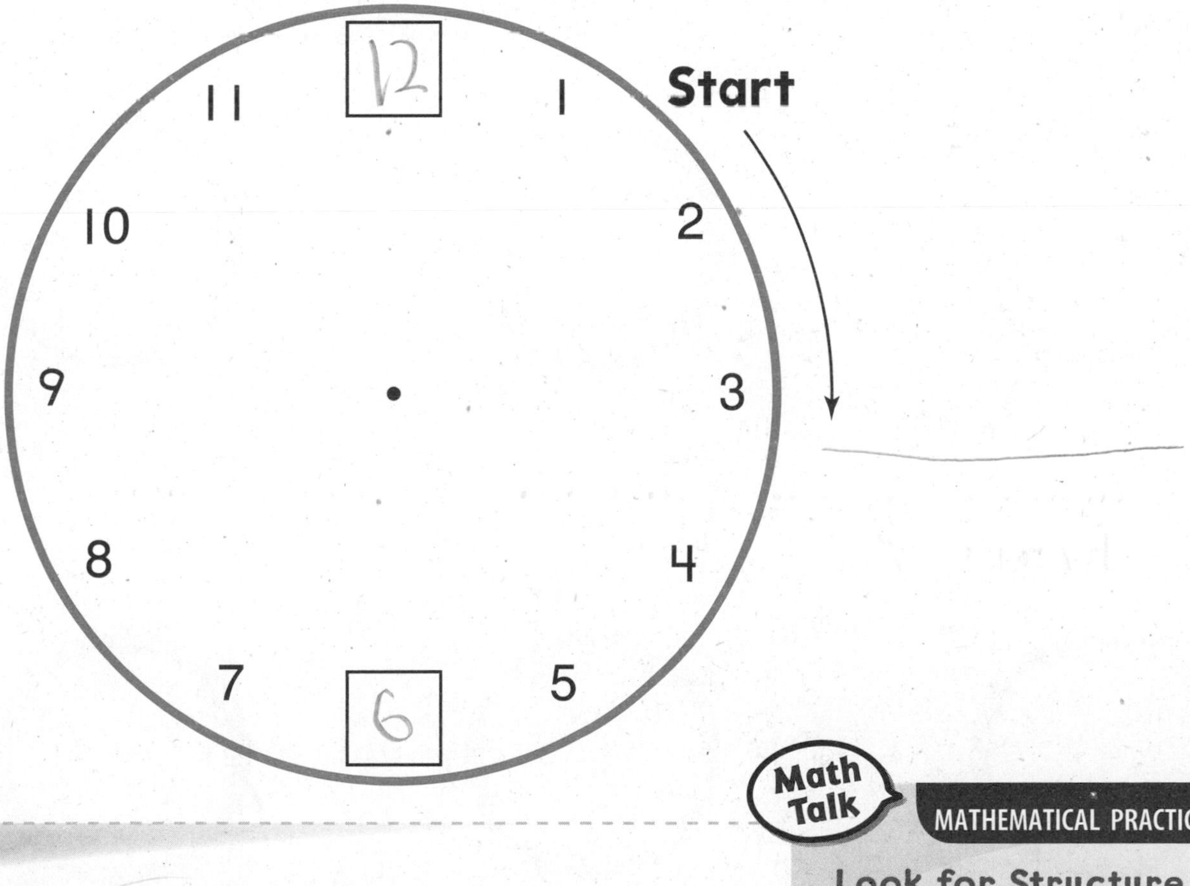

FOR THE TEACHER • In the top workspace, have children write the unknown numbers in the squares on the green yarn. In the bottom workspace, have children write the unknown numbers on the clock face.

Math Talk MATHEMATICAL PRACTICES 7

Look for Structure
How are a clock face and ordering numbers alike?

Model and Draw

What does this clock show?

The **hour hand** points to the 3.
It is 3 o'clock.

Say three o'clock.

Write 3:00.

Share and Show

MATH BOARD

Look at where the hour hand points.
Write the time.

1.

9:00

2.

1:00

3.

11:00

4.

6:00

5.

7:00

6.

5:00

Name Sarah Lee

On Your Own

MATHEMATICAL PRACTICE 6 **Make Connections** Look at where the hour hand points. Write the time.

7.

4:00

8.

10:00

9.

6:00

10.

12

11.

1:00

12.

3:00

13. THINKSMARTER On Rae's clock, the hour hand points to the 9. Circle Rae's clock.

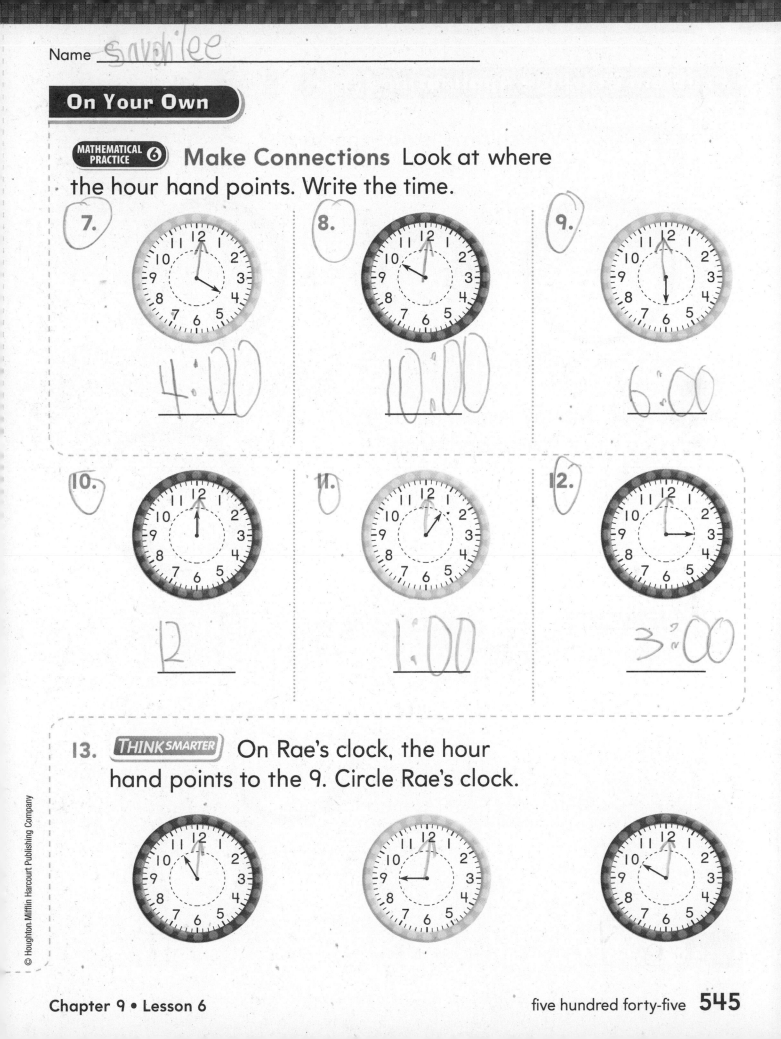

Problem Solving • Applications Real World

WRITE Math

Math on the Spot

14. THINK SMARTER Which time is **not** the same? Circle it.

1:00

I o'clock

15. GO DEEPER Manny leaves for school at 8 o'clock. Write and draw to show 8 o'clock.

____

16. THINK SMARTER Look at the hour hand. What is the time?

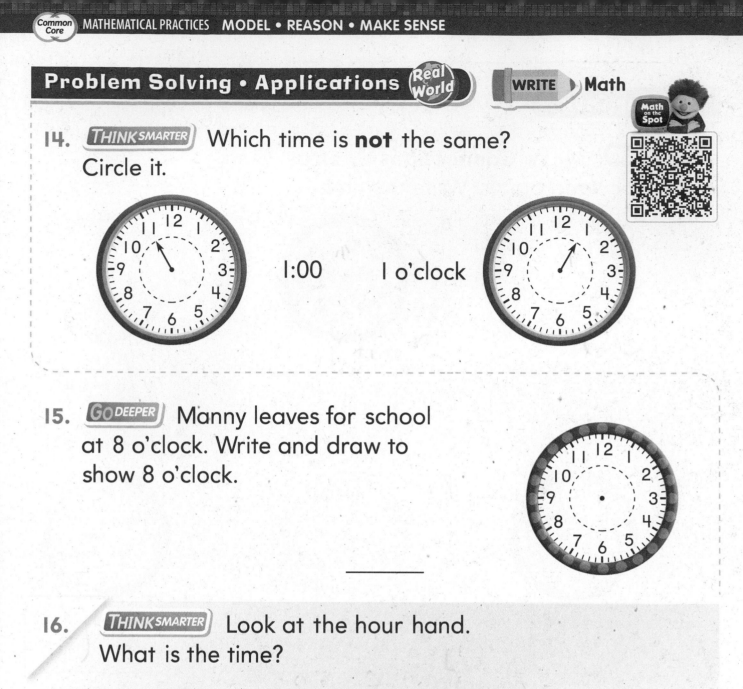

- ○ 7:00
- ○ 8 o'clock
- ○ 9 o'clock
- ○ 12:00

TAKE HOME ACTIVITY • Have your child describe what he or she did in this lesson.

Name ______________________

Time to the Hour

Common Core — **COMMON CORE STANDARD—1.MD.B.3**
Tell and write time.

**Look at where the hour hand points.
Write the time.**

1.

______

2.

______

3.

______

Problem Solving — Real World

Solve.

4. Which time is **not** the same? Circle it.

7:00 7 o'clock

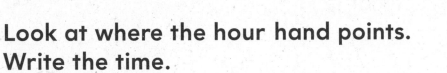

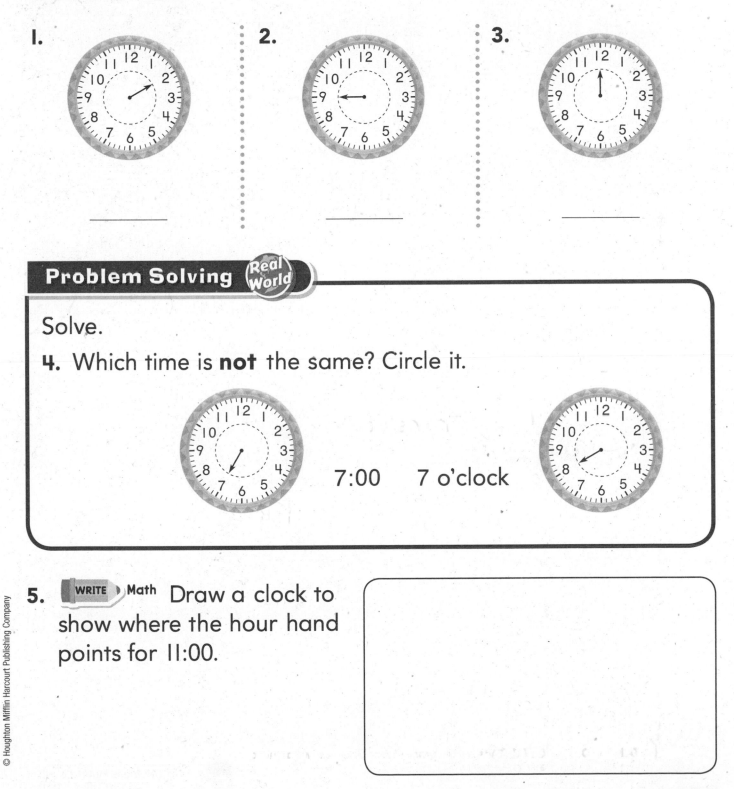

5. WRITE Math Draw a clock to show where the hour hand points for 11:00.

Lesson Check (1.MD.B.3)

1. Look at the hour hand. What is the time? Write the time.

____

2. Look at the hour hand. What is the time? Write the time.

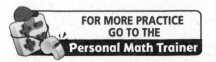

____ o'clock

Spiral Review (1.NBT.C.4)

3. What is the sum? Write the number.

$40 + 30 =$ ______

4. What is the sum? Write the number.

$53 + 30 =$ ______

FOR MORE PRACTICE GO TO THE Personal Math Trainer

Name ____________________

Time to the Half Hour

Essential Question How do you tell time to the half hour on a clock that has only an hour hand?

Common Core **Measurement and Data—1.MD.B.3**
MATHEMATICAL PRACTICES MP1, MP2, MP8

Listen and Draw

Circle **4:00**, **5:00**, or **between 4:00 and 5:00** to describe the time shown on the clock.

4:00

between 4:00 and 5:00

5:00

4:00

between 4:00 and 5:00

5:00

4:00

between 4:00 and 5:00

5:00

Math Talk MATHEMATICAL PRACTICES 2

Reasoning Use **before** and **after** to describe the time shown on the middle clock.

FOR THE TEACHER • Have children look at the hour hand on each clock to decide which choice best describes the time shown.

As an **hour** passes, the hour hand moves from one number to the next number.

> The hour hand is halfway between the 7 and the 8.

When a **half hour** has passed, the hour hand points halfway between two numbers.

half past 7:00

Share and Show MATH BOARD

Look at where the hour hand points.
Write the time.

1.

1:30
half past 1:00

2.

4:30
half past 4:00

3.

11:30
half past 11:30

4.

3:30
half past 3:00

Name ____________________

On Your Own

MATHEMATICAL PRACTICE 2 **Use Reasoning** Look at where the hour hand points. Write the time.

5.

5:30
half past 5:00

6.

10:30
half past 10:00

7.

2:30
half past 2:00

8.

9:30
half past 9:00

9. THINK SMARTER Maya starts reading at half past 8. Circle the clock that shows the time Maya starts reading.

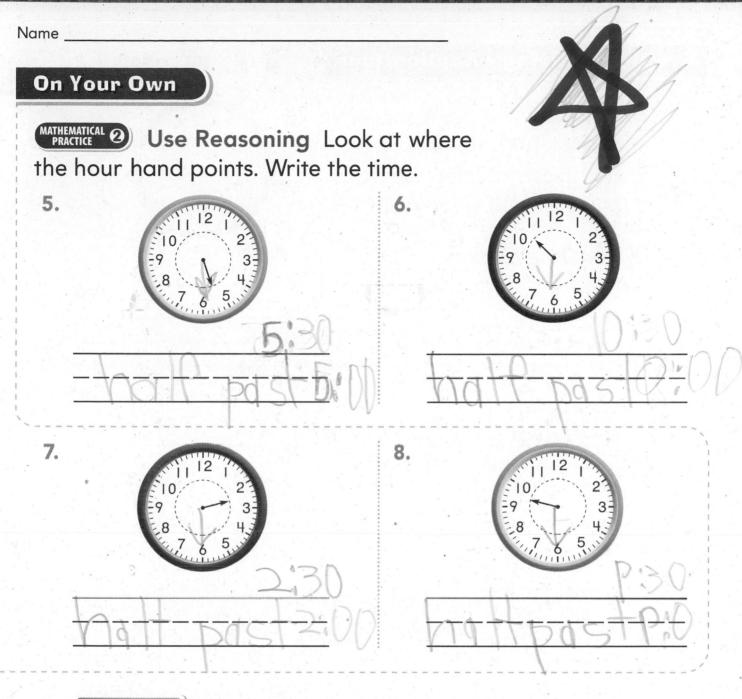

Problem Solving • Applications Real World

WRITE Math

10. THINK SMARTER Tim plays soccer at half past 9:00. He eats lunch at half past 1:00. He sees a movie at half past 2:00.

Math on the Spot

Look at the clock.
Write what Tim does.

____

Tim ______________________________.

11. GO DEEPER Tyra has a piano lesson at 5:00. The lesson ends at half past 5:00. How much time is Tyra at her lesson? Circle your answer.

half hour

hour

12. THINK SMARTER What time is it? Circle the time that makes the sentence true.

The time is

half past 5:00
6:00
half past 6:00

.

TAKE HOME ACTIVITY • Say a time, such as half past 10:00. Ask your child to describe where the hour hand points at this time.

Name ____________________

Time to the Half Hour

Common Core — COMMON CORE STANDARD—1.MD.B.3
Tell and write time.

Look at where the hour hand points. Write the time.

1.

____

2.

____

3.

____

Problem Solving (Real World)

Solve.

4. Greg rides his bike at half past 4:00. He eats dinner at half past 6:00. He reads a book at half past 8:00.

Look at the clock.
Write what Greg does.

Greg ____________.

5. WRITE Math Draw clocks to show where the hour hand points for 5:00 and half past 5:00.

Lesson Check (1.MD.B.3)

1. Look at the hour hand. What is the time?
Write the time.

____

---

2. Look at the hour hand. What is the time?
Write the time.

____

Spiral Review (1.NBT.A.1, 1.NBT.B.2b)

3. What number does the model show?
Write the number.

______

---

4. How many tens and ones make this number?

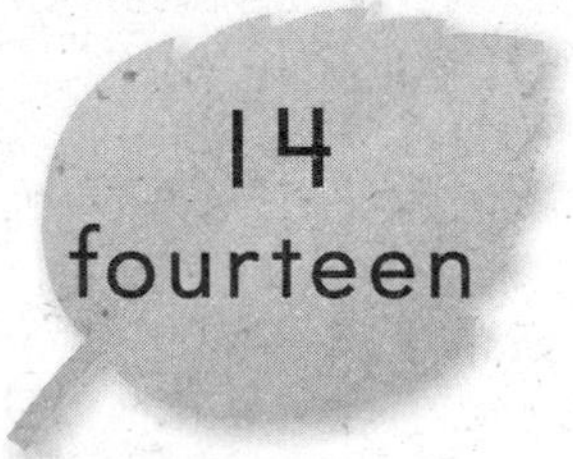

____ ten ____ ones

FOR MORE PRACTICE GO TO THE **Personal Math Trainer**

Name ______________________________

Tell Time to the Hour and Half Hour

Essential Question How are the minute hand and hour hand different for time to the hour and time to the half hour?

Common Core **Measurement and Data—1.MD.B.3**

MATHEMATICAL PRACTICES MP2, MP5, MP6

Listen and Draw (Real World)

Each clock has an hour hand and a minute hand. Use what you know about the hour hand to write the unknown numbers.

It is 1:00.

The hour hand points to the _____.

The minute hand points to the _____.

It is half past 1:00.

The hour hand points between the _____ and the _____.

The minute hand points to the _____.

FOR THE TEACHER • Read the time on the first clock and have children identify where the hour hand and minute hand point. Then repeat for the second clock.

Math Talk MATHEMATICAL PRACTICES 5

Use Tools Look at the top clock. Explain how you know which is the minute hand.

Model and Draw

An hour has 60 **minutes**.

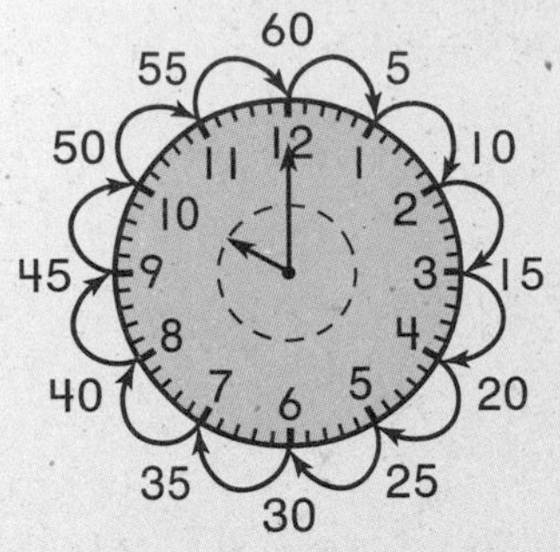

The clocks show 10:00.

A half hour has 30 minutes.

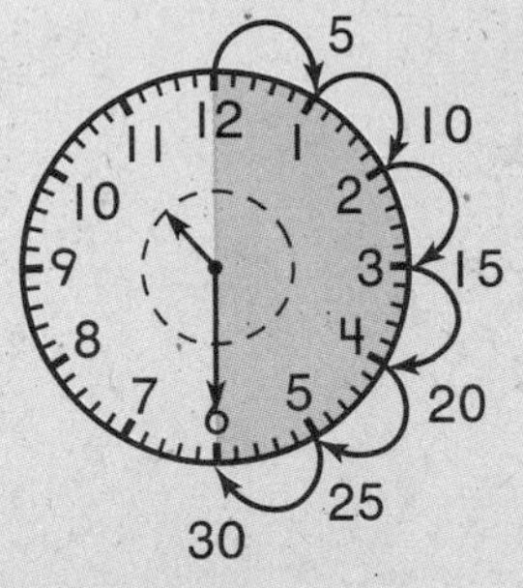

The clocks show half past 10:00. The **minute hand** has moved from the 12 to the 6.

30 minutes after 10:00

Share and Show MATH BOARD

Write the time.

1.

2.

3.

Name ______________________________

On Your Own

MATHEMATICAL PRACTICE 6 **Attend to Precision** Write the time.

4.

5.

6.

7.

8.

9.

Circle your answer.

10. Sara goes to the park when both the hour hand and the minute hand point to the 12. What time does Sara go to the park?

1:00 12:00 12:30

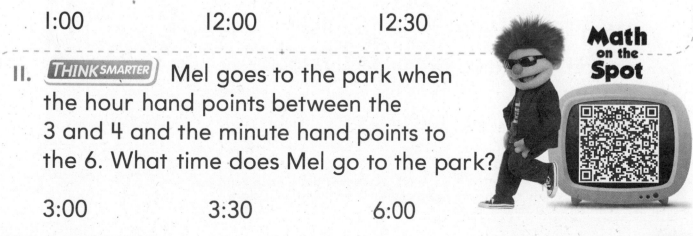

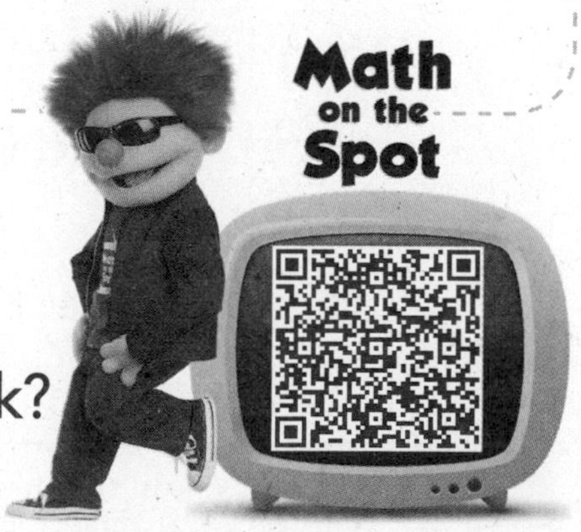

11. THINK SMARTER Mel goes to the park when the hour hand points between the 3 and 4 and the minute hand points to the 6. What time does Mel go to the park?

3:00 3:30 6:00

Problem Solving • Applications Real World

WRITE Math

Solve.

12. Linda wakes up at 6:30. Draw to show what time Linda wakes up.

13. David left school at 3:30. Circle the clock that shows 3:30.

14. GO DEEPER The hour hand points halfway between the 2 and 3. Draw the hour hand and the minute hand. Write the time.

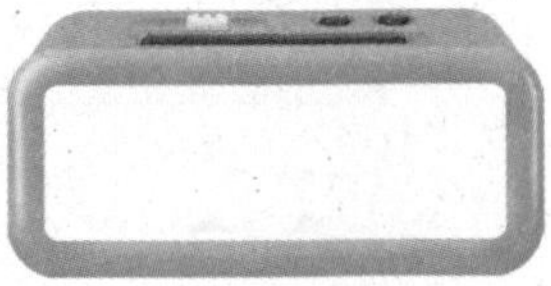

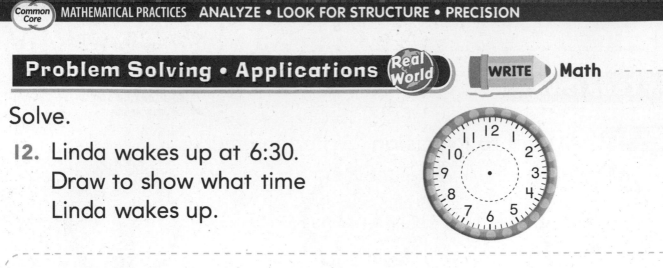

15. THINK SMARTER Choose all the ways that name the time on the clock.

- ○ half past 7:00
- ○ half past 6:00
- ○ 8:30
- ○ 7:30

TAKE HOME ACTIVITY • At times on the half hour, have your child show you the minute hand and the hour hand on a clock and tell what time it is.

Name ____________________

Tell Time to the Hour and Half Hour

COMMON CORE STANDARD—1.MD.B.3
Tell and write time.

Write the time.

1.

2.

3.

4.

5.

6.

Problem Solving Real World

Solve.

7. Lulu walks her dog at 7 o'clock. Bill walks his dog 30 minutes later. Draw to show what time Bill walks his dog.

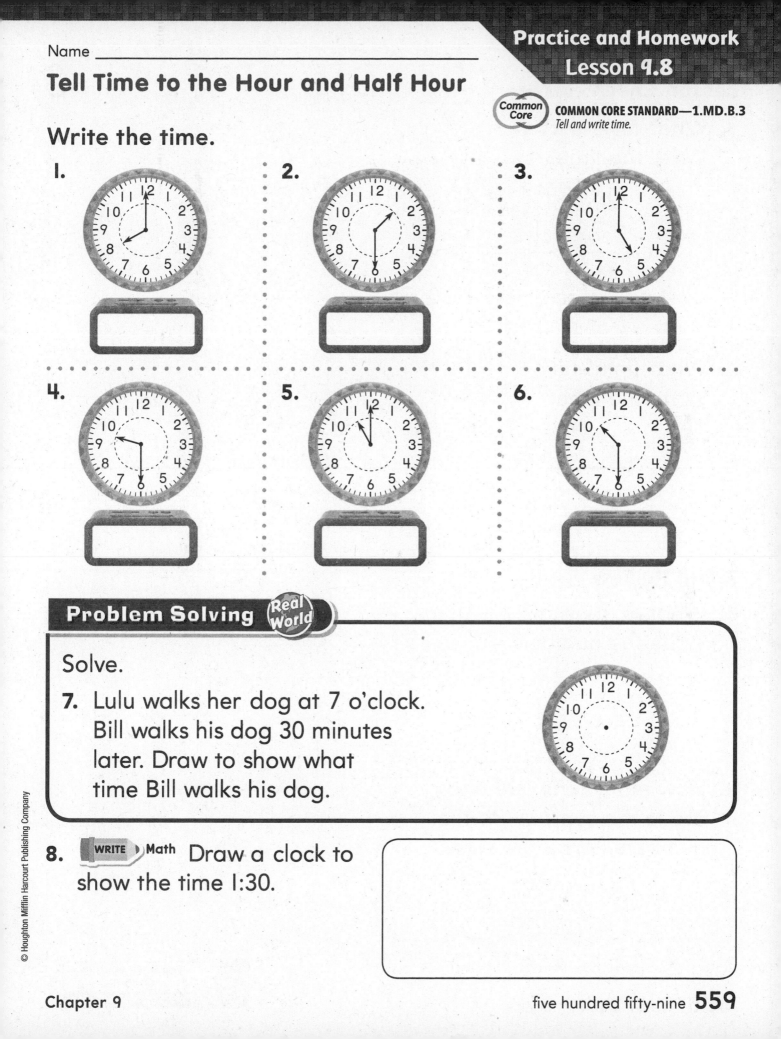

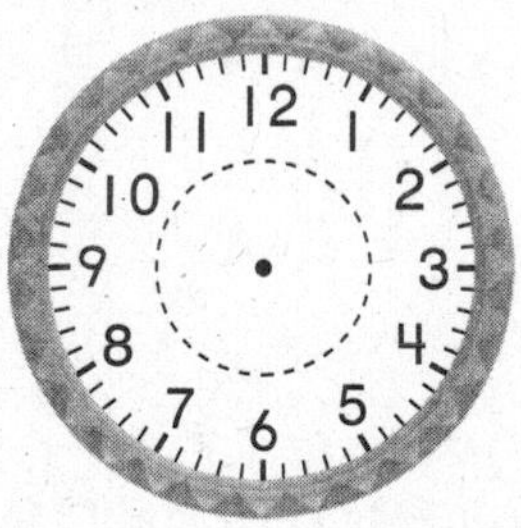

8. WRITE Math Draw a clock to show the time 1:30.

Lesson Check (1.MD.B.3)

1. What time is it?
Write the time.

____

2. What time is it?
Write the time.

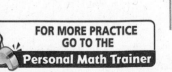

____

Spiral Review (1.NBT.C.4)

3. What is the sum?
Write the number.

$$48 + 20 = \_\_\_$$

4. How many tens and ones are in the sum? Write the numbers. Write the sum.

$$\begin{array}{r} 67 \\ +\ 25 \\ \hline \end{array}$$

____ tens ____ ones

Name ______________________________

Practice Time to the Hour and Half Hour

Essential Question How do you know whether to draw and write time to the hour or half hour?

Common Core **Measurement and Data—1.MD.B.3**
MATHEMATICAL PRACTICES MP1, MP4, MP8

Listen Real World

Circle the clock that matches the problem.

Math Talk MATHEMATICAL PRACTICES 8

Generalize Describe how you know which clock shows 1:30.

FOR THE TEACHER • Read the following problems. Barbara goes to the store at 8:00. Circle the clock that shows 8:00. Have children use the top workspace to solve. Then have children solve this problem: Barbara takes Ria for a walk at 1:30. Circle the clock that shows 1:30.

Model and Draw

Where should you draw the minute hand to show the time?

Share and Show

MATH BOARD

Use the hour hand to write the time.
Draw the minute hand.

1.

2.

3.

4.

✓5.

✓6.

Name ____________________

On Your Own

MATHEMATICAL PRACTICE 4 **Use Diagrams** Use the hour hand to write the time. Draw the minute hand.

7.

8.

9.

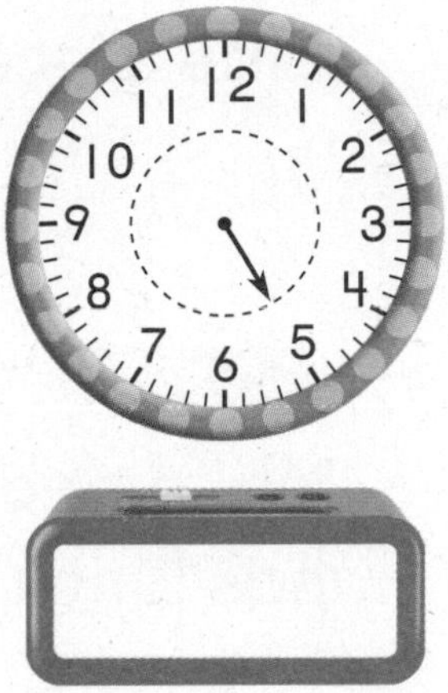

10.

11.

12.

13. THINKSMARTER **What is the error?** Zoey tried to show 6:00. Explain how to change the clock to show 6:00.

Math on the Spot

____

____

____

Problem Solving • Applications Real World

WRITE Math

Solve.

14. Vince goes to a baseball game at 4:30. Draw to show what time Vince goes to a baseball game.

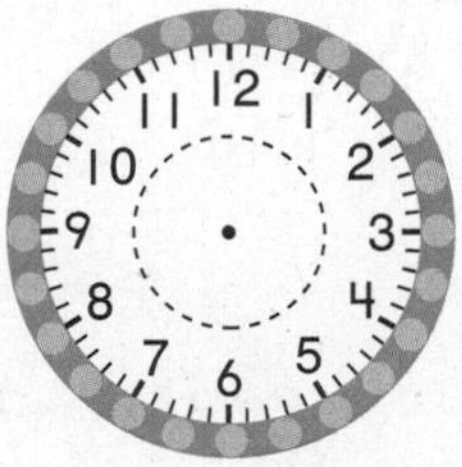

15. GO DEEPER Brandon has lunch at 1 o'clock. Write and draw to show what time Brandon has lunch.

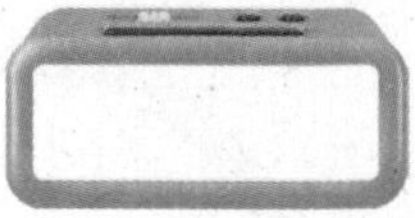

16. THINK SMARTER Juan tried to show 8:30. He made a mistake.

What did Juan do wrong? Explain his mistake.

TAKE HOME ACTIVITY • Show your child a time to the hour or half hour on a clock. Ask him or her what time it will be in 30 minutes.

Name ____________________

Practice Time to the Hour and Half Hour

Common Core **COMMON CORE STANDARD—1.MD.B.3**
Tell and write time.

Use the hour hand to write the time. Draw the minute hand.

1.

2.

3.

Problem Solving Real World

Solve.

4. Billy played outside for a half hour. Write how many minutes Billy played outside.

____ minutes

5. WRITE Math Draw a clock to show a time to the hour. Draw another clock to show a time to the half hour. Write each time.

Lesson Check (1.MD.B.3)

1. Write the time.

______

Spiral Review (1.NBT.C.6, 1.MD.A.2)

2. What is the difference?
Write the number.

$80 - 30 =$ ____

3. Use ■. Amy measures the eraser with ■.
About how long is the eraser?

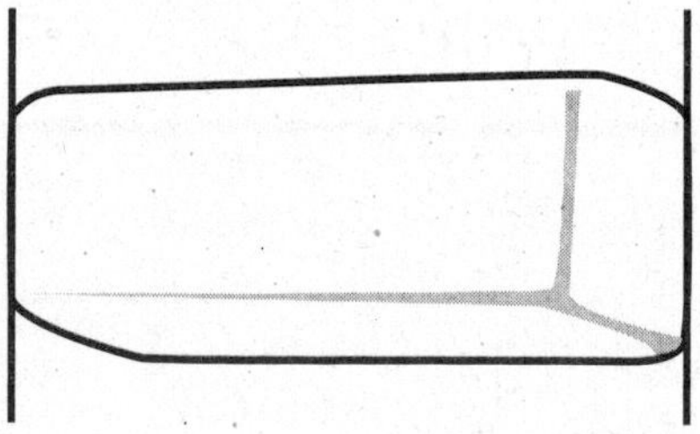

about ____ ■ long

FOR MORE PRACTICE GO TO THE **Personal Math Trainer**

Name ______________________________

Chapter 9 Review/Test

Personal Math Trainer
Online Assessment and Intervention

1. Match each word on the left to a drawing on the right.

shortest •

longest •

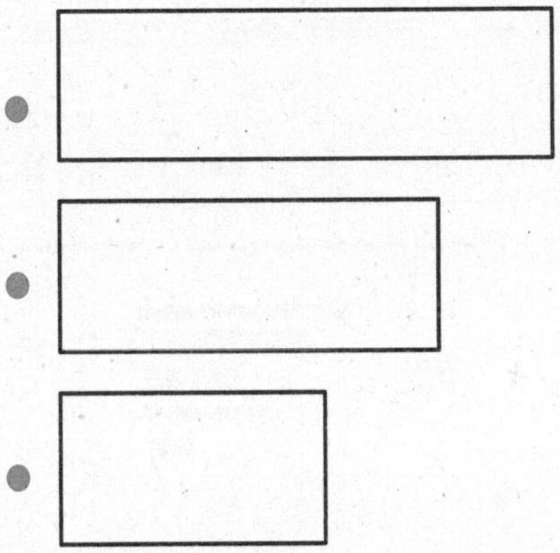

2. Is the first line shorter than the second line? Choose Yes or No.

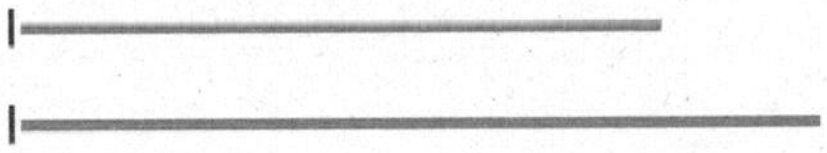

○ Yes ○ No

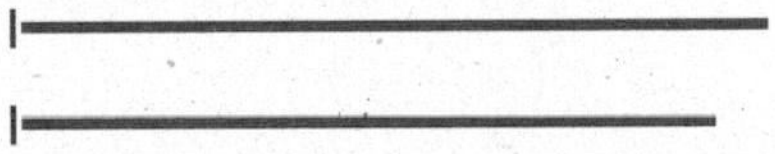

○ Yes ○ No

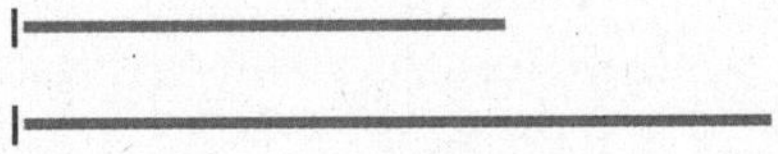

○ Yes ○ No

3. The crayon is about 5 tiles long. Draw tiles below the crayon to show its length.

GO DIGITAL Assessment Options Chapter Test

4. Use the 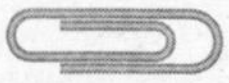 below. About how long is the ?

about ______ 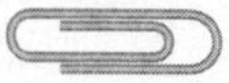

---

5. Measure the . Use 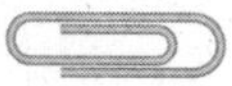.

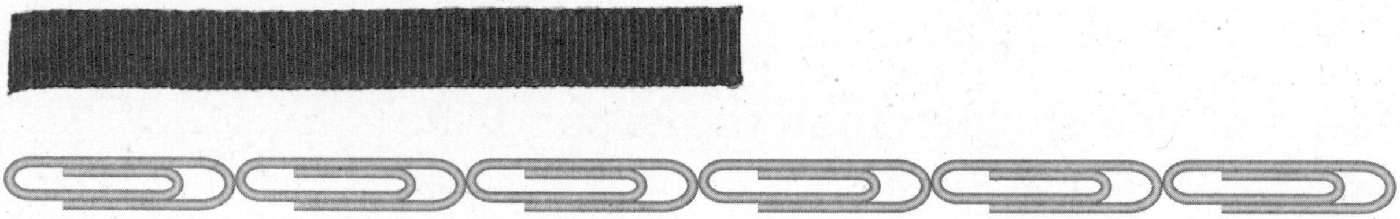

about ______ 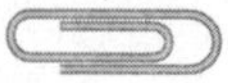

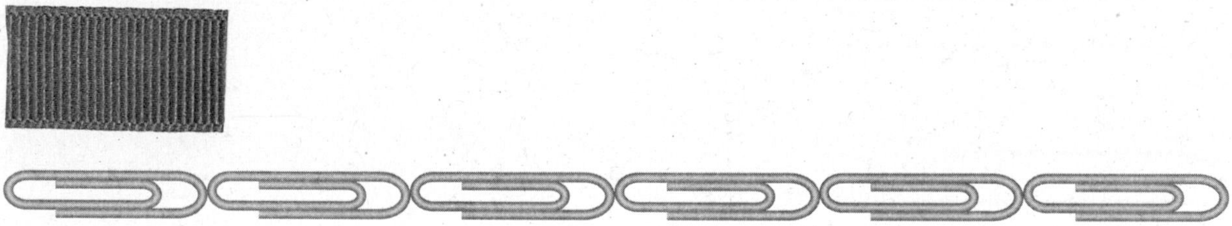

about ______ 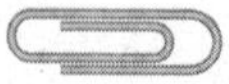

about ______ 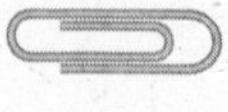

Name ______________________________

6. Look at the hour hand. What is the time?

○ 9:00
○ 10 o'clock
○ 11 o'clock
○ 12:00

7. What time is it? Circle the time that makes the sentence true.

The time is [1:30 / 2:00 / 2:30].

8. Choose all the ways that name the time on the clock.

○ half past 6:00
○ half past 11:00
○ 6:00
○ 11:30

9. Draw the hand on the clock to show 9:30.

10. GO DEEPER Lucy tried to show 5:00. She made a mistake.

Draw hands on the clock to show 5:00.

What did Lucy do wrong? Explain her mistake.

Personal Math Trainer

11. THINK SMARTER + The is shorter than the .
The  is longer than the  .
Draw the length of the .

Chapter 10

Represent Data

Curious About Math with Curious George

How many days will it snow or rain this week where you live? How can you find out?

Name ______________________________

Show What You Know

Personal Math Trainer
Online Assessment and Intervention

Make a Concrete Graph

Sort a handful of ■ and ■. Make a concrete graph. (K.MD.B.3)

Square Colors								
■								
■								

1. How many ■ are there? __________

More, Fewer

2. Shade to show a set of fewer. (1.NBT.B.3)

Draw Equal Groups

3. Draw a ○ below each picture to show the same number of objects. (K.CC.C.6)

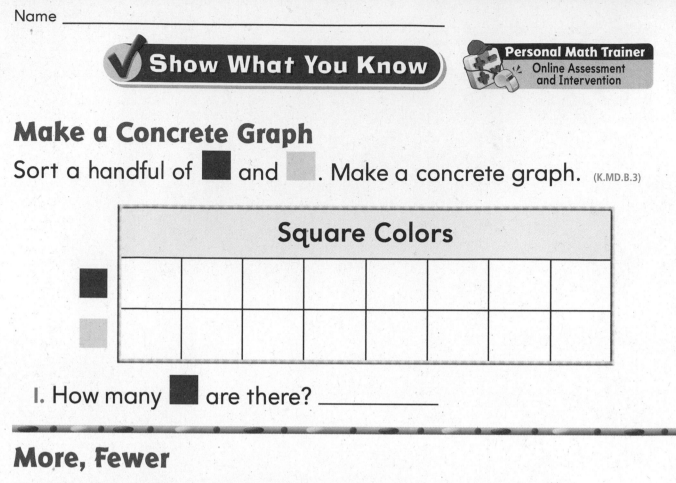

This page checks understanding of important skills needed for success in Chapter 10.

Name ______________________________

Vocabulary Builder

Review Words

graph
more
fewer
most
fewest

Visualize It

Complete the chart.
Mark each row with a ✔.

Word	I Know	Sounds Familiar	I Do Not Know
graph			
more			
fewer			
most			
fewest			

Understand Vocabulary

Use the review words. Label the groups.

1.

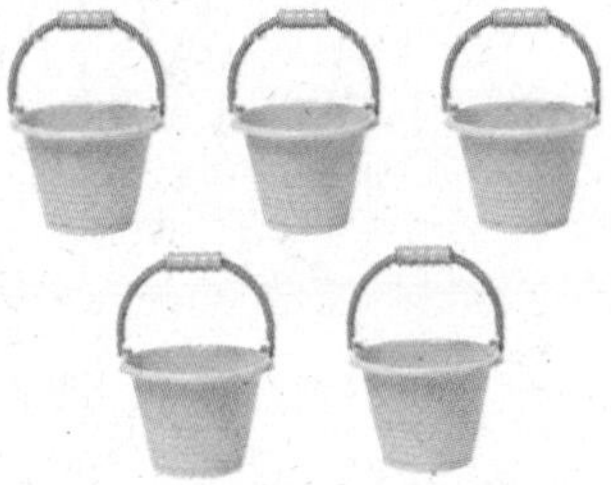

______________ ______________

2.

______________ ______________

GO DIGITAL
• Interactive Student Edition
• Multimedia eGlossary

Game

Graph Game

Materials • 16 • 16 • 16

Play with a partner.

1. Spin the .
2. Put 1 cube of that color in the correct row of your graph.
3. Take turns. Play until each partner has 5 turns.
4. The player who went last spins again to get a color.
5. The player with more cubes of that color wins. Spin again if you both have the same number of cubes of that color.

Player 1

Player 2

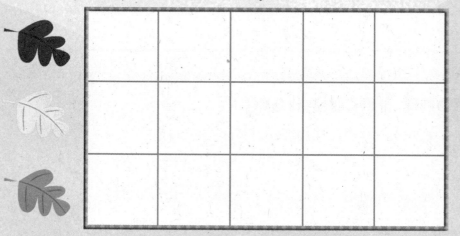

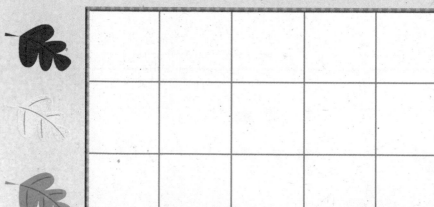

Chapter 10 Vocabulary

bar graph

gráfica de barras

4

fewer

menos

19

longest

el más largo

33

more

más

38

picture graph

gráfica con dibujos

41

shortest

el más corto

48

tally chart

tabla de conteo

55

tally mark

marca de conteo

56

3 **fewer** 🐦

Flowers in the Garden

Kinds of Flowers		0	1	2	3	4	5	6	7
daisies									
sunflowers									

Number of Flowers

$5 - 3 = 2$

There are **more** ⭐.

longest

shortest

Our Favorite Activity at the Fair

| | animals | ☥ | ☥ | ☥ | ☥ | ☥ | | |
| | rides | ☥ | ☥ | ☥ | ☥ | ☥ | ☥ | ☥ |

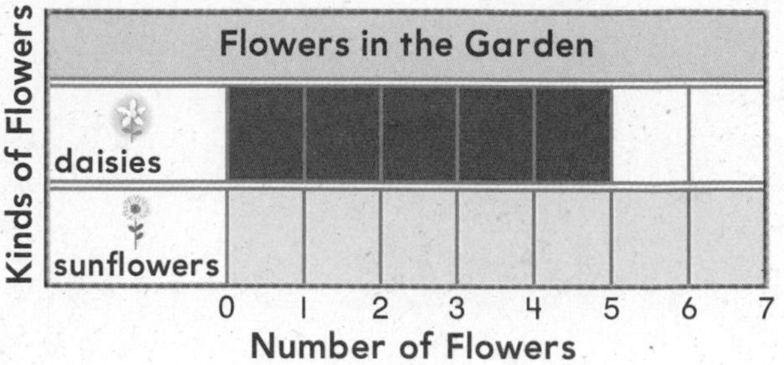

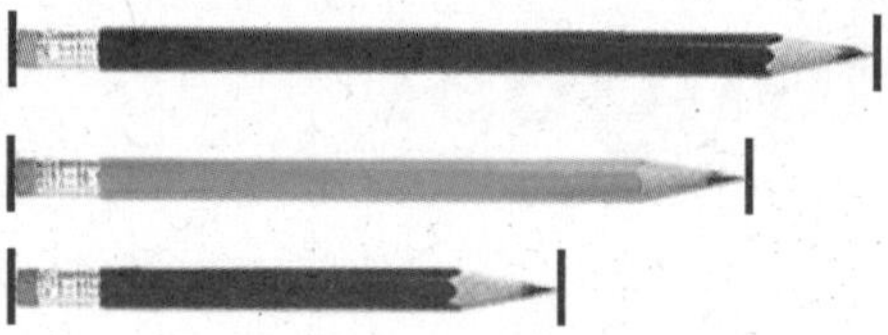

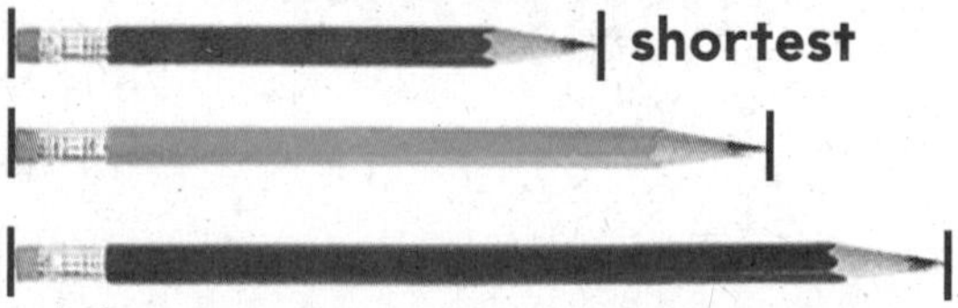

Each ☥ stands for 1 child.

‖‖‖

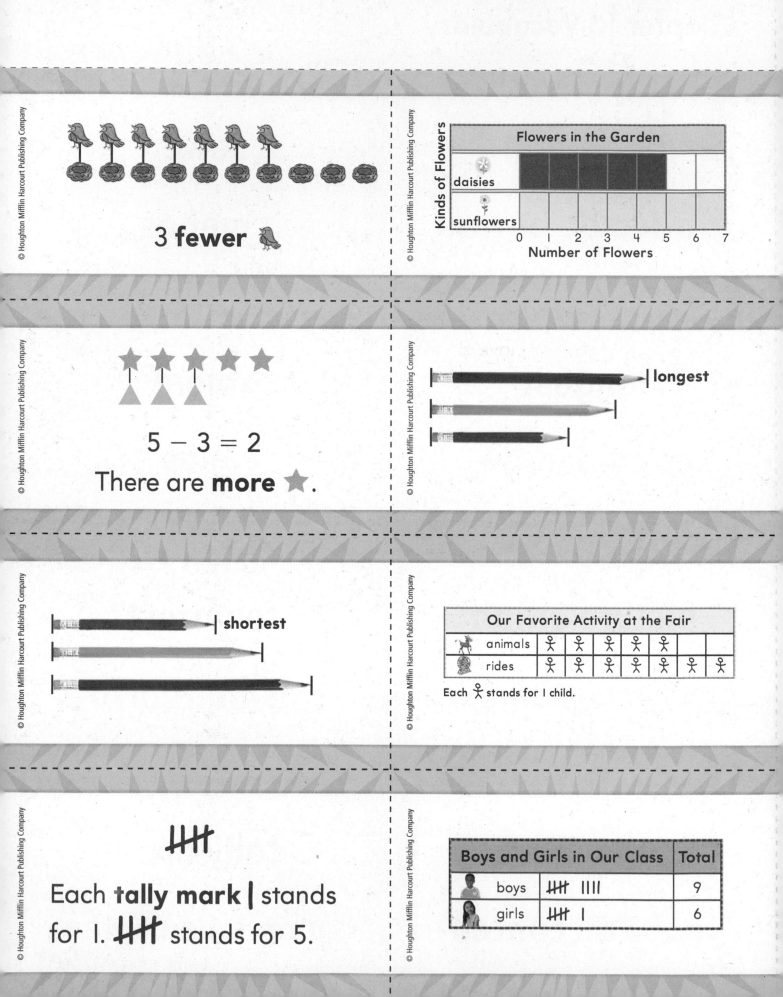

Each **tally mark |** stands for 1. ‖‖‖ stands for 5.

Boys and Girls in Our Class		Total
boys	‖‖‖ ‖‖‖	9
girls	‖‖‖	6

© Houghton Mifflin Harcourt Publishing Company

Picture It

Word Box
bar graph
fewer
longest
more
picture graph
shortest
tally chart
tally mark

Materials

timer

How to Play

Play with two other players.

1. Choose a secret word from the Word Box. Do not tell the other players.
2. Set the timer.
3. Draw pictures to show clues for the secret word.
4. The first player to guess the word before time runs out gets 1 point.
5. Take turns.
6. The first player to score 5 points wins.

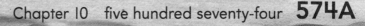

Journal

The Write Way

Reflect

Choose one idea. Draw and write about it.

- Tell the difference between a picture graph and a bar graph.
- Explain how to read a tally chart.

Name _____

Read Picture Graphs

Essential Question What do the pictures in a picture graph show?

Common Core Measurement and Data—
1.MD.C.4
MATHEMATICAL PRACTICES
MP3, MP4

Listen and Draw Real World Hands On

Use ▪ ▪. Draw to show the cubes.
Write how many more ▪.

_____ more ▪

Math Talk MATHEMATICAL PRACTICES 4

Represent Describe how you can use your picture to compare the cubes.

FOR THE TEACHER • Read the following problem. There are 2 green cubes and 4 blue cubes. How many more blue cubes are there than green cubes?

Chapter 10

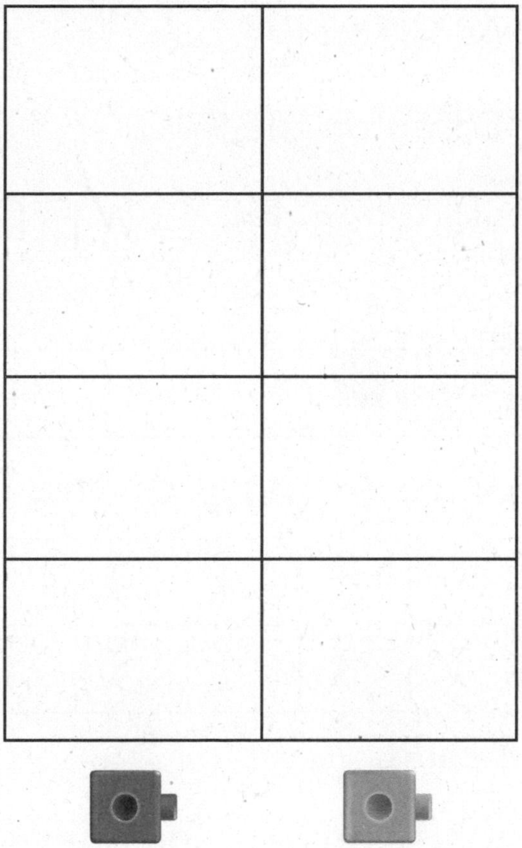

Model and Draw

Children at the Playground

| swings | ☺ | ☺ | ☺ | ☺ | |
| slide | ☺ | ☺ | | | |

Each ☺ stands for 1 child.

There are __4__ children on the 🛝.

There are __2__ children on the 🛝.

There are more children on the __swings__.

A **picture graph** uses pictures to show information.

Share and Show MATH BOARD

Our Favorite Activity at the Fair

| | animals | ☺ | ☺ | ☺ | ☺ | ☺ | | |
| | rides | ☺ | ☺ | ☺ | ☺ | ☺ | ☺ | ☺ |

Each ☺ stands for 1 child.

Use the picture graph to answer the question.

1. Which activity did more children choose? Circle.

2. How many children chose 🐴? ____ children

✓ 3. How many children chose 🎡? ____ children

✓ 4. How many fewer children chose 🐴 than 🎡? ____ fewer children

Name ______________________________

On Your Own

What We Drink for Lunch								
milk	🧍	🧍	🧍	🧍	🧍	🧍	🧍	🧍
juice	🧍	🧍	🧍					
water	🧍	🧍	🧍	🧍	🧍			

Each 🧍 stands for 1 child.

Use the picture graph to answer the question.

5. How many children drink MILK?

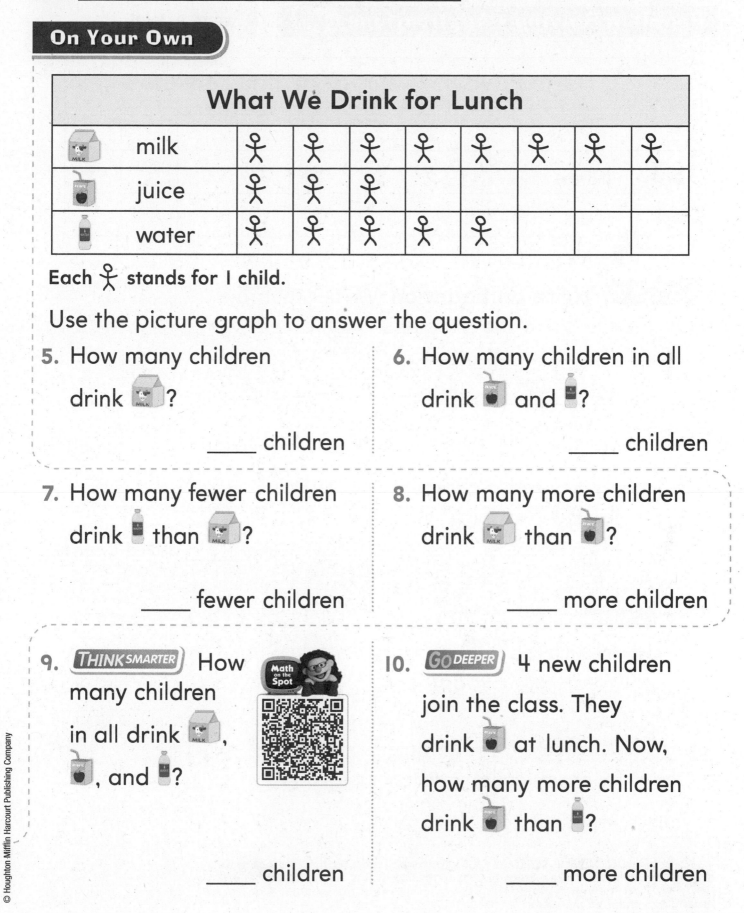

_____ children

6. How many children in all drink JUICE and WATER?

_____ children

7. How many fewer children drink WATER than MILK?

_____ fewer children

8. How many more children drink MILK than JUICE?

_____ more children

9. THINK SMARTER How many children in all drink MILK, JUICE, and WATER?

Math on the Spot

_____ children

10. GO DEEPER 4 new children join the class. They drink JUICE at lunch. Now, how many more children drink JUICE than WATER?

_____ more children

Problem Solving • Applications Real World

WRITE Math

Our Favorite Animal at the Zoo								
zebras	🧍	🧍	🧍	🧍	🧍			
lions	🧍	🧍	🧍	🧍	🧍	🧍	🧍	🧍
seals	🧍							

Each 🧍 stands for 1 child.

MATHEMATICAL PRACTICE 4 **Write an Equation** Write a number sentence to solve the problem.

11. How many children chose zebras and seals altogether?

    ___ ◯ ___ ◯ ___

    ___ children

12. How many more children chose lions than seals?

    ___ ◯ ___ ◯ ___

    ___ more children

13. GO DEEPER How many more children chose lions than zebras and seals altogether?

    ___ ◯ ___ ◯ ___

    ___ more children

14. THINK SMARTER Use the graph at the top. How many children chose lions?

    ☐

TAKE HOME ACTIVITY • Keep track of the weather for one week by drawing a picture each day to show if it is sunny, cloudy, or rainy. At the end of the week, ask your child what the weather was like for most of the week.

Name ____________________

Read Picture Graphs

COMMON CORE STANDARD—1.MD.C.4
Represent and interpret data.

Our Favorite Outdoor Activity								
 biking								
 skating								
 running								

Each  stands for 1 child.

Use the picture graph to answer the question.

1. How many children chose ?

_______ children

2. How many children chose  and  altogether?

_______ children

Problem Solving Real World

Write a number sentence to solve the problem.
Use the picture graph at the top of the page.

3. How many more children chose  than ?

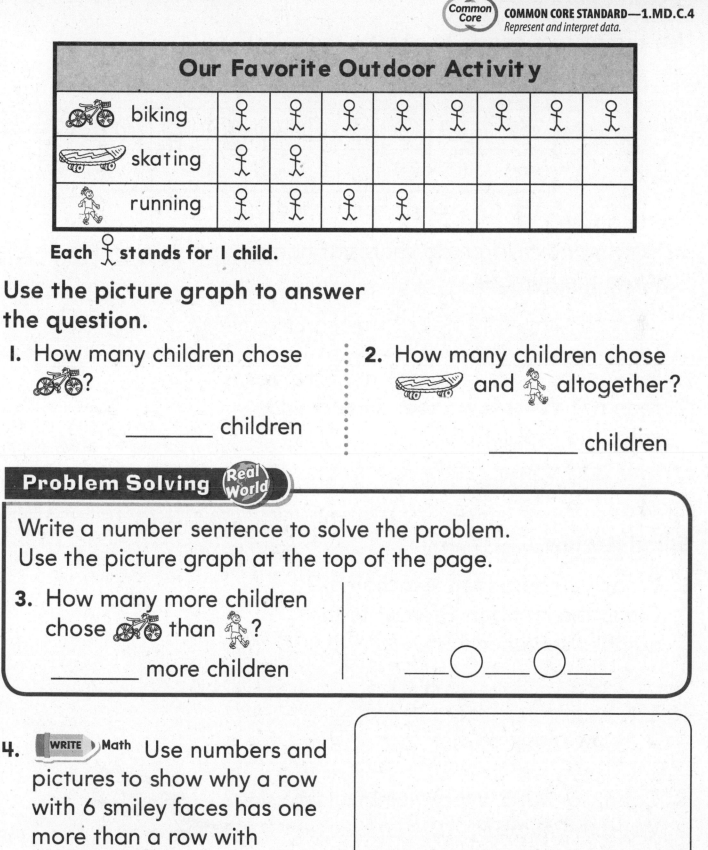

_______ more children

___ ◯ ___ ◯ ___

4. WRITE Math Use numbers and pictures to show why a row with 6 smiley faces has one more than a row with 5 smiley faces.

Lesson Check (1.MD.C.4)

Use the picture graph to answer the question.

Do you do chores at home?								
yes	☺	☺	☺	☺	☺	☺	☺	☺
no	☺	☺	☺	☺	☺	☺		

Each ☺ stands for 1 child.

1. How many children do chores at home? Write the number.

   ____ children

2. How many more children answered yes than no? Write a number sentence to solve the problem.

   ____ more children

   ____ ◯ ____ ◯ ____

Spiral Review (1.NBT.A.1, 1.NBT.C.5)

3. What number is ten less than 82? Circle the number. Then write the number sentence.

   92   83   81   72

   ____ − 10 ____

4. Count forward. What number is missing? Write the number.

   110, 111, 112, ______, 114

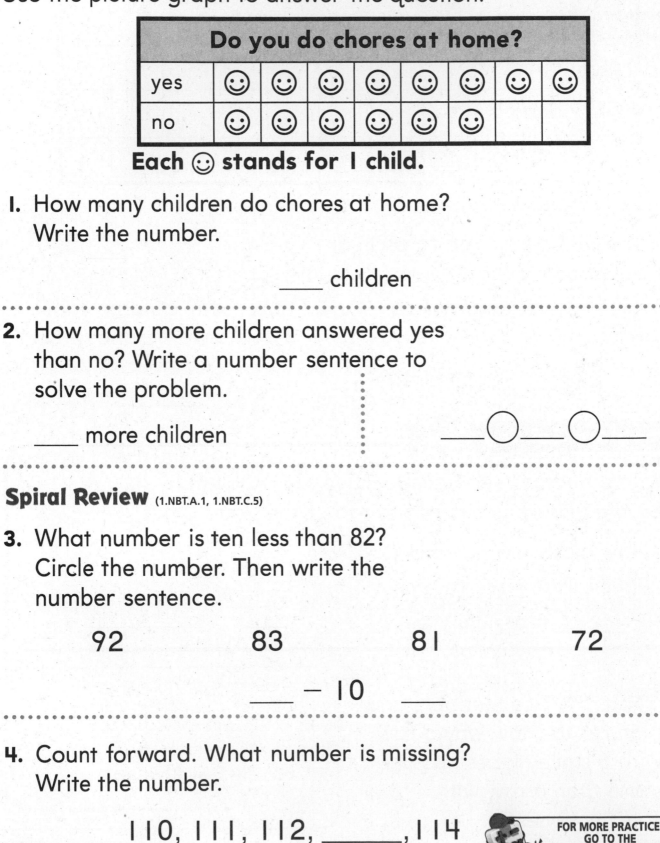

Name ______________________________

Make Picture Graphs

Essential Question How do you make a picture graph to answer a question?

Common Core **Measurement and Data—1.MD.C.4**
MATHEMATICAL PRACTICES
MP3, MP4 , MP6

Listen and Draw

Real World · Hands On

Use ● to solve the problem.
Draw to show your work.

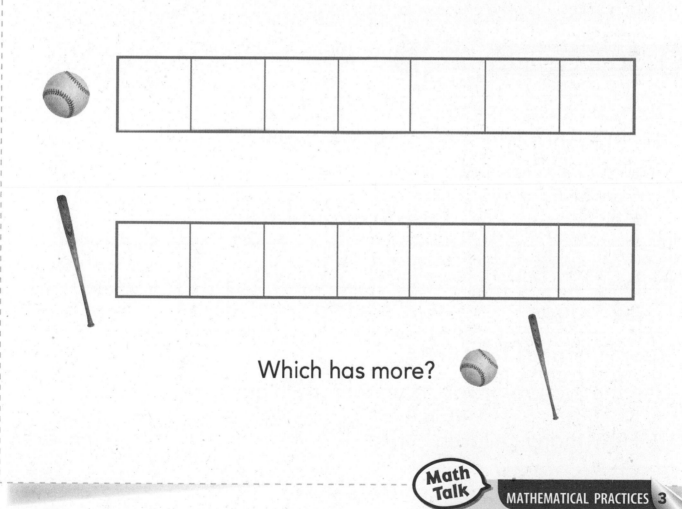

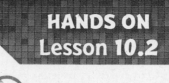

Which has more? 

Math Talk MATHEMATICAL PRACTICES 3

Compare Describe what the picture graph shows.

FOR THE TEACHER • Read the following problem. Asaf has 6 baseballs. He has 4 bats. Does he have more baseballs or bats? Have children draw circles to show the baseballs and bats. Then have them circle the object with more.

Model and Draw

Are there more black or white sheep in the picture? Make a picture graph to find out.

Sheep in the Meadow					
black	◯				
white					

Each ◯ stands for 1 sheep.

There are more ______________ sheep.

Share and Show MATH BOARD

Do more children like cats or dogs?
Ask 10 friends which pet they like better.
Draw 1 circle for each child's answer.

Our Favorite Pet										
cats										
dogs										

Each ◯ stands for 1 child.

Use the picture graph to answer each question.

1. How many children chose cats? ____ children

2. How many children chose dogs? ____ children

3. Which pet did more children choose? Circle.

Name ______________________________

On Your Own

Which activity do the most children like best?
Ask 10 friends. Draw 1 circle for each child's answer.

Our Favorite Activity										
reading										
computer										
sports										

Each ◯ stands for 1 child.

MATHEMATICAL PRACTICE 4 **Use Graphs** Use the picture graph to answer the question.

4. How many children chose reading?

____ children

5. How many children chose computer and sports?

____ children

6. Which activity did the most children choose? Circle.

7. Did all your classmates make picture graphs that look the same? Circle **yes** or **no**.

Math on the Spot

8. THINK SMARTER Write your own question about the graph.

____

9. GO DEEPER Look at the question you wrote. Answer your question.

____

Problem Solving • Applications Real World

WRITE Math

Matt made this picture graph to show the paint colors his friends like best.

Favorite Paint Color					
 blue	○	○	○	○	○
 red	○	○	○		
 green	○	○			

Each ○ stands for 1 child.

10. How many children chose a paint color?

____ children

11. How many fewer children chose  than ?

____ fewer children

Personal Math Trainer

12. THINKSMARTER+ Complete the picture graph to show the number of flowers.

Flowers in the Vase					

Each ○ stands for 1 flower.

TAKE HOME ACTIVITY • Ask your child to make a picture graph showing how many glasses of water each family member drinks in a day. Discuss how to find who drinks the most water.

Name ______________________________

Make Picture Graphs

Common Core — **COMMON CORE STANDARD—1.MD.C.4**
Represent and interpret data.

Which dinosaur do the most children like best? Ask 10 friends.
Draw 1 circle for each child's answer.

Our Favorite Dinosaur										
 Tyrannosaurus										
 Triceratops										
 Apatosaurus										

Each ○ stands for 1 child.

Use the picture graph to answer the question.

1. How many children chose  ?

_____ children

2. Which dinosaur did the most children choose? Circle.

Problem Solving Real World

3. Write your own question about the graph.

____

____

____

4. WRITE Math Write a question that can be answered by making a picture graph.

____

____

____

Lesson Check (1.MD.C.4)

Use the picture graph to answer the question.

Which Hand Do You Use to Eat?								
left	○	○	○					
right	○	○	○	○	○	○	○	○

Each ○ stands for 1 child.

1. How many children use their right hand? Write the answer.

   ____ children

2. How many more children use their right hand than their left? Write a number sentence to solve the problem.

   ____ more children

   ____ ○ ____ ○ ____

Spiral Review (1.OA.C.6, 1.NBT.C.6)

3. Write the sum.

   $6 + 3 =$ ____

4. Write the difference. Write how many tens.

   $60 - 20 =$ ____

   ____ tens

FOR MORE PRACTICE GO TO THE **Personal Math Trainer**

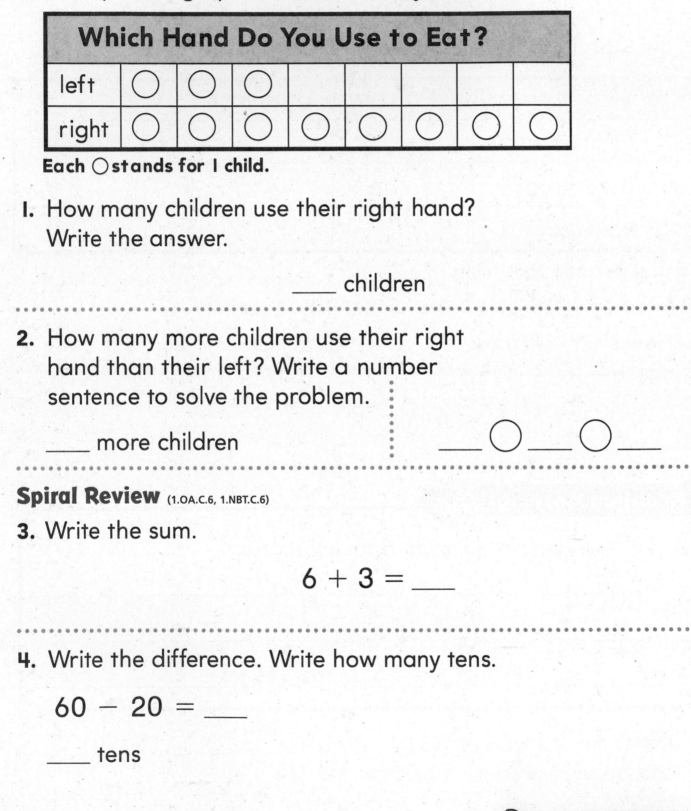

Name ______________________________

Read Bar Graphs

Essential Question How can you read a bar graph to find the number that a bar shows?

Common Core **Measurement and Data—1.MD.C.4**
MATHEMATICAL PRACTICES
MP3, MP4, MP5

Listen Real World Hands On

Write a question about the graph.
Use ● to help solve the problem.

Type of Sneaker We Are Wearing											
 laces	○	○	○	○	○	○	○	○	○	○	
 no laces	○	○	○	○	○	○					

Each ○ stands for 1 child.

____

____

____

FOR THE TEACHER • Read the following problem. Emma's class made this picture graph. What question could Emma's class answer using the graph? Write the question and the answer.

Math Talk MATHEMATICAL PRACTICES 3

Apply Describe how the class made this picture graph.

Model and Draw

In a **bar graph,** each bar shows information. You can compare the lengths of the bars.

What title describes this graph?

Touch the end of a bar. Look down to see the number of children.

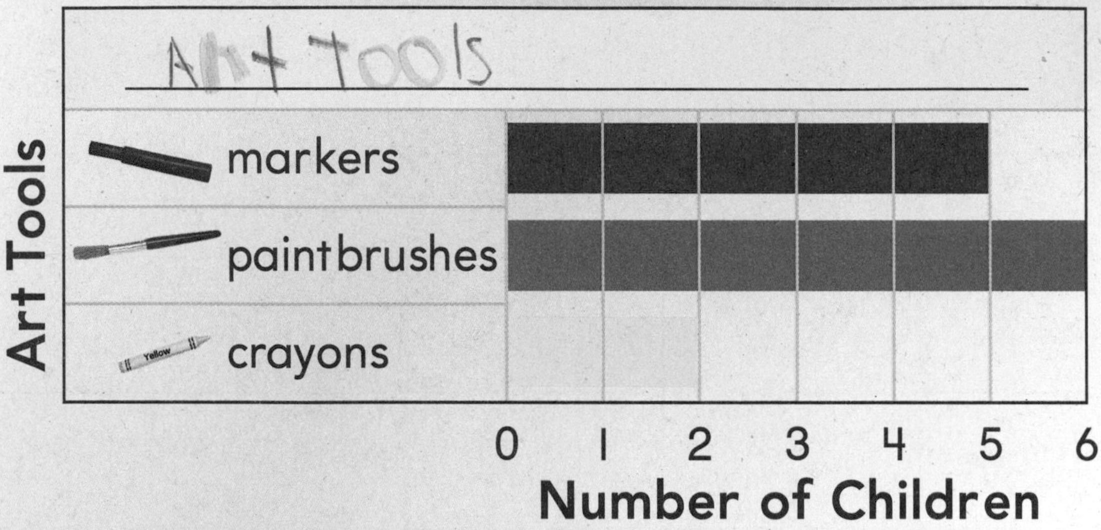

Share and Show MATH BOARD

Use the bar graph to answer the question.

1. How many children chose ?

6 children

2. How many children chose ?

2 children

3. How many more children chose  than ?

4 more children

4. Which art tool did the fewest children choose? Circle.

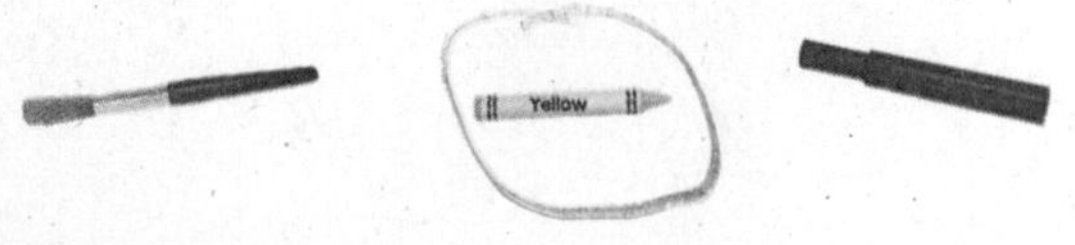

5. Which art tool did the most children choose? Circle.

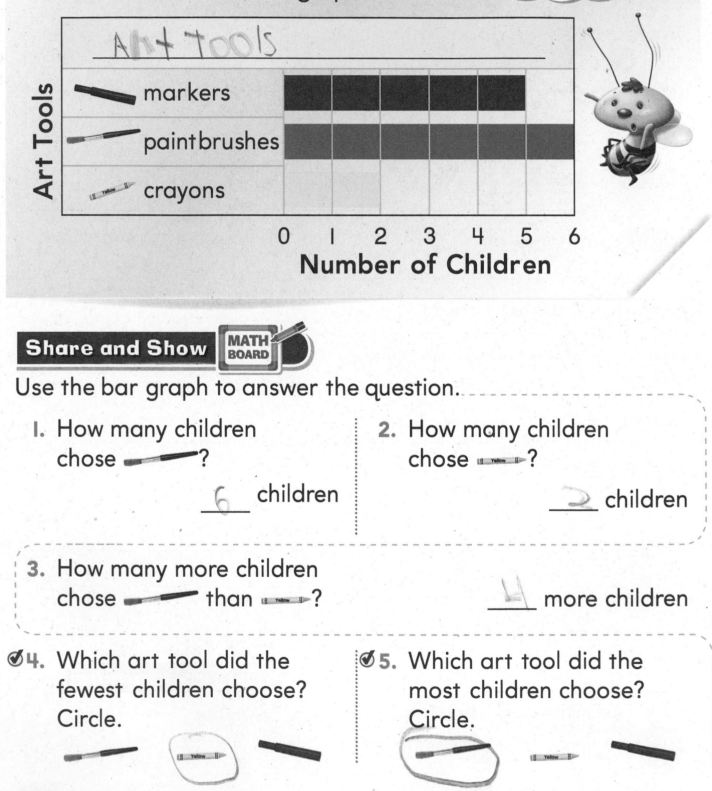

Name ______________________

On Your Own

MATHEMATICAL PRACTICE 4 **Use Graphs** Use the bar graph to answer the question.

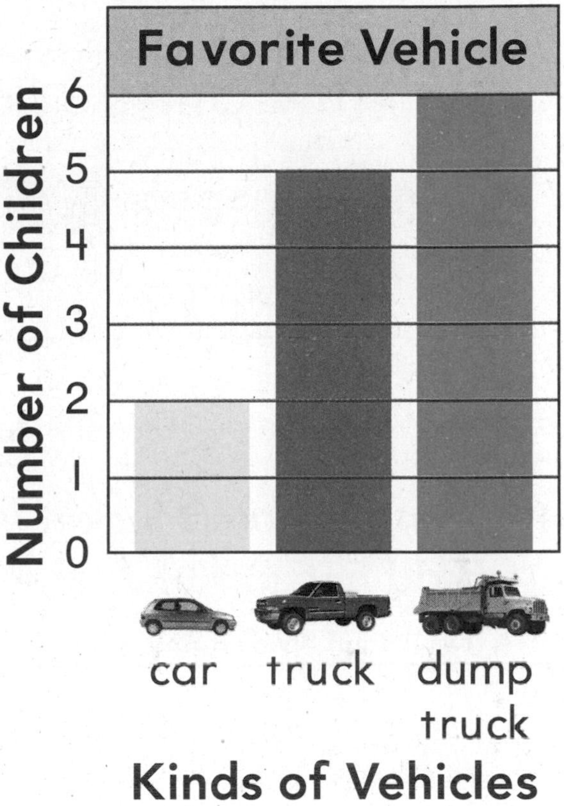

6. How many children chose ?

2 children

7. How many children chose ?

6 children

8. How many children in all chose  and ?

8 children

9. How many more children chose  than ?

3 more children

10. Which vehicle did the most children choose? Circle.

11. THINKSMARTER Order the vehicles from least to most votes. Write 1 for the least votes and 3 for the most votes.

Math on the Spot

 ____  ____  ____

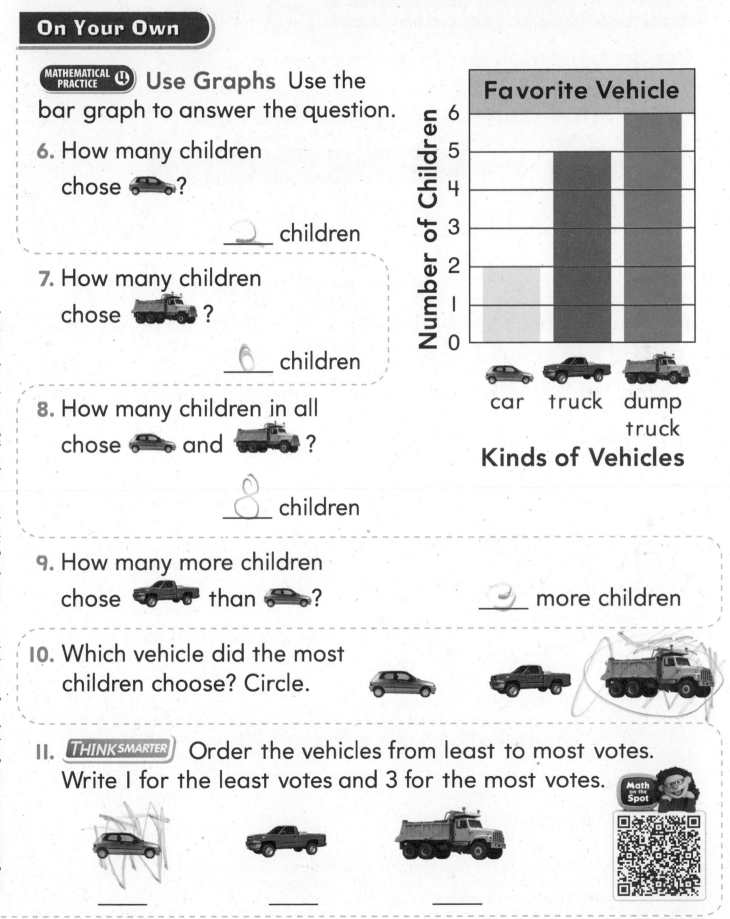

Problem Solving • Applications Real World WRITE Math

Use the bar graph to answer the question.

How Our Jackets Are Fastened

Fasteners

zippers

buttons

0 1 2 3 4 5
Number of Jackets

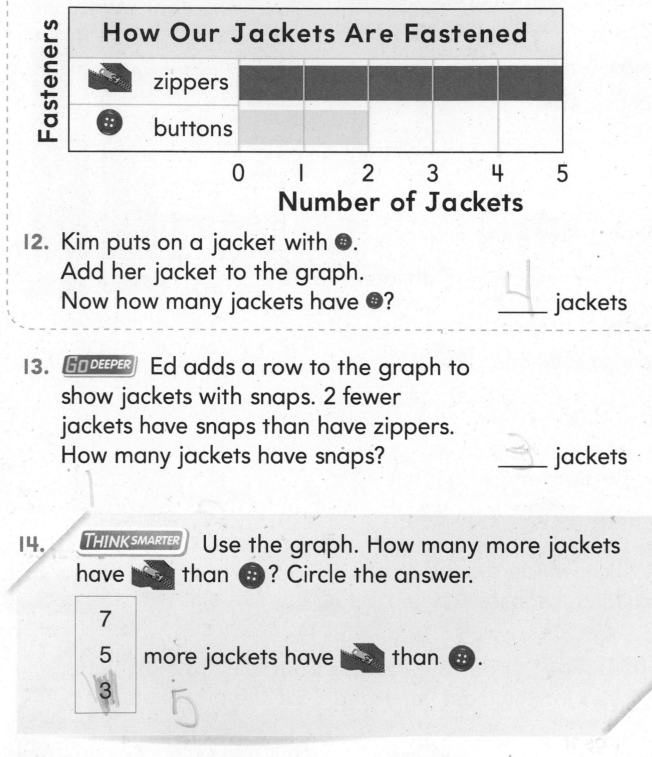

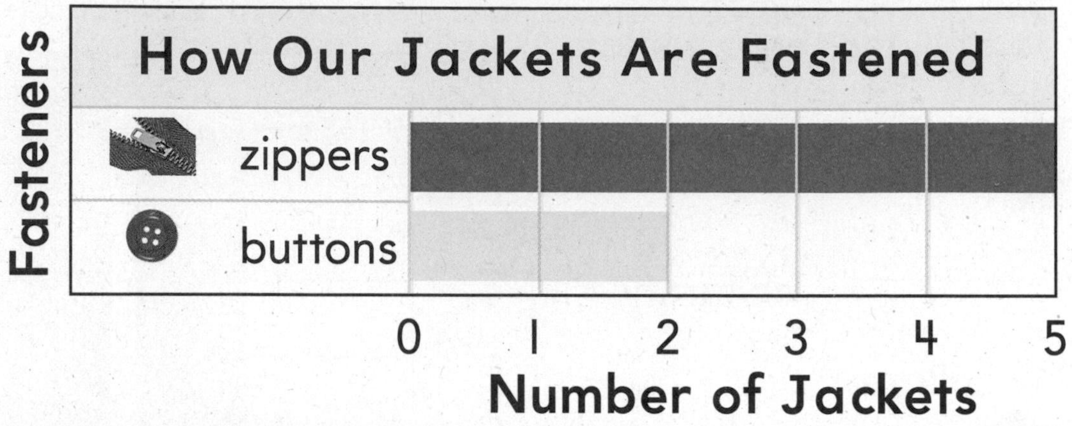

12. Kim puts on a jacket with ●.
Add her jacket to the graph.
Now how many jackets have ●?

____4____ jackets

13. **GO DEEPER** Ed adds a row to the graph to
show jackets with snaps. 2 fewer
jackets have snaps than have zippers.
How many jackets have snaps?

____3____ jackets

14. **THINK SMARTER** Use the graph. How many more jackets
have 🤐 than ●? Circle the answer.

7

5 more jackets have 🤐 than ●.

3

TAKE HOME ACTIVITY • Have your child look through newspapers
and magazines for examples of bar graphs. Talk about what
information is shown in each graph you find.

Name ______________________________

Read Bar Graphs

COMMON CORE STANDARD—1.MD.C.4
Represent and interpret data.

Use the bar graph to answer the question.

1. How many children chose ?

_______ children

2. How many more children chose than ?

_______ more children

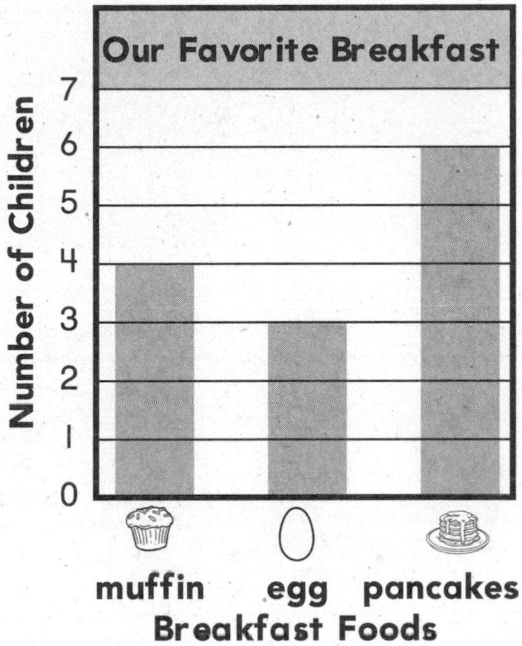

Problem Solving Real World

Use the bar graph to answer the question.

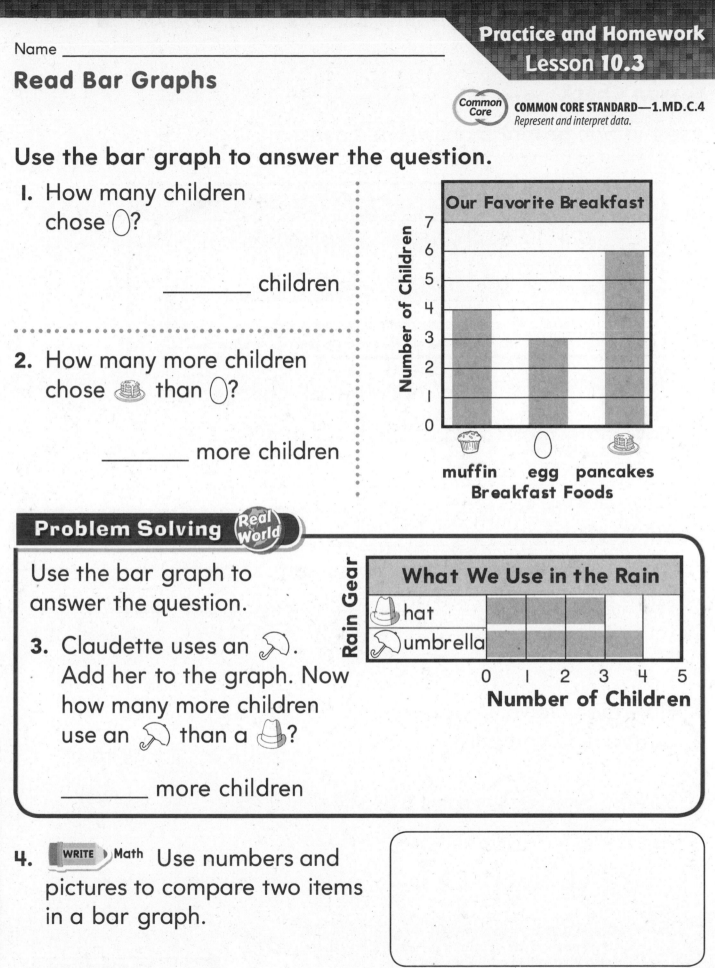

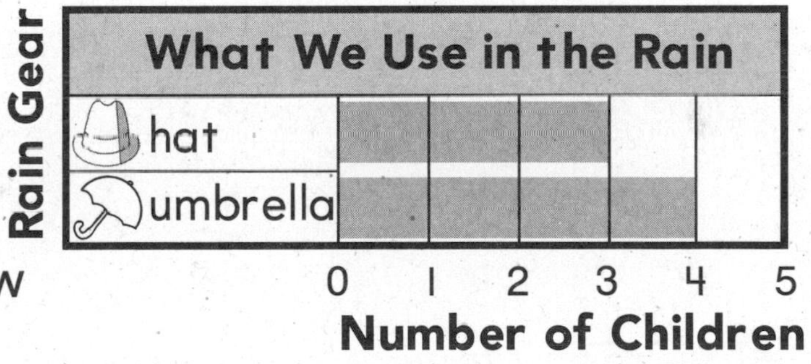

3. Claudette uses an . Add her to the graph. Now how many more children use an than a ?

_______ more children

4. WRITE Math Use numbers and pictures to compare two items in a bar graph.

Lesson Check (1.MD.C.4)

Use the bar graph to answer the question.

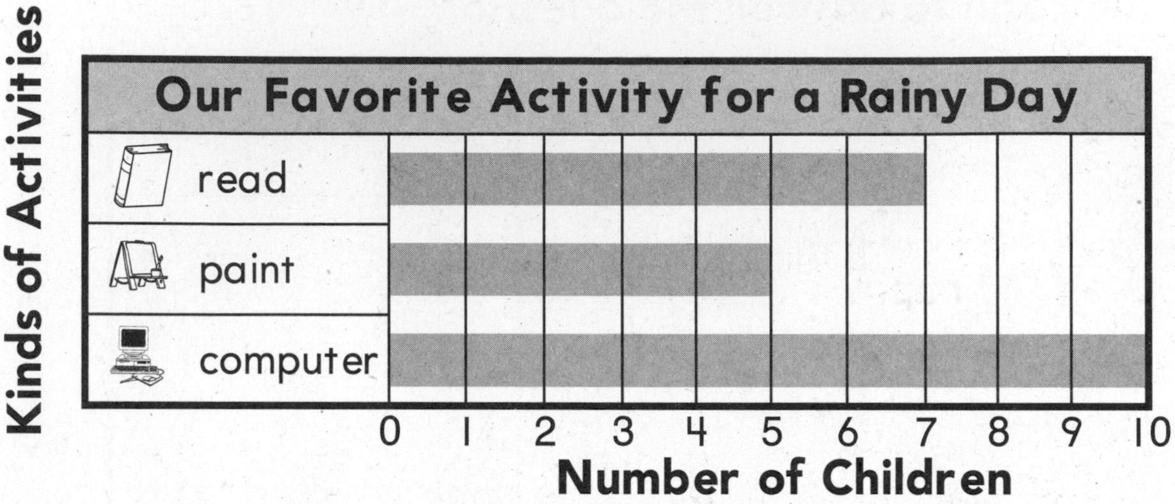

1. How many more children chose computer than paint?

____ more children

Spiral Review (1.OA.B.4, 1.OA.D.8)

2. Write a subtraction sentence you can solve by using 9 + 7 = 16.

____ – ____ = ____

3. How many fewer baseballs are there? Subtract to compare.

7 – 5 = ____

____ fewer

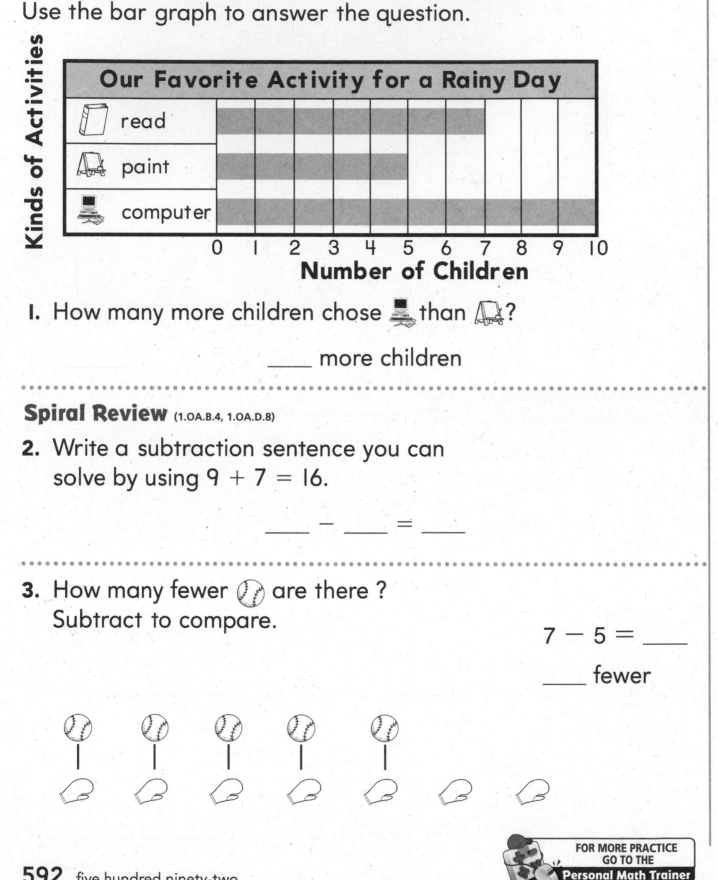

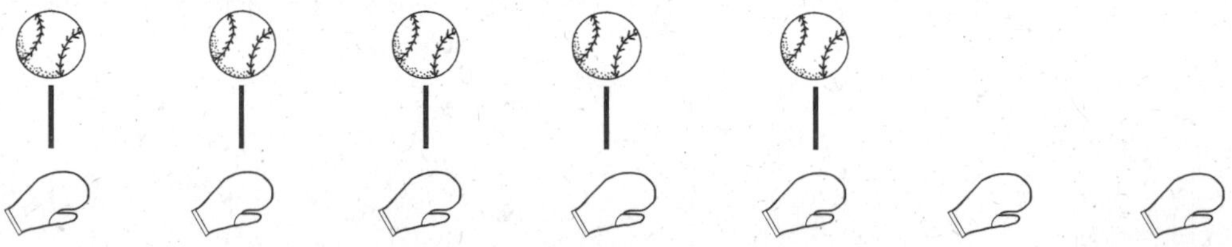

FOR MORE PRACTICE GO TO THE Personal Math Trainer

Name ____________________

Make Bar Graphs

Essential Question How does a bar graph help you compare information?

Common Core Measurement and Data—1.MD.C.4
MATHEMATICAL PRACTICES
MP3, MP4, MP8

Listen and Draw Real World Hands On

Use ▪ to model the problem.
Color 1 box for each food item to complete the graph.

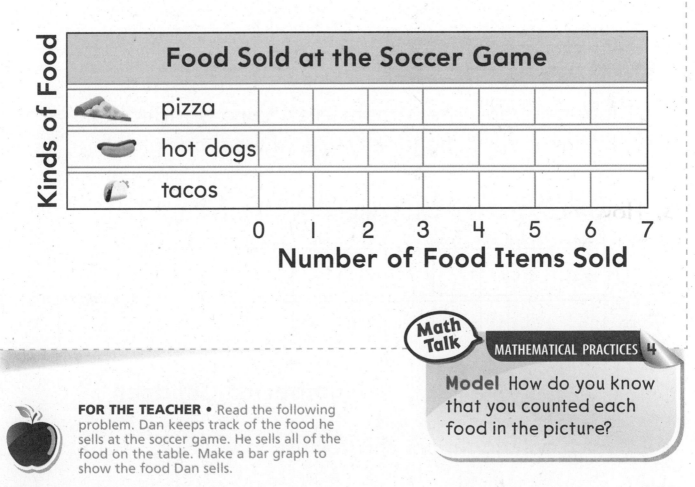

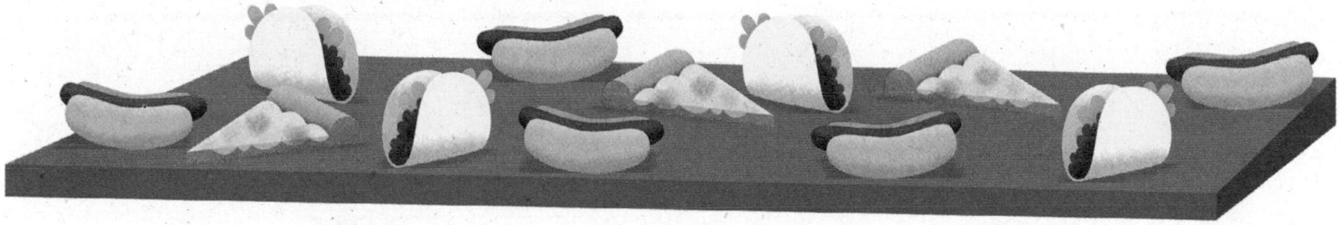

Food Sold at the Soccer Game

Kinds of Food							
pizza							
hot dogs							
tacos							

0 1 2 3 4 5 6 7

Number of Food Items Sold

Math Talk MATHEMATICAL PRACTICES 4

Model How do you know that you counted each food in the picture?

FOR THE TEACHER • Read the following problem. Dan keeps track of the food he sells at the soccer game. He sells all of the food on the table. Make a bar graph to show the food Dan sells.

Model and Draw

Are there more daisies or sunflowers in the garden?
Make a bar graph to find out.
Shade 1 box for each flower in the picture.

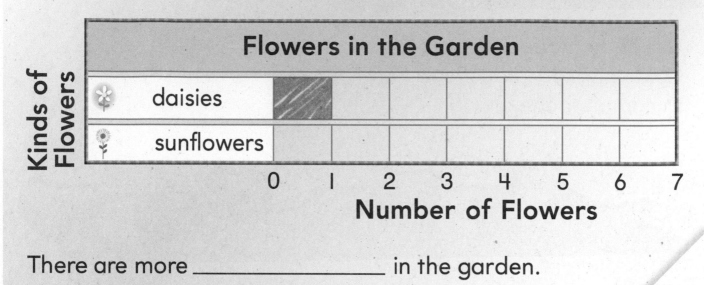

Flowers in the Garden

Kinds of Flowers							
daisies							
sunflowers							
	0–1	1–2	2–3	3–4	4–5	5–6	6–7

0 1 2 3 4 5 6 7
Number of Flowers

There are more ________________ in the garden.

Share and Show MATH BOARD

Do more children write with their left hand or right hand?
Ask 10 friends which hand they use. Make a bar graph.

Hand We Use to Write

Writing Hand										
left										
right										

0 1 2 3 4 5 6 7 8 9 10
Number of Children

1. Which hand do more children use to write? ________________

Name ______________________________

On Your Own

MATHEMATICAL PRACTICE 8 **Draw Conclusions**

Do children like , , or  best?

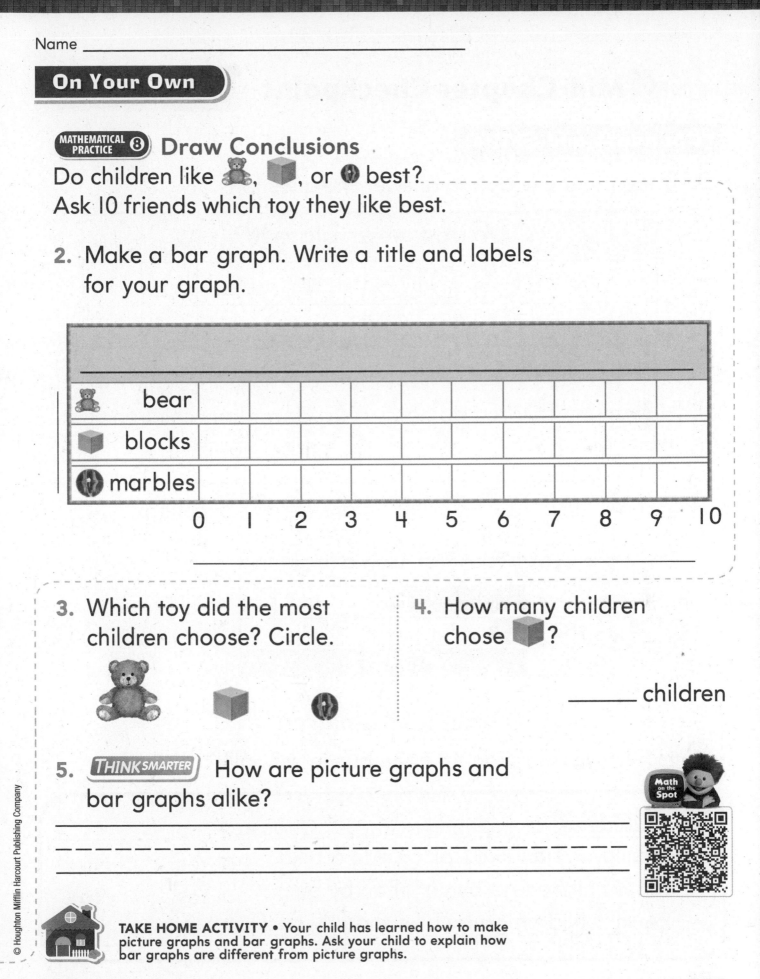

Ask 10 friends which toy they like best.

2. Make a bar graph. Write a title and labels for your graph.

____

 bear										
 blocks										
 marbles										

0 1 2 3 4 5 6 7 8 9 10

____

3. Which toy did the most children choose? Circle.

4. How many children chose ?

_____ children

5. **THINKSMARTER** How are picture graphs and bar graphs alike?

____

____

____

Math on the Spot

TAKE HOME ACTIVITY • Your child has learned how to make picture graphs and bar graphs. Ask your child to explain how bar graphs are different from picture graphs.

Name ______________________

Mid-Chapter Checkpoint

Personal Math Trainer
Online Assessment and Intervention

Concepts and Skills

Use the picture graph to answer the questions. (1.MD.C.4)

Do you wear glasses?								
yes	○	○	○					
no	○	○	○	○	○	○	○	○

Each ○ stands for 1 child.

1. How many children do not wear glasses? ____

2. How many children wear glasses? ____

THINK SMARTER Use the bar graph to answer the questions. (1.MD.C.4)

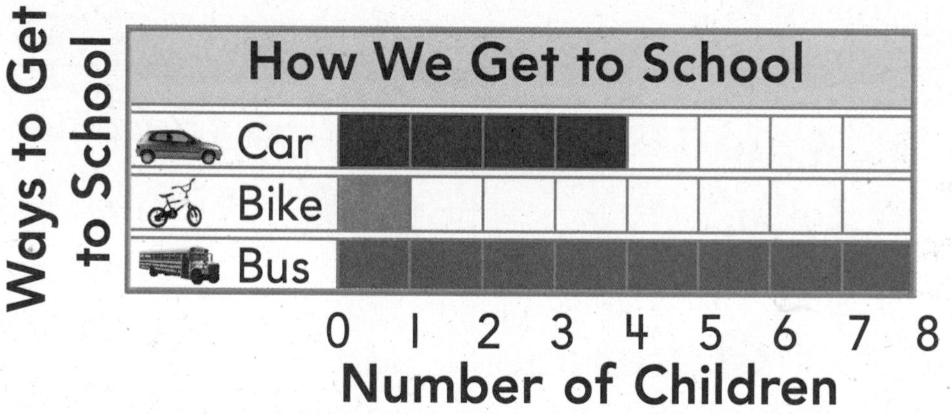

3. How many children take the bus to school? ____

4. THINK SMARTER Is the sentence true? Choose Yes or No.

5 children ride in a car or ride a bike.	○ Yes	○ No
More children go by car than by bus.	○ Yes	○ No
Fewer children go by bike than by car.	○ Yes	○ No

Name ______________________________

Make Bar Graphs

Common Core — COMMON CORE STANDARD—1.MD.C.4
Represent and interpret data.

Which is your favorite meal?

1. Ask 10 friends which meal they like best.
   Make a bar graph.

Our Favorite Meal

Meal										
breakfast										
lunch										
dinner										

0 1 2 3 4 5 6 7 8 9 10

Number of Children

2. How many children chose breakfast?

   _______ children

3. Which meal was chosen by the most children?

   ____

Problem Solving — Real World

4. What if 10 children chose breakfast?
   How many children could choose lunch or dinner?

   _______ children

5. WRITE Math Use words and pictures to show how to make a bar graph about favorite storybooks.

Lesson Check (1.MD.C.4)

Use the bar graph to answer the question.

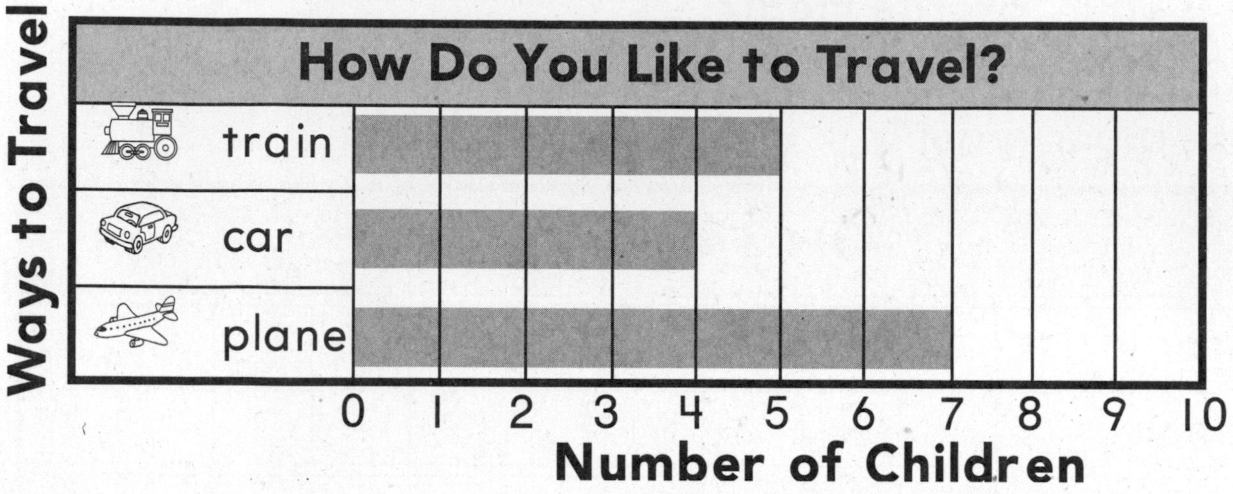

1. How many more children chose  than ?

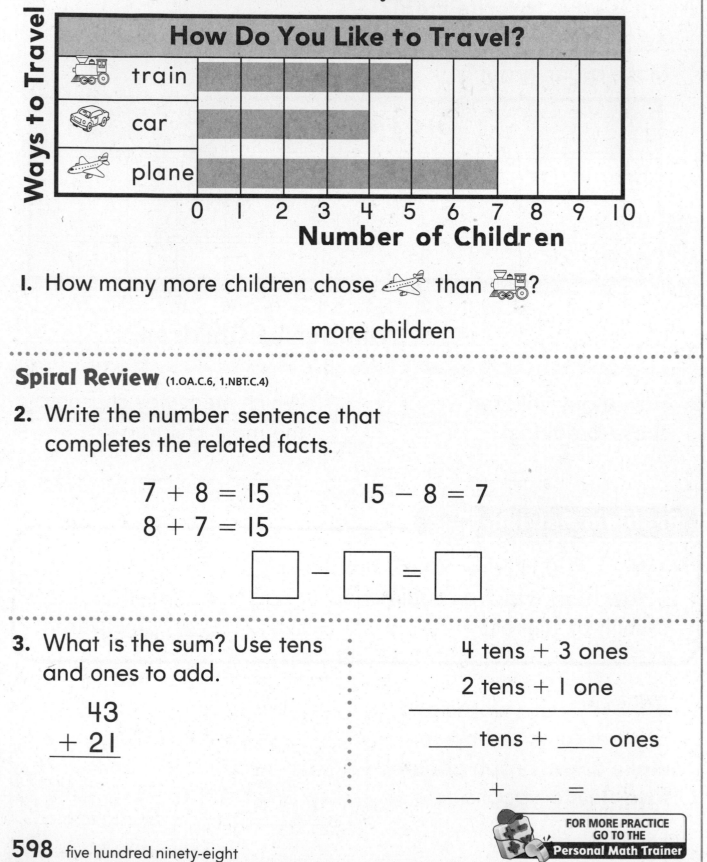

____ more children

Spiral Review (1.OA.C.6, 1.NBT.C.4)

2. Write the number sentence that completes the related facts.

$7 + 8 = 15$ $15 - 8 = 7$

$8 + 7 = 15$

$\square - \square = \square$

3. What is the sum? Use tens and ones to add.

$$\begin{array}{r} 43 \\ +\ 21 \\ \hline \end{array}$$

4 tens + 3 ones

2 tens + 1 one

____ tens + ____ ones

____ + ____ = ____

FOR MORE PRACTICE GO TO THE **Personal Math Trainer**

Name ______________________

Read Tally Charts

Essential Question How do you count the tallies on a tally chart?

Common Core **Measurement and Data—1.MD.C.4**

MATHEMATICAL PRACTICES MP2, MP3, MP4

Listen and Draw (Real World) (Hands On)

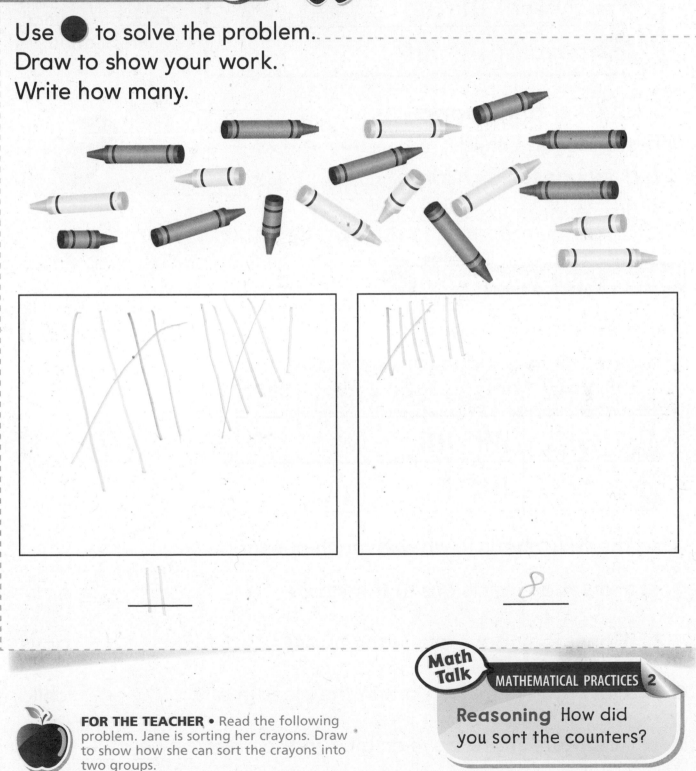

Use ● to solve the problem.
Draw to show your work.
Write how many.

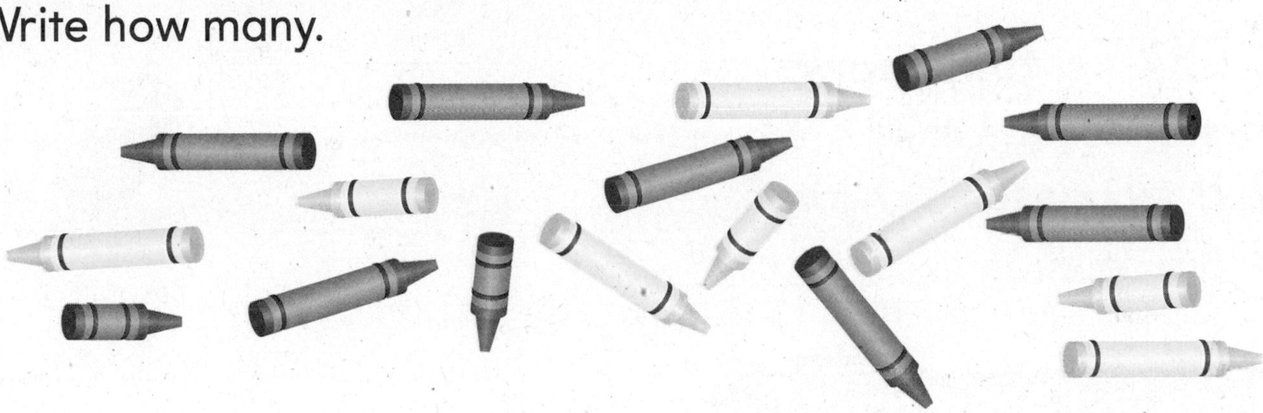

11 ______ 8 ______

Math Talk MATHEMATICAL PRACTICES 2

Reasoning How did you sort the counters?

FOR THE TEACHER • Read the following problem. Jane is sorting her crayons. Draw to show how she can sort the crayons into two groups.

Model and Draw

Do more children like chicken or pizza better?

Food We Like		Total
 chicken	|||	3
 pizza	𝍸 |||	8

You can use a **tally chart** to collect information.

Each | is a **tally mark.**
It stands for 1 child.
𝍸 stands for 5 children.
More children like pizza.

Share and Show

MATH BOARD

Complete the tally chart.

Boys and Girls in Our Class		Total
 boys	𝍸 ||||	9
 girls	𝍸		6

Use the tally chart to answer each question.

1. How many girls are in the class? 6 girls

2. How many boys are in the class? 9 boys

3. How many children are in the class in all? 15 children

4. Are there more boys or girls in the class? doys

Name ______________________

On Your Own

Complete the tally chart.

Our Favorite Sport		Total
t-ball	~~||||~~	5
soccer	~~||||~~ II	7
swimming	III	3

Use the tally chart to answer the question.

5. How many children chose soccer? __7__ children

6. How many more children chose t-ball than swimming? __2__ more children

7. Which sport did the most children choose? Circle.

8. THINK SMARTER Write your own question about the tally chart.

How many more children

9. GO DEEPER Sam asked some other children which sport they like. They all chose swimming. Now the most children chose swimming. How many children did Sam ask? ______ children

Problem Solving • Applications | Real World | WRITE Math

Our Favorite Season		Total
❄ winter	\|\|\|\|	4
☀ summer	⊮⊮ ⊮⊮	10
🍁 fall	\|\|\|\|	4

Remember to write the total.

MATHEMATICAL PRACTICE 2 Connect Symbols and Words
Complete each sentence about the tally chart.
Write **greater than, less than,** or **equal to.**

10. The number of tallies for ☀ is _____ the number of tallies for ❄.

11. The number of tallies for ❄ is _____ 3 _____ the number of tallies for 🍁.

12. The number of tallies for 🍁 is _____ the number of tallies for ☀.

13. **GO DEEPER** The number of tallies for ☀ is _____ the number of tallies for both ❄ and 🍁.

14. **THINK SMARTER** Look at the chart. How many tallies in all?

○ ⊮ \|\|\| ○ ⊮ ⊮ \|\|\|\|

○ ⊮ ⊮ ○ ⊮ ⊮ ⊮ \|\|\|

🏠 **TAKE HOME ACTIVITY** • Together with your child, make a tally chart showing how many times you all say the word "eat" during a meal. Then have your child write the number.

Name ______________________________

Read Tally Charts

Common Core **COMMON CORE STANDARD—1.MD.C.4**
Represent and interpret data.

Complete the tally chart.

Our Favorite Vegetable		Total
 beans	𝍷𝍷𝍷𝍷	
 corn	𝍸 𝍷𝍷𝍷	
 carrots	𝍸	

Use the tally chart to answer each question.

1. How many children chose  ? ____ children

2. How many more children chose  than  ? ____ more children

Problem Solving Real World

Complete each sentence about the tally chart.
Write **greater than**, **less than**, or **equal to**.

3. The number of children who chose  is ____________________ the number who chose  .

4. The number of children who chose  is ____________________ the number who chose  .

5. WRITE Math Use words, numbers, or pictures to show how to group and count tally marks for the number 8.

Lesson Check (1.MD.C.4)

Use the tally chart to answer each question.

Our Favorite Pet	
 dog	𝍸 II
 cat	𝍸
 fish	II

1. How many children chose  ?

____ children

2. How many more children chose  than ?

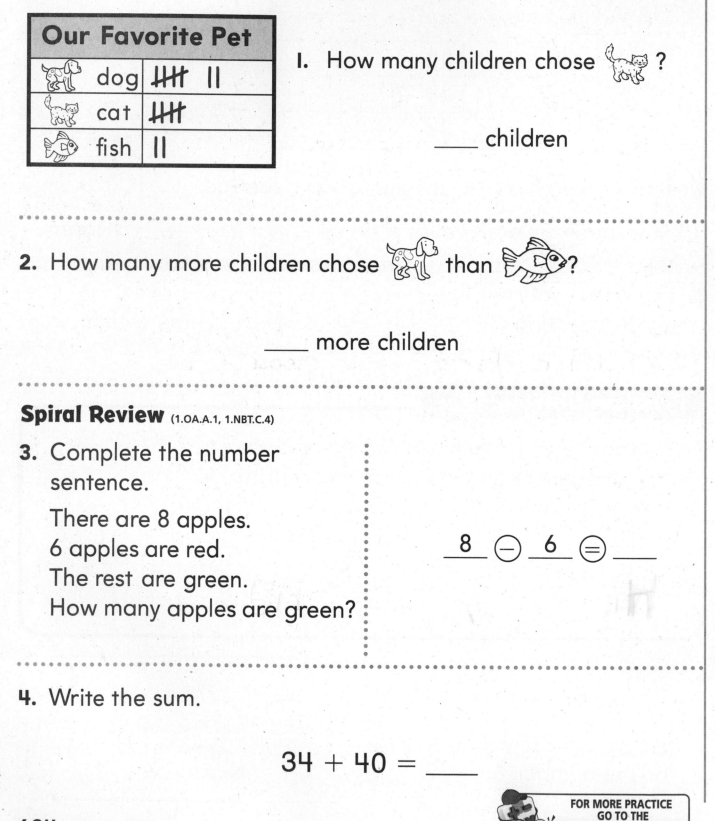

____ more children

Spiral Review (1.OA.A.1, 1.NBT.C.4)

3. Complete the number sentence.

There are 8 apples.
6 apples are red.
The rest are green.
How many apples are green?

$8 \ominus 6 \ominus$ ____

4. Write the sum.

$34 + 40 =$ ____

FOR MORE PRACTICE GO TO THE Personal Math Trainer

Name ___________________________

Make Tally Charts

HANDS ON
Lesson 10.6

Essential Question Why is a tally chart a good way to show information that you have collected?

Common Core **Measurement and Data—1.MD.C.4**
MATHEMATICAL PRACTICES MP1, MP3, MP4

Listen Real World

Complete the tally chart.

Our Favorite Game			Total
	card game	𝍸	
	puzzle	|||	
	board game	𝍸 𝍸	

Use the tally chart to answer the question.

Which game did the most children choose? Circle.

Which game did the fewest children choose? Circle.

Math Talk MATHEMATICAL PRACTICES 1

Analyze How do you know which game is the favorite?

FOR THE TEACHER • Read the following problem. Ava asks the children in her class which of three games they like the best. She makes a tally mark to show each child's answer. Which game did the most children choose? Which did the fewest children choose?

Model and Draw

How can you make a tally chart to show the boats at the lake?

Decide if each boat has a sail.

Boats at the Lake		Total
boats with sails	‖	
boats without sails		

Share and Show MATH BOARD

Use the picture to complete the tally chart. Then answer each question.

Fish in the Tank		Total
zebra fish		
angel fish		

1. How many are in the tank?

2. How many more than are there?

 _____ more

3. How many and are in the tank?

 _____ fish

© Houghton Mifflin Harcourt Publishing Company

Name ______________________________

On Your Own

Which of these snacks do most children like the best?
Ask 10 friends. Make 1 tally mark for each child's answer.

Our Favorite Snack		Total
 pretzel		
 apple		
 yogurt		

Use the tally chart to answer each question.

4. How many children chose ?

____ children

5. How many children chose ?

____ children

6. Which snack do most children like best? Circle.

7. **THINK SMARTER** What if 6 children out of the 10 chose ? Which snack would be the favorite? Circle it.

8. **Explain** Write your own question about the tally chart.

____

____

Problem Solving • Applications Real World

WRITE Math

MATHEMATICAL PRACTICE 1 **Analyze Relationships** Jenna asked 10 friends to choose their favorite subject. She will ask 10 more children.

Our Favorite School Subject		Total
math	~~IIII~~ I	
reading	II	
science	II	

9. Predict. Which subject will children most likely choose? ____________

10. Predict. Which subject will children least likely choose? ____________

11. THINK SMARTER How can you prove if your prediction is good? Try it.

____

12. THINK SMARTER Complete the tally chart to show the number of votes.

Fruit We Like		Total
apple	IIII	4
banana		5
grapes		2

TAKE HOME ACTIVITY • With your child, survey friends and family to find out their favorite food. Draw tally marks to record the results and then prepare the food.

Name ______________________

Make Tally Charts

Common Core **COMMON CORE STANDARD—1.MD.C.4**
Represent and interpret data.

Which color do most children like best? Ask 10 friends. Make 1 tally mark for each child's answer.

Favorite Color		Total
red		
blue		

1. How many children chose red?

   ____ **children**

2. How many children chose blue?

   ____ **children**

Problem Solving Real World

Jason asked 10 friends to choose their favorite game. He will ask 10 more children.

Our Favorite Game	
tag	I
kickball	~~IIII~~ II
hopscotch	II

3. Predict. Which game will children most likely choose? ____________

4. Predict. Which game will children least likely choose? ____________

5. WRITE Math Write a question that can be answered by making a tally chart.

   ____

   ____

Lesson Check (1.MD.C.4)

1. Which insect did the most children choose?
Circle the answer.

Our Favorite Insect		Total
 ladybug	III	3
 bee	I	1
 butterfly	~~IIII~~ II	7

Spiral Review (1.NBT.B.2b, 1.NBT.B.3)

2. Circle the number that is greater than 54.
Write the number.

45 50 54 57

____ is greater than 54.

____ > 54

3. Use the model. Write the number three different ways.

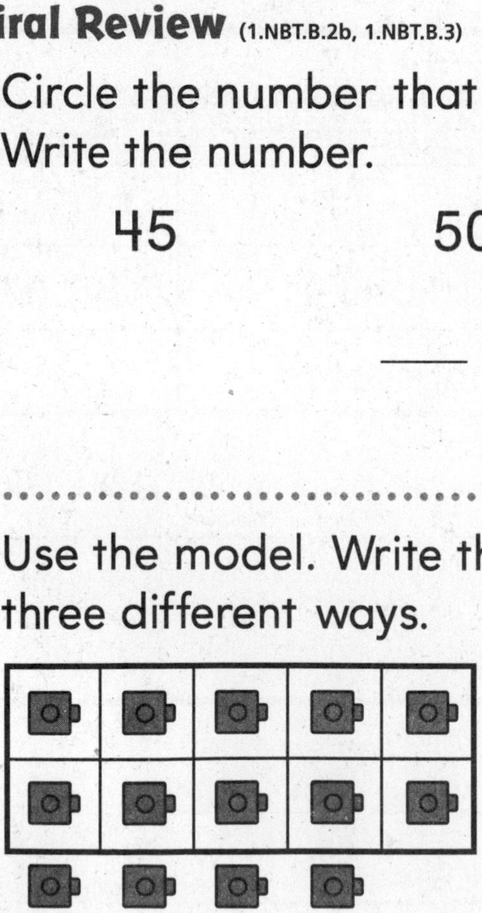

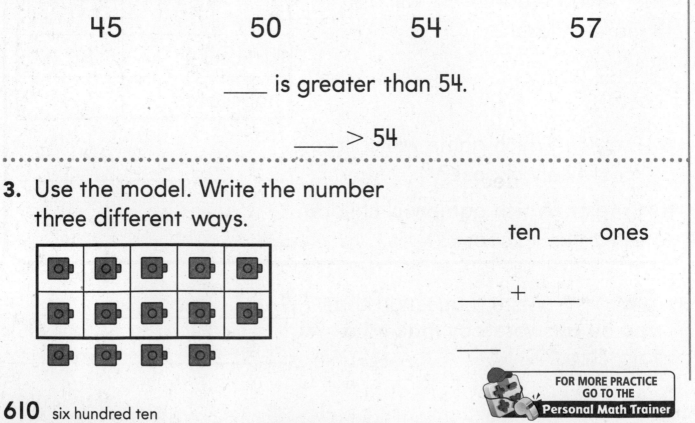

____ ten ____ ones

____ + ____

____

FOR MORE PRACTICE GO TO THE Personal Math Trainer

Name ______________________________

Problem Solving • Represent Data

Essential Question How can showing information in a graph help you solve problems?

Common Core **Measurement and Data—1.MD.C.4**
MATHEMATICAL PRACTICES MP3, MP5, MP6

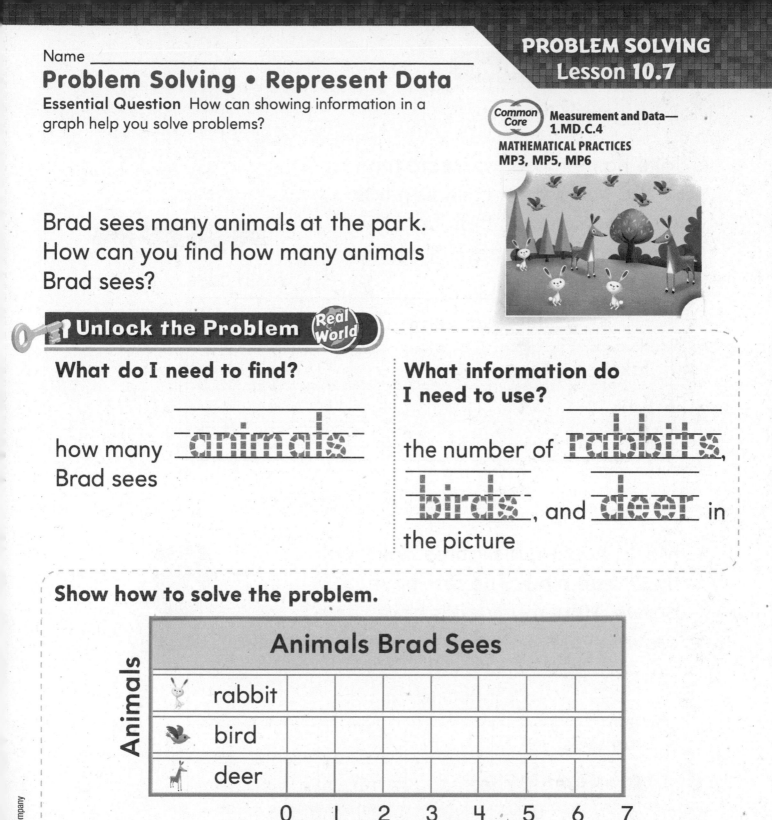

Brad sees many animals at the park. How can you find how many animals Brad sees?

Unlock the Problem (Real World)

What do I need to find?

how many animals Brad sees

What information do I need to use?

the number of rabbits, birds, and deer in the picture

Show how to solve the problem.

Animals Brad Sees

Animals							
rabbit							
bird							
deer							

0 1 2 3 4 5 6 7

Number of Animals

____ + ____ + ____ = ____ animals

HOME CONNECTION • Your child learned how to represent data from a picture in a bar graph. Have your child explain why it is easier to use data in a bar graph than in a picture.

Try Another Problem

Make a graph to solve.

- What do I need to find?
- What information do I need to use?

1. Jake has 4 more train cars than Ed. Ed has 3 train cars. Ben has 2 fewer train cars than Ed. How many train cars does Jake have?

____ train cars

Our Train Cars

Children								
Jake								
Ed								
Ben								

0 1 2 3 4 5 6 7 8

Number of Train Cars

2. Marla has 8 dolls. Three dolls have blue eyes. The rest have brown. How many dolls have brown eyes?

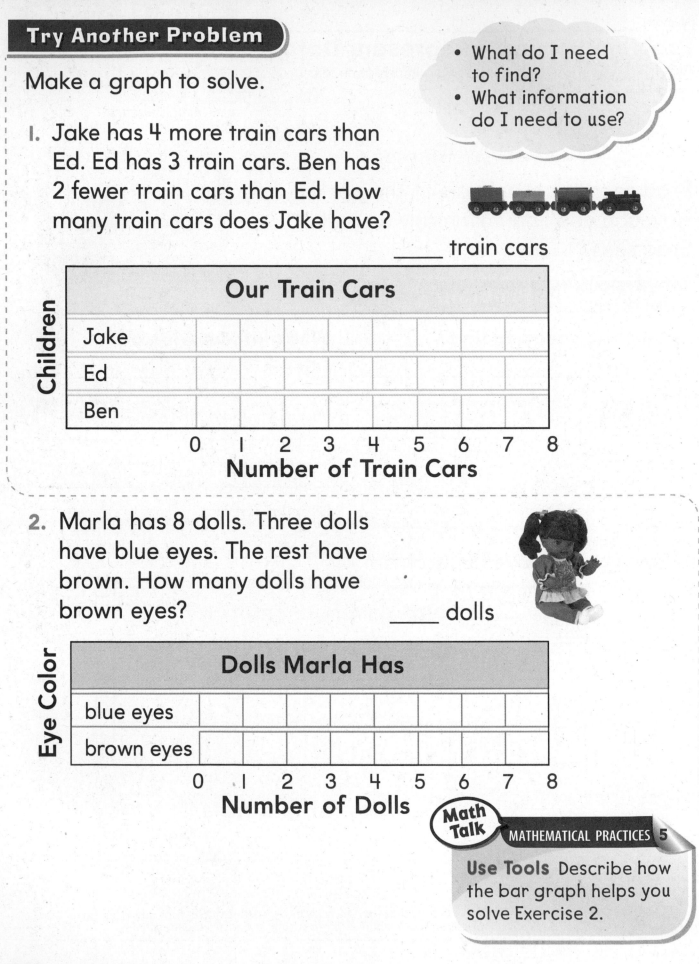

____ dolls

Dolls Marla Has

Eye Color								
blue eyes								
brown eyes								

0 1 2 3 4 5 6 7 8

Number of Dolls

Math Talk MATHEMATICAL PRACTICES 5

Use Tools Describe how the bar graph helps you solve Exercise 2.

Name ______________________________

Share and Show MATH BOARD

MATHEMATICAL PRACTICE 6 **Make Connections** Find out about the eye color of your classmates.

3. Write a question you can ask your friends.

____

4. Ask 10 friends your question. Make a tally chart.

______________________________		Total

5. THINK SMARTER Use the tally chart to make a bar graph.

Math on the Spot

______________________________								

0 1 2 3 4 5 6 7 8

____

6. Explain What did you learn from the graph?

____

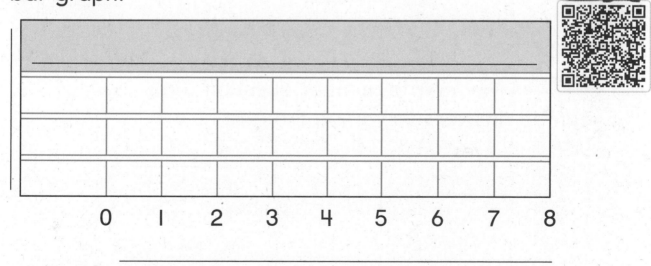

On Your Own

WRITE Math

What is your favorite fruit? Nina asked 20 children this question. Then she made a bar graph. But Nina spilled paint on the graph.

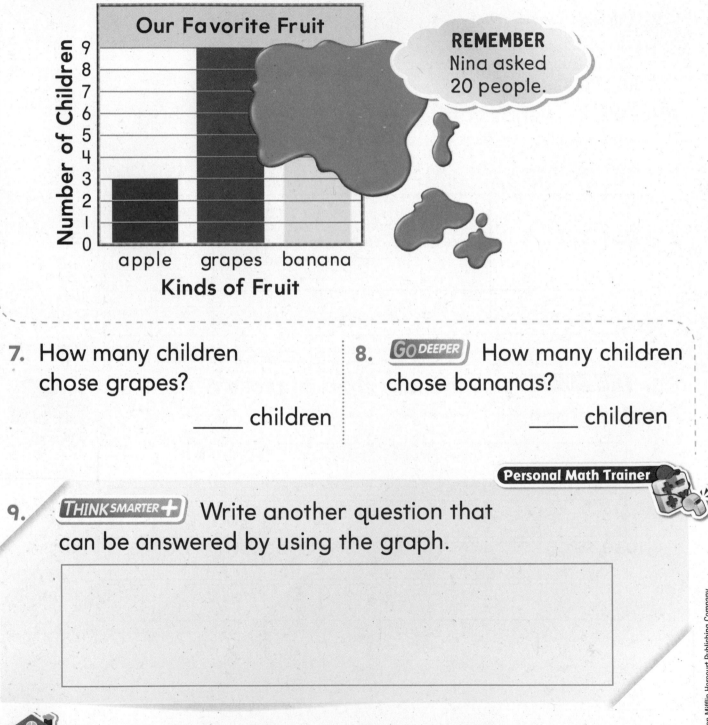

REMEMBER Nina asked 20 people.

7. How many children chose grapes?

____ children

8. GO DEEPER How many children chose bananas?

____ children

Personal Math Trainer

9. THINK SMARTER + Write another question that can be answered by using the graph.

TAKE HOME ACTIVITY • Work with your child to make a tally chart and a bar graph showing the favorite color of 10 family members or friends. Talk about the results.

Name ______________________________

Problem Solving • Represent Data

COMMON CORE STANDARD—1.MD.C.4
Represent and interpret data.

Bella made a tally chart to show the favorite sport of 10 friends.

Our Favorite Sport	
Soccer	𝍸 I
Basketball	III
Baseball	I

Use the tally chart to make a bar graph.

Our Favorite Sport

Kinds of Sports								
Soccer								
Basketball								
Baseball								
	0 1	2	3	4	5	6	7	8

Number of Children

Use the graph to solve.

1. How many friends chose soccer?

____ friends

2. How many friends chose soccer or basketball?

____ friends

3. WRITE Math Write the names of 3 types of animals. Count the letters in each name. Make a bar graph showing the letter for each animal.

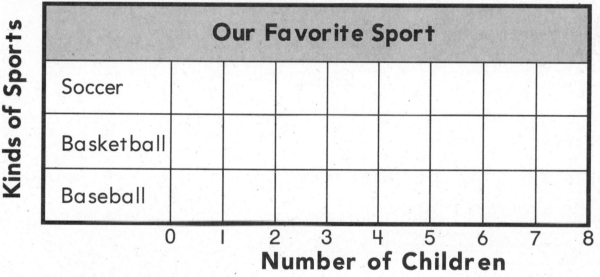

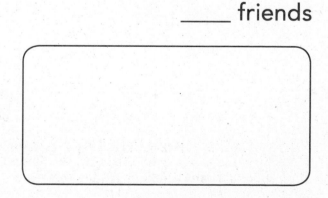

Lesson Check (1.MD.C.4)

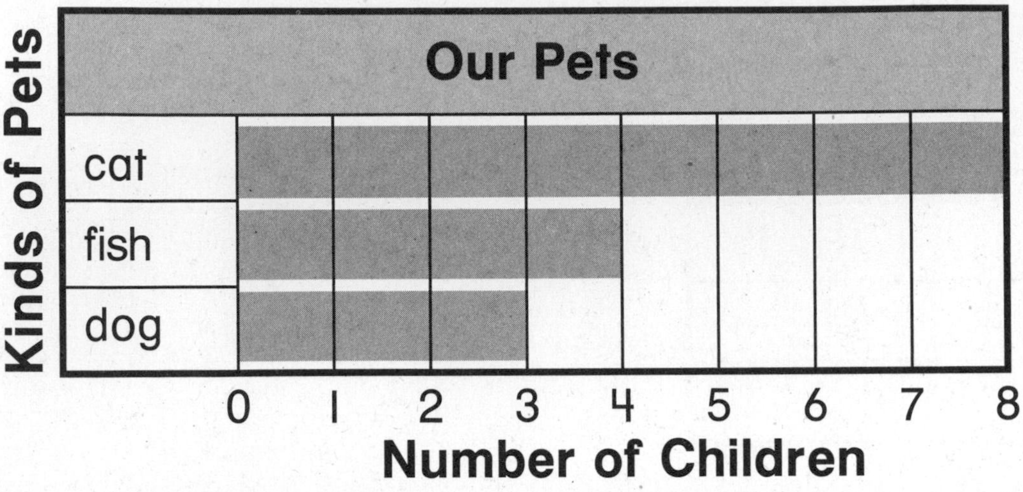

1. Use the graph. How many more children have fish than a dog?

____ more

Spiral Review (1.MD.A.1, 1.MD.B.3)

2. Which ribbon is the shortest? Color the shortest ribbon.

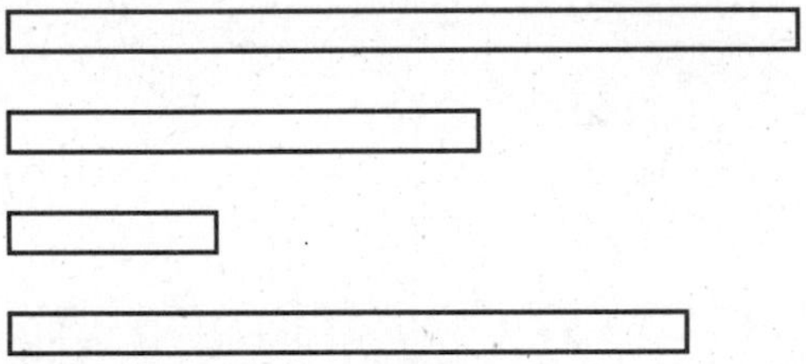

3. Look at the hour hand. Write the time.

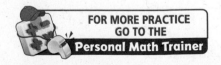

____

Name ___________________________

✓ Chapter 10 Review/Test

Personal Math Trainer
Online Assessment and Intervention

Use the picture graph to answer the questions.

Each stands for 1 child.

1. How many children chose RED?

☐

---

2. Is the sentence true? Choose Yes or No.

More children like blue than red.	○ Yes	○ No
5 children like red.	○ Yes	○ No
2 more children like blue than red.	○ Yes	○ No

---

3. 1 more child gets a BLUE. Draw what the blue row looks like now.

GO DIGITAL Assessment Options Chapter Test

Use the bar graph to answer the questions.

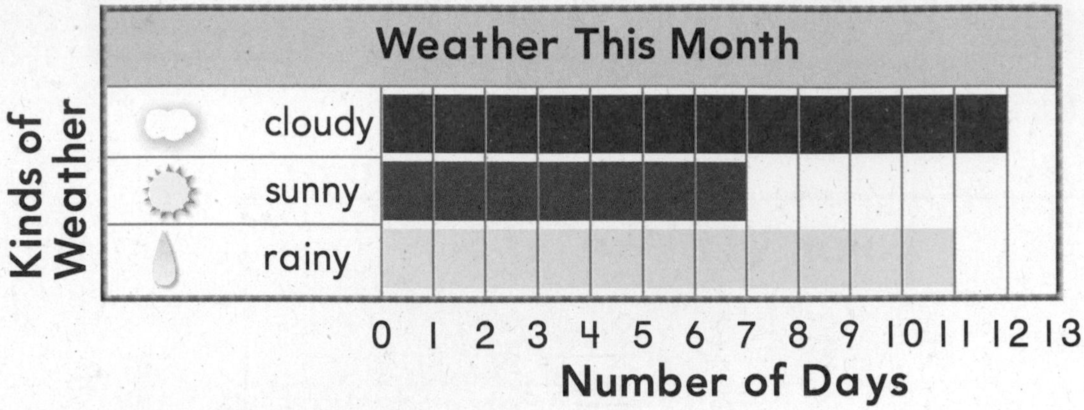

4. How many days were sunny?

☐

5. Compare rainy and sunny days. Circle the number that makes the sentence true.

There were [4 / 5 / 7] more rainy days than sunny days.

6. Ann says the graph shows 1 more rainy day than cloudy days. Is she correct?

Choose Yes or No.

○ Yes ○ No

Explain your answer.

Name ______________________________

Use the tally chart to answer the questions.

Sam's Cars and Trucks		Total
 cars		8
 trucks	𝍸 I	6

7. How many  does Sam have?

☐

8. Draw tally marks for the number of cars that the chart shows.

☐

9. Circle the words that make the sentence true.

The number of tally marks for  is

greater than
less than
equal to

the number of tally marks for .

Personal Math Trainer

10. THINK SMARTER + Chung visits the zoo.
He sees 2 . He sees 4 more  than .
He sees 3 fewer  than . Make a bar graph.

What Chung Sees

Kind of Animal						
 lion						
 elephant						
 monkey						

0 1 2 3 4 5 6

Number of Animals

Use the bar graph to answer the question.

11. GO DEEPER How many more  does Chung see than  and  altogether?

______ more 

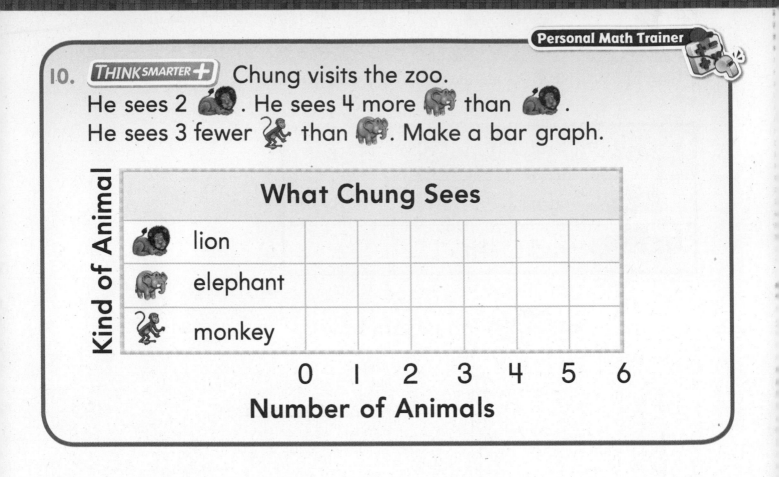

12. Write another question that can be answered by the bar graph.

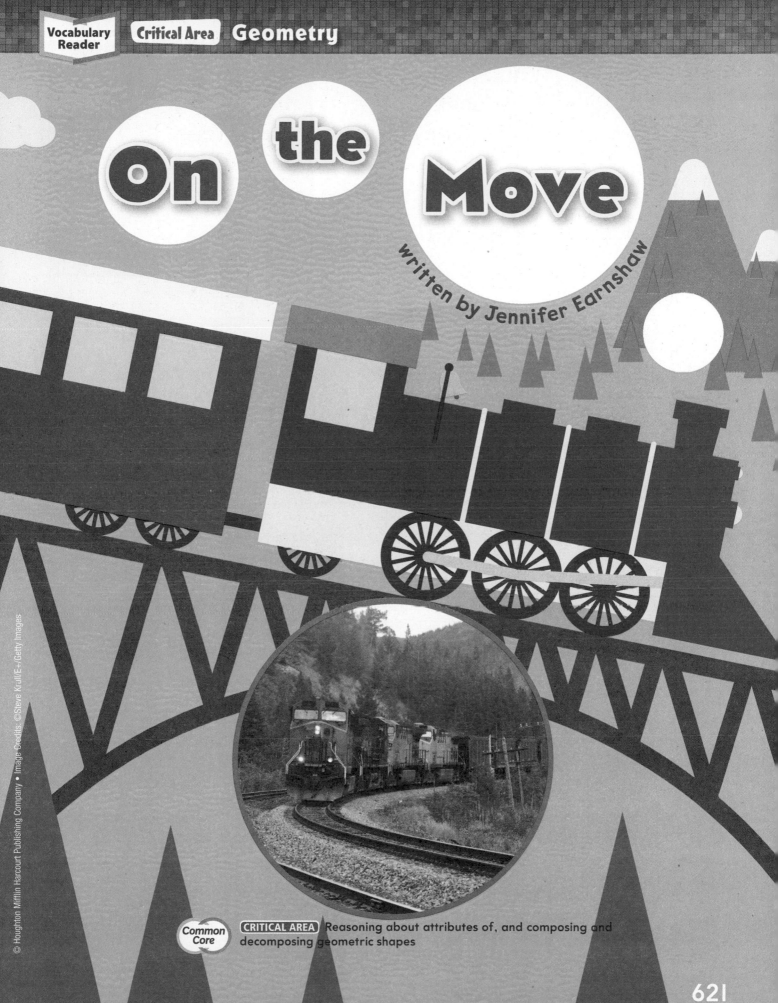

On the Move

written by Jennifer Earnshaw

Common Core

CRITICAL AREA Reasoning about attributes of, and composing and decomposing geometric shapes

The train car waits for the engine.

Name some shapes you see.

Social Studies

What will this train bring?

The big truck travels up the road.

Name some shapes you see.

Social Studies

What will this truck bring?

The ship loads at the dock.

Name some shapes you see.

Social Studies

What will this ship bring?

These trucks drive across town.

Name some shapes you see.

Social Studies

What will these trucks bring?

The airplane arrives at the airport.

Name some shapes you see.

Social Studies

What will this airplane bring?

Name ______________________________

Write About the Story

Think of another kind of truck that takes goods from one place to another. Draw a picture. Use circles, squares, triangles, or rectangles in your drawing.

Vocabulary Review

circle triangle
square rectangle

truck

WRITE Math Write about your drawing.

Figure It Out

1. Draw an airplane.
   Use some triangles and circles in your drawing.

2. Draw a train.
   Use some rectangles and circles in your drawing.

MATH BOARD Choose two shapes to use to draw a ship. Draw the ship.

Chapter 11

Three-Dimensional Geometry

Curious About Math with Curious George

What three-dimensional shapes do you see in the sand castle?

Name ____________________

Show What You Know

Personal Math Trainer
Online Assessment and Intervention

Alike and Different

Circle the objects that are alike. (K.MD.A.1)

I.

2.

Identify Three-Dimensional Shapes

Color the  blue. Color the  red.
Color the  yellow. (K.G.B.4)

3.

4.

5.

Sort by Size

Mark an X on the object that does not belong. (K.MD.B.3)

6.

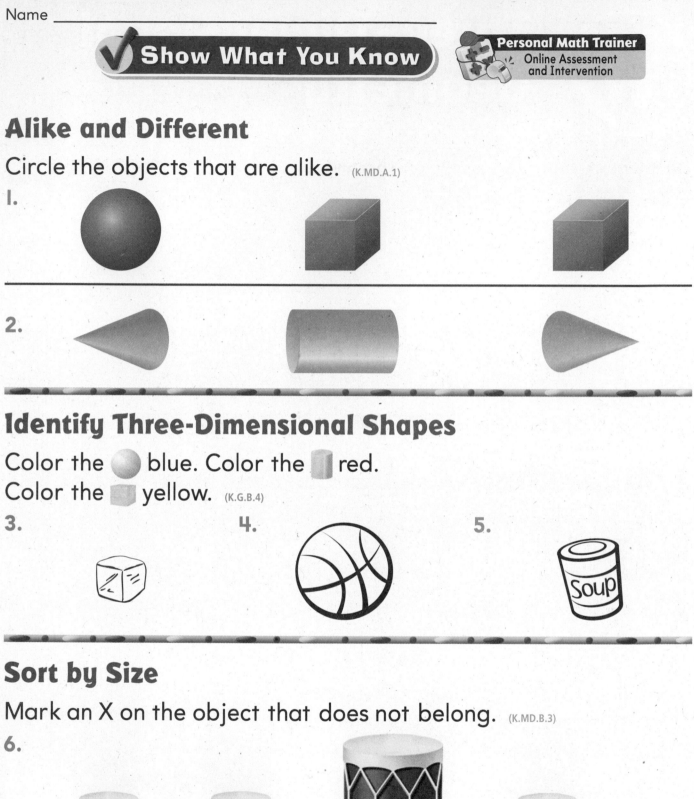

This page checks understanding of important skills needed for success in Chapter II.

Name ______________________________

Vocabulary Builder

Review Words

cone
cube
cylinder
sphere

Visualize It

Write review words to name the shapes.

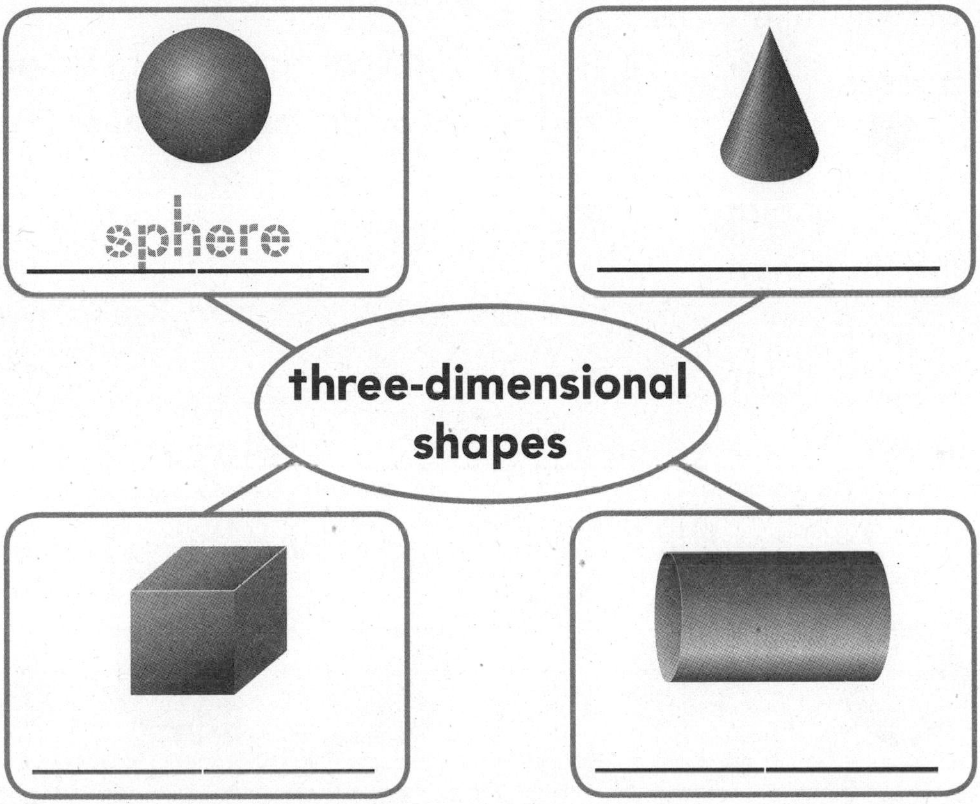

Understand Vocabulary

Look at the three-dimensional shapes.
Color the sphere . Color the cube .
Color the cylinder .

1.

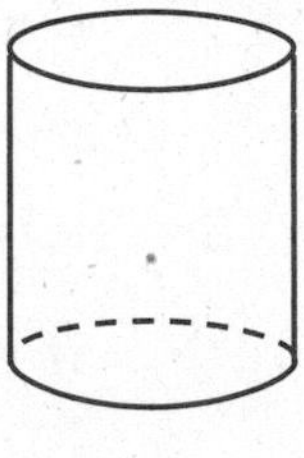

2.

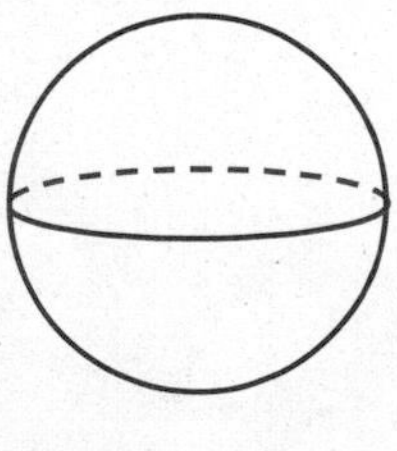

3.

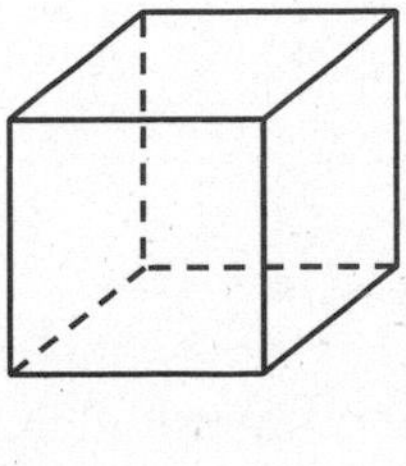

GO DIGITAL
• Interactive Student Edition
• Multimedia eGlossary

Chapter 11 Game

Shape Match Bingo

Materials • 9 ● • 9 ● • spinner

Play with a partner. Take turns.

1. One player uses ●. The other player uses ●.
2. Spin the spinner. Use a counter to cover a space with that shape.
3. If you cannot cover a space, your turn is over.
4. The first player to cover all of his or her spaces wins.

Player 1

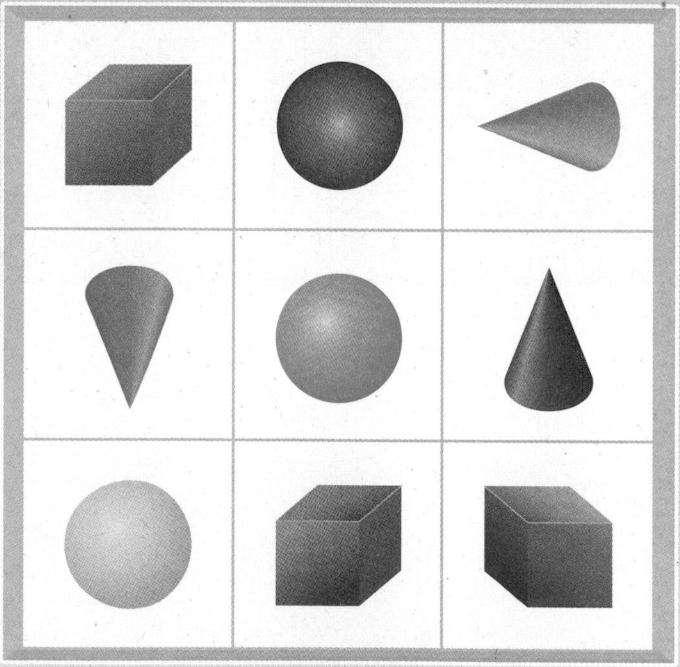

Player 2

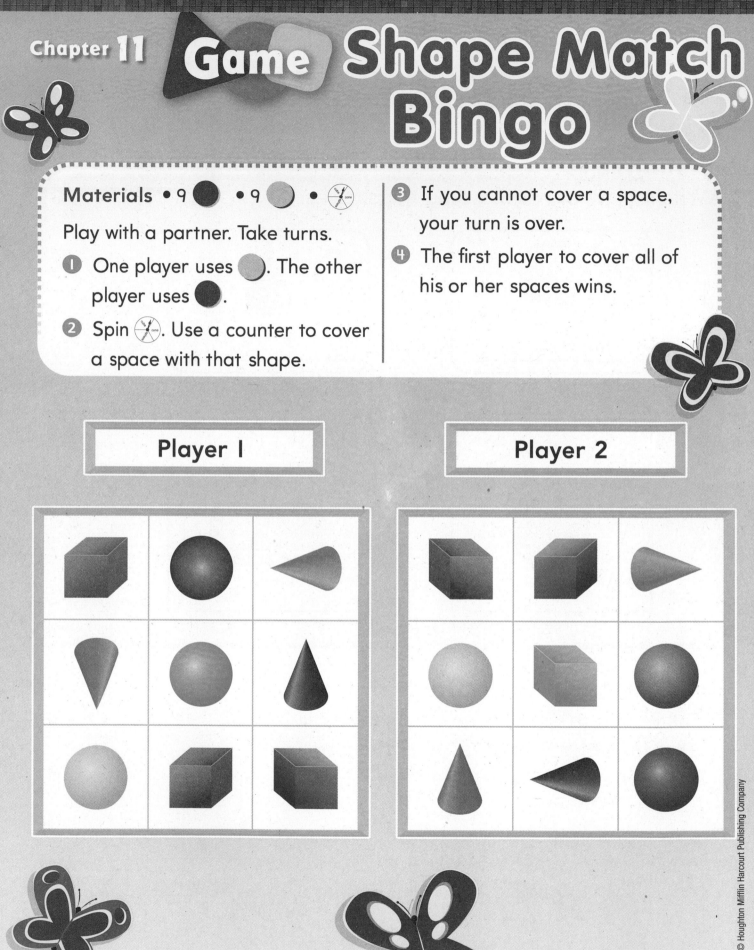

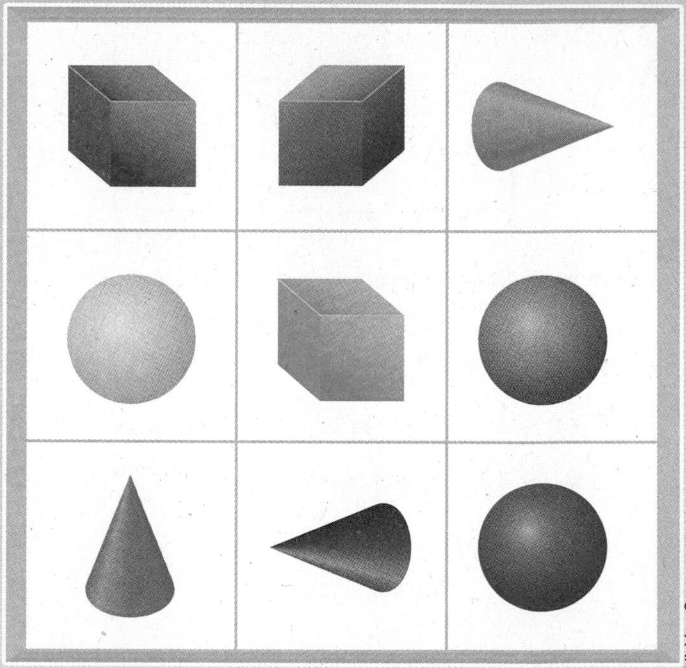

Chapter 11 Vocabulary

bar graph gráfica de barras 4	**cone** cono 7
cube cubo 10	**curved surface** superficie curva 11
cylinder cilindro 12	**flat surface** superficie plana 20
rectangular prism prisma rectangular 46	**sphere** esfera 50

© Houghton Mifflin Harcourt Publishing Company

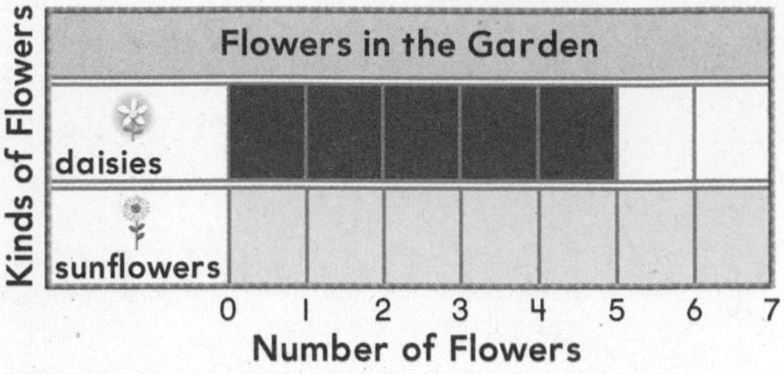

© Houghton Mifflin Harcourt Publishing Company

Some three-dimensional shapes have a **curved surface.**

© Houghton Mifflin Harcourt Publishing Company

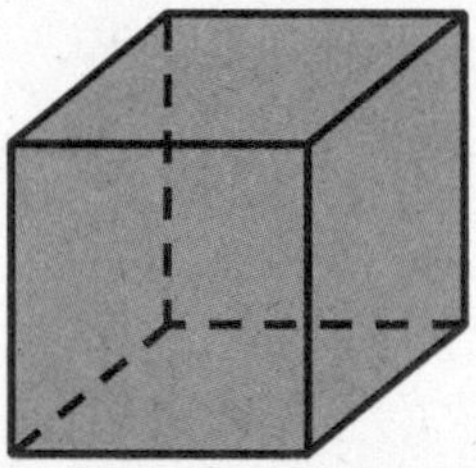

© Houghton Mifflin Harcourt Publishing Company

Some three-dimensional shapes have only **flat surfaces.**

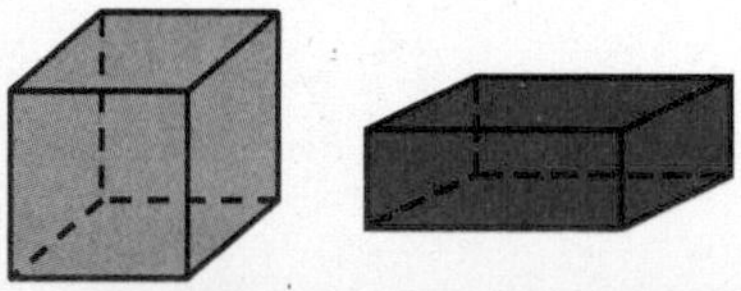

© Houghton Mifflin Harcourt Publishing Company

© Houghton Mifflin Harcourt Publishing Company

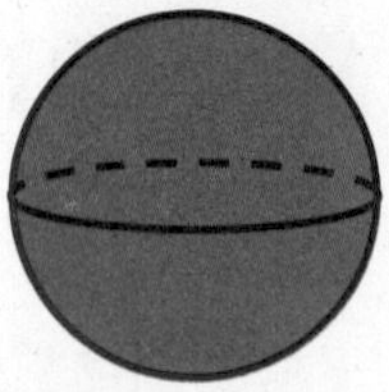

© Houghton Mifflin Harcourt Publishing Company

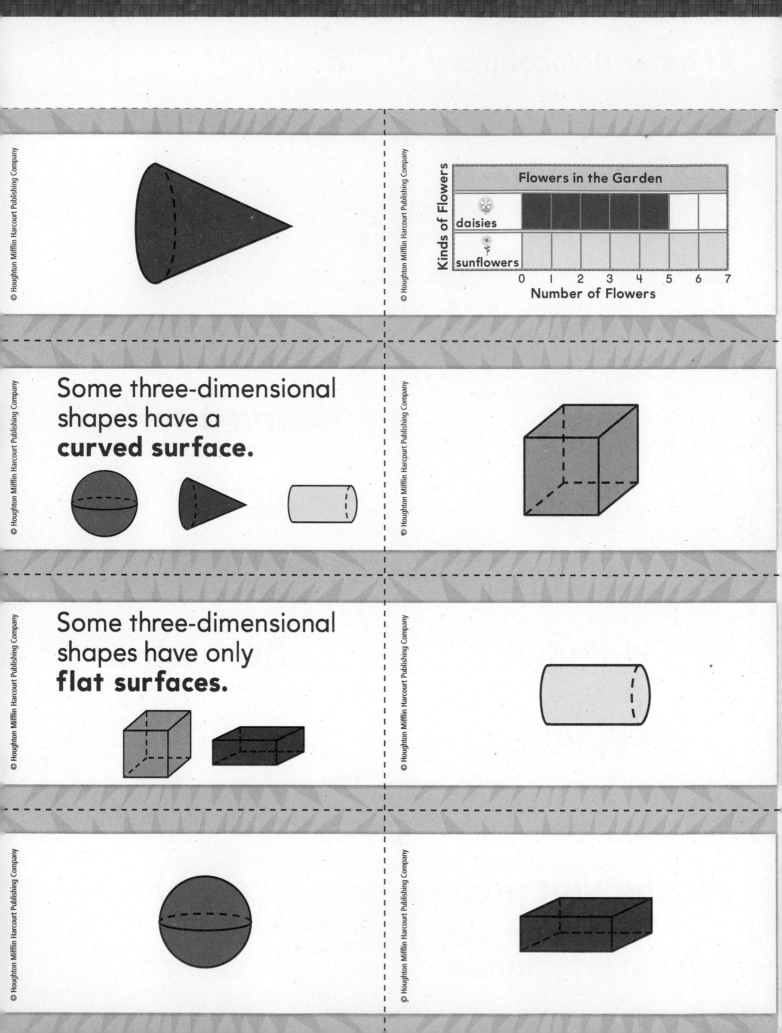

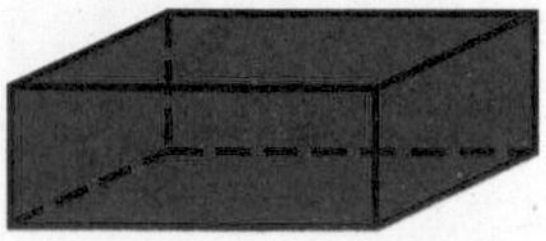

Going on a Train Trip

Word Box
bar graph
cone
cube
curved surface
cylinder
flat surface
rectangular prism
sphere

For 2 players

Materials

- 1
- 1
- 1
- Clue Cards

How to Play

1. Choose a and put it on START.
2. Toss the to take a turn. Move your that many spaces.
3. If you land on these spaces:
   Red Space Take a Clue Card. Answer the question. If you are correct, keep the Clue Card and move ahead 1. If you are not correct, return the Clue Card to the bottom of the pile.
   Blue Space Follow the directions on the space.
4. Collect 5 Clue Cards. Move around the track as many times as you need to. Then, follow the closest center path to reach FINISH.
5. The first player to reach FINISH wins.

Game

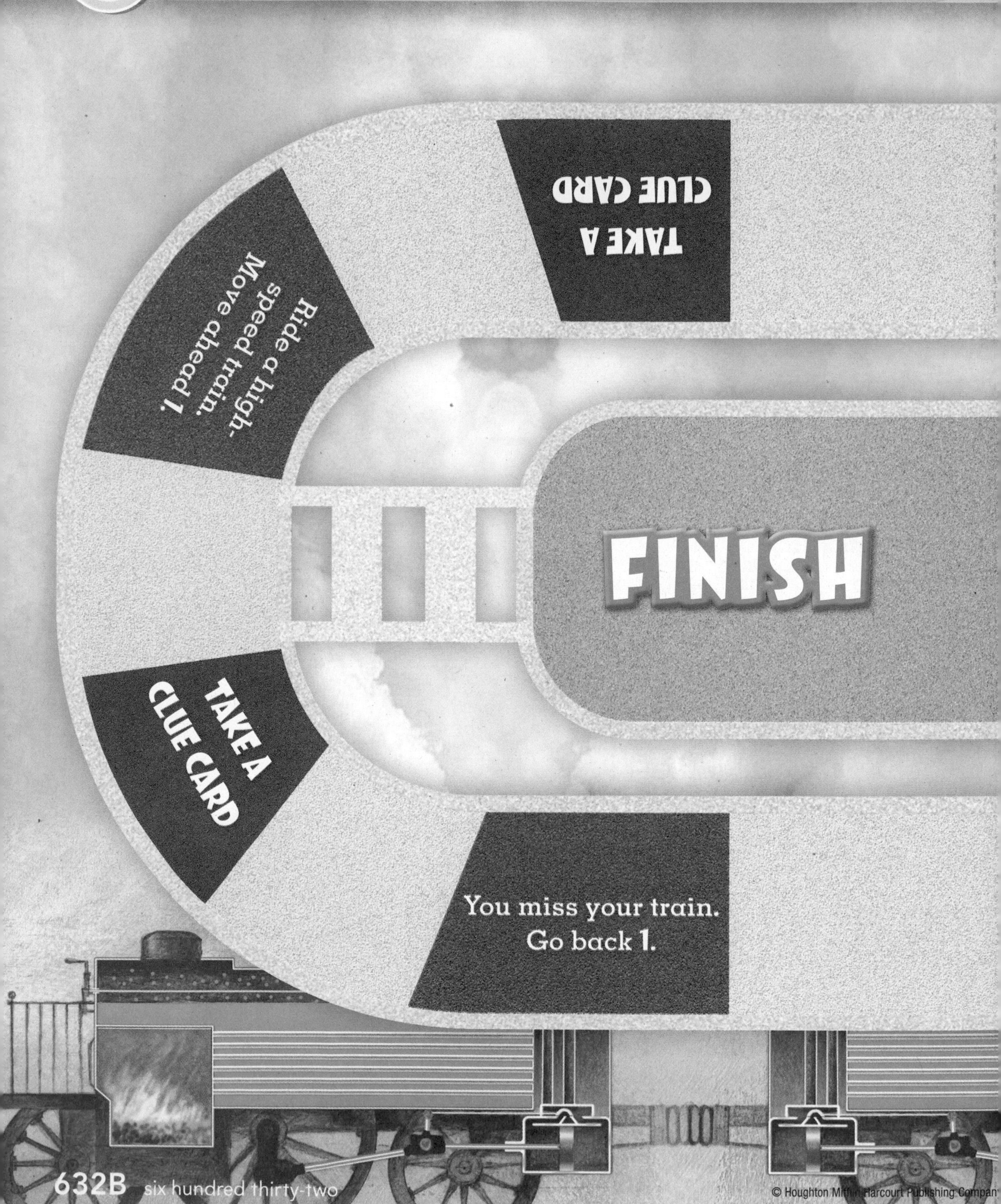
TAKE A CLUE CARD
Ride a high-speed train. Move ahead 1.
FINISH
TAKE A CLUE CARD
You miss your train. Go back 1.

Game

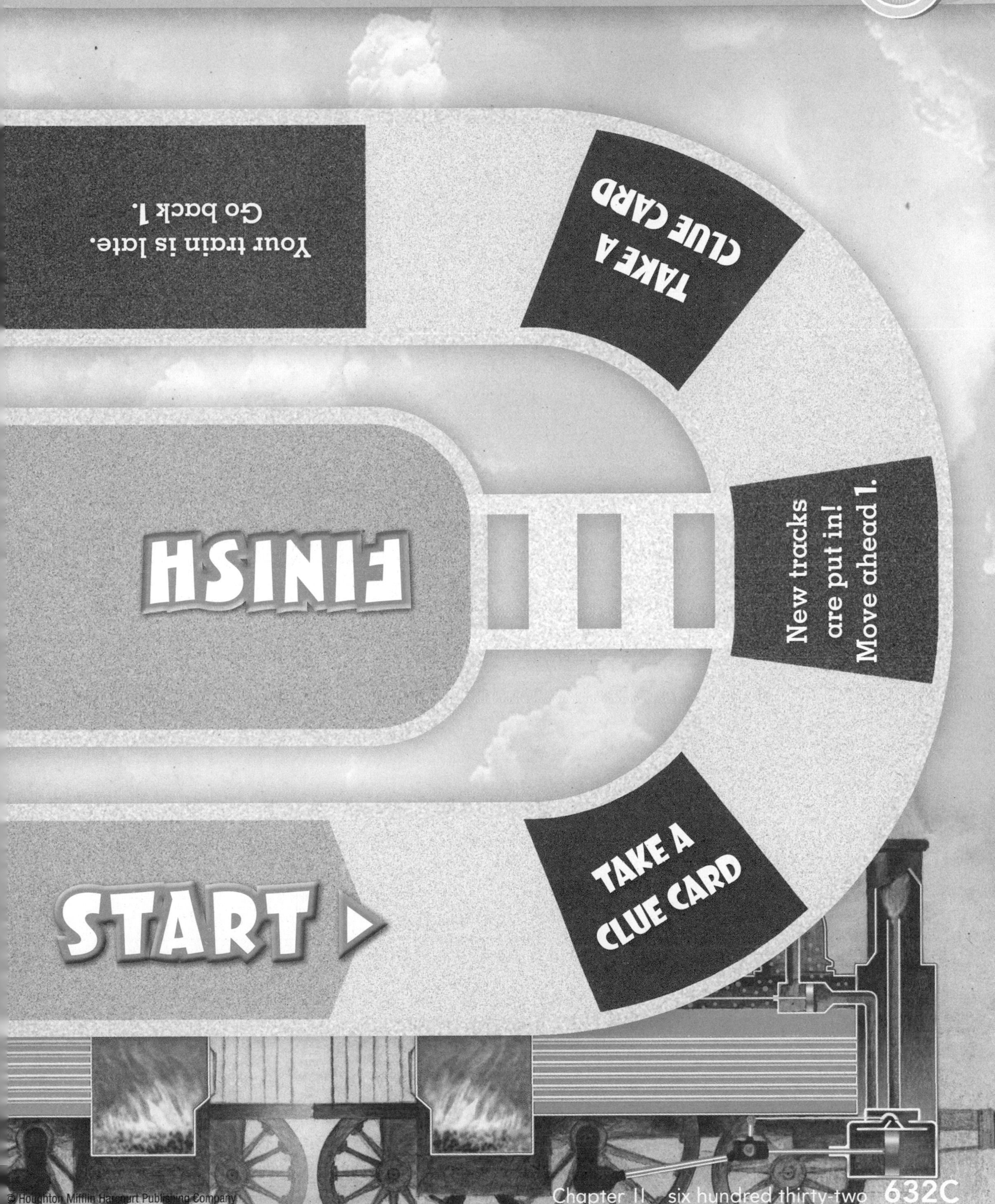

Your train is late.
Go back 1.
TAKE A CLUE CARD
FINISH
New tracks are put in! Move ahead 1.
START
TAKE A CLUE CARD

Journal

The Write Way

Reflect

Choose one idea. Draw and write about it.

- Tell about **two** of these words.

  cone   cube   cylinder   sphere

- Compare a curved surface to a flat surface. Tell how they are alike and how they are different.

Name ______________________________

Three-Dimensional Shapes

Essential Question How can you identify and describe three-dimensional shapes?

Common Core **Geometry—1.G.A.1**

MATHEMATICAL PRACTICES
MP4, MP6, MP8

Listen and Draw

Draw to sort the three-dimensional shapes.

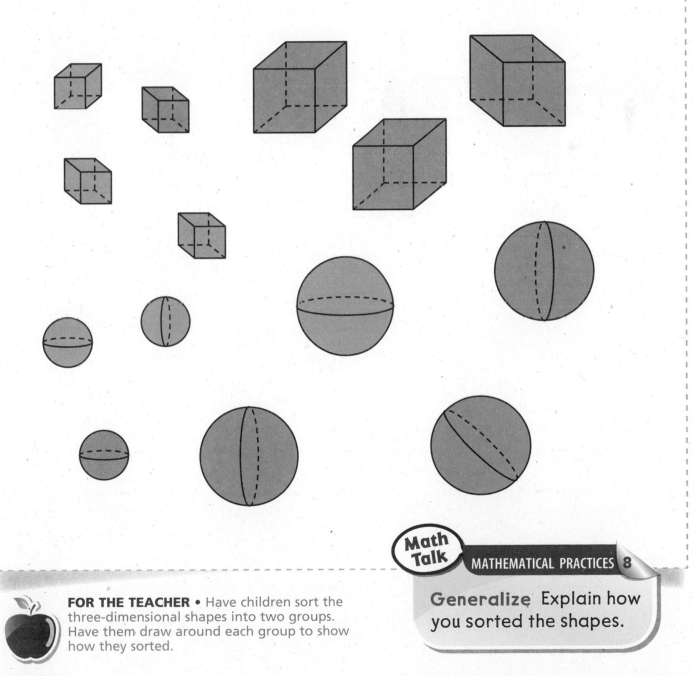

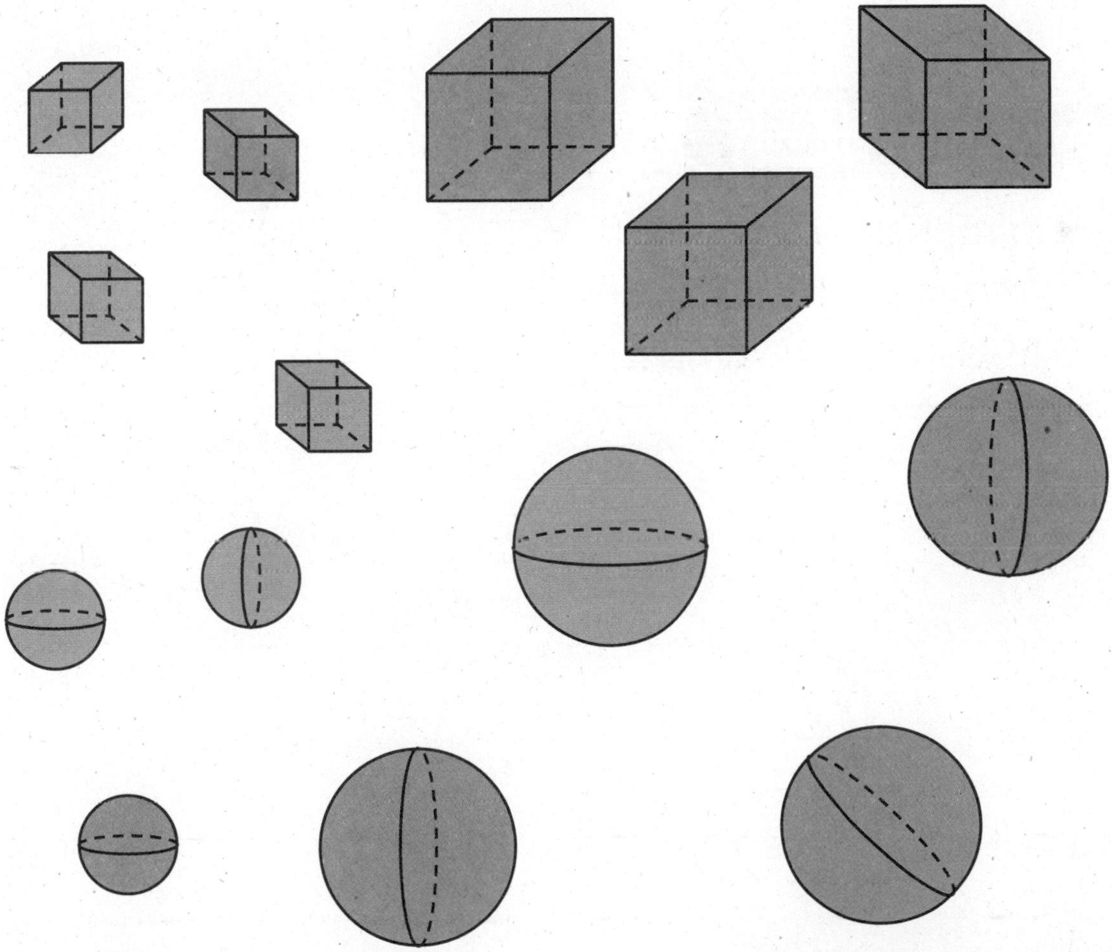

Math Talk MATHEMATICAL PRACTICES 8

Generalize Explain how you sorted the shapes.

FOR THE TEACHER • Have children sort the three-dimensional shapes into two groups. Have them draw around each group to show how they sorted.

Model and Draw

These are three-dimensional shapes.

Why is a cube a special kind of rectangular prism?

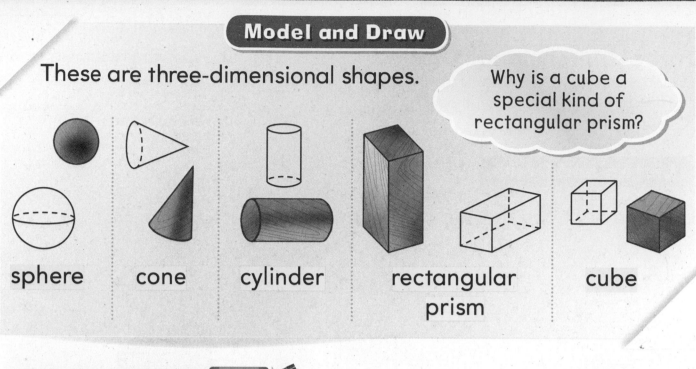

Share and Show

MATH BOARD

Use three-dimensional shapes.
Sort the shapes into three groups.
Name and draw the shapes.

1. only flat surfaces

2. only a curved surface

✓ 3. both flat and curved surfaces

Name ______________________________

On Your Own

MATHEMATICAL PRACTICE 4 **Use Models** Use three-dimensional shapes. Write the number of flat surfaces for each shape.

4. A rectangular prism has 6 flat surfaces.

5. A cube has _____ flat surfaces.

6. A cylinder has _____ flat surfaces.

7. A sphere has _____ flat surfaces.

Exercises 4–7 can help you write the shape names.

GO DEEPER Write to name each shape.

8.

sphere

9.

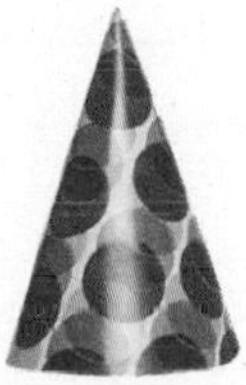

cone

10.

cube

11.

cyinder

12.

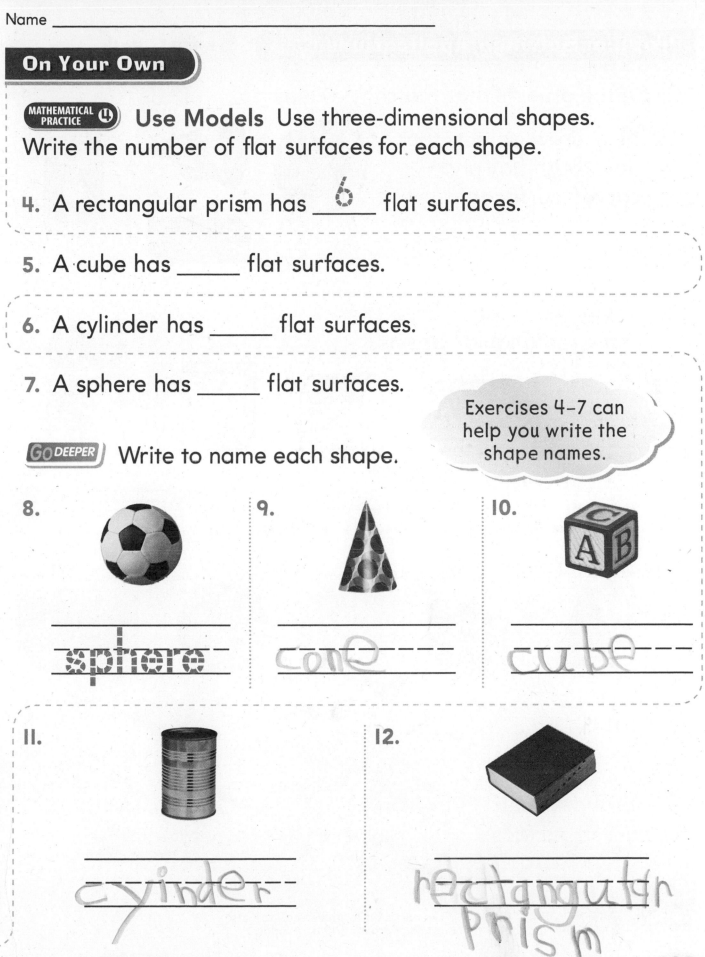

rectangulter prism

Problem Solving • Applications Real World

WRITE Math

Circle the objects that match the clues.

13. Kelly drew objects that have both flat and curved surfaces.

14. THINK SMARTER Sandy drew some rectangular prisms.

Math on the Spot

Personal Math Trainer

15. THINK SMARTER + Match each shape to the group where it belongs.

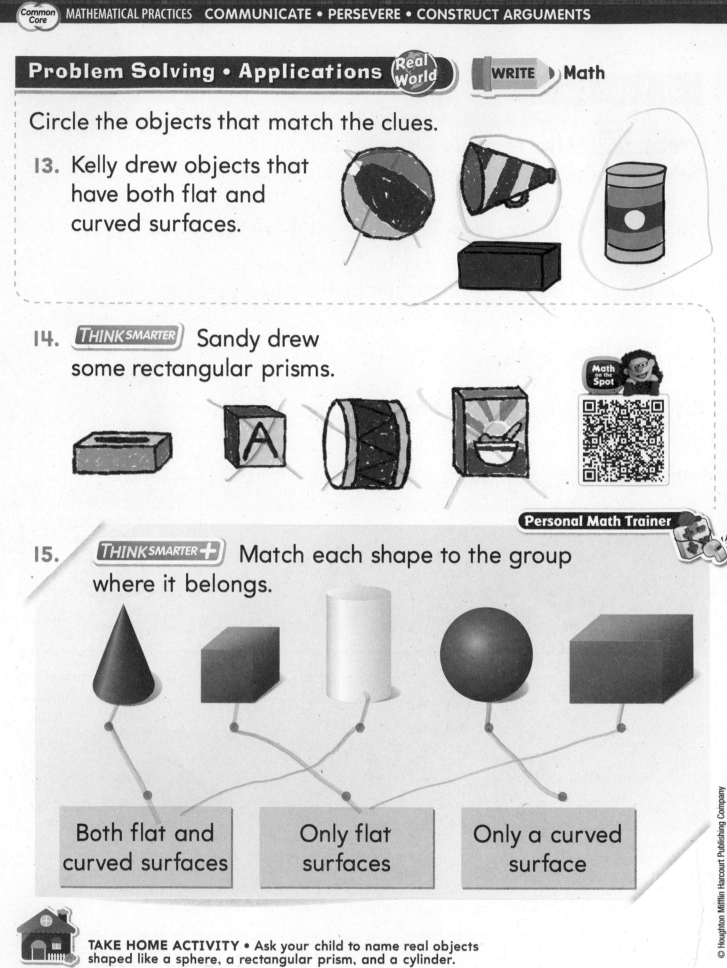

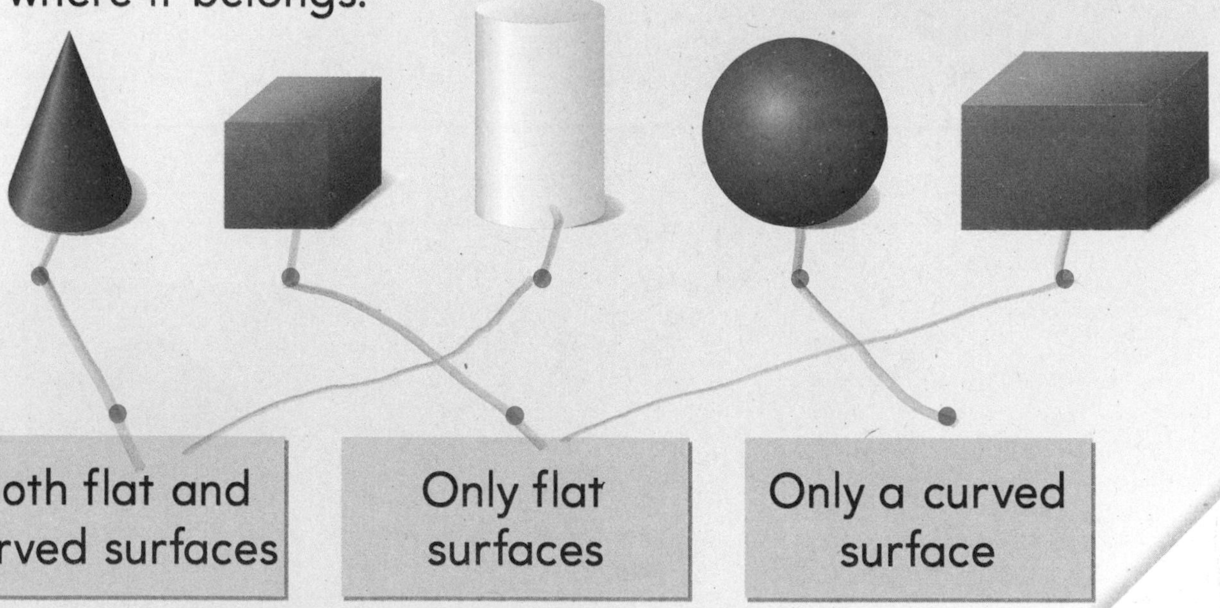

Both flat and curved surfaces	Only flat surfaces	Only a curved surface

TAKE HOME ACTIVITY • Ask your child to name real objects shaped like a sphere, a rectangular prism, and a cylinder.

Name ______________________________

Three-Dimensional Shapes

COMMON CORE STANDARD—1.G.A.1
Reason with shapes and their attributes.

Use three-dimensional shapes. Write the number of flat surfaces for each shape.

1. A cylinder has __ flat surfaces.

2. A rectangular prism has __ flat surfaces.

3. A cone has __ flat surface.

4. A cube has __ flat surfaces.

Problem Solving Real World

5. Circle the object that matches the clue.
Mike finds an object that has only a curved surface.

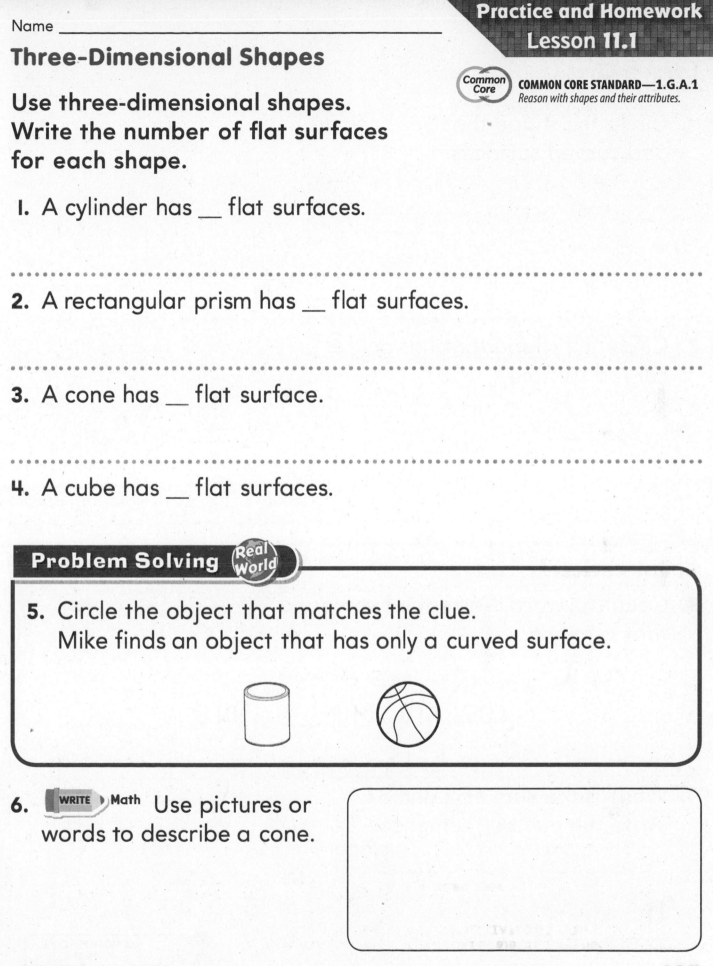

6. WRITE Math Use pictures or words to describe a cone.

Lesson Check (1.G.A.1)

1. Circle the shape that has both flat and curved surfaces.

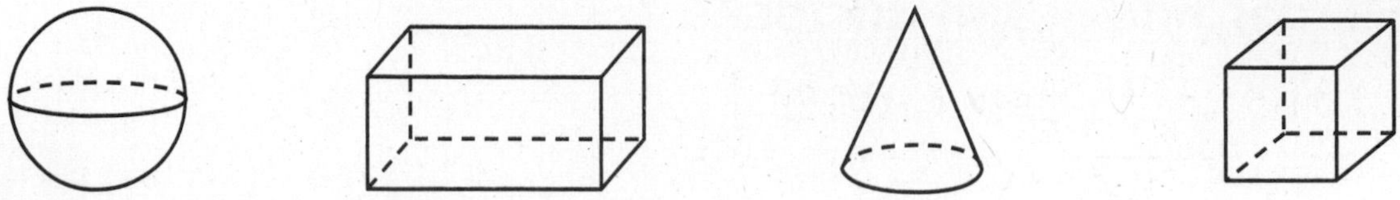

2. Circle the shape that has only a curved surface.

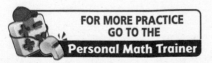

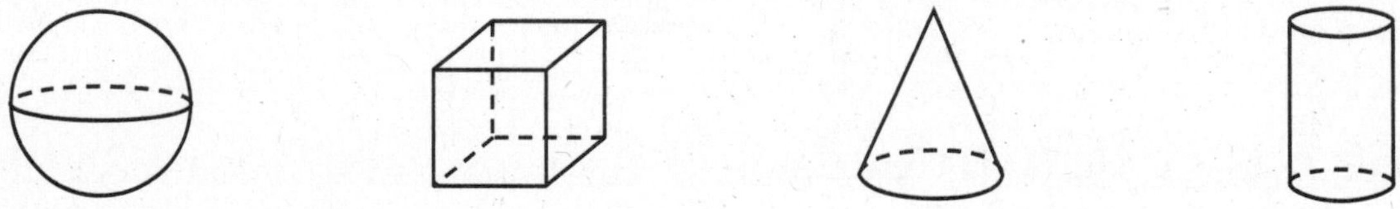

Spiral Review (1.OA.C.6, 1.NBT.A.1)

3. Count forward. Write the number that is missing.

109, 110, 111, ____, 113

4. What is the sum of 2 and 3? Write the number sentence.

____ ◯ ____ = ____

FOR MORE PRACTICE GO TO THE **Personal Math Trainer**

Name ______________________

Combine Three-Dimensional Shapes

Common Core Geometry—1.G.A.2

MATHEMATICAL PRACTICES
MP1, MP2, MP3, MP6

Essential Question How can you combine three-dimensional shapes to make new shapes?

Listen and Draw

Real World

Hands On

Trace to draw the new shape.
Write to name the new shape.

Mandy

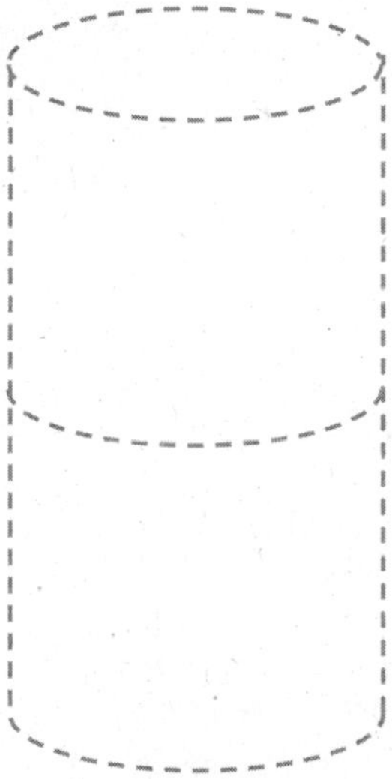

____

Carl

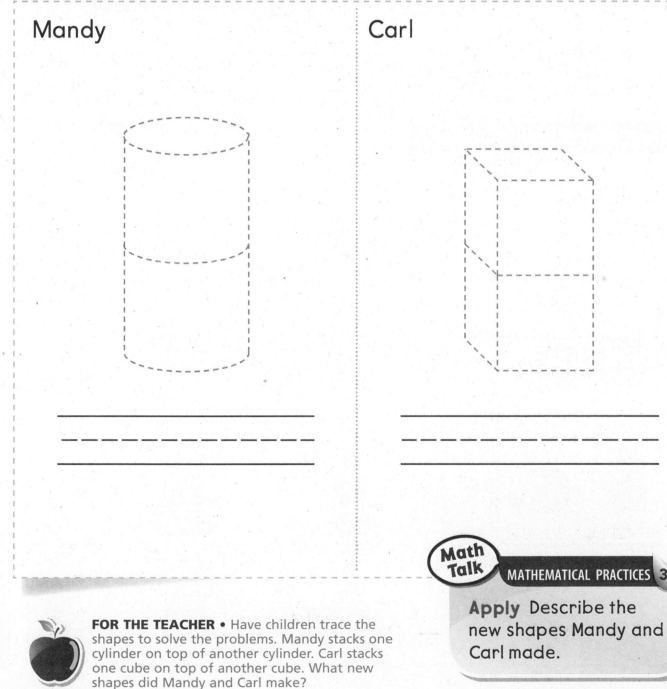

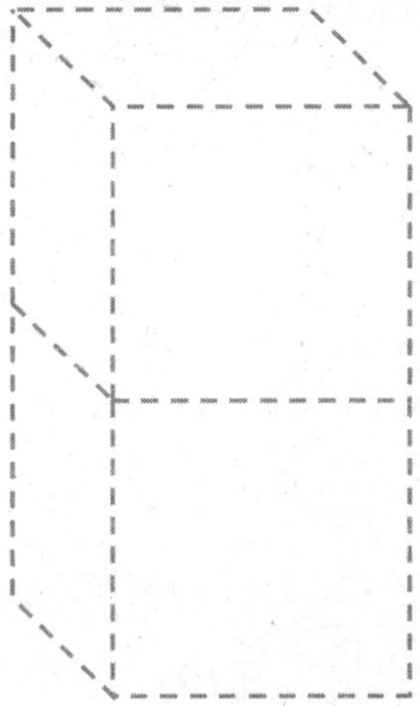

____

Math Talk MATHEMATICAL PRACTICES 3

Apply Describe the new shapes Mandy and Carl made.

FOR THE TEACHER • Have children trace the shapes to solve the problems. Mandy stacks one cylinder on top of another cylinder. Carl stacks one cube on top of another cube. What new shapes did Mandy and Carl make?

Model and Draw

You can put shapes together to make a new shape.

What other new shapes could you make?

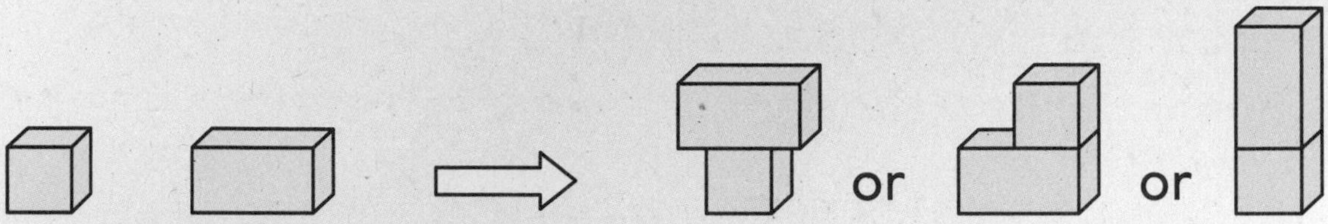

Share and Show MATH BOARD

Use three-dimensional shapes.

Combine.	Which new shape can you make? Circle it.
1. 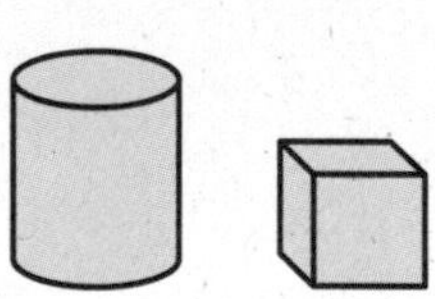	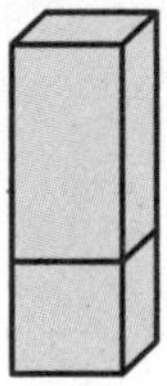 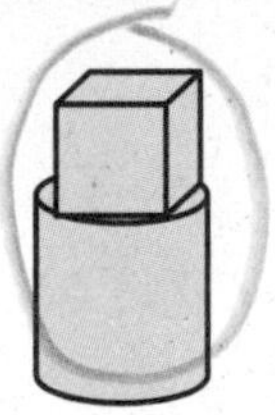
2. 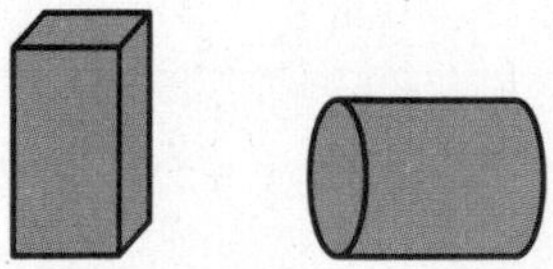	 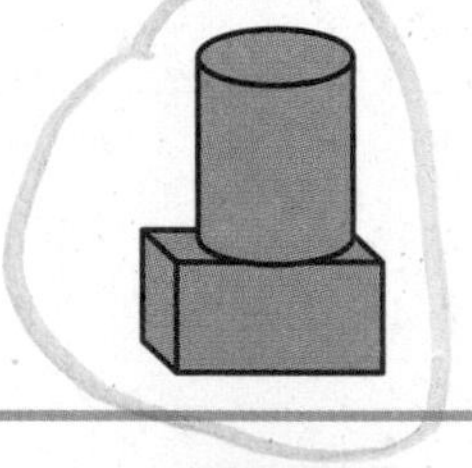
3. 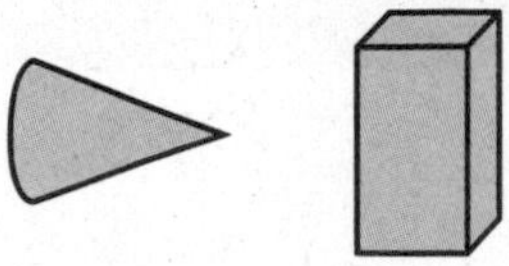	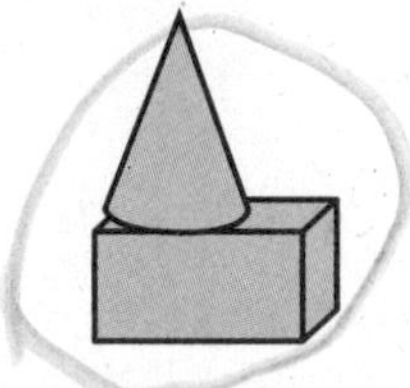 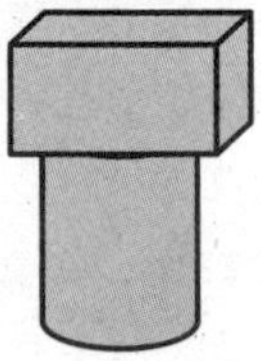

Name ______________________________

On Your Own

MATHEMATICAL PRACTICE 6 **Attend to Precision**

Use three-dimensional shapes.

Combine.	Which new shape can you make? Circle it.
4. 	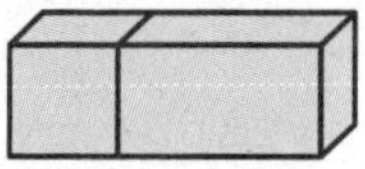 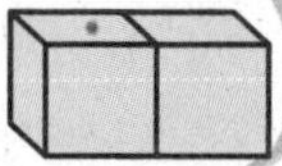
5. 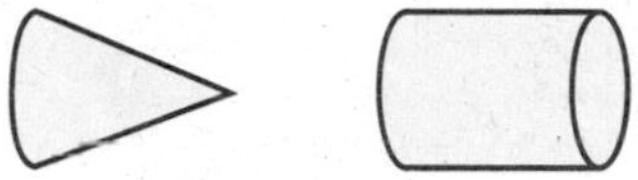	 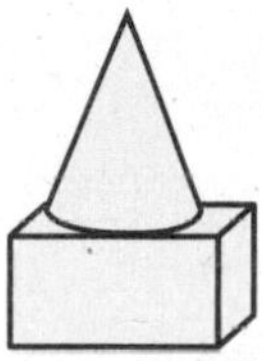
6. 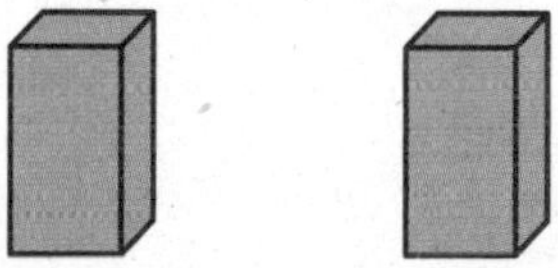	 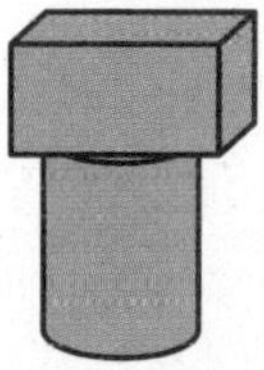
7. 	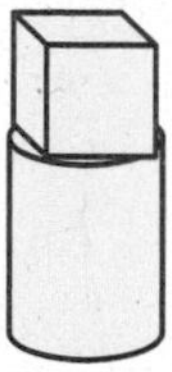 
8. THINK SMARTER 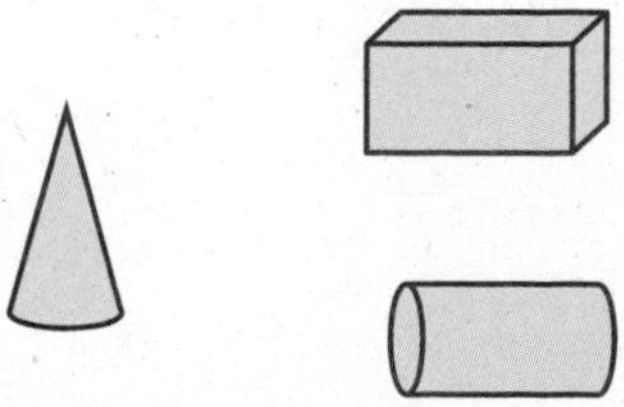	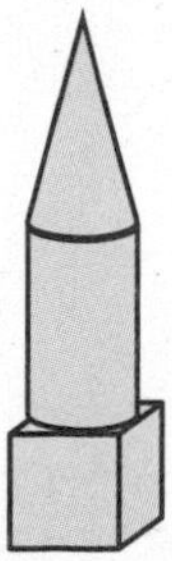 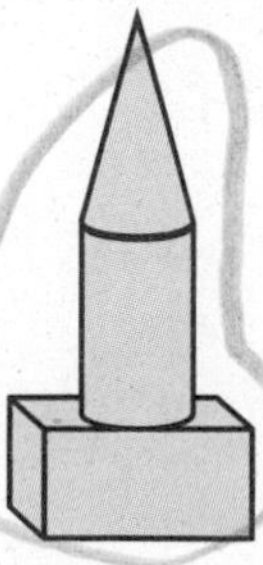

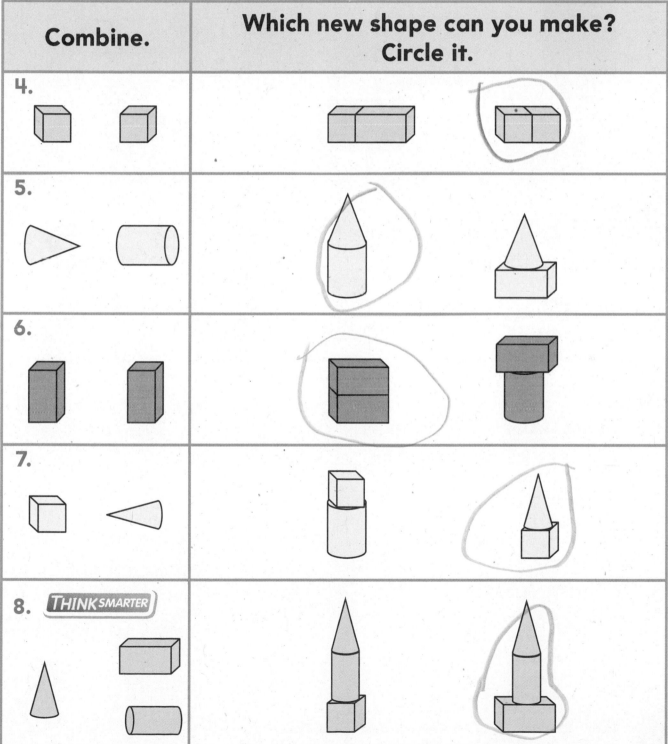

Problem Solving • Applications Real World WRITE Math

GO DEEPER Circle the shapes you could use to model the ice cream cone.

9.

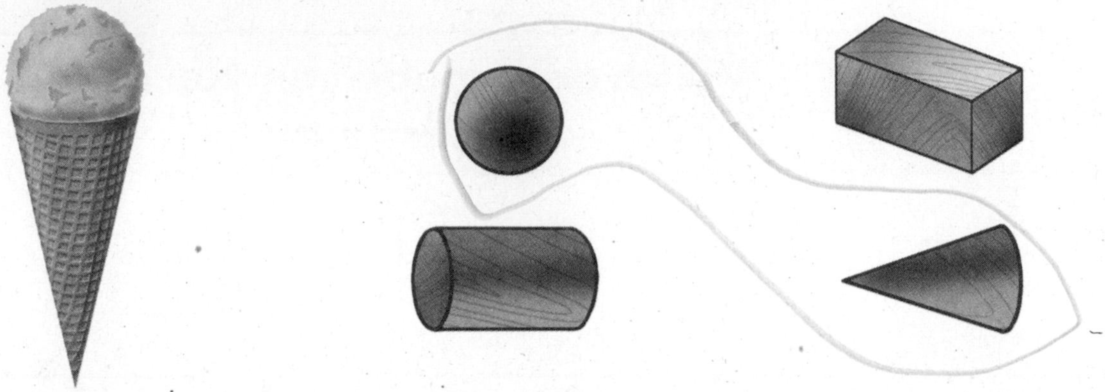

10. THINK SMARTER Circle the ways that make the same shape.

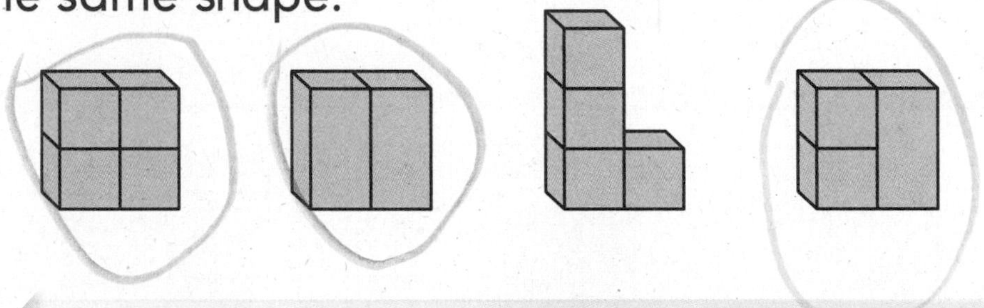

11. THINK SMARTER Combine 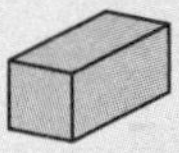 and .
Choose all the new shapes you can make.

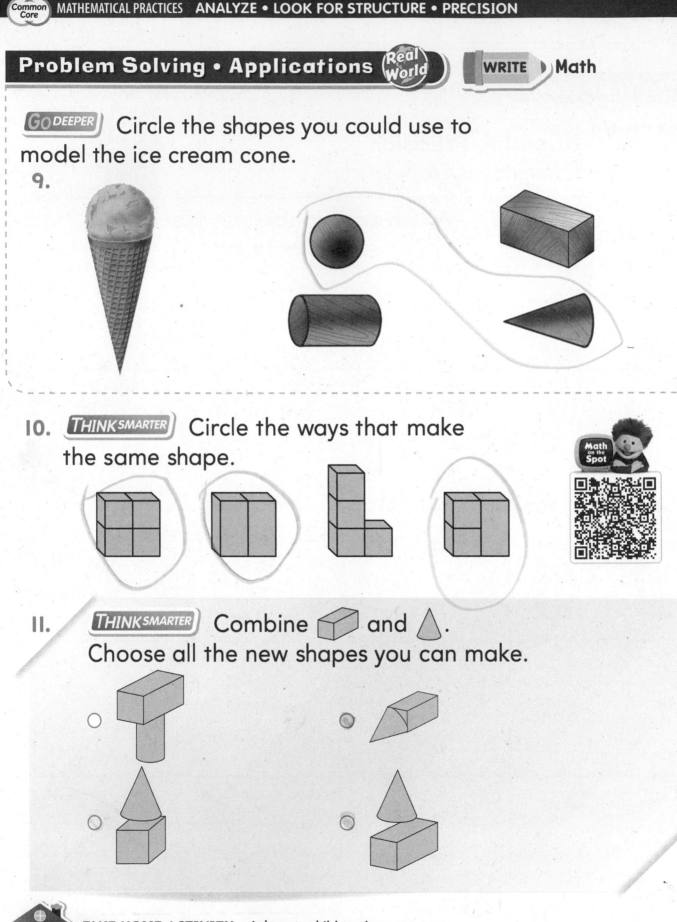

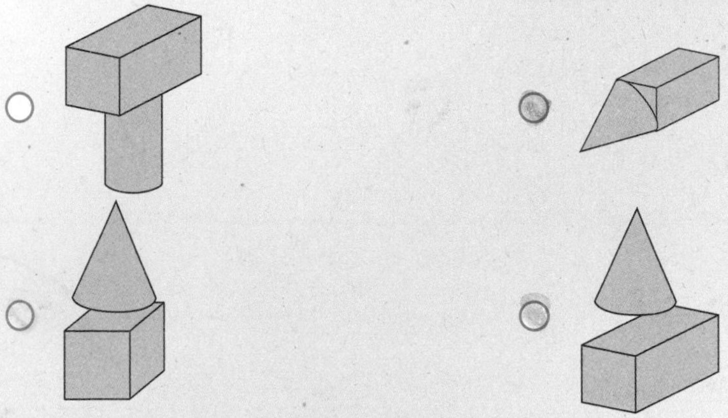

TAKE HOME ACTIVITY • Ask your child to show you two different new shapes he or she can make by combining a soup can and a cereal box.

Name ______________________________

Practice and Homework
Lesson 11.2

Combine Three-Dimensional Shapes

Common Core **COMMON CORE STANDARD—1.G.A.2**
Reason with shapes and their attributes.

Use three-dimensional shapes.

Combine.	Which new shape can you make? Circle it.
1. 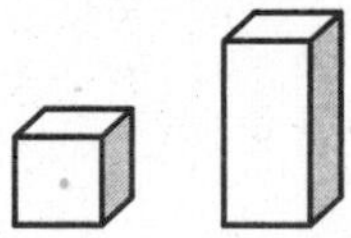	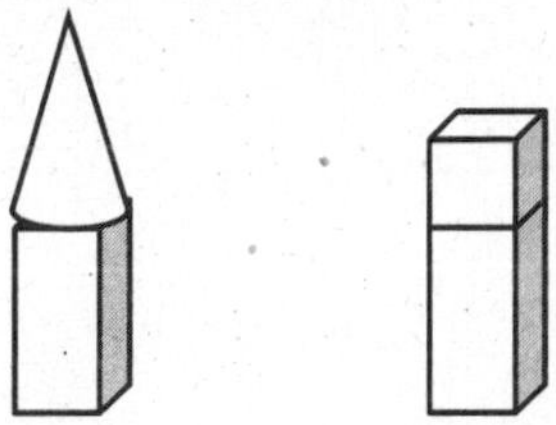
2. 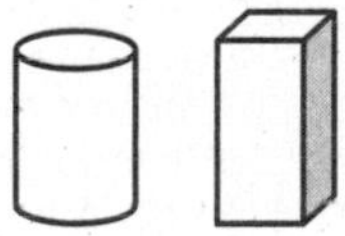	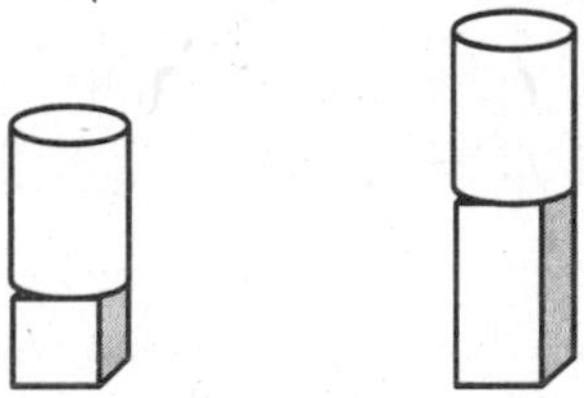

Problem Solving Real World

3. Circle the shapes you could use to model the bird feeder.

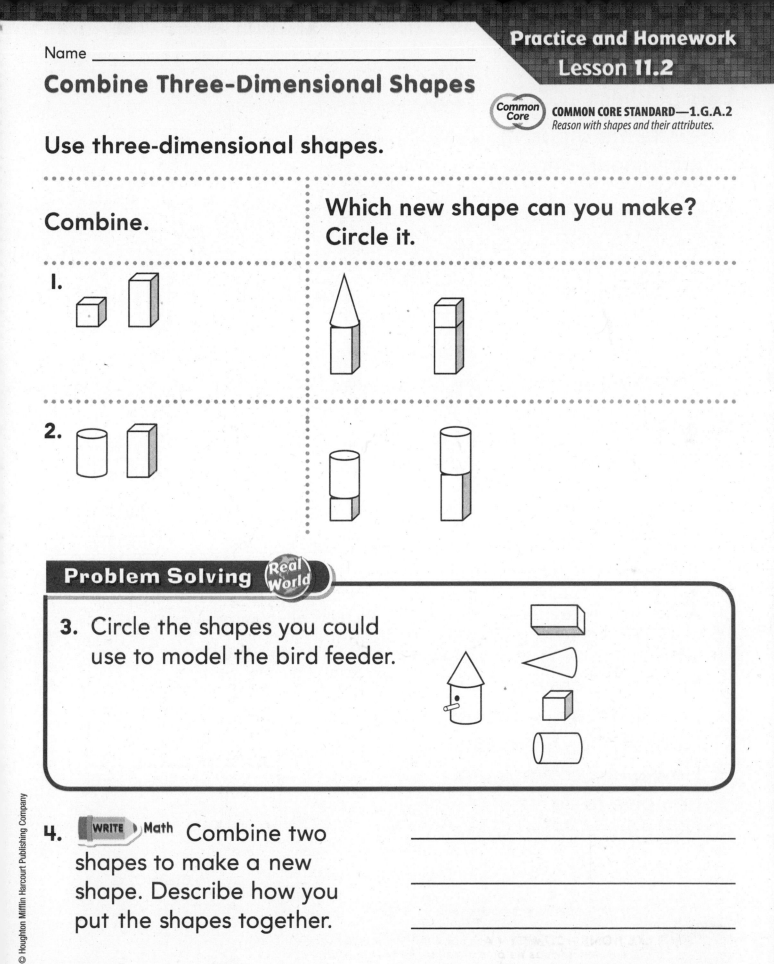

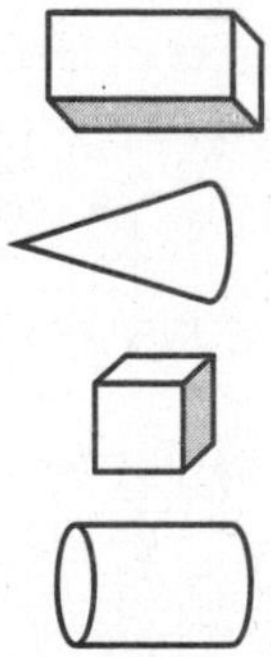

4. WRITE Math Combine two shapes to make a new shape. Describe how you put the shapes together.

____

____

____

____

Lesson Check (1.G.A.2)

1. Circle the shape that combines ⬭ and △.

· ·

Spiral Review (1.OA.A.1, 1.NBT.C.4)

2. Write the sum. Write how many tens.

40 + 20 = ___ ___ tens

· ·

3. Emi has 15 crayons.
She gives some crayons to Jo.
Now she has 9 crayons.
How many crayons did
Emi give to Jo?
Use the model to solve.

___ crayons

FOR MORE PRACTICE
GO TO THE
Personal Math Trainer

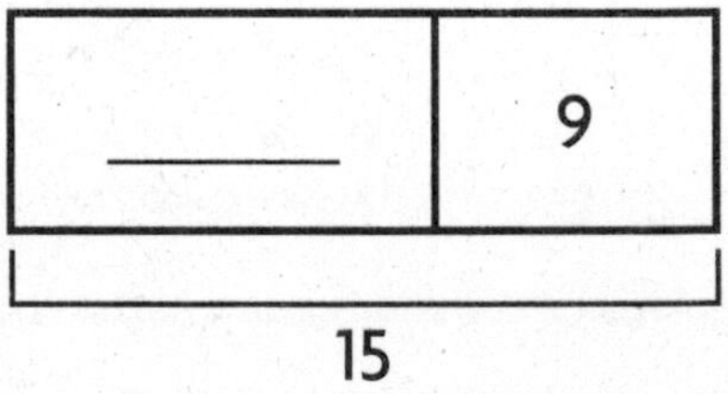

Name ______________________________

HANDS ON
Lesson 11.3

Make New Three-Dimensional Shapes

Essential Question How can you use a combined shape to build new shapes?

Common Core **Geometry—1.G.A.2**

MATHEMATICAL PRACTICES
MP1, MP2, MP3, MP5

Listen and Draw Real World

Draw to copy the shape.

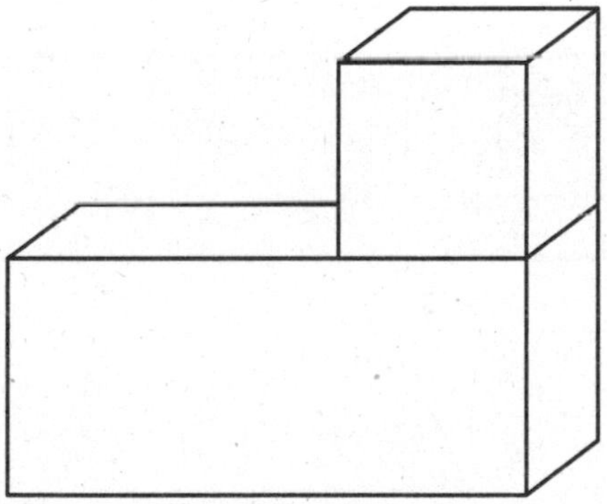

FOR THE TEACHER • Leila put a box on top of another box. Draw to copy the new shape Leila made.

Math Talk MATHEMATICAL PRACTICES 1

Describe how to draw to copy the new shape.

Model and Draw

Circle a new shape you can make. **Explain** why you cannot make the other shape.

Step 1 Build. **Step 2** Repeat. **Step 3** Combine.

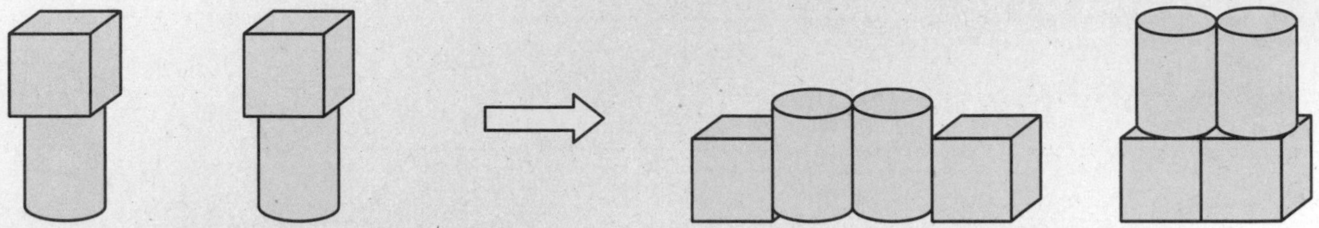

Share and Show MATH BOARD

Use three-dimensional shapes.

Build and Repeat.	Combine. Which new shape can you make? Circle it.
1. 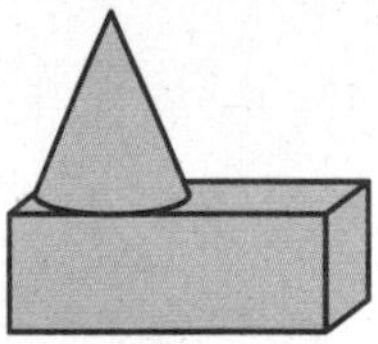	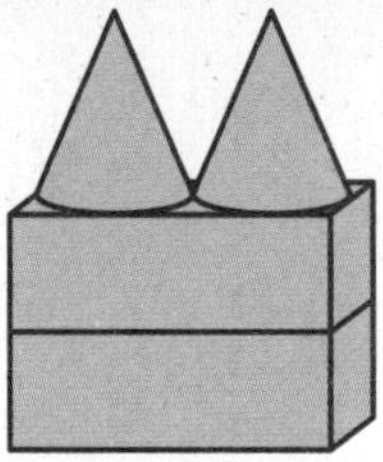 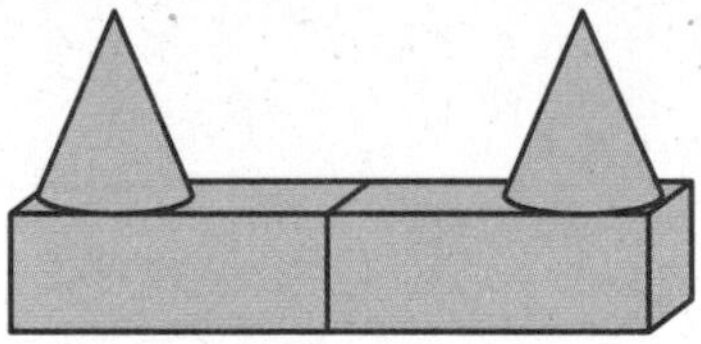
✓2. 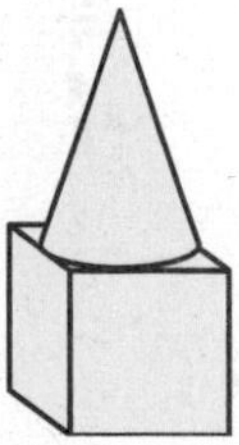	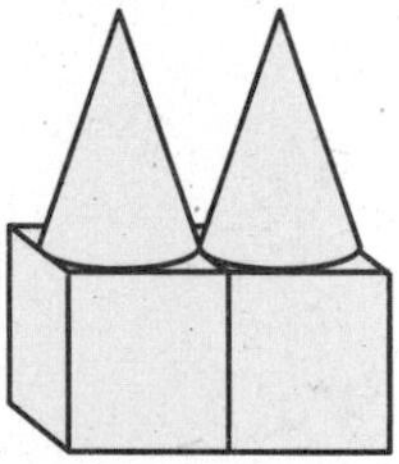 
✓3. 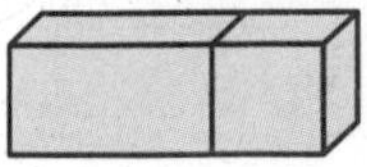	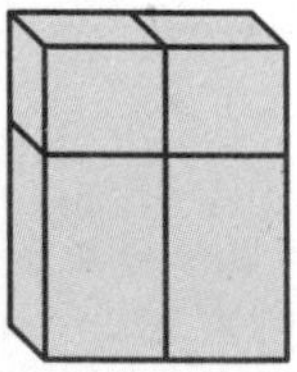 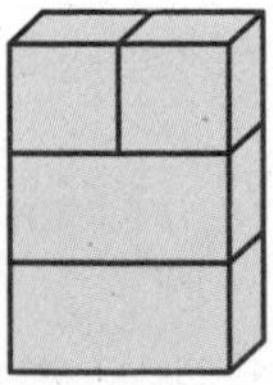

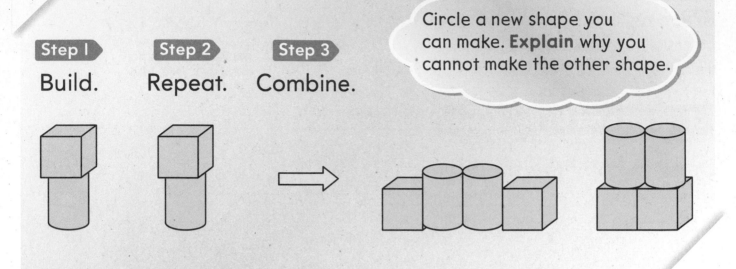

Name ______________________________

On Your Own

MATHEMATICAL PRACTICE 5 **Use a Concrete Model**

Use three-dimensional shapes.

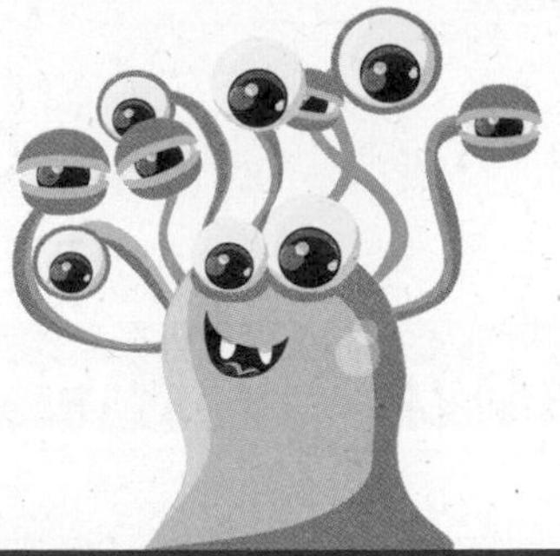

Build and Repeat.	Combine. Which new shape can you make? Circle it.
4. 	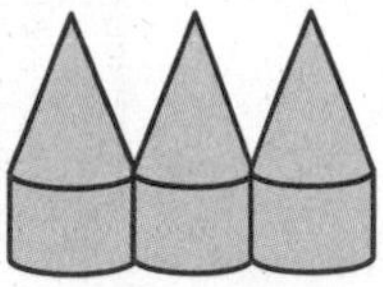 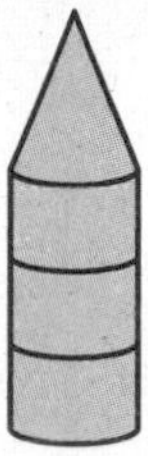
5. 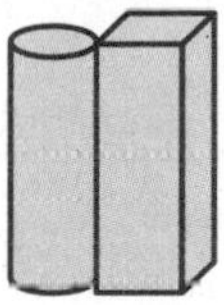	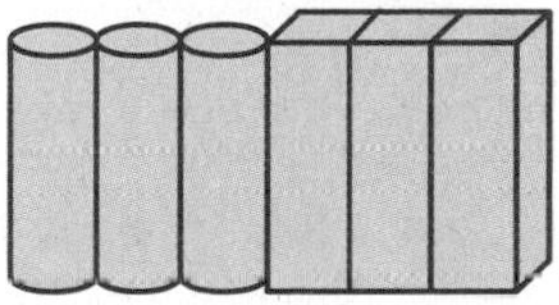 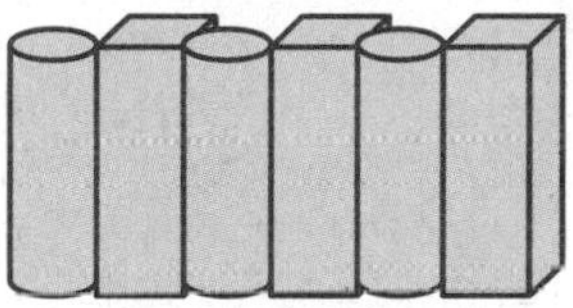
6. 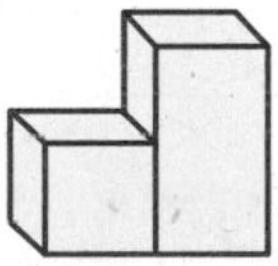	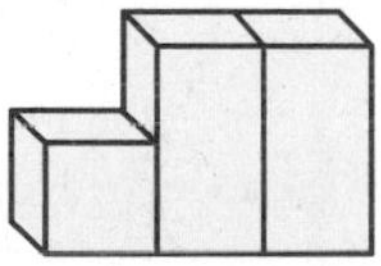 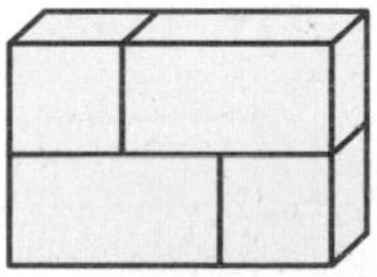

7. THINK SMARTER Look at the shape.

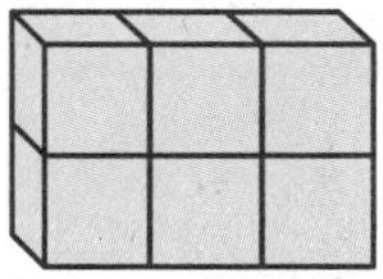

How many  are used to make the shape?

_____ 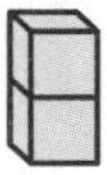 make the shape.

How many  are used to make the shape?

_____  make the shape.

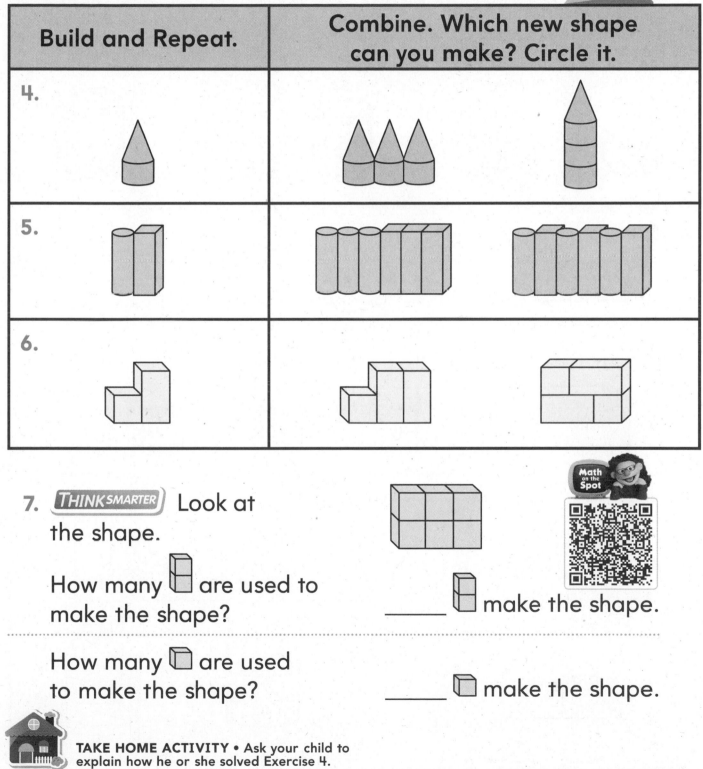

TAKE HOME ACTIVITY • Ask your child to explain how he or she solved Exercise 4.

Name ____________________

Mid-Chapter Checkpoint

Personal Math Trainer
Online Assessment and Intervention

Concepts and Skills

1. Circle the rectangular prisms. (1.G.A.1)
2. Draw a line under the shapes that have both flat and curved surfaces. (1.G.A.1)

Use three-dimensional shapes. (1.G.A.2)

Combine.	Which new shape can you make? Circle it.
3. 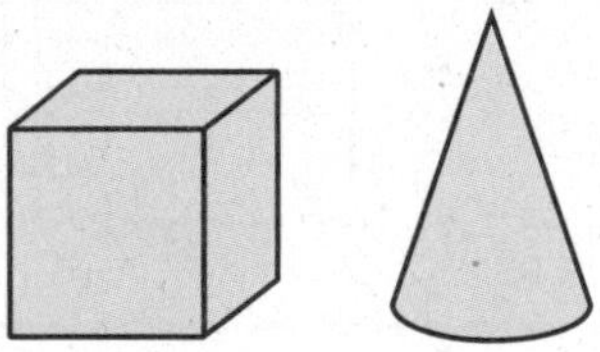	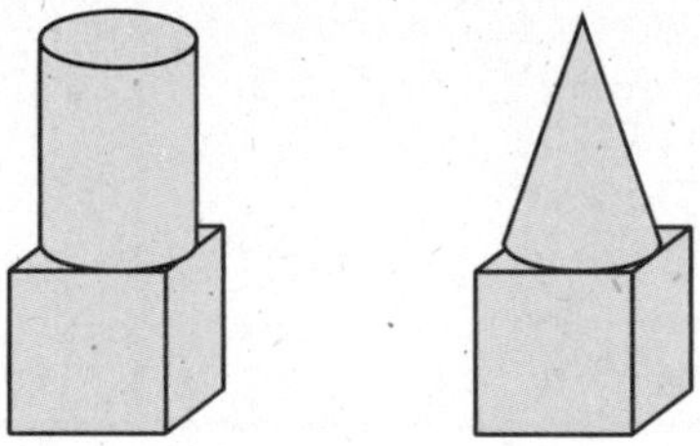

4. THINK SMARTER Which new shape can you make? (1.G.A.2)

Combine 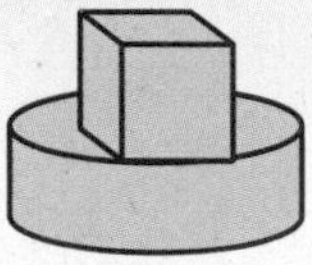 and 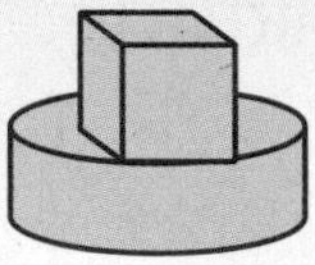.

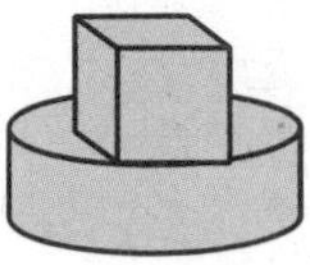 ○
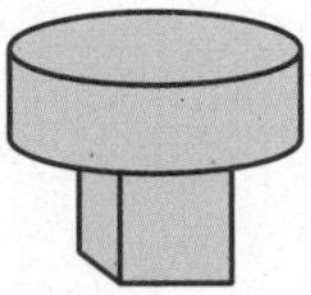 ○
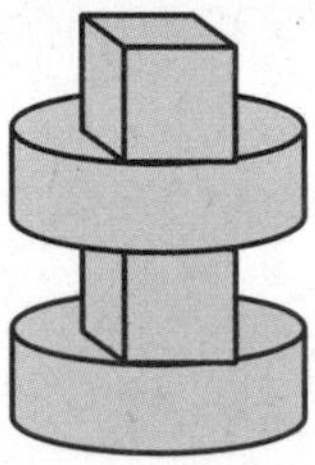 ○
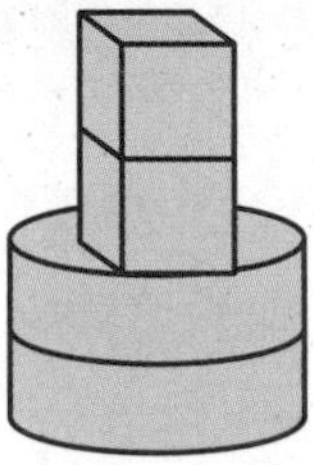 ○

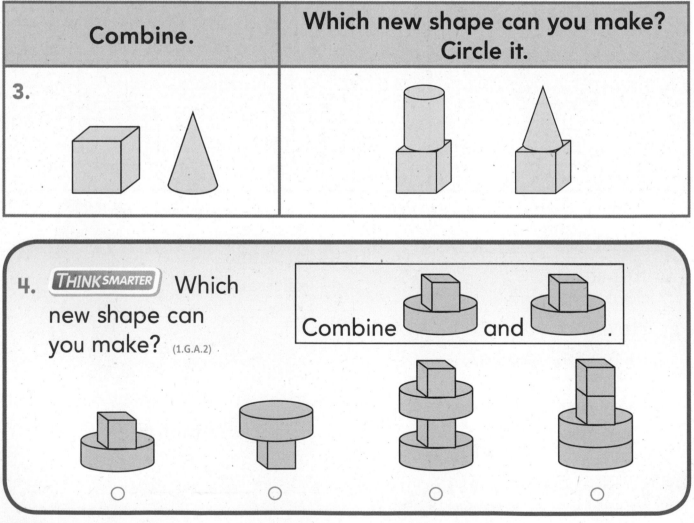

Name ____________________

Make New Three-Dimensional Shapes

Common Core

COMMON CORE STANDARD—1.G.A.2
Reason with shapes and their attributes.

Use three-dimensional shapes.

Build and Repeat.	Combine. Which new shape can you make? Circle it.
1. 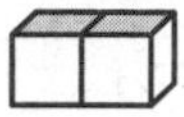	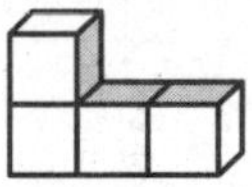 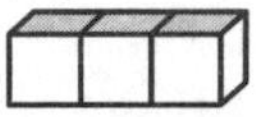
2. 	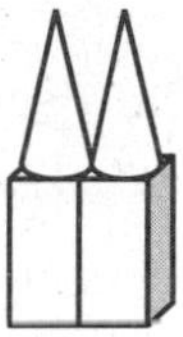 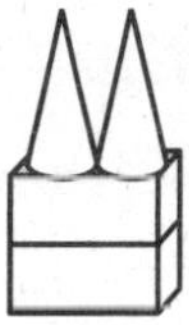

Problem Solving Real World

3. Dave builds this shape. Then he repeats and combines. Draw a shape he can make.

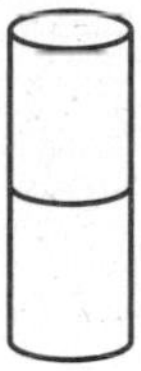

4. WRITE Math Use a cube and a cylinder to build a new shape. Repeat. Draw to show how you can combine these two new shapes to make a larger shape.

Lesson Check (1.G.A.2)

1. Which new shape can you make? Circle the shape.

Combine 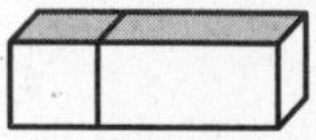 and 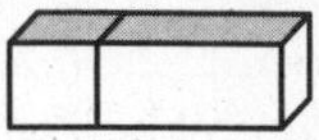.

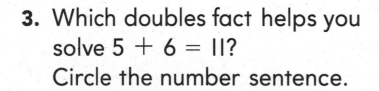

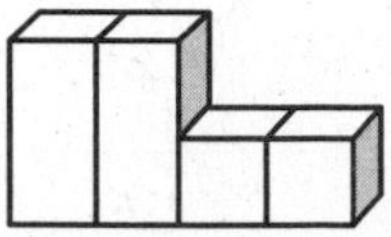

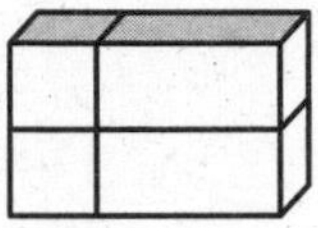

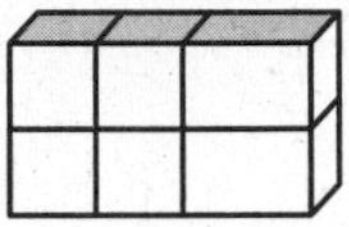

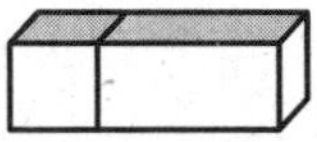

Spiral Review (1.OA.B.4, 1.OA.C.6)

2. Which addition fact helps you solve 15 − 6 = ____? Write the number sentence.

____ + ____ = ____

3. Which doubles fact helps you solve 5 + 6 = 11? Circle the number sentence.

3 + 3 = 6   4 + 4 = 8

5 + 5 = 10   7 + 7 = 14

Name ______________________________

Problem Solving • Take Apart Three-Dimensional Shapes

Essential Question How can acting it out help you take apart combined shapes?

Common Core **Geometry—1.G.A.2**

MATHEMATICAL PRACTICES
MP1, MP6, MP7, MP8

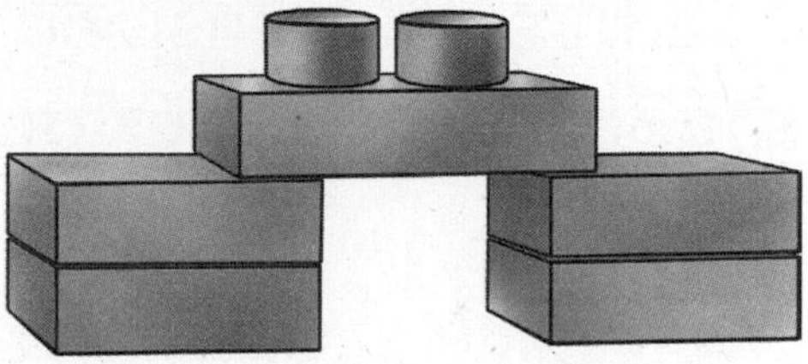

Mike has , 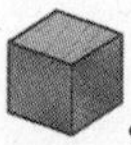, , and . He chose some shapes to build a bridge. Which shapes did Mike use to build the bridge?

Unlock the Problem (Real World)

What do I need to find?

which shapes Mike chose to build the bridge

What information do I need to use?

Mike has these shapes.

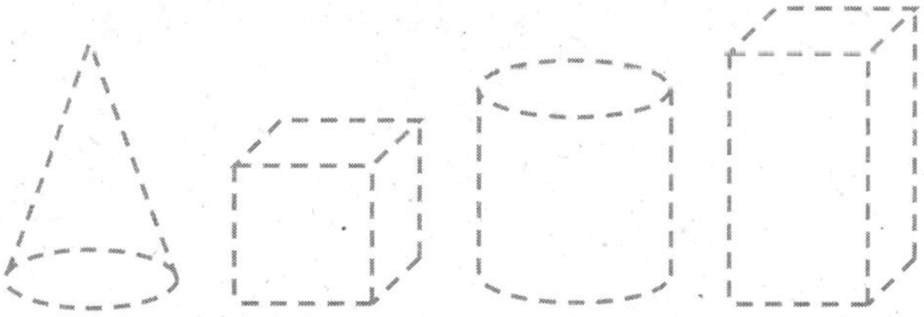

Show how to solve the problem.

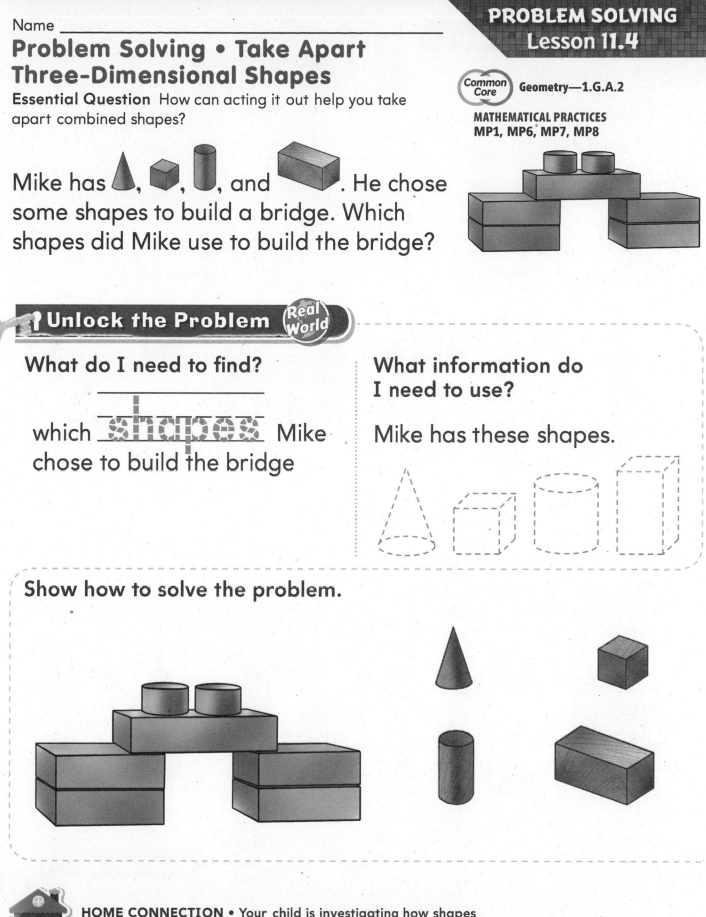

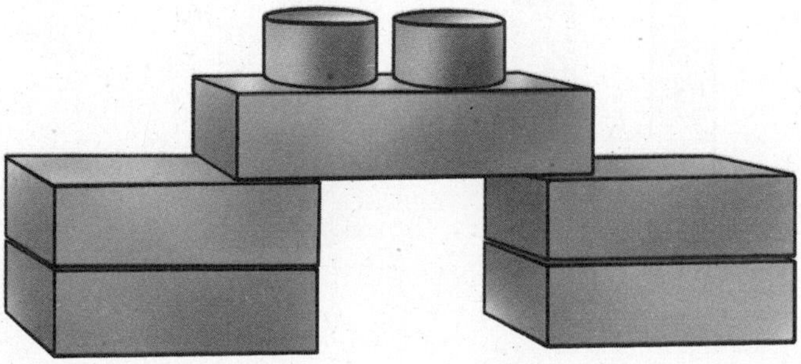

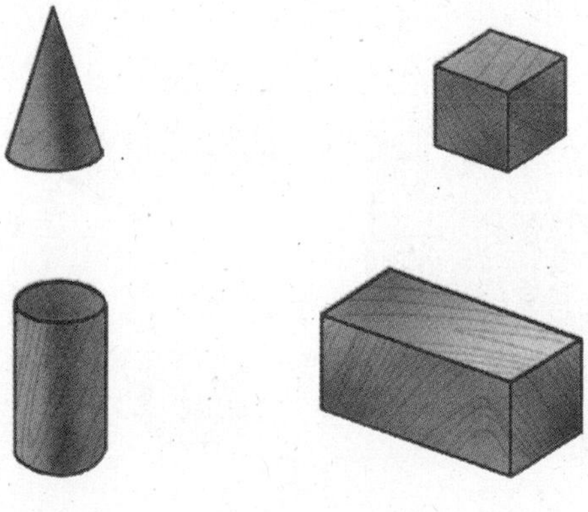

HOME CONNECTION • Your child is investigating how shapes can be taken apart. Being able to decompose shapes into smaller parts provides a foundation for future work with fractions.

Try Another Problem

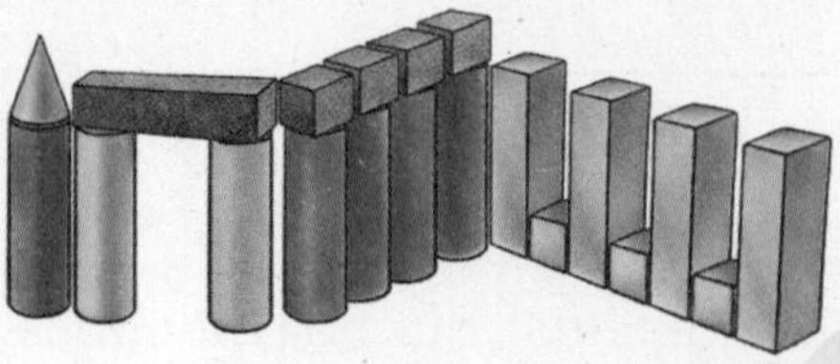

Kim used shapes to build this castle.

Use three-dimensional shapes. Circle your answer.

- What do I need to find?
- What information do I need to use?

1. Which shapes did Kim use to build the tower?

2. Which shapes did Kim use to build this wall?

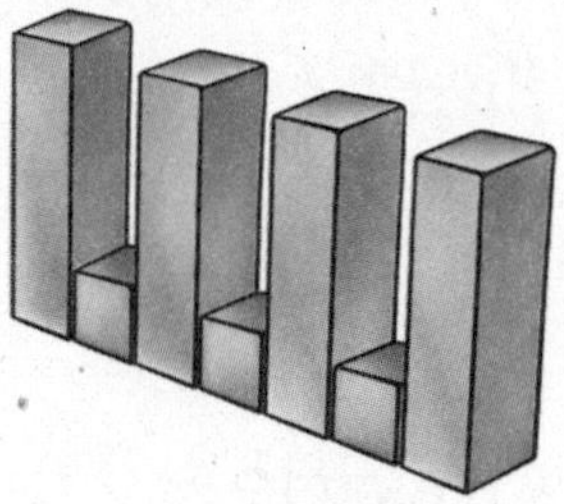

3. Which shapes did Kim use to build this wall?

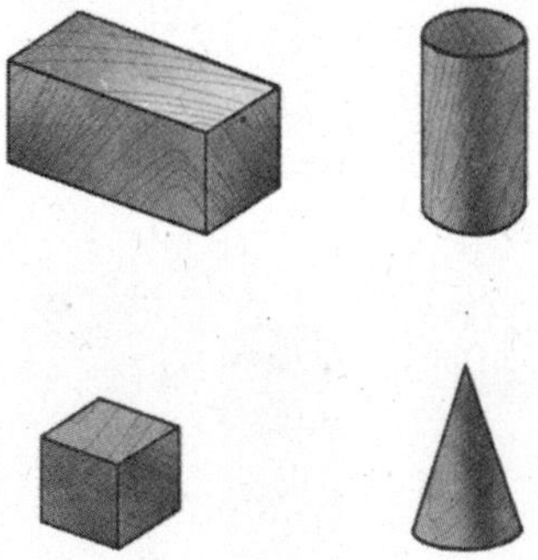

4. Which shapes did Kim use to build the gate?

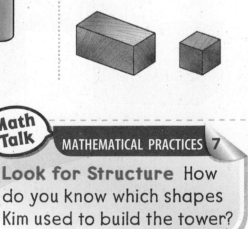

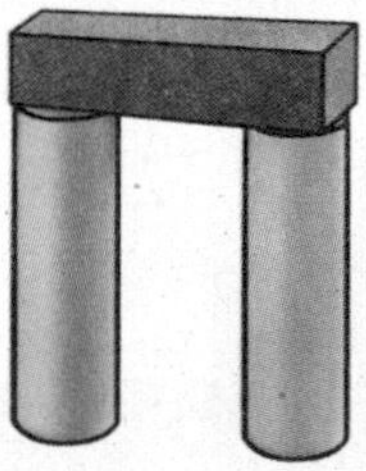

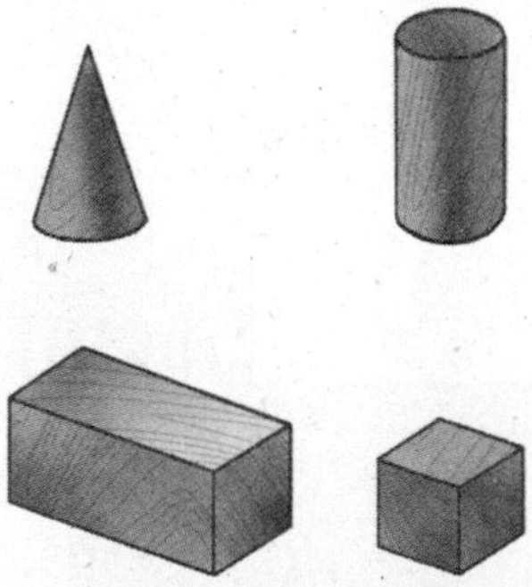

Math Talk — MATHEMATICAL PRACTICES 7

Look for Structure How do you know which shapes Kim used to build the tower?

Name ______________________________

Share and Show MATH BOARD

MATHEMATICAL PRACTICE 1 **Analyze** Use three-dimensional shapes. Circle your answer.

5. Zack used shapes to build this gate. Which shapes did Zack use?

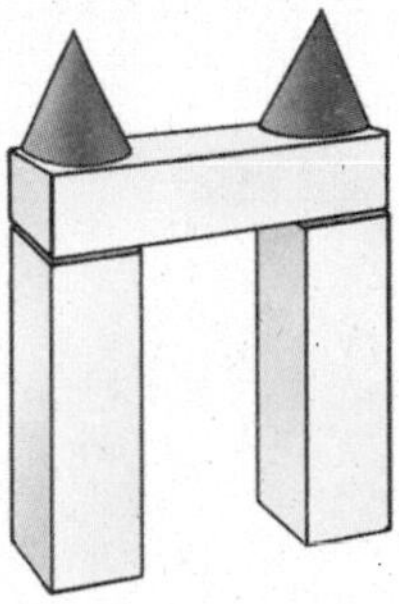

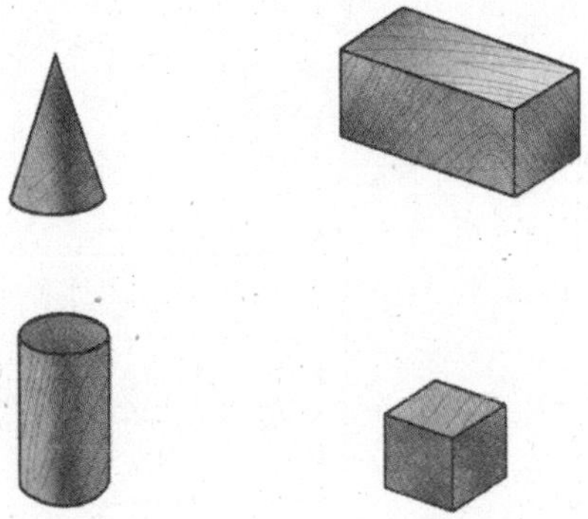

6. Chris used shapes to build this wall. Which shapes did Chris use?

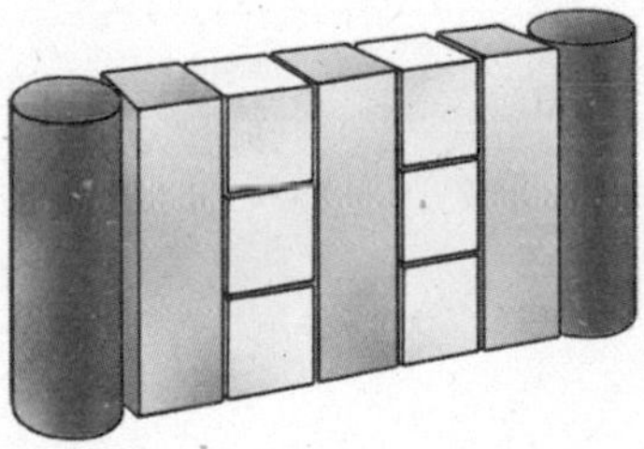

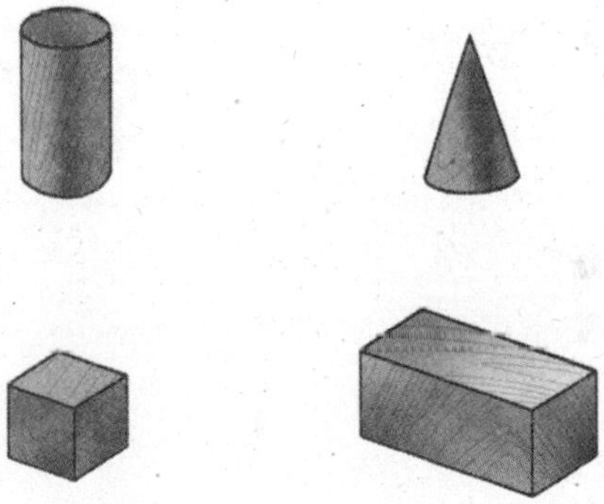

7. THINK SMARTER Rosa uses , , , and  to build a tower. Draw to show a tower Rosa could build.

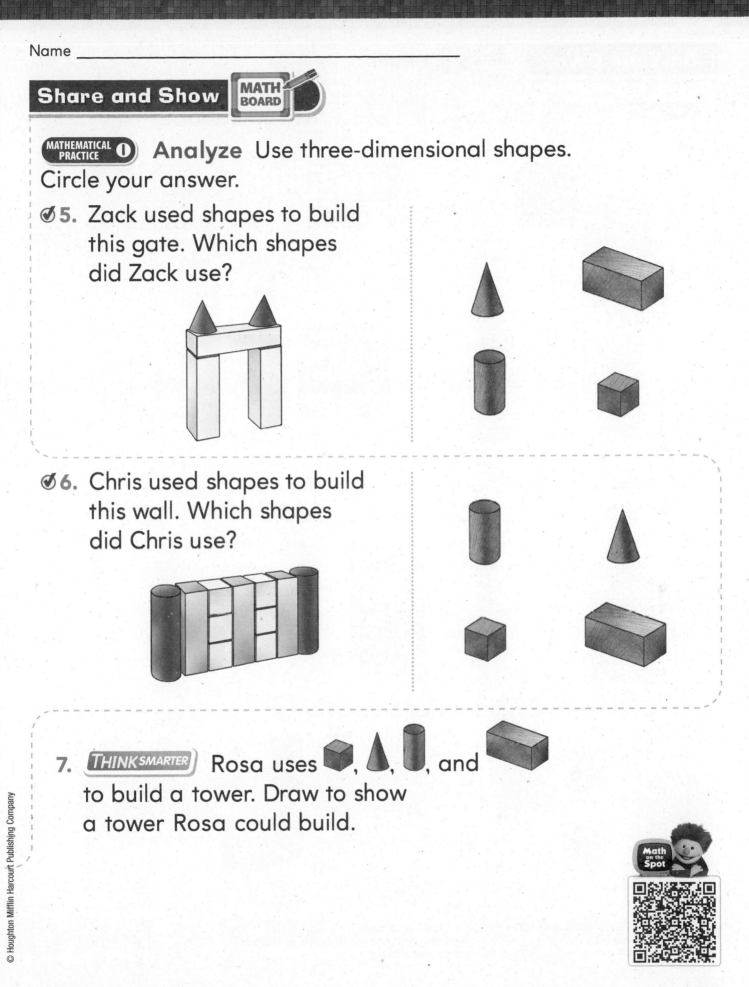

Math on the Spot

On Your Own

WRITE Math

GO DEEPER Circle the ways that show the same shape.

8.

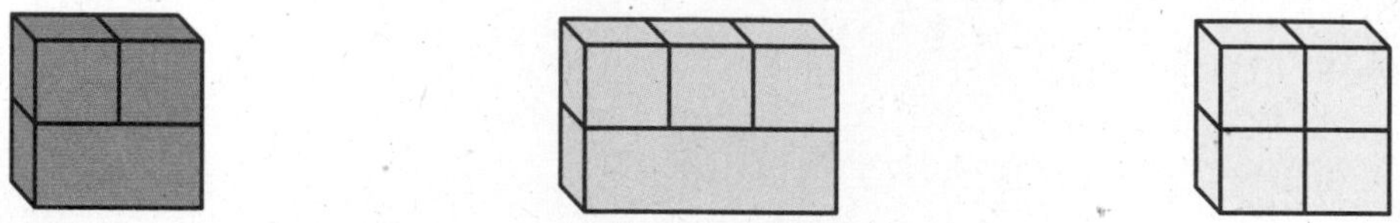

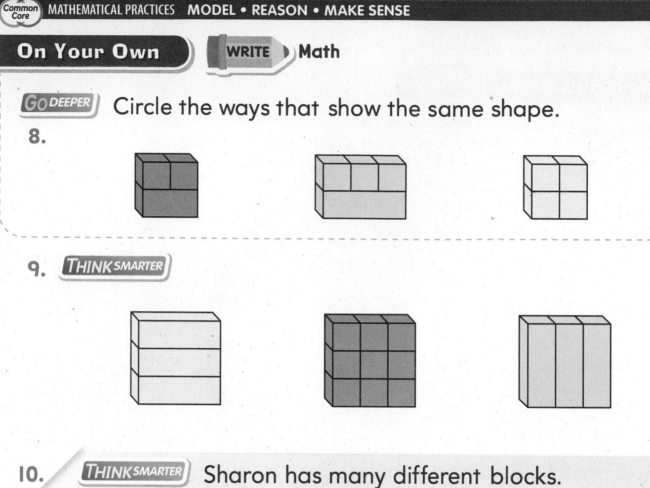

9. THINK SMARTER

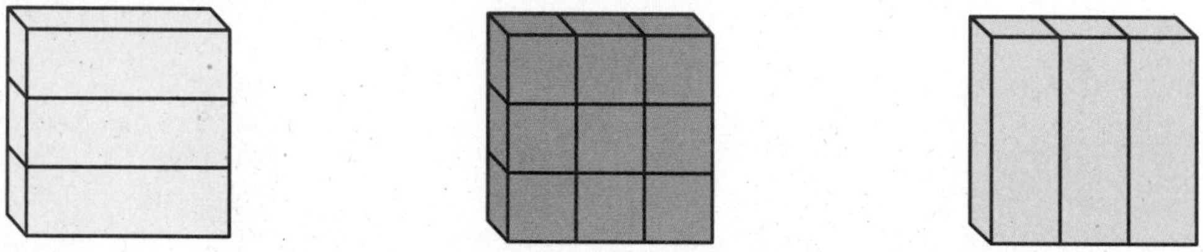

10. THINK SMARTER Sharon has many different blocks. She built this shape with her blocks.

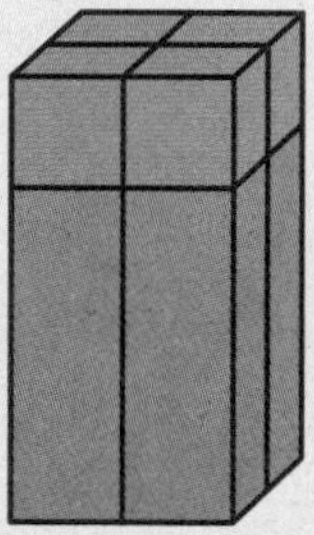

Choose all the shapes Sharon used.

○ 

○ 

○ 

○ 

TAKE HOME ACTIVITY • Use real items such as a soup can (cylinder) and a cereal box (rectangular prism) to build a shape. Ask your child to name the shapes you used.

Name ____________________________

Problem Solving • Take Apart Three-Dimensional Shapes

COMMON CORE STANDARD—1.G.A.2
Reason with shapes and their attributes.

Use three-dimensional shapes. Circle your answer.

1. Paco used shapes to build this robot. Circle the shapes he used.

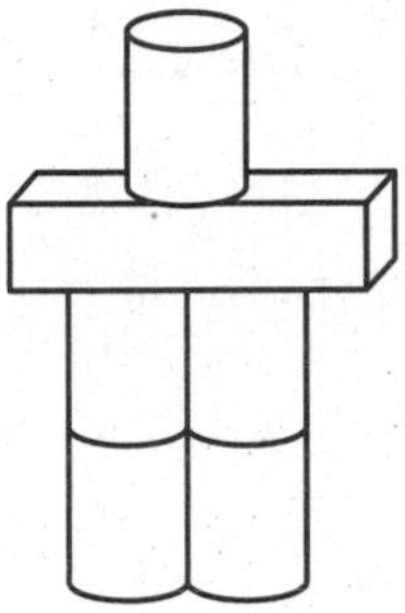

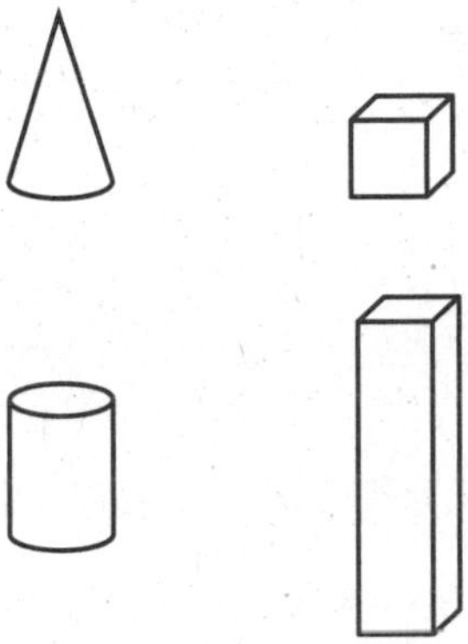

Problem Solving Real World

2. Circle the ways that show the same shape.

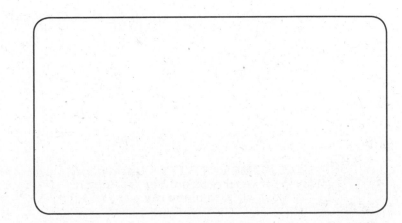

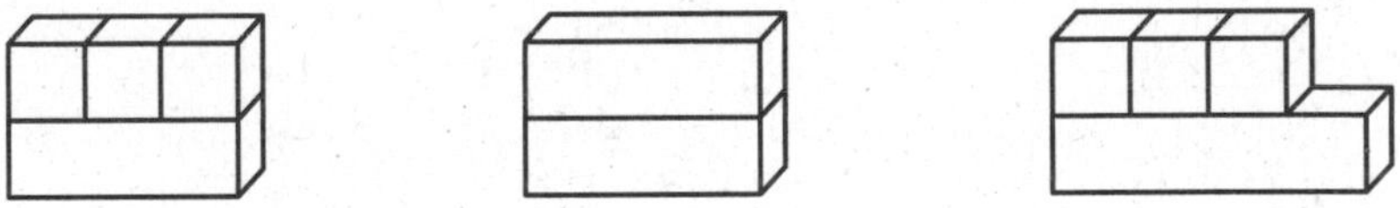

3. WRITE Math Draw a picture of a house made from shapes. Write the shape names you used.

Lesson Check (1.G.A.2)

1. Lara made this picture frame. Circle the shapes she used to make the frame.

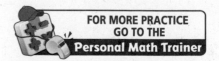

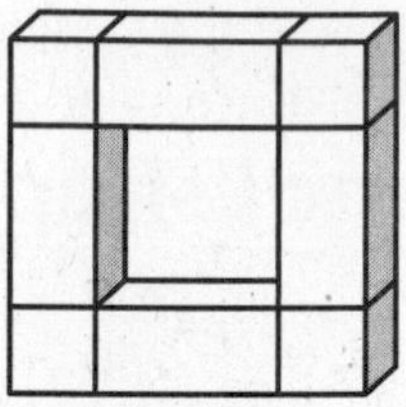

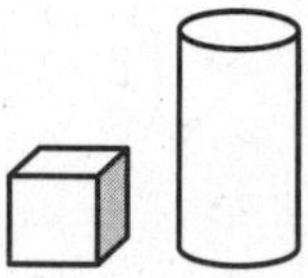 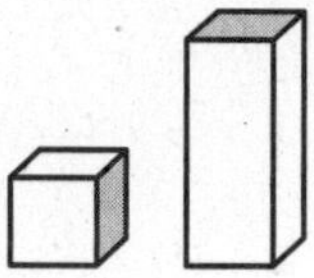 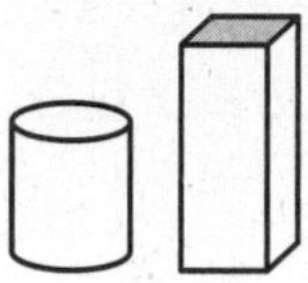 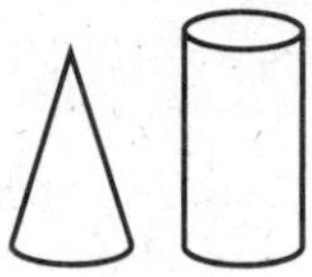

Spiral Review (1.NBT.B.3, 1.NBT.C.6)

2. Compare each pair of numbers. Write <, >, or =.

13 ◯ 31 | 13 ◯ 13 | 31 ◯ 13 | 31 ◯ 31

3. Subtract. What is the difference? Write the number.

$$60 - 30 = \_\_\_\_$$

Name ____________________

Two-Dimensional Shapes on Three-Dimensional Shapes

Essential Question What two-dimensional shapes do you see on the flat surfaces of three-dimensional shapes?

Common Core Geometry—1.G.A.1

MATHEMATICAL PRACTICES
MP1, MP4, MP6

Listen and Draw

Real World

Hands On

Use a cone.

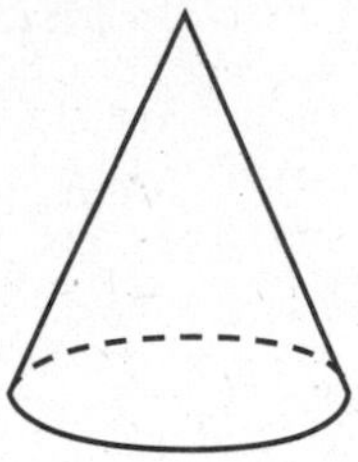

Math Talk MATHEMATICAL PRACTICES 1

Analyze What other shape could you use to draw the same kind of picture?

FOR THE TEACHER • Read the following problem and have children use the workspace to act it out. Lee places a cone on a piece of paper and draws around its flat surface. What did Lee draw?

Model and Draw

Trace around the flat surfaces of the three-dimensional shape to find the two-dimensional shapes.

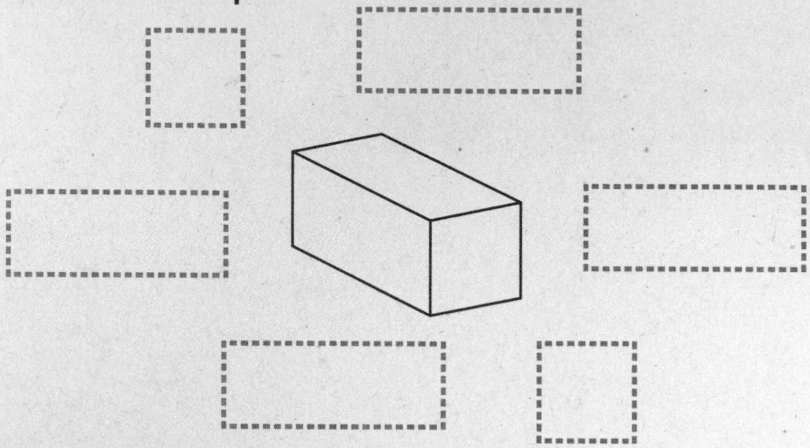

Share and Show

MATH BOARD

Use three-dimensional shapes. Trace around the flat surfaces. Circle the shapes you draw.

1. 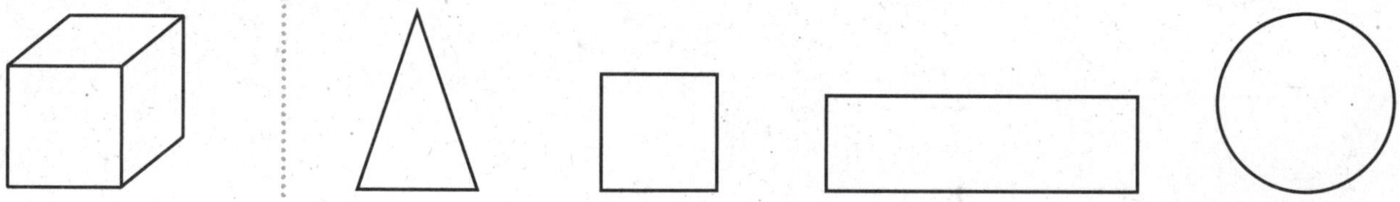

✓ 2. 

✓ 3. 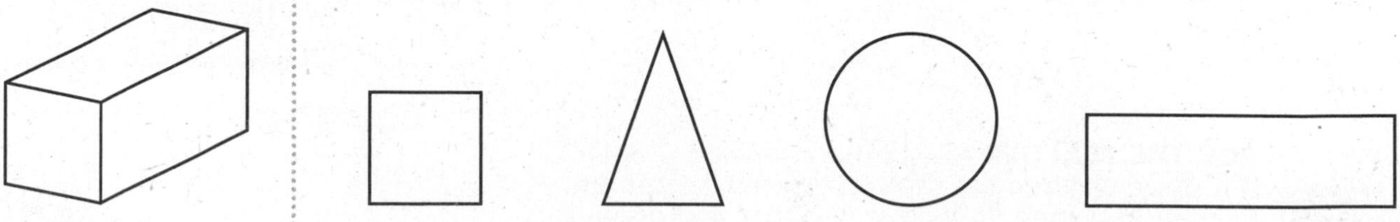

Name ______________________________

On Your Own

MATHEMATICAL PRACTICE 6 **Make Connections** Circle the objects you could trace to draw the shape.

4.

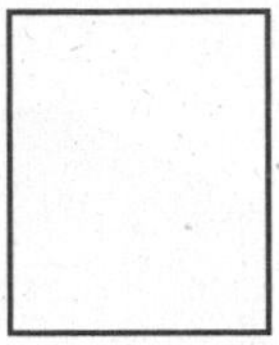

5.

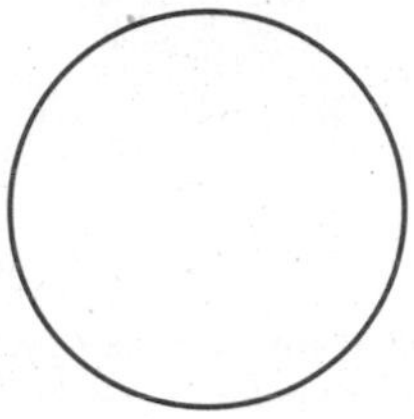

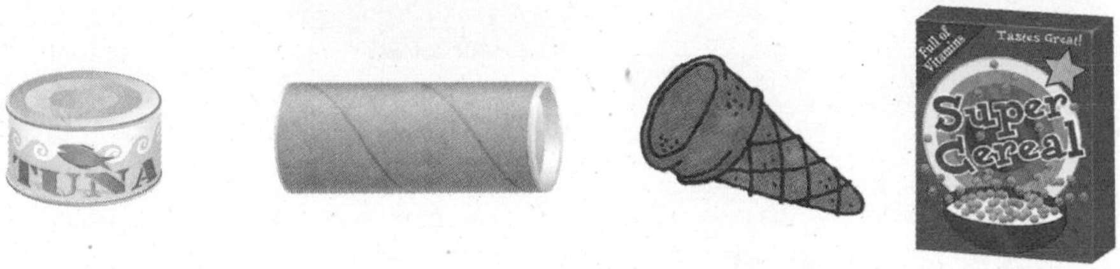

6.

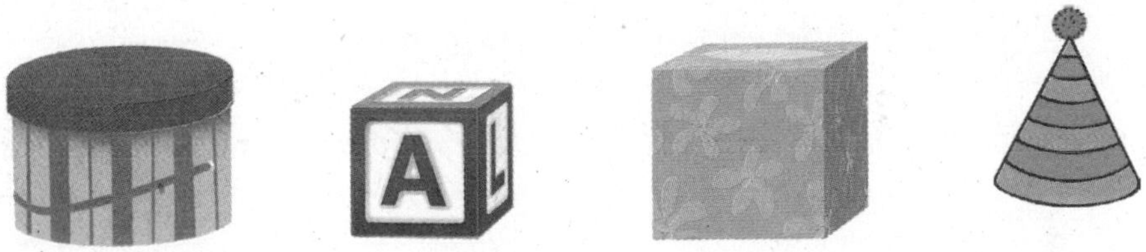

7.

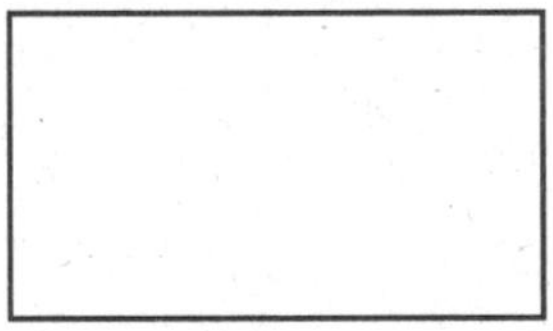

8. THINKSMARTER Draw a shape you would make if you traced this object.

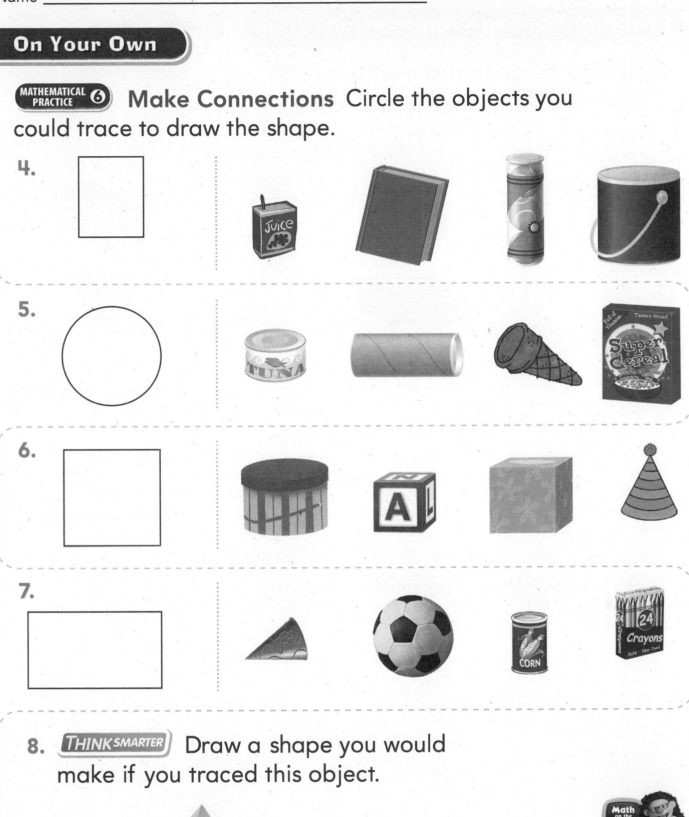

Math on the Spot

Problem Solving • Applications Real World

WRITE Math

Circle the shape that the pattern will make if you fold it and tape it together.

9.

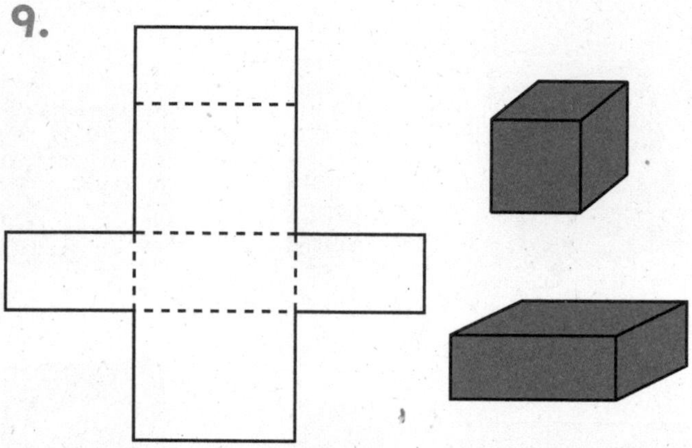

10.

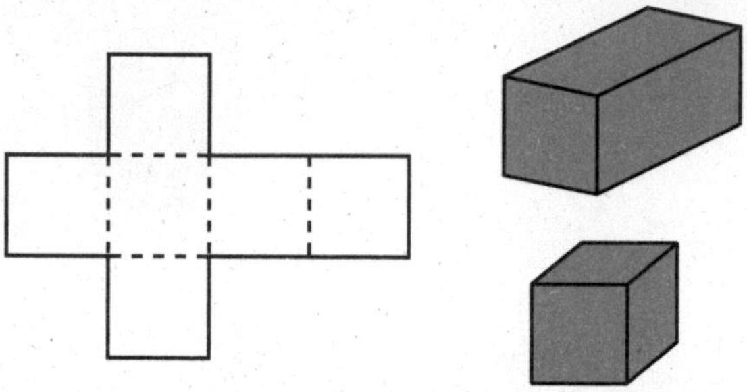

Personal Math Trainer

11. THINKSMARTER+ Kei wants to trace a ▭.
She finds these objects.
Which object should she use?

globe jar box

____

What would happen if Kei used the  to trace a shape?

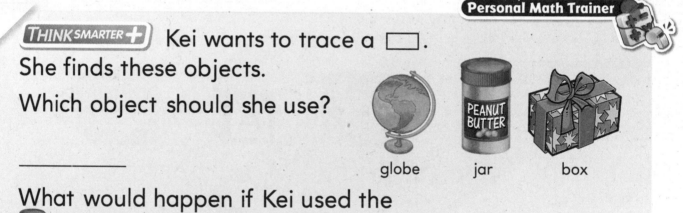

TAKE HOME ACTIVITY • Collect a few three-dimensional objects, such as boxes, that are shaped like rectangular prisms or cubes. Ask your child what two-dimensional shapes are on those objects.

Name ______________________________

Two-Dimensional Shapes on Three-Dimensional Shapes

Common Core **COMMON CORE STANDARD—1.G.A.1**
Reason with shapes and their attributes.

Circle the objects you could trace to draw the shape.

1. 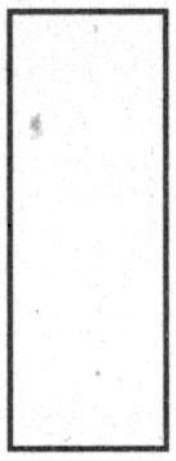

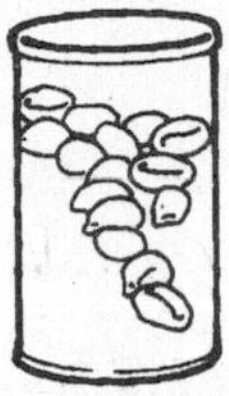

2. 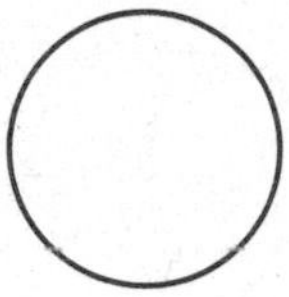

Problem Solving Real World

3. Look at this shape. Draw the shape you would make if you traced this object.

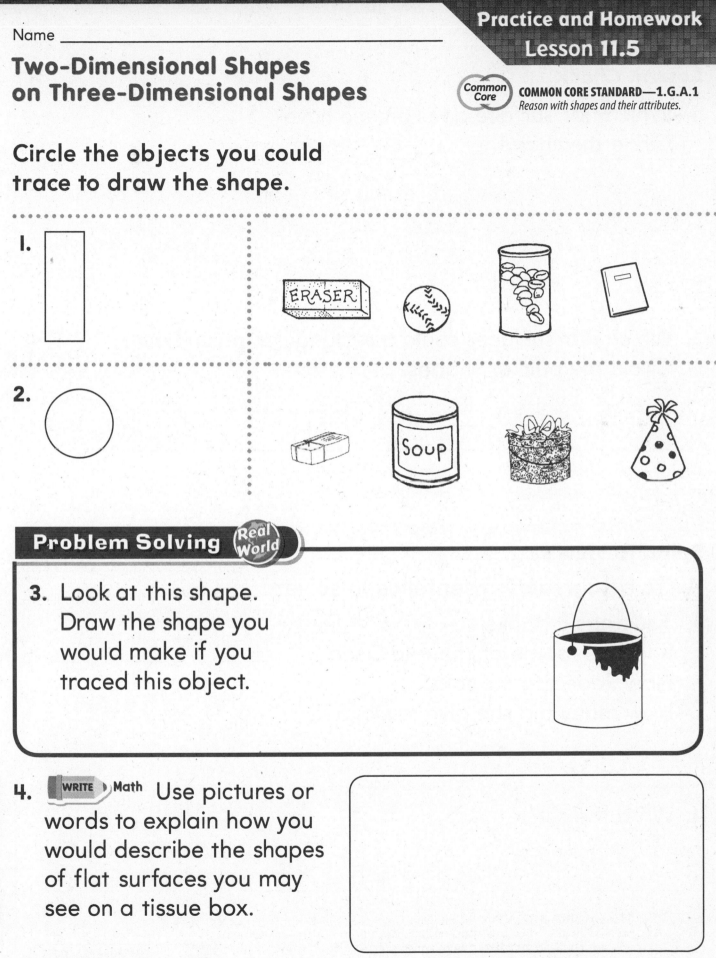

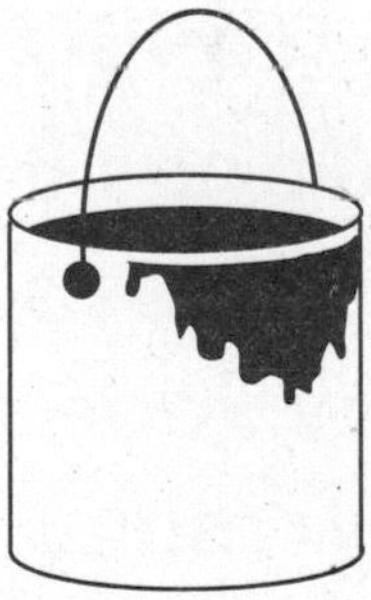

4. WRITE Math Use pictures or words to explain how you would describe the shapes of flat surfaces you may see on a tissue box.

Lesson Check (1.G.A.1)

1. Which flat surface does a cone have?
Circle the shape.

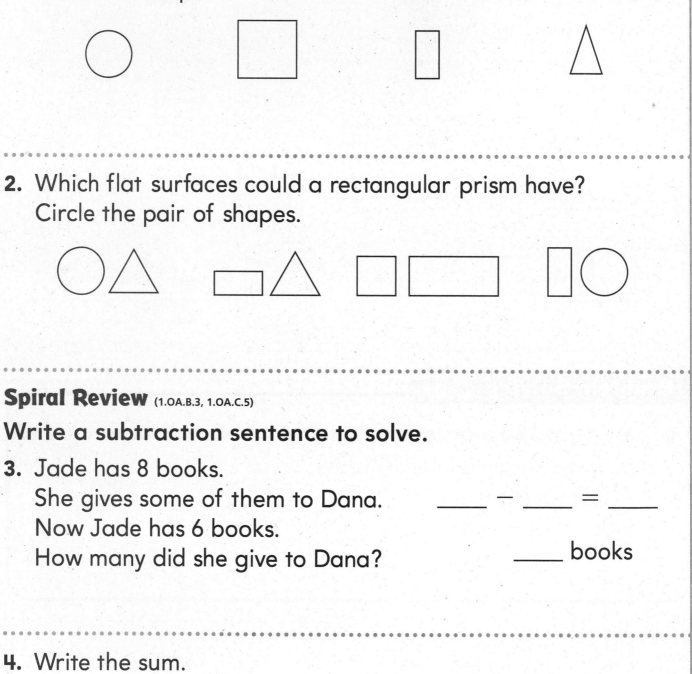

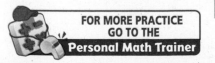

2. Which flat surfaces could a rectangular prism have?
Circle the pair of shapes.

Spiral Review (1.OA.B.3, 1.OA.C.5)

Write a subtraction sentence to solve.

3. Jade has 8 books.
She gives some of them to Dana.
Now Jade has 6 books.
How many did she give to Dana?

____ – ____ = ____

____ books

4. Write the sum.

3 + 0 = ____

FOR MORE PRACTICE GO TO THE **Personal Math Trainer**

Name ______________________________

Chapter 11 Review/Test

Personal Math Trainer
Online Assessment and Intervention

1. Match each shape to the group where it belongs.

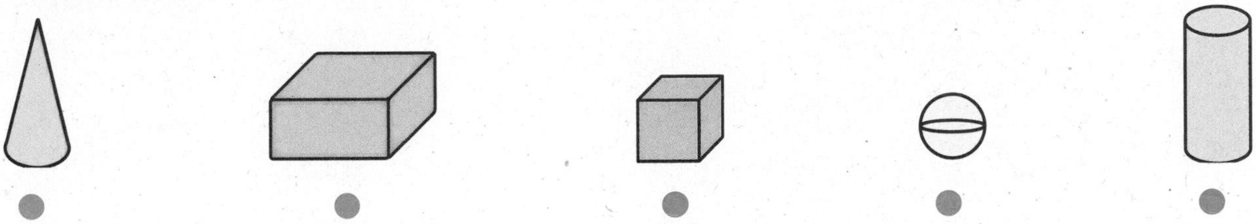

Only flat surfaces	Only a curved surface	Both flat and curved surfaces

2. Combine  and 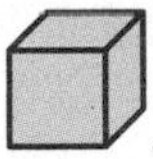. Choose all the new shapes you can make.

○ 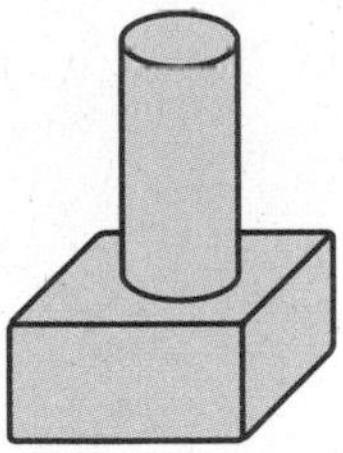

○ 

○ 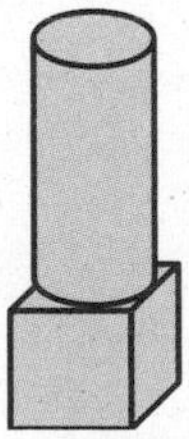

○ 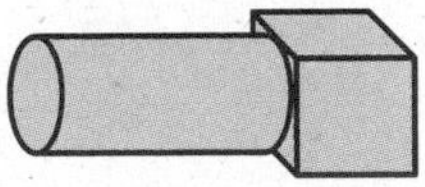

○ 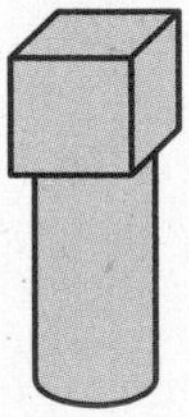

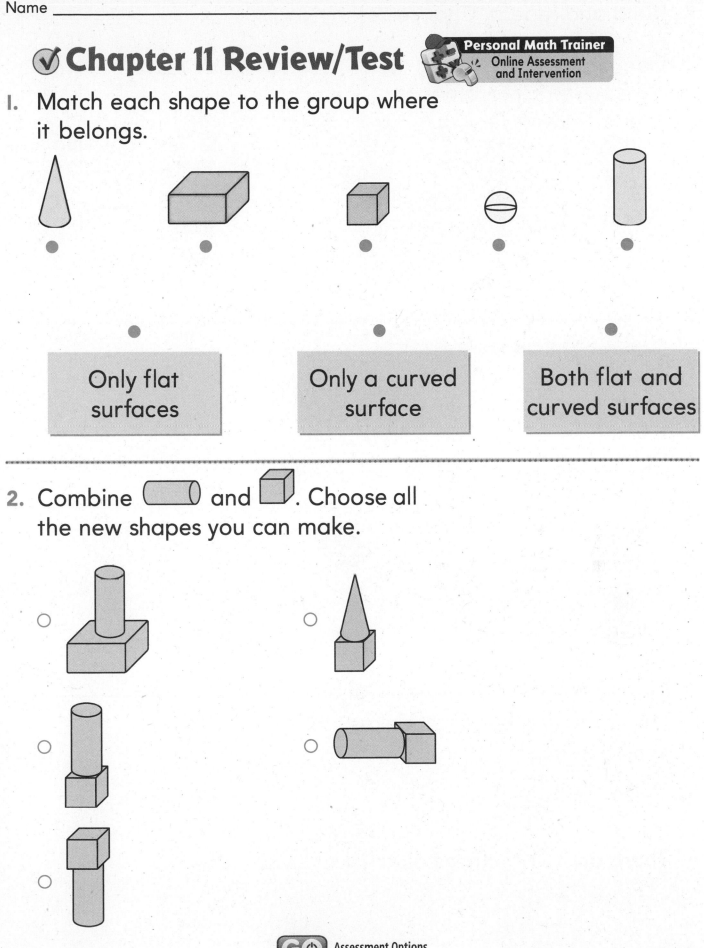

GO DIGITAL Assessment Options Chapter Test

3. Build and repeat. Choose Yes or No.

Can two  make ? ○ Yes ○ No

Can two 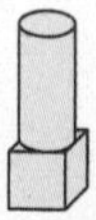 make 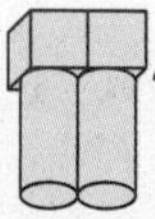? ○ Yes ○ No

Can two 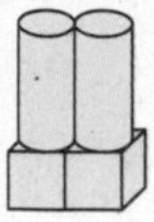 make 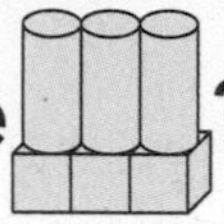? ○ Yes ○ No

---

4. Damon built this shape.

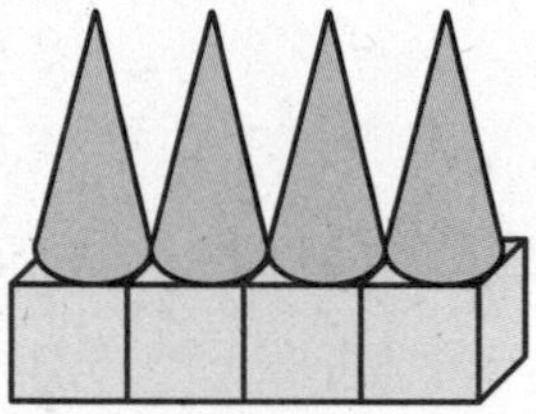

Choose all the shapes Damon used.

○  ○ 

○ 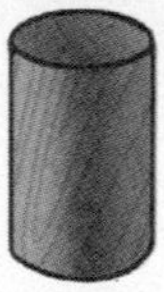 ○ 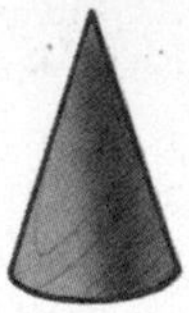

---

5. Circle the number that makes the sentence true.

There are [0 / 1 / 2] circles on a 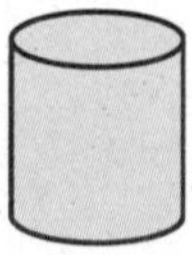.

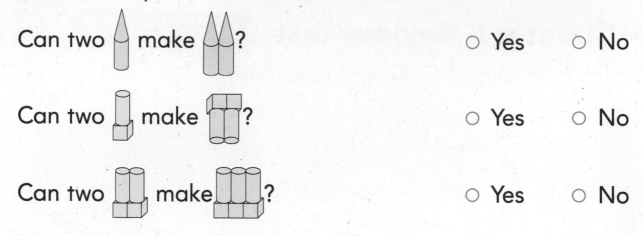

Name ______________________

6. GO DEEPER Sara wants to trace a ○. She finds these objects.

Draw the object Sara should trace.

What would happen if she used the  to trace a shape?

7. Which shape has only 2 flat surfaces?

○ 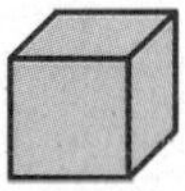

○ 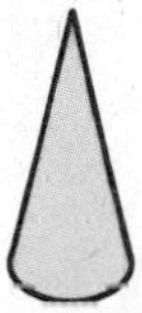

○ 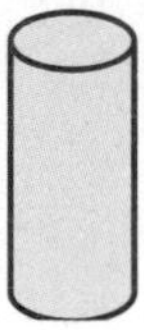

○ 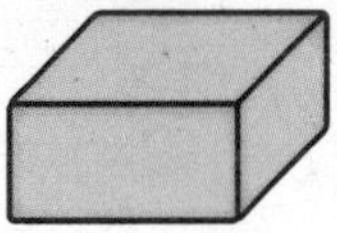

8. Look at the shape.

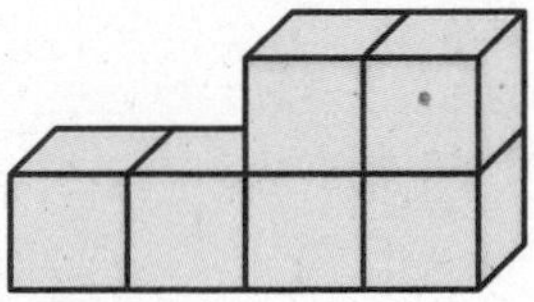

How many  are used to make the shape?

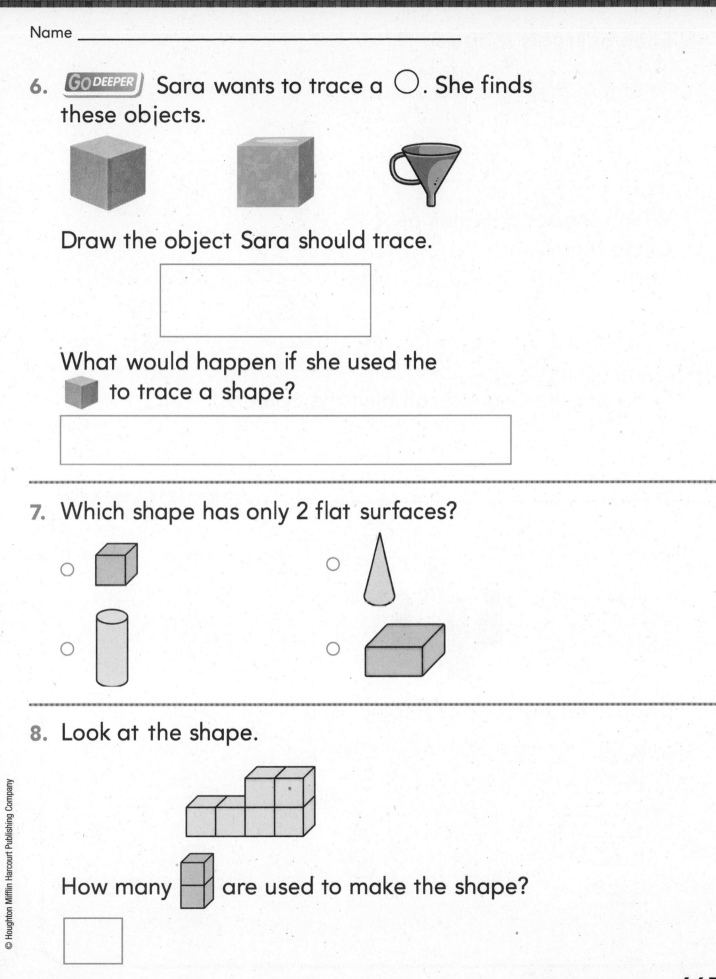

9. Ellen built this shape.

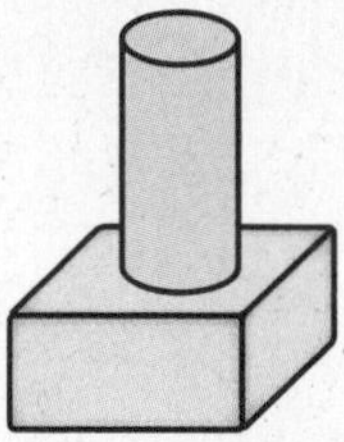

Which shapes did Ellen use?
Circle them.

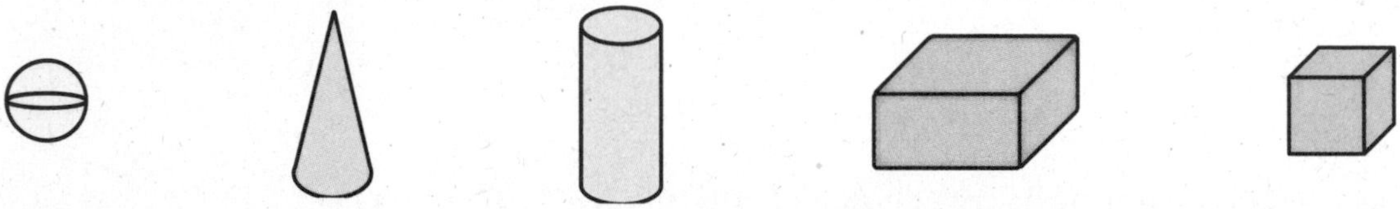

Draw another way to combine the objects.

Personal Math Trainer

10. THINK SMARTER + Hector built this shape.

Choose all the shapes Hector used.

○ 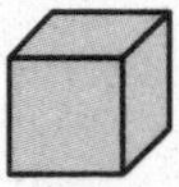

○ 

○ 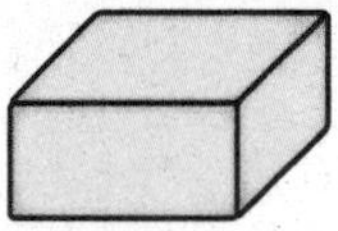

○ 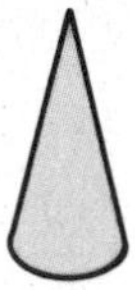

○ 

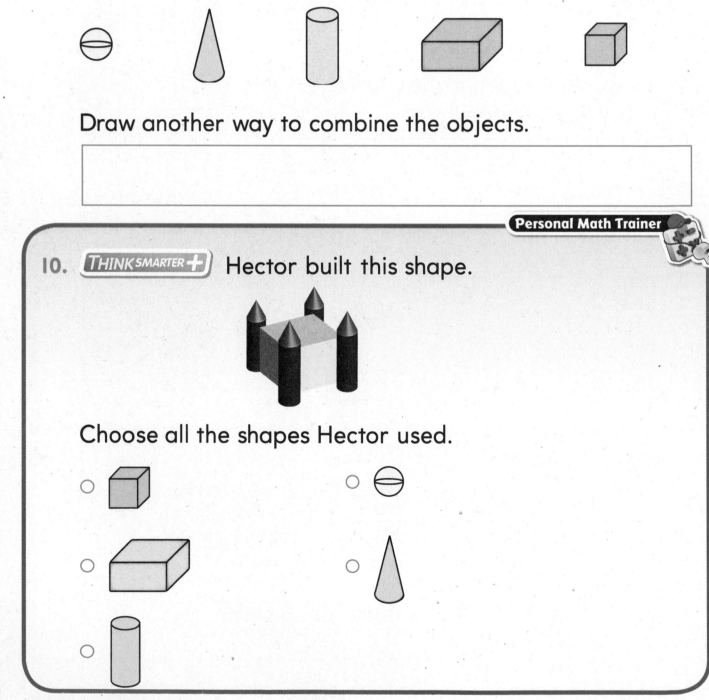

Chapter 12

Two-Dimensional Geometry

Curious About Math with Curious George

Shapes can be found in many places. What shapes might you see on a playground?

Name ______________________________

Show What You Know

Personal Math Trainer
Online Assessment and Intervention

Sort by Shape

Circle the shape that belongs in each group. (K.G.A.2)

1.

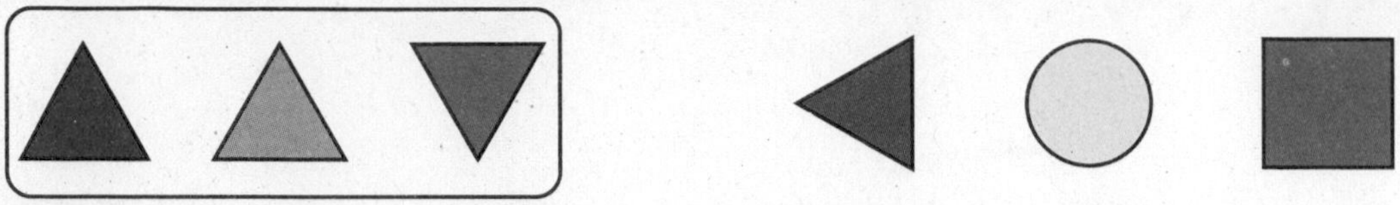

2.

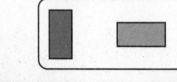

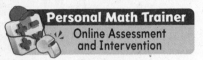

Sort Shapes

Circle the shapes with 4 sides. (K.G.A.2)

3.

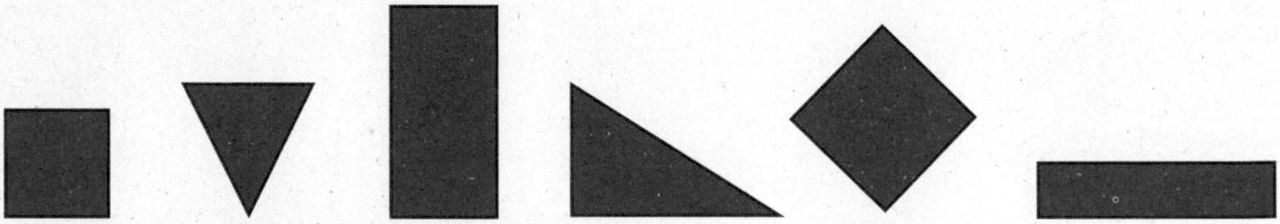

Identify Two-Dimensional Shapes

Color each square blue. Color each rectangle yellow. Color each circle red. (K.G.A.3)

4.

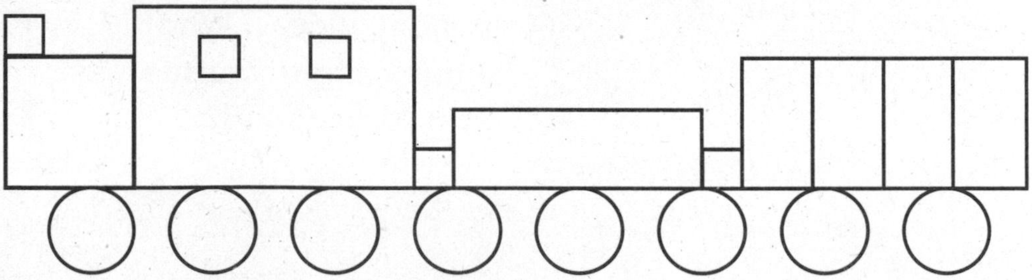

This page checks understanding of important skills needed for success in Chapter 12.

Name ______________________________

Review Words
- circle
- hexagon
- rectangle
- square
- triangle

Vocabulary Builder

Visualize It

Complete the chart.
Mark each row with a ✓.

Word	I Know	Sounds Familiar	I Do Not Know
circle			
hexagon			
rectangle			
square			
triangle			

Understand Vocabulary

Write the number of each shape.

1. ____ circles
2. ____ squares
3. ____ triangles

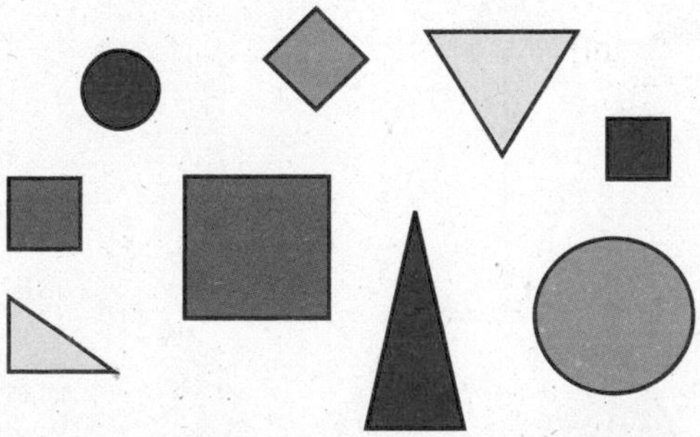

• Interactive Student Edition
• Multimedia eGlossary

Chapter 12

Game Rocket Shapes

Materials

• spinner • 6 squares • 8 circles • 14 triangles

Play with a partner.
Take turns.

1. Spin the spinner.
2. Name the shape you spin.
3. Place that shape on the rocket if you can.
4. If you cannot place the shape, your turn is over.
5. The first player to cover a whole rocket wins.

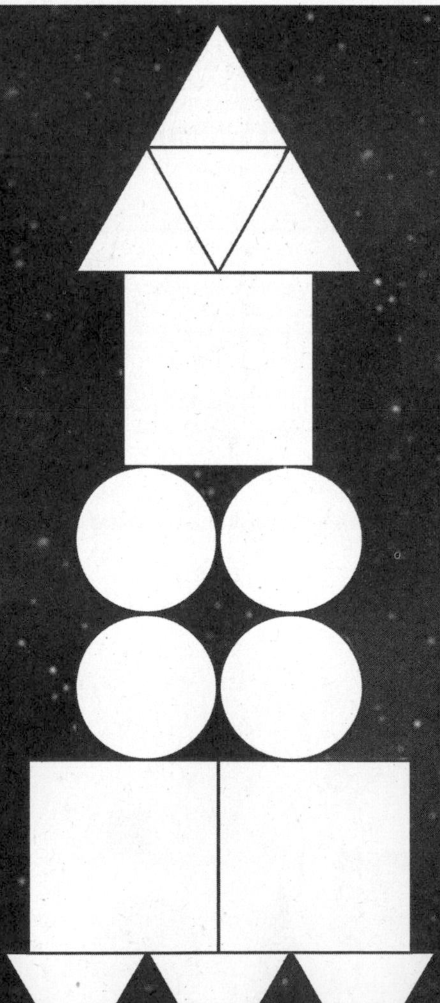

Player 1

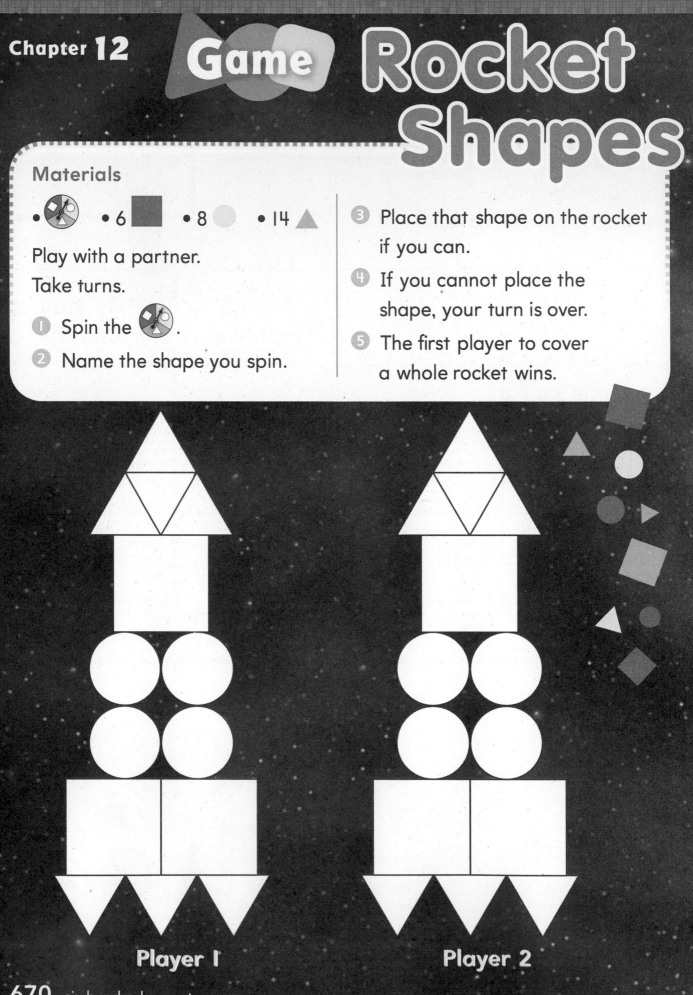

Player 2

Chapter 12 Vocabulary

circle círculo 5	**equal parts** partes iguales 18
fourth of cuarto de 21	**fourths** cuartos 22
half of mitad de 24	**halves** mitades 25
hexagon hexágono 26	**quarter of** cuarta parte de 43

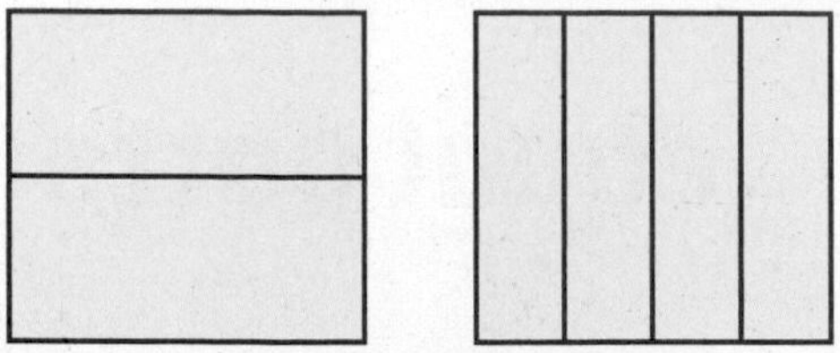

These show **equal parts,** or equal shares.

© Houghton Mifflin Harcourt Publishing Company

© Houghton Mifflin Harcourt Publishing Company

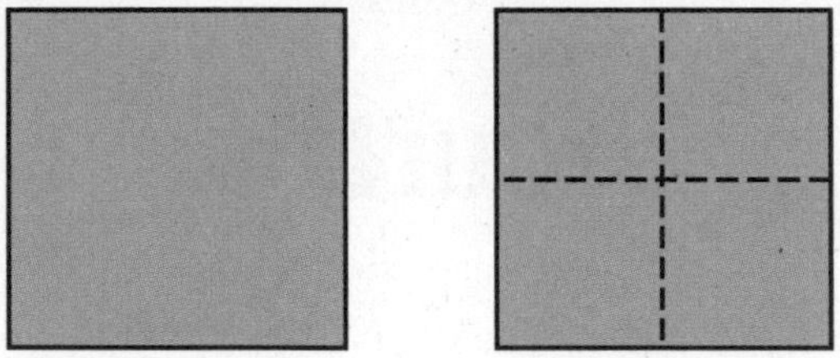

1 whole   4 **fourths,** or 4 quarters

© Houghton Mifflin Harcourt Publishing Company

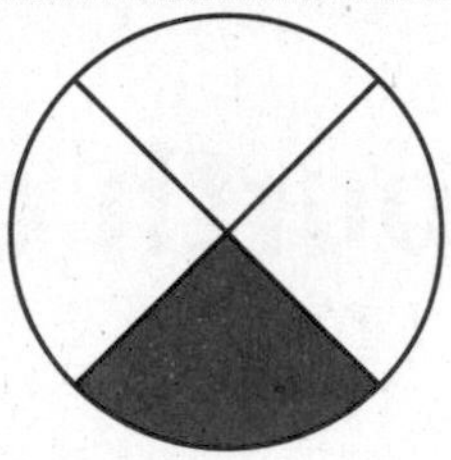

A **fourth of** this shape is shaded.

© Houghton Mifflin Harcourt Publishing Company

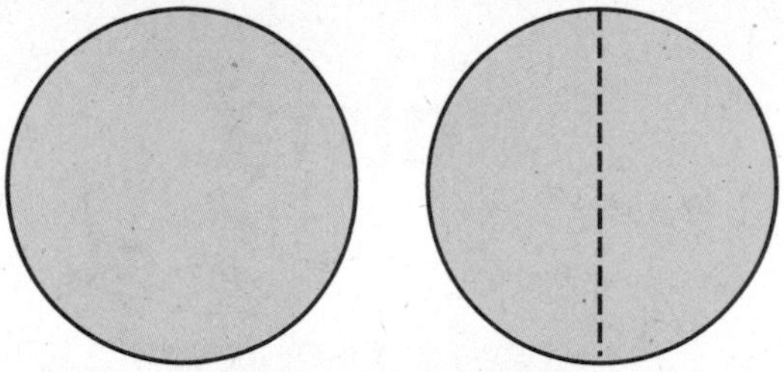

1 whole   2 **halves**

© Houghton Mifflin Harcourt Publishing Company

Half of this shape is shaded.

© Houghton Mifflin Harcourt Publishing Company

A **quarter of** this shape is shaded.

© Houghton Mifflin Harcourt Publishing Company

quarters

cuartas partes

44

rectangle

rectángulo

45

side

lado

49

square

cuadrado

51

trapezoid

trapecio

58

triangle

triángulo

59

unequal parts

partes desiguales

60

vertex

vértice

61

© Houghton Mifflin Harcourt Publishing Company

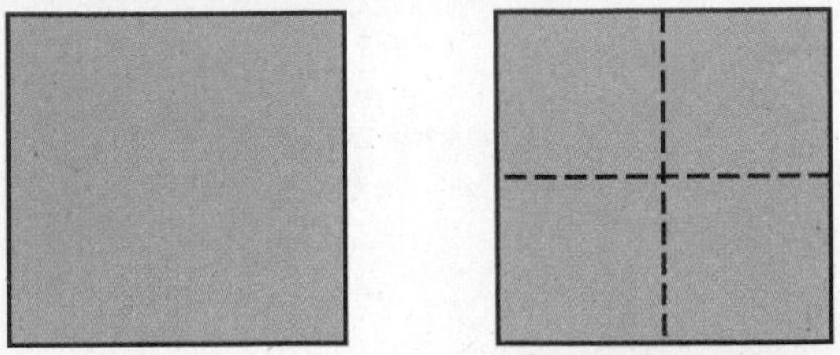

1 whole

4 fourths,
or 4 **quarters**

© Houghton Mifflin Harcourt Publishing Company

© Houghton Mifflin Harcourt Publishing Company

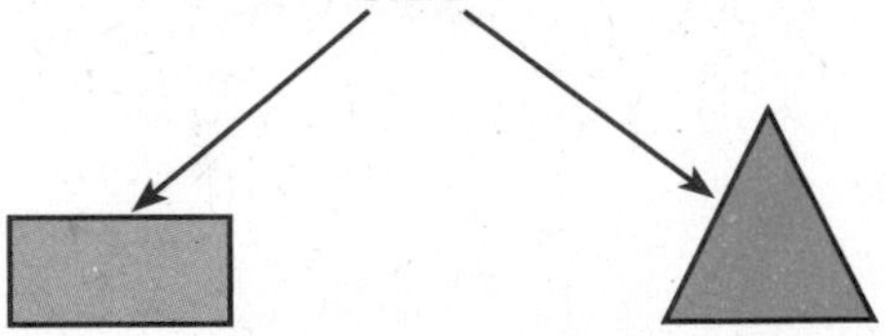

© Houghton Mifflin Harcourt Publishing Company

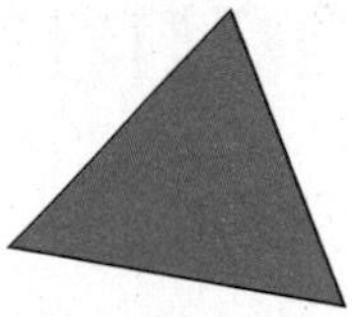

© Houghton Mifflin Harcourt Publishing Company

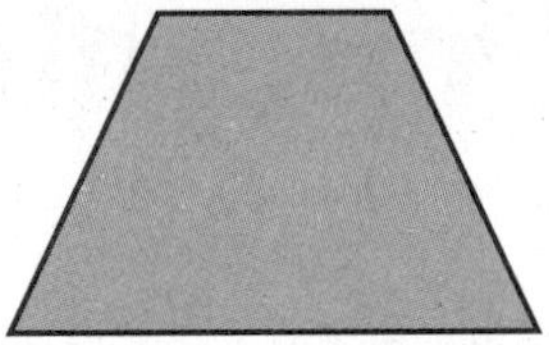

© Houghton Mifflin Harcourt Publishing Company

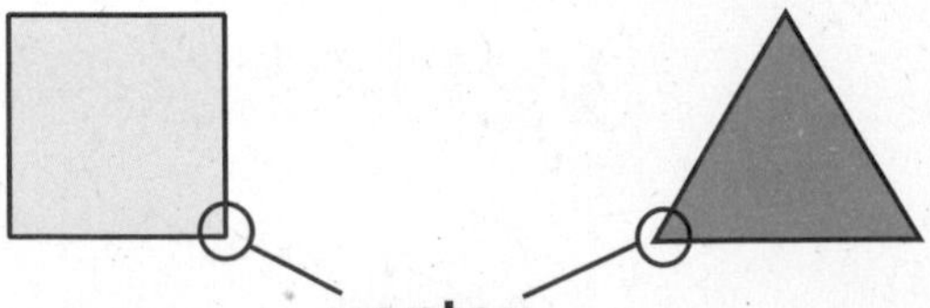

© Houghton Mifflin Harcourt Publishing Company

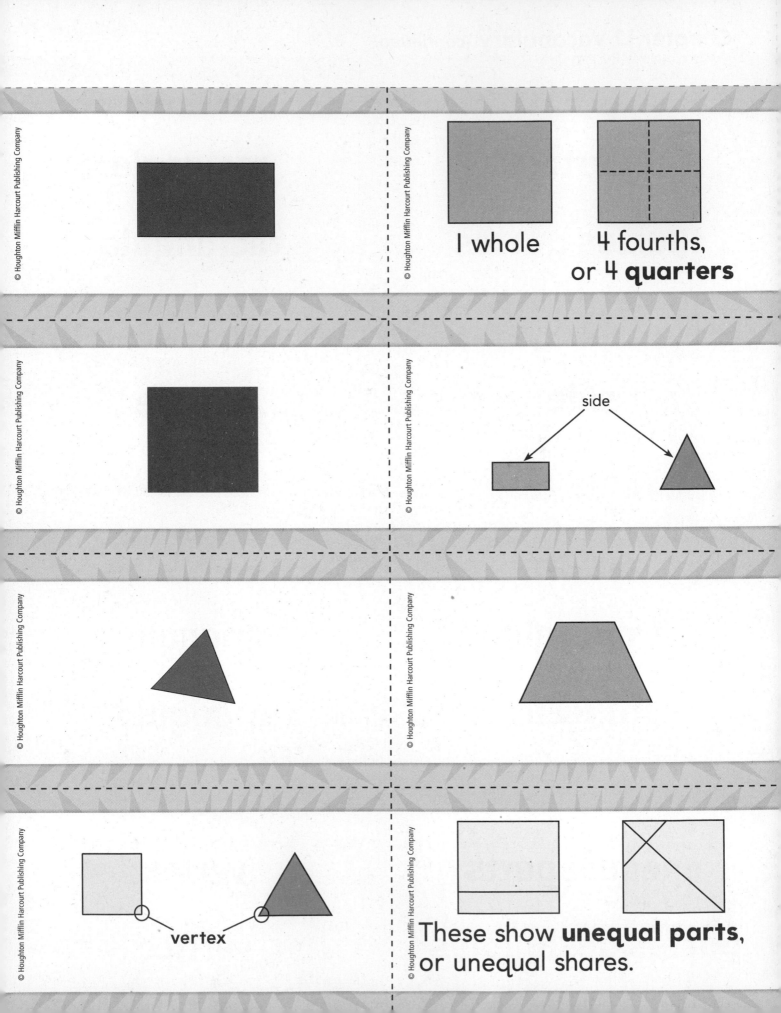

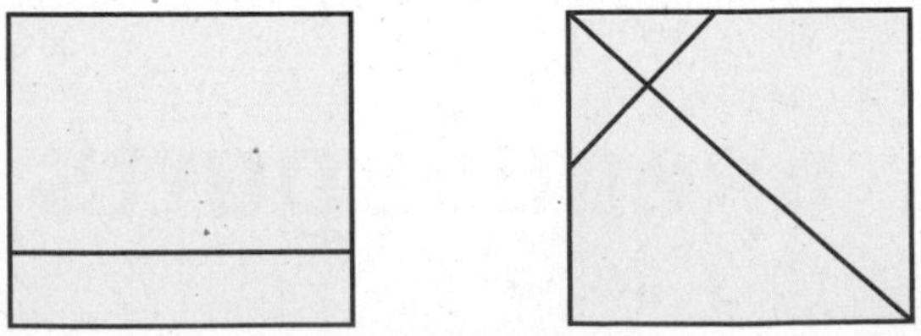

These show **unequal parts**, or unequal shares.

Game

Guess the Word

Word Box

- circle
- equal parts
- fourth of
- fourths
- half of
- halves
- hexagon
- quarter of
- quarters
- rectangle
- side
- square
- trapezoid
- triangle
- unequal parts
- vertex

Materials

timer

How to Play

Play with a partner.

1. Choose a math word from the Word Box. Do not tell your partner.
2. Set the timer.
3. Give a one-word clue.
4. Your partner tries to guess the secret word.
5. Repeat with a new one-word clue until your partner guesses correctly or time runs out.
6. Take turns.
7. The first player to correctly guess 5 words wins.

The Write Way

Reflect

Choose one idea. Draw and write about it.

- Tell about two of your favorite shapes.
- Explain how you can combine shapes to make a new shape.

Name ______________________________

Sort Two-Dimensional Shapes

Essential Question How can you use attributes to classify and sort two-dimensional shapes?

Common Core Geometry—1.G.A.1

MATHEMATICAL PRACTICES
MP6, MP7, MP8

Listen and Draw (Real World)

Draw to sort the shapes.
Write the sorting rule.

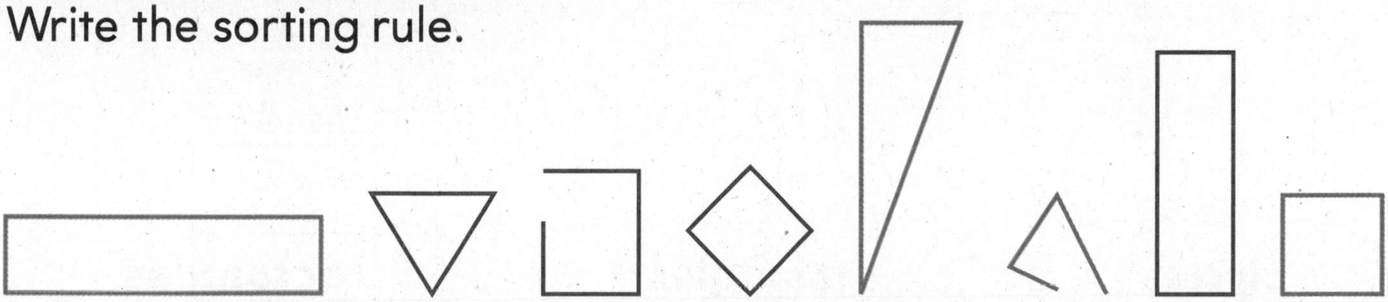

______________________________ ______________________________

FOR THE TEACHER • Read the following aloud. Devon wants to sort these shapes to show a group of triangles and a group of rectangles. Draw and write to show how Devon sorts the shapes.

Math Talk — MATHEMATICAL PRACTICES 6

Explain Are there shapes that did not go in your groups?

Model and Draw

Here are some ways to sort two-dimensional shapes.

A **square** is a special kind of rectangle.

curved and closed shapes

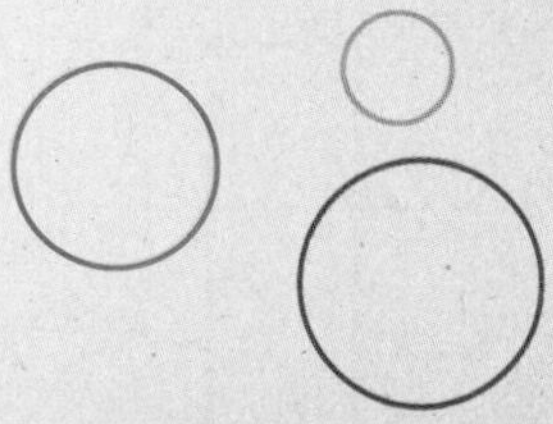

circles

closed shapes with ____ **sides**

triangles

closed shapes with ____ **vertices**

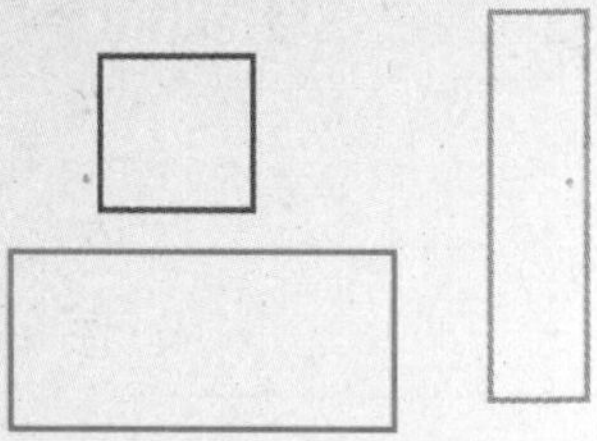

rectangles

Share and Show

MATH BOARD

THINK
Vertices (corners) are where the sides meet.

Read the sorting rule. Circle the shapes that follow the rule.

1. 4 vertices (corners)

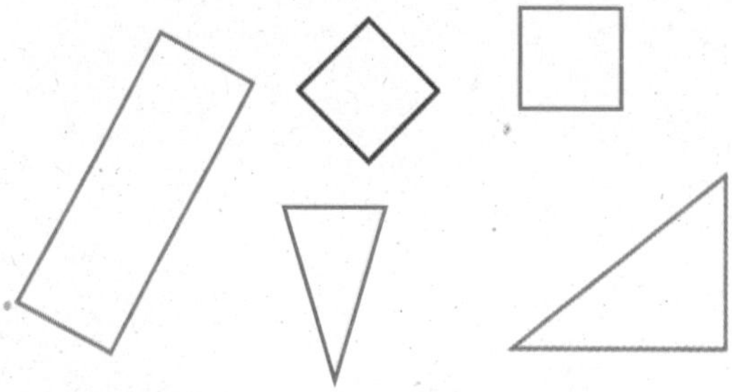

2. **not** curved

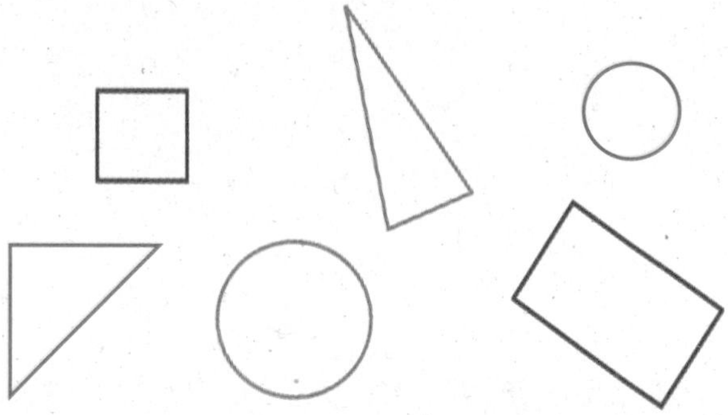

3. only 3 sides

4. more than 3 sides

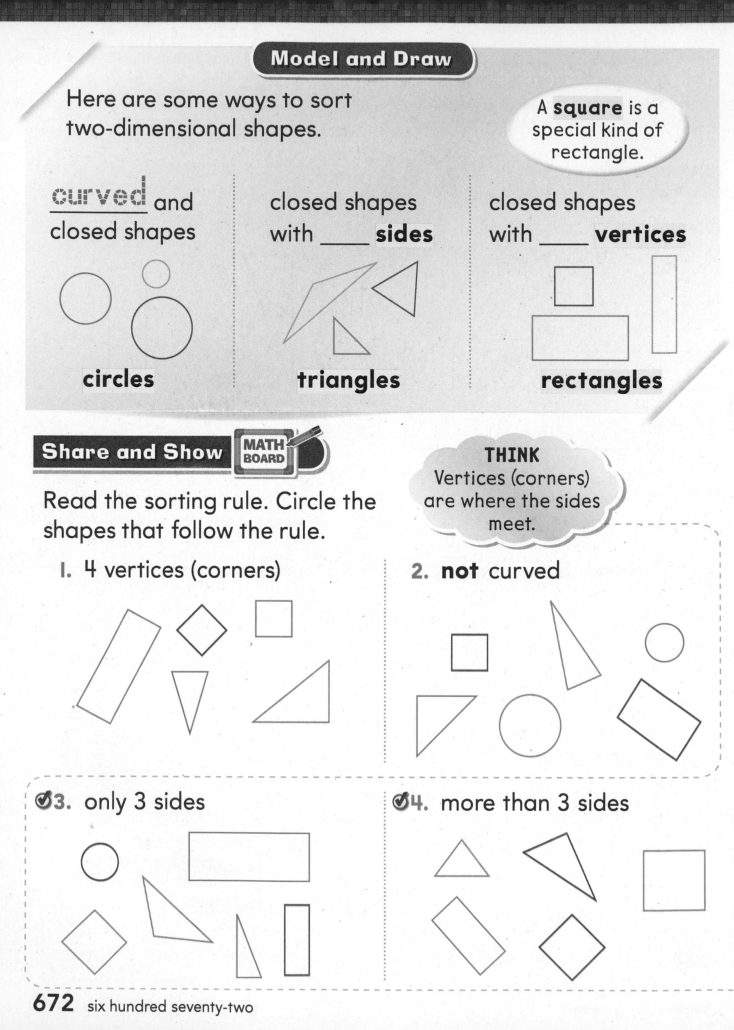

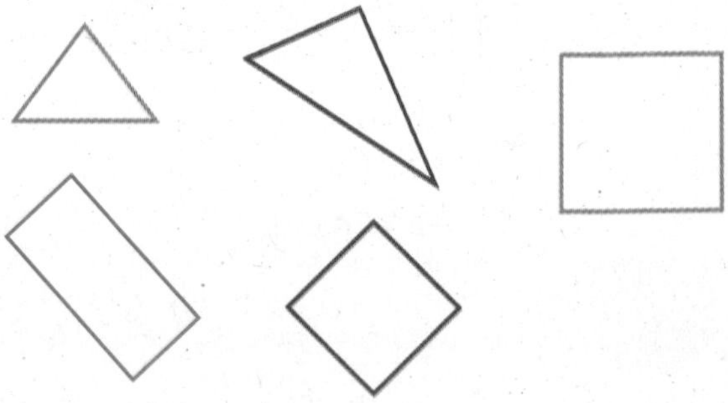

Name ______________________________

On Your Own

REMEMBER
Read the sorting rule first.

MATHEMATICAL PRACTICE 6 **Use Math Vocabulary**
Circle the shapes that follow the rule.

5. curved

6. only 3 vertices (corners)

7. 4 sides

8. 4 sides are the same length

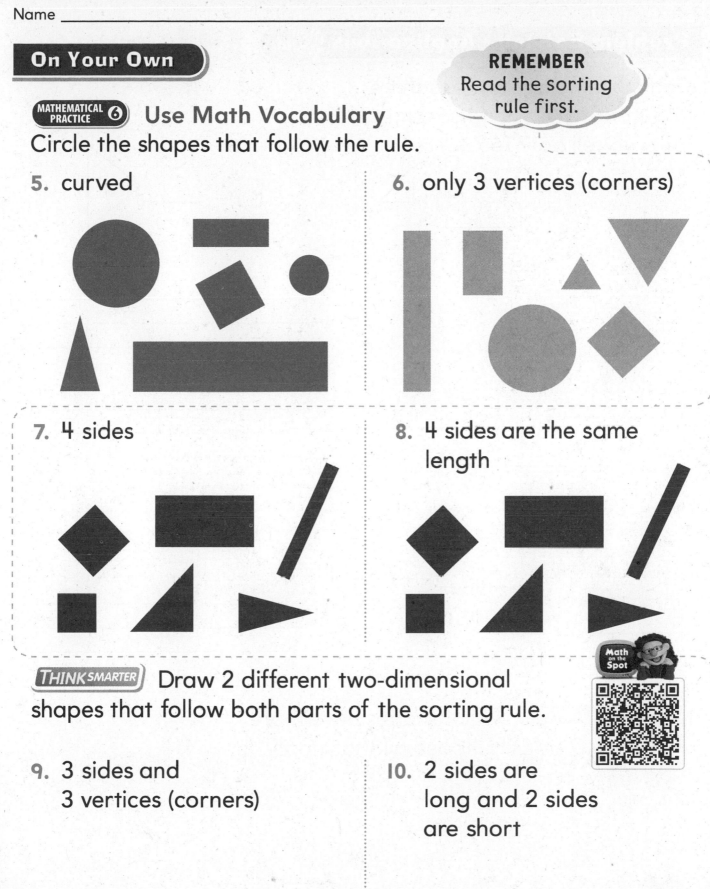

THINK SMARTER Draw 2 different two-dimensional shapes that follow both parts of the sorting rule.

9. 3 sides and 3 vertices (corners)

10. 2 sides are long and 2 sides are short

Problem Solving • Applications | Real World | WRITE Math

Ted sorted these shapes three different ways. Write sorting rules to tell how Ted sorted.

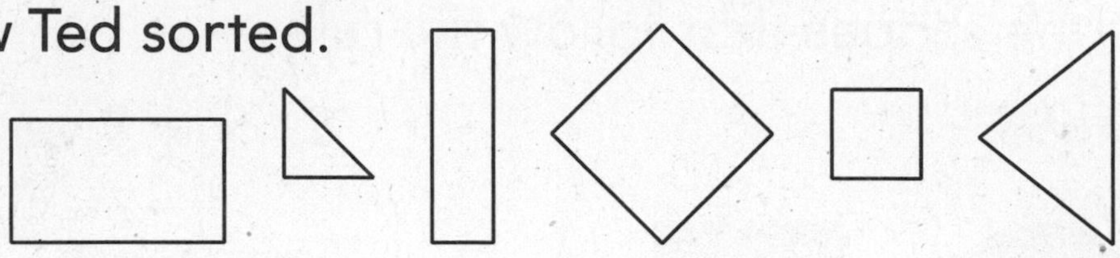

11.

- - - - - - - - - - - - - - -

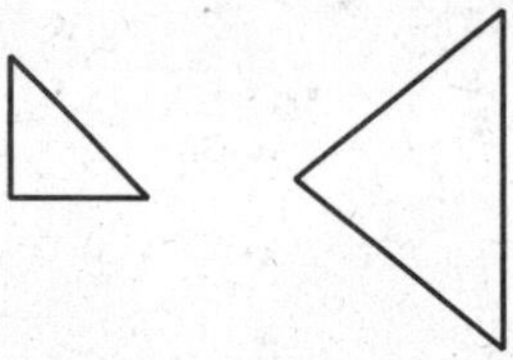

12.

- - - - - - - - - - - - - - -

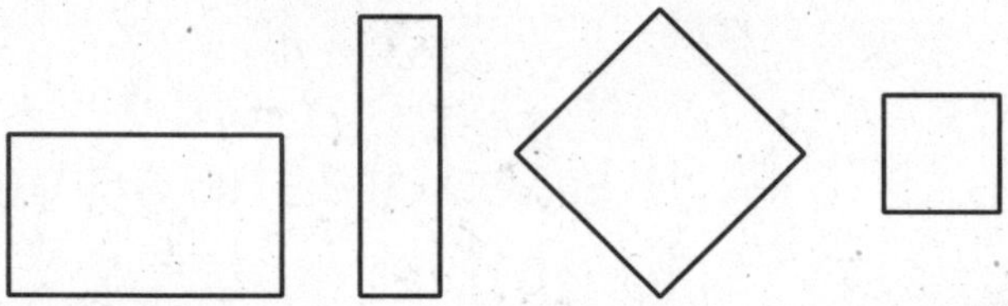

13. THINK SMARTER

- - - - - - - - - - - - - - -

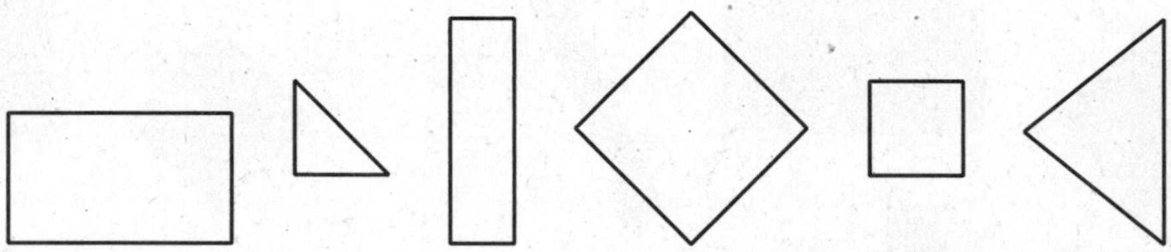

14. THINK SMARTER Which shapes have more than 3 sides? Choose all that apply.

○ ▭ ○ △ ○ ▢ ○ ▱ ○ ⬠

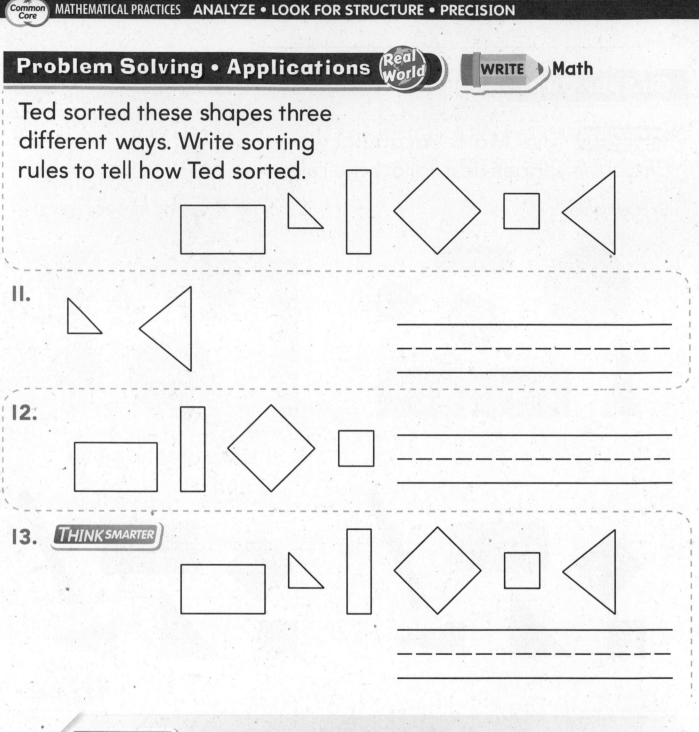

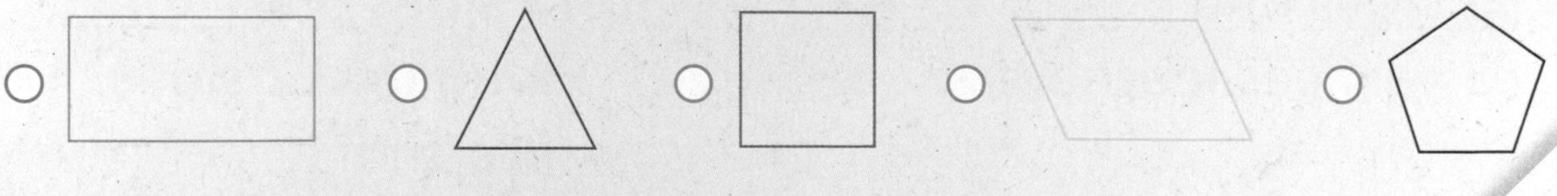

TAKE HOME ACTIVITY • Gather some household objects such as photos, buttons, and napkins. Ask your child to sort them by shape.

Name ______________________________

Sort Two-Dimensional Shapes

Common Core **COMMON CORE STANDARD—1.G.A.1**
Reason with shapes and their attributes.

Read the sorting rule. Circle the shapes that follow the rule.

1. **not** curved

2. 4 vertices

Problem Solving Real World

3. Katie sorted these shapes. Write a sorting rule to tell how Katie sorted.

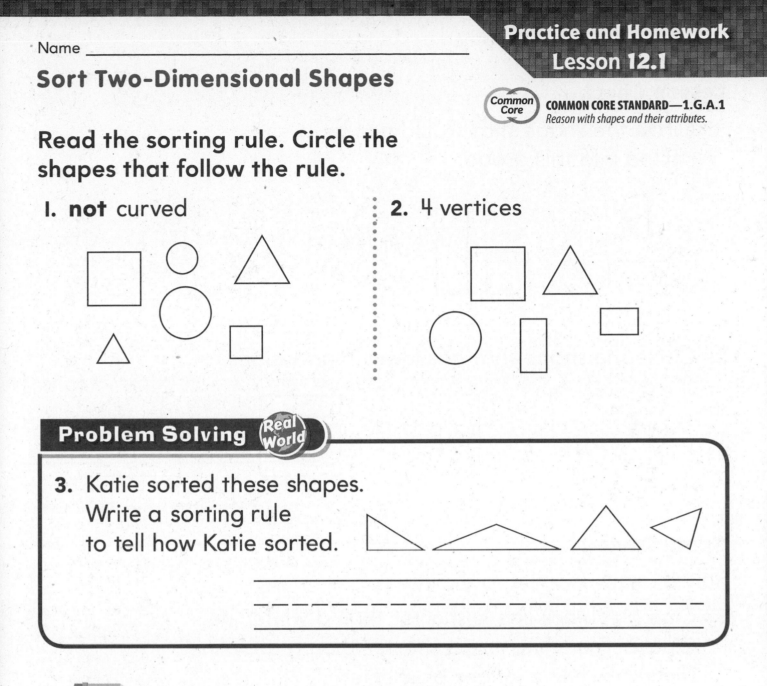

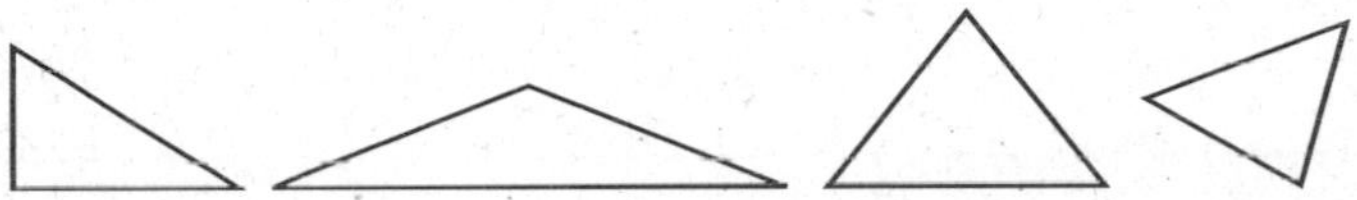

____

4. WRITE Math Explain how you would name a sorting rule for 1 square, 1 rectangle, and 1 triangle.

____

____

____

____

Lesson Check (1.G.A.1)

1. Circle the shape that would **not** be sorted into this group.

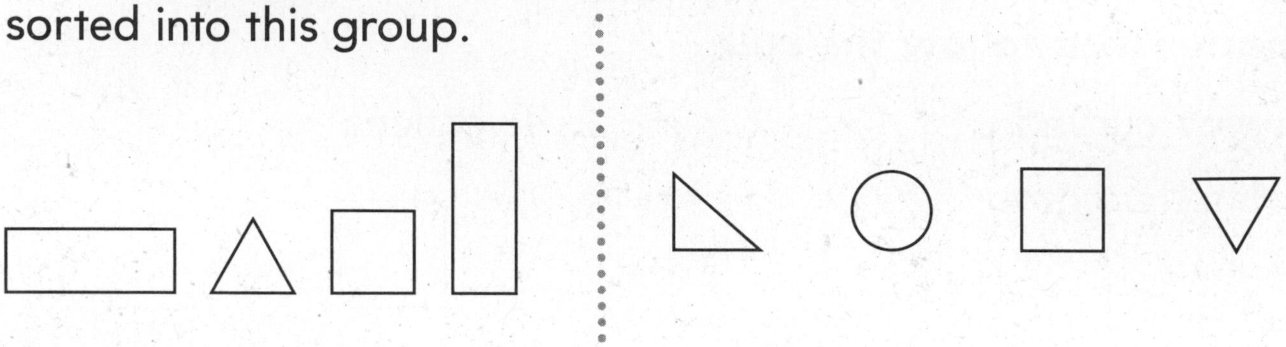

2. Circle the shape that has fewer than 4 sides.

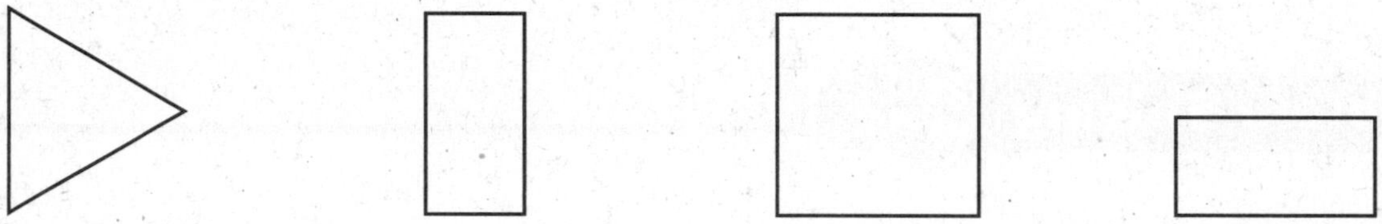

Spiral Review (1.MD.A.1)

Solve. Draw or write to explain.

3. Clue 1: A black line is shorter than a white line.
Clue 2: The white line is shorter than a gray line.
Is the black line longer or shorter than the gray line? ____________________

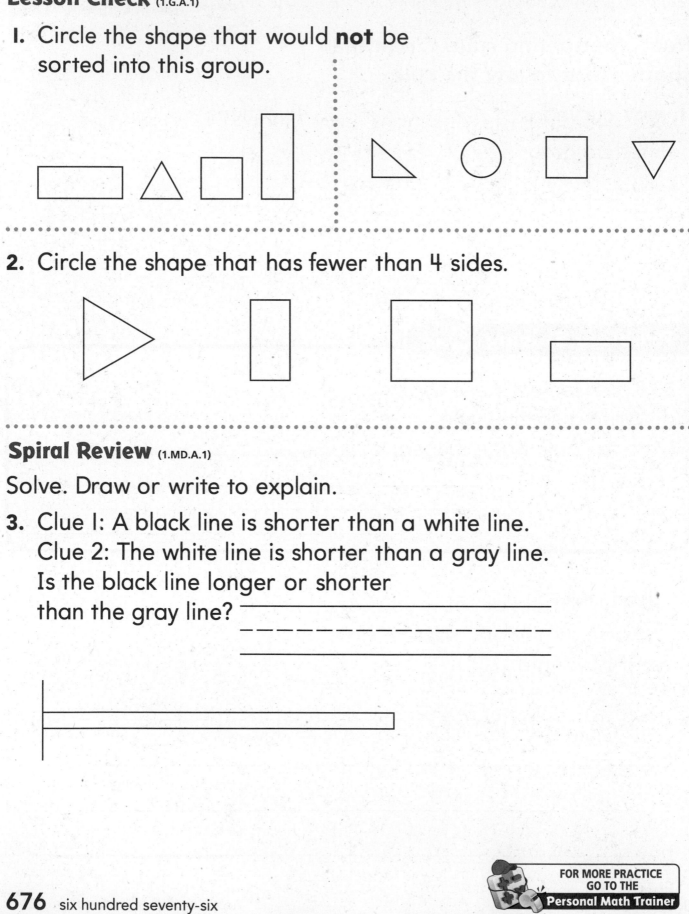

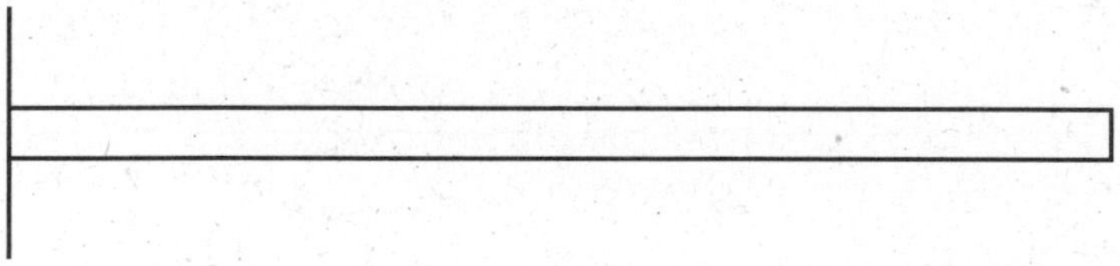

FOR MORE PRACTICE GO TO THE Personal Math Trainer

Name ______________________________

Describe Two-Dimensional Shapes

Essential Question What attributes can you use to describe two-dimensional shapes?

Common Core **Geometry—1.G.A.1**

MATHEMATICAL PRACTICES
MP6, MP7, MP8

Listen and Draw

Hands On

Use two-dimensional shapes. Sort them into two groups. Draw to show your work.

curved	straight

Math Talk MATHEMATICAL PRACTICES 7

Look for Structure How did you sort the shapes into two groups? Name the shapes in each group.

FOR THE TEACHER • Have children sort two-dimensional shapes into groups that are curved and straight. Have them draw the shapes to show how they sorted.

Model and Draw

Some shapes have straight sides and vertices (corners).

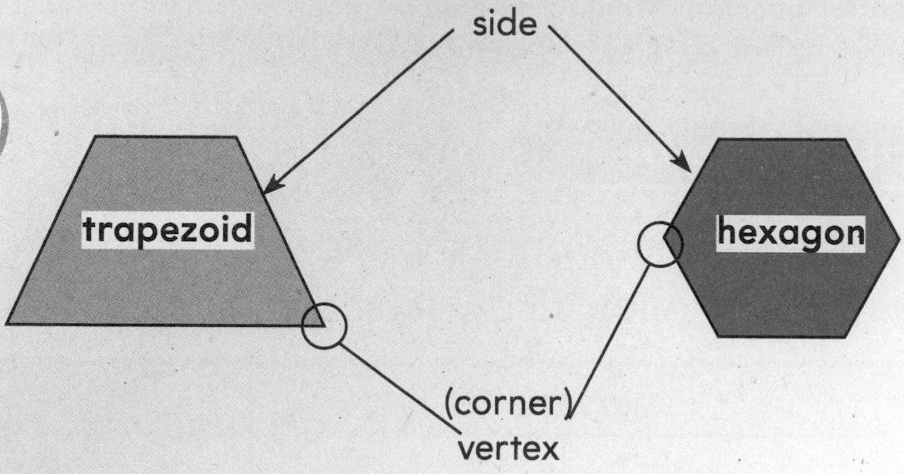

Share and Show

MATH BOARD

Use two-dimensional shapes.
Draw and write to complete the chart.

	Shape	Draw the shape.	Number of Straight Sides	Number of Vertices (Corners)
1.	hexagon			
2.	rectangle			
3.	square			
✓4.	trapezoid			
✓5.	triangle			

Name ____________________

On Your Own

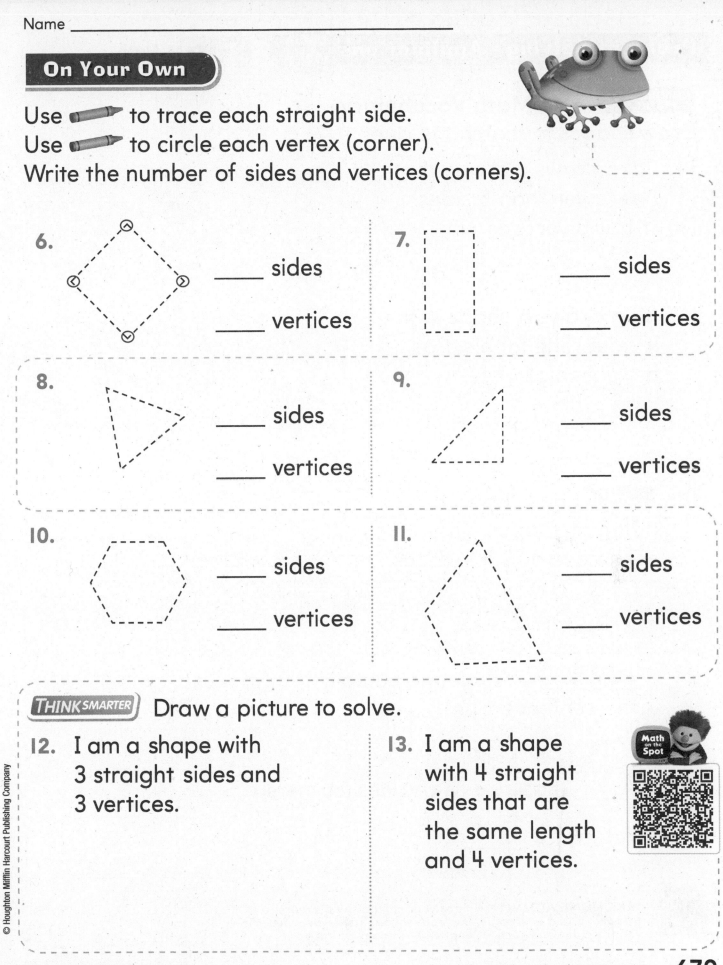

Use [crayon] to trace each straight side.
Use [crayon] to circle each vertex (corner).
Write the number of sides and vertices (corners).

6. 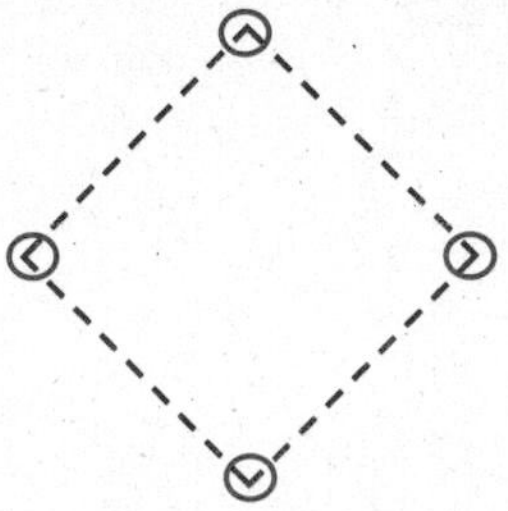

____ sides

____ vertices

7. 

____ sides

____ vertices

8. 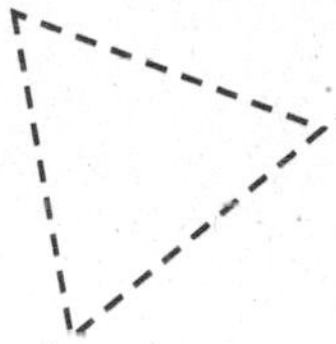

____ sides

____ vertices

9. 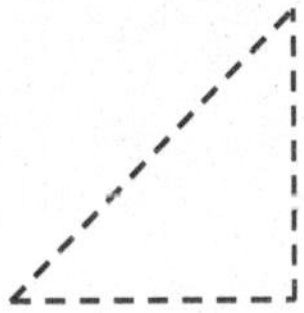

____ sides

____ vertices

10. 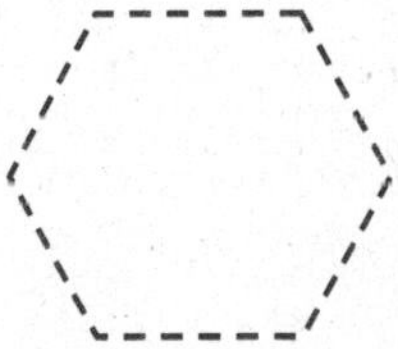

____ sides

____ vertices

11. 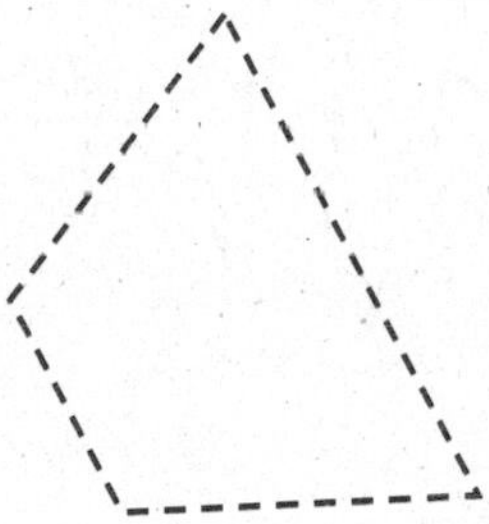

____ sides

____ vertices

THINK SMARTER Draw a picture to solve.

12. I am a shape with 3 straight sides and 3 vertices.

13. I am a shape with 4 straight sides that are the same length and 4 vertices.

Math on the Spot

Problem Solving • Applications Real World

WRITE Math

MATHEMATICAL PRACTICE 6 **Use Math Vocabulary**

Draw shapes to match the clues.

14. Jake draws a shape that has fewer than 5 sides. It has 3 vertices.

15. Meg draws a shape with 4 sides. She labels it as a trapezoid.

16. GO DEEPER Ben draws two different shapes. They each have only 4 vertices.

17. THINK SMARTER Circle the number that makes the sentence true.

A  has

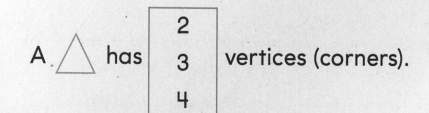

2
3
4

vertices (corners).

TAKE HOME ACTIVITY • Have your child draw a square, a trapezoid, and a triangle. For each shape, have him or her show you the sides and vertices and tell how many of each.

Name ______________________

Describe Two-Dimensional Shapes

Practice and Homework
Lesson 12.2

COMMON CORE STANDARD—1.G.A.1
Reason with shapes and their attributes.

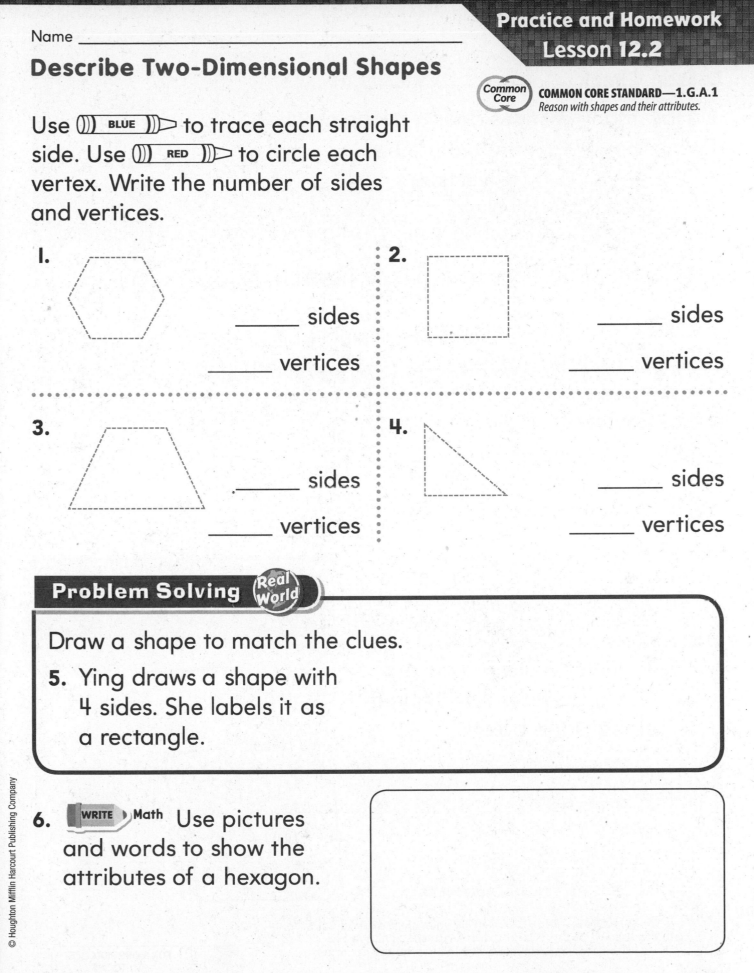

Use BLUE to trace each straight side. Use RED to circle each vertex. Write the number of sides and vertices.

1. 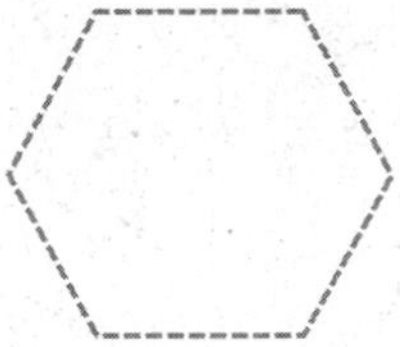

_____ sides

_____ vertices

2. 

_____ sides

_____ vertices

3. 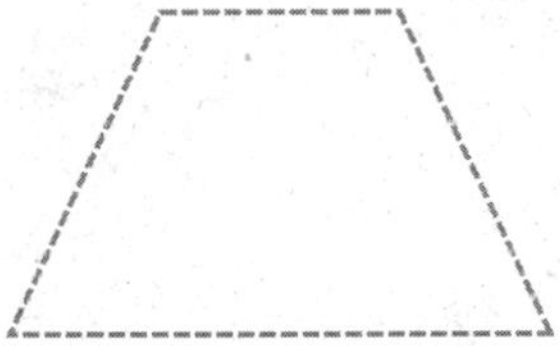

_____ sides

_____ vertices

4. 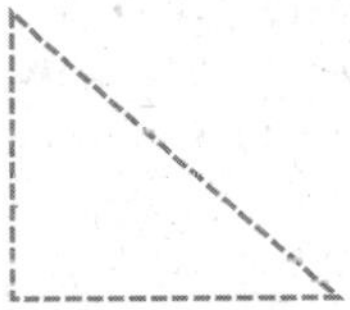

_____ sides

_____ vertices

Problem Solving (Real World)

Draw a shape to match the clues.

5. Ying draws a shape with 4 sides. She labels it as a rectangle.

6. WRITE Math Use pictures and words to show the attributes of a hexagon.

Lesson Check (1.G.A.1)

1. How many vertices does a triangle have?

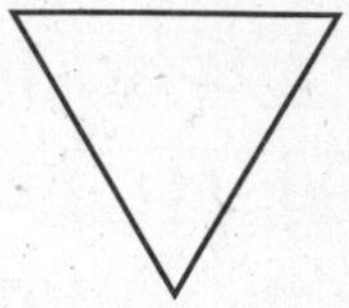

____ vertices

2. How many vertices does a 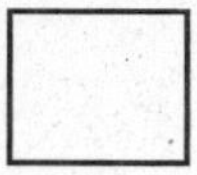 have?

____ vertices

Spiral Review (1.OA.C.5, 1.MD.A.2)

3. Circle the greater addend. Count on to find the sum.

$$\begin{array}{r} 2 \\ +\ 9 \\ \hline \end{array}$$

4. Corey measures a crayon box with his paper clip ruler. About how long is the box?

about ____ 

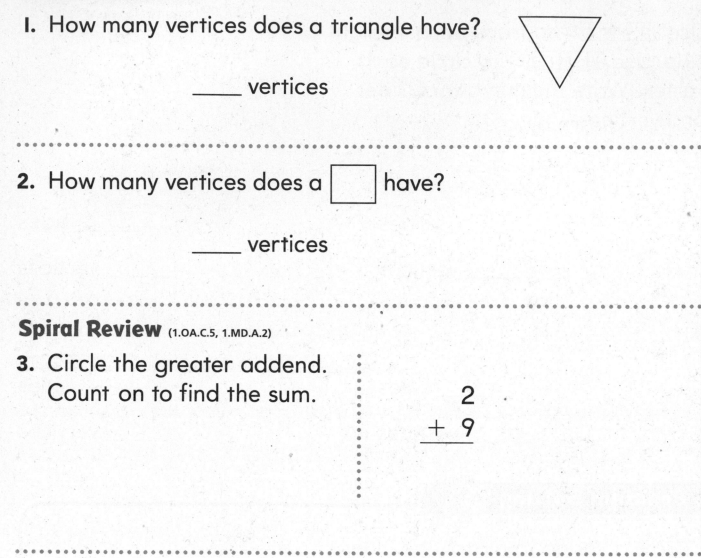

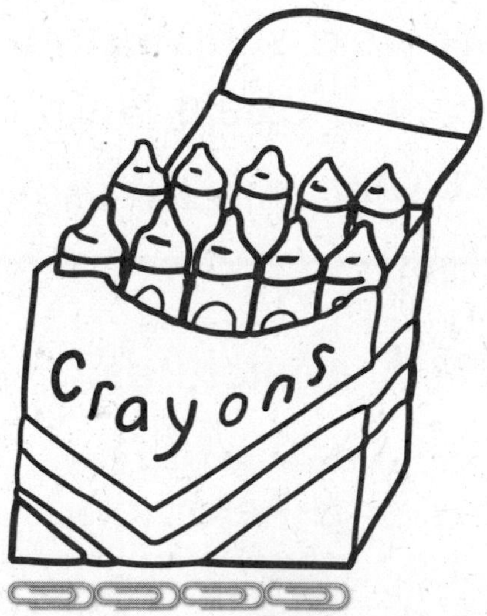

FOR MORE PRACTICE GO TO THE **Personal Math Trainer**

Name ____________________

Combine Two-Dimensional Shapes

Essential Question How can you put two-dimensional shapes together to make new two-dimensional shapes?

Common Core **Geometry—1.G.A.2**

MATHEMATICAL PRACTICES
MP5, MP6

Listen and Draw

Hands On

Use pattern blocks. Draw to show your work.

Math Talk MATHEMATICAL PRACTICES 5

Use Tools Describe the new shape Karen made.

FOR THE TEACHER • Have children use pattern blocks to act out the following problem. Karen has some pattern blocks. She puts two triangles together. Draw a new shape Karen could make.

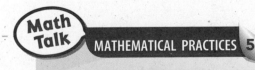

Model and Draw

How many do you need to make a ?

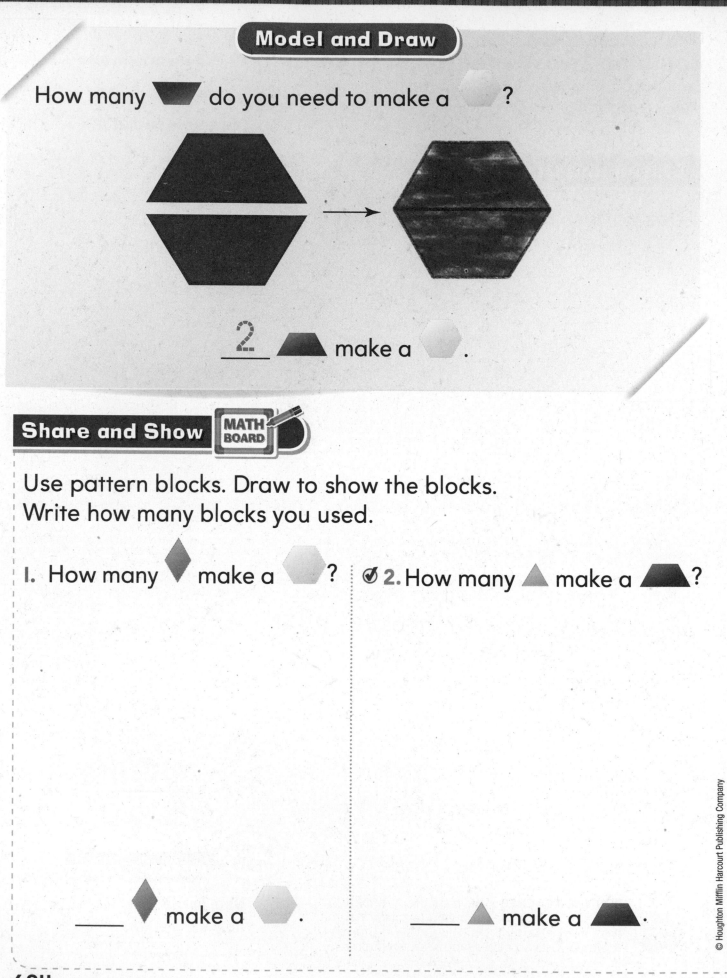

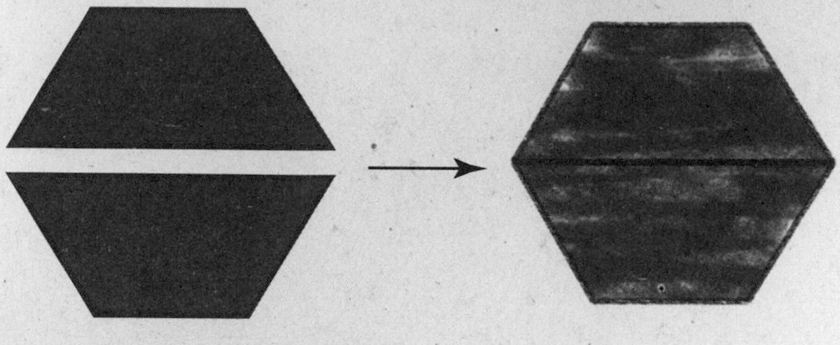

2 make a .

Share and Show MATH BOARD

Use pattern blocks. Draw to show the blocks.
Write how many blocks you used.

1. How many make a ?

____ make a .

✓ 2. How many make a ?

____ make a .

Name ____________________

On Your Own

MATHEMATICAL PRACTICE 5 **Use a Concrete Model** Use pattern blocks. Draw to show the blocks. Write how many blocks you used.

3. How many  make a ?

____  make a .

4. How many  make a ?

____  make a .

5. THINK SMARTER Use me two times to make this shape. Which block am I? Circle a block to show your answer.

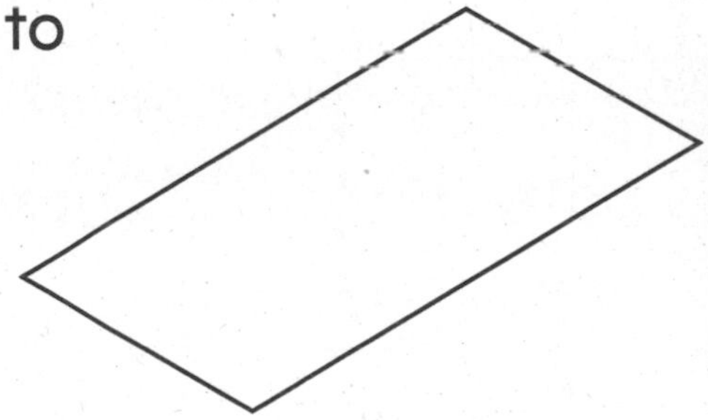

6. GO DEEPER Use these pattern blocks to make the shape. Write how many times you used each block.

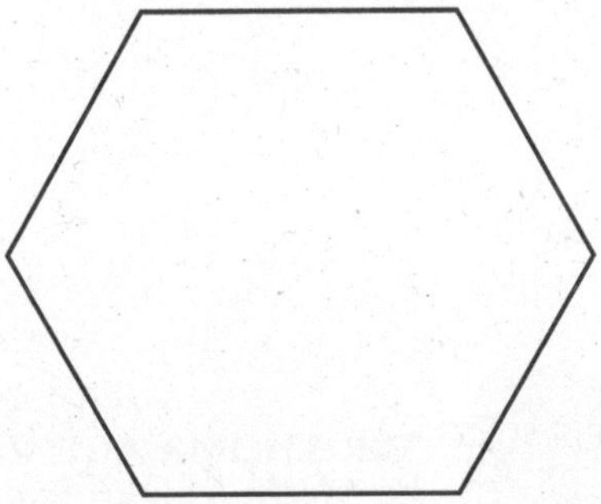

____ ____ ____

Problem Solving • Applications WRITE ▸ Math

GO DEEPER Use pattern blocks.
Draw to show your answer.

7. 2 ▲ make a ◆.

How many ▲ make 3 ◆?

___ ▲ make 3 ◆.

8. **THINK SMARTER +** How many ▲ make a ▰?

Use pattern blocks. Draw to show the blocks you used.

Personal Math Trainer

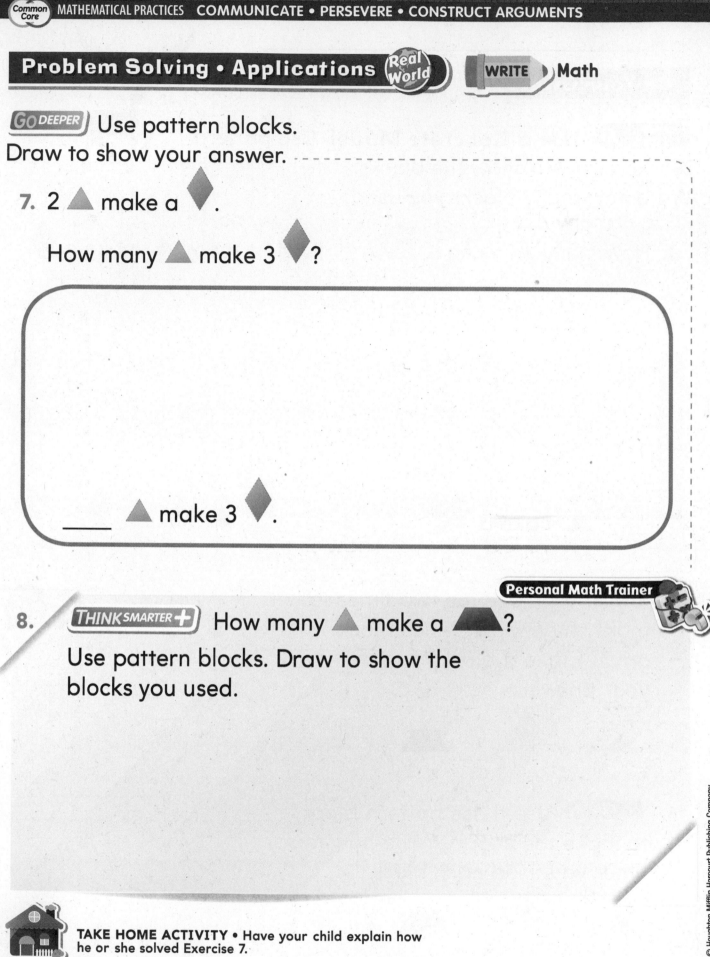

TAKE HOME ACTIVITY • Have your child explain how he or she solved Exercise 7.

Name ______________________________

Combine Two-Dimensional Shapes

Common Core **COMMON CORE STANDARD—1.G.A.2**
Reason with shapes and their attributes.

Use pattern blocks. Draw to show the blocks. Write how many blocks you used.

1. How many  make a 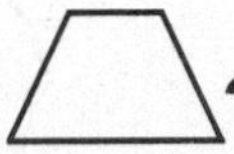?

_____  make a 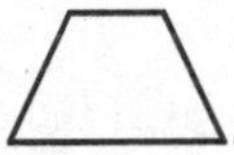.

2. How many  make a ?

_____  make a .

Problem Solving Real World

Use pattern blocks. Draw to show your answer.

3. 2 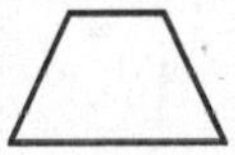 make a .

How many 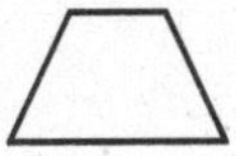 make 4 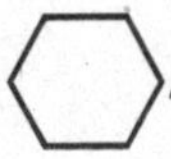?

_____ 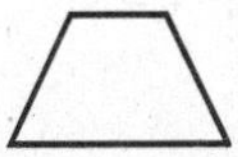 make 4 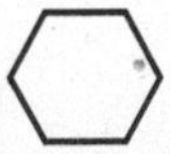.

4. WRITE Math Draw the shapes you could put together to make a rectangle.

Lesson Check (1.G.A.2)

1. How many △ do you use to make a ⬡?

   ______ △ make a ⬡.

2. How many ◇ do you use to make a ⬡?

   ______ ◇ make a ⬡.

Spiral Review (1.MD.A.2, 1.MD.B.3)

3. Use 📎. Which string is about 5 📎 long? Circle the string that is about 5 📎 long.

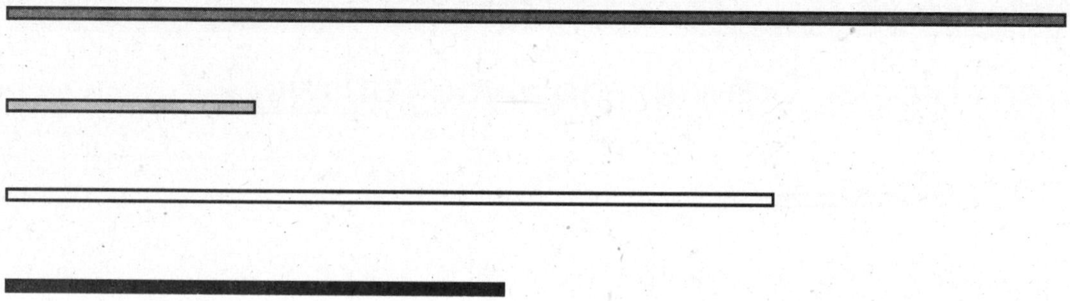

4. Look at the hour hand. Write the time.

______

FOR MORE PRACTICE GO TO THE **Personal Math Trainer**

Lesson 12.4

Name ____________________

Combine More Shapes

Essential Question How can you combine two-dimensional shapes to make new shapes?

Common Core Geometry—1.G.A.2

MATHEMATICAL PRACTICES
MP1, MP4

Listen and Draw

Hands On

Use shapes to fill each outline.
Draw to show your work.

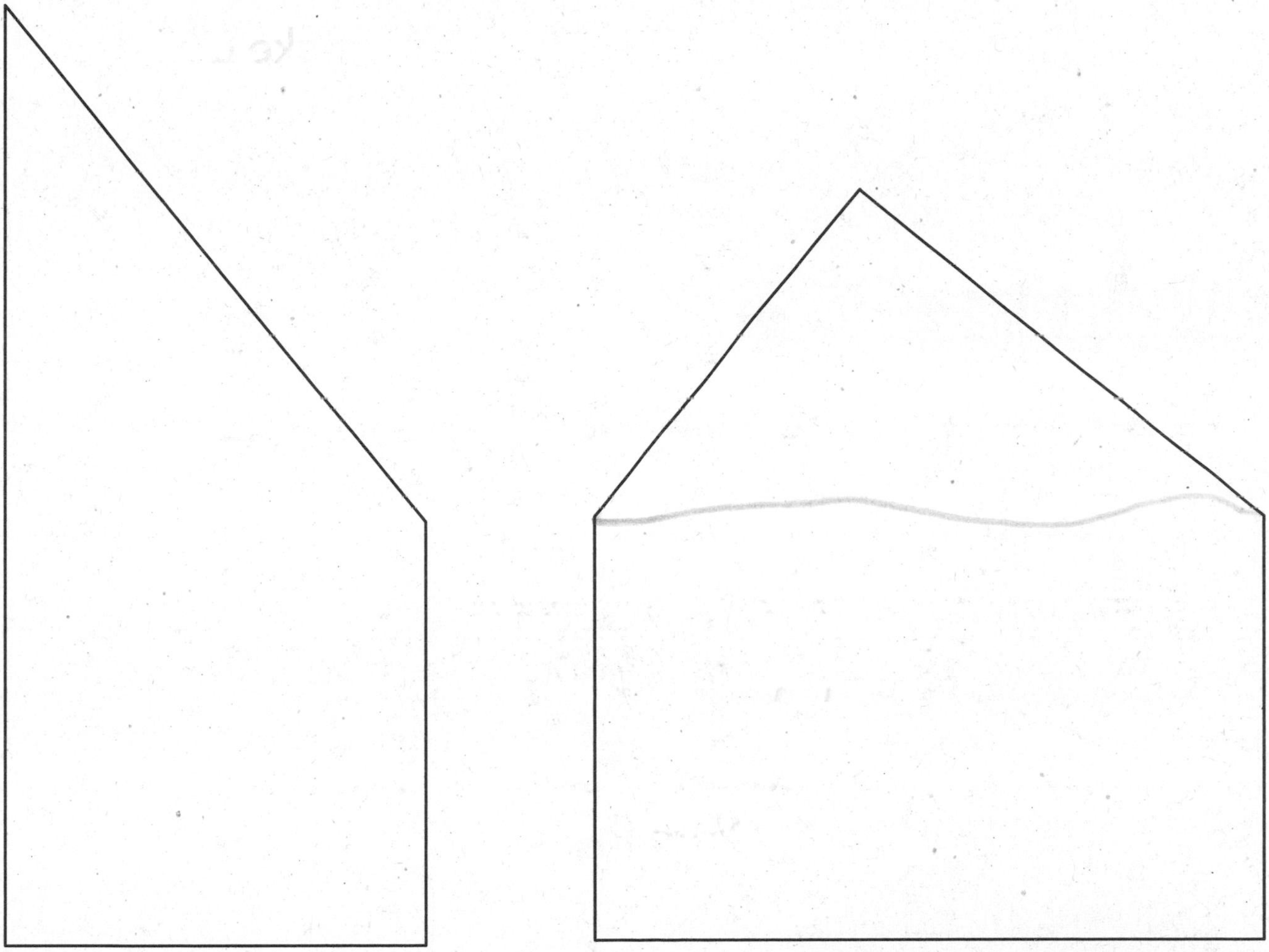

Math Talk MATHEMATICAL PRACTICES 4

Represent Use the outline on the left to describe how two shapes can make another shape.

FOR THE TEACHER • Have children use two shapes to fill the outline on the left, and draw a line to show the two shapes. Then have children use three shapes to fill the outline on the right, again drawing lines to show the shapes.

Model and Draw

Combine shapes to make a new shape.

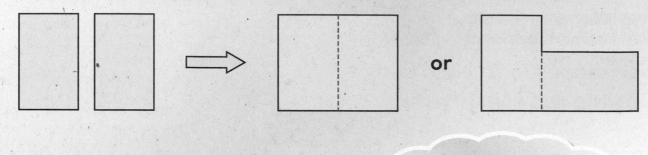

How else could you combine 2  ?

Share and Show MATH BOARD

Circle two shapes that can combine to make the shape on the left.

1.  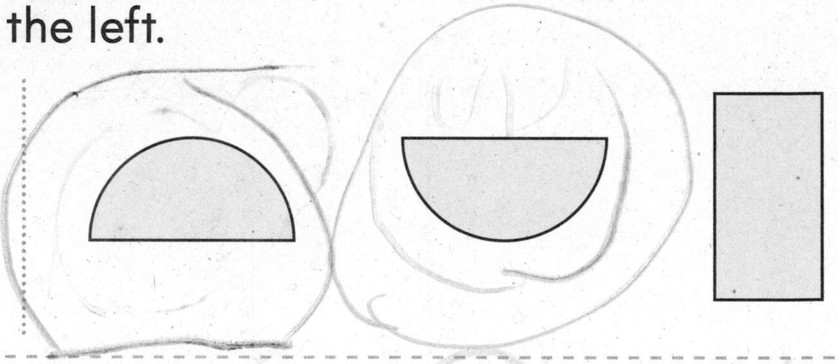

2.  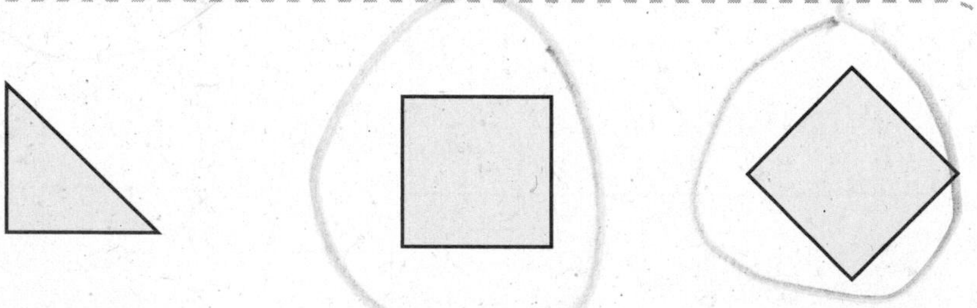

3. 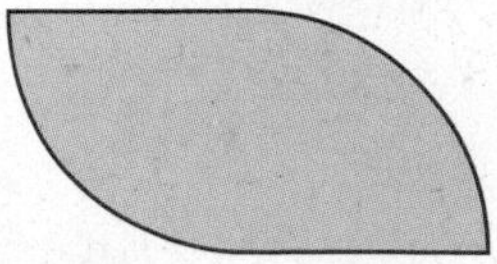 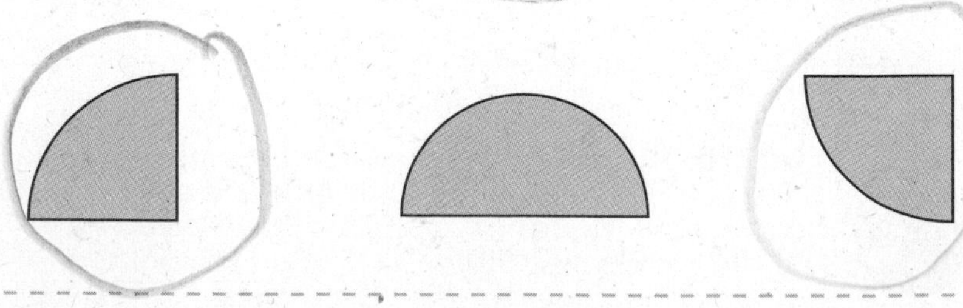

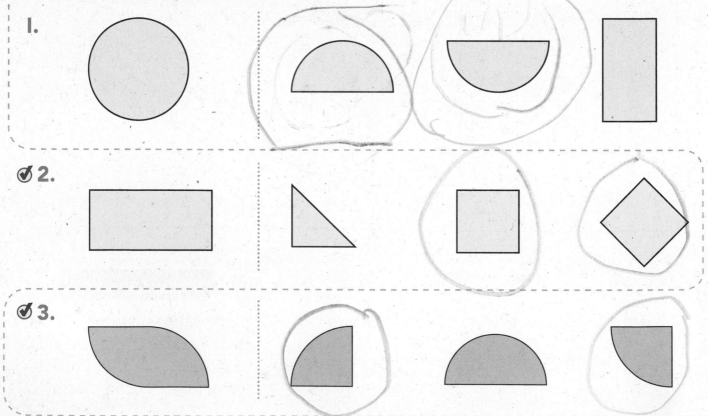

Name ______________________________

On Your Own

MATHEMATICAL PRACTICE 4 **Use Diagrams** Circle two shapes that can combine to make the shape on the left.

4.

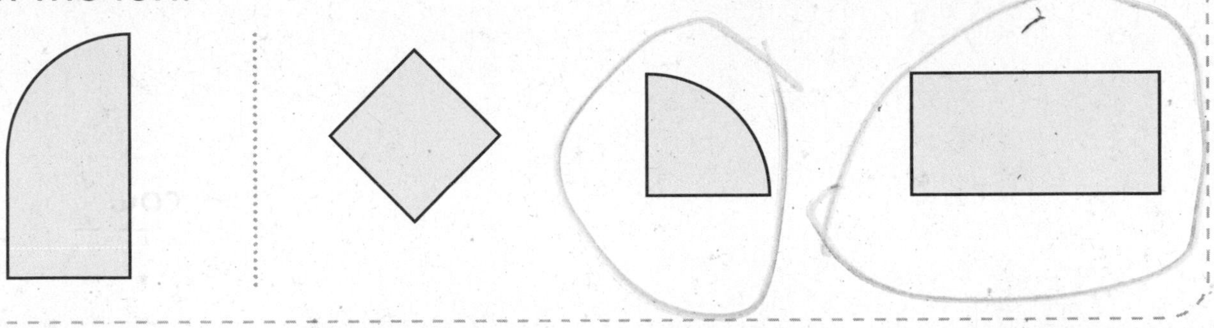

5.

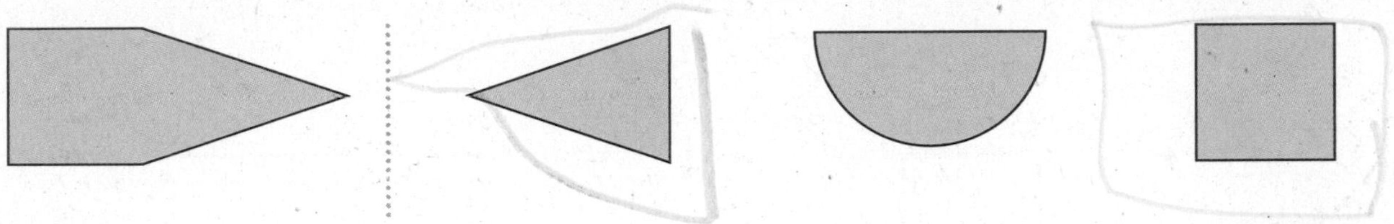

THINKSMARTER Draw lines to show two different ways to combine the shapes on the left to make new shapes on the right.

6.

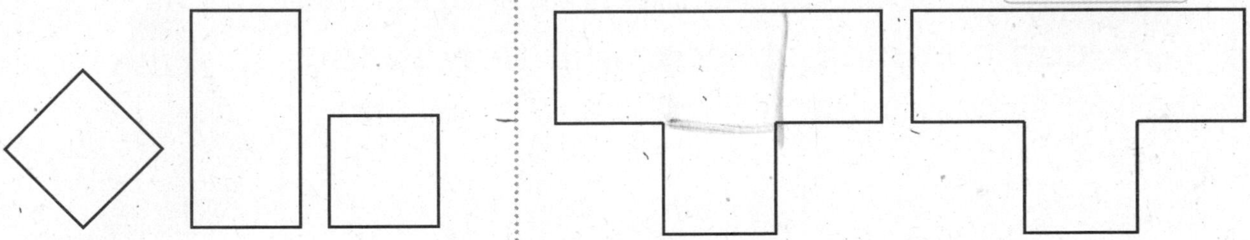

7.

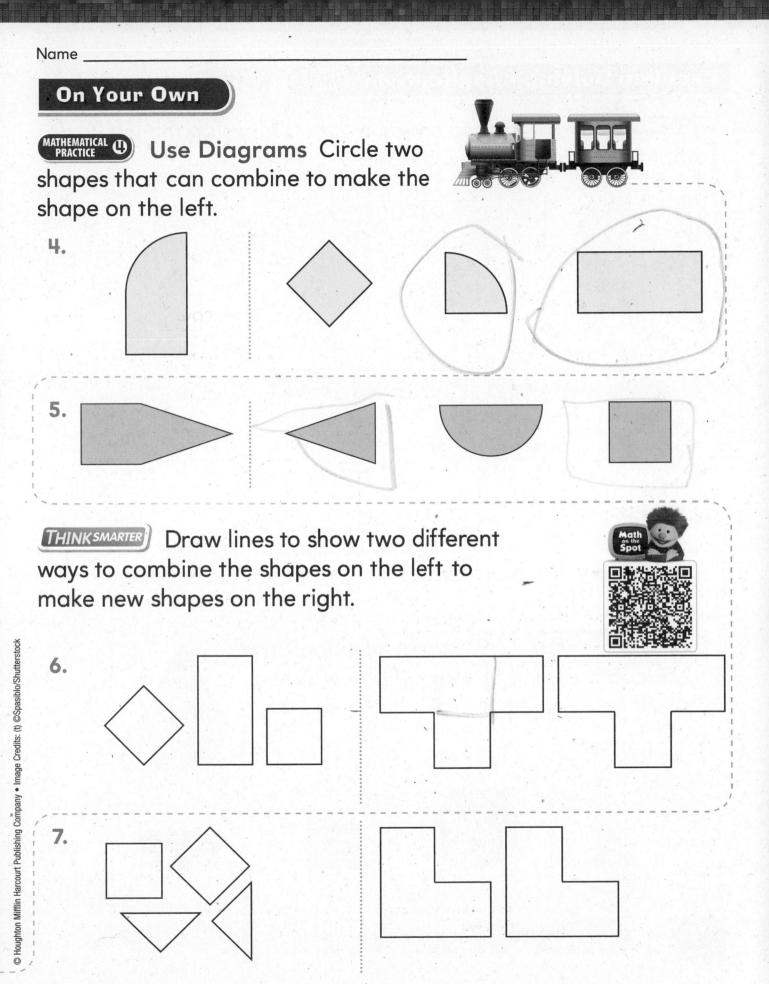

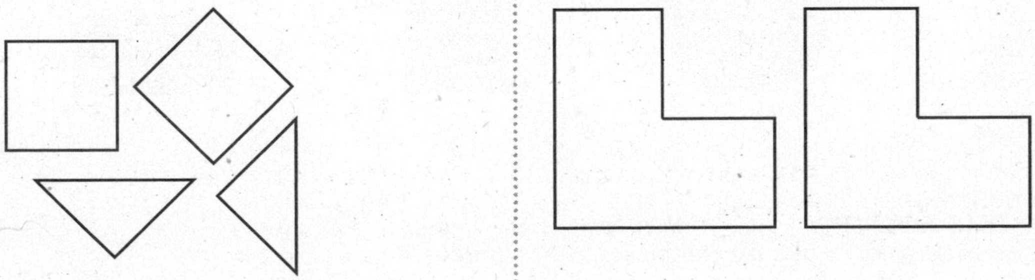

Problem Solving • Applications Real World

WRITE Math

THINKSMARTER Draw lines to show how the shapes on the left combine to make the new shape.

8.

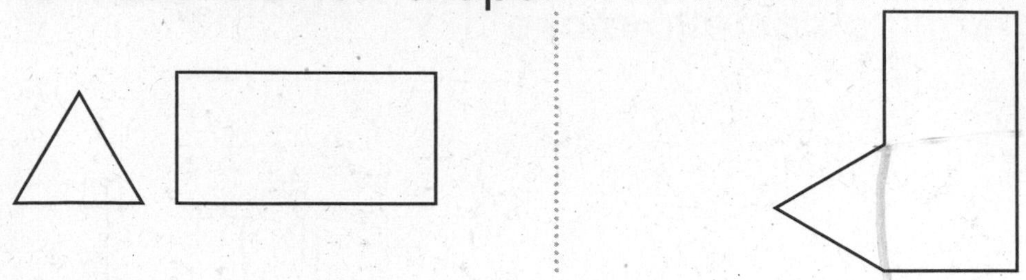

9.

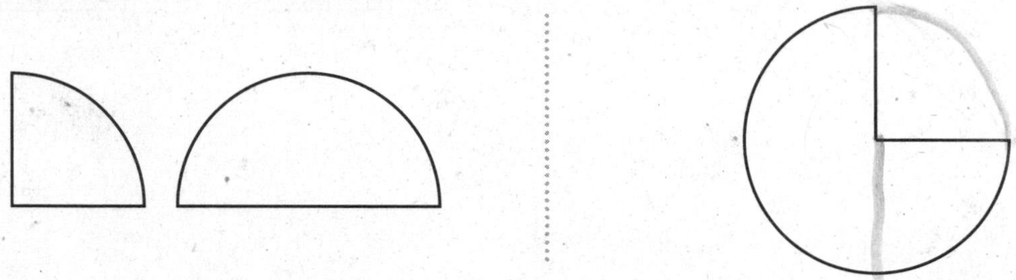

10.

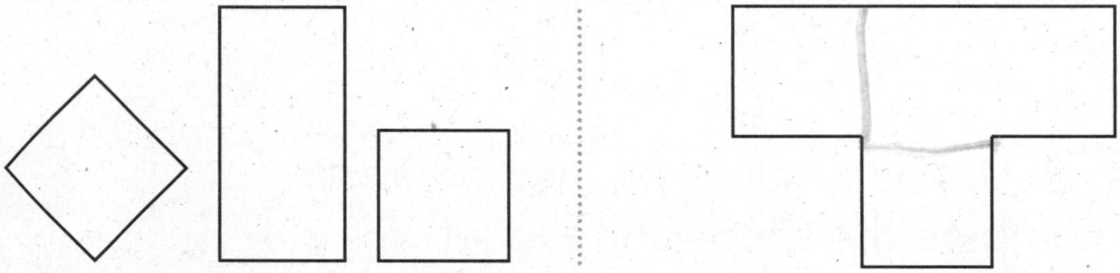

11. THINKSMARTER Circle the two shapes that can combine to make this new shape.

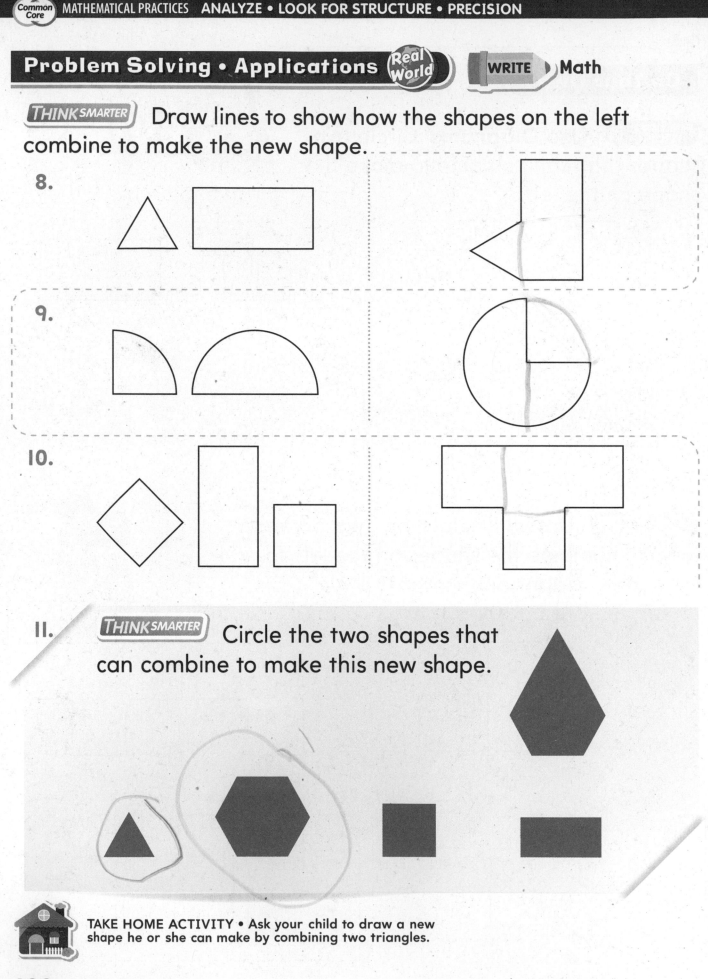

TAKE HOME ACTIVITY • Ask your child to draw a new shape he or she can make by combining two triangles.

Name ______________________________

Combine More Shapes

Practice and Homework
Lesson 12.4

Common Core — **COMMON CORE STANDARD—1.G.A.2**
Reason with shapes and their attributes.

Circle two shapes that can combine to make the shape on the left.

1.

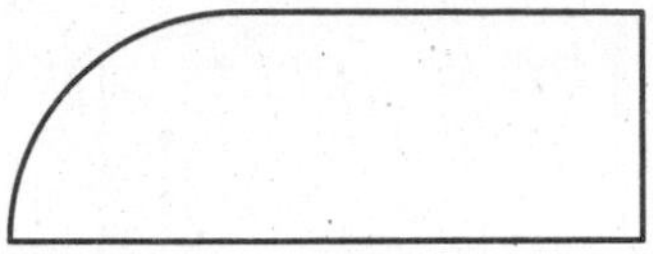

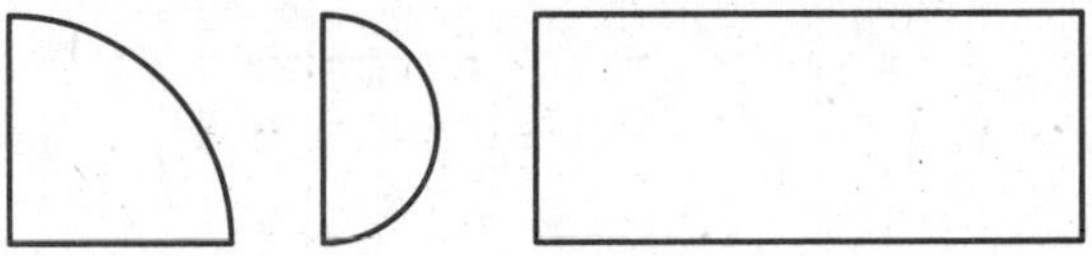

2.

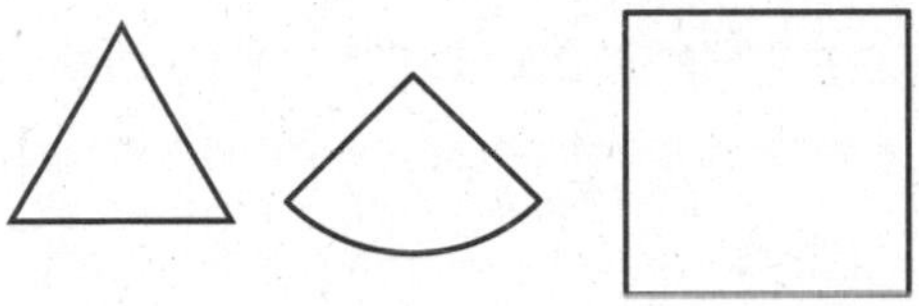

Problem Solving Real World

3. Draw lines to show how the shapes on the left combine to make the new shape.

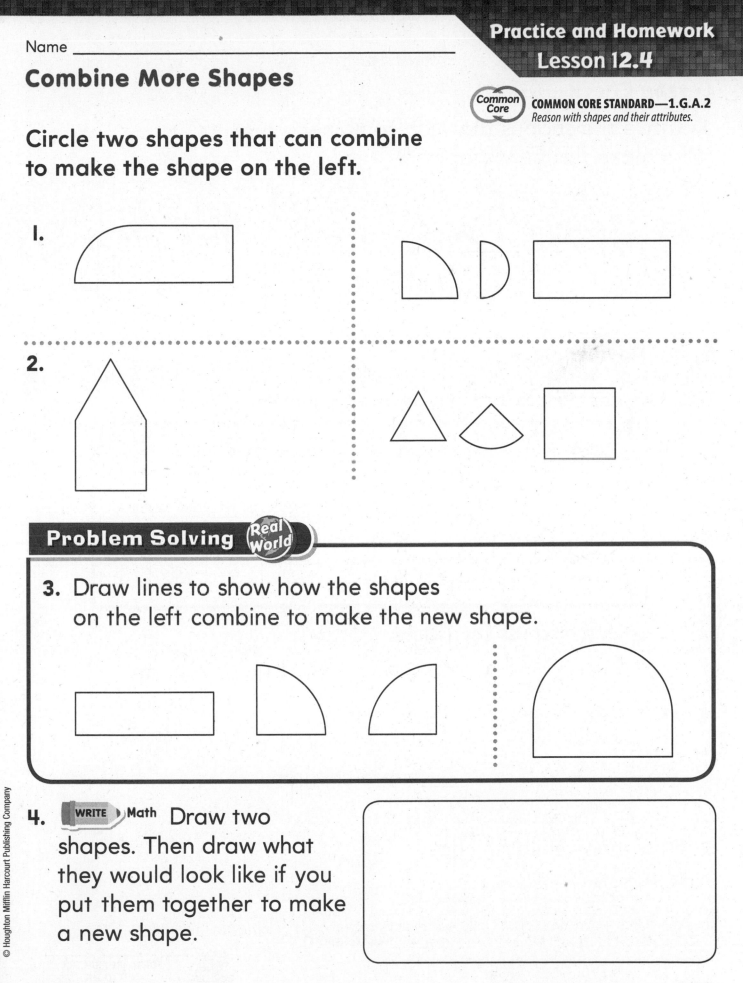

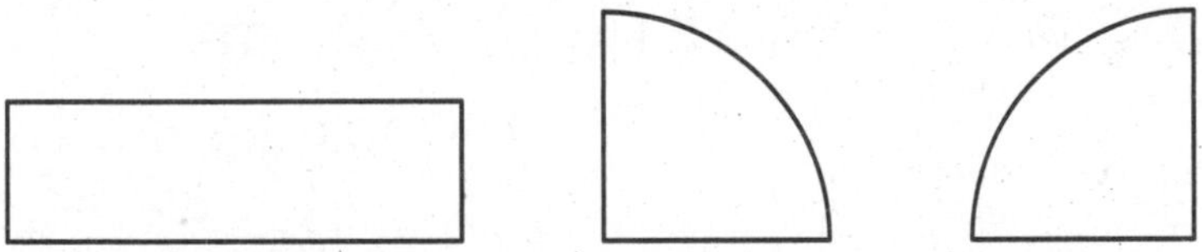

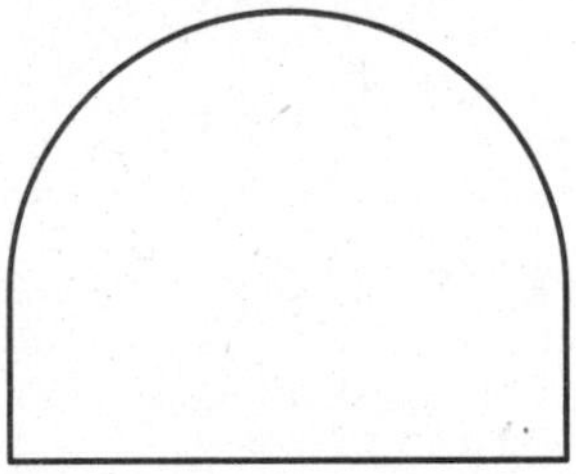

4. WRITE Math Draw two shapes. Then draw what they would look like if you put them together to make a new shape.

Lesson Check (1.G.A.2)

1. Circle the shapes that can combine to make this new shape.

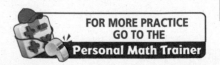

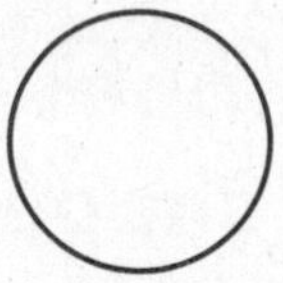

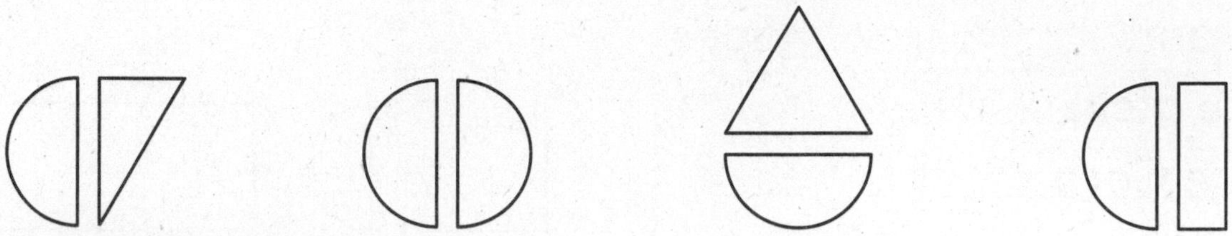

Spiral Review (1.MD.C.4)

Use the picture graph to answer each question.

Our Favorite Activity						
Swimming	🧍	🧍	🧍			
Dancing	🧍	🧍	🧍	🧍		
Drawing	🧍	🧍	🧍	🧍	🧍	🧍

Each 🧍 stands for 1 child.

2. How many more children chose [crayon] than [swimming]?

____ more children

3. How many children chose [dancing] and [swimming]?

____ children

FOR MORE PRACTICE GO TO THE **Personal Math Trainer**

Name ____________________

Problem Solving • Make New Two-Dimensional Shapes

Essential Question How can acting it out help you make new shapes from combined shapes?

Common Core **Geometry—1.G.A.2**

MATHEMATICAL PRACTICES
MP1, MP4

Cora wants to combine shapes to make a circle. She has .
How can Cora make a circle?

Unlock the Problem

What do I need to find?

how Cora can make a
circle

What information do I need to use?

Cora uses this shape.

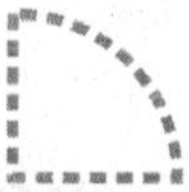

Show how to solve the problem.

Step 1 Use shapes. Combine to make a new shape.

Step 2 Then use the new shape.

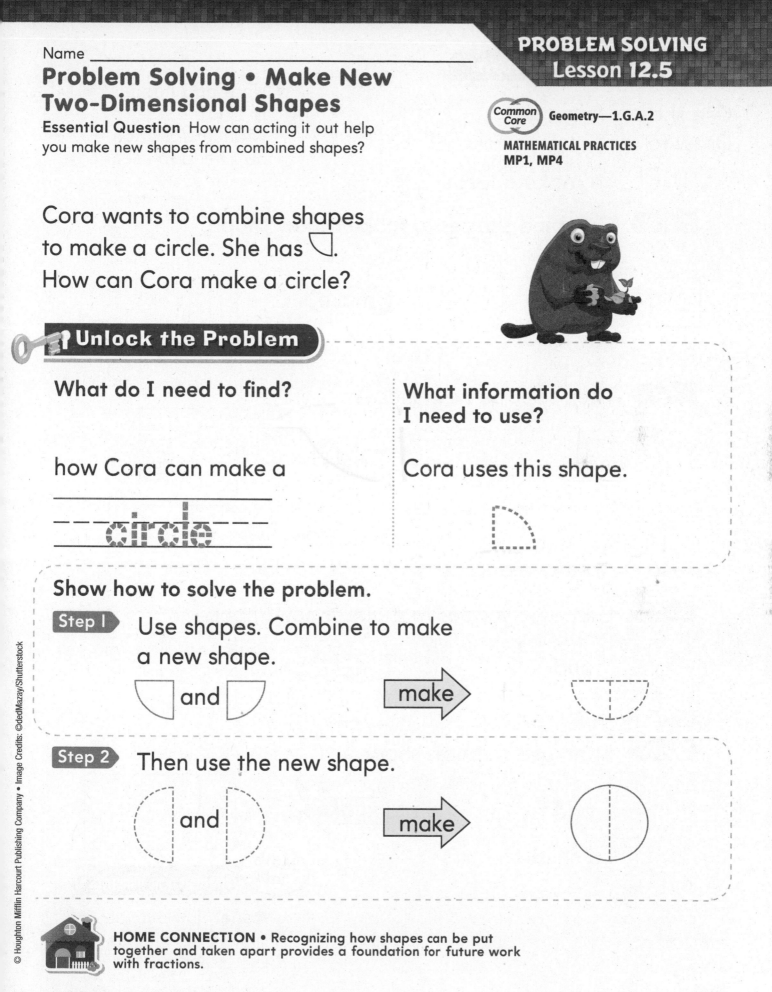

HOME CONNECTION • Recognizing how shapes can be put together and taken apart provides a foundation for future work with fractions.

Try Another Problem

Use shapes to solve.
Draw to show your work.

- What do I need to find?
- What information do I need to use?

1. Use ☐ to make a larger ☐.

 Step 1 ▷ Combine shapes to make a new shape.

 ☐ and ☐ make ▷ ▯

 Step 2 ▷ Then use the new shape.

 and make ▷ ☐

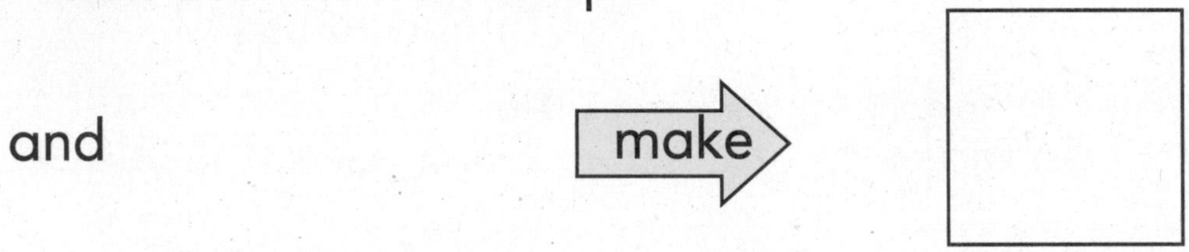

2. Use ◺ to make a ▭.

 Step 1 ▷ Combine shapes to make a new shape.

 ◺ and ◺ make ▷ ☐

 Step 2 ▷ Then use the new shape.

 and make ▷ ▭

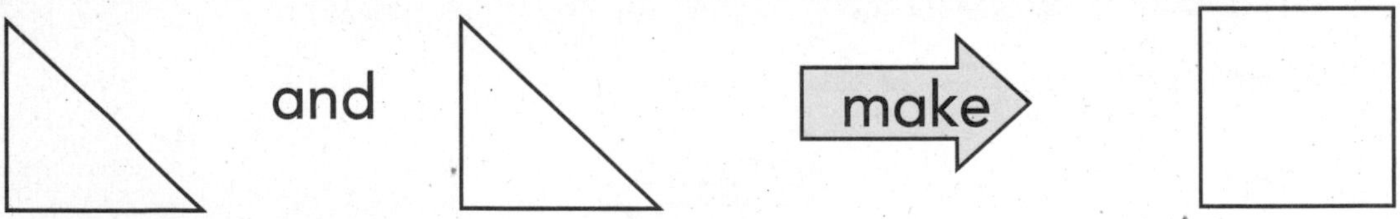

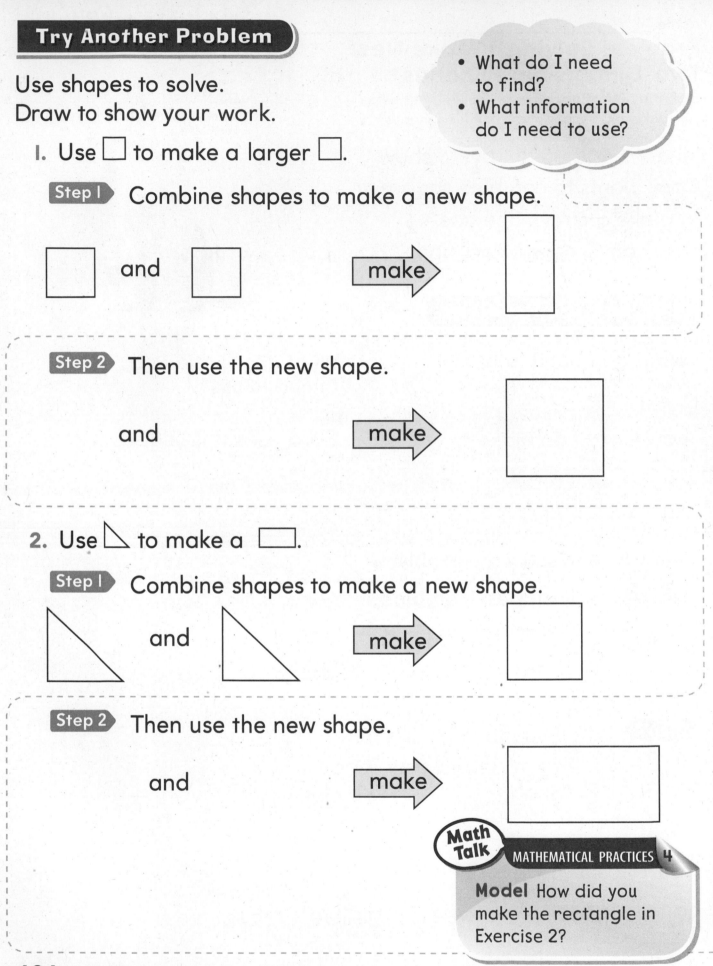

Math Talk MATHEMATICAL PRACTICES 4

Model How did you make the rectangle in Exercise 2?

Name ______________________________

Share and Show MATH BOARD

MATHEMATICAL PRACTICE 1 **Analyze Relationships** Use shapes to solve. Draw to show your work.

3. Use to make a .

Step 1 Combine shapes to make a new shape.

 and 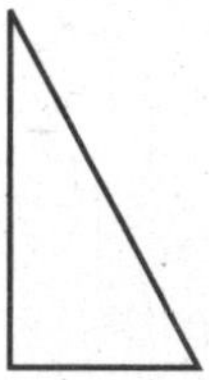

make

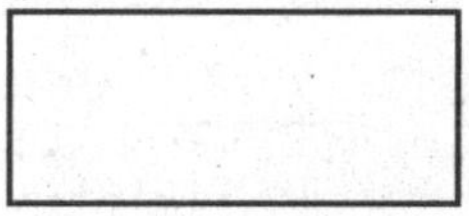

Step 2 Then use the new shape.

and

make

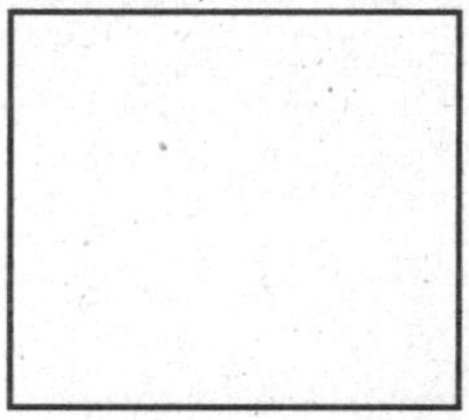

4. THINK SMARTER Use and to make a .

Math on the Spot

Step 1 Combine shapes to make a new shape.

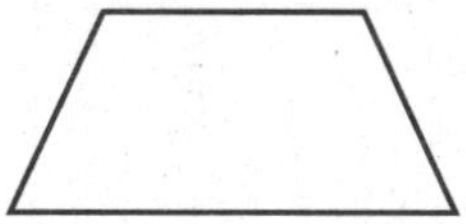 and 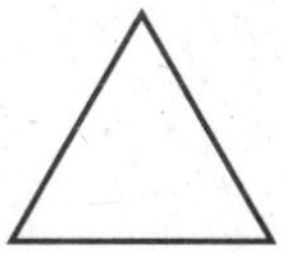

make

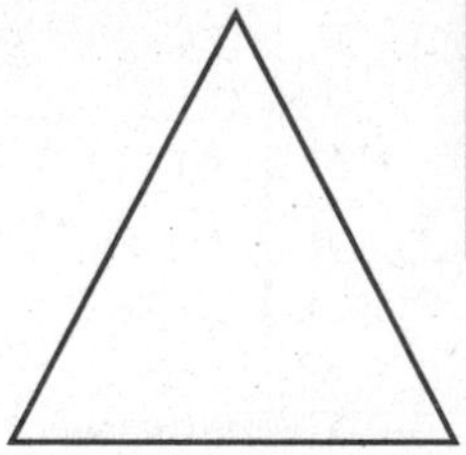

Step 2 Then use the new shape.

and

make

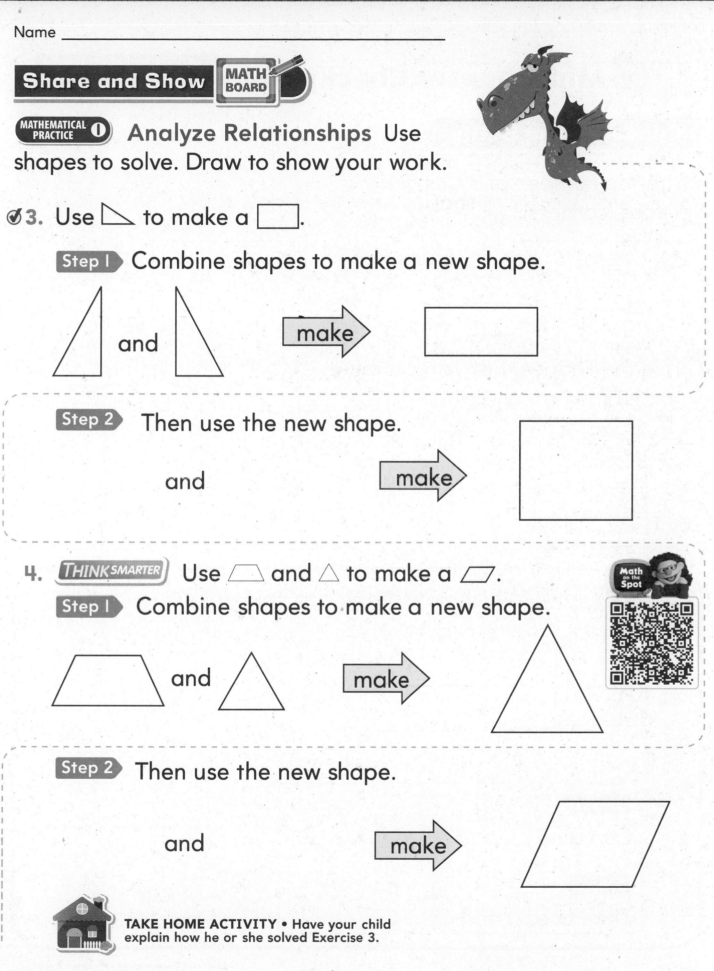

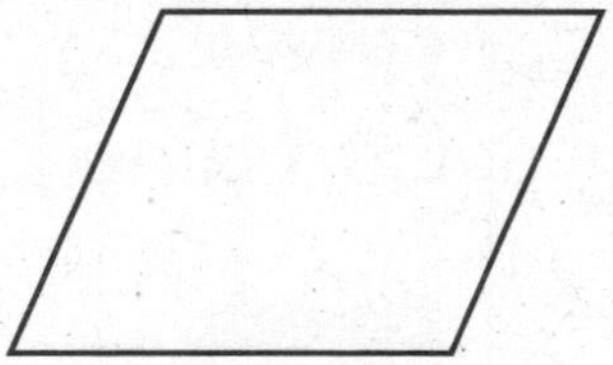

TAKE HOME ACTIVITY • Have your child explain how he or she solved Exercise 3.

Name ______________________________

Mid-Chapter Checkpoint

Personal Math Trainer
Online Assessment and Intervention

Concepts and Skills

Write the number of sides and vertices (corners). (1.G.A.1)

1. 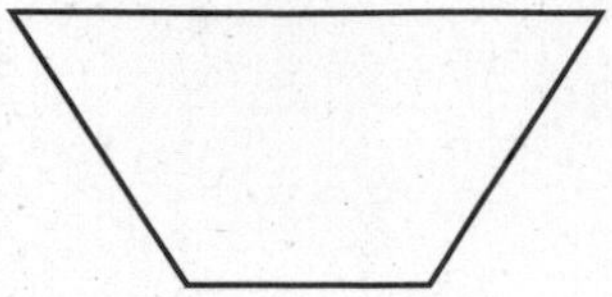

____ sides

____ vertices

2. 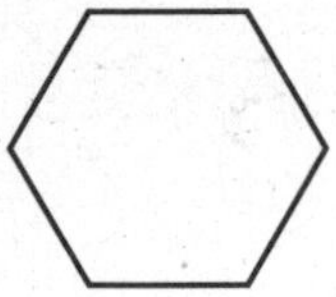

____ sides

____ vertices

Circle the shapes that can combine to make the new shape. (1.G.A.2)

3. 

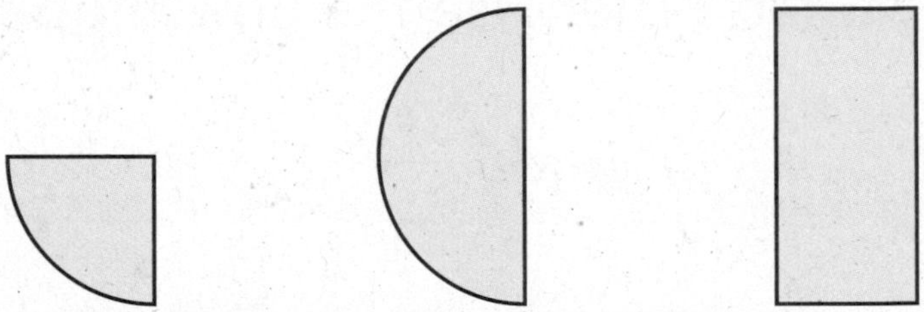

4. THINKSMARTER Which new shape can you make? (1.G.A.2)

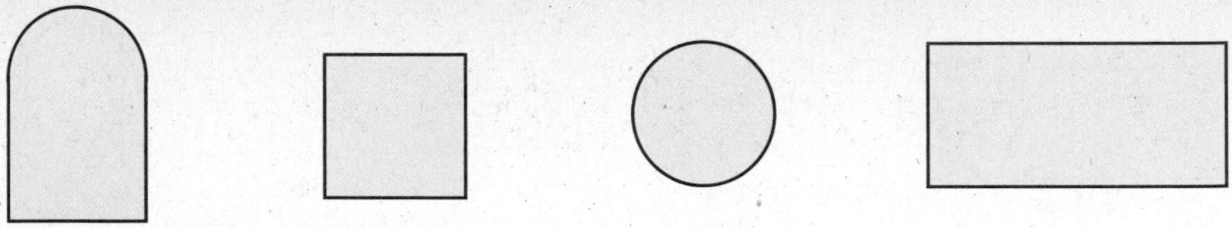

○ ○ ○ ○

Step 1

Combine  and 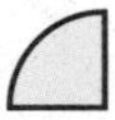 to make 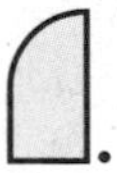.

Step 2

Then use  and 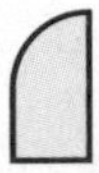.

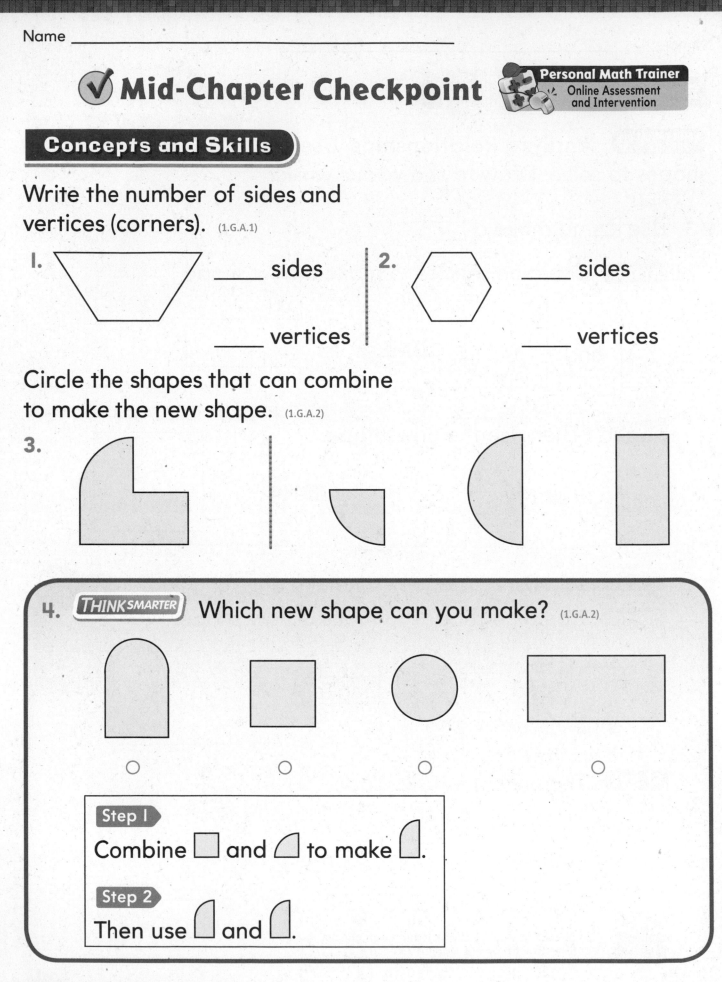

Name _____

Problem Solving • Make New Two-Dimensional Shapes

Common Core **COMMON CORE STANDARD—1.G.A.2**
Reason with shapes and their attributes.

Use shapes to solve.
Draw to show your work.

1. Use ☐ to make a ▭.
 Step 1. Combine shapes to make a new shape.

 ☐ and ☐ make➔ ▭

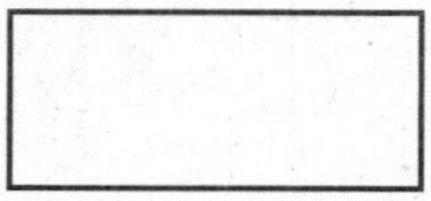

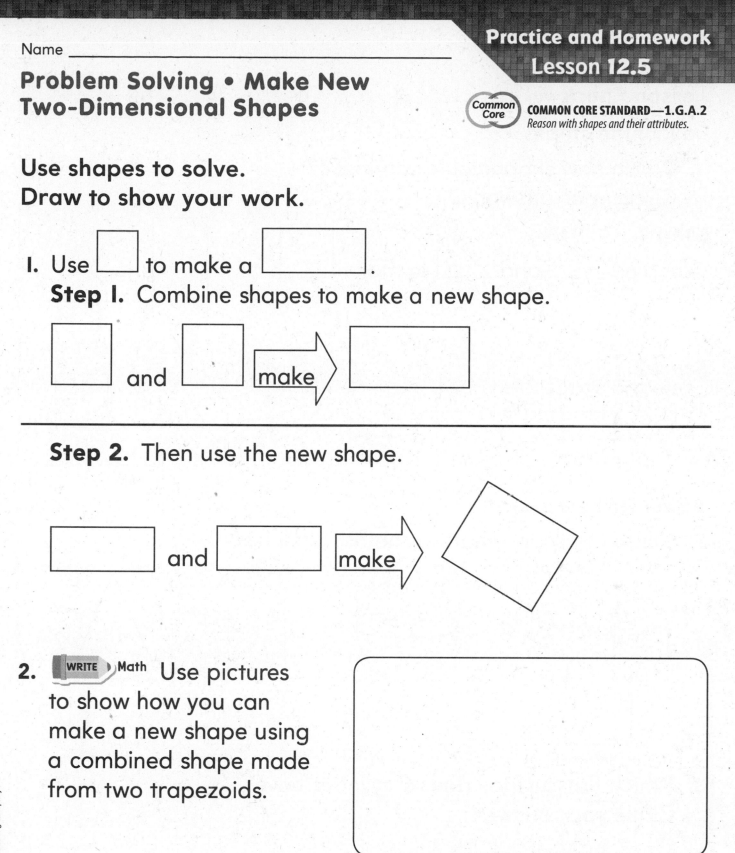

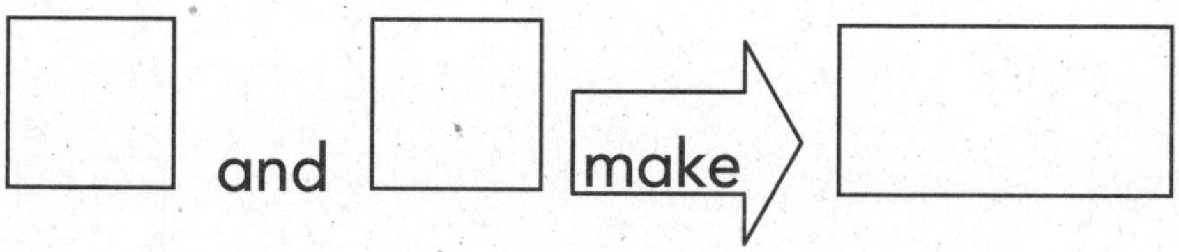

 Step 2. Then use the new shape.

 ▭ and ▭ make➔ ◇

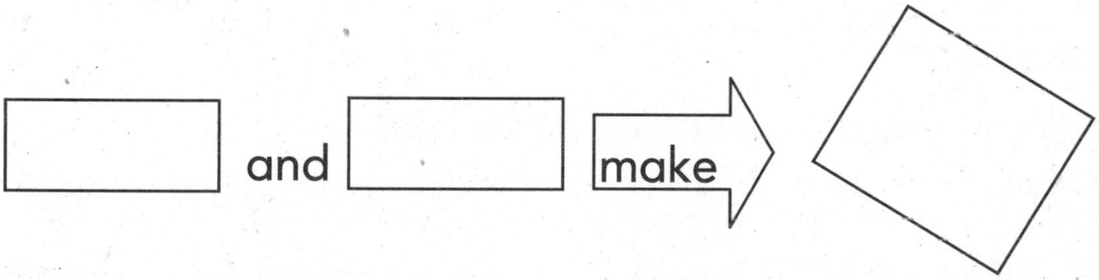

2. ✏️ WRITE Math Use pictures to show how you can make a new shape using a combined shape made from two trapezoids.

Lesson Check (1.G.A.2)

Follow the steps.

1. Which new shape could you make?
 Circle your answer.

Step 1.
Combine △ and △ to make ☐ .

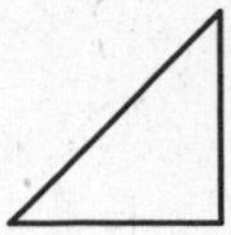

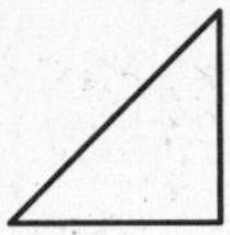

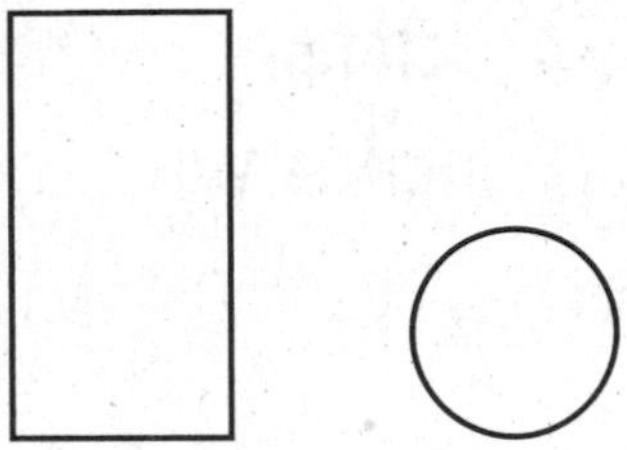

Step 2.
Then use ☐ and ☐ .

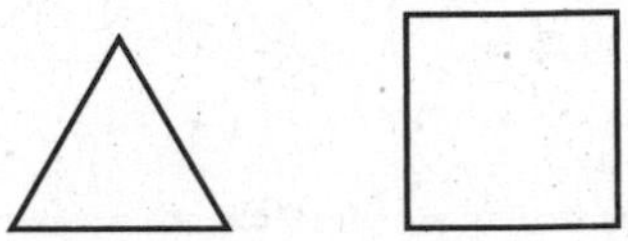

Spiral Review (1.G.A.1)

2. Circle the shape that has no flat surfaces.

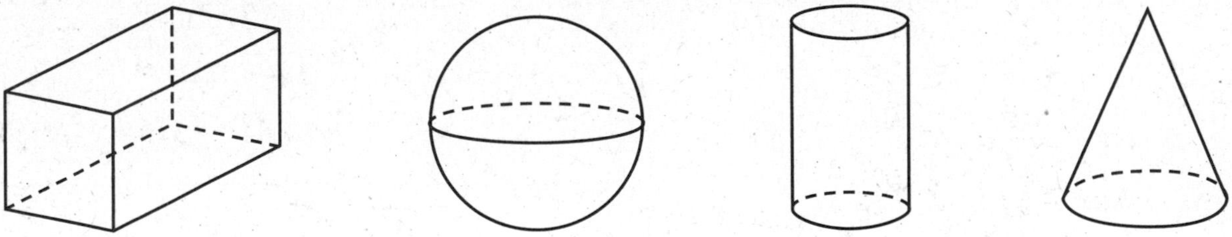

3. Which flat surface does a cylinder have?
 Circle your answer.

© Houghton Mifflin Harcourt Publishing Company

FOR MORE PRACTICE
GO TO THE
Personal Math Trainer

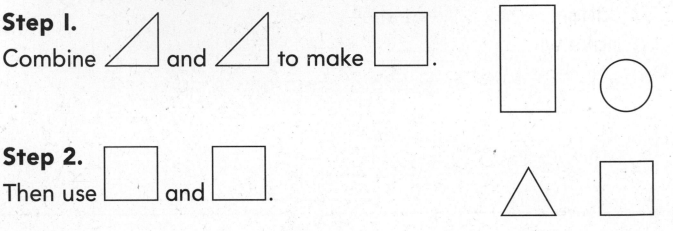

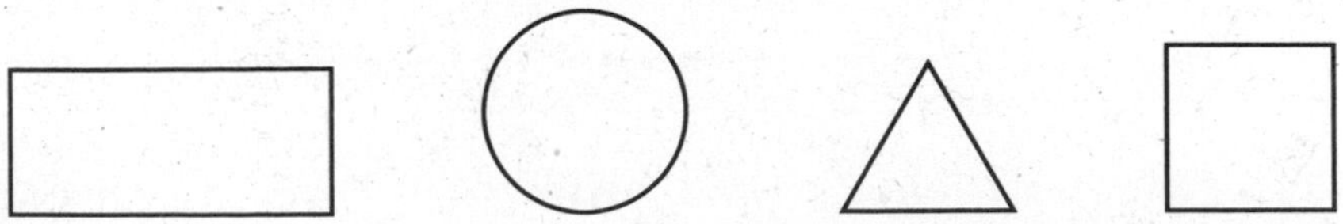

Name _____

Find Shapes in Shapes

Essential Question How can you find shapes in other shapes?

Common Core Geometry—1.G.A.2

MATHEMATICAL PRACTICES
MP4, MP5

Listen and Draw

Use pattern blocks. What shape can you make with 1 ⬡ and 2 ▲? Draw to show your shape.

FOR THE TEACHER • Have children explore making new shapes with the given pattern blocks. Discuss different shapes that can be made using the same pattern blocks.

Math Talk

MATHEMATICAL PRACTICES 5

Use Tools Can you use the same pattern blocks to make a different shape?

Model and Draw

Which two pattern blocks make this shape?

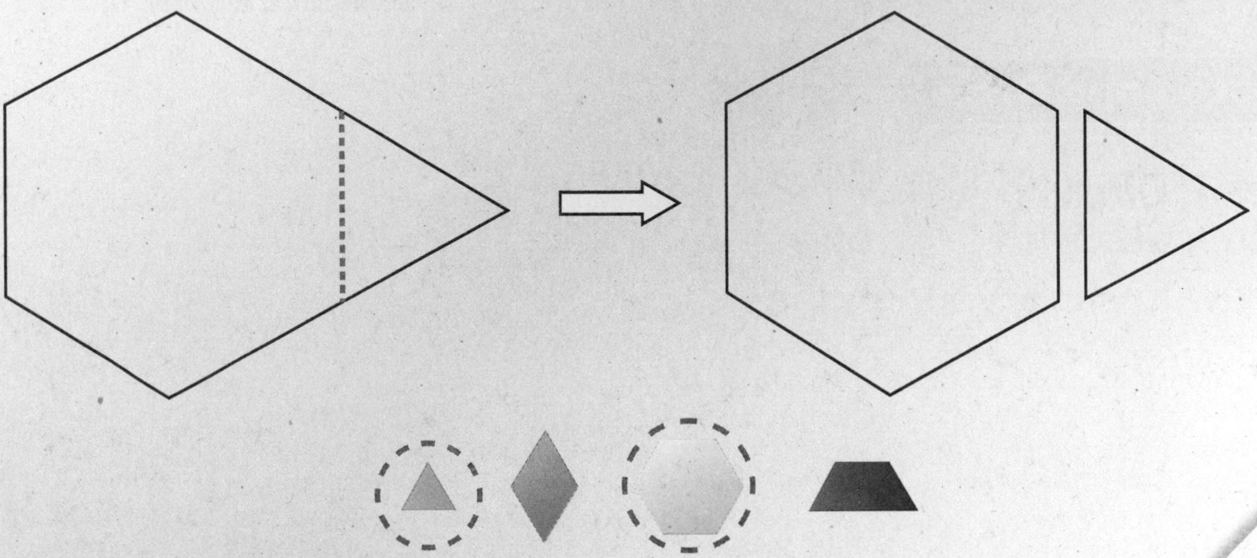

Share and Show

MATH BOARD

Use two pattern blocks to make the shape.
Draw a line to show your model. Color the shapes.
Circle the blocks you use.

1.

2.

Name ________________________________

On Your Own

MATHEMATICAL PRACTICE 5 **Use a Concrete Model**

Use two pattern blocks to make the shape. Draw a line to show your model. Color the shapes. Circle the blocks you use.

3.

4.

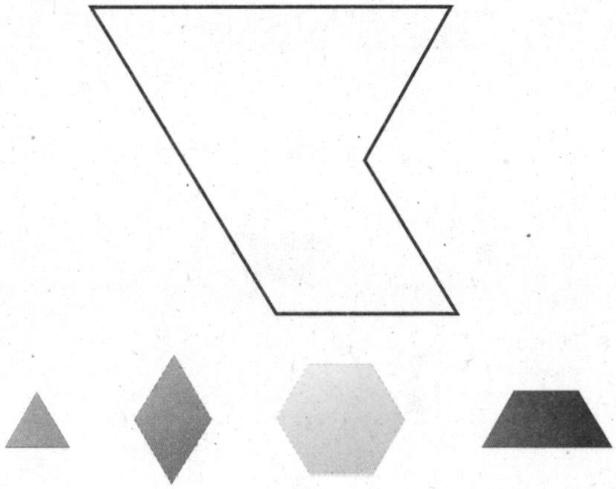

5.

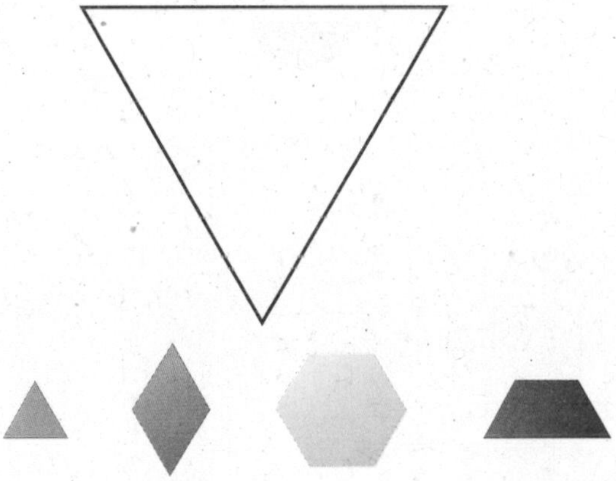

6.

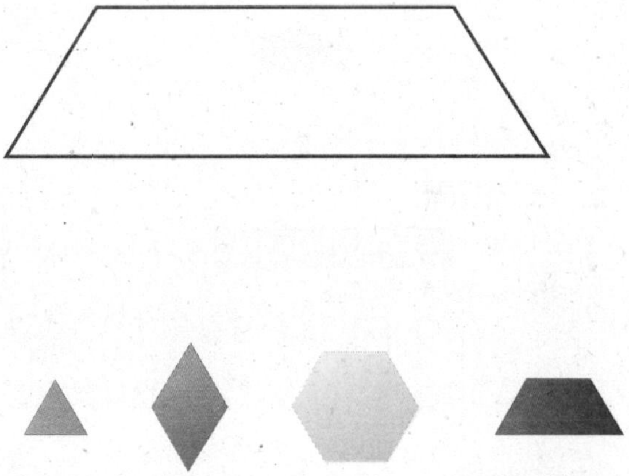

7. THINK SMARTER Use three pattern blocks to make the shape. Draw lines to show your model. Color the shapes. Circle the blocks you use.

Math on the Spot

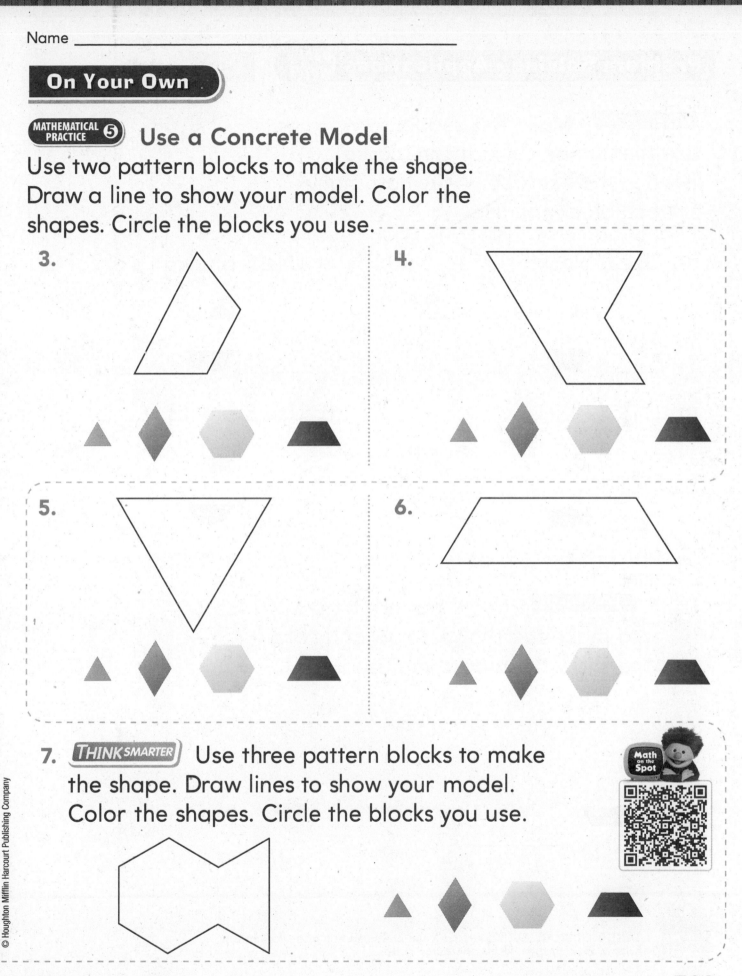

Problem Solving • Applications (Real World) WRITE ✏ Math

THINK SMARTER Make this shape.
Use the number of pattern blocks
listed in the exercise. Write how many
of each block you use.

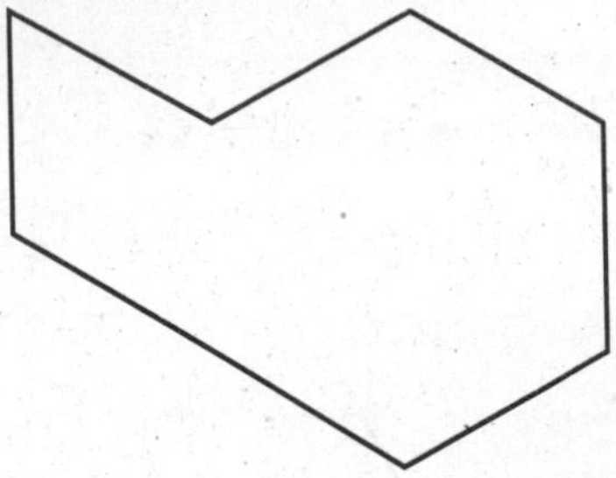

8. Use 3 blocks.

____ ▲ ____ ▱

____ ▽ ____ ⬡

9. Use 5 blocks.

____ ▲ ____ ▱

____ ▽ ____ ⬡

10. Use 7 blocks.

____ ▲ ____ ▱

____ ▽ ____ ⬡

11. Use 8 blocks.

____ ▲ ____ ▱

____ ▽ ____ ⬡

12. THINK SMARTER Use 4 pattern blocks
to make the shape. Draw and color
to show the blocks you used.

▽ ▲ ▱ ⬡

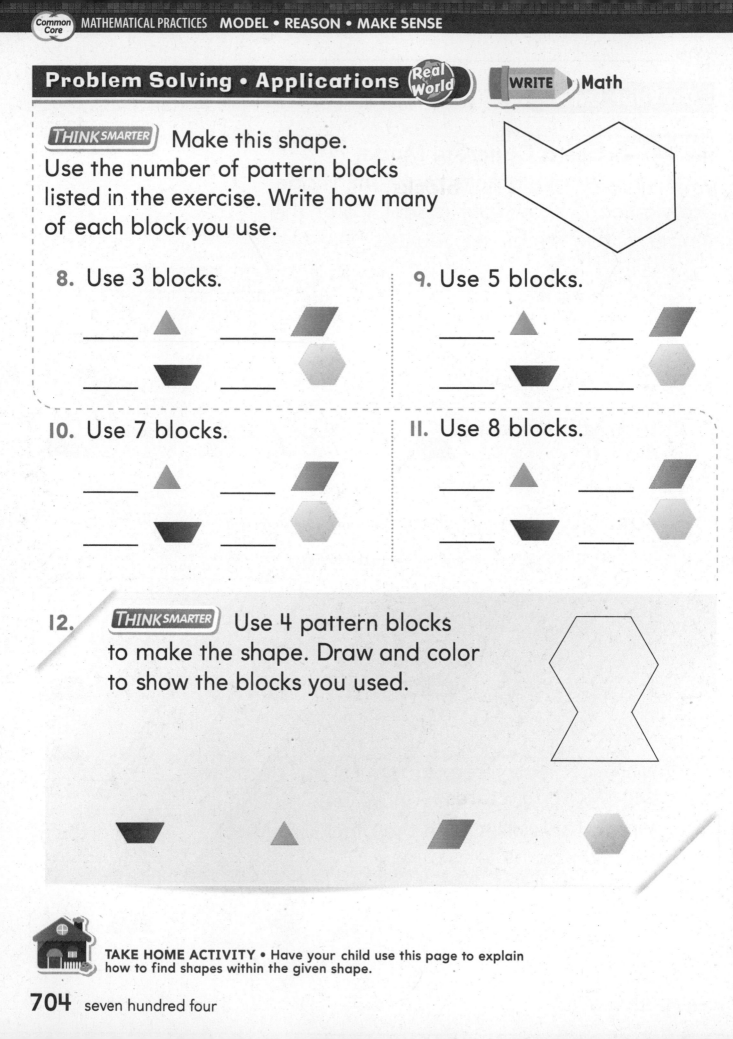

TAKE HOME ACTIVITY • Have your child use this page to explain
how to find shapes within the given shape.

Name ______________________________

Find Shapes in Shapes

Common Core **COMMON CORE STANDARD—1.G.A.2**
Reason with shapes and their attributes.

Use two pattern blocks to make the shape. Draw a line to show your model. Circle the blocks you use.

1.

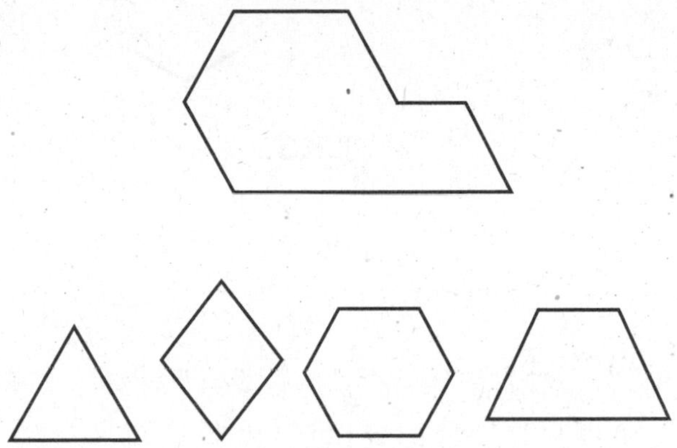

2.

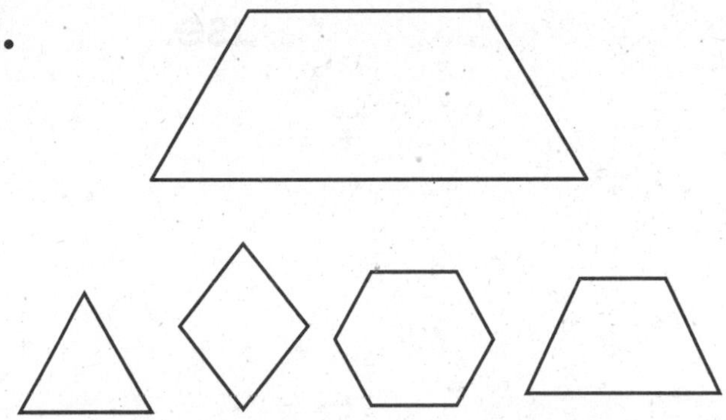

Problem Solving Real World

Make the shape to the right. Use the number of pattern blocks listed in the exercise. Write how many of each block you use.

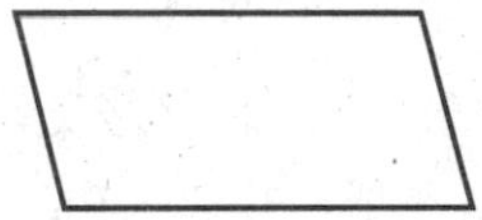

3. Use 3 blocks.

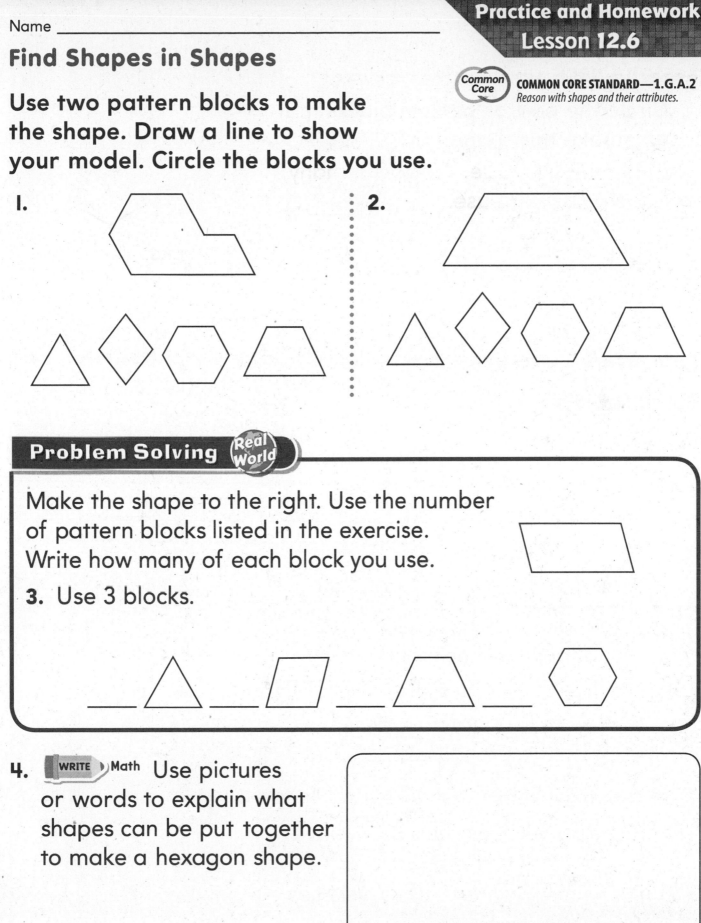

4. WRITE Math Use pictures or words to explain what shapes can be put together to make a hexagon shape.

Lesson Check (1.G.A.2)

1. Circle the pair of pattern blocks that can make this shape.

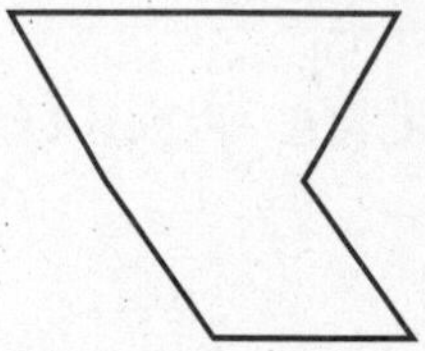

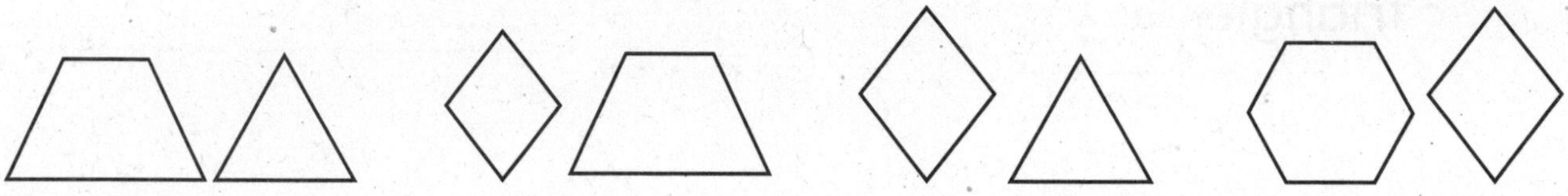

Spiral Review (1.MD.B.3, 1.MD.C.4, 1.G.A.1)

2. Write the time.

____

3. Write tally marks to show the number 8.

____

4. How many vertices does a  have?

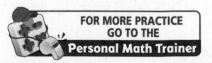

____ vertices

FOR MORE PRACTICE GO TO THE **Personal Math Trainer**

Name ______________________

Take Apart Two-Dimensional Shapes

Essential Question How can you take apart two dimensional shapes?

Common Core Geometry—1.G.A.2

MATHEMATICAL PRACTICES
MP1, MP7

Listen and Draw Real World

Color rectangles orange.
Color triangles purple.

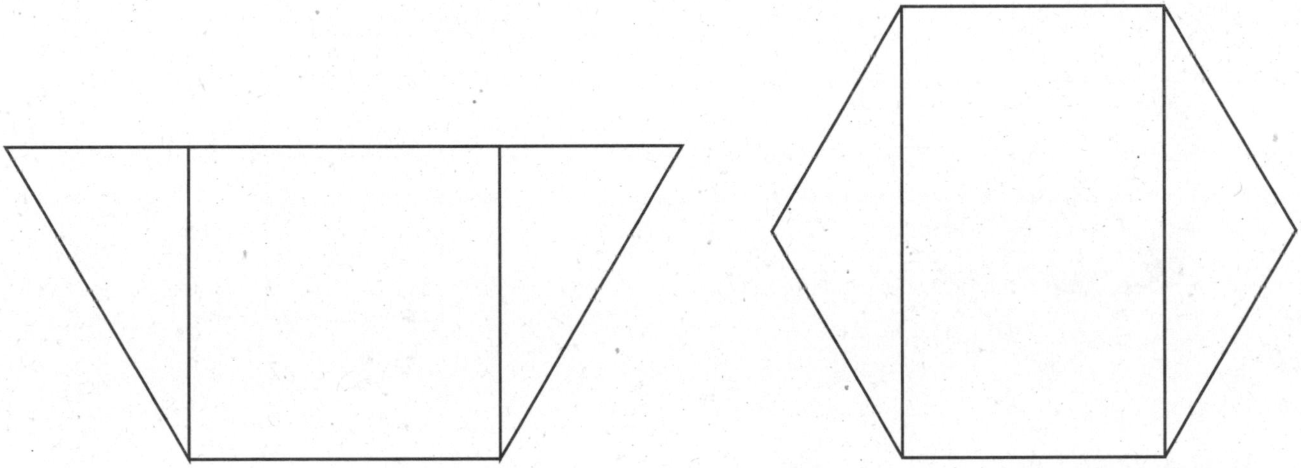

Math Talk

MATHEMATICAL PRACTICES 7

Look for Structure
What shapes did Angelina make?

FOR THE TEACHER • Read the following aloud. Angelina put some triangles and rectangles together. She drew pictures to show what she made. Color to show how Angelina put the shapes together.

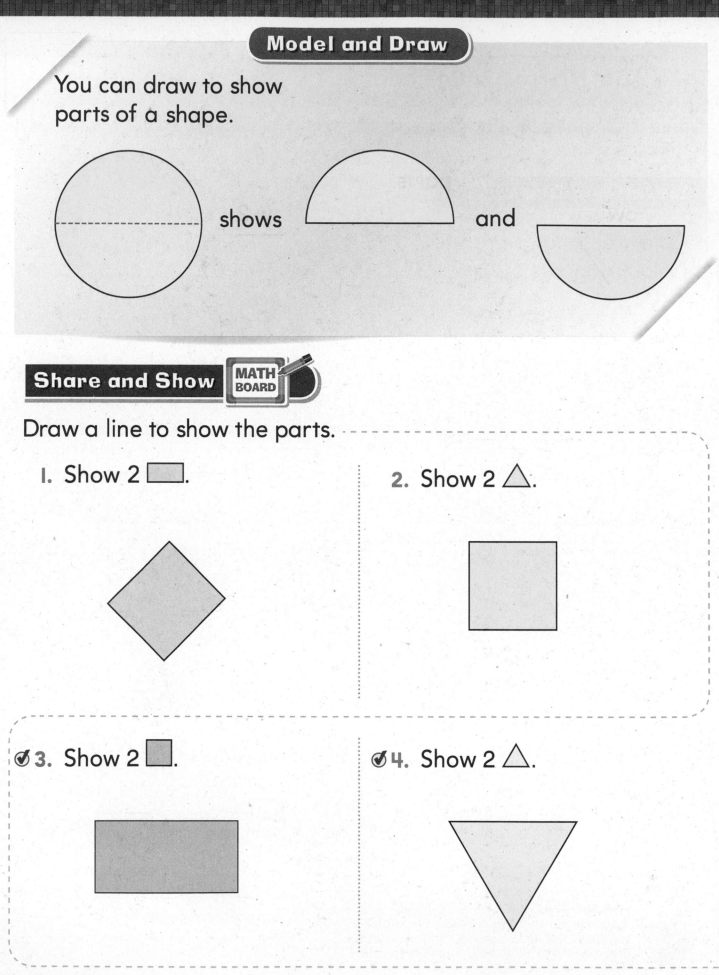

Model and Draw

You can draw to show parts of a shape.

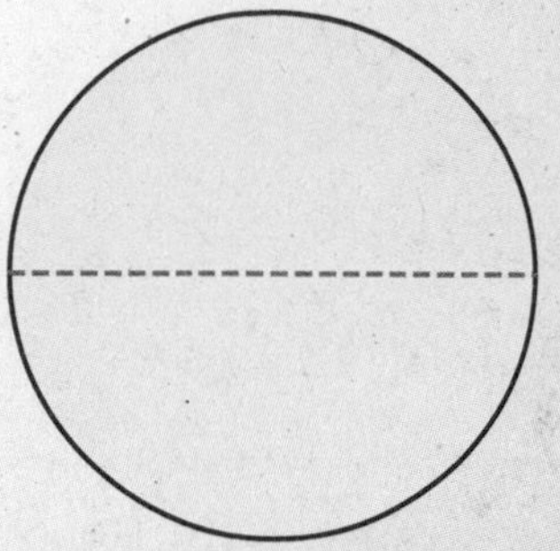

shows

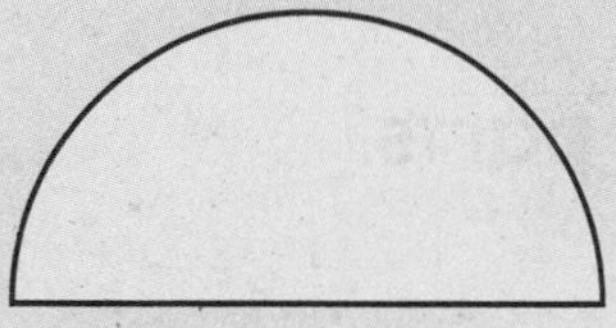

and

Share and Show MATH BOARD

Draw a line to show the parts.

1. Show 2 ▭.

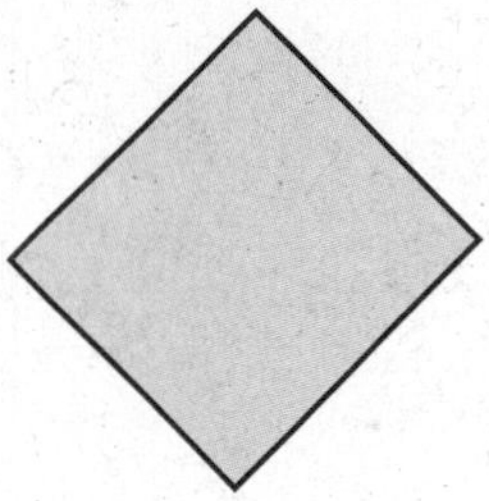

2. Show 2 △.

3. Show 2 □.

4. Show 2 △.

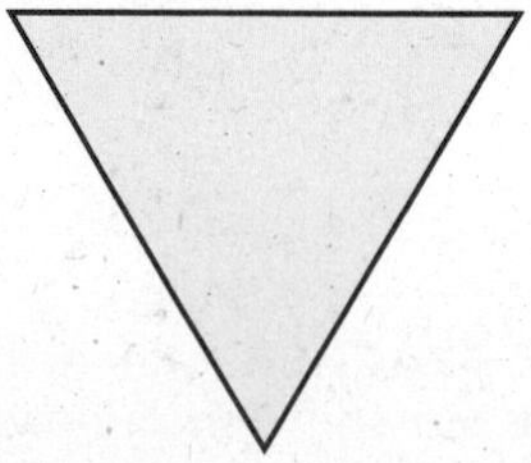

Name ______________________________

On Your Own

MATHEMATICAL PRACTICE 7 **Identify Relationships**

Draw a line to show the parts.

5. Show 2 △.

6. Show 2 ▭.

7. Show 1 ▭ and 1 □.

8. Show 1 △ and 1 ⏢.

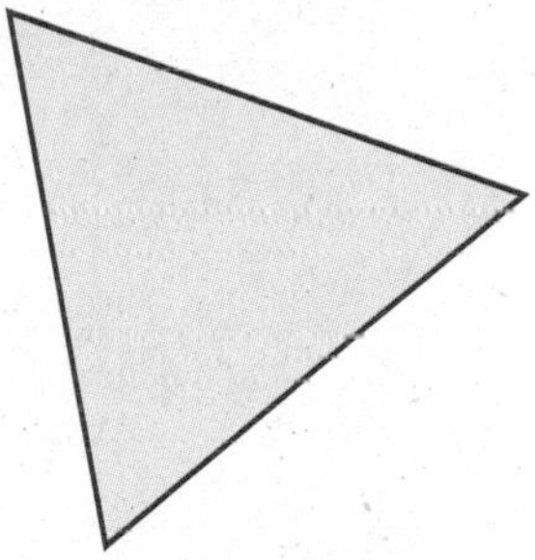

THINK SMARTER Draw two lines to show the parts.

9. Show 3 △.

10. Show 2 △ and 1 ⏢.

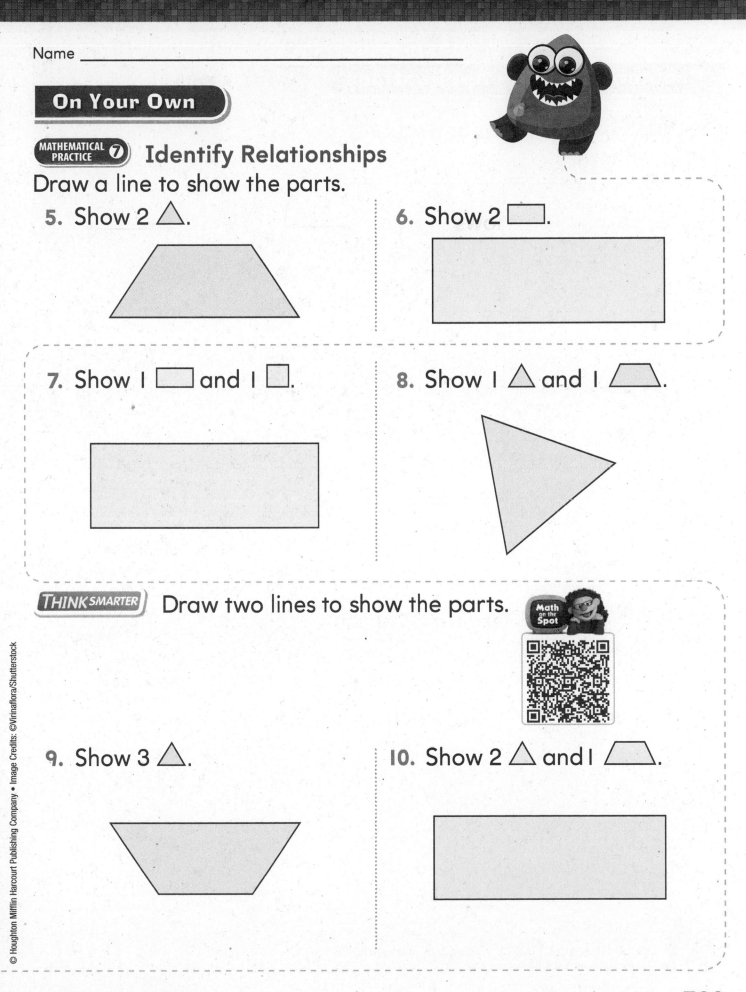

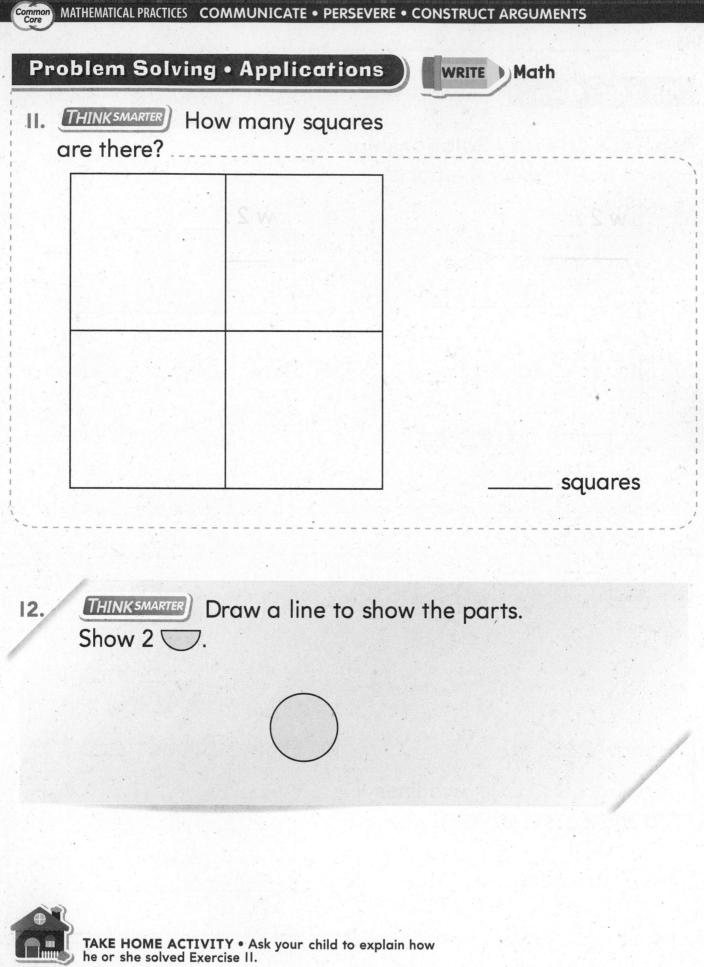

Problem Solving • Applications

WRITE Math

11. THINK SMARTER How many squares are there?

_____ squares

12. THINK SMARTER Draw a line to show the parts.
Show 2 .

TAKE HOME ACTIVITY • Ask your child to explain how he or she solved Exercise 11.

Name ______________________

Take Apart Two-Dimensional Shapes

Common Core **COMMON CORE STANDARD—1.G.A.2**
Reason with shapes and their attributes.

Draw a line to show the parts.

1. Show 2 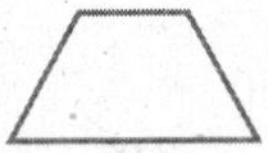.

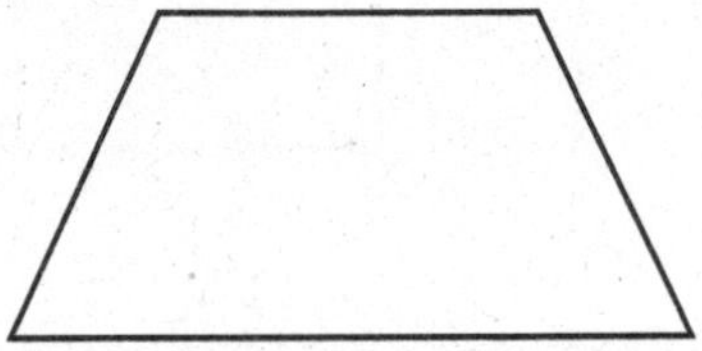

2. Show 2 .

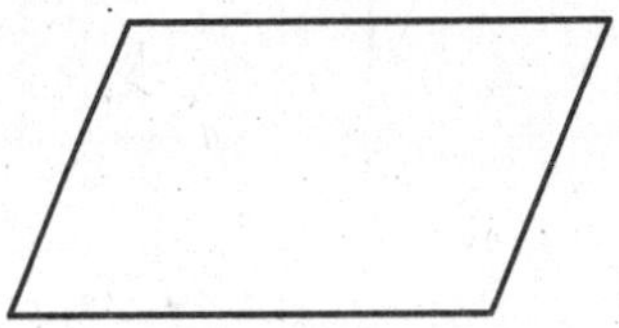

Problem Solving Real World

3. How many triangles are there?

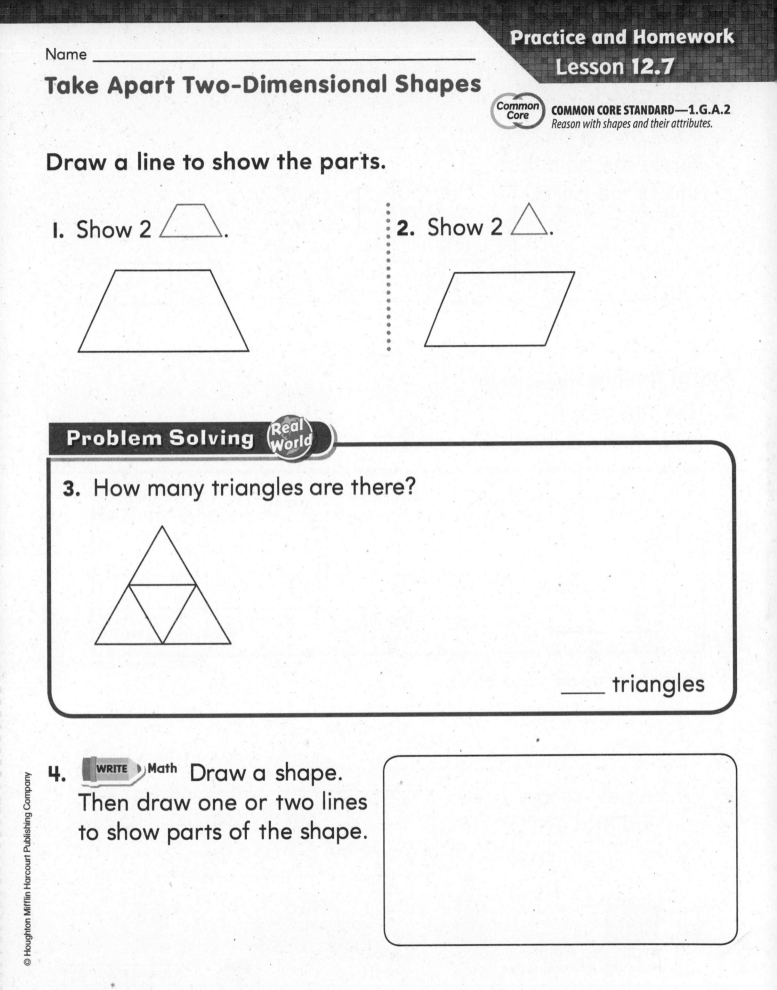

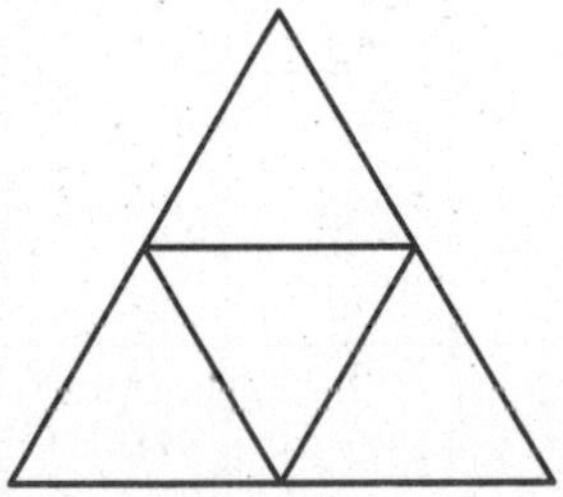

____ triangles

4. WRITE Math Draw a shape. Then draw one or two lines to show parts of the shape.

Lesson Check (1.G.A.2)

1. Look at the picture.
Circle the pair that shows the parts.

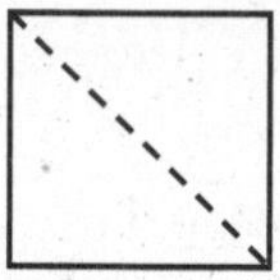

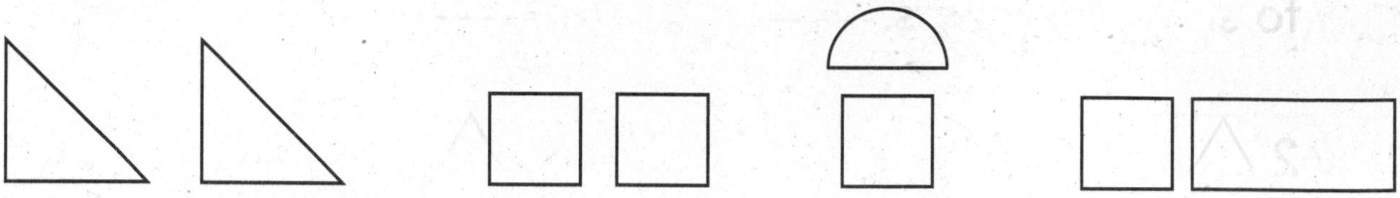

Spiral Review (1.MD.C.4, 1.G.A.2)

2. Use the graph.
How many children chose  ?

Our Favorite Sport							
soccer							
baseball							
tennis							

Each  stands for 1 child.

____ children

3. Which new shape can you make?
Circle your answer.

Combine 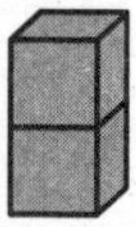 and 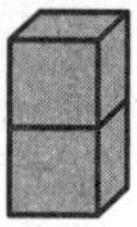 .

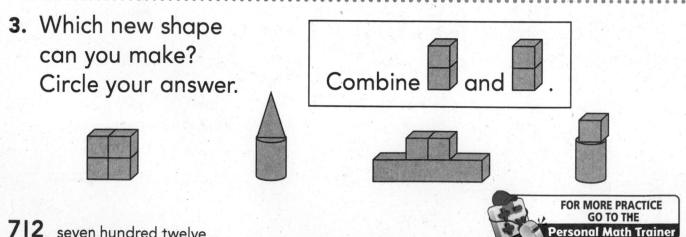

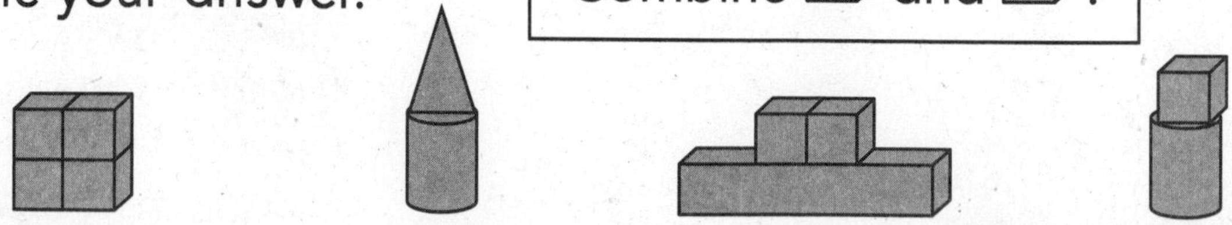

FOR MORE PRACTICE GO TO THE **Personal Math Trainer**

Name ________________________________

Equal or Unequal Parts

Essential Question How can you identify equal and unequal parts in two-dimensional shapes?

Common Core **Geometry—1.G.A.3**

MATHEMATICAL PRACTICES
MP1, MP3, MP6

Listen and Draw

Draw to show the parts.

Show 2 △.

Show 3 △.

Math Talk MATHEMATICAL PRACTICES 6

Explain how the triangles shown in each square compare.

FOR THE TEACHER • Have children draw lines to show two triangles in one square and three triangles in the other square.

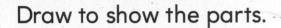

Model and Draw

These show **equal parts**, or **equal shares**.

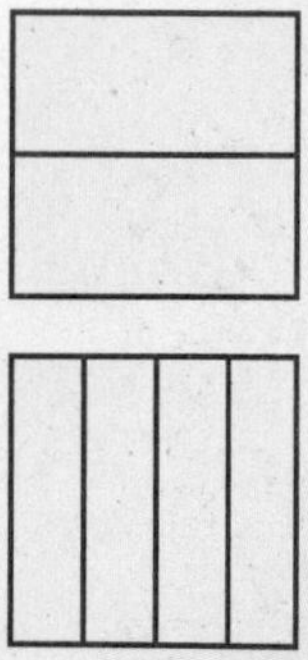

How can you describe equal shares?

These show **unequal parts**, or **unequal shares**.

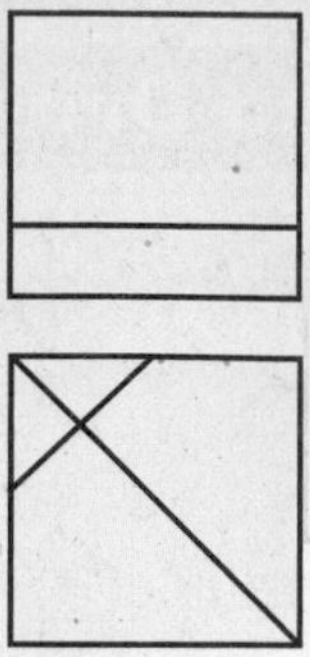

Share and Show MATH BOARD

THINK
Are the parts the same size?

Circle the shape that shows equal parts.

1.

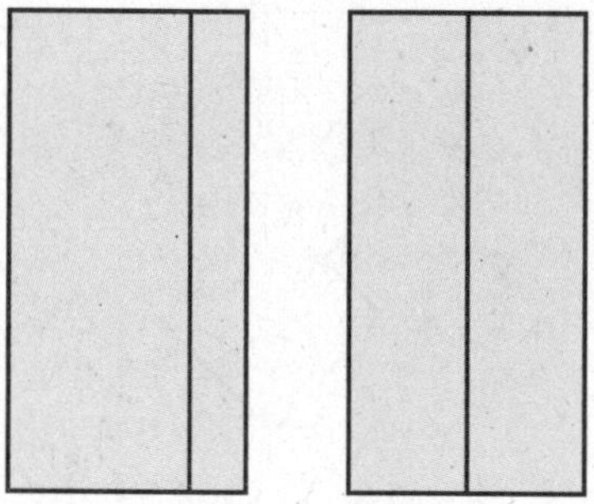

2.

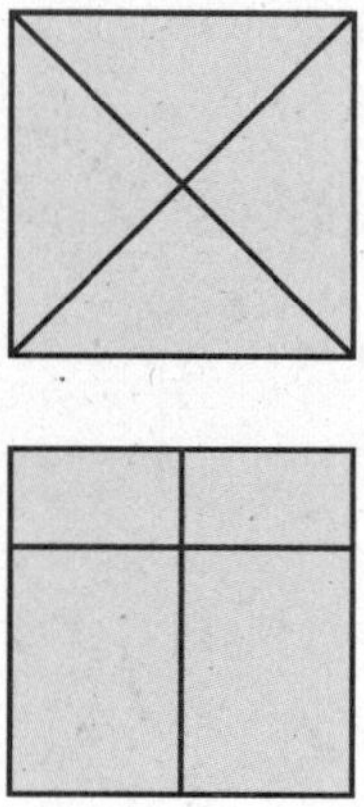

✓3.

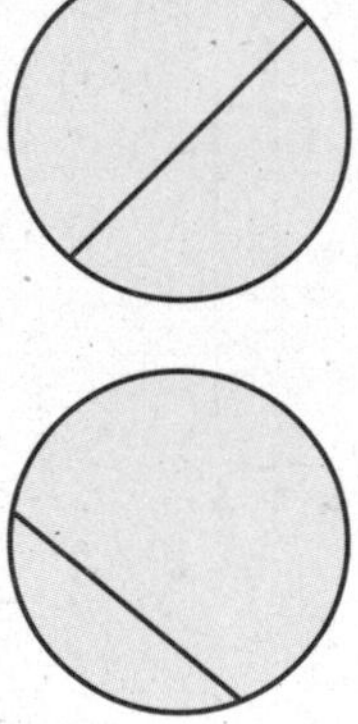

Circle the shape that shows unequal parts.

4.

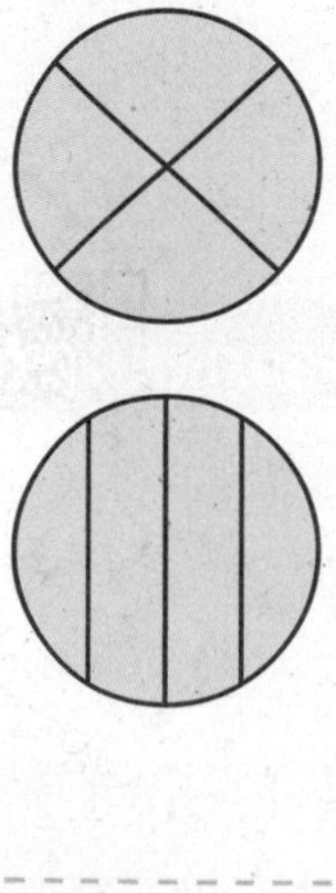

5.

✓6.

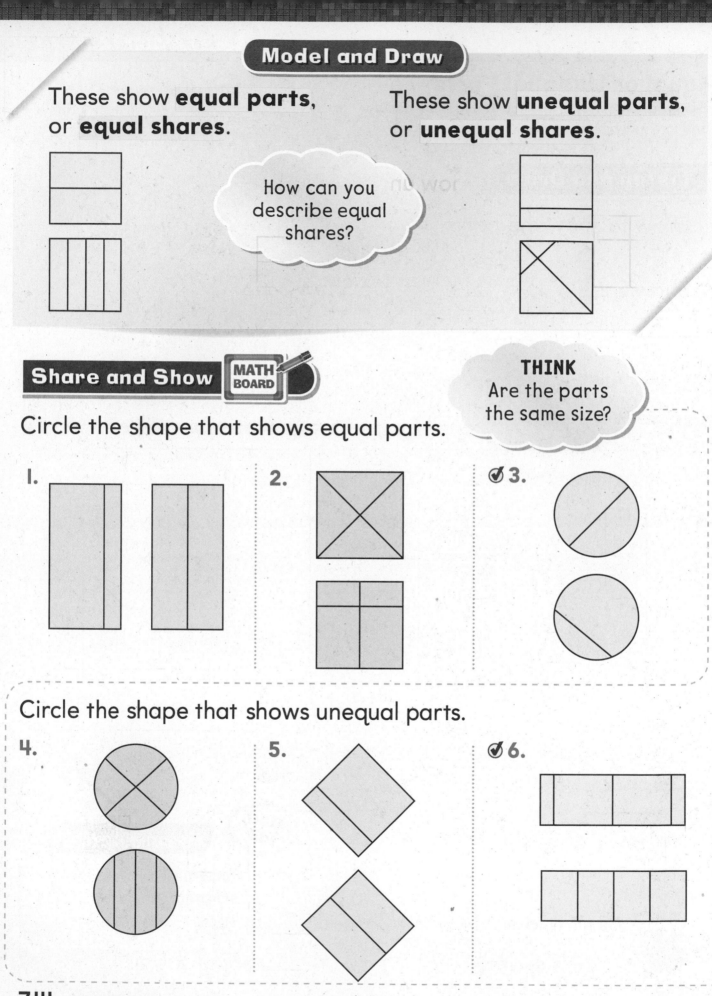

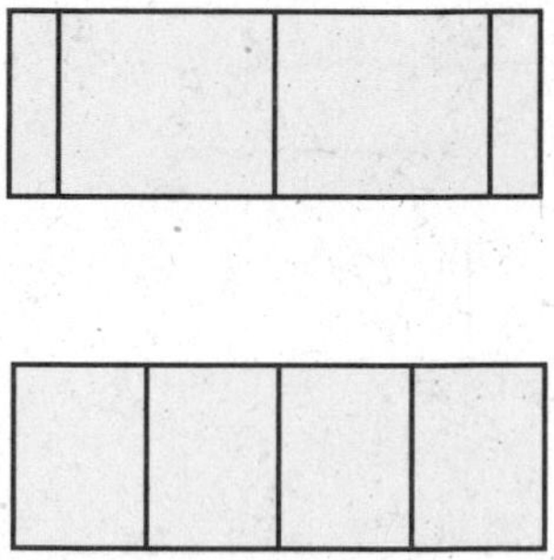

Name ____________________

THINK
Equal shares means the same as equal parts.

On Your Own

MATHEMATICAL PRACTICE 6 **Use Math Vocabulary**

Color the shapes that show unequal shares.

7. 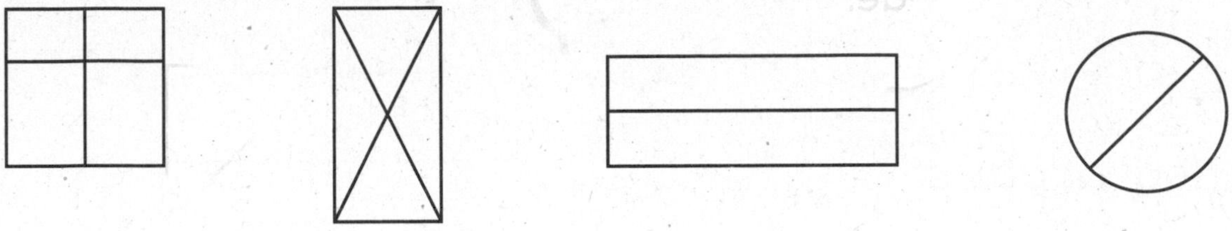

8. 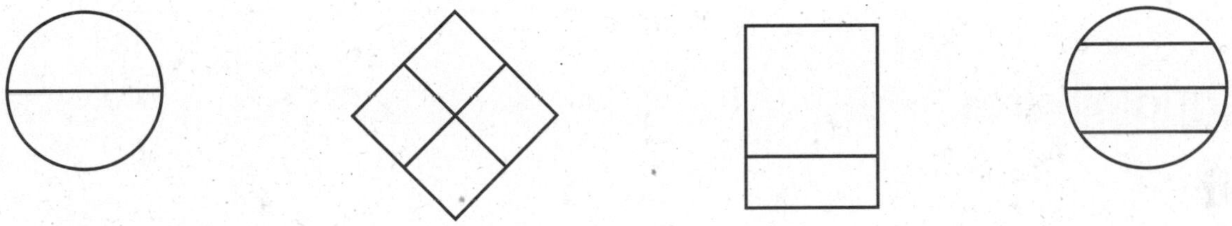

Color the shapes that show equal shares.

9. 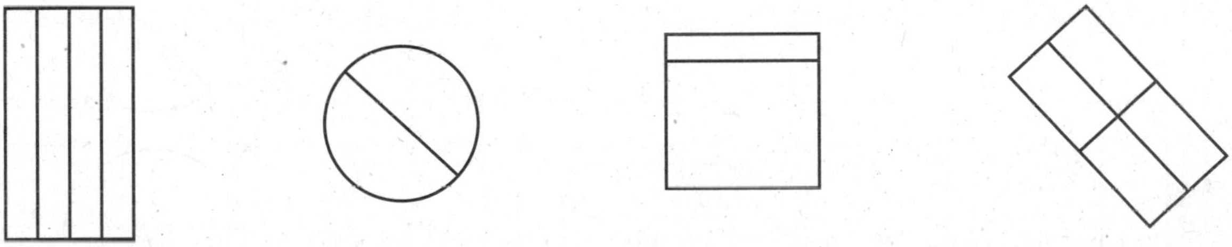

10. 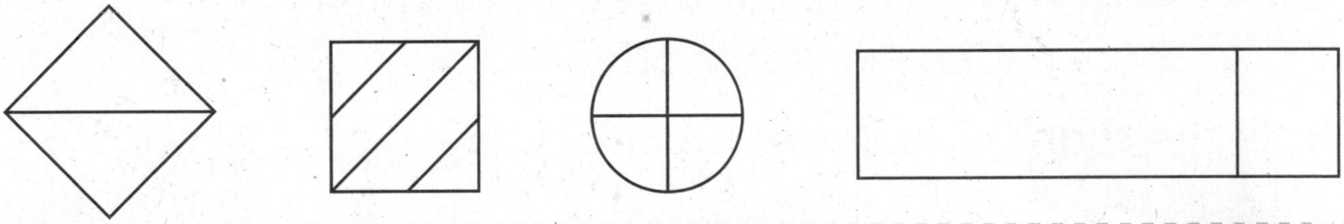

THINK SMARTER Write the number of equal shares.

11. 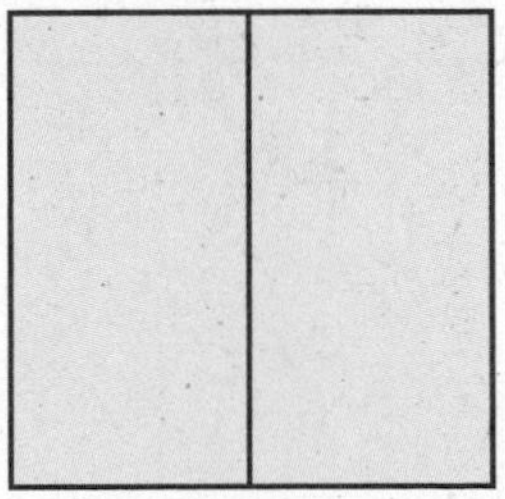

____ equal shares

12. 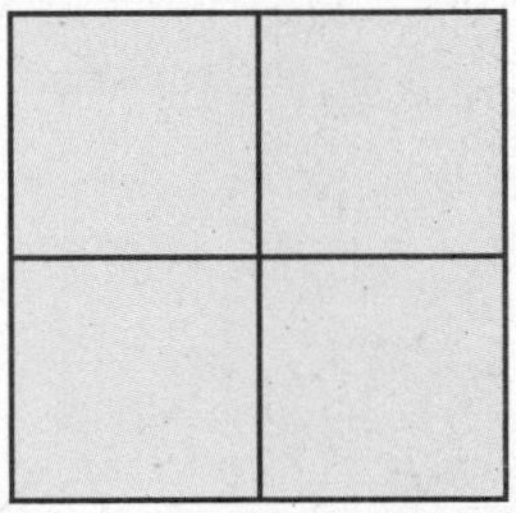

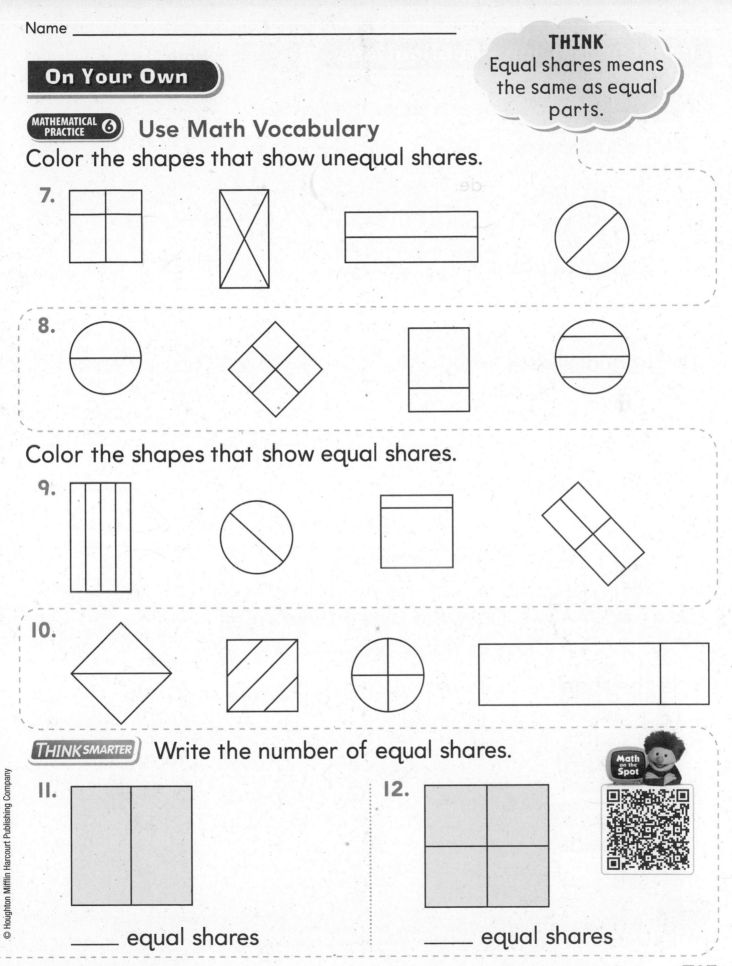

____ equal shares

Math on the Spot

Problem Solving • Applications

WRITE Math

THINK SMARTER Draw lines to show the parts.

13. 2 equal parts

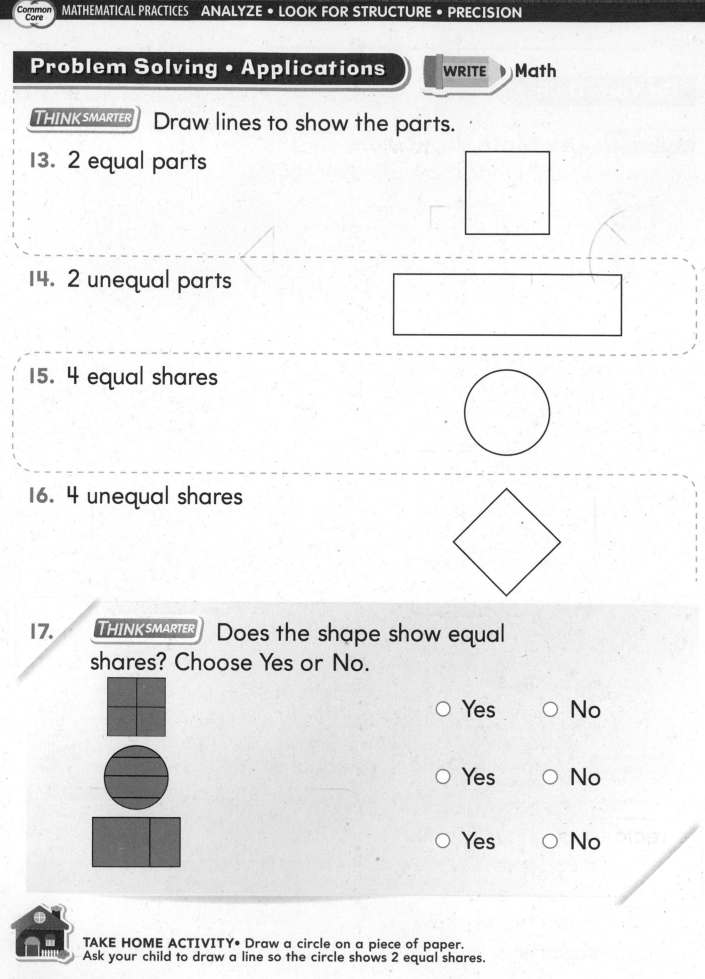

14. 2 unequal parts

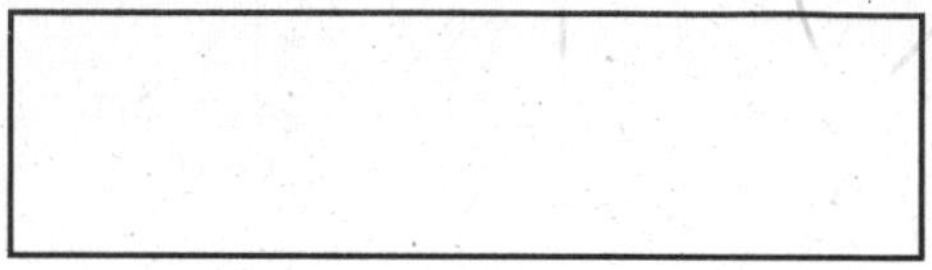

15. 4 equal shares

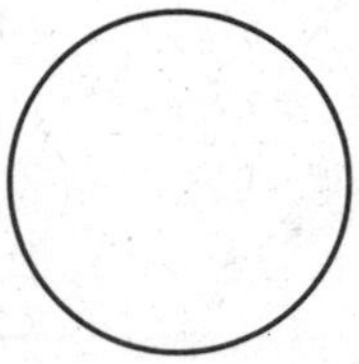

16. 4 unequal shares

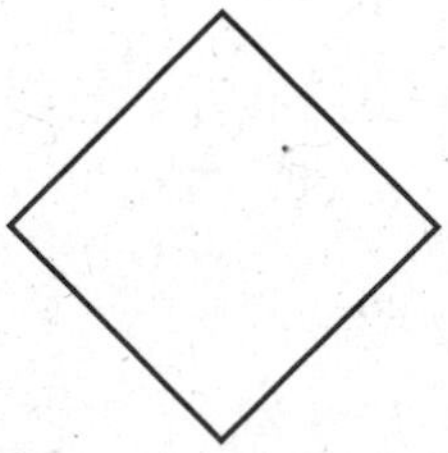

17. THINK SMARTER Does the shape show equal shares? Choose Yes or No.

○ Yes ○ No

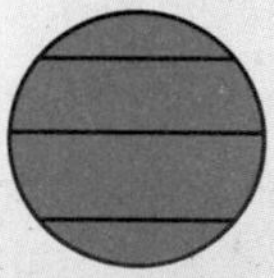

○ Yes ○ No

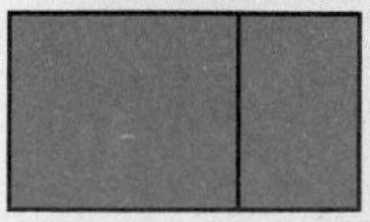

○ Yes ○ No

TAKE HOME ACTIVITY • Draw a circle on a piece of paper. Ask your child to draw a line so the circle shows 2 equal shares.

Name ______________________________

Equal or Unequal Parts

Common Core — COMMON CORE STANDARD—1.G.A.3
Reason with shapes and their attributes.

Color the shapes that show unequal shares.

1.

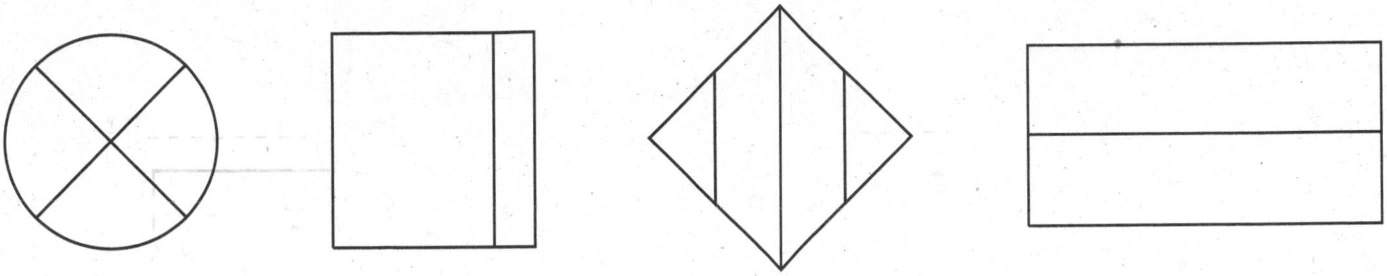

Color the shapes that show equal shares.

2.

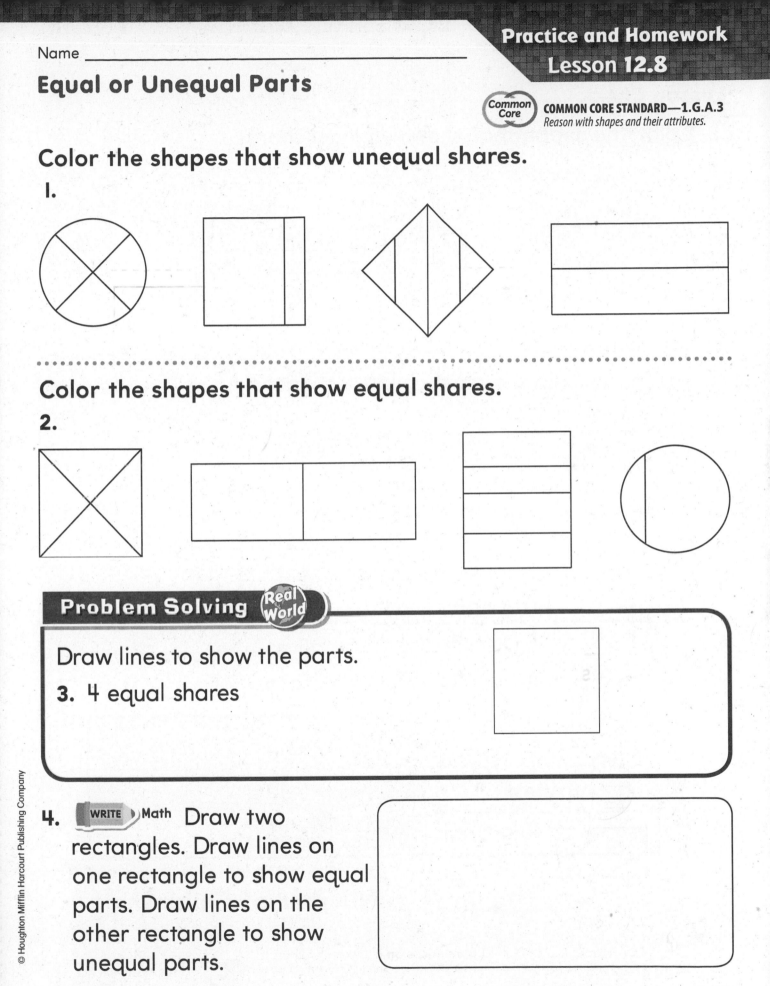

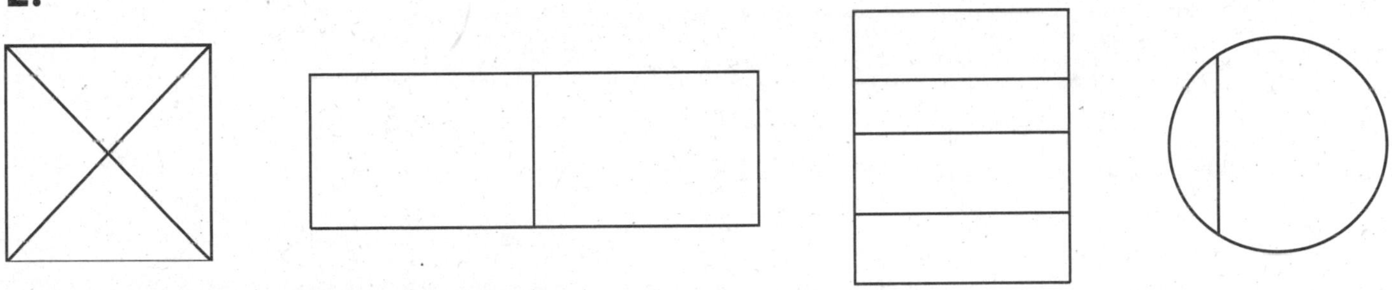

Problem Solving — Real World

Draw lines to show the parts.

3. 4 equal shares

4. WRITE Math Draw two rectangles. Draw lines on one rectangle to show equal parts. Draw lines on the other rectangle to show unequal parts.

Lesson Check (1.G.A.3)

1. Color the shape that shows unequal shares.

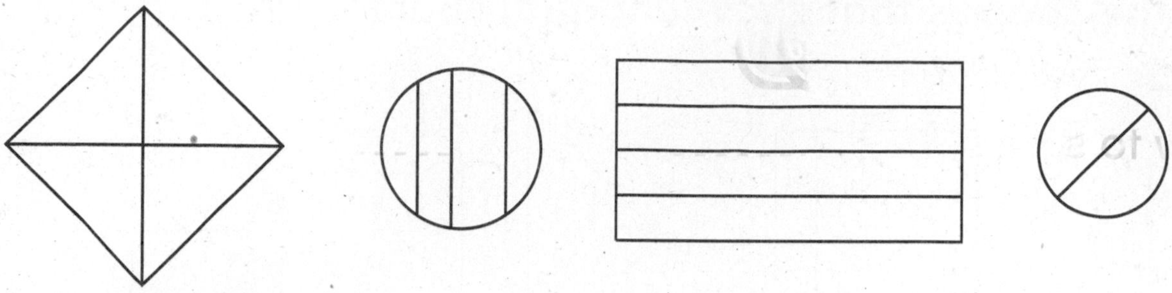

Spiral Review (1.MD.C.4)

2. Which food did the most children choose?
Circle your answer.

Our Favorite Breakfast		Total
eggs	||||	4
waffles	|||	3
pancakes	~~||||~~ |	6

3. Use the graph. How many children chose ?

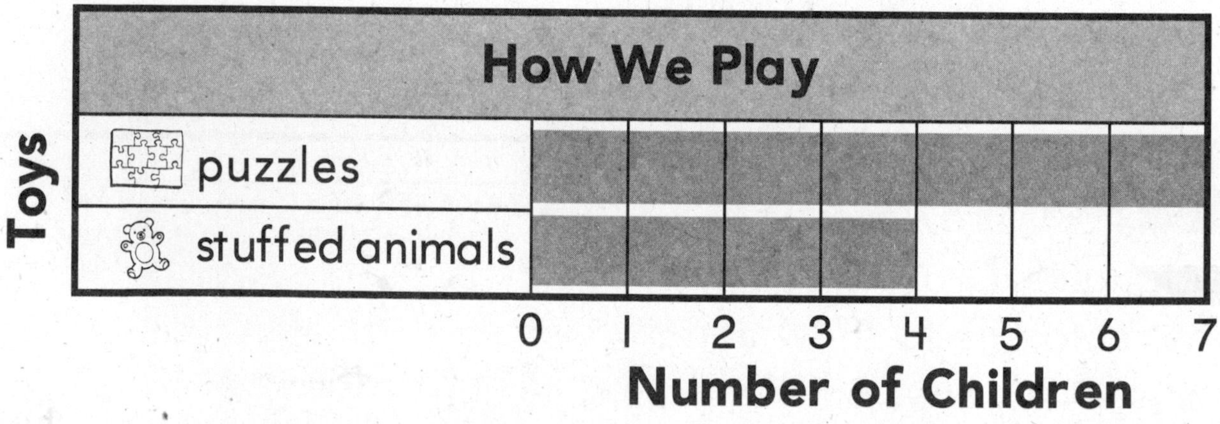

____ children

FOR MORE PRACTICE GO TO THE **Personal Math Trainer**

Name ____________________

Halves

Essential Question How can a shape be separated into two equal shares?

Common Core Geometry—1.G.A.3

MATHEMATICAL PRACTICES
MP1, MP4, MP6

Listen and Draw Real World

Draw to solve.

Math Talk MATHEMATICAL PRACTICES

Analyze Will all four friends get the same amount of sandwich?

FOR THE TEACHER • Have children draw to solve this problem: Two friends share the sandwich on the left. How can they cut the sandwich so each gets an equal share? Then have children solve this problem: Two other friends share the sandwich on the right. How could this sandwich be cut a different way so each friend gets an equal share?

Model and Draw

The 2 equal shares make 1 whole.

2 equal shares

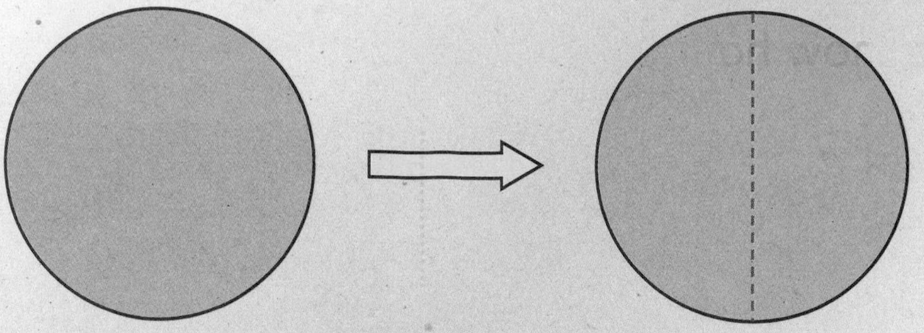

1 whole

2 **halves**

Is **half of** the circle larger or smaller than the whole circle?

Share and Show MATH BOARD

Draw a line to show halves.

1. 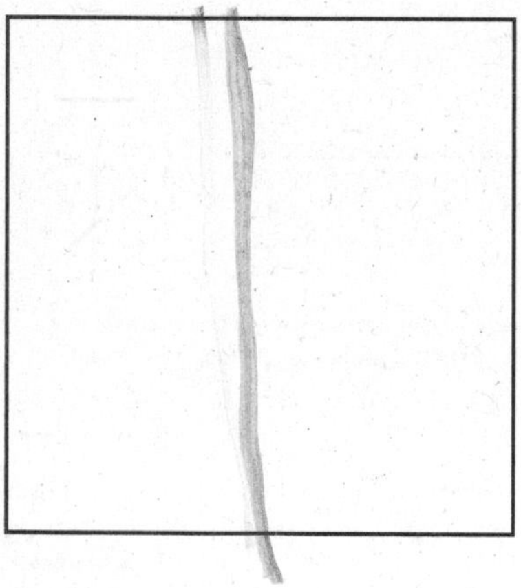

✓ 2. 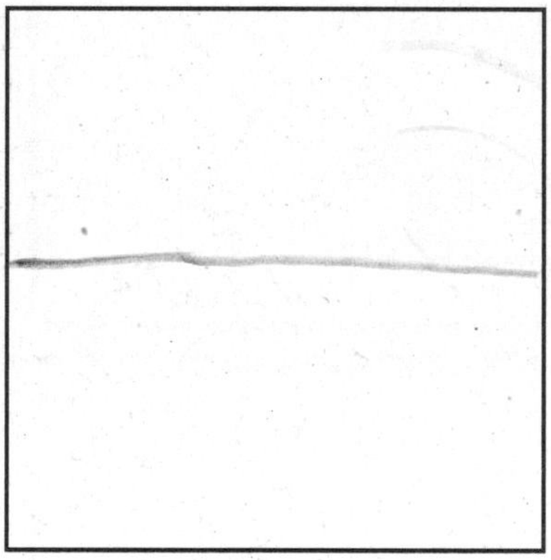

3. 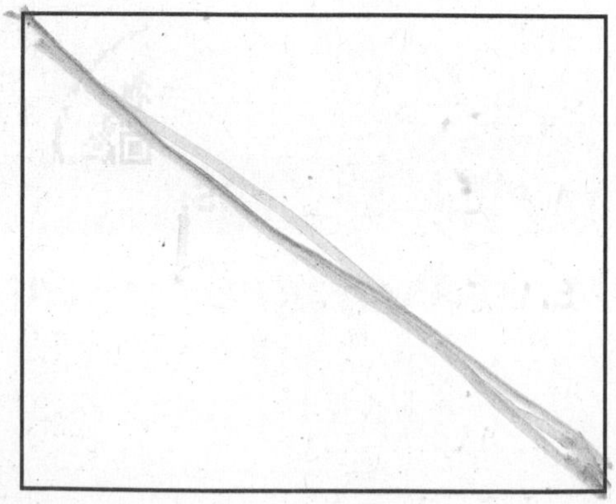

✓ 4. 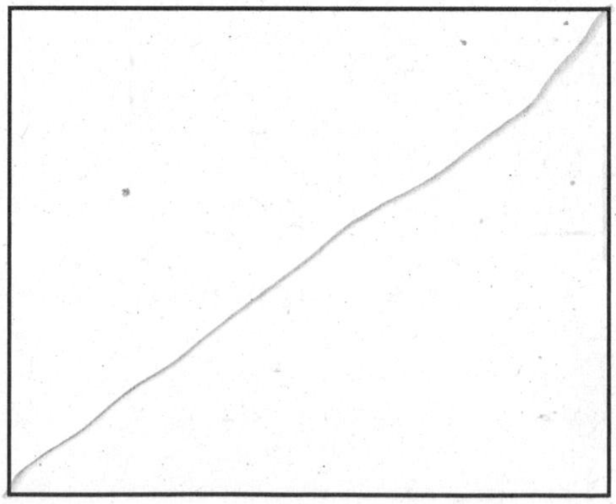

Name ______________________________

On Your Own

THINK
Halves are equal shares.

MATHEMATICAL PRACTICE 1 Analyze Relationships

Circle the shapes that show halves.

5. 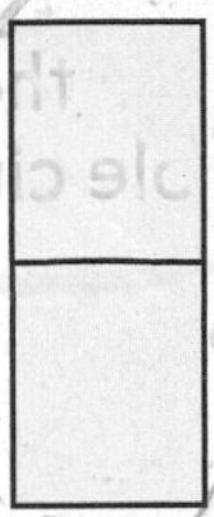

6. 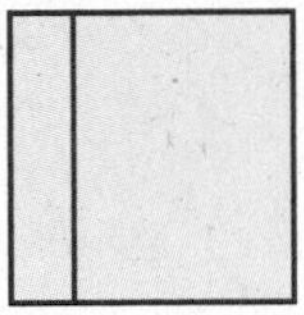

7. 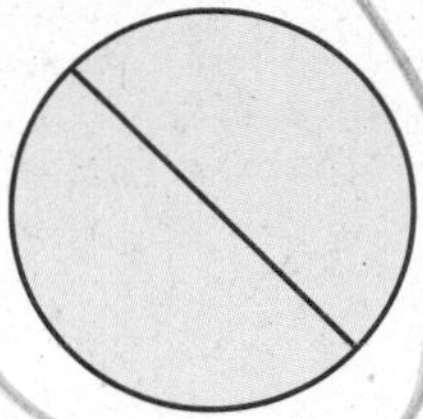

8. 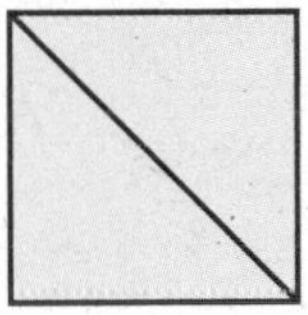

9. 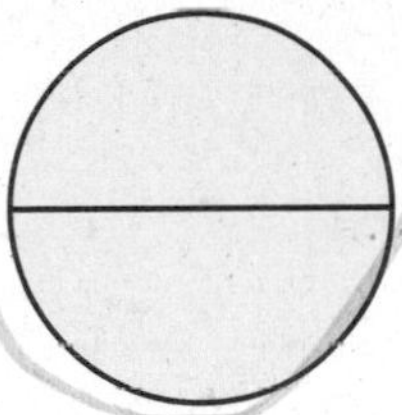

10. 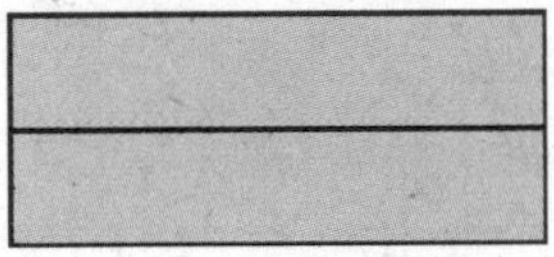

11. 

12. 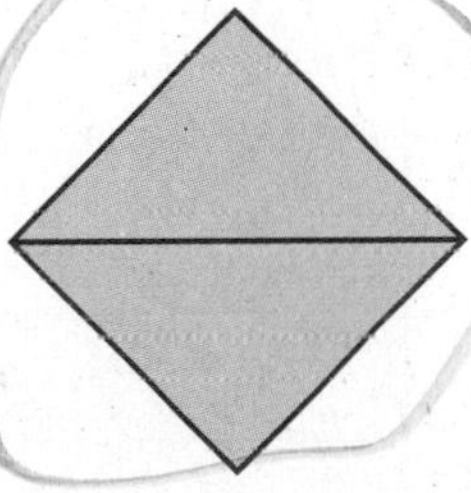

13. 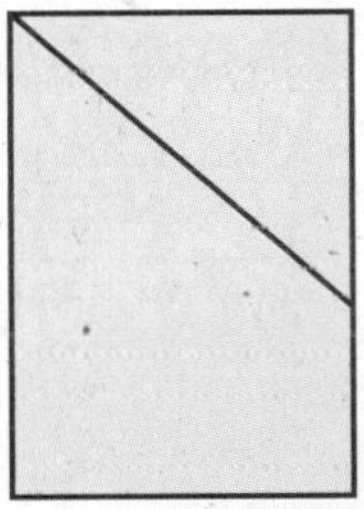

14. THINKSMARTER Use the picture. Write numbers to solve.

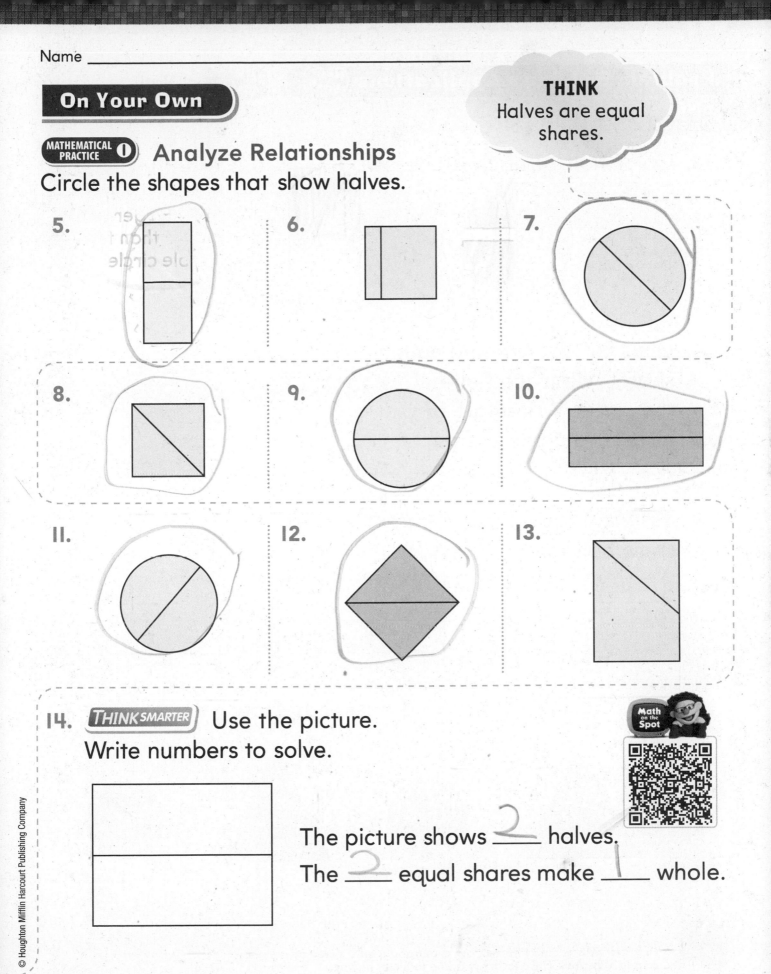

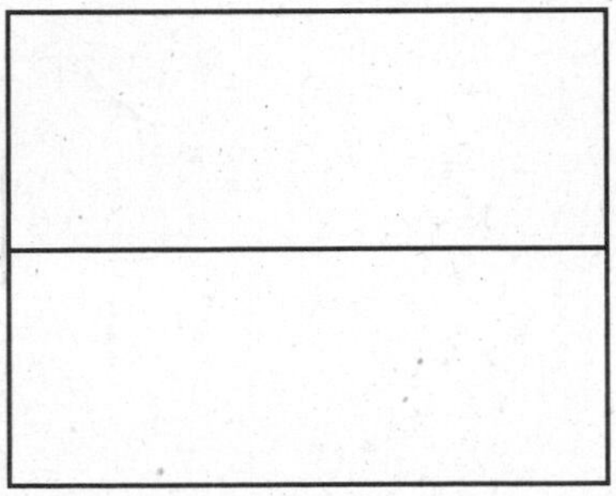

Math on the Spot

The picture shows __2__ halves.

The __2__ equal shares make __1__ whole.

Problem Solving • Applications Real World

WRITE Math

Draw or write to solve.

15. Color half of each shape.

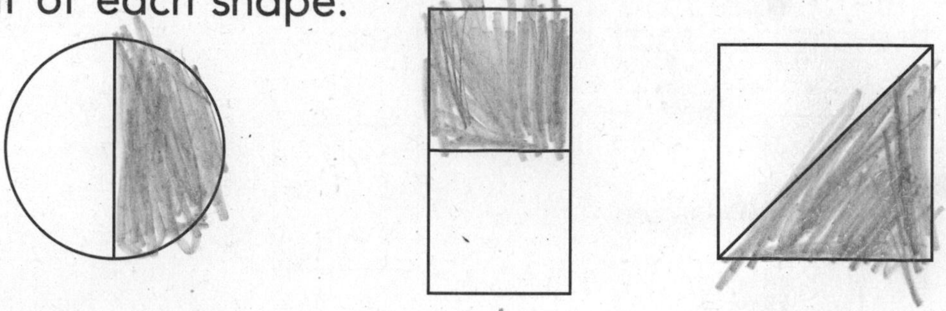

16. Linus cut a circle into equal shares. He traced one of the parts. Write **half of** or **halves** to name the part.

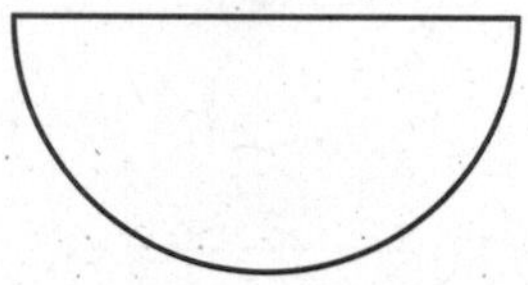

half

_______________ a circle

17. GO DEEPER Draw three different ways to show halves.

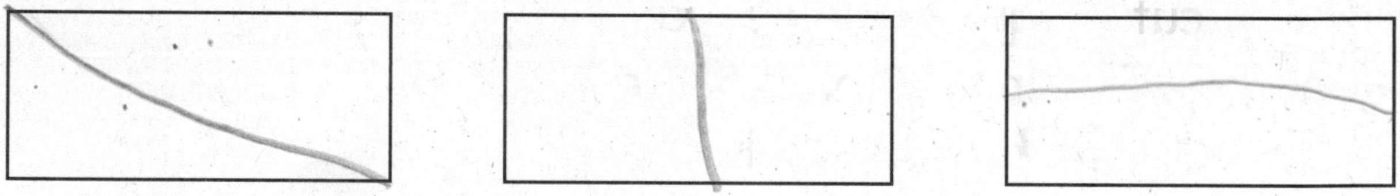

18. THINK SMARTER Circle the shapes that show halves.

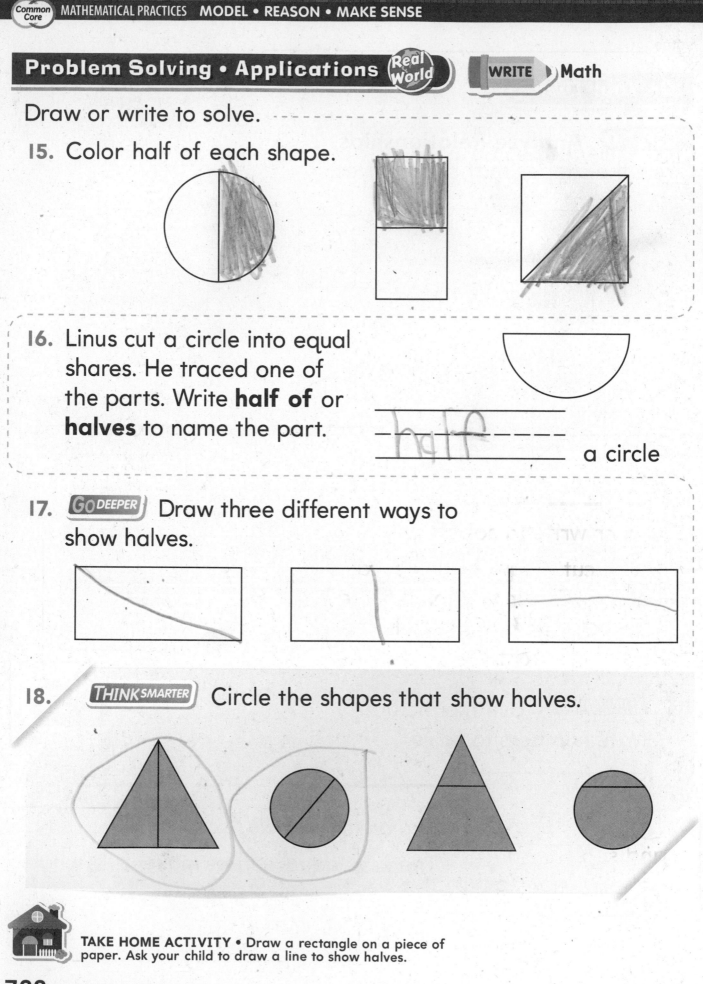

TAKE HOME ACTIVITY • Draw a rectangle on a piece of paper. Ask your child to draw a line to show halves.

Name ______________________________

Halves

COMMON CORE STANDARD—1.G.A.3
Reason with shapes and their attributes.

Circle the shapes that show halves.

1. 

2. 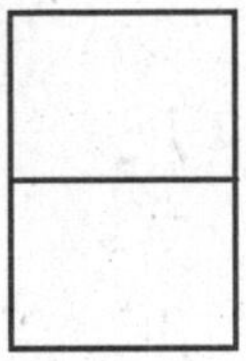

3. 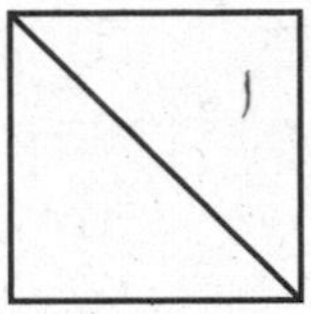

4. 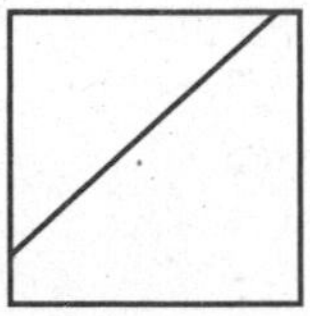

5. 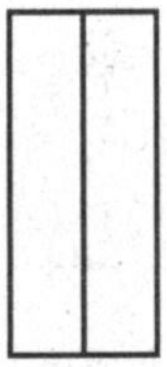

6. 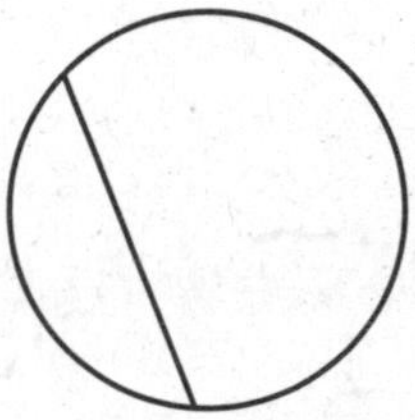

Problem Solving Real World

Draw or write to solve.

7. Kate cut a square into equal shares. She traced one of the parts. Write **half of** or **halves** to name the part.

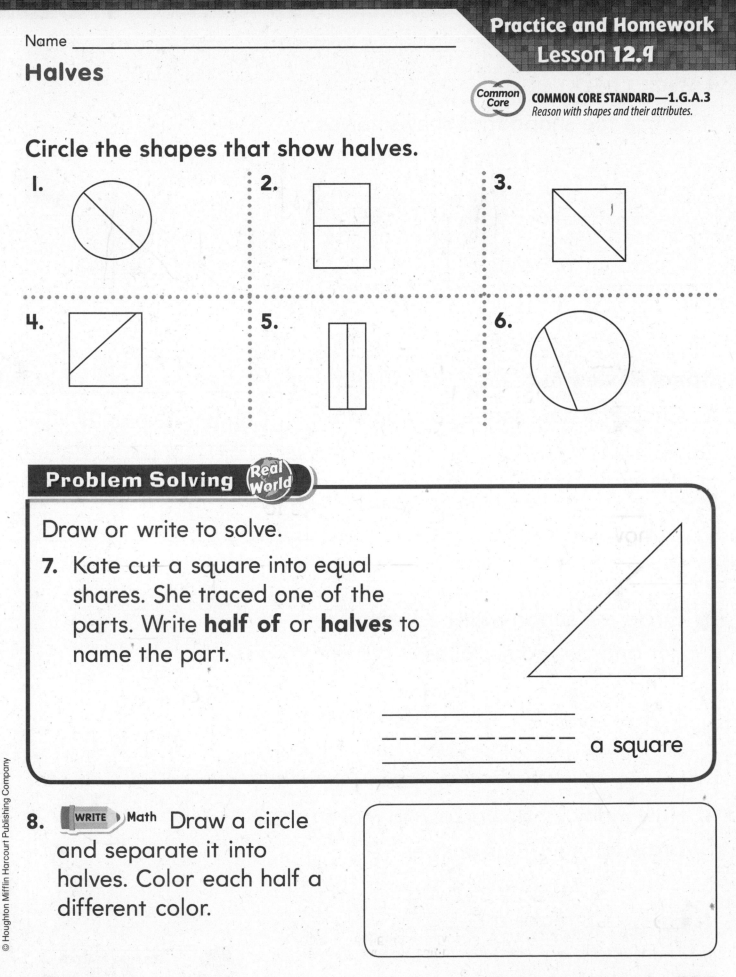

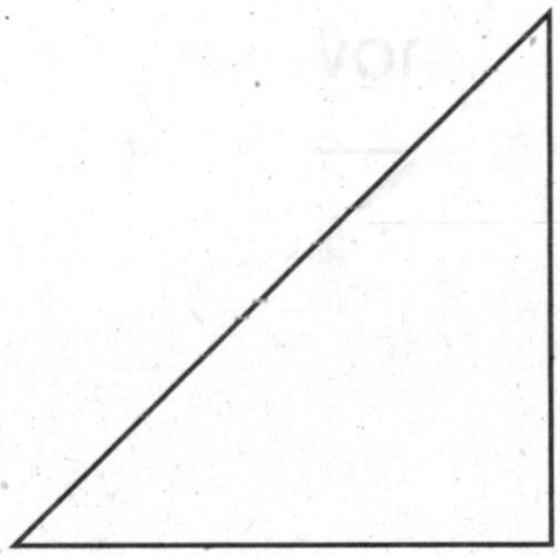

______________ a square

8. WRITE Math Draw a circle and separate it into halves. Color each half a different color.

Lesson Check (1.G.A.3)

1. Circle the shape that shows halves.

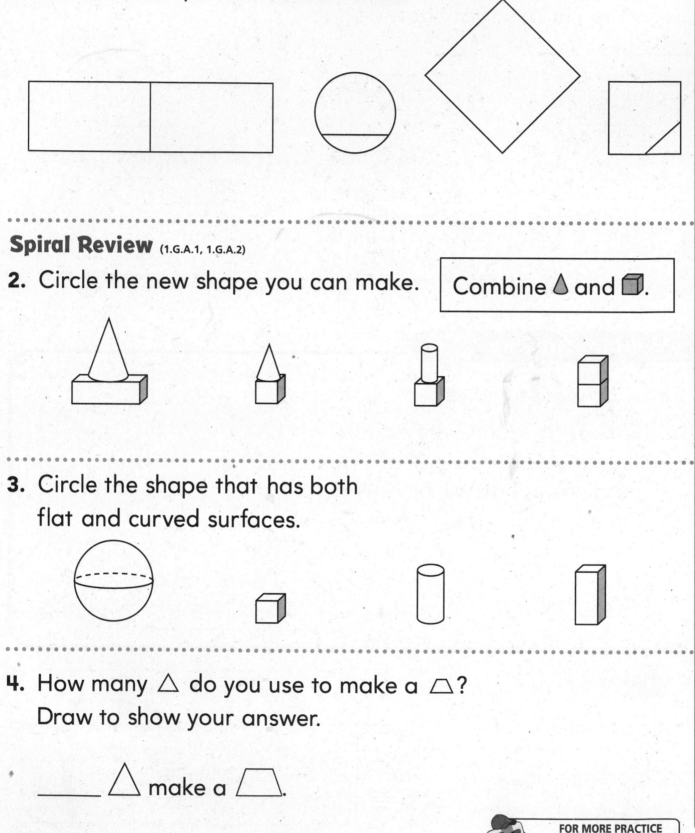

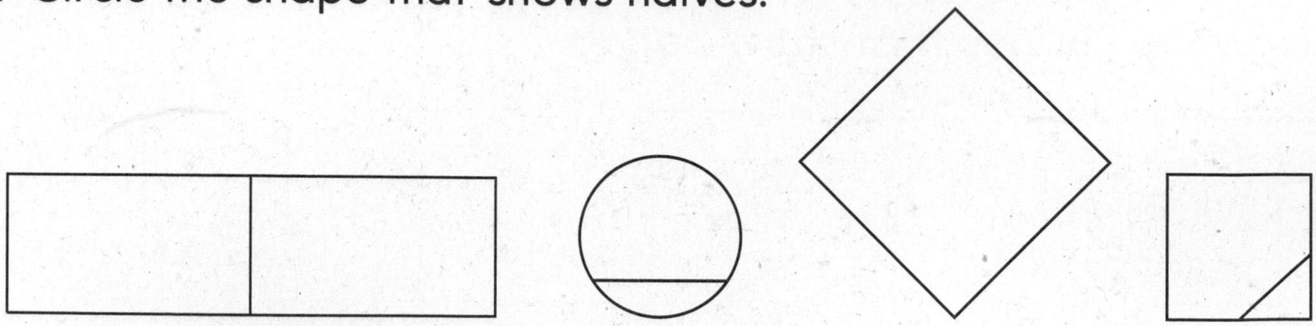

Spiral Review (1.G.A.1, 1.G.A.2)

2. Circle the new shape you can make.

Combine  and 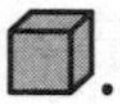.

3. Circle the shape that has both flat and curved surfaces.

4. How many △ do you use to make a ⏢? Draw to show your answer.

_____ △ make a ⏢.

FOR MORE PRACTICE GO TO THE **Personal Math Trainer**

Name ____________________

Fourths

Essential Question How can a shape be separated into four equal shares?

Common Core Geometry—1.G.A.3

MATHEMATICAL PRACTICES
MP1, MP4, MP6

Listen and Draw Real World

Use what you know about halves.
Draw to solve. Write how many.

There are ____ equal shares.

Math Talk MATHEMATICAL PRACTICES 6

Explain How did you decide how to cut the pizza?

FOR THE TEACHER • Read the following problem. Two friends will share a pizza. Then two more friends come. Now four friends will share the pizza. How can the pizza be cut so each friend gets an equal share? How many equal shares are there?

Model and Draw

The 4 equal shares make 1 whole.

4 equal shares

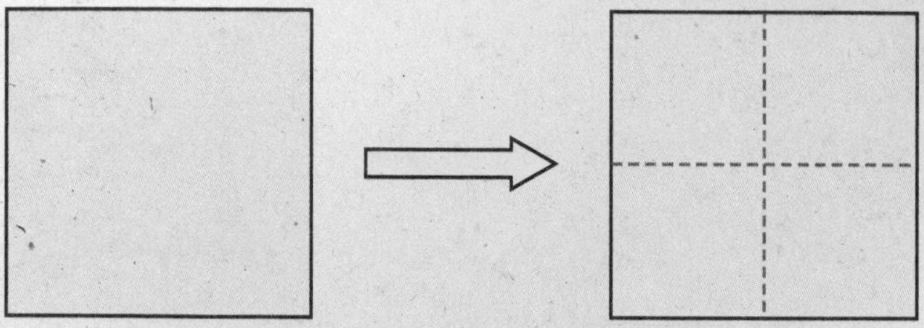

How can you describe one of the 4 equal shares?

1 whole

4 **fourths**, or
4 **quarters**

Share and Show MATH BOARD

Color a **fourth of** the shape.

1. 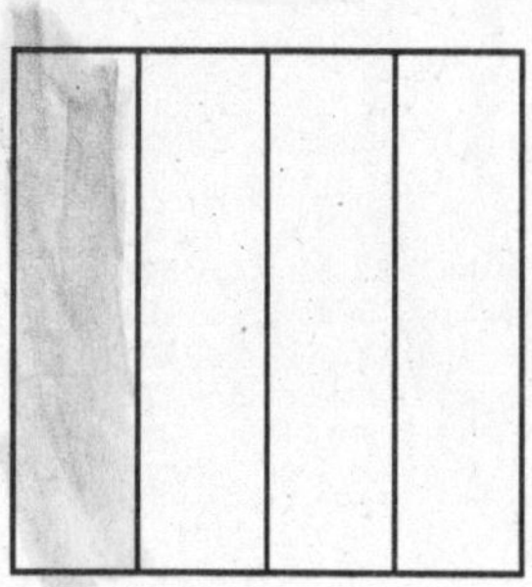

2. 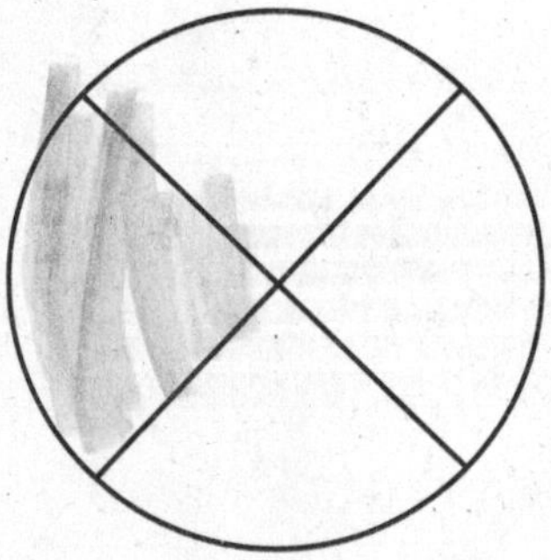

✓3. 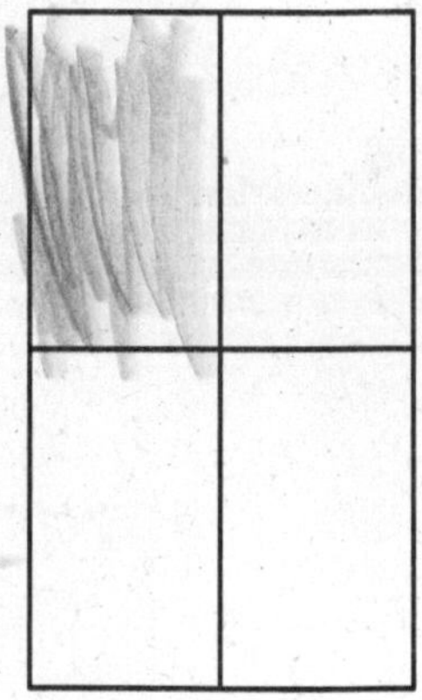

Color a **quarter of** the shape.

4. 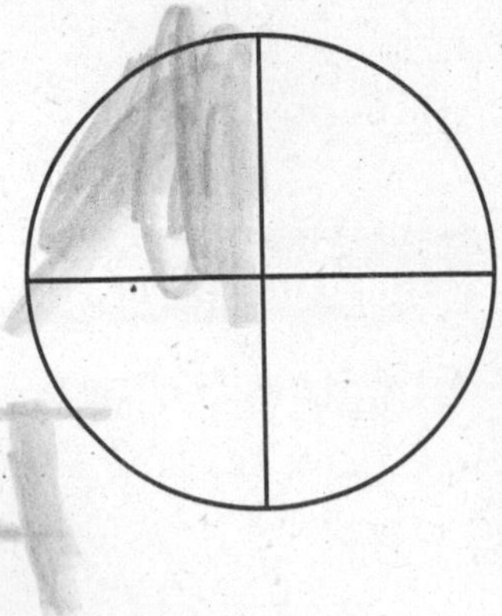

5. 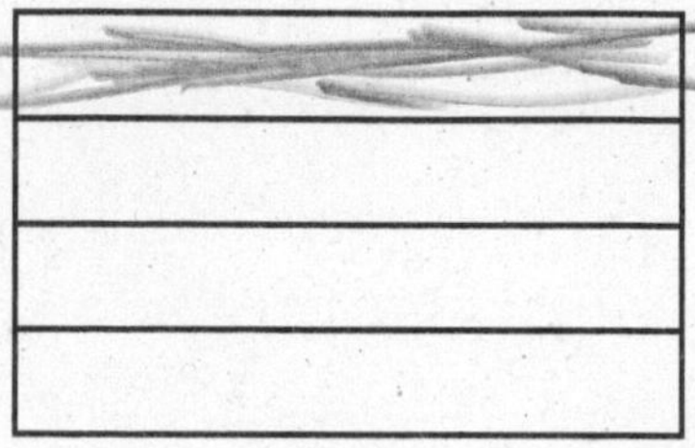

✓6. 

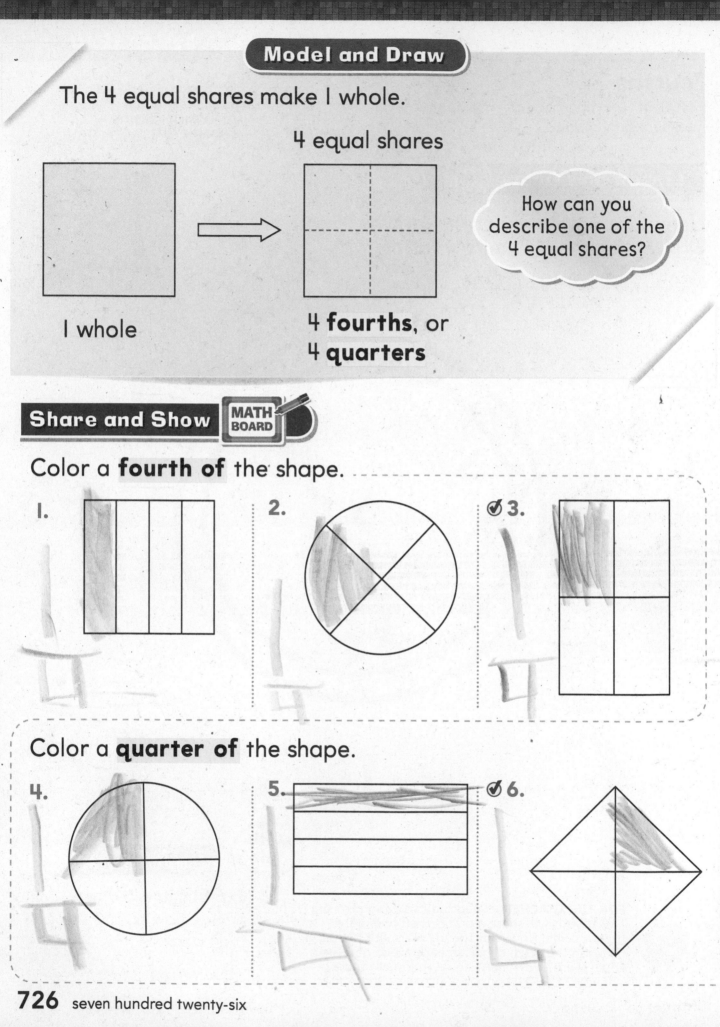

Name ______________________________

On Your Own

MATHEMATICAL PRACTICE 4 **Use Diagrams** Circle the shapes that show fourths.

7.

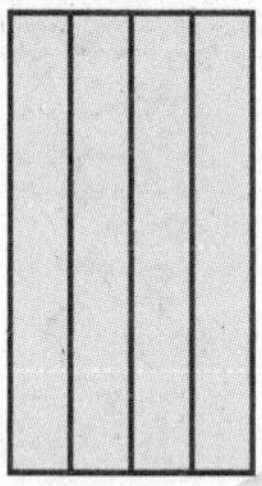

8.

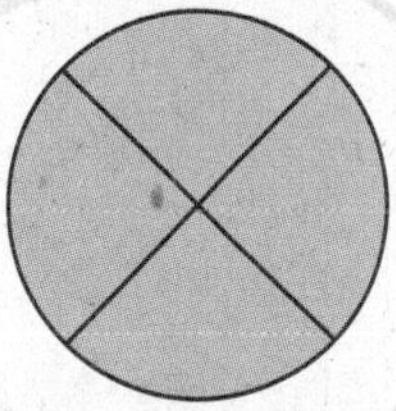

9.

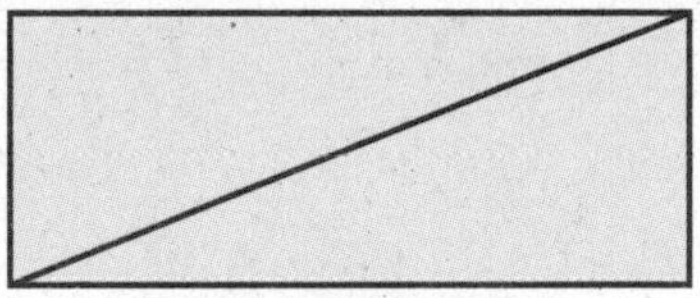

10.

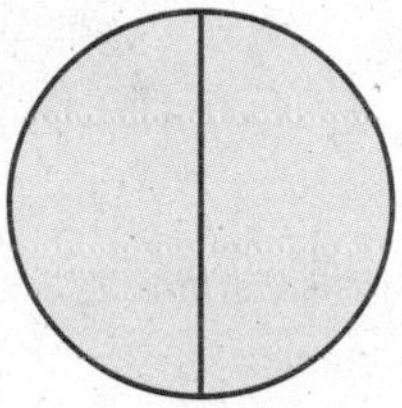

11.

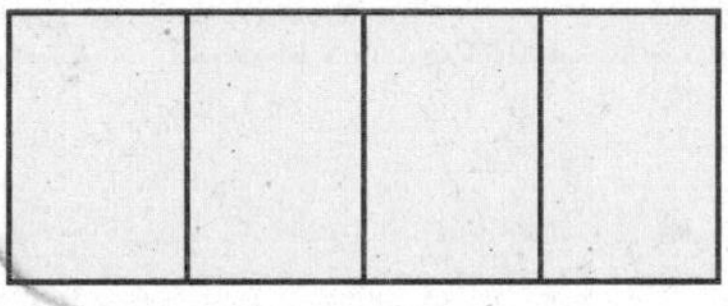

12.

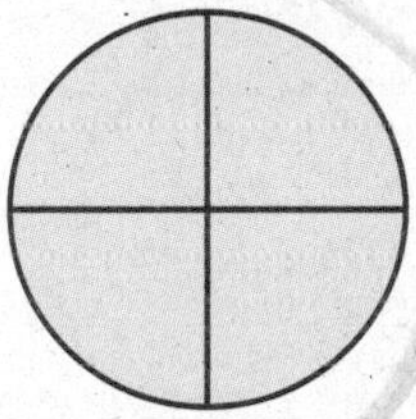

13.

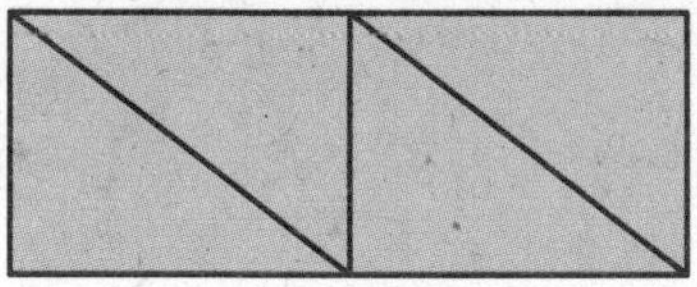

14.

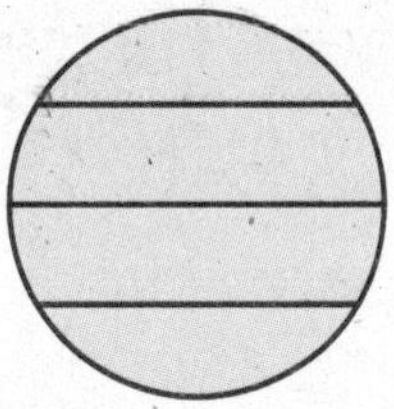

15.

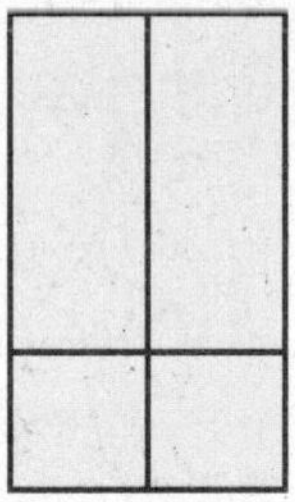

16. **GO DEEPER** Draw three different ways to show fourths.

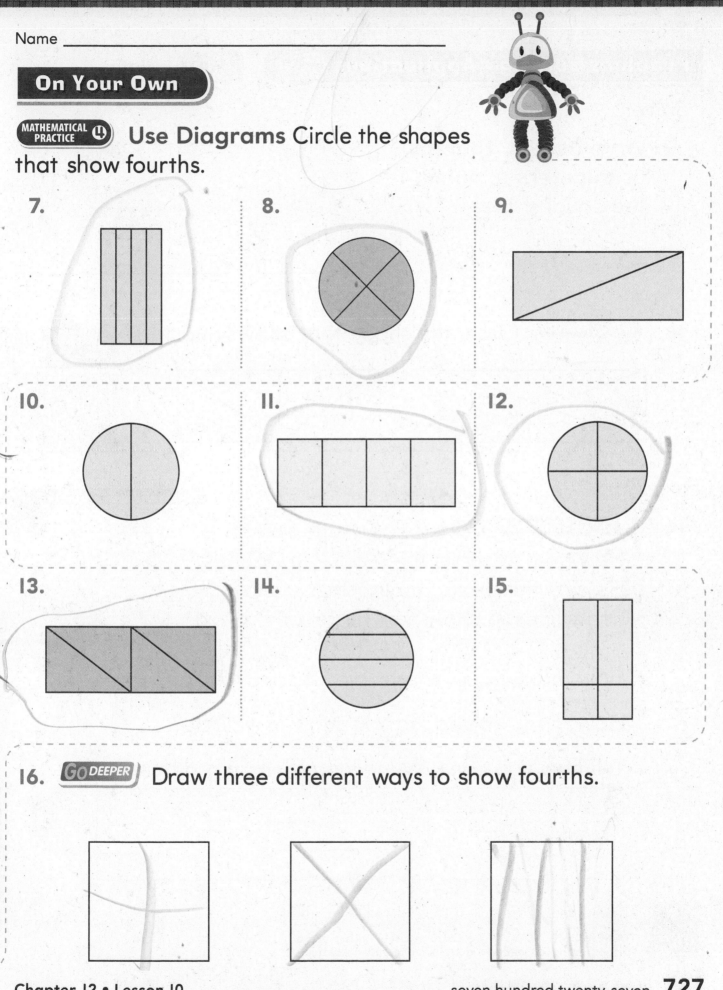

Problem Solving • Applications Real World

WRITE Math

Solve.

17. Write **halves, fourths,** or **quarters** to name the equal shares.

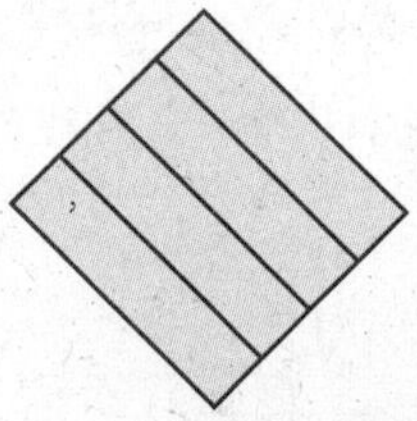

________ ____________

18. THINKSMARTER Circle the shape that shows quarters.

Math on the Spot

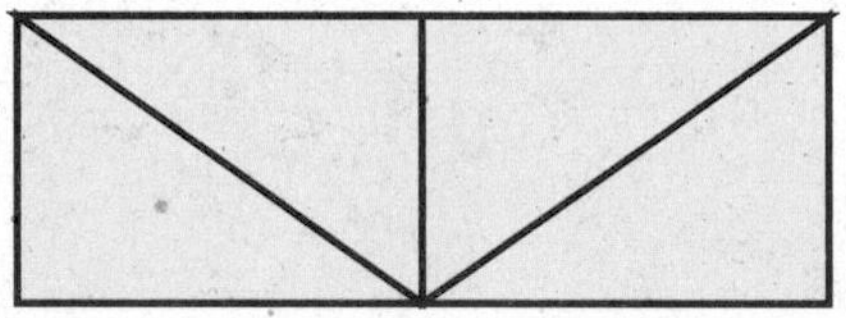

Personal Math Trainer

19. THINKSMARTER+ Alano has a small pizza. He wants to share the pizza with friends. He cuts the pizza into fourths. Draw lines to show how he cuts the pizza.

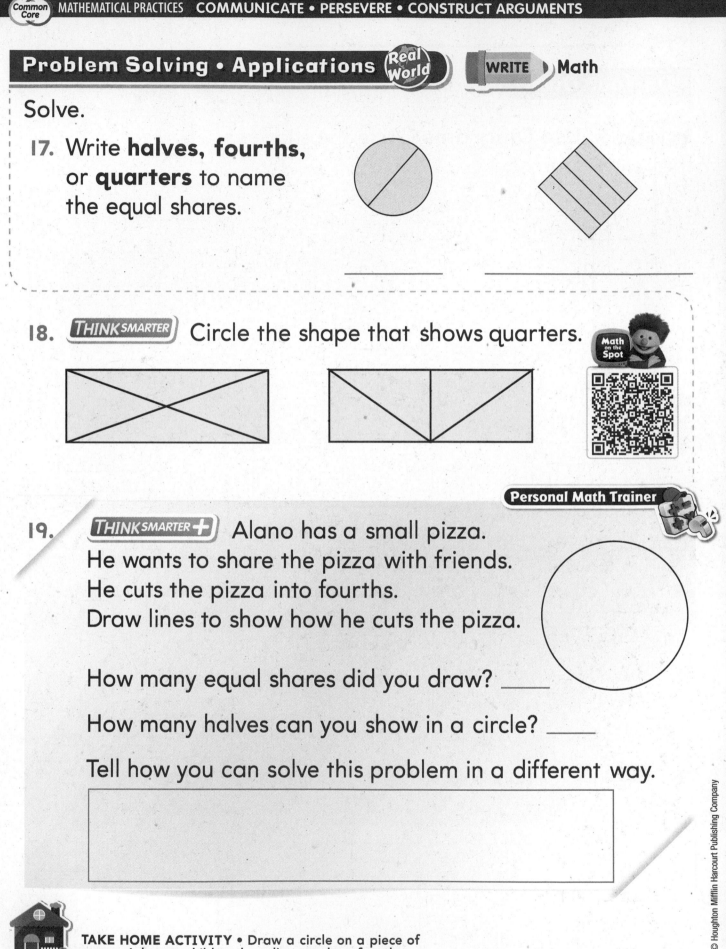

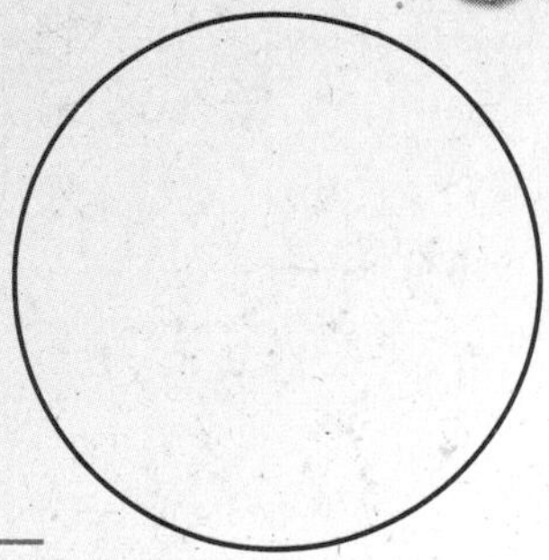

How many equal shares did you draw? ____

How many halves can you show in a circle? ____

Tell how you can solve this problem in a different way.

TAKE HOME ACTIVITY • Draw a circle on a piece of paper. Ask your child to draw lines to show fourths.

Name ______________________________

Fourths

COMMON CORE STANDARD—1.G.A.3
Reason with shapes and their attributes.

Circle the shapes that show fourths.

1. 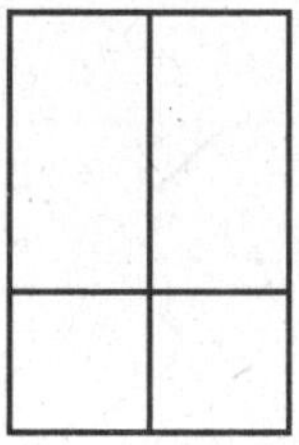

2. 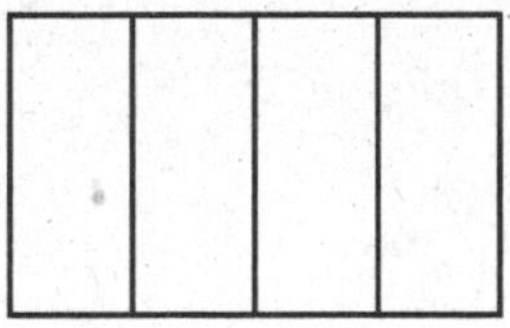

3. 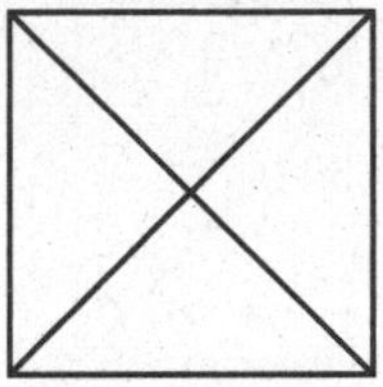

4. 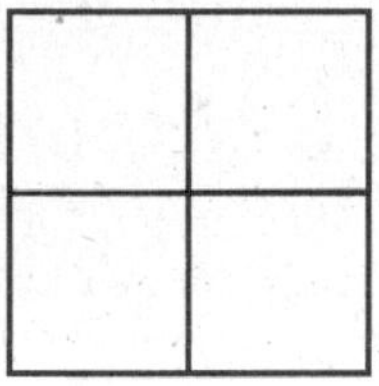

5. 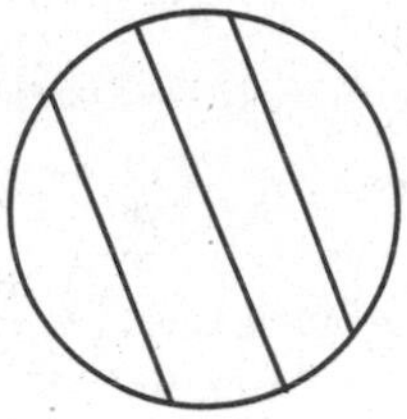

6. 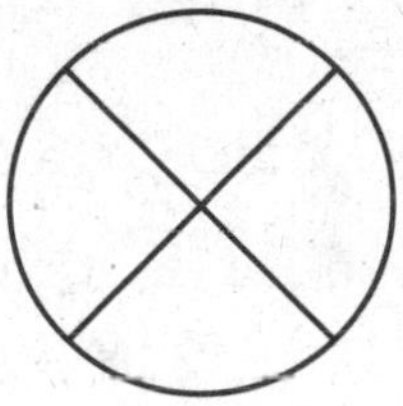

Problem Solving Real World

Solve.

7. Chad drew a picture to show a quarter of a circle. Which shape did Chad draw? Circle it.

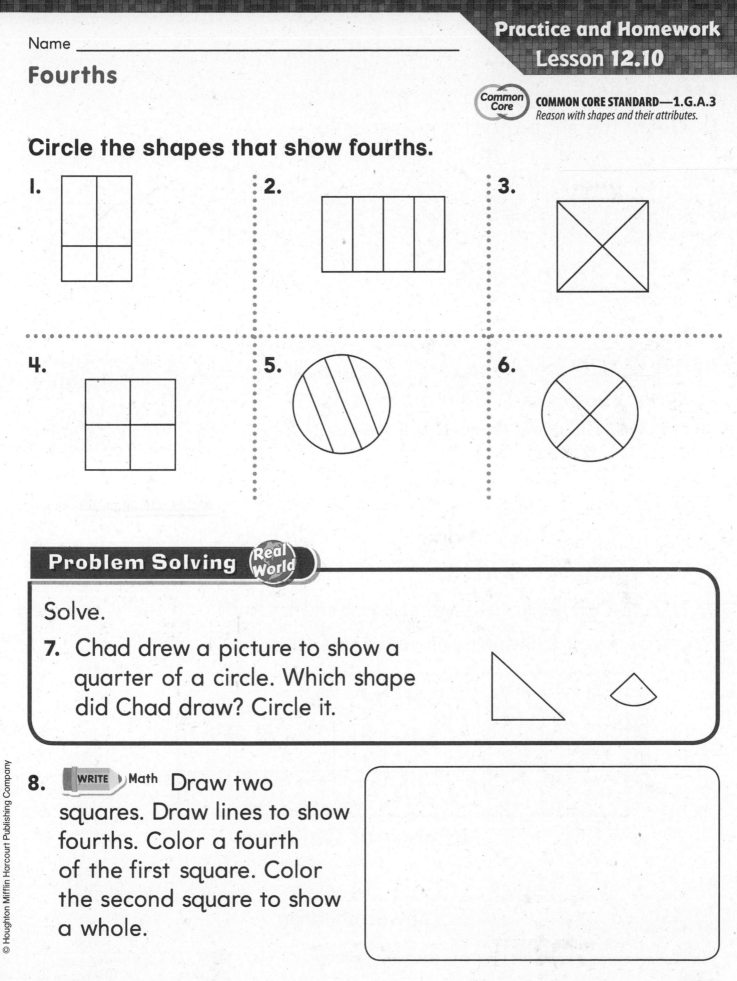

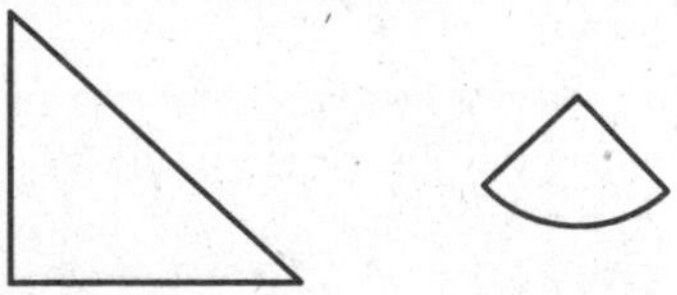

8. WRITE Math Draw two squares. Draw lines to show fourths. Color a fourth of the first square. Color the second square to show a whole.

Lesson Check (1.G.A.3)

1. Circle the shape that shows fourths.

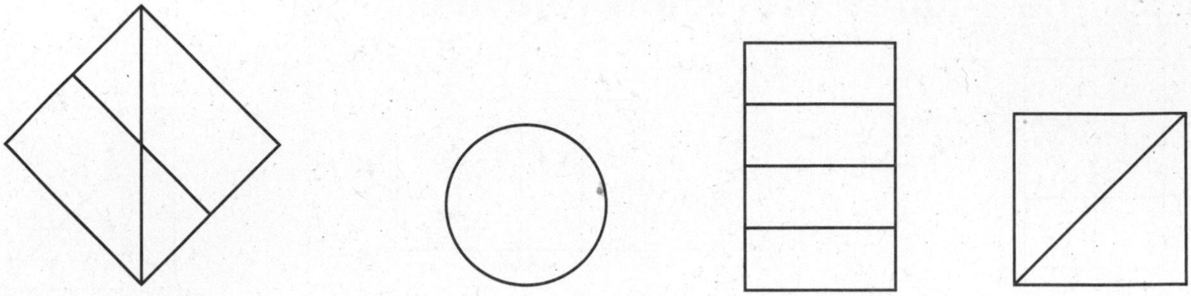

Spiral Review (1.MD.C.4, 1.G.A.2)

2. What shapes did Leila use to build the wall? Circle the shapes she used.

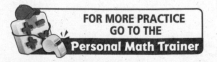

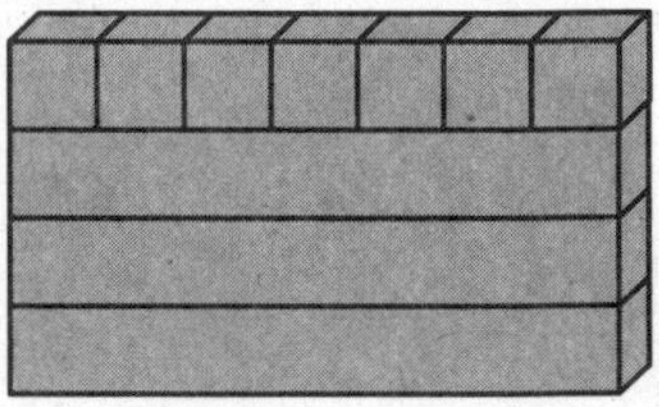

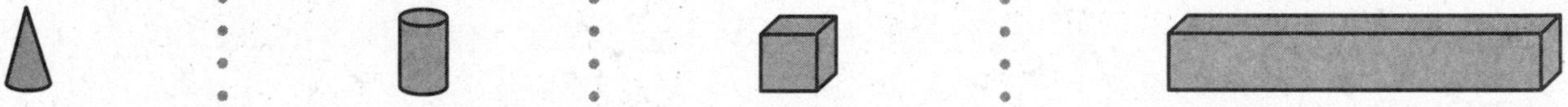

3. Use the graph to answer the question. How many fewer children answered **yes** than **no**?

Do You Have a Pet?							
Answer: yes	○	○	○	○			
Answer: no	○	○	○	○	○	○	

Number of Children

____ fewer children

FOR MORE PRACTICE GO TO THE **Personal Math Trainer**

Name ____________________

Chapter 12 Review/Test

Personal Math Trainer
Online Assessment and Intervention

1. Which shapes have only 3 sides?
Choose all that apply.

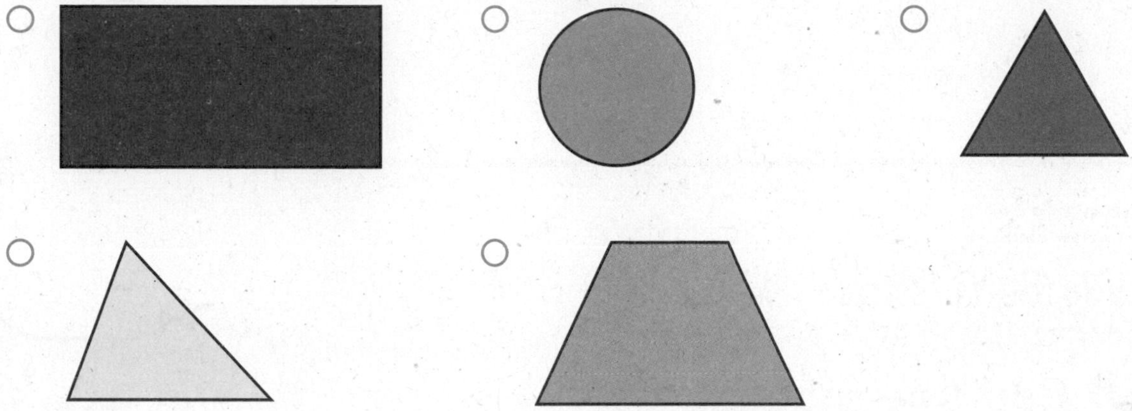

2. Circle the number that makes the sentence true.

A  has 2 / 3 / 4 vertices (corners).

3. How many  make a ?

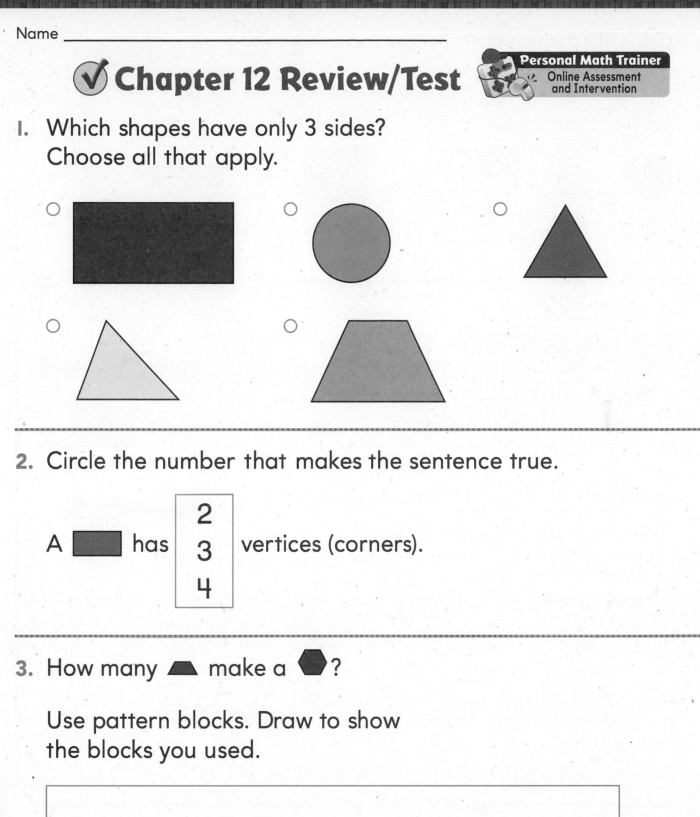

Use pattern blocks. Draw to show the blocks you used.

GO DIGITAL Assessment Options Chapter Test

4. Circle two shapes that can combine to make this new shape.

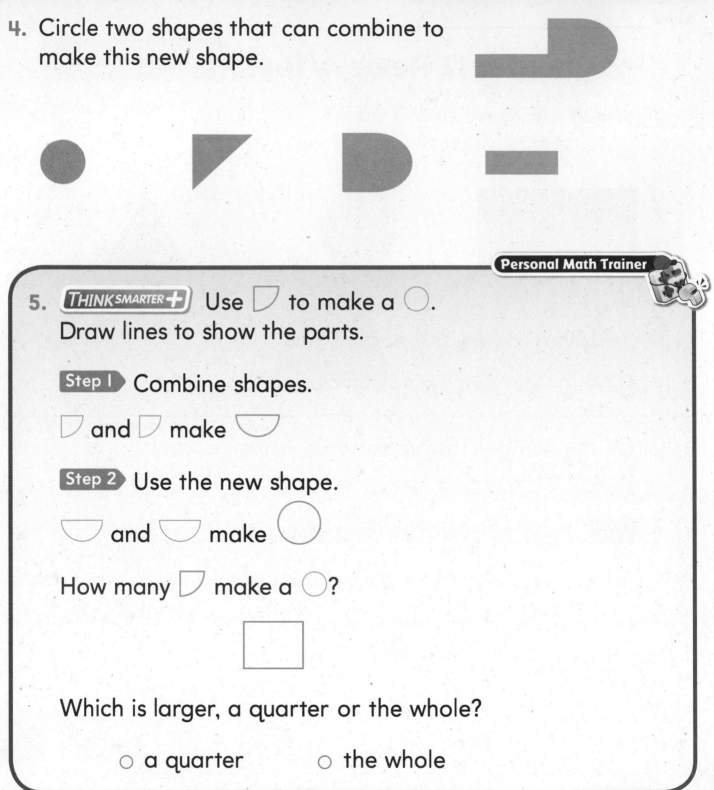

Personal Math Trainer

5. THINK SMARTER+ Use  to make a .
Draw lines to show the parts.

Step 1 Combine shapes.

 and  make 

Step 2 Use the new shape.

 and  make 

How many  make a ?

Which is larger, a quarter or the whole?

○ a quarter ○ the whole

Name ______________________________

6. Use 4 pattern blocks to make the shape. Draw to show the blocks you used.

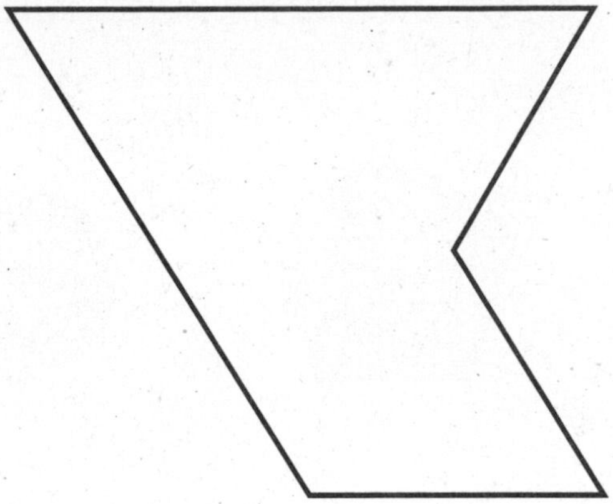

7. Draw a line to show the parts. Show 2 .

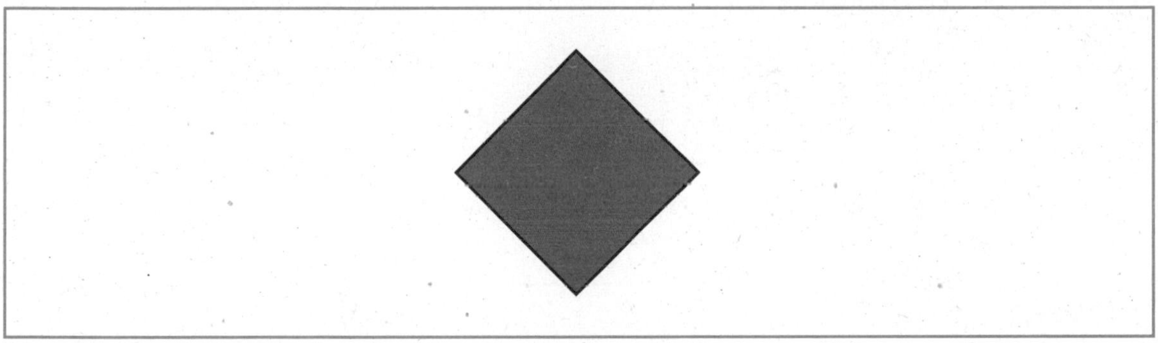

8. Does the shape show equal shares? Choose Yes or No.

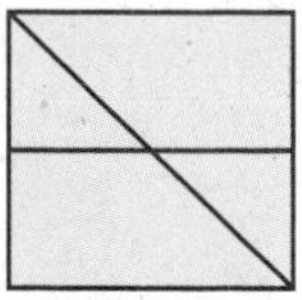

○ Yes ○ No

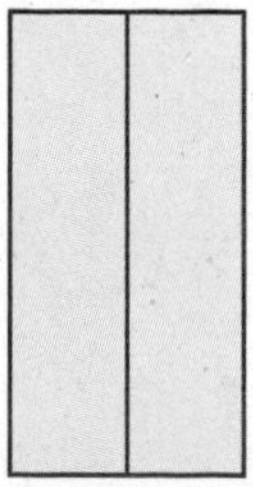

○ Yes ○ No

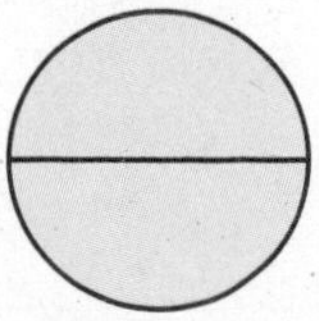

○ Yes ○ No

9. Circle the shapes that show halves.

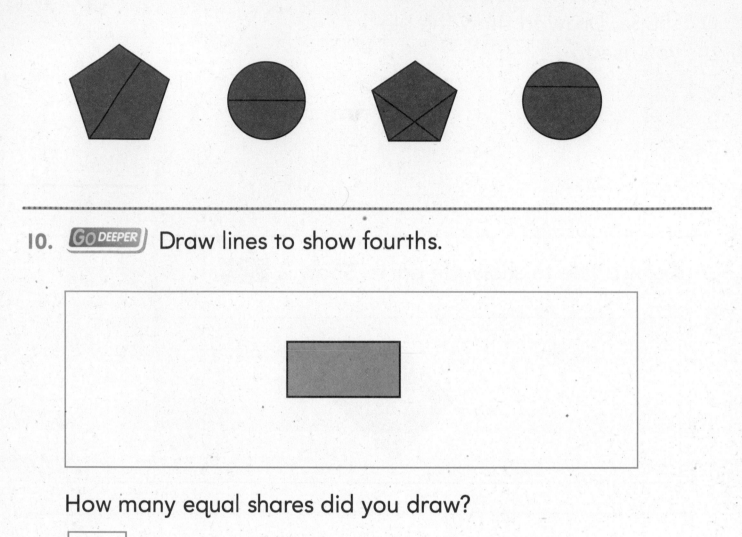

10. GO DEEPER Draw lines to show fourths.

How many equal shares did you draw?

☐

How many halves can you show in a rectangle?

☐

Tell how you can solve this problem in a different way.

Picture Glossary

add sumar

3 + 2 = 5

addend sumando

1 + 3 = 4

addend (arrows point to the 1 and the 3)

addition sentence enunciado de suma

2 + 1 = 3 is an **addition sentence.**

bar graph gráfica de barras

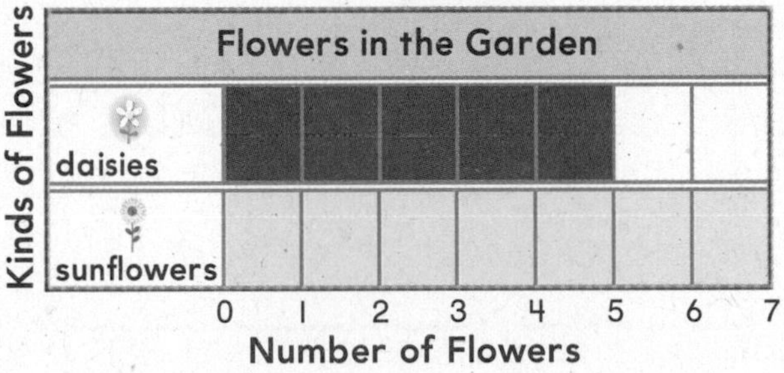

circle círculo

compare comparar

Subtract to **compare** groups.

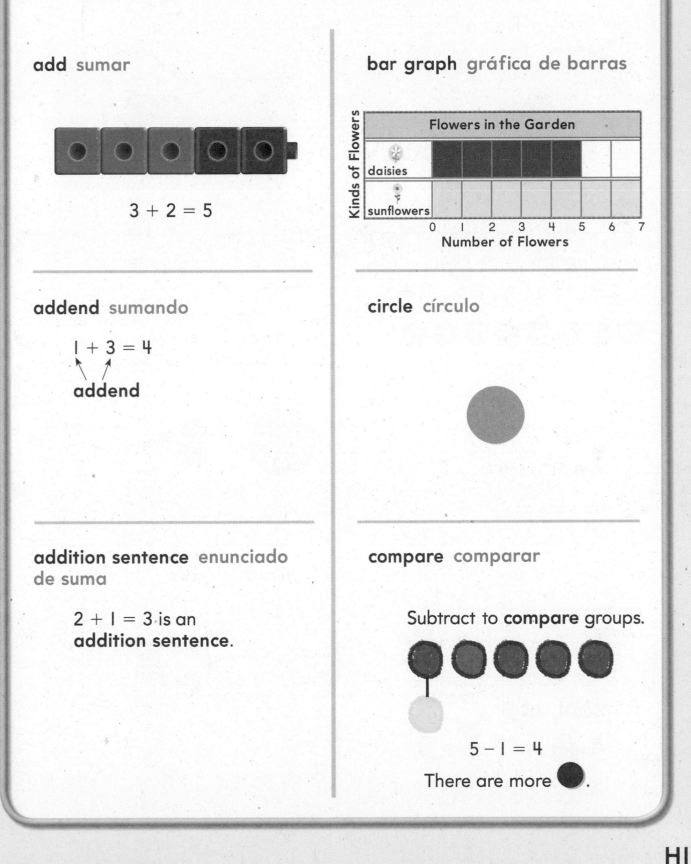

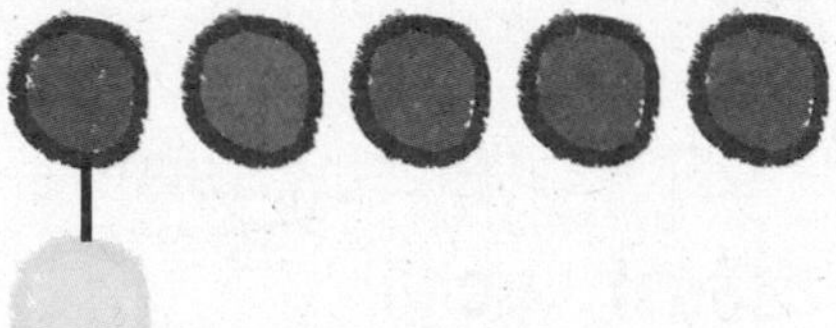

5 − 1 = 4

There are more ●.

cone cono

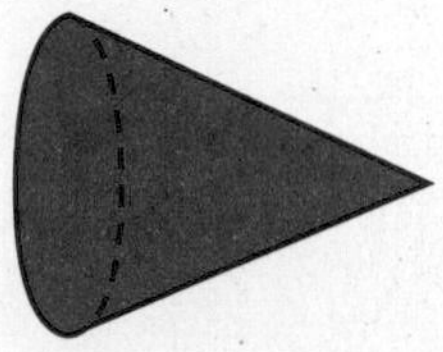

count back contar hacia atrás

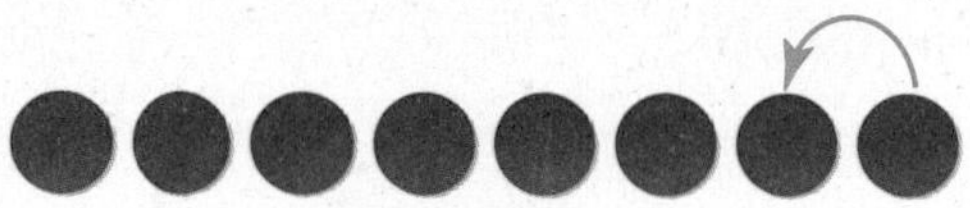

8 – 1 = 7

Start at 8.

Count back 1.

You are on 7.

count on contar hacia adelante

4 + 2 = 6

Say 4.

Count on 2.

5, 6

cube cubo

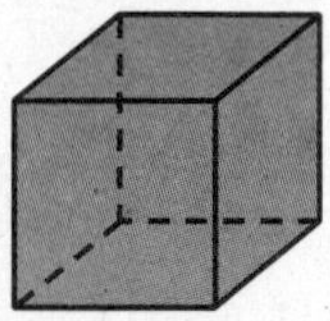

curved surface superficie curva

Some three-dimensional shapes have a **curved surface**.

cylinder cilindro

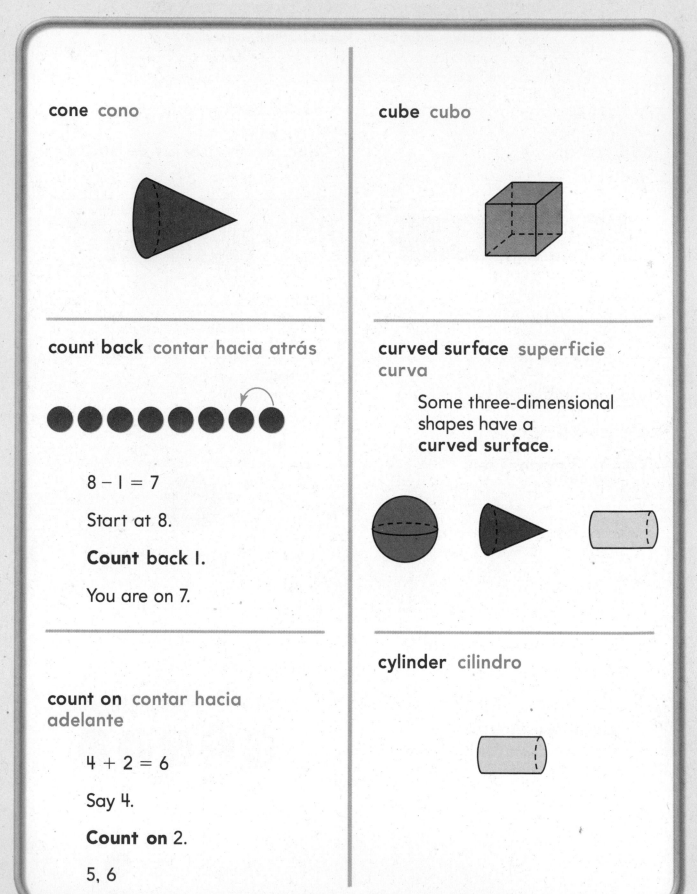

difference diferencia

$4 - 3 = 1$

The **difference** is 1.

digit dígito

13 is a two-digit number.

The 1 in 13 means 1 ten.
The 3 in 13 means 3 ones.

doubles dobles

$5 + 5 = 10$

doubles minus one dobles menos uno

$5 + 5 = 10$, so $5 + 4 = 9$

doubles plus one dobles más uno

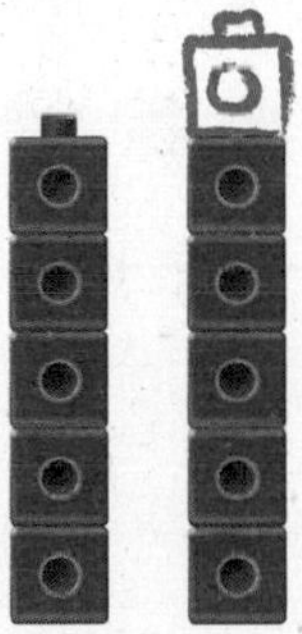

$5 + 5 = 10$, so $5 + 6 = 11$

equal parts partes iguales

These show **equal parts**, or equal shares.

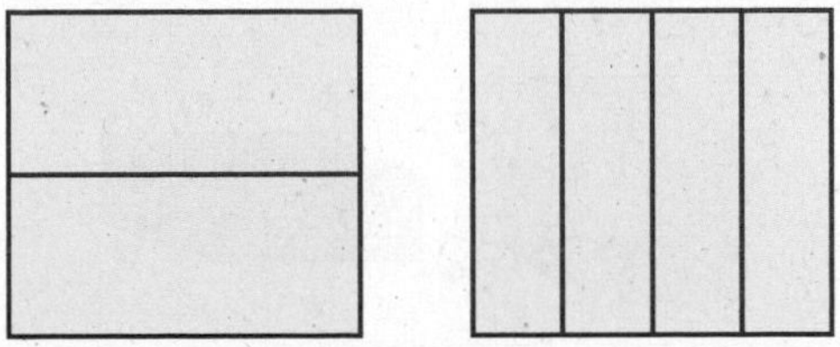

equal shares porciones iguales

These show equal parts, or **equal shares**.

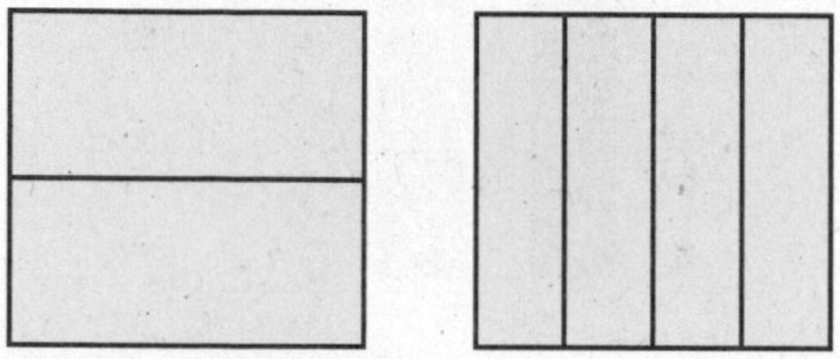

fewer menos

3 **fewer**

flat surface superficie plana

Some three-dimensional shapes have only **flat surfaces**.

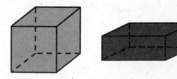

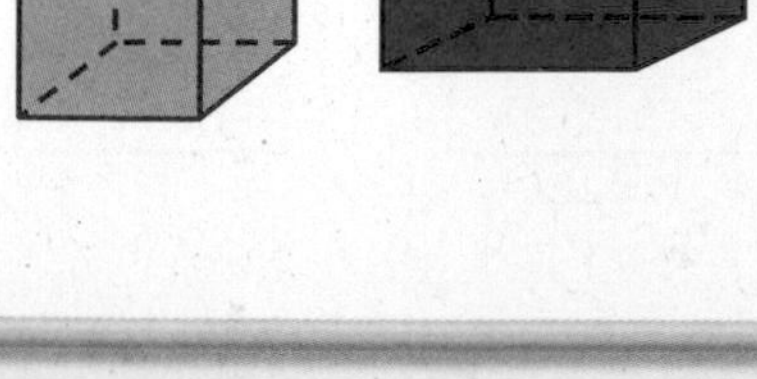

fourth of cuarto de

A **fourth of** this shape is shaded.

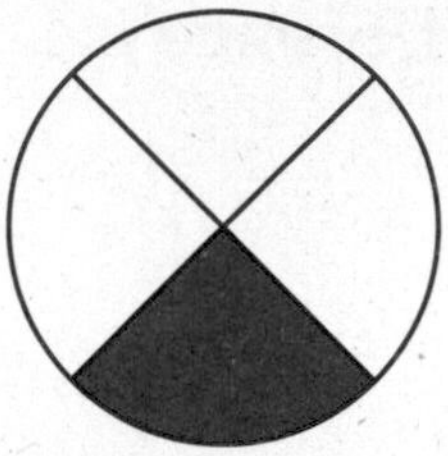

fourths cuartos

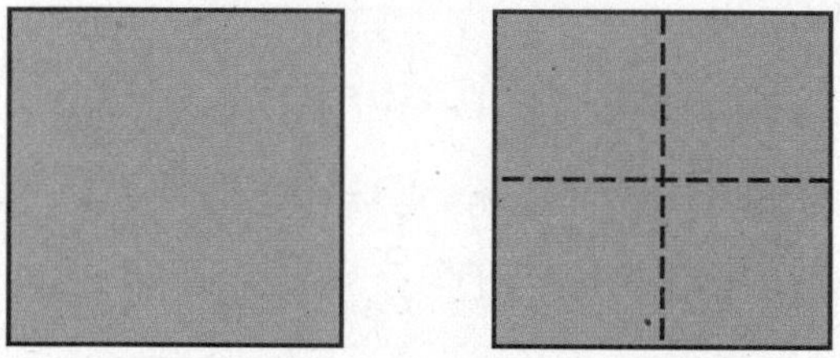

I whole

4 **fourths**, or 4 quarters

half hour media hora

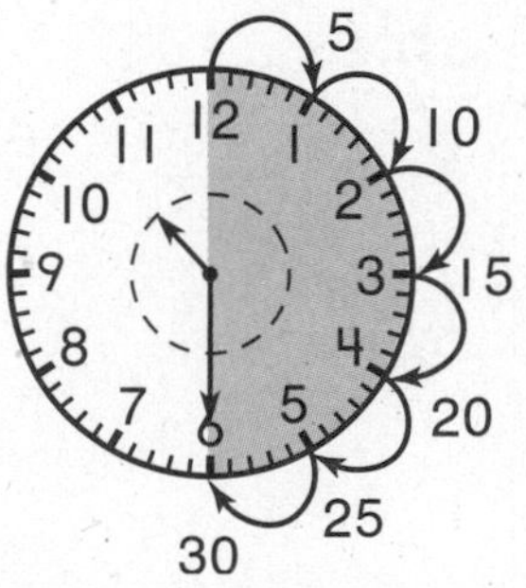

A **half hour** has 30 minutes.

half of mitad de

Half of this shape is shaded.

halves mitades

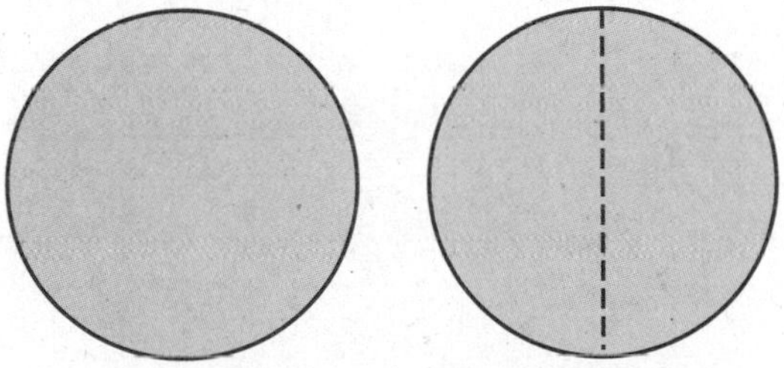

I whole 2 **halves**

hexagon hexágono

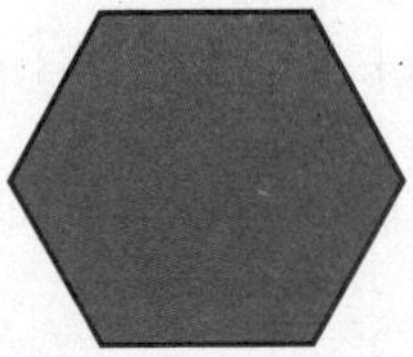

hour hora

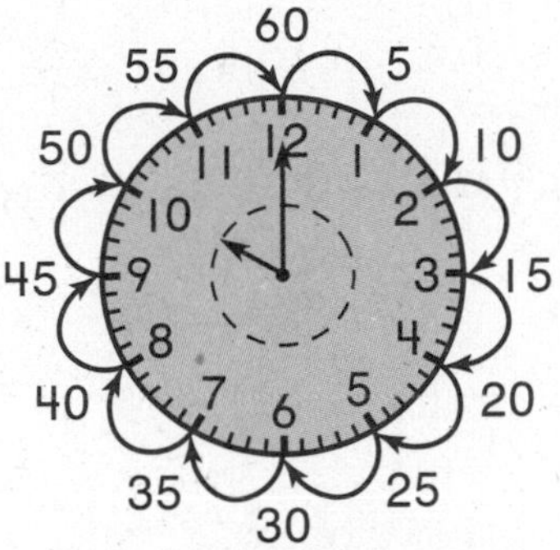

An **hour** has 60 minutes.

hour hand horario

hundred centena

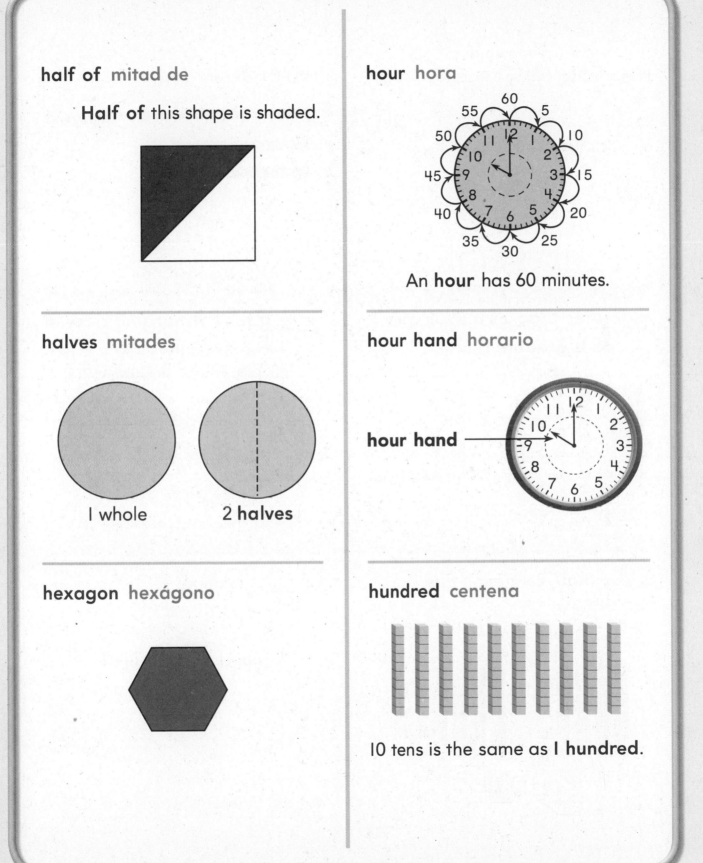

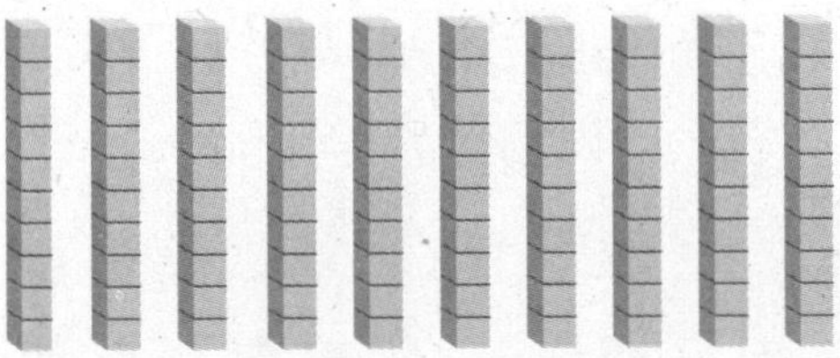

10 tens is the same as **I hundred**.

is equal to (=) es igual a

2 plus 1 **is equal to** 3.

$2 + 1 = 3$

is greater than es mayor que

35 **is greater than** 27.

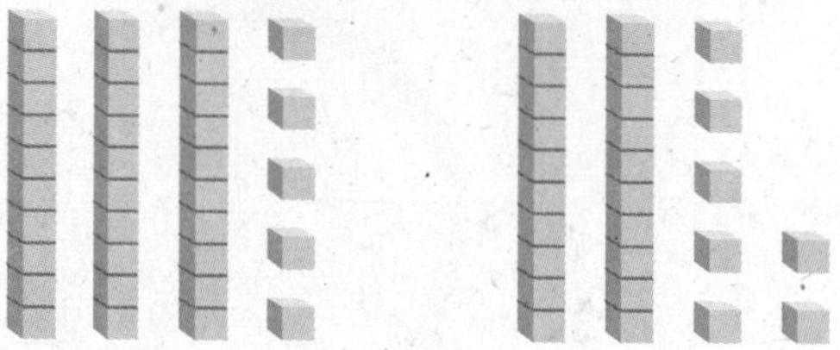

$35 > 27$

is less than es menor que

43 **is less than** 49.

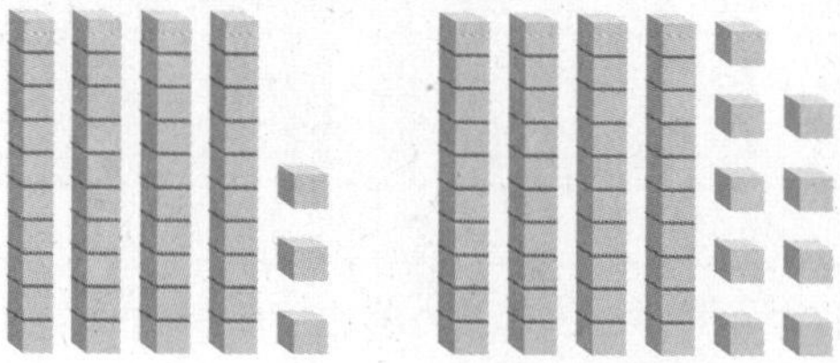

$43 < 49$

longest el más largo

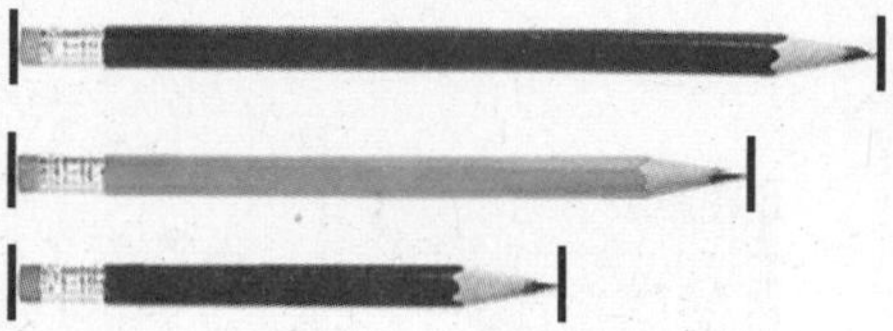

make a ten formar una decena

Move 2 counters into the ten frame. **Make a ten.**

$$\begin{array}{r} 8 \\ +\ 4 \\ \hline 12 \end{array}$$

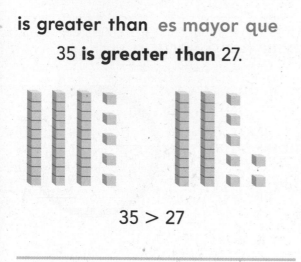

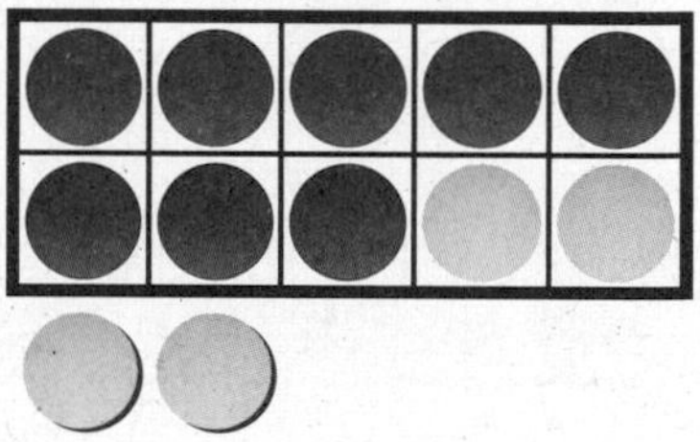

minus (−) menos

4 **minus** 3 is equal to 1.

$4 - 3 = 1$

minute hand minutero

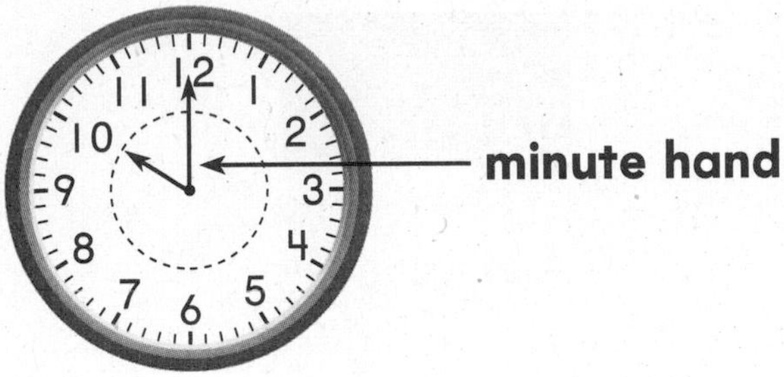

minutes minutos

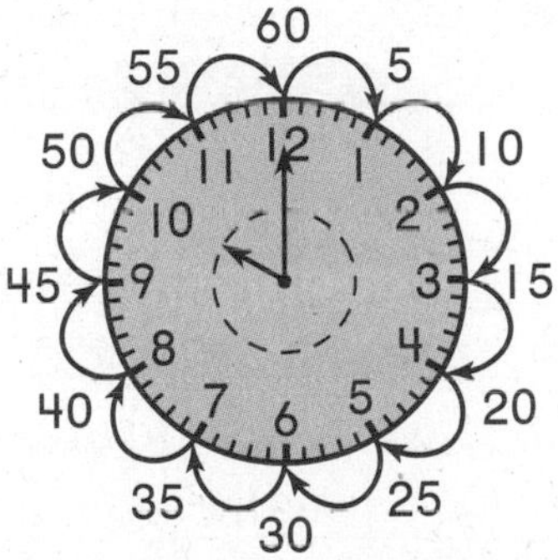

An hour has 60 **minutes.**

more más

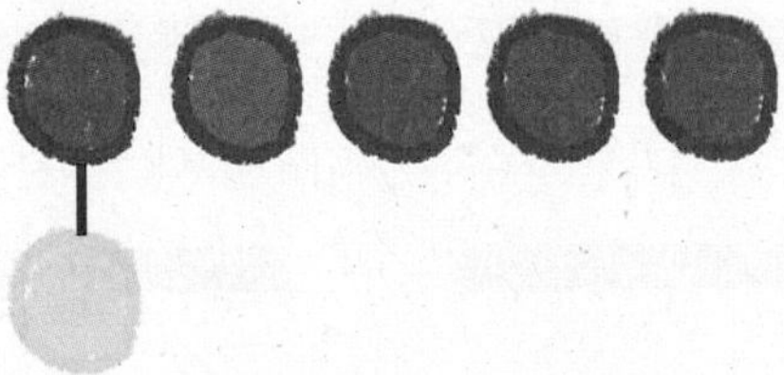

5 − 1 = 4

There are **more** ●.

ones unidades

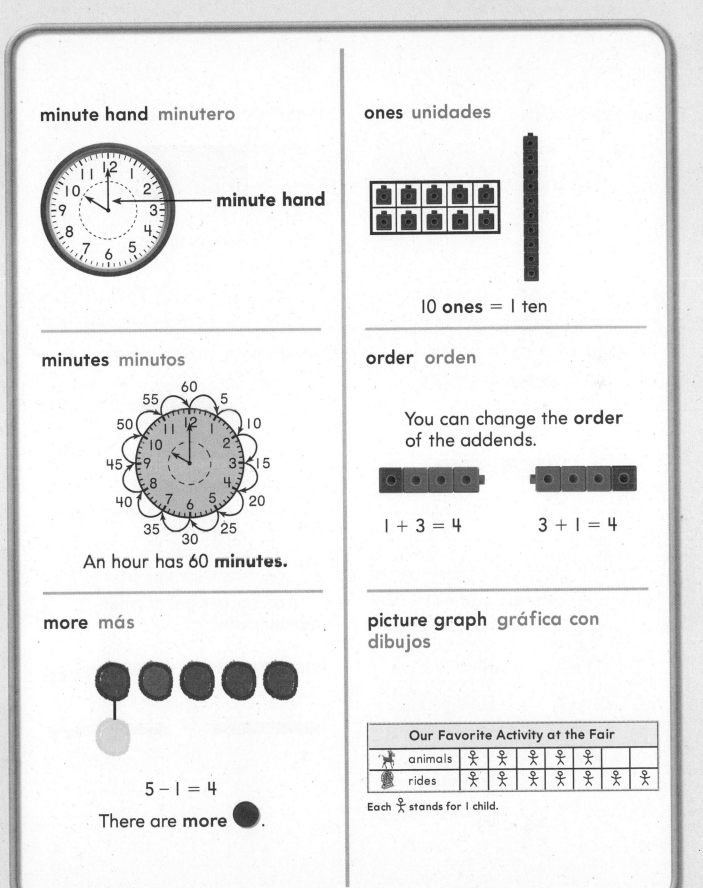

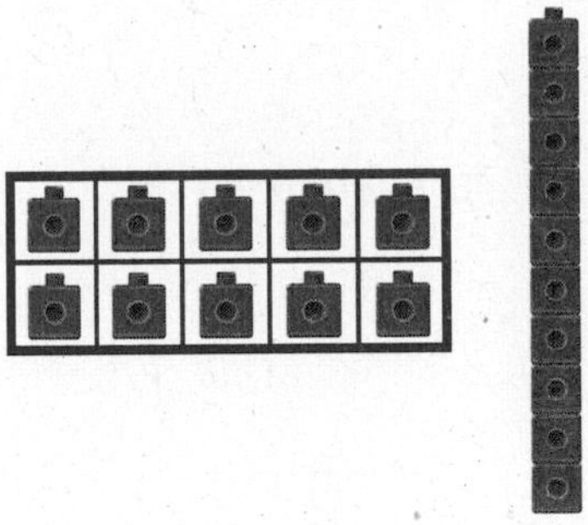

10 **ones** = 1 ten

order orden

You can change the **order** of the addends.

1 + 3 = 4   3 + 1 = 4

picture graph gráfica con dibujos

Our Favorite Activity at the Fair							
animals	🯅	🯅	🯅	🯅	🯅		
rides	🯅	🯅	🯅	🯅	🯅	🯅	🯅

Each 🯅 stands for 1 child.

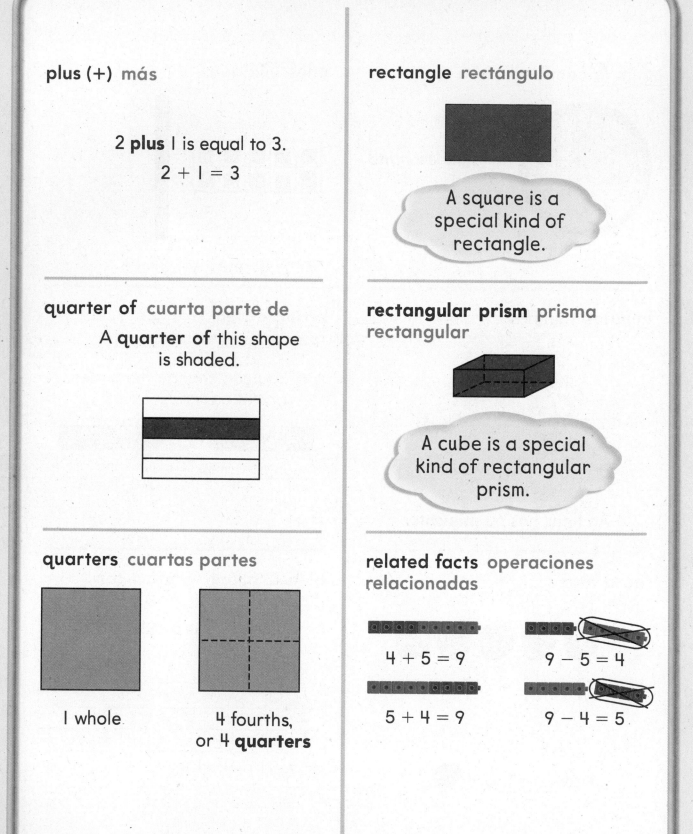

plus (+) más

2 **plus** 1 is equal to 3.

2 + 1 = 3

quarter of cuarta parte de

A **quarter of** this shape is shaded.

quarters cuartas partes

1 whole

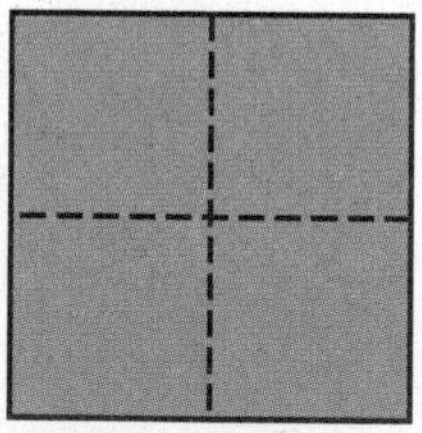

4 fourths, or 4 **quarters**

rectangle rectángulo

A square is a special kind of rectangle.

rectangular prism prisma rectangular

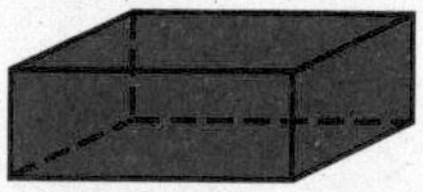

A cube is a special kind of rectangular prism.

related facts operaciones relacionadas

4 + 5 = 9

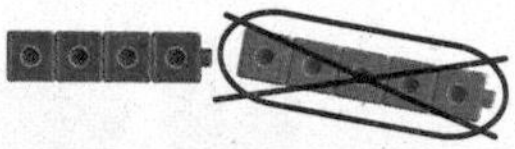

9 − 5 = 4

5 + 4 = 9

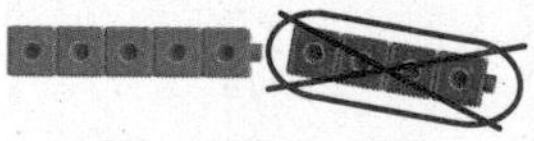

9 − 4 = 5

shortest el más corto

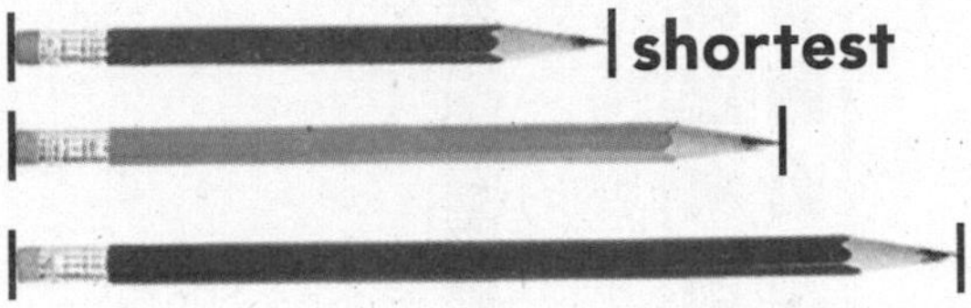

side lado

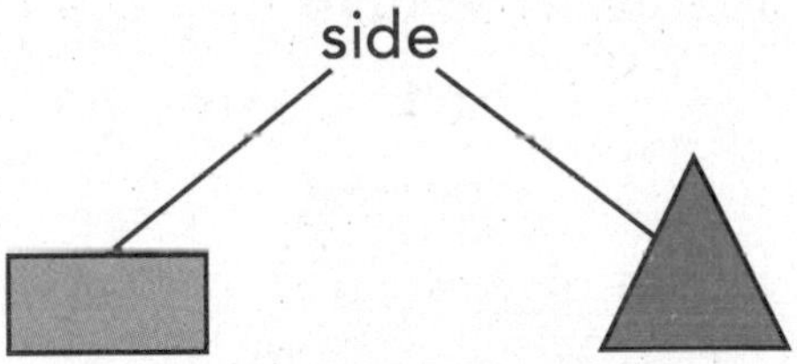

sphere esfera

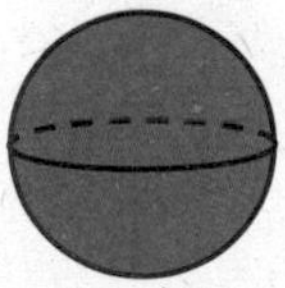

square cuadrado

subtract restar

Subtract to find out how many.

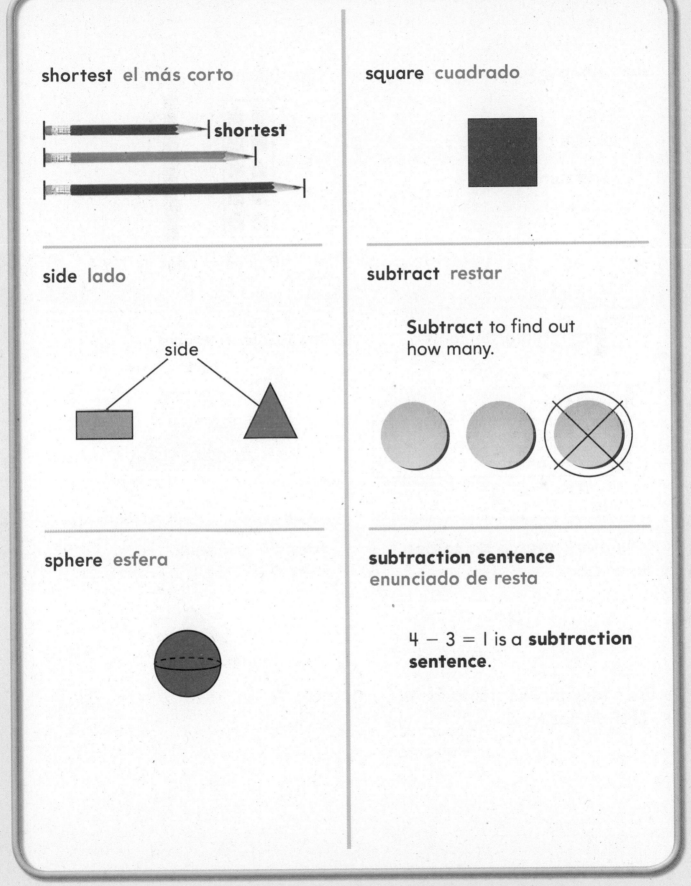

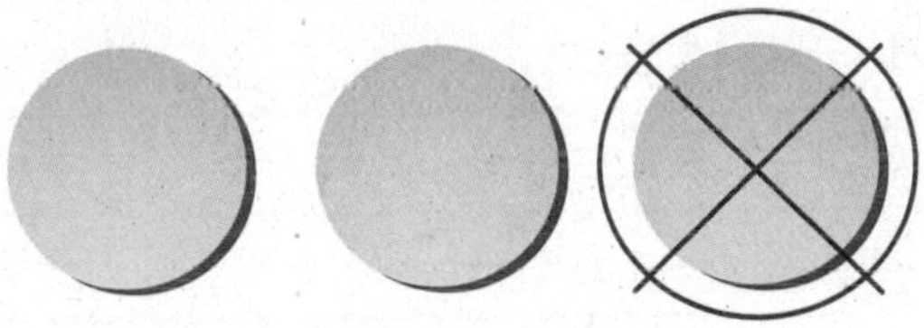

subtraction sentence
enunciado de resta

4 − 3 = 1 is a **subtraction sentence**.

sum suma o total

2 plus 1 is equal to 3.

The **sum** is 3.

tally chart tabla de conteo

Boys and Girls in Our Class		Total
boys	𝍸 IIII	9
girls	𝍸 I	6

tally mark marca de conteo

Each **tally mark** | stands for 1.
𝍸 stands for 5.

ten decena

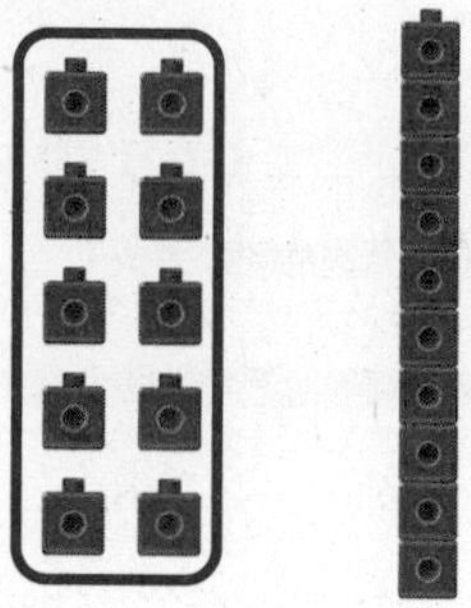

10 ones = 1 **ten**

trapezoid trapecio

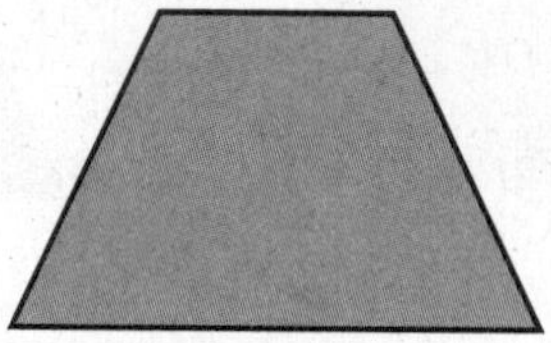

triangle triángulo

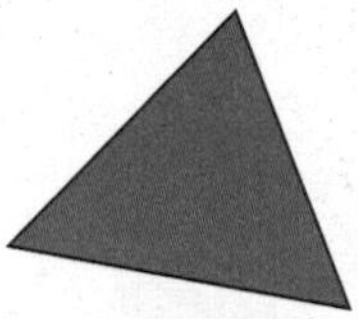

unequal parts partes desiguales

These show **unequal parts**, or unequal shares.

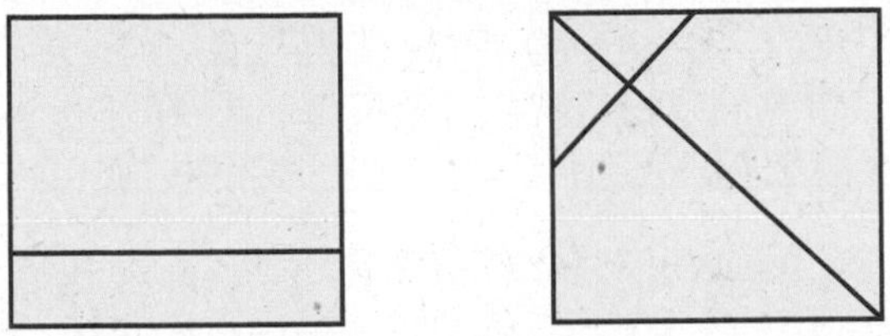

unequal shares porciones desiguales

These show unequal parts, or **unequal shares**.

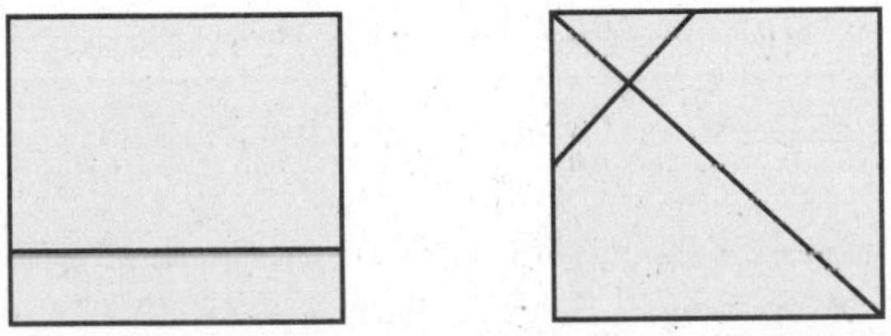

vertex vértice

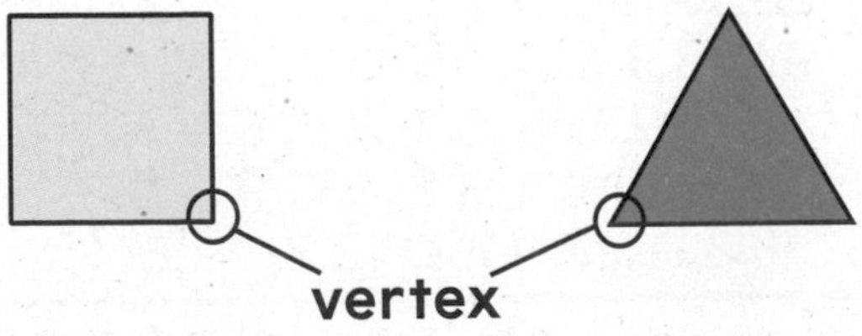

zero 0 cero

When you add **zero** to any number, the sum is that number.

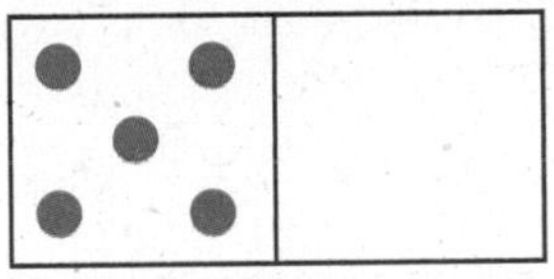

$5 + \mathbf{0} = 5$

COMMON CORE STATE STANDARDS

Standards You Will Learn

Mathematical Practices		Some examples are:
MP1	Make sense of problems and persevere in solving them.	Lessons 1.1, 1.2, 1.3, 1.4, 2.1, 2.2, 2.3, 2.4 2.5, 2.6, 3.2, 3.4, 3.12, 4.3, 4.6, 5.1, 5.2, 5.5, 6.8, 7.3, 7.5, 8.1, 8.7, 8.8, 8.10, 9.1, 9.2, 9.3, 9.5, 9.7, 9.9, 10.6, 11.2, 11.3, 11.4, 11.5, 12.4, 12.5, 12.7, 12.8, 12.9, 12.10
MP2	Reason abstractly and quantitatively.	Lessons 1.5, 2.1, 2.2, 2.5, 3.7, 3.8, 3.9, 3.10, 3.12, 4.1, 4.4, 4.5, 4.6, 5.1, 5.6, 5.9, 5.10, 6.2, 6.4, 6.7, 6.10, 7.4, 7.5, 8.2, 8.6, 8.7, 8.8, 8.9, 8.10, 9.3, 9.4, 9.7, 9.8, 10.5, 11.2, 11.3
MP3	Construct viable arguments and critique the reasoning of others.	Lessons 2.5, 2.7, 2.8, 3.10, 3.11, 4.2, 4.6, 5.7, 6.3, 6.4, 7.2, 7.5, 8.1, 8.3, 8.9, 8.10, 9.1, 9.2, 9.4, 9.5, 10.1, 10.2, 10.3, 10.4, 10.5, 10.6, 10.7, 11.2, 11.3, 12.8
MP4	Model with mathematics.	Lessons 1.1, 1.2, 1.3, 1.4, 1.5, 1.7, 2.1, 2.2, 2.3, 2.4, 2.5, 2.6, 2.7, 2.8, 2.9, 3.1, 3.9, 3.12, 4.1, 4.2, 4.3, 4.4, 4.5, 4.6, 5.1, 5.3, 5.4, 5.6, 5.7, 6.4, 6.5, 6.6, 6.7, 6.8, 6.9, 6.10, 7.3, 7.4, 8.3, 8.4, 8.5, 9.2, 9.9, 10.1, 10.2, 10.3, 10.4, 10.5, 10.6, 11.1, 11.5, 12.4, 12.5, 12.6, 12.9, 12.10
MP5	Use appropriate tools strategically.	Lessons 1.1, 1.2, 1.3, 1.4, 2.3, 2.4, 3.2, 3.3, 3.4, 3.6, 3.7, 3.8, 4.3, 4.4, 4.5, 5.2, 5.8, 6.1, 6.2, 6.3, 6.6, 6.9, 7.1, 7.2, 8.4, 8.6, 9.4, 9.6, 9.8, 10.3, 10.7, 11.3, 12.3, 12.6
MP6	Attend to precision.	Lessons 1.2, 1.7, 1.8, 2.6, 2.9, 3.1, 3.2, 3.5, 3.11, 4.1, 4.3, 5.7, 5.9, 5.10, 6.3, 6.4, 6.6, 6.7, 6.8, 6.10, 7.4, 7.5, 8.1, 8.3, 8.4, 8.5, 8.7, 8.8, 9.1, 9.3, 9.6, 9.8, 10.2, 10.7, 11.1, 11.2, 11.4, 11.5, 12.1, 12.2, 12.3, 12.8, 12.9, 12.10

Standards You Will Learn

Mathematical Practices		Some examples are:
MP7	Look for and make use of structure.	Lessons 1.5, 1.6, 1.7, 1.8, 2.8, 3.3, 3.4, 3.5, 3.6, 4.2, 5.2, 5.3, 5.4, 5.5, 5.6, 5.8, 5.9, 6.1, 6.5, 6.8, 6.9, 7.1, 7.2, 8.2, 8.7, 8.9, 9.6, 11.4, 12.1, 12.2, 12.7
MP8	Look for and express regularity in repeated reasoning.	Lessons 1.5, 1.6, 1.7, 2.7, 2.9, 3.2, 3.3, 3.11, 5.2, 5.3, 5.4, 5.5, 6.1, 6.2, 6.5, 7.3, 8.3, 8.8, 8.10, 9.3, 9.7, 9.9, 10.4, 11.1, 11.4, 12.1, 12.2
Domain: Operations and Algebraic Thinking		**Student Edition Lessons**
Represent and solve problems involving addition and subtraction.		
1.OA.A.1	Use addition and subtraction within 20 to solve word problems involving situations of adding to, taking from, putting together, taking apart, and comparing, with unknowns in all positions, e.g., by using objects, drawings, and equations with a symbol for the unknown number to represent the problem.	Lessons 1.1, 1.2, 1.3, 1.4, 1.7, 2.1 2.2, 2.3, 2.4, 2.5, 2.6, 2.8, 4.6, 5.1, 5.7
1.OA.A.2	Solve word problems that call for addition of three whole numbers whose sum is less than or equal to 20, e.g., by using objects, drawings, and equations with a symbol for the unknown number to represent the problem.	Lesson 3.12
Understand and apply properties of operations and the relationship between addition and subtraction.		
1.OA.B.3	Apply properties of operations as strategies to add and subtract. *Examples: If $8 + 3 = 11$ is known, then $3 + 8 = 11$ is also known. (Commutative property of addition.) To add $2 + 6 + 4$, the second two numbers can be added to make a ten, so $2 + 6 + 4 = 2 + 10 = 12$. (Associative property of addition.)*	Lessons 1.5, 1.6, 3.1, 3.10, 3.11

Standards You Will Learn

Standards You Will Learn		Student Edition Lessons
Domain: Operations and Algebraic Thinking		
Understand and apply properties of operations and the relationship between addition and subtraction.		
1.OA.B.4	Understand subtraction as an unknown-addend problem.	Lessons 4.2, 4.3
Add and subtract within 20.		
1.OA.C.5	Relate counting to addition and subtraction (e.g., by counting on 2 to add 2).	Lessons 3.2, 4.1
1.OA.C.6	Add and subtract within 20, demonstrating fluency for addition and subtraction within 10. Use strategies such as counting on; making ten (e.g., $8 + 6 = 8 + 2 + 4 = 10 + 4 = 14$); decomposing a number leading to a ten (e.g., $13 - 4 = 13 - 3 - 1 = 10 - 1 = 9$); using the relationship between addition and subtraction (e.g., knowing that $8 + 4 = 12$, one knows $12 - 8 = 4$); and creating equivalent but easier or known sums (e.g., adding $6 + 7$ by creating the known equivalent $6 + 6 + 1 = 12 + 1 = 13$).	Lessons 1.8, 2.9, 3.3, 3.4, 3.5, 3.6, 3.7, 3.8, 3.9, 4.4, 4.5, 5.2, 5.3, 5.4, 5.8, 5.10, 8.1
Work with addition and subtraction equations.		
1.OA.D.7	Understand the meaning of the equal sign, and determine if equations involving addition and subtraction are true or false.	Lesson 5.9

Standards You Will Learn		Student Edition Lessons
Domain: Operations and Algebraic Thinking		
Work with addition and subtraction equations.		
1.OA.D.8	Determine the unknown whole number in an addition or subtraction equation relating three whole numbers.	Lessons 2.5, 2.7, 5.5, 5.6
Domain: Number and Operations in Base Ten		
Extend the counting sequence.		
1.NBT.A.1	Count to 120, starting at any number less than 120. In this range, read and write numerals and represent a number of objects with a written numeral.	Lessons 6.1, 6.2, 6.9, 6.10
Understand place value.		
1.NBT.B.2	Understand that the two digits of a two-digit number represent amounts of tens and ones. Understand the following as special cases:	Lessons 6.6, 6.7
	a. 10 can be thought of as a bundle of ten ones — called a "ten."	Lessons 6.5, 6.8
	b. The numbers from 11 to 19 are composed of a ten and one, two, three, four, five, six, seven, eight, or nine ones.	Lessons 6.3, 6.4
	c. The numbers 10, 20, 30, 40, 50, 60, 70, 80, 90 refer to one, two, three, four, five, six, seven, eight, or nine tens (and 0 ones).	Lesson 6.5
1.NBT.B.3	Compare two two-digit numbers based on meanings of the tens and ones digits, recording the results of comparisons with the symbols $>$, $=$, and $<$.	Lessons 6.8, 7.1, 7.2, 7.3, 7.4

Standards You Will Learn

Standards You Will Learn		Student Edition Lessons
Domain: Number and Operations in Base Ten		
Use place value understanding and properties of operations to add and subtract.		
1.NBT.C.4	Add within 100, including adding a two-digit number and a one-digit number, and adding a two-digit number and a multiple of 10, using concrete models or drawings and strategies based on place value, properties of operations, and/or the relationship between addition and subtraction; relate the strategy to a written method and explain the reasoning used. Understand that in adding two-digit numbers, one adds tens and tens, ones and ones; and sometimes it is necessary to compose a ten.	Lessons 8.2, 8.4, 8.5, 8.6, 8.7, 8.8, 8.9, 8.10
1.NBT.C.5	Given a two-digit number, mentally find 10 more or 10 less than the number, without having to count; explain the reasoning used.	Lesson 7.5
1.NBT.C.6	Subtract multiples of 10 in the range 10–90 from multiples of 10 in the range 10–90 (positive or zero differences), using concrete models or drawings and strategies based on place value, properties of operations, and/or the relationship between addition and subtraction; relate the strategy to a written method and explain the reasoning used.	Lessons 8.3, 8.10
Domain: Measurement and Data		
Measure lengths indirectly and by iterating length units.		
1.MD.A.1	Order three objects by length; compare the lengths of two objects indirectly by using a third object.	Lessons 9.1, 9.2

Standards You Will Learn

		Student Edition Lessons
Domain: Measurement and Data		
Measure lengths indirectly and by iterating length units.		
1.MD.A.2	Express the length of an object as a whole number of length units, by laying multiple copies of a shorter object (the length unit) end to end; understand that the length measurement of an object is the number of same-size length units that span it with no gaps or overlaps. *Limit to contexts where the object being measured is spanned by a whole number of length units with no gaps or overlaps.*	Lessons 9.3, 9.4, 9.5
Tell and write time.		
1.MD.B.3	Tell and write time in hours and half-hours using analog and digital clocks.	Lessons 9.6, 9.7, 9.8, 9.9
Represent and interpret data.		
1.MD.C.4	Organize, represent, and interpret data with up to three categories; ask and answer questions about the total number of data points, how many in each category, and how many more or less are in one category than in another.	Lessons 10.1, 10.2, 10.3, 10.4, 10.5, 10.6, 10.7
Domain: Geometry		
Reason with shapes and their attributes.		
1.G.A.1	Distinguish between defining attributes (e.g., triangles are closed and three-sided) versus non-defining attributes (e.g., color, orientation, overall size); build and draw shapes to possess defining attributes.	Lessons 11.1, 11.5, 12.1, 12.2

Standards You Will Learn

Student Edition Lessons

Domain: Geometry		
Reason with shapes and their attributes.		
1.G.A.2	Compose two-dimensional shapes (rectangles, squares, trapezoids, triangles, half-circles, and quarter-circles) or three-dimensional shapes (cubes, right rectangular prisms, right circular cones, and right circular cylinders) to create a composite shape, and compose new shapes from the composite shape.	Lessons 11.2, 11.3, 11.4, 12.3, 12.4, 12.5, 12.6, 12.7
1.G.A.3	Partition circles and rectangles into two and four equal shares, describe the shares using the words *halves, fourths*, and *quarters*, and use the phrases *half of*, *fourth of*, and *quarter of*. Describe the whole as two of, or four of the shares. Understand for these examples that decomposing into more equal shares creates smaller shares.	Lessons 12.8, 12.9, 12.10

Index

A

B

C

D

N

O

P

Q

R

T

U

V

W

Z